Judy Garland

The Day-by-Day Chronicle of a Legend

Scott Schechter

Taylor Trade Publishing
Lanham • New York • Boulder • Toronto • Oxford

First Taylor Trade Publishing edition 2006
Originally published in 2002 by Cooper Square Press. Reprinted by permission.

This Taylor Trade Publishing paperback edition of *Judy Garland* is an original publication. It is published by arrangement with the author.

Published by Taylor Trade Publishing
An imprint of The Rowman & Littlefield Publishing Group, Inc.
4501 Forbes Boulevard, Suite 200, Lanham, Maryland 20706

Distributed by NATIONAL BOOK NETWORK

Library of Congress Cataloging-in-Publication Data

The Cooper Square Press edition of this book was previously catalogued by the Library of Congress as follows:

Schechter, Scott.
Judy Garland : the day-by-day chronicle of a legend / Scott Schechter.— 1st Cooper Square Press ed.
p. cm.
Includes bibliographical references and index.
1. Garland, Judy. 2. Singers—United States—Biography. I. Title.
ML420.G253 S3 2002
782.42164'092—dc21

2001008721

ISBN-10: 0-8154-1205-3 (cloth : alk. paper)
ISBN-13: 978-1-58979-300-2 (pbk : alk. paper)
ISBN-10: 1-58979-300-5 (pbk : alk. paper)

The paper used in this publication meets the minimum requirements of American National Standard for Information Sciences—Permanence of Paper for Printed Library Materials, ANSI/NISO Z39.48-1992.
Manufactured in the United States of America.

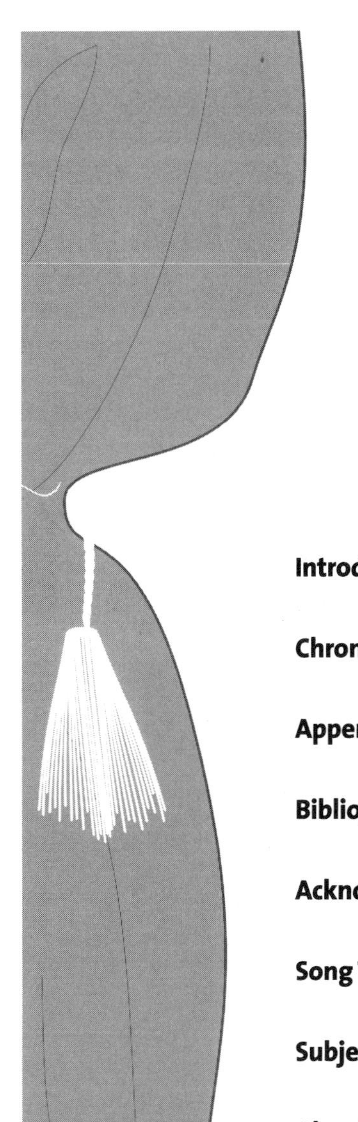

Contents

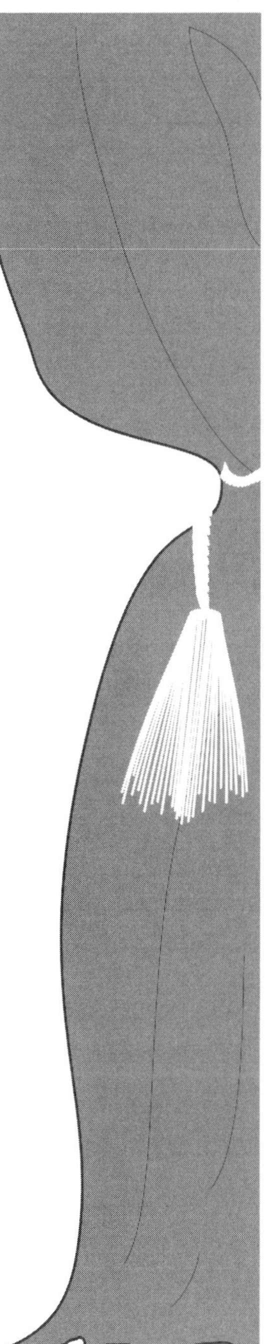

Judy in *Strike Up The Band* (1940): The "(I Ain't Got) Nobody (And Nobody's Got Me)" number in the library, surrounded by books full of information. (Courtesy of Photofest.)

Introduction

"I was born to sing and try to take people's minds off their troubles for awhile . . . if I can." —**Judy Garland**, May 10, 1964

"I've been working for 43 years. If I'd been as ill or as sick as they've printed, I wouldn't have been able to be working for 43 years. So I think it's time to put an end to all of this foolishness." —**Judy Garland**, March 6, 1967

"I'd like to explain myself a little. So much of the past that has been written about me, has been so completely, just 'authored': not even correct. . . . I think that the nicest thing to say is that I enjoy my work, that I'm a very happy woman, a very healthy woman, and that I look forward to my shows every night, and am having a marvelous life. I've had press agents that I've paid, to whom I've said 'Why don't they put that in a magazine?' And they've said 'No, they're not interested in that. That's not news. You have to do something terrible.' I don't believe you do. I think it might be awfully smashing news for people to find out that I'm a very contented, healthy, happy woman." —**Judy Garland**, August 1967

For much of the time that Judy was with us (nearly twelve days into her forty-seventh year), she was misunderstood. Her passing, and the years that have followed, have only improved the scenario somewhat. As an example of this, I am reminded of one of her many "comebacks" *after* she passed away, when she was the darling of the book publishing industry in 1975. One of the three major tomes released that year featured a cover photo of Judy in her most famous movie role. While I was looking through it in the store, a lad even younger than I said to his friend while pointing at my book—"Hey, it's Dorothy! . . . She killed herself, didn't she?" I had to suppress the urge to clobber him with the hefty, near–coffee-table size volume (well, it *was* a hardcover, and would have done a bit too much damage), until I quickly realized the kid had simply stated the two things everyone *thought* they knew about her.

Judy Garland was not about either of those two images. In actuality, she was one of the strongest, most aware, in-tune, intelligent, warmest, wittiest, wisest, sophisticated, and drop-dead funniest human beings. I realize this is not the image of Judy the world favors—preferring to see her as victim, instead of as the ultimate survivor—but anyone willing to do the research would find another Garland not usually spoken about. This Judy is the one who overcame one obstacle after another in order to spend the last forty-five of her forty-seven years sharing her gifts with the world. Working nearly non-stop, she produced a body of work perhaps unequaled in the entertainment industry: forty films; sixty TV shows; 100 single recordings and a dozen albums; several hundred radio shows; and easily 1,500 concert, nightclub, theatre, charity, military, and vaudeville performances.

To show the span of Judy's career (starting in the era of silent films, and ending at the time of 70mm stereo movies, color television, and man walking on the moon), one need only realize that Judy worked with everyone: from 1920s crooner Rudy Vallee to 1960s rocker Johnny Rivers; from 1930s singer Allan Jones to his son, singer Jack Jones, of "The Love Boat Theme" fame; and from legendary comedian Fanny Brice to today's superstar-legend who portrayed her on stage and screen, Barbra Streisand. That's an astounding body of work, and a length of time spent in a fleeting business, for a so-called "unreliable" performer. It might surprise many to realize that the longest period Judy did not work—other than before and after the three times she gave birth—was a six-month period in 1966–1967, and that was only due to tax problems with the IRS. Judy Garland *lived* to sing, as her daughter Lorna Luft once explained. It's easy to accept this statement, and to believe that her life was about her *art* and *not* her tribulations, when looking at her life closely.

This book presents that close look by presenting a record of Judy's existence on nearly a day-to-day basis. Yes, the hospitals and husbands are mentioned, but only in the context of her life and art, and not the other way around. It should become clear that, yes, the lady "lived" . . . but mostly . . . the woman *worked.* As we're looking at her life as it unfolded, we'll also get to read Judy's own thoughts from interviews she gave over the years, and also how contemporary critics—who often aren't respected unless they're ripping someone apart—fell all over themselves for nearly forty-five years to praise the gifts of France Ethel Gumm/Judy Garland—the gifts of incomparable Voice, Heart, and Soul—from 1924, until only three months before her passing in 1969.

As an added "bonus," there's a brief summary of the career highlights hit after her passing, as well as a recommendation for collecting on CDs and videos, her work . . . her Legacy . . . *THE LEGEND'S LEGACY.*

There is no doubt that due to this rich legacy of work she left the world, her impact will continue for all time. New generations keep watching *The Wizard of Oz*, fall in love with Dorothy, and want to see more of her. The world has recently changed and undergone several horrific tragedies. There are fewer things of which we can be certain. Yet, along with knowing that our country and the world will survive, it can also be stated as fact that, as the star of the one movie seen by more people than any other in movie history, Judy Garland will live forever.

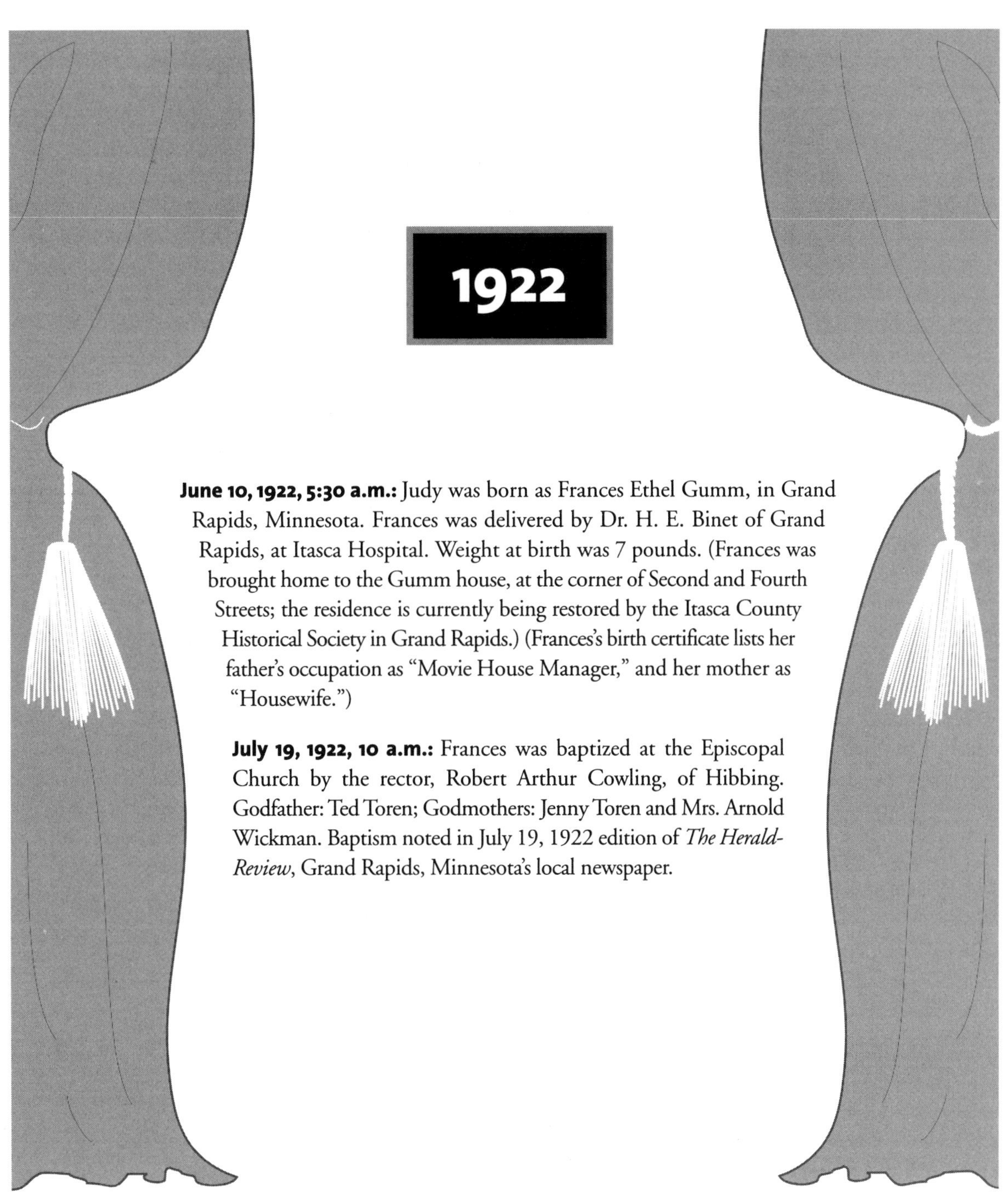

1922

June 10, 1922, 5:30 a.m.: Judy was born as Frances Ethel Gumm, in Grand Rapids, Minnesota. Frances was delivered by Dr. H. E. Binet of Grand Rapids, at Itasca Hospital. Weight at birth was 7 pounds. (Frances was brought home to the Gumm house, at the corner of Second and Fourth Streets; the residence is currently being restored by the Itasca County Historical Society in Grand Rapids.) (Frances's birth certificate lists her father's occupation as "Movie House Manager," and her mother as "Housewife.")

July 19, 1922, 10 a.m.: Frances was baptized at the Episcopal Church by the rector, Robert Arthur Cowling, of Hibbing. Godfather: Ted Toren; Godmothers: Jenny Toren and Mrs. Arnold Wickman. Baptism noted in July 19, 1922 edition of *The Herald-Review*, Grand Rapids, Minnesota's local newspaper.

1923

June 10, 1923: Frances's first birthday.

December 1923: Frances's first noted/known performance. At the age of only one-and-a-half, she sang "Jingle Bells" in her sister's neighborhood talent show.

No other performances noted for this year.

1924

Spring 1924: Mary Jane and Virginia Gumm (Frances's sisters) put on a circus in their garage. Frances was in the sideshow with another girl as Siamese twins. Later, Frances sang "Tie Me To Your Apron Strings Again."

May or June 1924: Frances's "formal" public-singing debut: Itasca Dry Goods Company, annual Style Show, Grand Rapids, Minnesota.

June 10, 1924: Frances's second birthday.

December 26, 1924: Frances's theatrical (and thus "official") stage debut, age two-and-a-half, at her father's movie house, "The New Grand Theater," in Grand Rapids, Minnesota, during the evening performance. (*The Grand Rapids Herald-Review* of December 24, 1924, had announced that the performance would feature "'Baby Frances, two years of age.") Frances's segment of the show opened with "When My Sugar Walks Down The Street," which she sang with her sisters (and would later film the number for the "Born In A Trunk" sequence of *A Star Is Born* in 1954; though the song would be cut from the film. The footage can be seen on the DVD of the film from Warner Home Video); Frances then performed a tap-dance routine (during a three-song segment by her sisters). Following this routine, Frances reappeared for her solo, "Jingle Bells," which she

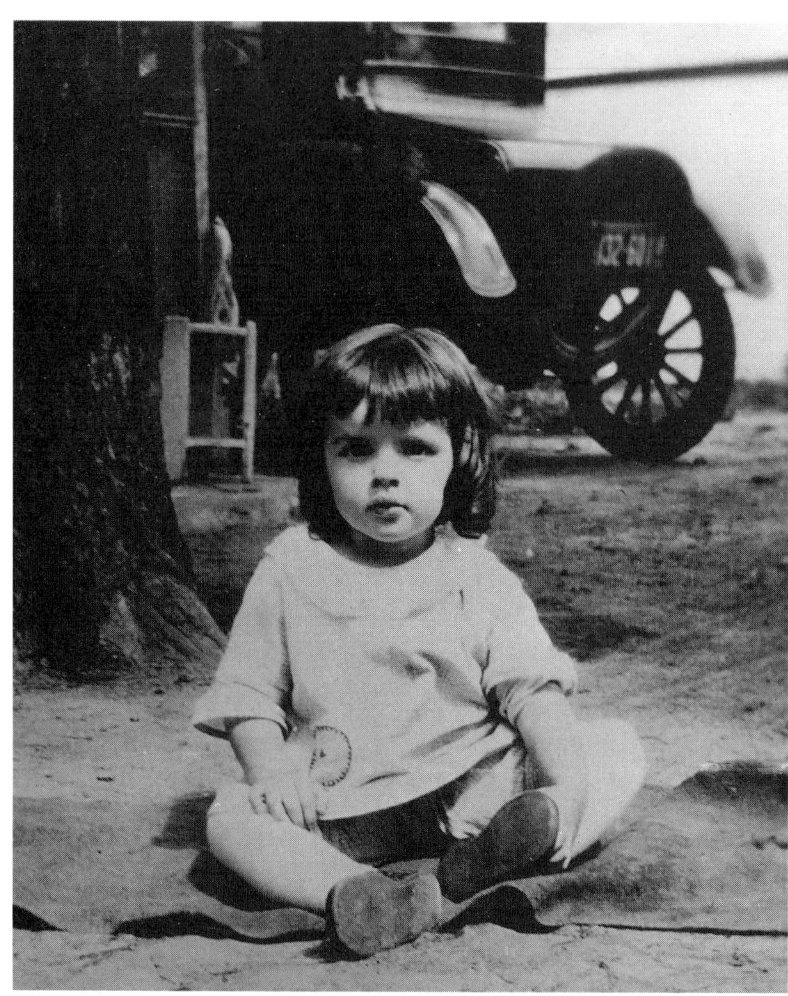

"There's no place like home." In her own backyard: Frances Ethel Gumm, Grand Rapids, Minnesota, 1924, age two. (Courtesy of Photofest.)

proceeded to sing several times, until her father carried her off-stage, still singing and ringing her little bell, to the audience's roar. (Even then she wanted to "Sing 'em all, and stay all night!") Back stage she exclaimed: "I wanna sing some more!"

December 31, 1924: Frances's first review was published, in *The Herald-Review* of Grand Rapids, Minnesota, covering her December 26 debut:

> *Herald-Review*: "Gumm Children Please" (Headline): "The three young daughters of Mr. And Mrs. Frank Gumm delighted a large audience at the New Grand theater last Friday night with 20 minutes of singing and dancing. . . . The work of Frances, the two-year-old baby, was a genuine surprise. The little girl spoke and sang so as to be heard by everyone in the house and she joined in the dancing both alone and with her older sisters. The audience expressed their appreciation of the work of all three girls by vigorous applause."

1925

January 3, 1925: "The Gumm Sisters" perform at a private party for Alice King, held at the home of W.C. Tyndall, Grand Rapids, Minnesota.

January 30, 1925: Frances interrupts an Amateur Night, at the New Grand Theater, by repeating her performance from the month before (Christmas Eve 1924)—singing chorus after chorus of "Jingle Bells." When she came on again at the finale of this show, the audience declared her the winner, though her father, as owner of the theater, would not allow her to accept the award.

March 7, 1925: "The Gumm Sisters" perform at a private birthday party for Laverne Mueller, at the Mueller home, Grand Rapids, Minnesota.

March 29, 1925: Frances's debut as a solo performer—two-and-three-quarters years old—New Grand Theater, Grand Rapids, Minnesota.

March 31, 1925 *or* April 1, 1925 (Both dates have been noted): Itasca Dry Goods Company show; Grand Rapids, Minnesota. Frances danced and modeled children's wear.

May 23, 1925: "The Gumm Sisters"; the New Grand Grand Rapids, Minnesota. (It is believed that the girls appeared in *The Kinky Kids Parade*, impersonating Al Jolson, in blackface.)

(Between 1924 and 1926, The Gumms would frequently appear in nearby towns such as Virginia, Hibbing, and Cohasset, as well as other theaters in Deer River, and Coleraine.)

June 7, 1925: "The Gumm Family" performed at a picnic at Pokegema Lake, Minnesota.

June 10, 1925: Frances's third birthday.

July 15, 1925: "The Gumm Sisters" performed at the Lyceum Theater, in Deer River, Minnesota. (This was Frances's first theatrical/legitimate professional performance outside of Grand Rapids, Minnesota, and most likely her first "paying" engagement, as her other "theater" appearances had all been at her father's "New Grand." It is at this point that one might consider Frances a "professional" performer, although it would still be some time before her family—her mother in particular—would pursue "the show business" for

Judy, with any real drive or planning. Although, according to her sisters, Judy knew at the age of two-and-a-half just what she wanted to be when she grew up: "the world greatest entertainer," naturally!)

August 20, 1925: "The Gumm Sisters" performed at a picnic at Pokegema Lake, Minnesota.

August 21, 1925: "The Gumm Sisters" performed at a party for Frances's sisters, Mary Jane and Virginia Gumm, held at the Gumm home, in Grand Rapids, Minnesota.

October 26, 1925: Frances performed at the Degree of Honor District Convention, Oddfellows Hall, Grand Rapids, Minnesota.

October 30, 1925: "The Gumm Sisters" performed at the First Annual Merchants Fall Festival, Legion Hall, Grand Rapids, Minnesota.

December 24, 1925 to December 26, 1925: "The Gumm Sisters" performed at the New Grand Theater, Grand Rapids, Minnesota.

January 1, 1926: "The Gumm Sisters" performed at the New Grand Theater, Grand Rapids, Minnesota.

January 9, 1926: "The Gumm Sisters" performed at the Garden Theater, Hibbing, Minnesota.

February 10, 1926: "The Gumm Sisters" performed at the Grand Rapids Women's Club Benefit for Permanent Boys and Girls Scout Camp Fund, held at the New Grand Theater, Grand Rapids, Minnesota.

February 22, 1926: "The Gumm Sisters" performed at the seventeenth anniversary of the Canisteo Lodge #271 and Washington's Birthday Dance, Masonic Order, Coleraine, Minnesota.

March 26, 1926: Frances appeared at the Second Annual Spring Style Show, held at the Itasca Dry Goods Store, Grand Rapids, Minnesota. (According to the review in *The Independent* newspaper, possibly written by her father Frank Gumm, Frances emerged from a large hatbox, and danced the Charleston.)

April 24, 1926: "The Gumm Sisters" sang at a Weiner and Marshmallow Roast, at the Big Spring, Grand Rapids, Minnesota.

April 30, 1926 to May 1, 1926: Frances performed with her entire family, under the stage name "Jack and Virginia Lee and Kiddies," the Garick Theater, Virginia, Minnesota.

May 13, 1926 to May 14, 1926: "The Gumm Sisters" performed between the two acts of the Annual Spring Play, *Adam and Eve*, at the Grand Rapids High School auditorium in Grand Rapids, Minnesota.

May 14, 1926: "The Gumm Sisters" performed at the New Grand Theater, Grand Rapids, Minnesota.

May 28, 1926 to May 29, 1926: Frances and her family did their stage act, "Jack and Virginia Lee and Kiddies," the Grand Theater, Bemidji, Minnesota.

June 8, 1926 to July 17, 1926: Gumm family working/vacation trip to California. (The Gumms played in the following towns along the way: Devil's Lake, North Dakota; Harve, Shelby, Whitefish, and Kalispell, Montana; Idaho; Cashmere and Leavenworth, Washington; then they vacationed in Seattle; Portland; and San Francisco before they continued their vacationing in Los Angeles. During what could be considered the first real "tour" of her career, Frances performed "In A Little Spanish Town," in Egyptian costume.) Engagements were as follows (note slight variations in the family's "billing"):

June 9, 1926: "Jack and Virginia and Three Little Lees," the Grand Theater, Devil's Lake, North Dakota. (This was Judy's first time on an actual stage *outside* her home town of Grand Rapids, Minnesota, one day before her fourth birthday.)

June 10, 1926: Frances' fourth birthday.

June 13, 1926: "Jack and Virginia Lee and Three Kiddies," the Lyric Theater, Harve, Montana

June 14, 1926: "Jack and Virginia Lee with Three Little Lees," the Liberty Theater, Shelby, Montana.

June 17, 1926: "Jack and Virginia Lee and Three Little Lees," the Liberty Theater, Kalispell, Montana.

June 18, 1926 to June 19, 1926: "Jack and Virginia Lee and Three Little Lees," the Orpheum Theater, Whitefish, Montana.

June 21, 1926: "Jack and Virginia Lee and The Three Little Lees," the Royal Theater, Cashmere, Washington.

June 22, 1926: "Jack and Virginia Lee and Three Kiddies," the Liberty Theater, Leavenworth, Washington.

July 10, 1926: Judy's first performance in California: the Earlanger's Mason Theater, Los Angeles, California. Special Saturday Afternoon Kiddies Matinee, at which "The Gumm Sisters" performed. (The theater was presenting the show *Topsy and Eva* starring the Duncan Sisters, the act that had inspired the Gumm Sisters. The Duncan Sisters were so impressed with the Gumms—especially Frances—that they insisted the family keep in touch with them.)

July 17, 1926: The Gumm family returned home to Grand Rapids, Minnesota.

July 25, 1926: Frances and her sisters performed at Kom-on-in Beach, at Trout Lake, Minnesota (by the campfire).

August 23, 1926: Frances and her sisters performed at a party for Mr. and Mrs. Harry Glyer, held at the Gumm home.

August 26, 1926: Frances and her sisters performed at a TaffyPull, given for Beverly Delaney, at the Gumm home.

August 28, 1926 to August 29, 1926: "The Three Little Gumm Girls" performed at the New Grand Theater, Grand Rapids, Minnesota.

September 4, 1926: "The Gumm Sisters" performed at the Farmers Club, Wendago, Minnesota.

October 3, 1926: Frances and her sisters performed at a dinner given for the Gumm family, at the home of Sadie Messer, Swan River, Minnesota.

October 4, 1926: "The Gumm Sisters" performed at the Annual District Convention, Grand Rapids, Minnesota.

October 8, 1926 to October 10, 1926: "The Gumm Family" performed together for the last time on the stage of their theater (as they decided to move to California), in "Gala Farewell Shows." (These would be Frances's last appearances on the first stage on which she had ever appeared).

October 13, 1926: "The Gumm Family" performed at a Costume Bridge Party held for the Gumm family, at the home of Mr. and Mrs. R.D. Burgess, Grand Rapids, Minnesota.

October 14, 1926: Frances and her sisters performed at the Episcopal Guild Church Dinner for the Gumm Family, Grand Rapids, Minnesota.

October 15, 1926: Frances and her sisters performed at a Halloween Bridge Party, held at the home of Mr. and Mrs. Gilbert, Grand Rapids, Minnesota.

October 17, 1926: "The Gumm Family" performed at a George O'Brien Dinner, Grand Rapids, Minnesota.

October 20, 1926: (Afternoon): Frances and her sisters performed at a party given in their honor by Carrie Mueller, at the Mueller home, Grand Rapids, Minnesota. (Evening): Frances and her sisters performed at a Bridge Dinner, held at the home of Mr. Hugh Logan, Grand Rapids, Minnesota.

October 21, 1926: "The Gumm Family" performed at a dinner held at the home of the Bassard Family, Grand Rapids, Minnesota.

October 24, 1926: "The Gumm Family" gave their last known performance in Grand Rapids, when they performed at a bridge party held at the home of the Powers Family.

October 27, 1926: Gumms leave Grand Rapids, Minnesota, to move to Los Angeles, California.

November 1926 to April 1927: The Gumms lived at 3154 Glen Manor, in the Atwater district of Los Angeles. During this time, "The Gumm Sisters" made an appearance at the Biltmore Hotel (earning 50 cents each), and joined the Meglin Kiddies (a.k.a. The Ethel Meglin Dance Studio/Booking Agency).

December 1926: Around Christmas, "The Gumm Sisters" were three of the "100 Clever Children in the Twinkletoe Kiddie Revue," at Loew's State on Broadway, in Los Angeles.

1927

February 26, 1927: "The Gumm Family" performed at The Order of the Eastern Star Annual Ball, Shrine Civic Auditorium, Los Angeles, California.

March 1927: The Gumm family moved to Lancaster, California, living at 1207 Cedar Street, in Newgrove. Their phone number was: Lancaster 1101. At this time, Frank bought and began managing the Lancaster Theater.

March 17, 1927: "The Gumm Sisters" performed at the Al Malaikah Temple Shrine Luncheon, The Biltmore Hotel, Los Angeles, California.

April 24, 1927: "The Gumm Family" performed at the Order of the Eastern Star Charity Ball, held at The Shrine Civic Auditorium, Los Angeles, California.

May 4, 1927: "The Gumm Sisters" performed at the Kiwanis Club Meeting, Biltmore Hotel, Los Angeles, California.

May 11, 1927: "The Gumm Family" performed at the All Souls Church Mississippi Flood Food Benefit, Wilshire Masonic Hall, Los Angeles, California.

May 21, 1927 and May 22, 1927: (matinee and 9 p.m.): The family's first performances at their new theater, "The New Lancaster Theater": "The Gumm Sisters" (Frank and Ethel are on the bill also) perform "Bye, Bye, Blackbird"; "When The Red, Red Robin Comes Bob, Bob, Bobbin' Along"; and "In A Little Spanish Town."

> The local newspaper the *Ledger-Gazette* stated: "The little daughters completely won the hearts of the audience with their songs and dances."

June 10, 1927: Frances's fifth birthday.

July 3, 1927 and July 4, 1927: "The Gumm Family", Lancaster Theater. The family sang "Rocky Mountain Moonlight," written by Ethel.

July 17, 1927: The first solo billing of "Frances Ethel Gumm," Lancaster Theater, Lancaster, California.

August 28, 1927 to August 29, 1927: "The Three Little Gumm Girls," the New Lancaster Theater, Lancaster, California.

October 9, 1927, *or* October 14, 1927: "The Gumm Family," Antelope Valley Fair, Lancaster.

October 22, 1927: "The Gumm Sisters" performed at the Los Angeles Express "Better Babies" Entry Party, Los Angeles, California.

November 22, 1927 to November 23, 1927: "The Gumm Sisters" performed at the Valley Theater (The new name for Frank Gumm's theater.)

December 2, 1927: "The Gumm Sisters," Valley Theater, Lancaster. Frances solos during the show (known as the "Kinky Kid Parade"), and includes her impression of Al Jolson singing "Mammy" while in blackface.

December 4, 1927 to December 5, 1927: "The Gumm Sisters," Valley Theater, Lancaster.

December 17, 1927: *Snow White and the Seven Dwarfs*, Lancaster Grammar School. (Frances played one of the dwarfs.)

December 25, 1927: "The Gumm Sisters," the Valley Theater.

1928

January 1, 1928 to January 2, 1928: "The Gumm Family" performed at their Valley Theater, Lancaster.

February 28, 1928 to February 29, 1928: The Lancaster Department Store Spring Style Show (a.k.a. Mrs. Wheeler's Dancing School Style Show), the Valley Theater, Lancaster, California. (Frances Ethel Gumm and Alberta Gustoff performed in the "Tin Soldier Dance.")

March 2, 1928: "The Gumm Family" performed at the cast party for *The First Year*, held at their home, Lancaster, California.

March 18, 1928 to March 19, 1928: "The Gumm Family" performed at their Valley Theater, Lancaster.

March 19, 1928: Frances and her sisters perform at a dinner for the Devine Family, held at the Gumm home, Lancaster.

March 23, 1928: "The Gumm Family" performed at their Valley Theater, Lancaster.

March 27, 1928: Frances and her sisters perform at a birthday party for their father, Frank Gumm, at the Gumm home in Lancaster.

April 13, 1928: Frances and her sisters perform at a party for Jerry and Dyna Valry, held at the Gumm family home in Lancaster.

May 2, 1928 to May 4, 1928: "The Gumm Family" perform at their Valley Theater, Lancaster.

May 12, 1928: "The Gumm Sisters" participate on a float in the Annual Health Parade, Lancaster, California.

May 29, 1928: Frances sings at a dinner held at the home of Joseph A. Martin.

June 3, 1928: "The Gumm Family" perform at the Antelope Valley Day Picnic, Frazier Mountain Park, California.

June 8, 1928: Frances's sixth birthday party, held at the Gumm home. "The Gumm Sisters" perform.

June 10, 1928: Frances's sixth birthday.

June 10, 1928 to June 11, 1928: "The Gumm Sisters" perform at their Valley Theater, Lancaster, California.

July 2, 1928: Frances and her sisters perform at Virginia Gumm's birthday party, held at the Gumm's home in Lancaster.

July 24, 1928: "Baby Frances Gumm" performed at The Kiwanis Club, Lancaster, California.

August 1928 to October 1928: KFI Radio, Los Angeles, *The Kiddies Hour* (a.k.a. *The Children's Hour*). Frances's radio debut, age six. Recordings from these shows are not known to exist. Songs included: "Avalon Town," "You're The Cream In My Coffee," and, for cowboy star William S. Hart, "There's A Long, Long Trail A-Winding" during a September broadcast. "The Gumm Sisters" performed on a regular basis. The show later moved to KNX.

> The Lancaster newspaper *The Ledger-Gazette* reported on the radio debut in the August 17 issue: "Lancaster was again featured in Radioland, when the three little Gumm sisters broadcasted over KFI during *The Kiddies Hour*. Local listeners report that their numbers went over very well, and that the announcer publicly complimented them very highly. Big Brother Ken was so pleased with the performance that he has asked them to put on the entire hour program next Wednesday, beginning at five p.m."

August 26, 1928 to August 27, 1928: "The Gumm Sisters" performed at their Valley Theatre, Lancaster.

August 27, 1928: "The Gumm Family" performed at the Kiwanis Division meeting, held at the Lancaster High School Auditorium, Lancaster.

September 14, 1928: "The Gumm Sisters" performed at their Valley Theater, Lancaster.

September 18, 1928: "The Gumm Sisters" performed with "The Meglin Kiddies" at the Ladies Aid Charity Fete, at the Pickfair, Beverly Hills, California.

September 21, 1928: Frances and her sisters performed at an after theater party, held at the home of S. H. Savage.

September 24, 1928: Frances and her sisters performed at Mary Jane Gumm's thirteenth birthday party, held at the Gumm home, Lancaster.

September 28, 1928: "The Gumm Sisters" (with "The Meglin Kiddies"), Montebello Community Center.

October 12, 1928: "The Gumm Sisters" (with "The Meglin Kiddies"), The Los Angeles General Children's Hospital Ward; Los Angeles, California.

October 15, 1928: Frances and her sisters perform at a farewell party for A.R. Freeman, held at the Gumm home, Lancaster, California.

October 28, 1928: "The Gumm Sisters" with "The Meglin Kiddies" perform at the "Los Angeles Kiddie Coop" Fund Breakfast Club Luncheon Benefit; the Breakfast Club, Los Angeles, California. (There were 76 numbers featuring 300 pupils.)

November 4, 1928: Frances and her sisters performed at a dinner for "The Gumm Family", held at the home of Charles Geary, Lancaster.

November 4, 1928 to November 5, 1928: "The Gumm Sisters" performed at their Valley Theater, Lancaster, California.

November 21, 1928: "The Gumm Sisters," Kiwanis Club Lunch, I.O.O.F. Hall, Lancaster, California.

December 1, 1928: "The Gumm Sisters" with "The Meglin Kiddies" performed at the Los Angeles General Hospital Children's Ward, Los Angeles, California.

December 13, 1928: The Shrine Auditorium, Los Angeles, California. *The Los Angeles Examiner's All-Star Christmas Benefit.* Stars included Joan Crawford, Myrna Loy, Tom Mix, Dolores Del Rio, and the "100 Meglin Kiddies," (including Frances) who performed for the near-capacity crowd of 6,500.

Friday, December 21, 1928 to Thursday, December 27, 1928: Loew's State Theater, Los Angeles, California. Christmas Show, with 115 Meglin Kiddies pupils: Frances appeared as Cupid, stopping the show with "I Can't Give You Anything But Love, Baby."

> *The Los Angeles Record* stated: "We have no names with which to lay tribute to. One small miss shook these well-known rafters with her songs a la Sophie Tucker."

December 30, 1928 to December 31, 1928: "The Gumm Sisters" recreated their Loew's State Theater routines on the stage of their Valley Theater, Lancaster, California.

1929

January 2, 1929: Frances and her sisters performed at a New Year's Celebration Party, held at the Gumm home in Lancaster.

January 23, 1929: "The Gumm Sisters" performed with "The Meglin Kiddies" (75 pupils in all) at the Old Soldier's Home, Sawtelle, California.

February 13, 1929: Kiwanians Association Club Meeting; Kiwanis Hall, Lancaster, California. Frances delighted the audience with an impression of Fanny Brice (and performed with her sisters.)

February 28, 1929: Grammar school, Lancaster. *Cinderella in Flowerland.* Frances played "Bonnie Bee" (Her sister Virginia played title role, and her other sister Mary Jane played the Prince.)

February 29, 1929: *The Los Angeles Evening Express* newspaper's seventh annual "Better Babies Exposition/Contest"; Broadway Department Store, Los Angeles. "Baby Frances Ethel Gumm" won twelfth runner up, and honorable mention in the talent contest, winning a $10.00 gift certificate from the Broadway Department Store.

March 1, 1929: *The Ledger-Gazette* announces that

> "Mrs. Frank Gumm and daughters leave next week for Los Angeles where they will reside indefinitely in order that the girls may pursue special studies. They will spend their weekends in Lancaster, Mrs. Gumm furnishing the music at the theater. Mr. Gumm will continue to reside at the family home on Cedar Avenue."

(Frances, her mother and sisters, moved into an upstairs apartment at 1814 1/2 South Orchard, near Washington Boulevard and Vermont Avenue, near the downtown Los Angeles theatrical district.)

March 21, 1929 to March 27, 1929: Meglin Kiddies recital (30 pupils, including "The Gumm Sisters."); Grauman's Egyptian Theater, Los Angeles.

April 1, 1929: "The Gumm Sisters" with "The Meglin Kiddies"; Screen Stars Gambol: Benefit for Loyola University; Shrine Auditorium, Los Angeles, California.

April 7, 1929: Meglin Kiddies Revue, Figueroa Playhouse; Los Angeles, California. "The Gumm Sisters" performed, and the show also included solos by Frances.

May 12, 1929: Performance at the Valley Theater, Lancaster, California.

May 16, 1929 and May 17, 1929, 8:00 p.m.: Second Annual Minstrel Show, the Valley Theater, Lancaster, California. "Gumm Family/Gumm Sisters." Songs included: "When We Turn Out The Home Town Band"; "Old Man River"(sung by "The Gumm Sisters" in blackface); and "Hello Sunshine" (finale, with entire Company.)

Early June 1929: "The Gumm Sisters" with "The Meglin Kiddies"; The Annual Milk Fund; Shrine Auditorium, Los Angeles, California.

June 9, 1929 and June 10, 1929: "The Gumm Sisters" at the Valley Theater, Lancaster, California. (Reprise of the May 16 and May 17 Minstrel Show).

June 10, 1929: Frances's seventh birthday.

June 11, 1929 through June 13, 1929: Judy Garland's Film Debut; Frances's first time in front of a movie camera. "The Gumm Sisters" sang "That's The Good Old Sunny South," performing "live" (no pre-recording), in the two-reel short, *The Big Revue.* This was a Mayfair Pictures, Inc. production, filmed at the Tec-Art Studios in Hollywood. The eighteen-minute, two-reel short premiered at the Fox Belmont Theater in Hollywood, on August 14, 1929. This film still exists—"The Gumm Sisters" song is available in excerpted form on *The Concert Years* video cassette on the LaserLight label; and is available in its entirety on the laser disc box set: *Judy Garland: The Golden Years At MGM* released in March 1995. Seeing and hearing a just-turned seven year-old Judy Garland—a.k.a. Frances Gumm—who clearly has "it" even at that age, certainly makes one grateful for the somewhat recent invention of sound film.

June 25, 1929: "The Gumm Sisters" with "The Meglin Kiddies"; Elks Lodge; Ventura, California.

July 15, 1929: "The Three Gumm Sisters"; the Lone Pine Theater, Lone Pine, California.

July 16, 1929 and July 17, 1929: "The Three Gumm Sisters"; The Bishop Theater, Bishop, California (400-seat capacity). An ad for this engagement shows a photo of the girls in their movie debut costumes, and says "Extra Added Attraction . . . The Three Gumm Sisters (*in Person*). Now with the famous Meglin Kiddies of Los Angeles, and available only during vacation times, will appear in *Harmony Songs, Tap, and Acrobatic Dances*." (The ad also stated "A Guaranteed Attraction. . . . On the same bill with Metro-Goldwyn-Mayer's 6-reel feature picture *A Single Man*, starring Aileen Pringle and Lew Cody. Also two-reel comedy *Thundering Tupees* and MGM oddity *The Persian Wedding*.") The sisters performed their current act, which included: "That's The Good Old Sunny South" from *The Big Revue* film, and Frances did an impression of Ted Lewis, singing "Wear A Hat With A Silver Lining," and "Little Pal." Frances received her first individual praise, from the local newspaper: "All do so well in their specialties that the discrimination of special mention is hardly just: but the remarkable work of Baby Frances particularly appeals to hearers because of her diminutive size and few years."

July 21, 1929: "The Gumm Sisters"; Elks Lodge; San Fernando, California.

July 24, 1929: "Baby Frances Gumm"; Kiwanis Club Meeting; Kiwanis Hall, Lancaster, California.

July 28, 1929: Frances (with Eugene Taylor), Valley Theater, Lancaster. (The Lancaster paper stated ".... The kiddies sang and danced exceptionally well, and created a riot with the audience when they finished their skit with the 'bowery number.' ")

August 14, 1929: Movie premiere of Judy Garland's film debut, *The Big Revue*, held at the Fox Belmont Theater, Hollywood, California. (Eighteen-minute, two-reel short.)

August 15, 1929 to August 21, 1929: Meglin Kiddies "56 Clever Tots," and Stephen Fetchit (the Headliner), in Fannchon and Marco Show; Loew's State Theater, Los Angeles, California. ("The Gumm Sisters" were featured, but received no special notice.)

August 25, 1929 to August 26, 1929: "The Gumm Sisters"; the Valley Theater, Lancaster, California.

Fall 1929: "The Three Gumm Sisters" audition for Gus Edwards at MGM Studios.

September 24, 1929: "The Gumm Sisters" perform at PTA Meeting; Lancaster, California.

September 30, 1929: "The Three Gumm Sisters"; Kiwanis Club; Lancaster, California.

October 6, 1929: "The Gumm Sisters" with "The Meglin Kiddies"; Benefit for The Knights of Columbus; Covin, California.

October 19, 1929: (*Afternoon*) Frances; Jazz Cafe; Lancaster, California (Frances sings a song at reopening of candy shop). (*Evening*) Frances and Virginia; Haubrich's Department Store (opening of new music department); Lancaster, California (Frances and Virginia sang three songs). (Ethel Gumm played the piano, and *The Ledger-Gazette* reported that "a drawing of coupons for prizes was presided over by W. S. Mumaw, Baby Gumm assisting and winning the first prize.")

November 8, 1929: *The Ledger-Gazette Newspaper* (Lancaster, California) announced that "The Gumm Sisters" were in Los Angeles, rehearsing with an organization known as "The Hollywood Starlets," run by Flynn O'Malley. (The announcement also stated that Judy's father was installing RCA Photophone sound equipment in his Valley Theater).

November 11, 1929: "The Gumm Sisters" performed at the American Legion Armistice Day.

November 1929 to December 1929: (Radio) *Big Brother Ken's Kiddie Hour* Radio Show; KNX (or KFI) Radio, Los Angeles, California (Monday afternoons). The girls did special Christmas shows with Big Brother Ken, where the Gumm sisters used their new name, "The Hollywood Starlets Trio." It's understandable why the girls would be willing to change their name: O'Malley's "Starlets" got them a flurry of work, in a brief period, ranging from the ridiculous—a department store appearance—to the sublime—three more movie shorts.

On the set of one of her first films, *The Wedding of Jack and Jill,* filmed November–December 1929. Frances (far left, in the balloon-pants and feather-cap "Arabian Nights" costume), age seven, had a solo with an incredible title: "Hang Onto A Rainbow." (Courtesy of Photofest.)

November 16, 1929: "Big Brother Ken's Toyland Revue": Grand Opening of the Toy Department at Walker's Department Store, Los Angeles, California ("The Gumm Sisters" performed: billed here in error as "The *Gunn* Sisters.")

November 1929 to December 1929: (Films) Judy and her sisters filmed three movie shorts with "The Vitaphone Kiddies" for "Vitaphone Varieties," a subsidiary of Warner Brothers. These were filmed at First National Studios (Vitaphone), in Burbank, California, in two-color Technicolor. The first—*A Holiday in Storyland*—found "The Gumm Sisters" singing "When The Butterflies Kiss The Buttercups Goodbye" (as "The 3 Kute Kiddies"), and Baby Frances (Judy) has her *first screen solo*: "Blue Butterfly." In the second film—*The Wedding of Jack and Jill*—Baby Gumm solos on "Hang Onto A Rainbow." In the third short—*Bubbles* (filmed in December 1929)—"The Gumm Sisters" sing the first number of the film's dream sequence: "The Land Of Let's Pretend," dressed as moonmaidens (Judy has two solo lines, during which she is given a close-up); thereafter, they are merely seen in the background. (The soundtrack portion only of the first two films still exist; *both* audio and film exist of the last short, in a black and white print, found at The Library Of Congress—All of this surviving material is available on the *Judy Garland: The Golden Years at MGM* laser disc box set, released by MGM/UA Home Video, in March 1995. Excerpts from these songs were also included in the four-CD box set from 32 Records, called *JUDY*, released on October 13, 1998.)

November 19, 1929: "Baby Gumm"; "Book Week Pageant"; Lancaster High School Auditorium, Lancaster, California.

November 23, 1929: "Big Brother Ken's Toyland Revue"; Walker's Department Store, Los Angeles, California.; "The Gumm Sisters."

November 24, 1929: "The Gumm Sisters"—under their current new name "Hollywood Starlets Trio"—performed at their Valley Theater, Lancaster, California. (Frances sang "Wear A Hat With A Silver Lining.")

November 30, 1929: "Big Brother Ken's Toyland Revue"; Walker's Department Store; Los Angeles, California.; "The Gumm Sisters."

Early December 1929: (Film Showing) *The Big Revue*, Judy's film debut, was shown at a Warner Brothers theater, in Los Angeles, California.

December 4, 1929: "The Gumm Sisters"; Kiwanis Organization Dinner.

December 6, 1929: Frances and her sisters performed at a joint Spelling Bee and Kiwanis Meeting; Lancaster High School, Lancaster, California.

December 7, 1929: "Big Brother Ken's Toyland Revue"; Walker's Department Store, Los Angeles, California.; "The Gumm Sisters."

December 8, 1929: "The Gumm Sisters"; American Legion Post; Filmore, California.

December 13, 1929: "The Gumm Sisters"; American Legion Organization; Filmore, California.

December 21, 1929 to December 27, 1929: "The Hollywood Starlets Trio" (a.k.a. "The Gumm Sisters"); State Theater, Long Beach, California.

December 22, 1929: "The Gumm Family"; The Munz Country Club; Antelope Valley, California.

December 23, 1929: "The Hollywood Starlets Trio" (a.k.a. "The Gumm Sisters"); Annual Christmas Dinner Dance; The Los Angeles Country Club; Beverly Hills, California (Christmas Entertainment).

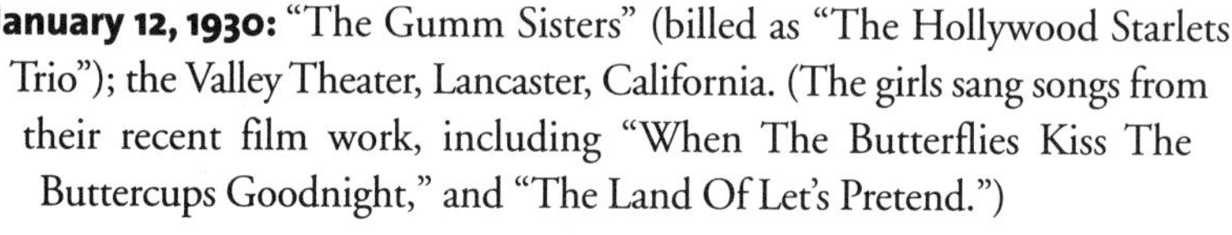

1930

January 12, 1930: "The Gumm Sisters" (billed as "The Hollywood Starlets Trio"); the Valley Theater, Lancaster, California. (The girls sang songs from their recent film work, including "When The Butterflies Kiss The Buttercups Goodnight," and "The Land Of Let's Pretend.")

January 13, 1930: (Radio) "The Gumm Sisters"; *Big Brother Ken* appearances continued, over KNX Radio; Los Angeles, California (appearances continued on following Mondays).

February 7, 1930: "The Hollywood Starlets Trio" ("The Gumm Sisters"); PTA Benefit; Burbank High School; Burbank, California.

February 28, 1930: Baby Frances and Mary Jane Gumm; *The Gypsy Rover* High School Operetta; Lancaster High School; Lancaster, California. (Frances appeared as one of the "little children," and during one scene, as the children climbed up into the lap of "Sir Toby Lyon," Frances fell down; and to the delight of the audience, climbed right up again . . . as she would be doing the rest of her life.)

March 4, 1930: "Eighth Annual Los Angeles Evening Express 'Better Babies' Exposition," held this year at Paramount Studios, Hollywood, California. "Baby Frances Ethel Gumm" (Judy) was named "Second Place Winner," and won a porcelain doll from Mary Pickford. Also included in the contest was an audition for studio chief B. P. Schulberg. (Another report on this event states that Frances was only one of fifty finalists, but didn't even win a merchandise certificate this time out.)

March 7, 1930: *Goldilocks*, Grammar School Operetta/School Play; Frances plays the lead, Virginia plays "the Wood God"; Lancaster Grammar School; Lancaster, California.

March 15, 1930: Frances participated in the "Children's Fashion Revue," at Walker's Department Store; Lancaster, California.

March 17, 1930: "The Gumm Family" performed for their guests at a St. Patrick's Day Party, held at their home, Lancaster, California.

March 26, 1930: Frances won first prize in two events that were tied in with Jean Rutledge's eleventh birthday in Lancaster: a Recitation Program, and Easter Egg Hunt (Frances's prize in the latter was for finding the most Easter eggs.)

March 28, 1930: "The Gumm Sisters" performed for the Knights of Pythius (most likely in Lancaster, California).

March 31, 1930: "The Gumm Sisters" participated in Mrs. May Burk's Music Pupil's Recital at the Lancaster High School auditorium; Lancaster, California.

April 1930: (Movie Premiere) Movie premiere of "The Gumm Sisters," *A Holiday in Storyland*; Warner's Downtown and Hollywood Theaters; Los Angeles, California.

April 18, 1930: "The Gumm Sisters" performed at the Knights of Pythius District Convention.

April 23, 1930: Frances and her sisters performed at the "Third Annual Antelope Valley Jubilee," held at the Lancaster High School auditorium; Lancaster, California.

May 2, 1930: "The Gumm Sisters" performed at their Valley Theater, Lancaster, California.

May 9 1930 to May 10, 1930: "The Gumm Sisters" film, *A Holiday in Storyland,* was shown at the Valley Theater, Lancaster, California; They also performed in support of the film. This was the first known screening of a Gumm Sisters/Judy film at Frank Gumm's own movie theater: his theater hadn't been equipped with sound until February 16, 1930; One can only imagine Mr. Gumm's joy as he got to see his daughter's sing on screen "When The Butterflies Kiss The Buttercup Goodnight" and Frances's—Judy's—first film solo "Blue Butterfly," at his very own theater. This was certainly one film that must have been played over and over by Frank during those two days, as well as being difficult to return to the film company.

May 16, 1930: (*Morning*): "The Gumm Sisters" performed at "Big Brother Frolic" sponsored by Big Brother Ken, held at Walker Department Store, Los Angeles, California.; (*Evening*): Episcopal ProCathedral Annual Service, Los Angeles; Frances Gumm was there as a delegate from St. Paul's Church of Lancaster, California.

May 20, 1930: Frances and her sisters performed at the Easter Star "Sunshine Chapter" sixteenth birthday held at Masonic Hall; Lancaster, California.

May 22, 1930: Frances; Piano Class Recital of Mrs. J. C. Shapland; Lancaster High School; Lancaster, California (Frances was mistress of ceremonies, then at the close of show sang a ballad and did a dance.)

May 24, 1930: "The Hollywood Starlets Trio" ("The Gumm Sisters") performed at the Annual Milk Fund Benefit at the Shrine Auditorium; Los Angeles, California.

June 10, 1930: Frances's eighth birthday was celebrated at the Lancaster High School "plunge," and it was reported she received "many lovely gifts."

June 21, 1930: "The Gumm Sisters" appeared at the "Big Brother Frolic," sponsored by Big Brother Ken; Walker's Department Store; Los Angeles, California.

June 28, 1930: "The Hollywood Starlets Trio" ("The Gumm Sisters") performed in San Fernando, California.

July 4, 1930 *or* July 5, 1930: "The Hollywood Starlets Trio" ("The Gumm Sisters"); Hotel Del Coronado; San Diego, California.

> *The San Diego News* called the girls "the highlight of a (Hollywood Starlets) presentation. Their smallest member is a feisty little miss who also sang solo in a surprisingly powerful voice and all but stopped the show."

July 17, 1930 to July 23, 1930: (Vaudeville) "The Hollywood Starlets Trio" ("The Gumm Sisters"); Million Dollar Theater, Los Angeles, California.

July 23, 1930: Frances performed at a patio party held for her at the Fine Foods Cafe; Hollywood, California.

August 1, 1930 to August 2, 1930: "The Gumm Sisters" film, *The Wedding of Jack and Jill*, was shown at the Valley Theater (Frank Gumm's Theater); Lancaster, California. "The Gumm Sisters" performed on stage, in support of the film, and Judy's father got to see and hear his daughter sing her solo "Hang Onto A Rainbow" on the big screen.

August 5, 1930: (*Afternoon*): "Baby Gumm" (Judy) performed at a party for Paula Orlo; Blossom Room, Hotel Roosevelt, Los Angeles, California; (*Evening*): Elks Anniversary Show; Elks Hall, San Fernando, California.

August 14, 1930 to August 20, 1930: (Vaudeville) "The Hollywood Starlets Trio" ("The Gumm Sisters"); Million Dollar Theater, Los Angeles, California.

August 21, 1930 to August 27, 1930: (Vaudeville) "The Gumm Sisters"/"Hollywood Starlets" in a Fanchon and Marco Show; Loew's State Theater, Los Angeles, California.

Or August 23, 1930 to August 29, 1930: "The Hollywood Starlets Trio" at the State Theater, Long Beach, California. (Alternate engagements have been noted for these dates.)

September 13, 1930: "The Gumm Sisters" performed at a Big Brother Ken Show; Pantages Theater, Los Angeles, California.

September 20, 1930: "The Gumm Sisters" performed at a Big Brother Ken Show; Pantages Theater, Los Angeles, California.

September 23, 1930: "The Gumm Sisters" performed for the American Legion.

September 27, 1930: "The Gumm Sisters" performed at a Big Brother Ken Show; Pantages Theater, Los Angeles, California.

October 4, 1930: "The Gumm Sisters" performed at a Big Brother Ken Show; Pantages Theater, Los Angeles, California.

October 11, 1930: "The Gumm Sisters" performed at a Big Brother Ken Show; Pantages Theater, Los Angeles, California.

October 12, 1930: "The Gumm Sisters" performed at an Antelope Valley Band Concert, "Pioneer Day"; San Bernadino, California.

October 27, 1930: "The Gumm Family"; Kiwanis Organization: Kiwanis Inter-Club Relationship Meeting; Beacon Tavern, Victorville; Barstow, California. (Gumm Sisters, with Kiwanis Quartet—and Frank—sing with band; Ethel Gumm may have performed also.)

November 8, 1930: "The Gumm Sisters" performed at a Big Brother Ken Show; Walker's Department Store; Los Angeles, California.

November 14, 1930: "The Gumm Sisters"; *The Old Sleuth* (a school play); Lancaster Grammar School; Lancaster, California. (The sisters sang "My Baby Comes For Me," between the acts of the play).

November 15, 1930: "The Gumm Sisters" performed at a *Big Brother Ken* show; Walker's Department Store; Los Angeles, California.

November 21, 1930: "The Gumm Sisters" performed at a *Big Brother Ken* show; Walker's Department Store; Los Angeles, California.

November 28, 1930: "The Gumm Sisters" performed at a *Big Brother Ken* show.

December 19, 1930: "The Gumm Sisters" performed at the Hollywood Dance Studio Christmas Follies; Old Soldiers' Home, Sawtelle, California.

1931

January 10, 1931: "The Gumm Sisters" performed at the opening of Big Brother Ken's Dance Studio.

January 11, 1931 to January 12, 1931: "The Three Gumm Sisters" performed at the Valley Theater, Lancaster, California. (A theater ad mentions the girl's "harmony songs and dance numbers.")

January 17, 1931: (Vaudeville) "The Gumm Sisters" with "The Meglin Kiddies"; Pantages Theater, Los Angeles, California.

January 24, 1931: (Vaudeville) "The Gumm Sisters" with "The Meglin Kiddies"; Pantages Theater, Los Angeles, California.

January 31, 1931: (Vaudeville) "The Gumm Sisters" / "The Meglin Kiddies'; Pantages Theater, Los Angeles, California (Saturday matinee; last appearance with the Meglin organization). Also on the same afternoon: (Radio) "The Gumm Sisters"; KFVD Radio; Hollywood, California (afternoon broadcast at the Hal Roach Studio).

February 1931: (Vaudeville) "The Hollywood Starlets Trio" ("The Gumm Sisters"); Savoy Theater, San Diego, California.

February 18, 1931 *or* February 21, 1931: (Benefit) "The Hollywood Starlets Trio" ("The Gumm Sisters"); *either* the Savoy Theater *or* the Russ Auditorium; San Diego, California (midnight matinee for the Red Cross Drought Relief Fund).

March 21, 1931: Blue Gate Cottage Benefit: Big Brother Ken Junior Matinee; Fox Wilshire Theater, Beverly Hills, California.

March 24, 1931 to March 25, 1931: "The Gumm Sisters" performed at the Farmer's Institute Meeting, held at the Lancaster Grammar School, Lancaster, California.

March 30, 1931: "The Gumm Sisters" performed for the Kiwanis Club, Kiwanis Hall, Lancaster, California.

April 1, 1931 to April 2, 1931: "The Gumm Family"; Agricultural conference; Union Hall, Lancaster, California.

(Judy's early boyfriends in Lancaster at this time included: Eddie White; Buddy Welch; and Gayland Reed, remembered as Judy's "first love.")

April 3, 1931: "The Gumm Sisters" performed at Kiwanis Club Meeting, Kiwanis Hall, Lancaster, California.

May 1 or 3, 1931: "The Gumm Sisters featuring Babe Gumm" had an audition for Universal Pictures and Carl Laemmle, at the Hollywood Dance Studio.

May 10, 1931: "The Gumm Sisters" performed at the Auxiliary American Legion Show, at the Veteran's Hospital; San Fernando, California.

May 15, 1931: *In a Florist's Windows* and *The Magic Wood* Grammar School Operettas; Lancaster Grammar School Auditorium; Lancaster, California. (Frances Gumm played "Fairie Sunbeam.")

June 10, 1931: Frances's ninth birthday.

June 12, 1931: Frances's ninth birthday party held on the lawn of the Gumm family's new, larger house, on the corner of Cedar and Newgrove.

July 10, 1931 to July 17, 1931: (Vaudeville) "The Gumm Sisters"; Maurice Kusell's "Stars of Tomorrow" juvenile revue; Wilshire-Ebell Theater, Los Angeles, California. ("The Gumm Sisters" were featured in three song and dance numbers including "Puttin' On The Ritz" where they played "Harlem Crooners," "Garden Of Beautiful Flowers," in which they played "gardenettes," and "Floatin' Down The Mississippi." Frances was also featured in two solos, and was teamed with Miss Betty Jean Allen for "A Plantation Melody"; the show's eight-piece orchestra was under direction of Ethel Gumm. After the show, Judy and her sisters sang at the opening night party at director James Cruze. Maurice Kussell introduced them to George Frank of the Frank and Dunlap Talent Agency—James Cagney was a client—who signed Frances as the agency's first child performer. The five-year contract was for stage, screen, radio, and even television. She was also renamed "Frances Gayne." The "option clause" was exercised shortly after, and "Frances Gayne" was released, after her father thought her "too young.")

August 15, 1931: Frances (Judy) had an audition at Universal Studios, Universal City, California.

August 30, 1931 to August 31, 1931: Frances appeared at her father's Valley Theater, Lancaster, California.

September 4, 1931: (Press Release) *The Ledger-Gazette* of Lancaster announced Frances's contract signing with the Frank and Dunlap Talent agency, and that she would appear:

September 6, 1931 to Monday, September 7, 1931: Valley Theater, Lancaster, California; Frances (using her temporary new name of "Gayne") in "a group of song specialties."

September 15, 1931: Frances; PTA event; Lancaster High School Auditorium; Lancaster, California. (A newspaper account: "Little Frances Gumm captivated the audience with her two lively songs.")

September 20, 1931: Frances; Valley Theater, Lancaster, California. ("Frances Gumm will appear again in a group of popular song numbers, Sunday afternoon at 4, and in the evening at 9:30.")

October 3, 1931: (Personal Appearance) Frances performed at the Eastern Star State Chapter Conclave; Bakersfield, California. (Billing was either "Francis Gayne" or "Baby Marie Gumm.")

October 5, 1931: (Personal Appearance) Frances and Frank Gumm; Eastern Star Sunshine Chapter Banquet; Order of the Eastern Star Lodge; Tehachapi, California. (Frances sang "For You, For You"; billing was either "Francis Gumm" or "Baby Marie Gumm.")

October 6, 1931: (Personal Appearance) Frances and Frank Gumm; Order of the Eastern Star Lodge; Bakersfield, California (Frances sang "Sweet And Lovely" before 1,000 people.)

October 14, 1931: (Personal Appearance) "Baby Marie Gumm" (Judy) performed at American Legion; Hollywood, California.

October 23, 1931: (Personal Appearance) "Frances Gayne" (Judy) performed at the Eastern Star State Grand Chapter Banquet; Coronado, California.

November 20, 1931: "The Gumm Sisters" performed at Maurice L. Kusell's Pupil Recital; Old Soldier's Home; Sawtelle, California.

November 22, 1931: "The Gumm Sisters" performed at Maurice L. Kusell's Pupil Recital; American Legion Post; Covina, California.

November 30, 1931: "Baby Gumm" performed at Knights of Columbus.

December 12, 1931 *or* December 21, 1931: Frances and Ethel; Eastern Star Sunshine Chapter Meeting; Eastern Star Lodge; Lancaster, California.

December 16, 1931: Frances performed at the Kiwanis Club Meeting; I.O.O.F. Hall, Lancaster, California.

December 24, 1931 to December 30, 1931: (Vaudeville) Frances; *Maurice L. Kusell's All Star Kiddie Revue*; Warner Brothers Downtown Hollywood Theater, Hollywood, California ("Little singer at Hollywood Theater," with Jess Stafford's orchestra, in Christmas Show.)

December 30, 1931: (Personal Appearance, at midnight) "The Gumm Sisters" performed at the California Protective Artists Association Benefit for Unemployed; Shrine Auditorium; Los Angeles, California.

December 31, 1931: "The Gumm Family" performed at the Elks New Years Eve Ball; San Fernando, California.

1932

January 23 or 25, 1932: Frances; Coconut Grove, Ambassador Hotel nightclub; Los Angeles, California (impromptu appearance at "Tea Dance"; with Jimmie Grier and his Orchestra.)

January 28, 1932: Frances and Mary Jane Gumm performed for the Kiwanis Club at Kiwanis Hall, Lancaster, California.

February 16, 1932: "The Gumm Sisters" performed at Five Friends Plan Dance; Fox Film Studios; Los Angeles, California.

March 19, 1932 *or* March 21, 1932: Frances; Coconut Grove "Tea Dance", Ambassador Hotel nightclub; Los Angeles, California (with Jimmie Grier and his Orchestra).

April 10, 1932: Frances; Talent Show; Lancaster High School; Lancaster, California.

April 15, 1932: "Baby Gumm" with "Bob Weir and His Bandits"; General Aid Society; High School Auditorium; Lancaster, California.

April 17, 1932 to April 18, 1932: Frances; Valley Theater, Lancaster, California.

April 24, 1932 to April 25, 1932: Frances; Valley Theater, Lancaster, California.

April 30, 1932: "The Gumm Sisters"; Maurice L. Kusell's Benefit for the Jewish Educational Fund; Philharmonic Auditorium, Los Angeles, California.

May 1, 1932 to May 2, 1932: Frances; Valley Theater, Lancaster, California.

May 21, 1932: Frances; Annual May Musicale of the PTA; Lancaster High School Auditorium; Lancaster, California. (Frances sang "Only God Can Make A Tree" and "Cherie.")

May 22, 1932 to May 23, 1932: Frances and her sisters sang at their father's Valley Theater, Lancaster, California.

May 24, 1932: "The Gumm Sisters" performed for *The Los Angeles Examiner* Cooking School/Prudence Penny Tuesday Cooking Matinee at the Barker Brothers Department Store, Los Angeles, California.

May 29, 1932 to May 30, 1932: "Baby Gumm" (Judy) and Galen Reed performed at the Valley Theater, Lancaster, California. (Galen was reportedly Judy's "first love.")

June 10, 1932: Frances's tenth birthday.

June 14, 1932: "The Gumm Sisters"; Benefit for Unemployed; Shrine Auditorium, Los Angeles, California.

Vaudeville Tour (under management of Fanchon and Marco), summer tour of twelve theaters; Gumm Sisters:

July 7, 1932 or July 8, 1932 to July 10, 1932: "The Gumm Sisters"; Orange Theater, Orange, California.

July 11, 1932 to July 13, 1932: "The Gumm Sisters"; Fox West Coast Theater, Santa Ana, California.

July 14, 1932 to July 16, 1932: "The Three Gumm Sisters"; Fox Dome Theater, Venice, California.

July 22, 1932 to July 28, 1932: "The Three Gumm Sisters"; Fox West Coast Theater, Long Beach, California (This engagement was possibly extended from July 29–31, 1932.)

August 5, 1932 to August 6, 1932: "The Gumm Sisters" (mistakenly billed as "The Three *Gum* Sisters"); Fox Cabrillo Theater, San Pedro, California. (This engagement was possibly extended from August 7–10.)

August 11, 1932 to August 13, 1932: "The Three Gumm Sisters"; Manchester Theater, Los Angeles, California.

August 14, 1932 to August 15, 1932: "The Gumm Sisters"; Fox Boulevard Theater, Los Angeles, California. (There may have been two other engagements that followed this one, running up through August 23, 1932.)

August 25, 1932 to August 31, 1932: "The Gumm Sisters"; Paramount Theater, Los Angeles, California. Though the tour headlined comic Fuzzy Knight, and "The Gumm Sisters" only did their twenty-minute routine five times a day—six times a day on weekends—Frances was singled out at the Paramount, receiving her *first review* from *Variety*, at age ten. (It is believed to be their first notice in *any* theatrical paper.)

August 30, 1932: The issue of *Variety* released that day carried the review:

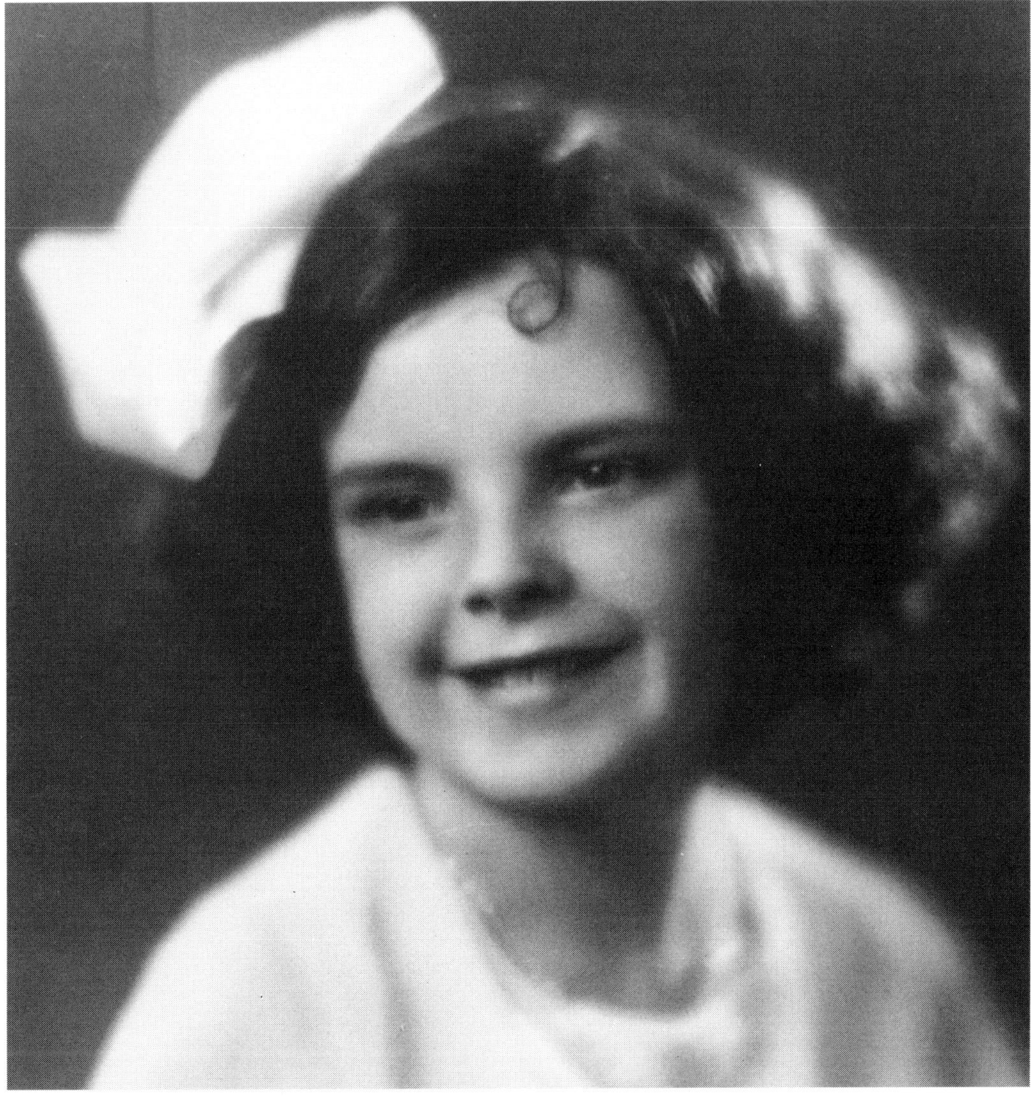

Vaudeville sensation "Baby" Gumm was stopping shows on a regular basis and even getting rave reviews from *Variety* by 1932, not long after this portrait was taken in Los Angeles. (Courtesy of Photofest.)

> "Gumm sisters, harmony trio, socked with two numbers. Selling end of trio is the ten-year-old sister with a pip of a lowdown voice. Kid stopped the show, but wouldn't give more."

(In returning home to Lancaster, for the start of school year, Ethel Gumm had to cancel four weeks of engagements, including two weeks in San Francisco.)

(Frances and her best friend Muggsie put their footprints in cement, at the corner of Newgrove and Fig, Lancaster, California; fall 1932. The footprints still exist in a Lancaster visitor center.)

September 18, 1932: "The Gumm Sisters" performed for the Southern California Dance Teachers Association Dinner Celebration; Biltmore Hotel, Los Angeles, California.

October 7, 1932 to October 8, 1932: "The Gumm Family" performed at the Second Annual Alfalfa Festival at I.O.O.F. Hall, Lancaster, California.

October 26, 1932: "The Gumm Sisters" performed at a "Stage and Screen Spectacle" Benefit for Mt. Sinai Hospital; Shrine Auditorium, Los Angeles, California.

October 29, 1932: (Radio) "The Gumm Sisters"; Broadcast with Uncle Tom Murray and the Hollywood Hillbillies; KFI and KECA Radio, Los Angeles, California. . . . *And* . . . "The Gumm Sisters" performed at "The Little Club"; their opening of season dance, held at the Coconut Grove; Ambassador Hotel, Los Angeles, California.

October 30, 1932 to October 31, 1932: "The Gumm Sisters"; Valley Theater, Lancaster, California.

November 5, 1932: "The Gumm Sisters"; Maurice L. Kusell's Protege Review; Barker Brothers Store Auditorium; Los Angeles, California.

November 22, 1932: Morning: "The Three Gumm Sisters"; Junior Red Cross Girl's League Canned Goods Drive; Evening: (Trade Show) "The Three Gumm Sisters"; musical program for the Southern California Gas Company Dinner; Held at the home of Mrs. W.S. Mumaw, Lancaster, California.

December 8, 1932: "Baby Gumm" (Frances) performed at Elks Meeting; San Fernando, California.

December 16, 1932 to December 17, 1932: "Baby Gumm"; Fox Arlington Theater, Santa Barbara, California.

December 29, 1932 to January 4, 1933: "Baby Gumm"; Maurice L. Kusell's Juvenile Christmas Revue; the Million Dollar Theater, Los Angeles, California. (*The Los Angeles Record* stated that Frances was "astounding. Her singing all but knocks one for a loop, her dancing is snappy and clever. She handles herself onstage like a veteran pro.")

1933

January 1, 1933 to January 4, 1933: "Baby Gumm" (Judy) concluded her engagement that started on December 29, 1932: Maurice L. Kusell's Juvenile Christmas Revue at The Million Dollar Theater, Los Angeles, California.

January 21, 1933: "The Gumm Sisters" performed at the Menorah Center Monster Ball; Menorah Center.

January 29, 1933: Frances; Valley Theater, Lancaster, California (Frances and a Kussell student by the name of either Clarke or Claire Williams—both names are mentioned, on different dates—were featured in a "stage specialty.")

February 3, 1933 to February 5, 1933: Frances; Strand Theater, Long Beach, California (As Ethel Gumm could not be with Frances for this engagement, Aunt Norma allowed Frances to experiment with her stage name, coming up with "Gracie Gumm"—"Radio's Youthful Star.")

February 6, 1933 to February 7, 1933: "Baby Gumm" and Claire Williams; Valley Theater, Lancaster, California.

February 14, 1933: Frances; Lancaster Campfire Girls, Valentine's Day Party; Lancaster, California.

February 18, 1933: "The Gumm Sisters"; Rainbow Girls Valentine's Day Dance; Lancaster, California.

March 6, 1933: Frances; Campfire Girls Event; Lancaster, California.

March 16, 1933: Frances; Campfire Girls St. Patrick's Day Lunch; Lancaster, California.

April 1, 1933: (Radio) Frances; Unknown radio station, Beverly Hills, California.

April 7, 1933: Frances; the Little Club event at the Coconut Grove; Ambassador Hotel; Los Angeles, California.

April 14, 1933: Frances; the Little Club event at the Coconut Grove; Ambassador Hotel; Los Angeles, California.

April 20, 1933: (Radio) Frances; KFI Radio, Los Angeles (Frances sang with Al Pierce and his gang.)

May 5, 1933 *or* May 6, 1933: (Personal Appearance) "The Gumm Sisters'; Reception/Open House for the Hamburger Memorial Home for Jewish Orphans (a home for Jewish working girls); Los Angeles, California. (The girls were mistakenly billed as "The *Gunn* Sisters.")

May 10, 1933 *or* May 12, 1933: "The Gumm Sisters" and Clark Williams; Antelope Valley Joint Union High Promenade; Lancaster High School, Lancaster, California ("The Gumm Sisters" and Clark Williams, for junior class promenade.)

May 11, 1933: Frances; Valley Theater, Lancaster, California. (Easter Star Spring Fashion Revue; special musical numbers were sung by Frances, with Paul Brown's Orchestra.)

May 13, 1933 to May 14, 1933: (Vaudeville) Frances; Garfield Theater, Alhambra, California (This weekend engagement, which Frank Gumm brought her to, saw Frances experiment with her name yet again, this time as third on the bill: "Another Great Score!! Orpheum Big Time Vaudeville—*Alice Gumm*")

May 19, 1933 to May 20, 1933 *or* May 25, 1933 to May 26, 1933: (Vaudeville) Frances; Fairfax Theater, West Hollywood, California.

June 4, 1933: "The Gumm Sisters"; Dancing Teachers Business Association Demonstration Recital; Alexandria Hotel; Los Angeles, California.

June 10, 1933: Frances's eleventh birthday, and: "The Gumm Sisters" performed at The Scions Annual Spring Dance and Frolic; Pollyanna Tea Rooms; West Lake, California. (The girls were billed as "The *Gum* Sisters.")

June 14, 1933: "The Gumm Sisters"; Kiwanis Club meeting; Kiwanis Hall, Lancaster, California.

June 16, 1933 to July 1933: (Radio) Frances; *Junior Hi Jinx* radio show, KFWB Radio, Los Angeles, California. (Show was every Friday at 7:45 p.m. beginning June 16 through July; the other Gumm sisters joined Frances on the series. The sisters' appearance on the show brought them two rave reviews from *The Los Angeles Examiner* newspaper.)

July 5, 1933: Frances and "The Gumm Sisters"; Lancaster Rainbow for Girls Compliment for Mary Jane and Virginia Gumm; Lancaster, California.

July 16, 1933: (Audition) "The Gumm Sisters"; RKO vaudeville circuit booking agents King and Winkler auditioned the sisters at the Gumm home on Cedar Street, Lancaster, California. (They were so impressed that they booked the sisters into one of their theaters the very next day):

July 17, 1933: (Vaudeville) "The Three Gumm Sisters"; Monday Night Guest Artist Vaudeville; RKO Hillstreet (*or* "Hill*crest*") Theater, Los Angeles, California. (Frances's solo was "Rain, Rain, Go Away," and MGM casting agent Ben Piazza expressed interest in her, although nothing became of this.)

July 20, 1933 to July 26, 1933: Frances; Warner Brothers Downtown Theater, Los Angeles, California (Last name listed as "*Gum.*")

July 29, 1933 to July 30, 1933: "The Gumm Sisters"; the Strand Theater, Long Beach, California.

Late July 1933: (Party) "The Gumm Sisters"; Order of Rainbow farewell party for "The Gumm Sisters"; They sang, and Frances had solos; Lancaster, California.

(The Gumm family moved to 2605 Ivanhoe Drive, Los Angeles, California, in late July. Frank still spent a lot of time in Lancaster managing his movie house.)

August 2, 1933 to August 8, 1933: (Vaudeville) "The Gumm Family" (Frank opens for "The Gumm Sisters"; Ethel at piano); Golden Gate Theater, San Francisco, California.

> The girls earned their second review from *Variety*; Appearing in the August 8, 1933 issue, this time it was negative: " "The Gumm Sisters," with Mama Gumm at the piano, and Papa Gumm in advance, deuced. Three girls of assorted sizes who sing in mediocre voice and style, with majority of the burden falling to the youngest one, a mere tot, who lustily shouted three numbers, decidedly not of her type. And much too long."
>
> However, that summer, the trade paper *Junior Professional* had stated: "This remarkable tot has twice the charm and genuine ability of all the (child movie stars) put together."
>
> *San Francisco Chronicle's* George C. Warren also raved during this engagement at the Golden Gate about "The Gumm Sisters," who harmonize, and have a strong-voiced small woman, who imitates and sings in a big way."

Interesting that Frances was called a "woman," which was becoming an increasing occurrence as the power and emotion of her voice forced many to refuse to believe they were being thrilled by a child.

August 9, 1933 to August 15, 1933 *or* August 10, 1933 to August 16, 1933: (Vaudeville) "The Gumm Sisters"; Fox West Coast Theater, Long Beach, California.

August 24, 1933 to August 30, 1933: (Vaudeville) "The Gumm Sisters"; Warner Brothers Theater, Hollywood, California. (The girls were billed as "Harmony at its best," in this show that featured Teddy Joyce.)

August 31, 1933 to September 6, 1933: (Vaudeville) "The Gumm Sisters"; Warner Brothers Downtown Theater. (The girls appeared second on the bill, mentioned as "Harmony Supreme"; the "Gumm" name was misspelled in ads as "*Drumm.*")

> They earned their third *Variety* review, which, like the second one, was negative: "The Gumm Sisters, three harmony warblers, with Mother Gumm accompanying at the piano. Two of the sisters are grownup, while the third is a precocious juve whose mild attempts at comedy add nothing to the offering."

September 8, 1933 to September 9, 1933: (Vaudeville) "The Gumm Sisters"; Fox Riverside Theater, Riverside, California. (The girls were billed as "The *Gum* Sisters.")

September 12, 1933: (Vaudeville)"The Three Gumm Sisters"; the Garfield Theater, Alhambra, California.

September 21, 1933 *or* September 23, 1933: "The Gumm Family"; Acadia Club of Los Angeles Dinner, Lodge 437; Mason Temple Hall, Los Angeles, California.

October 14, 1933: "The Gumm Sisters"; the Casa Del Adobe; Lancaster, California.

October 21, 1933: Frances; Lawlor's Hollywood Professional School Recital; Hollywood Conservatory Auditorium; Los Angeles, California. (Frances and her sister Jimmie started school there in the fall of

1933. This recital also featured Mickey Rooney, who was enrolled in the school as well, making this the first time the two future MGM stars would share a stage.)

October 26, 1933: "The Three Gumm Sisters"; Safeway Employees' Association Benefit; American Legion Stadium, Hollywood, California.

November 3, 1933: "The Gumm Sisters"; Open House Program at Hamburger Memorial Home for Jewish Orphans; Hollywood, California.

November 10, 1933: Frances sang at an after-theater party held at the Gumm home, Silverlake district of Los Angeles, California.

November 18, 1933: "The Three Gumm Sisters"; All Star Midnight Matinee, Los Angeles B'nai B'rith Lodge Benefit; Grauman's Egyptian Theater, Hollywood, California.

November 21, 1933: "The Gumm Sisters" sang at Dorothy Granger's twenty-first birthday party.

November 23, 1933: Frances; Million Dollar Revue—American Jewish Congress Benefit; Shrine Auditorium; Los Angeles, California.

December 14, 1933: "The Three Gumm Sisters"; Lawlor's 1933 Christmas Revue; Hollywood Conservatory Auditorium, Hollywood, California.

1934

February 2, 1934: (Radio) Frances; KHJ radio show *Friday Nite Frolics*, broadcast "live" from the stage of the Paramount Theater, Los Angeles, California.

February 8, 1934 to February 13, 1934: (Vaudeville) "The Gumm Sisters"; Orpheum Theater, Los Angeles, California. (the Gumms were one of seven acts on this vaudeville bill.)

(Early in 1934, Frank and Ethel Gumm bought a home a block away from the one at 2605 Ivanhoe; this new one was at 2671 Lakeview Terrace East, in Silver Lake, California.)

February 1934 through March 1934: Vaudeville Tour, Paramount circuit: "The Gumm Sisters."

February 16, 1934 to February 22, 1934: (Vaudeville) "The Gumm Sisters"; Paramount Theater, Seattle, Washington. (Frank Gumm met his family on February 22, and drove them to their next stops.)

February 24, 1934: (Vaudeville) "The Gumm Sisters"; Mt. Baker Theater, Bellingham, Washington. (Billed as "The Three *Glumm* Sisters.")

February 25, 1934: (Vaudeville) "The Gumm Sisters"; Empire *or* the Mercy's Capitol Theater, Yakima, Washington. (Billed as "A Great Trio.")

February 27, 1934: (Vaudeville) "The Gumm Sisters"; Liberty Theater, Wenatchee, Washington. (Billing at theater was: "Three Gumm Sisters [Trio Unusual].")

March 1, 1934 to March 4, 1934: (Vaudeville) "The Gumm Sisters"; Orpheum Theater, Spokane, Washington. (The local *Spokesman-Review* paper said: "The Three Gumm Sisters are harmony singers in a dainty bit of vocal entertainment that features the youngster of the lot in a clever imitation of Helen Morgan. The crowd gave the girls a great hand.")

March 5, 1934 to March 7, 1934: (Vaudeville) "The Gumm Sisters"; Liberty Theater, Lewiston, Idaho. (Gumms were billed as "Radio's Sweethearts." This was the end of the tour, though on the way home, they played):

March 9, 1934 to March 15, 1934: (Vaudeville) "The Gumm Sisters"; Fox Theater, San Francisco.

March 15, 1934: Frances sang at the Club Oasis; San Francisco.

April 12, 1934 to April 18, 1934: Frances; the Gilmore Circus; the New Spreckels Theater, San Diego, California (billed as "Baby Gumm," among 23 stars of the Gilmore Circus). *The San Diego Union-Tribune* stated "Little Miss Frances Gumm, a child, sang 'Why Darkies Were Born' in such a fashion that she shared the encore honors with 'The Sheriff' who is the star performer of the show.")

April 15, 1934: (Radio) Frances; Midnight *Frolic* broadcast (*Friday Nite Frolics* radio broadcast over KHJ), by Gilmore troupe, Agua Caliente Hotel, Agua, Mexico.

April 19, 1934 to April 25, 1934: Frances; State Theater, Long Beach, California. (This was another engagement with the Gilmore Circus, and the local paper said "Frances Gumm, a charming youngster who is the 'baby' of the troupe, sings 'That's What a Darkie Is,' and 'Dinah' in a singularly grownup little voice.")

April 26, 1934 to May 2,1934 *or* April 28, 1934 to April 29, 1934: "The Gumm Sisters"; Gilmore Circus, Shrine Auditorium, Los Angeles, California (Mary Jane and Virginia joined Frances for this appearance).

May 3, 1934 to May 9, 1934: (Vaudeville) "The Gumm Sisters"; "Big Stage Show"; Million Dollar Theater, Los Angeles, California.

May 18, 1934 to May 20, 1934: (Vaudeville) "The Gumm Sisters" *either Movie Star Frolics*, Gilmore Stadium, Los Angeles, California (billed as "Trio Musicale") *or* the St. Catherine Hotel Avalon; Santa Catalina Island, California.

June 2, 1934 to June 3, 1934: (Personal Appearance) "The Gumm Sisters"; St. Catherine Hotel, Catalina Island (weekend professional engagement).

June 10, 1934: Frances's twelfth birthday.

June 17, 1934: "The Gumm Sisters" sang at Farewell Reception/Open House (leaving for tour), held at Gumm home, Silverlake District of Los Angeles, California.

June 1934 to October 1934: (Vaudeville) Gumm Sisters Cross-Country Tour.

June 22, 1934 to June 28, 1934: (Vaudeville) "The Gumm Sisters"; Tabor Grand Theater, Denver, Colorado. (Opening song at the time was "Avalon Town"; a ten-piece orchestra played. There was a lighting cue mishap on opening night: the spot was on wrong side of stage at entrance: thus, the Gumms spent the number chasing it, and vice versa.)

June 29, 1934 to July 12, 1934: (Nightclub) "The Gumm Sisters"; Blakeland Inn, Denver *or* Littleton, Colorado (This club had been raided on the night of June 28, the night before "The Gumm Sisters" opened. Even though the club was closed by the police, the owner stayed open for himself and his friends, and was so impressed by the Gumms, that he not only paid them for the week, but also got them a booking in Colorado Springs).

July 4, 1934: Gumm Sisters; S.S. Broadmoor; Yacht Club Marina; Colorado Springs, Colorado.

July 15, 1934: "The Gumm Sisters"; "Guest Artist Night" at Old Mexico Nite Club; "A Century Of Progress" exhibition on the grounds of the World's Fair; New Beach Island, Chicago, Illinois.

July 18, 1934: "The Gumm Sisters"; Belmont Theater, Chicago. (One night engagement as a fill-in for another act.)

July 19, 1934: Frances; World's Fair, Chicago, Illinois. (Frances was selected as guest of honor and star performer for the "Eighth Children's Day"; "A Century Of Progress" exhibition.)

July 24, 1934 to August 14, 1934: (Nightclub) "The Gumm Sisters"; Old Mexico Cafe, on the fairgrounds of the World's Fair, Chicago. (Three-week engagement; Gumms were billed as "Blue Harmony"; received first week's pay upon arrival—it was the last money they were paid: the club folded near the end of the third week.)

August 17, 1934 to August 23, 1934: (Vaudeville) "The Gumm Sisters"; the Oriental Theater, Chicago. This was a huge break: as a last-minute fill-in, the girls played the second show on August 17, just as they were heading back home. Headliner George Jessel was so enthused by their talent, and the audience's response, that for their next show, he changed their last name, which had gotten a laugh from the audience, to "The *Garland* Sisters," from New York's *World Telegram's* drama critic Robert Garland. (Though strangely enough, an existing ad still shows their billing as "The Gumm Sisters.") The act consisted of two songs sung by the trio and Frances's solo of "Bill" from *Show Boat*; Ethel Gumm played piano for all three songs. (Admission was only twenty-five cents until 6:30 p.m.)

August 19, 1934 to August 21, 1934: (Nightclub) "The Gumm Sisters"; Chez Paree Club, Chicago (three midnight shows; appeared with singer Morton Downey; three shows only, as management found out Frances was a minor). (The great "break" of working with George Jessel led to Jessel lining up other Chicago engagements.)

August 24, 1934 to August 30, 1934: (Vaudeville) "The Gumm Sisters"; Marbro Theater, Chicago. (Newspaper ad shows billing as "The *Glumm* Sisters.")

August 31, 1934 to September 3, 1934: "The *Garland* Sisters"; the Uptown Theater, Chicago, Illinois. (The girls were signed by the local William Morris office, which booked the remainder of the tour, until mid October):

September 7, 1934 to September 13, 1934: (Vaudeville) "The Gumm Sisters"; Michigan Theater, Detroit, Michigan. (The first "official" and agreed-upon *billing* of "*3 Garland Sisters*: Grace—Beauty—Songs.")

Portrait of Frances (far right), her sisters, and their mother Ethel in Chicago, August 1934, just after their biggest break to date and as they made the tranformation from Gumm to Garland. (Courtesy of Photofest.)

September 14, 1934 to September 20, 1934: (Vaudeville) "The *Garland* Sisters"; Riverside Theater, Milwaukee, Wisconsin.

September 27, 1934 to October 3, 1934: (Vaudeville) "The *Garland* Sisters"; Tower Theater, Kansas City, Missouri.

October 5, 1934 to October 7, 1934: (Vaudeville) "The *Garland* Sisters"; Dubinsky's Electric Theater, St. Joseph, Missouri.

October 9, 1934 to October 11, 1934: (Vaudeville) "The *Garland* Sisters"; Dubinsky's Jefferson Theater, Jefferson City, Missouri. (Last stop of tour.)

October 24, 1934: (Personal Appearance/Night Club/Radio) "The *Garland* Sisters"; Florentine Room, Beverly Wilshire Hotel, Los Angeles, California (the girls sang with Vincent Lopez and His Orchestra).

November 1, 1934 to November 7, 1934: (Personal Appearance) "The *Garland* Sisters"; Grauman's Chinese Theater, Hollywood, California. (The girls appeared prior to the film *The Count of Monte Cristo*.) This was another monumental appearance for Frances, as she received her fourth review from *Variety* (in the November 6 issue):

> "Hardly a new act, this trio of youngsters has been kicking around the coast for two years, but has just found itself. As a trio, it means nothing, but with the youngest, Frances, 13 (sic), featured, it hops into class entertainment; for if such a thing is possible, the girl is a combination of Helen Morgan and Fuzzy Knight. Possessing a voice that, without a p.a. system, is audible throughout a house as large as the Chinese, she handles ballads like a veteran, and gets every note and word over with a personality that hits audiences. For comedy, she effects a pan like Knight, and delivers her stuff in the same manner as the comic. Nothing slow about her on hot stuff, and to top it off, she hoofs. Other two sisters merely form a background. Kid, with or without her sisters, is ready for the East. Caught on several previous shows, including the 5,000 seat Shrine Auditorium here, she never failed to stop the show, her current engagement being no exception."

November 9, 1934 to November 11, 1934: (Vaudeville) "The Gumm Sisters"; Strand Theater, Long Beach, California (billed as "The Gumm Sisters direct from Grauman's Chinese"). (This was the same theater where Frances had appeared as "Gracie Gumm" the year before. This engagement was the last time the girls used the Gumm family name.)

November 14, 1934 to November 20, 1934: (Vaudeville) "The Garland Sisters"; Orpheum Theater, Los Angeles, California. (Return engagement, and from this engagement on, the sisters use the Garland name.)

November 25, 1934: "The Garland Sisters" sing at a party for Dr. and Mrs. Marcus Rabwin, held at the home of Mr. and Mrs. S.E. Rykoff. (Dr. Marcus Rabwin was one of the most important men in Judy's life, second only in importance to her father: He had convinced Judy's parents to let her be born when they were actually thinking of abortion, as they didn't want any more children. Rabwin would be a constant throughout Judy's life, and as late as a year or two before her passing, he was still running to her side whenever needed, to treat her, to help her. He most likely was the only person at her funeral to have known her for, literally, her entire life.)

December 7, 1934: (Personal Appearance) "The Gumm Sisters"; Valley Theater, Lancaster, California. (The girls last appearance at their father's Lancaster theater.)

December 8, 1934: (Vaudeville) "The Garland Sisters"; *Irving Strouse's Sunday Nite Vaudeville Frolics*; Wishire-Ebell Theater, Los Angeles, California. (The girls were billed as the "Garland Trio.")

> *The Los Angeles Times* noted "the Garland Sisters scored a hit, with the youngest member of the trio practically stopping the show with her singing."

Even more raptuous was critic W. E. Oliver in his review for the *Los Angeles Evening Express*: "12 Year Old Girl Is Sensation At Frolics" (Headline): "Little Frances . . . sang in a way that produced in the audience sensations that haven't been equaled in years. Not your smart, adult-aping prodigy is this girl, but a youngster who had the divine instinct to be herself on stage, along with a talent for singing, a trick of rocking the spectators with rhythms, and a capacity for putting emotion into her performance that suggests what Bernhardt must have been at her age. It isn't the cloying, heavy sentiment her elders so often strive for, but simple, sincere feeling that reaches the heart. The three girls together are an act anyone would want to see. Frances alone is a sensation, and last Saturday's audience realized it by the way they encored. Much of her individual style of singing was culled by the little girl from her parent's old act, although she must have the divine spark to be able to sing as she did . . . she would make any show."

December 14, 1934: "The Garland Sisters"; *Los Angeles Evening Examiner* Christmas Benefit; Shrine Auditorium, Los Angeles, California.

December 23, 1934: (Vaudeville) *Irving Strouse's Sunday Nite Vaudeville Frolics*; Hollywood Playhouse, Hollywood, California. (In various ads, the billing appeared as "Garland 3", and "Frances Garland," as well as "Frances Garland Trio.")

George C. Warren of the *San Francisco Chronicle* wondered if Frances was a child in his review: "The Garland Trio made a great hit last night, especially the small member of the three, called 'little Francis' (sic) on the program, but whose singing and action seem much more mature than the short frock and the bare legs indicate. She is very clever whether she is young or old, and deserved the applause."

San Francisco's *Call-Bulletin* decided she was a youngster when they raved: "Frances (has become) the talk of the town in no time at all... as much the sweetheart of the stage as Shirley Temple is of the screen, with less renown, and, naturally, with more maturity in her appeal, but no less charm."

1935

December 25, 1934 to January 1, 1935: (Vaudeville) Curran Theater, San Francisco, California. Los Angeles *Frolics* show, billed as *Irving Strouse's January Vaudeville Frolics* with 60 members, including "Frances Garland and her Sisters" or "Frances Garland Trio."

January 10, 1935: (Screen Test) "The Garland Sisters" successfully tested and were signed to Universal Studios, for *The Great Ziegfeld* film. However, when the property was sold that spring to MGM, the girls were dropped from the picture.

January 13, 1935: "Frances Garland"; *Irving Strouse's Sunday Nite Vaudeville Frolics*; Wilshire-Ebell Theater, Los Angeles.

January 18, 1935: "The Garland Sisters" performed at Carl Laemmle's sixty-eighth birthday party; Universal Studios, Universal City, California.

January 26, 1935: "The Garland Sisters" sang at Tommy Hick's thirteenth birthday party held at the Hick's home, North Hollywood, California.

February 28, 1935: "The Garland Sisters"; Big Time Revue Vaudeville Night; Wilshire Theater, Santa Monica, California.

March 7, 1935 to March 13, 1935: "The Garland Sisters"; Paramount Theater, Los Angeles, California. (Photograph exists of the only on-stage performance photo of the sisters, and only photo of a family marquee—"The Garland Sisters.") The girls were earning $110.00 a week at this point, a huge amount in 1935, no doubt helped by reviews like their fifth notice from *Variety*:

> "Garland Sisters, three femmes, one of whom, Frances, is still a child and about 80% of the combination, are excellent harmonists, but it remained for the youngster to tie things up in a knot. Girl looks like a bet for pictures and should make rapid headway. However, she should be coached more proficiently in her foreign tongue songs, particularly the German, as her pronunciation is none too accurate. Otherwise, the kid is tops and deserved everything she drew today."

March 14, 1935 to March 20, 1935: "The Garland Sisters"; Warfield Theater, San Francisco, California.

March 29, 1935: (Recording) "The Garland Sisters"; Decca Records, Los Angeles, California. The girls cut three test records for Decca. With Ethel Gumm at the piano, the girls sang "Moonglow"; on her own, Frances sang "Bill" and a medley of "On the Good Ship Lollipop"/"The Object of My Affection"/ "Dinah." Unfortunately, the tests were rejected, and the recordings are not thought to exist and may have possibly been erased or destroyed. This was Judy Garland's first time in front of a recording studio microphone. (Test sheet lists artist as "Francis Garland"; and "Matrix # DLA 158," for "Bill.")

Early April 1935: Frank Gumm lost lease on his movie theater, because he owed $2,000 in back rent. The family was now living together at 842 North Mariposa Avenue, near 20th Century Fox studios. Frank leased a new theater, shortly after, in Lomita, twenty miles from Los Angeles.

April 7, 1935: "The Garland Sisters"; *Miniature Flashes of Hollywood*, Lawlor's School Spring Musical Play; Masonic Temple Auditorium, Hollywood, California.

April 12, 1935: "The Garland Sisters"; *The Lawlor Professional Revue of 1935*; Grammar School Auditorium, Lancaster, California.

April 13, 1935: "The Garland Sisters"; B'nai B'rith Annual Midnight Matinee Benefit; Grauman's Egyptian Theater, Hollywood.

April 19, 1935 to April 21, 1935: "The Gumm Sisters"; the Strand Theater, Long Beach, California.

April 26, 1935 to May 2, 1935: "The Garland Sisters"; Million Dollar Theater, Los Angeles, California.

May 3, 1935 to May 9, 1935: "Three Garland Sisters"; Orpheum Theater, San Francisco, California.

May 11, 1935: "The Gumm Sisters"; the Sisterhood of Temple Israel Mother and Children's Day; Temple Israel, Hollywood, California.

May 15, 1935 to June 5, 1935: (Vaudeville) "The Garland Sisters"; Paramount Theater, Los Angeles, California. This one-week engagement was extended to three. One critic said Frances was "about as talented an entertainer as one could imagine," and she earned her sixth *Variety* review:

> "Class act on bill is the Three Garland Sisters, which, for the Paramount booking seems to have concentrated heavily on Francis (sic) the youthful member of the family. Girls do only a couple of harmony numbers, leaving the rest of performance to kid sister, who is talented beyond doubt, and who scores heavily with her rendition of 'Eili, Eili' plus a couple of songs in foreign tongue."

June 8, 1935: "The Garland Sisters"; Lomita Theater, Lomita, California. (Frank Gumm's theater. Judy's mother and father began using the Garland name around this time, with ads calling Frank's theater

"*Garland's Lomita Theater.*") This was the first appearance of the girls on the stage of their father's last movie house. Their second—and final—known appearance would be six days later.

June 10, 1935: Frances's thirteenth birthday.

June 14, 1935: "The Garland Sisters" and Frankie Darro; Lomita Theater, Lomita, California. (Premiere of the movie *Burn 'Em Up Borneo.*) This was the last time the girls appeared at one of their father's theaters.

June 15, 1935 to July 26, 1935: (Personal Appearance) "The Garland Sisters"; Cal-Neva Lodge, Lake Tahoe, Nevada. It was during this engagement that Frances adopted the name *Judy*, from the new Hoagy Carmichael song. Also, agent Al Rosen heard her sing here, and would shortly be responsible for leading Judy to MGM. (Though interest had actually been building there for some time.)

August 6, 1935 to August 7, 1935: Possible engagement: "The Garland Sisters"; Hotel Miramar; Santa Monica, California.

August 12, 1935: (Film): "The Garland Sisters"; *La Fiesta de Santa Barbara*, filmed on location in Santa Barbara; Garland Sisters sing "La Cucaracha" in all-star Technicolor short. This was the girls' final film, and actually the last job ever for the sisters as a team, and was completed in only half a day. MGM wouldn't release the film until 1936. (The entire short is on the laser disc of the Jean Harlow movie *Libiled Lady.* The Garland Sisters' song is on the 1995 Judy/MGM laser disc box set.)

August 27, 1935: "Children's Day," Pan-Pacific Exposition; Open-air Theater, San Diego, California: this was the *first billing of "Judy Garland."*

September 13, 1935: (Audition) Judy Garland successfully auditioned for the head of Metro-Goldwyn-Mayer (MGM), Louis B. Mayer. Judy's father took her to the studio (in her play clothes), as mother Ethel was playing piano at the Community Playhouse. Metro's musical mastermind Roger Edens soon replaced Frank at the piano; Edens, who would become one of Judy's greatest musical influences later said her voice that day had "unbelieveable control, full power in the high register and shimmering warmth in the low." (Judy sang "Zing! Went The Strings Of My Heart," and "Eili, Eili.")

September 16, 1935: (Contract) MGM issues order to legal department to prepare contract "for the services of Judy Garland as an actress." The contract—spanning seven years, commencing October 1, 1935—called for an initial salary of $100.00 a week, with options every six months for the first year, then once a year for the remaining six years. (The memo also called for correspondence to be addressed to "the artist . . . care of her agents, Al Rosen Agency, 6404 Hollywood Blvd.") The order for the contract also listed an incorrect, or made-up, birth date, of January 10, 1923, six months later than Judy's actual birthday of June 10, 1922, and mentioned that she was "living with her parents at 842 North Mariposa, Los Angeles. Telephone—Normandie 5156." It also allowed her to negotiate for radio broadcasts, but MGM had to give consent before Judy rendered services. (The actual, final version of this first MGM contract ran nineteen pages.)

September 27, 1935: (Contract) Judy's MGM contract was approved by Los Angeles Superior Court (as Judy was a minor). Frank and Ethel accompanied her to the court house where MGM had the first known photographs of their new star taken. (One of these photos appeared in the 1975 book *Rainbow.*)

October 1, 1935: Judy's first day at MGM. (Judy's days at the studio were mostly taken up by her schooling and her vocal coaching by Roger Edens. The full studio machinery had not yet been activated.)

Early October 1935 (a Saturday, most likely October 5 or October 12): Judy's first MGM assignment: singing between halves at the University of Southern California Football Game, at the Los Angeles Coliseum, Los Angeles, California. (Judy sang "Fight on for Good Old USC." She was halfway through when the home team raced out on the field early; the fans' cheers drowned her out, and she was forced to stop midsong. Another source lists this day as September 30, 1935 and taking place at USC, not at Los Angeles Coliseum.)

Mid October 1935: In a letter Frank Gumm wrote to an old family friend John Perkins of Lancaster, California, he mentioned:

> Babe got her seven year contract with M.G.M. and it started October 1 at $150 (sic) per week and the last year she gets $1,000 a week as the salary advances every six months; a very attractive deal. Of course, its all on six months' options and she has to make good or they have the privilege of letting her go at the end of each six months' period . . . She is set for the first six months though and her first picture will probably be *This Time It's Love* in which Robert Montgomery and Jessie Matthews will be the stars and baby plays opposite Buddie Ebson (sic) a 6 foot 2 comedian that made a big hit with his sister in the new *Broadway Melody of 1936.* The picture goes into production in January next to be released about next April. Babe, or "Judy" as she is now called, will broadcast Saturday night, October 19 with Wallace Beery on the Shell Chateau hour from 6:30 to 7:30 P.M.

The film Frank mentioned would not happen, but the radio show did—although that was postponed by one week.

October 26, 1935: (Radio) Judy's first "official" MGM related work, and her national radio network debut: an appearance on Wallace Beery's *Shell Chateau Hour*, NBC Radio Network, broadcast "live," from the KFI Studios in Los Angeles, California, 6:30–7:30 p.m. Judy is introduced by Beery as "a girl here who I think is going to be the sensation of pictures. She's only twelve years old. . . ." (of course Judy was thirteen and four-plus months old), and following some scripted banter ("I wanna be a singer, Mr. Beery; And I wanna act, too!"), Judy sings "Broadway Rhythm." Her parents, and sister Jimmie sat in front row of the audience. (Recording of this show still exists, and is the earliest surviving solo recording of Judy aside from the films she made when she was seven years old. Though not on CD, this performance was on several LPs, including an album on the Star-Tone label. No mention is made of her signing her MGM contract, though she would return to the show three weeks later.)

October 27, 1935: Judy sang at a party for Mr. and Mrs. Sam Katz's wedding anniversary, given by Louis B. Mayer, at the Cafe Trocadero, West Los Angeles, California.

October 31, 1935: (Publicity) Judy's first "publicity party": a Halloween party (where she first met Jackie Cooper).

November 3, 1935: Judy sang at Frank Fay Opportunity Night; Cafe Trocadero; West Los Angeles, California.

November 10, 1935: Judy sang at a party for Mr. and Mrs. Nicholas Schenck, given by Louis B. Mayer; Cafe Trocadero; West Los Angeles, California.

November 16, 1935: (Radio) *Shell Chateau Hour*, NBC, 6:30–7:30 p.m., broadcast "live" from KFI Studios, Los Angeles, California. Judy sings "Zing! Went The Strings Of My Heart," and chats with host Wallace Beery, who said during the introduction: "Since her last appearance here she signed a seven-year contract with the MGM Studios [though of course the contract had been signed before Judy's first appearance on the show] . . . and the minute she was signed, Sam Katz wrote her into his new picture, *Yours and Mine*. (Judy would never appear in this film. Judy also sang a reprise of "Zing!") Ethel was the only family member in the audience, as father Frank Gumm had been taken to the hospital that day, though a radio was placed by his bedside to listen to Judy. (Wallace Beery's introduction and Judy's performance of "Zing!" sans the reprise, is available on the four-CD box set *Judy* released on October 13, 1998, on the 32 Records label; the reprise still exists in private collections.) Judy was taken directly from this radio show, to sing at The MGM Club Dance, at La Monica Ballroom, Santa Monica, California, despite her father being in the hospital.

From the first gallery publicity portrait sitting for MGM's newest "featured contract player," Judy Garland, November 1935. One wonders if the haunting look in her eyes reflects the pain she felt at being fed through the glamour mill at the tender age of thirteen or true anguish from the very recent loss of her father. (Courtesy of Photofest.)

November 17, 1935: Judy's father, Frank Gumm, died of spinal meningitis. Judy lost the one person she felt was on her side, and would spend the rest of her life searching for the same type of unconditional support she had received from her dad. Judy later called the death of her father "the most terrible thing that ever happened to me in my life."

Mid to late November 1935: Judy's first publicity portrait sitting at the "Gallery" studios, in MGM.

November 25, 1935: Judy sang at the Helpers Dinner; Biltmore Hotel, Los Angeles, California.

November 27, 1935: (Record) Judy recorded two more songs—"No Other One" and "All's Well"—for Decca Records, at their Los Angeles studios. Decca would reject these songs, just as they had the ones made on March 29, 1935. (These recordings are thought to no longer exist.)

November 28, 1935: Judy sang at the Charity Benefit for Los Angeles Orphans; Cafe Trocadero, West Hollywood, California.

December 1935: MGM decided to loan Judy to Hal Roach, for an *Our Gang Follies* film, then reversed their decision at the last minute.

December 1, 1935: Judy sang at Will Rogers Memorial Fund Benefit; Shrine Auditorium, Los Angeles, California.

December 12, 1935: Judy sang at *Los Angeles Examiner* Christmas Benefit; Shrine Auditorium, Los Angeles, California.

December 18, 1935: Judy sang at Elks Movie Star Benefit; Fox Rosemary Theater, Ocean Park, California.

December 30, 1935: Publicity photo shot on this date of Judy with Mickey Rooney and Jane Withers.

1936

Early 1936: Judy continued her daily lessons and training (and schooling) at MGM, six days a week, Monday through Saturday.

Early 1936: Judy, her mother, and sister Jimmie (older sister Suzan had married) moved to a house at 180 South McCadden Place, right in the middle of Hollywood (reported as "respectable rather than glamorous," though it had Judy's first swimming pool).

March 10, 1936: (Film) *This Time It's Love* had evolved into *Born to Dance*: Cole Porter was writing the songs, when on this date, he noted in his diary that to his "great joy" the casting would include "Buddy Ebsen opposite Judy Garland," though Judy would be written out of the film.

Spring 1936: (Film) Judy and fellow MGM contract player Deanna Durbin were teamed in a one-reel test, shown only to an MGM exhibitor's convention. (This film is not known to exist.) Judy would later joke that she was seen having a dirty face, that she was holding an apple and that she was "Queen of Transelvania."

Early June 1936: (Personal Appearance) Judy was sent by MGM on her very first trip to New York, for promotional appearances. While there:

June 10, 1936: Judy celebrated her fourteenth birthday, and two days later:

June 12, 1936: (Record) Judy recorded her first released recordings: "Stompin' At The Savoy," backed with "Swing, Mr. Charlie," for *Decca Records*. Recorded in New York City, at Decca's main studio at 50 West 57th Street, with Bob Crosby and his Orchestra. This record (#848) listed Judy's age as thirteen (instead of fourteen), and was released in July 1936. (Bob Crosby's manager did not want Crosby's name on "the same record label with this unknown girl," so no orchestra is listed on the label.) Judy would sign a long-term recording contract with Decca in 1937, and all of her recordings for the label are available on *The Complete Decca Masters, Plus* from *MCA Records*, a four-CD box set that contains all seventy-nine singles Decca released during Judy's 1936–1947 years with the label, along with eleven alternate versions. Featuring a lavish and well-written booklet, and superb digital sound, this set is highly recommended.

Mid June 1936: MGM called Judy back to Hollywood (canceling some East Coast radio shows) to again team with Deanna Durbin in a one reel short, *Every Sunday*, to test their appeal to audiences.

June 30, 1936: Judy prerecorded her two songs for *Every Sunday* ("Waltz with a Swing/ Americana"; and a reprise of "Americana" with Durbin). This is the first time Judy recorded on the mammoth and legendary recording stages of MGM.

Early July 1936: Judy films her scenes and songs for *Every Sunday* over a few days. (The short was released on November 28, 1936; by that time Judy would already have a successful feature-length film in release.)

July 1936: (Record) Judy Garland's first recording available to the public, was released by Decca Records: "Stompin' At The Savoy", backed with "Swing, Mr. Charlie" (recorded June 12, 1936: see that date for more info).

July 1936: MGM agreed to loan Judy to 20th Century Fox for her first feature-length film: *Pigskin Parade*, to begin filming in August 1936.

August 4, 1936: An MGM Inter-Corporate Memo was drawn on this date, to loan Judy to 20th Century Fox studios. (See "Early August 1936 to September 15, 1936," below.)

August 6, 1936: (Radio) *The Shell Chateau Hour*, NBC Radio Network, 6:30–7:30 p.m., broadcast live, from WEAF studio, Los Angeles. On her third and final appearance on this show, Judy sang "Revival Day" and "After You've Gone" (her first time singing a song which would become associated with her later in her career). (This appearance is known to exist in private collections.)

Early August 1936 to September 15, 1936: (Film) Judy spent five weeks at 20th Century Fox Studios, making her first feature-length film, *Pigskin Parade*, in a supporting role as "Sairy Dodd." The part was written especially for Judy, who appears in half a dozen scenes and sings three songs (an additional song, "Hold That Bulldog", would be cut prior to release), including two powerful solos: "The Texas Tornado" and "It's Love I'm After."

September 15, 1936: Judy attended Jackie Cooper's fourteenth birthday party, at his home.

End of September 1936: Judy's option was again picked up by MGM.

October 1936: *Pigskin Parade* played its initial engagements (wide release was in November: *Variety* review appeared in their November 18, 1936 issue), winning Judy some good notices, including these:

> *The New York Sun* said "[The film features her] piquant face and surprising voice . . . one of the film's biggest assets."
>
> *The Hollywood Reporter* stated: "One of the loftiest highlights is little Judy, who captured the preview audience with a brace of nifty songs."

(*Pigskin* would become one of the top moneymakers of the year, and would win an Academy Award Nomination for Stuart Erwin—who played Judy's brother—in the new Best Supporting Actor category.)

Late 1936: Judy was written into *Broadway Melody of 1937* (which eventually became, due to delays, *Broadway Melody of 1938*). (Judy spent the rest of 1936 as she had the preceding fourteen months or so: reporting to Metro at 9 a.m.—after receiving her morning call from Mary Schroeder, the studio's "Special Services Department" representative, who would act as Judy's aid, giving her the assignments, interviews, photo session shoots, etc., for the day. Judy would then spend the day having her school hours and her vocal coaching with her musical mentor, Roger Edens. Her main performing at this moment, until early 1937—when her hectic work schedule would begin—consisted of mainly singing at parties and benefits.)

1937

January 5, 1937: (Radio) *Jack Oakie's College*, CBS Radio Network. (Judy was billed as "the little girl with the big voice"; another guest was George Jessel, who had given Judy her last name in Chicago, back in 1934.)

February 1, 1937: A milestone in Judy's career. At Clark Gable's thirty-sixth birthday party, Judy performed her first public rendition of her version of the song that would become her first major hit, with a special opening written by Edens: "Dear Mr. Gable, You Made Me Love You." (There were some original lyrics relating to the entertainment industry, which would be changed into the version we know now by February 22, 1937.) This song would become her first hit record and would stay in her repertoire (minus the "Dear Mr. Gable" material) up through her final concert. The same night as the Gable party, Judy introduced the number officially at a benefit at the Trocadero.

February 2, 1937: (Radio) *Ben Bernie and All the Lads*, NBC Radio Network/WJZ, Blue Network (30 Minute Show). Judy sang "Oh Say Can You Swing" (an Edens routine).

February 22, 1937: MGM Dinner-Dance. (Judy sang "Dear Mr. Gable, You Made Me Love You.")

February 23, 1937: (Radio) *Jack Oakie's College*, CBS Radio Network, Los Angeles. Judy was now added to this 60-minute weekly series as a series regular. (This was her first of three radio series on which she would become a series regular: the next would start in November of 1937; Finally, there was Bob Hope's radio show during the 1939–1940 season. Judy would appear on only one television series as a regular: Her own variety series for CBS during the 1963–1964 season.) Judy introduced the "Dear Mr. Gable, You Made Me Love You" song nationally on this broadcast. (Judy's other solos during her sixteen-week stint as series regular would include: "Some Of These Days"; "Slap That Bass"; "They Can't Take That Away From Me"; "Play, Orchestra, Play"; "Always"; "There's A Lull In My Life"; and "Alabamy Bound." All of Judy's appearances on the Oakie series are believed to still exist. It has been widely rumored that Jack Oakie's widow completed negotiations to allow for the release of the material on CD. To date, no announcement has been made regarding release, but it is believed the release will ultimately be a two-disc, fifty-song collection. The label was once believed to be Capitol Records; however, a more likely company would be MCA Records, who have had their own successes with compilations of early Garland material recorded for Decca Records.)

March 2, 1937: (Radio) *Jack Oakie's College*. Judy, as a series regular, sang "Something In The Air," and, in tribute to Sophie Tucker (whom she was about to work with), "Some Of These Days."

March 5, 1937: The first noted date of Judy's first work on her first MGM feature, *Broadway Melody of 1938*. On this day, Judy recorded the song, "Everybody Sing," with Sophie Tucker, one of Judy's four scheduled solos (although two of them—"Your Broadway And My Broadway" and "Yours And Mine"—would be cut from the film before release. A different rendition/arrangement of "Yours And Mine," sung by Judy, would play over the opening credits. The "cut" renditions are available on the two-CD set, *Judy Garland: Collector's Gems from the MGM Films*, a Turner Classic Movies/Rhino Records label release; # R2 72543; issued on October 1, 1996. Additional takes of "Everybody Sing" are heard on the 1995 MGM laser disc set on Judy.) This was Judy's first time on MGM's recording stage—for an MGM feature-length film—to create the vocals to which she would lip-synch on camera. (Meredith Howard was Judy's MGM "Publicity Aide" at this time—her first publicist.)

March 9, 1937: (Radio) *Jack Oakie's College*. Judy's weekly appearance (though she would miss the next two weeks, due to work on *Broadway Melody*). (A guest this week was George Jessel.) On this show, Judy sang "The Dixieland Band" as "The Oakie-land Band" in honor of the host.

March 14, 1937: Recording session at MGM for *Broadway Melody of 1938*. The song, "Your Broadway and My Broadway" was recorded. (After being filmed some time following this recording session, the song would be cut. Only the audio exists today—available on the above mentioned *Collector's Gems* two-CD set; other takes can be heard on the 1995 MGM laser disc set. The footage is not known to exist.)

March 30, 1937: (Radio) *Jack Oakie's College*. Judy continued her weekly appearances with this show, having missed the shows on March 9 and March 16 due to work on *Broadway Melody* at MGM. She would now appear on every show until the series' last show on June 22, 1937. On this show, Judy sang "Goodnight, My Love" and "Slap That Bass."

April 6, 1937: (Radio) *Jack Oakie's College.* Judy's songs this week: "Let's Call The Whole Thing Off" with Jack Oakie; and "Smiles." (This performance of "Smiles" is on Volume One of the AEI Judy Garland LP series, now out of print, and has yet to be released on CD.)

April 13, 1937: (Radio) *Jack Oakie's College.* Judy's songs this week: "Blue Hawaii" and one unidentified number. (Also on this date: The Hollywood Reporter announced that Judy would star in a film called *Molly, Bless You* with Wallace Beery, Sophie Tucker, and Reginald Gardiner. It would never actually be made.)

April 16, 1937: "Yours And Mine" recorded at MGM (for *Broadway Melody of 1938* film). (This version would be cut, after filming, although a different version/arrangement of the song would be heard over the film's opening credits. Audio of recording session still exists on the two-CD *Collector's Gems*; footage of number is not known to exist.)

April 20, 1937: (Radio) *Jack Oakie's College.* Judy's songs this week: "Johnny One Note" and, in tribute to Irving Berlin, "Always."

April 27, 1937: (Radio) *Jack Oakie's College.* Judy's songs this week: "Swing High, Swing Low" and a second unidentified number.

Early May 1937: MGM's Exhibitor's gathering (Judy sang "Dear Mr. Gable, You Made Me Love You").

May 4, 1937: (Radio) *Jack Oakie's College.* Judy sang "The Birth Of The Blues" and "Trailing Along With A Trailer."

May 7, 1937: Recording session at MGM: Judy's first recording of "Dear Mr. Gable, You Made Me Love You" (the legendary vocal that would become her first film-song hit). (Different takes of this song can be heard on the 1995 MGM laser disc box set on Judy and on the Rhino Records six-CD box set *That's Entertainment*, in which the ending chorus is an alternate to the ending chorus heard in the finished film. The version as it appears in the film can be heard on the Rhino Records single CD *Judy Garland In Hollywood—Her Greatest Movie Hits, 1936–1963*, released in 1998.)

By now, Judy was heavily into the production of *Broadway Melody of 1938*, and was officially starting her day at 7 a.m. at her home, where she would be made up on the days she was filming, to be on the set at 9 a.m. This routine would continue until she reached eighteen; then she would have her 7 a.m. makeup call at MGM.

May 11, 1937: (Radio) *Jack Oakie's College.* Judy's weekly appearance as a regular. On this broadcast she sang "Alabamy Bound" and a special arrangement (sort of a sequel to "Dear Mr. Gable") of "They Can't Take That Away From Me." (This version of "They Can't Take That Away From Me" is on the CD, *Judy Garland on Radio, 1936-1944, Volume 1: All The Things You Are*, on the Vintage Jazz Classics, LTD Label, # VJC–1043, released in spring, 1993.)

May 18, 1937: (Radio) *Jack Oakie's College.* Judy's songs this week: "Suddenly" and "Play, Orchestra, Play," which included bits of "Blue Skies"; "April Showers"; "Look For The Silver Lining"; "Singing In The Rain"; and "I Got Rhythm."

May 25, 1937: (Radio) *Jack Oakie's College.* Judy's songs this week: "A Shine On Your Shoes/Shoe Shine Boy" and also "Swing High, Swing Low."

May 26, 1937: *The Hollywood Reporter* announced that Judy would star in the film *The Ugly Duckling.* (This would later become *Everybody Sing*, after being called *Swing Fever* for awhile, and had been planned as a Judy vehicle since late in 1936. Production would not start until August 1937.)

May 27, 1937: *The Hollywood Reporter* announced that Judy would be dropping out as vocalist on the Jack Oakie show (apparently because she was too busy at MGM. The Oakie show was being canceled anyway, and Judy would stay with the show through its final broadcast on June 22, 1937.)

Judy rehearsing with Buddy Ebsen for their dance in the finale of her first feature for MGM, *Broadway Melody of 1938*, filmed March through July 1937. (Courtesy of Photofest.)

June 1, 1937: (Radio) *Jack Oakie's College*. Judy's songs this week: "Dinah" and "Where Are You?"

June 8, 1937: (Radio) *Jack Oakie's College*. Judy's songs this week: "All God's Chillun Got Rhythm" and "Shine On Harvest Moon." (This same day, *The Hollywood Reporter* announced that Judy would star with Mickey Rooney and Freddie Bartholomew in *Thoroughbreds Don't Cry*. Bartholomew would later be replaced by Ronald Sinclair when the film went into production in August 1937.)

June 10, 1937: Judy's fifteenth birthday.

June 15, 1937: (Radio) *Jack Oakie's College*. Judy's songs this week: "There's A Lull In My Life" and "Johnny One Note."

June 22, 1937: (Radio) *Jack Oakie's College*. Judy's last appearance and the series' final show. Judy sang "There's A Lull In My Life" and, to promote the upcoming release of *Broadway Melody of 1938*, "Everybody Sing."

June 23, 1937: *The Hollywood Reporter* announced that Judy was losing popularity with her neighbors because she was practicing the saxophone, which she was to play in her next movie (she is never seen playing the sax in any of her films).

July 4, 1937: Louis B. Mayer's (Head of MGM) 4th of July party, which Judy attends.

July 16, 1937: (Radio) *Hollywood Hotel,* CBS (60 minutes). This show spotlighted the upcoming release of *Broadway Melody of 1938.*

End of July 1937: *Broadway Melody of 1938* film is finished at MGM and would be quickly released on August 20, 1937. (By the early 1990s, all of Judy's feature films had been released on VHS video cassette and laser disc with the exception of 1960's *Pepe,* in which only her singing voice is heard. Some of the VHS tapes of her films are out of print, as are all of the laser discs; few films are available on DVD; those that are available on DVD will be noted.)

Early August 1937: Judy begins work on her second feature for MGM, *Thoroughbreds Don't Cry,* her first film with Mickey Rooney (and the first time she'd be working on two films at the same time: by late August 1937, Judy would be in preproduction for *Everybody Sing*).

August 2, 1937: *The Hollywood Reporter* announced that MGM was shaping a story, *Listen, Darling* that would provide Judy with "her first starring role." (This film would not begin production until late July/early August 1938, a full year later.)

August 13, 1937: Judy's first MGM "preview" (or "test screening") of one of her films. *Broadway Melody of 1938* was screened at the Village Theater, in Westwood, California. Decca Records president Jack Kaap had flown in from New York to attend the premiere, and later that night in his suite at the Beverly Hills Hotel, he drew up what would become Judy Garland's first recording contract.

August 14, 1937: *The Hollywood Reporter's* review of *Broadway Melody* said,

> The sensational work of young Judy Garland causes wonder as to why she has been kept under wrap these many months. She sings two numbers that are showstoppers and does a dance with Buddy Ebsen. Hers is a distinctive personality well worth careful promotion. A certain picture star.

Here are excerpts from some of the other reviews Judy's work in *Broadway Melody* received:

> *The New York Times,* 9-3-37, Brosley Crowther: "Miss Garland particularly has a tour-de-force in which she addresses lyrical apostrophes to a picture of Clark Gable. She puts it over, in fact, with a bang."
>
> *The New York Herald-Tribune*: "A girl named Judy Garland does a heartwarming song about her love for Clark Gable, which the audience seemed to like."
>
> *Film Weekly*: "Judy Garland, youngest member of the cast, can best be described as a 'Tucker in her teens,' her torch singing being unquestionably first-rate. Even a rather silly song designed to boost Gable, takes on touching pathos when she puts it over. Obviously a 'find,' of whom more is going to be heard."
>
> *The Los Angeles Herald-Express*: "(Judy) really walks away with the picture. Here is not only a complete artist, but a personality that takes you by storm."

August 20, 1937: Judy issues her first public "Thank You" (to Sam Katz, Jack Cummings, and Roger Edens, for their hand in *Broadway Melody*) in a trade paper, which appeared in this day's issue of *The Hollywood Reporter.*

Summer 1937: Judy's mother, Ethel, changed Judy's agent. After briefly considering Abe Lastfogel of the William Morris Agency, Ethel replaced Al Rosen (Judy's first real agent, the one who helped get her into MGM), with Jesse Martin.

August 23, 1937: Judy was making personal appearances at the San Francisco Paramount Theater in connection with *Broadway Melody of 1938.*

August 26, 1937: MGM recording session. Judy recorded "Swing, Mr. Mendelson" for *Everybody Sing,* which had just started production. (Judy was also working on *Thoroughbreds Don't Cry.* An "extended version" of "Swing" can be heard on the *Collector's Gems* CD set.)

August 30, 1937: (Record) Judy's first recording contract with Decca Records (for an initial six months) was "sealed," with a recording session that produced one single (two songs): "Everybody Sing," from *Broadway Melody of 1938,* backed with "All God's Chillun Got Rhythm." The single would be released in September 1937 as Decca 78 single # 1432. (Judy would have some thirty sessions for Decca over the next ten years, producing a total of seventy-seven songs for the label along with the two cut for her first single in 1936, before she signed with the label.)

September 11, 1937: MGM recording session: "Sun Showers," from *Thoroughbreds Don't Cry.* (This song was cut after filming. The song still exists and is included in the *Collector's Gems* Rhino set; the footage is not known to exist.)

September 20, 1937: MGM recording session: "Got A Pair Of New Shoes," for *Thoroughbreds Don't Cry.* (There is a longer version recorded than the one used in the final film. This "extended version" can be found on the above-mentioned Rhino *Collector's Gems* two-CD set.)

September 24, 1937: (Record) Decca session, in Hollywood, that produced Judy's first hit single, "Dear Mr. Gable: You Made Me Love You," backed with "You Can't Have Everything." The single would be released the following month. (Spike Jones played the drums for this session.)

Late Summer/Early Fall 1937: Rehearsal recording made with Judy singing "Feeling Like A Million" to promote *Broadway Melody of 1938*; Roger Edens accompanies her on the piano. (This recording is found on the four-CD box set *Judy* on the 32 Records label, released October 13, 1998.)

October 4, 1937: MGM recording session: "Down on Melody Farm" (for *Everybody Sing*). (A longer version than heard in the film is available on the two-CD Rhino *Collectors' Gems* set.)

October 12, 1937: (Radio) *Ben Bernie and All the Lads,* NBC Radio, Los Angeles, WJZ Blue Network. (A 30-minute program.) Judy sang "They Can't Take That Away From Me" and "Got A Pair Of New Shoes" from her upcoming release, *Thoroughbreds Don't Cry.*

October 24, 1937: MGM recording session: "Got A Pair Of New Shoes" (finale version with Rooney and Sinclair) for *Thoroughbreds Don't Cry,* then a radio show: *Thirty Minutes in Hollywood* broadcast over WOR Radio, starring George Jessel. Judy sang "Dear Mr. Gable: You Made Me Love You" to plug *Broadway Melody of 1938,* which was now in wide release.

End of October 1937: Judy finishes production of *Thoroughbreds Don't Cry* at MGM. The film would be released on November 26, 1937.

November 4, 1937: (Radio) *New Faces of 1938,* NBC, WEAF, Red Network (60 minutes). This series' name would be changed to *Good News of 1938* with the next broadcast, and was produced in association with MGM. (This episode spotlighted *Broadway Melody of 1938,* with Judy singing her songs from the film. Judy would be added to its roster as a regular—or more appropriately as a *semi*-regular. There would be 11 additional appearances from November 1937 to May 1938.)

November 6, 1937, November 7, 1937, and November 8, 1937: Judy performing "Silent Night" was rehearsed, recorded, and filmed at MGM for the 1937 MGM Christmas Trailer. (This song is on the 1995 Judy laser disc box set, *The Golden Years At MGM.*)

November 18, 1937: (Radio) *Good News of 1938*, NBC. (Judy's songs not verified.)

November 19, 1937: Publicity photos were taken with Judy, Alan Jones, and Fanny Brice for their *Everybody Sing* movie.

November 25, 1937: (Radio) *Good News of 1938*, NBC. Judy sang "Got A Pair Of New Shoes" to promote *Thoroughbreds Don't Cry*, which was released the next day.

December 13, 1937: MGM recording session for *Everybody Sing*. The song, "Shall I Sing A Melody?" was recorded by Judy (the audio is found on the *Collectors' Gems* CD set).

December 21, 1937: The song "Why? Because!" was filmed by Judy and Fanny Brice (who played Baby Snooks for the only time on film) for *Everybody Sing*. (This was recorded "live" on the set, with no pre-recording done. The Rhino two-CD *Collectors* set utilized a partially alternate take, as the ending of the song is slightly different in the finished film.)

1938

Early January 1938: Judy finishes production of *Everybody Sing* at MGM. (Release date was February 4, 1938.) The following are excerpts from the notices:

> *Variety*, 1-26-38: "The diminutive Judy Garland takes a long leap forward to stardom. She has what it takes."
>
> *Film Weekly*: "Judy Garland is an extremely clever little comedian. She proves it in a delightful duet with Fanny Brice, and anyone who stands up to Miss Brice at her own comedy game is very good indeed. Also, Garland's is the number which lifts the picture into the 'excellent' class: her burlesque of 'Swing Low, Sweet Chariot,' complete with blacked face and 'Uncle Tom's Cabin' curls, is as good as anything I have seen in my recent film going."
>
> *Kinematograph Weekly* (British publication): "She has a sense of character, a sense of humor, and, above all, an amazing flair for hot rhythm."

January 6, 1938: (Radio) *Good News of 1938*, NBC. Judy's songs included "Smiles," "While Strolling Through The Park One Day," and "Suddenly."

Mid January 1938: Preview of *Everybody Sing* in Westwood, California.

January 20, 1938: (Radio) *Good News of 1938*, NBC. Judy sang "Smiles."

February 3, 1938: (Radio) *Good News of 1938*, NBC. Judy sang "Everybody Sing," appearing on the show with Allan Jones and Fanny Brice, her costars in *Everybody Sing*, to promote their film, which opened the next day.

February 4, 1938: World premiere of *Everybody Sing* at the Sheraton Theater in Miami Beach, Florida. (Judy stayed at the Roney Plaza Hotel while appearing at the theater's 8 and 10 p.m. shows.)

February 10, 1938: (Personal appearance) Judy's first appearance on a New York stage—the Loew's State in support of *Everybody Sing. Variety* raved "Youngster is a resounding wallop in her first vaudeville appearance [as Judy Garland]. Comes to the house with a rep in films and after a single date on the *Chase and Sanborn* radio show. Apparent from outset that girl is no mere flash, but has both the personality and the skill to develop into a box-office wow in any line of show business. Applause was solid, and she encored twice, finally begging off with an ingratiating and shrewd thank-you speech." (Judy's appearance grossed $10,000 more for the theater than their average weekly gross of that time.)

February 17, 1938: (Radio) *Good News of 1938*, NBC. Judy sang "Down On Melody Farm" from *Everybody Sing*. (It is likely that a recording from the soundtrack was used—and this may have been done on other occasions—as Judy was in New York, on tour in support of *Sing*.)

February 24, 1938: Judy's role in, and the production of, *The Wizard of Oz* are announced in *Variety*, page 3.

Late February 1938: (Personal appearance) Columbus, Ohio. Another appearance in support of *Everybody Sing*.

Early to mid March 1938: (Personal appearance) Chicago, in support of *Everybody Sing*. (While in Chicago, Judy and her mother stayed at The Palmer House. In a letter Judy's mother wrote to a family friend, dated March 15, 1938, we learn that Ethel had been answering all Judy's fan mail—about 100 letters a day—and Ethel had finally just hired a girl who "comes in three times a week for about four hours" to help with the mail.)

Mid to late March 1938: (Personal appearance) Pittsburgh, Pennsylvania. Appearance in support of *Everybody Sing*.

Late March 1938: (Personal appearance) Detroit, Michigan. Appearance in support of *Everybody Sing*.

Last few days of March 1938: Back to Chicago for more personal appearances in support of *Everybody Sing*.

March 28, 1938: Judy wrote a letter to L. B. Mayer's personal assistant, Ida Koverman, who had been an early supporter of Judy and largely responsible for her signing with MGM. Judy apologized for taking so long to write Koverman, and for how she had gone from a weeklong rest in NYC to the tour promoting *Everybody Sing*. Judy said that Manhattan "was as wonderful, as exciting, and as glamorous as ever," and concluded by sending love to Ida and Mayer, from herself, her mother, and Roger Edens.

April 2, and April 3, 1938: Last stop on promotional tour: Grand Rapids, Minnesota. This was Judy's only return trip to her hometown since she left with her family in the fall of 1926, and the last time she would ever be there. Judy and her mother spent two days there; Judy saw the house she was born in and the high school she would have attended. S. E. Heller arranged a luncheon at the Pokegama Hotel. Judy also appeared on stage between shows at the Rialto, the very first stage she ever sang on back on, December 26, 1924. While in Grand Rapids, Judy and her mother were guests of Mr. and Mrs. George O'Brien at their Riverside Hotel apartment.

April 4, 1938: Judy arrives home in Los Angeles.

April 7, 1938: (Radio) *Good News of 1938*, NBC (60 minutes). Judy sang "Stompin' At The Savoy" and "Why, Because?" with Fanny Brice from *Everybody Sing*.

Early April 1938: Judy goes into preproduction work on her next film, *Love Finds Andy Hardy*, with Mickey Rooney.

April 14, 1938: (Radio) *Good News of 1938*, NBC (60 Minutes). Judy's songs included "Why? Because" with Fanny Brice; "College Swing"; and a medley that included "The Notre Dame Victory Song," "On A Brave Old Army Team," "Fight For USC," and "Anchors Aweigh."

April 21, 1938: (Radio) *Good News of 1938*, NBC (60 Minutes). Judy's songs: "There's A Gold Mine in the Sky" and "My Heart Is Taking Lessons." (Recording of the later song still exists in private collections.)

April 25, 1938: (Record) Decca recording session in Hollywood producing one 78 single, "Cry, Baby, Cry," backed with "Sleep My Baby Sleep," released in May 1938, #1796. (Spike Jones played the drums for this session.)

April 28, 1938: (Radio) *Good News of 1938*, NBC (60 Minutes). Judy sings "Thanks For The Memory" (with special lyrics by Rodger Edens.)

May 5, 1938: (Radio) *Good News of 1938*, NBC (60 Minutes). Judy's songs included "How Deep Is The Ocean?"; "God's Country"; and "Serenade." (This was Judy's last appearance on the series. These three songs exist in private collections.)

Early to mid May 1938: Judy started filming *Love Finds Andy Hardy* at MGM.

May 16, 1938: Judy shot publicity stills with Mickey Rooney for *Love Finds Andy Hardy.*

May 24, 1938: Judy suffered three broken ribs, a sprained back, and a punctured lung, in an automobile accident. It appeared at first that Judy would be written out of *Andy Hardy*; however, her legendary powers of recovery were first put to the test at MGM, when . . .

June 10, 1938: Judy's sixteenth birthday, and the next day . . .

June 11, 1938: Judy returned to MGM to work on *Love Finds Andy Hardy.*

June 21, 1938: MGM recording session for *Love Finds Andy Hardy.* "It Never Rains, But What It Pours" and "Bei Mir Bist Du Schoen" were recorded by Judy. ("Bei Mir" would be cut before the film's release; the footage is not known to exist. It is possible that "Bei Mir" was not ever filmed. This song and the remixed, true *stereo* version of "It Never Rains" from the multitrack recording session can be heard on the Rhino *Collectors' Gems* two-CD set. These are the earliest known Judy Garland recordings to exist in *stereo* format. All of MGM's recording sessions were made in stereo—using microphones placed in multiple angles, and recorded onto individual stems/tracks. Many of these multiple stems would be transferred to audio tape in the early 1960s and be used for home video, CD, and even theatrical use starting in 1994. Not all of the stems survived, however, and so there are still many songs that can only be heard in mono instead of stereo. But, several songs, and even entire scores—supremely the ones from *Meet Me in St. Louis* and *Girl Crazy*—sound wonderfully rich and clear in true stereo today, thanks to MGM's devotion to quality, which dates back to the 1930s.)

June 24, 1938: MGM recording session. "In Between" and "Meet The Beat Of My Heart," both for *Love Finds Andy Hardy.* (Both are available in their originally recorded *stereo* versions, on the two-CD Rhino Records *Collector's Gems* set. This version of "Meet The Beat" is longer than the one used in the film.)

June 25, 1938: Judy filmed the two scenes that included the two songs recorded the day before, thus completing her work on *Love Finds Andy Hardy.* The film was released on July 22, 1938. Here are excerpts from her reviews:

> *Variety*, 7-13-38: "Newcomer to the Hardy group of players is Judy Garland, who tops off a slick performance by singing three good songs. Based on her showing, they will have to find a permanent place for Miss Garland in the future Hardy's."

Publicity photo of Judy with Mickey Rooney, taken on May 16, 1938, for *Love Finds Andy Hardy*. This was Judy's first of three appearances as the singing "Betsy Booth" (daughter of musical comedy star "Martha Booth") and her second of ten films she'd make with "the Mick." (Courtesy of Photofest.)

> *The Motion Picture Daily*: "[Judy comes] close to taking the [film's top] honors out of [co-star Mickey Rooney's] hands."
>
> *The Los Angeles Times*: "A fine foil . . . a very fine performance."

Late June 1938: Judy went into production on her next film at MGM, *Listen, Darling* (first announced for her in August 1937).

June 28, 1938: Wardrobe Tests for *Listen, Darling*.

July 8, 1938: Publicity photos were shot on the set of *Listen, Darling*.

July 8, 1938: (Radio Premiere) Premiere of the movie *Marie Antoinette* at the Cathay Circle Theater, in Hollywood, and broadcast over NBC Radio (60 Minutes). (The radio show is not known to exist.)

July 12, 1938: (Radio) *The Rinso Program, Starring Al Jolson*, CBS (30 Minutes). Judy substituted for Martha Raye, as she would again in 1966, in Las Vegas. Judy and Martha Raye also worked together on an episode of Judy's television series in January 1964. Perhaps most ironic is the fact that these two friends were once married to the same man, composer David Rose, who wrote "The Stripper." (Rose, in fact, left Raye to become Judy's first husband in 1941; Judy and Rose separated in 1943). Rose also scored *Little House on the Prairie* and *Bonanza*, which, ironically, were successful in beating their competition during the 1963–1964 television season, *The Judy Garland Show*. *The Rinso Program* radio show was also the first time Judy worked with the legendary performer Al Jolson, with whom she would be compared to in later years for the way she electrified audiences as he had done decades earlier. Judy would comment on this in 1968 saying, "I'm always being compared to Al Jolson, which doesn't help a woman's vanity!"

Judy's work during much of July and August 1938 was concentrated on the film *Listen, Darling*.

July 28, 1938: MGM recording session for *Listen, Darling*. "Ten Pins In The Sky" was recorded by Judy.

August 21, 1938, 6:30 to 10:15 p.m.: (Record) Judy recorded her next single for Decca, "It Never Rains, But What It Pours," from *Love Finds Andy Hardy*, backed with "Ten Pins In The Sky," from *Listen, Darling*. The 78 single, # 2017, was released in October 1938. (Spike Jones played the drums for this session, as he had for the September 24, 1937 and April 25, 1938 Decca sessions.)

August 27, 1938: Judy's first noted work on *The Wizard of Oz*—Judy's initial costume, hair and makeup tests (stills) were shot for *Oz*. The surviving shots show Judy looking more like *Alice in Wonderland* than Dorothy Gale as she modeled both blonde and red wigs and heavy make-up. (When shooting first started, MGM had initially decided to go with the blonde wig.)

September 8, 1938: (Radio) *Good News of 1939*, NBC (60 minutes). (Sponsored by Maxwell House.) Judy's songs included "In-Between," from *Love Finds Andy Hardy*, "My Lucky Star," and "Could You Pass In Love" arranged by Roger Edens (this last performance is available on the CD *Judy Garland on Radio, 1936–1944, Volume 1* on the Vintage Jazz Classics label, 1993).

Early to mid September 1938: Preproduction finally starts on *The Wizard of Oz* as Judy works on/finishes *Listen, Darling*.

September 16, 1938: MGM recording session for *Listen, Darling*. "Zing! Went The Strings Of My Heart." (The *stereo* version is available on the *Thoroughbreds Don't Cry/Listen, Darling* laser disc set and the Rhino six-CD *That's Entertainment* set. An alternate, unused swing version is on the Rhino *Collectors' Gems* set.)

September 22, 1938: Judy filmed the "Zing! Went The Strings Of My Heart" song to which she had recorded the vocal on September 16, for the *Listen, Darling* film. (All of Judy's songs at MGM, and beyond, are expertly lip-synched, as is still the custom today—just think of MTV videos. The only songs sung by Judy live on the set are a few lines of a "Swing, Mr. Mendelson, Swing" reprise sung to Allan Jones and Fanny Brice and the song "Why? Because!" also with Brice, from *Everybody Sing* [1938]; "Happy Birthday to You" in *Life Begins for Andy Hardy* [1941], in which, oddly enough, all her other songs were dropped before the film's release; and "It Never Was You," sung on a soundstage mock up of the London Palladium for Judy's last released movie *I Could Go On Singing* [1963].) Also on this date, Judy shot publicity photos with the cast of *Listen, Darling*.

September 26, 1938: MGM recording session for *Listen, Darling*. "On The Bumpy Road To Love" was recorded by Judy, Mary Astor, Freddie Bartholomew, and Scotty Beckett. (The *stereo* version can be heard on both the Rhino *Collectors' Gems* set, and the MGM/UA home video laser disc set of *Thoroughbreds Don't Cry/Listen, Darling*, which also has some alternate takes, etc.)

September 30, 1938: Judy's first recording session for *The Wizard Of Oz* at MGM. "If I Only Had The Nerve" and "We're Off To See The Wizard," both recorded with Bert Lahr, Ray Bolger, and Buddy Ebsen, the original Tin Man.

Early October 1938: Judy finally finishes *Listen, Darling* at MGM. (The film would be released almost immediately—October 16, 1938.)

October 6, 1938: MGM recording session for *Oz.* "The Jitterbug." (This song would be cut from the film before release; the song exists, the footage does not. There are surviving "home movies" shot on 16mm by the film's composer, Harold Arlen; these have been released on various *Oz* home video, laser disc, and DVD releases in 1989, 1993, and 1999 and synched with the audio of the song to form a rough "recreation" of the number.)

October 7, 1938: MGM recording session for *Oz.* "Over The Rainbow," Judy's signature/theme song is recorded for the first time ever (This is also, perhaps, the first "official public performance," certainly the first performance for "professional reasons"), although the filming of the song would be one of the last things shot for the movie, in March 1939.

October 11, 1938: MGM recording session for *Oz.* "We're Off To See The Wizard" is recorded with Judy and Ray Bolger, and with Judy, Ray Bolger, and Buddy Ebsen—the original Tin Man before his near-fatal allergic reaction to the makeup he was wearing forced him to be replaced by Jack Haley. Haley only recorded his solo in this song and his solos in other songs. In any "ensemble" songs with all four main characters singing together, Buddy Ebsen's voice is heard. That is his voice, still a part of *The Wizard of Oz.* Orchestras for the *Oz* recording sessions were between 35–38 pieces.) Also recorded on this day: "If I Were King Of The Forest" with Judy and cast.

October 12, 1938: On-set tests were done for *Oz* at MGM.

October 13, 1938: *Oz* started filming at MGM under direction of Richard Thorpe. First scene filmed: Dorothy and the Scarecrow in the cornfield, "If I Only Had A Brain." (The first day's shooting made the front page of *Daily Variety* the next day.)

October 15, 1938: *Oz* filming. The scenes in the Witch's castle tower room were shot.

October 17, 1938: Judy filmed a reprise of "Over The Rainbow" that would be cut from the film. The scene took place in the Wicked Witch's Castle as Dorothy was crying about missing Aunt Em. (The reprise was sung live on the set, with piano only, played by Roger Edens. The orchestra would be recorded on May 6, 1939, during a background scoring session. The footage is not known to exist; the audio has survived, and is available on both *The Ultimate Oz* laser disc box set released in 1993, the DVD released in 1999, and the two-CD Rhino Soundtrack package.)

Week of October 17, 1938: Scenes at the Wicked Witch's castle were filmed.

October 20, 1938: (Radio) *Good News of 1939*, NBC (60 minutes). Judy sang "Zing! Went The Strings of My Heart" and "On The Bumpy Road To Love," both from her just-released film *Listen, Darling.*

October 21, 1938: *Oz* scene was filmed. Dorothy and friends running down stairs to entrance hall of Wicked Witch's Castle.

October 24, 1938: *Oz* stops filming until November 4, as Buddy Ebsen had just collapsed from his aluminum makeup, and the film's producer, Mervyn LeRoy, unhappy with what he was seeing, fired director Thorpe and brought in George Cukor (on a temporary consulting basis).

October 26, 1938: Judy did new hair and makeup tests for *Oz*, under the direction of Cukor. (These stills included using her own hair with elaborate braids, and also some other blond wigs. Judy wore the dress she had been wearing during the two weeks of filming.)

October 30, 1938: Judy recorded "Merry Old Land Of Oz" with Jack Haley, the new Tin Man.

October 31, 1938: More *Oz* hair/makeup/wardrobe tests for Judy. (She was wearing the "original dress," and her "own hair and fall, before darkening.")

November 3, 1938: Cukor puts the finishing touches on the Dorothy the world knows and loves. (In his later direction of Judy, for their *A Star Is Born*, Judy and George must have relished—if not have been responsible for—the scene where the studio makeup department men turn Judy's character into an overly made-up, blonde starlet.)

November 4, 1938: *Oz* filming starts over under the direction of Victor Fleming, with the first scene filmed being the first scene, ironically, that had been filmed prior: Dorothy meeting the Scarecrow in the cornfield—the one we all see today. Not much was accomplished this day on Stage 26. During the first take of the day (at about 11 a.m.), the raven on the Scarecrow's shoulder became more temperamental than any other MGM star, truly "flying" into a rage. The rest of the day was wasted trying to get the bird down. No other filming was completed this day.

Week of November 7, 1938: The Cornfield sequence was completed with Judy and Ray Bolger followed by the scenes with the "talking trees." During the last three days of the week, through Saturday, November 12, the meeting of the Tin Man with Judy, Bolger, and Jack Haley was filmed—until it was realized that Haley's tin suit was shiny when it was supposed to be rusty, so three days of shooting were scrapped at a cost of more than $60,000. (That's an expensive piece of tin!)

November 16, 1938 to Friday, November 18, 1938: Scene of the first meeting of the Tin Man was refilmed with Judy, Bolger, and Haley, after the previous week's footage was scrapped.

November 19, 1938: "We're Off To See The Wizard" with Judy, Bolger, and Haley was shot. (Haley, oddly enough, had to lip-synch to Buddy Ebsen's voice, which was still on the vocal track and would never be rerecorded.)

Week of Monday, November 21, 1938 through Saturday, November 26, 1938: Judy and cast's "first meeting" with the Cowardly Lion was filmed.

Friday, November 25, 1938: Judy was officially promoted by MGM from "Featured Player" to "Star" and was presented with her own trailer dressing room. Members of the cast and crew gathered on the set to watch the presentation.

Week of Monday, November 28, 1938: Scenes in the "poppy fields" filmed with Judy and the other principals.

December 1, 1938: Scene in Wicked Witch's castle—where she is melted—was filmed with Judy and cast.

December 9, 1938 to December 30, 1938: Munchkinland sequence recorded and filmed.

December 9, 1938: MGM recording session with Judy for the Munchkinland sequence.

December 10, 1938: Scene in Witch's castle filmed.

December 14, 1938 to December 16, 1938: MGM recording session for *Oz* Munchkinland sequence. (Filming on this sequence started at this time.)

December 14, 1938: (Radio) *National Redemption Movement Program*, NBC Radio (30 minutes). Judy joined Mickey Rooney, Lewis Stone, and Jean Parker in a "Hardy Family" Sketch. (This show was a cel-

The most famous foursome ever (and Toto, too!): Jack Haley, Ray Bolger, Judy, and Bert Lahr make movie magic on the yellow brick road—and make history as stars of the one movie seen by more people than any other. (Courtesy of Photofest.)

ebration of the anniversary of the American Bill of Rights.) *Also, a second radio appearance*: *America Calling*, during which Judy sang "My Old Kentucky Home." (No other info is available about this program. A recording of this song survives in private collections.)

December 19, 1938: MGM recording session for *Oz* Munchkinland sequence.

December 22, 1938: MGM recording session for *Oz* Munchkinland sequence, including "Follow The Yellow Brick Road/You're Off To See The Wizard." *Also* recorded this day: the opening portion of "The Jitterbug" song was rerecorded with Jack Haley.

December 26, 1938: Christmas holiday; no work for Judy.

December 28, 1938: MGM recording session for *Oz*. "The Merry Old Land Of Oz" with Judy and cast. *Also* on this day: filming of the scene in the Munchkinland sequence where the Wicked Witch exits (during which Margaret Hamilton, as the Witch, was badly burned by some of the special effects; she would not return to work until mid February 1939.)

December 29, 1938: The very beginning of the Munchkinland sequence was filmed.

December 30, 1938: MGM recording session for *Oz*. More work on "The Merry Old Land Of Oz." This day was also spent completing the filming of the Munchkinland sequence.

1939

January 3, 1939: MGM recording session for *Oz*. Additional work on "The Merry Old Land of Oz" and filming for the "Haunted Forest" scene.

Early January 1939: A cold kept Judy away from MGM for about three days.

January 6, 1939: "Haunted Forest" scene filmed: "I'd turn back if I were you."

January 8, 1939: (Radio) *Hollywood Screen Guild Show*, CBS Radio (30 minutes). Judy sang "Shall I Sing A Melody" ("Sweet or Swing?") from *Everybody Sing* and "Thanks For The Memory" as the first guest on the premiere episode of this new show. (Performers fees were paid to The Motion Picture Relief Fund. Judy's performances from this show are on the LP and cassette *Judy Garland on Radio* on the Radiola label, released in 1974.) *Also* on this date, Judy appeared on the cover of the *Los Angeles Times* Sunday color section biting into an apple to promote *Oz*.

January 9, 1939, January 11, 1939, and January 13, 1939: Filming on "The Jitterbug" number for *Oz*. (This song was cut in final editing; the song exists, but the only surviving footage is silent footage available on both the *50th Anniversary* and on all *Oz* video editions from 1989 on, as well as the CDs from Rhino Records.)

January 12, 1939: Scene on Yellow Brick Road filmed after waking up from poppies.

January 14, 1939: Emerald City sequence filmed with Judy and cast, including Frank Morgan ("Who Rang That Bell?").

Third week of January 1939 (January 17, 19, and 20, 1939): Interior of Emerald City sequence filmed ("Merry Old Land of Oz.")

January 22, 1939: (Radio) Eddie Cantor's *Council of Stars* broadcast for The March of Dimes. (No other information available on this program.)

Last week of January 1939: The Wizard's balloon sequence was filmed for *Oz* with Judy ("Oh, now I'll never get home").

Late January to Mid February 1939: Filming of Emerald City sequences in the palace hallway, throne room, and foyer (which included filming the "If I Were King Of The Forest" song with Judy and cast). (Both Judy and Ray Bolger had missed several days during the second week of February due to illness.)

February 10, 1939: Judy attended Artie Shaw's opening at the Palomar nightclub in Hollywood. (Bandleader Shaw was Judy's first "adult" and "true" love—though he didn't return those feelings.)

(Around this time, Judy's MGM-appointed assistant was Betty Asher.)

Sometime during early winter to spring 1939, Judy and her mother had a large, four bedroom house built for themselves at 1231 Stone Canyon Road near Sunset Blvd. in the Bel Aire area of West Los Angeles. Jackie Cooper's mother, Mabel, was once again the decorator, as she was for their previous home. This new home had every possible game facility, from tennis and badminton courts to a swimming pool to garden walks and pinball machines. There was even a solarium with a complete suite for Judy on the top floor that contained a bedroom almost as large as a living room, big enough to entertain her friends, her own dressing room, and bath. There was a double bed, covered with cushions, in a little alcove, and a huge bookcase, which, when a hidden button was pressed, turned to reveal a secret Alice-In-Wonderland room for Judy. There was also a separate entrance leading to her quarters so she could have privacy.

Middle of February to February 17, 1939: Filming of The Wizard's "presentation" scenes ("A heart is not judged by how much you love, but by how much you are loved by others"). This marked director Victor Flemming's final days of work on *Oz*, as he left to salvage another 1939 classic that would also be released by MGM: *Gone With The Wind.*

Week of February 19, 1939 to February 25, 1939: Filming for the black-and-white Kansas scenes began; the farmhands scenes with Judy were filmed first.

February 25, 1939: Judy shot publicity photos for *Oz* with Ray Bolger and cast. (Her hair is not in braids, but in the longer style used in post-Emerald City scenes. Judy's close-up portraits with Toto were taken by MGM Photo Gallery chief Clarence Sinclair.)

Late February to the second week of March 1939: Principal photography of *Oz* completed by filming the scenes with "Miss Gulch," the scene with "Professor Marvel," some retakes on Judy's and Ray Bolger's first meeting in the cornfield, and, of course, "Over The Rainbow."

March 7, 1939: (Radio) *The Pepsodent Show Starring Bob Hope*, NBC (30 minutes). Judy's songs included "Franklin D. Roosevelt Jones"—which she would later sing in the film *Babes On Broadway* (1941)—"Sleep, My Baby, Sleep"; and a medley consisting of "Yankee Doodle Dandy"; "Stars And Stripes Forever"; "Columbia The Gem Of The Ocean." ("FDR Jones" exists in private collections.)

Mid March 1939: Only a few days after completing shooting on *Oz*, Judy left Los Angeles for a five week Personal Appearance Tour, which included return engagements in Cleveland, Ohio (where she broke the theater attendance record), and a return to New York.

April 6, 1939: (Radio) *Tune-Up Time,* CBS, New York, (45 minutes). Judy sang "FDR Jones" and "Sweet Sixteen." (It was amazing that MGM was allowing her to publicly admit her true "advanced" age. Another guest on this show was singer Kay Thompson, who from the middle 1940s on would become a major influence on Judy's style, her covocal arranger at MGM with Roger Edens, a lifelong friend and supporter, and, in 1946, daughter Liza Minnelli's godmother. This may have been their very first meeting. Judy's rendition of "Sweet Sixteen" from this show is on the CD *Judy Garland on Radio, 1936–1944, Volume 1: All The Things You Are* on Vintage Jazz Classics, 1993; Judy would soon record this song for Decca—see July 28, 1939.)

Judy and Toto pose between takes on the *Oz* set. There was a deep bond between the two, and Judy was a lifelong dog-lover and owner; twenty-five years later you could see her with a similar breed of terrier on episodes of *The Judy Garland Show*. (Courtesy of Photofest.)

Mid April 1939: (Personal Appearance) Return engagement at New York's Loew's State. Police had to be called in order to control the crowds, and she received an even more glowing review from *Variety*:

> "The impression of voice, singing style, and personality is all in her favor. Response heightens in intensity and volume as [she] proceeds. She's potent box office . . . a refreshing performer."

April 30, 1939: Judy returned to Los Angeles and went right into rehearsals for her next movie, *Babes in Arms*, which took only eleven weeks to complete. (The film had been planned as a vehicle for Judy and Mickey Rooney since the summer of 1938.)

Early May 1939: Judy filmed some retakes/pickup shots for *Oz* with "Glinda" (Billie Burke).

May 3, 1939: Costume tests for *Babes in Arms.*

May 6, 1939: Judy rehearsed the "Opera Vs. Jazz" number for *Babes in Arms.* She had a 10 a.m. call and was dismissed at 12:40 p.m.

May 8, 1939: Judy rehearsed the "Opera Vs. Jazz" and the "Good Morning" numbers for *Arms.* She had a 1 p.m. call and was dismissed at 4:55 p.m.

May 9, 1939: (Radio) Production notes for *Babes in Arms* note that the company had the day off since Judy was rehearsing for *The Pepsodent Show Starring Bob Hope*, NBC (30 minutes). (Judy's songs unidentified.)

One of the first known photographs of a theater marquee with "Judy Garland" in lights. This shot is from mid-April 1939, during her return engagement at the Loew's State, in Times Square, New York. Note the Wrigley's Spearmint gum billboard and the other theaters. (Courtesy of Photofest.)

May 10, 1939: Production notes for *Arms* show that Judy did prerecording for the "Opera Vs. Jazz" and "Rock-A-Bye-Baby" numbers (the latter is not known to be in final film or to exist.) Judy was on the set at 11:30 a.m.; had lunch from 1–2 p.m.; and was dismissed at 6 p.m. (Keep in mind that after filming, Judy often had other work to do at night—publicity appearances, interviews, radio shows, and making records, as well as getting home in time to have dinner and memorize the next day's shooting script, before bedtime and the early morning calls. Being a movie star at that time was a lot of hard work, and only handfuls of glamour.)

May 11, 1939: Judy did prerecording for "Good Morning," "Opera Vs. Jazz," and "Where or When." JG– Time called: 12:30 p.m. Time dismissed: 4:05 p.m.

May 12, 1939: Judy started filming *Babes in Arms,* on Stage 3. Name of Set: Int. Randall's Office ("Good Morning" song). Production notes for the day reveal: "JG– Time called: 9 a.m; arrived on set at 8:52 a.m.; 9:14–9:20—wait for Judy Garland, putting on wardrobe; 9:30–9:44—fix Judy's makeup and hair; lunch was from 12:30–1:30 p.m.; time dismissed: 5:40 p.m."

May 13, 1939: Scene filmed for *Arms.* Name of Set: Int. Randall's Office, Int. Moran Living Room. JG– Time called: 9 a.m.; lunch, 12:40–1:40 p.m.; time dismissed: 5:55 p.m.

May 15, 1939: MGM recording session for *Babes in Arms* movie. Judy completed "Good Morning," "Opera Vs. Jazz" duet/medley, and "Where or When." There was also filming this day: Int. Moran Living Room. Judy had a 9 a.m. call. The Assisant Director (AD) report shows: "9:00–9:17—wait for Judy Garland—she arrived on set 9 a.m.; but was putting on wardrobe. Meantime, rehearse without Judy; 9:17–9:20—wait for Judy Garland; lunch was 12:07–1:07; time dismissed: 6 p.m."

May 16, 1939: Judy worked on filming the scene, Int. Moran Living Room. "Judy's time called: 9 a.m.; 9:00–9:12—rehearsed to playback without Judy; 9:12–9:20—wait for Judy. She arrived on set at 9 a.m.; but was putting on wardrobe. Lunch was from 12:00–1:00 p.m.; 2:53–3:23—new set was arranged and lit (note that the company had to shoot around Judy until 4:30 p.m. since she had to finish her school work); Judy was dismissed at 6 p.m."

May 17, 1939: Judy continued filming the scene Int. Moran Living Room for *Arms.* JG– Time called: 8:30 a.m.; lunch was from 12:00–1:00 p.m.; time dismissed: 5:30 p.m.

May 18, 1939: Judy continued filming the scene Int. Moran Living Room and also worked on Int. Corridor—Backstage and Int Mickey's Bedroom. 9:00–9:15—wait for JG who had a 9:00 a.m. call. Judy arrived on set at 8:58 a.m.; but was putting on wardrobe and fixing hair; lunch was from 12:25–1:25 p.m.; time dismissed: 3:10 p.m.

May 19, 1939: AD reports for *Babes in Arms* show that on this date Judy was in school/did not work.

May 20, 1939: *Arms* filming. Int. Drugstore scene. JG– Time called: 9 a.m.; lunch was from 12:40–1:40 p.m.; time dismissed: 5:56 p.m.

May 22, 1939: *Arms* filming. Int. Mrs. Barton's Dressing Room, Int. Sorro's Office. JG– Time called 9 a.m.; lunch 12:38–1:38; AD reports show: "2:29–2:55—move to Int. Sorro's Office. Note: we could not finish this seq. in the dressing room until later on in afternoon after Judy Garland could finish her school work. She will be finished with same about 4:45"; "4:34–4:58—Move back to Int. Mrs. Barton's Dressing room—line and lite original setup that we had to abandon due to Judy Garland's schooling; 4:58–5:01—wait for Judy Garland—getting on wardrobe/fixing hair; dismissed at 6 p.m."

May 23, 1939: MGM recording session for *Babes in Arms* movie. Judy recorded two songs this day: "Babes In Arms" and "I Cried For You." AD indicates that filming on *Arms* continued (Int. Jim's Saloon, Ext. Moran Home), but noted that "JG was prerecording."

May 24, 1939: *Arms* filming. Int. Palace Theater. JG– Time called: 1 p.m.; time dismissed: 4 p.m.

May 25, 1939: *Arms* filming. Int. Patsy's Bedroom, Int. Judge Black's office. JG– Time called: 9 a.m.; time dismissed 1:30 p.m.; lunch 12:18–1:18; AD report: "1:25–1:30—Note: Judy Garland, who had a bad cold all morning, informed Bill Ryan that she could not work this afternoon."

May 26, 1939: AD report for *Arms* notes that Judy was ill and not working.

May 27, 1939: *Arms* filmed. Int. Patsy's Bedroom and Int. Bus ("I Cried For You" Number). JG– Time called: 9 a.m.; lunch 12:43–1:43; time dismissed: 6 p.m.

May 29, 1939: *Arms* filmed. Int. Judge Black's Office. JG– Time called: 9 a.m.; time dismissed: 3:15 p.m.

May 31, 1939: *Arms* AD notes that Judy was in school this day and did not film. Publicity portrait sitting photographs do exist with this date, though.

June 1, 1939: *Arms* AD notes that Judy was in school this day, and did not film.

June 2, 1939: *Arms* filmed. Ext. Country Road and Path. JG– Time called: 9 a.m.; lunch: 12:31–1:31 p.m.; time dismissed: 5:40 p.m.

June 3, 1939: *Arms* filmed Ext. Bus Terminal—Ext. Patsy's Home. JG–Time called: 9 a.m.; lunch: 12:35–1:35 p.m.; time dismissed: 5:55 p.m.

June 5, 1939: *Arms* AD notes that Judy was in school this day and did not film.

June 6, 1939: *Arms* filmed. Ext. Patsy's Home, Ext. Moran Home, Int. Patsy's Hall and Stairs. JG– Time called: 9 a.m.; lunch was 12:15–1:15 p.m.; time dismissed: 5:50 p.m.

June 7, 1939: *Arms* filmed. Ext. Moran Backyard ("Where or When" song). JG– Time called: 9 a.m.; lunch was 12:30–1:30 p.m.; time dismissed: 5:45 p.m.

June 8, 1939: *Arms* filmed. Ext. Moran Backyard ("Where or When" song). JG– Time called: 9 a.m.; lunch was 12:30–1:30 p.m.; time dismissed: 5:45 p.m.

June 9, 1939: *Arms* filming. Scene not noted. JG– Time called: 9 a.m.; lunch 12:20–1:20 p.m.; time dismissed: 6 p.m.

June 10, 1939: Judy's seventeenth birthday was spent filming Int. and Ext. Barn Theatre scenes. Judy had a 10 a.m. call time and was dismissed at 5:50 p.m. (Lunch time not noted.) Judy also celebrated her birthday at her new home with Artie Shaw and other friends. (There is also existing footage of a birthday "pool party" at Louis B. Mayer's home, with Mickey Rooney, Jackie Cooper, etc., complete with Judy cutting her birthday cake.)

June 12, 1939: *Arms* filmed. Int. and Ext. Barn Theatre scenes. JG–Time called: 9 a.m.; lunch 12:30–1:30 p.m.; time dismissed: 6 p.m.

June 13, 1939: *Arms* filmed. Int. and Ext. Barn Theatre scenes. JG– Time called: 9 a.m.; time dismissed: 5 p.m.

June 14, 1939: *Arms* filmed. Int. and Ext. Barn Theatre scenes. JG–Time called: 10 a.m.; time dismissed: 4:10 p.m.

June 15, 1939: *Arms* filmed. Int. Barn Theatre, Rosalie's Dress Room, and Night Int. Palace Theatre scenes. JG– Time called: 9 a.m.; lunch was 12:20–1:20 p.m.; time dismissed: 5:40 p.m.

Mid June 1939: First previews/test screenings of *Oz* film, held unannounced and inserted into a regular theater program outside greater Los Angeles.

June 16, 1939: *Arms* filmed Int. Barn (Opening Night) scene and rehearsed "Babes In Arms" number. JG– Time called: 9 a.m.; lunch was 12:50–1:50 p.m.; time dismissed: 4 p.m. There were publicity portraits with the cast of *Babes in Arms* that were also done on this day. This was also the day of the second *Oz* preview (First noted date of an *Oz* test screening) held at The Pomona Theater, Los Angeles.

June 17, 1939: For *Arms*, Judy rehearsed "Babes In Arms" number. (Filming was done this day on Ext Alley, Ext. Lamber yd., Ext. Moran Backyard–Moran Home.) JG–Time called: 9 a.m.; time dismissed:12:15.

June 19, 1939: For *Arms,* Judy rehearsed "Minstrel Number" and shot Int. Bus ("I Cried For You" song). JG– Time called: 9 a.m.; lunch: 1:10–2:10 p.m.; time dismissed: 6 p.m.

June 20, 1939: Judy rehearsed "Minstrel Number" for *Arms*. JG– Time called: 9 a.m.; lunch: 12:15–1:15 p.m.; time dismissed: 5:55 p.m.

June 21, 1939: Judy rehearsed "Minstrel Number" for *Arms*; JG–Time called: 9 a.m.; lunch: 12:10–1:10 p.m.; time dismissed: 5:25 p.m.

June 22, 1939: Judy rehearsed "Minstrel Number" and prerecorded "Babes In Arms" for *Arms*. JG– Time called: 9 a.m.; lunch: 12:00–1:00 p.m.; time dismissed: 6 p.m.

June 23, 1939: Judy rehearsed "Minstrel Number" and prerecorded "Babes In Arms" for *Arms*. JG– Time called: 9 a.m.; lunch: 12:00–1:00 p.m.; time dismissed: 4:10 p.m.

June 24, 1939: Judy rehearsed "Minstrel Man" and prerecorded "Minstrel Man." JG– Time called: 1 p.m.; time dismissed: 6 p.m.

June 26, 1939: *Arms* filming. Ext. Moran Backyard ("Babes In Arms" song). JG– Time called: 9 a.m.; lunch: 12:40–1:40 p.m.; time dismissed: 6 p.m.

June 27, 1939: *Arms* filming. Ext. Moran Backyard ("Babes In Arms" song), Ext. Alley ("Babes In Arms" song). Also, recording session for *Babes in Arms* movie. Judy recorded two lengthy songs this day, "Minstrel Show Sequence" (including "I'm Just Wild About Harry") and the "Finale" (including "God's Country"). JG– Time called: 9 a.m.; lunch: 12:15–1:15 p.m.; time dismissed: 6 p.m. (Also on this evening, another *Oz* test screening in San Luis Obispo.)

June 28, 1939: *Arms* filming. Ext. Lumber Yard ("Babes In Arms" number). JG– Time called: 9 a.m.; lunch: 12:30–1:30 p.m.; time dismissed: 5:30 p.m.

June 29, 1939: First was filming for *Arms*. Ext. School Yard ("Babes In Arms" number) JG– Time called: 1 p.m.; time dismissed: 10 p.m. AD notes say, "Judy Garland worked on *Good News* program between 4 p.m. and 6:30 p.m. (Radio): Maxwell House Coffee Time [NBC, (60 minutes)]." This program was dedicated to *The Wizard of Oz* to promote the upcoming release in August. This was the first time Judy sang "Over the Rainbow" on radio. (And the first time she sang it in public for that matter. The public would have to wait until September though, to be able to buy a copy of Judy's recording. Decca, Judy's record label, did not record the song until July 28. This entire radio broadcast—which features Harold Arlen playing "Rainbow" for Judy—is available on the CD *Behind The Scenes of* The Wizard Of Oz, available on the Vintage Jazz Classics label, either separately or packaged with the label's other Judy CD *All the Things You Are—Judy Garland On Radio, 1936–1944*. The portion with Arlen and Judy is on the *Judy* box set on the 32 Records label.)

June 30, 1939: *Arms* AD reports that "JG on *Wizard of Oz* retakes: (*Arms*) Company Not Working Due to Fact Judy Garland working on *Wizard of Oz* Retakes." (This would be the final work Judy would do on *Oz*.)

July 1, 1939: *Arms* filming. Ext. Barn Theatre ("Minstrel" number). JG– Time called: 9 a.m.; lunch: 12:30–1:30 p.m.; time dismissed: 5:45.

July 3, 1939: *Arms* filming. Ext. Barn Theatre ("Minstrel" Number). JG– Time called: 9 a.m.; lunch: 12:20–1:30 p.m.; dismissed: 6 p.m.

July 5, 1939: *Arms* filming. Ext. barn Theatre ("Minstrel" Number). JG– Time called: 10 a.m.; lunch: 12:30–1:30 p.m.; time dismissed: 7 p.m.

July 6, 1939: *Arms* filming. Ext. Barn Theatre ("Minstrel" Number) and Int. Backstage. JG– Time called: 9 a.m.; "10:30–11:12—wait for Judy—putting on 'Hi Yeller' makeup which was difficult to get to right shade. Also putting on body makeup and 'Hi Yeller' costume—Note: Cameraman found that Judy's face makeup was not dark enough makeup and had to be done over in a darker shade"; 11:12–11:24, rehearsal for Judy and Mickey in dance; lunch: 12:18–1:18 p.m.; time dismissed: 4:30 p.m.

July 7, 1939: *Arms* rehearsal, "God's Country" number. JG– Time called: 9 a.m.; lunch: 12:05–1:05 p.m.; time dismissed: 5:45 p.m.

July 8, 1939: *Arms* rehearsal, "God's Country" number. JG– Time called: 9 a.m.; time dismissed: 12:30 p.m.

July 10, 1939: *Arms* rehearsal, "God's Country" number. JG– Time called: 9 a.m.; lunch: 12:40–1:40 p.m.; time dismissed: 5:50 p.m.

July 11, 1939: *Arms* rehearsal, "God's Country" number. JG– time called: 9 a.m.; lunch: 12:20–1:20 p.m.; time dismissed: 5:20 p.m.

July 12, 1939: *Arms* rehearsal, "Gods Country" number, and MGM recording session for *Babes in Arms* (Judy's last session for this film). Prerecord "God's Country" (with a thirty-two piece orchestra). JG– Time called: 9 a.m.; lunch: 12:30–1:30 p.m.; time dismissed: 6 p.m.

July 13, 1939: *Arms* filming. Int. Madox Theatre ("Finale," shot on Stages 5 and 6). JG– Time called: 9 a.m.; lunch: 1:09–2:09 p.m.; time dismissed: 6 p.m.

July 14, 1939: *Arms* filming. Shot "God's Country" number. JG– Time called: 9 a.m.; lunch: 12:30–1:30 p.m.; time dismissed: 5:45 p.m. (Also on this date, Judy and her mother signed a modification to an existing agreement between Loews, Inc. [MGM] and Gleltman, Caopp, and Sadowsky, Inc. of New York to market silk, rayon, and wool dresses as tie-ins with *Oz*. Judy's mother signs the contract as "Ethel M. Garland." ("M" stood for Milne, her maiden name.)

July 15, 1939: *Arms* filming. Shot "God's Country" number. JG– Time called: 9 a.m.; lunch 12:30–1:30 p.m.; time dismissed: 6 p.m.

Also on July 15, 1939: (Record) A new one-year Decca Records contract was signed by Judy's mother Ethel (signature reads "Judy Garland by Ethel M. Garland." Judy was still a minor—she would not turn eighteen until June 10, 1940, a year away—and thus she could not legally sign contracts). The contract called for twelve songs to be recorded within the year, for which Judy would be paid a royalty advance of $250.00 per completed song. (She would actually record sixteen songs during this one-year period.) Her royalty rate was set as follows: where Judy sang on both sides of the single, she would get two cents for each single 78 record sold in the U.S. and Canada and 10 percent of the wholesale price in other countries; where Judy sang on only one side of the record, she would get one cent per disc sold in the

U.S. and Canada. Judy would also be paid 50 percent of whatever Decca would be paid for public performances or broadcasting. As far as songs to record, the contract states, "The Artist agrees to record such selections as Decca may choose within the Artist's repertoire."

July 17, 1939: *Arms* filming. Int. Madox Theatre ("Finale" on Stage 27). JG– Time called: 9 a.m.; lunch: 12:30–1:30 p.m.; time dismissed: 6 p.m.

July 18, 1939: *Arms* filming. Int. Madox Theatre ("Finale," on Stage 27) and Ext. Stage Door on Lot 2; JG– Time called: 9 a.m.; lunch: 12:30–1:30 p.m.; time dismissed: 6 p.m. This completed the actual filming of *Babes in Arms*, although there was some additional/final work done on August 2.

July 28, 1939: (Record) Decca Records recording session: four songs were recorded on this date. Judy's *first* made-for-records version of "Over The Rainbow." (This song was recently voted as "The Song of the Century" by the National Endowment for the Arts and the RIAA—Recording Industry Association of America.) Also recorded on this date: "The Jitterbug" from *Oz*—although by this date it had already "officially" been cut from the film; "In-Between" from Judy's film the year before—1938's *Love Finds Andy Hardy*; and "Sweet Sixteen," which Judy had sung on the April 6, 1939 Radio Show *Tune-Up Time*. "Rainbow" and "Jitterbug" were released as a 78 single—#2672—in September 1939, and—because of "Rainbow" obviously—the single reached the #5 spot on the Billboard chart the same month and became the year's biggest selling record. (In March 1940, the Decca versions of the *Oz* songs would be released as one of the first-ever original movie record "albums" compiled via a collection of 78 singles of songs from the film; although only "Rainbow" and "Jitterbug" actually featured Judy.)

July 29, 1939: (Record) Decca Records recording session, Hollywood, California. This session would produce three songs that, strangely enough, would not be released until 1943. The first two would appear on the *Judy Garland Second Souvenir Album*, a collection of 78 singles released on May 20, 1943; the third would only be released in England, on Decca's Brunswick label. The songs: "Zing! Went The Strings of My Heart" (Judy's first made-for-records version of the song that she sang both at her MGM audition and on the radio the night before her father died in 1935); "Fascinating Rhythm"; and "I'm Just Wild About Harry," featured in her *Babes in Arms* film, which had just finished production.

August 2, 1939: Judy's final work on *Babes in Arms*. Synchronizing on Stage 2A. JG– Time called: 1 p.m.; time dismissed: 2:30 p.m.

Early to mid August, 1939: Sneak Previews/Test Screenings for the just-completed *Babes in Arms*.

August 6, 1939: Judy left Los Angeles for a series of four one-day theater appearances in East Coast cities with Mickey Rooney to promote both *Oz* and their upcoming release of *Babes in Arms* en-route to the New York premiere of *Oz*.

August 9, 1939: Judy and Mickey Rooney opened at the Capitol Theater in Washington, D.C. There were four shows this day, beginning at 2 p.m. and running to mid-evening (which brought on a suit in Juvenile Court, as no girls under 18 were allowed at this time to appear on stage after 7 p.m.).

August 10, 1939: Judy and Mickey Rooney performed in Bridgeport, Connecticut.

August 11, 1939: Judy and Mickey Rooney performed in New Haven, Connecticut.

August 12, 1939: Judy and Mickey Rooney in Hartford, Connecticut—*and*—also on this date:

August 12, 1939: World Premiere "Engagement" (for five days, through Wednesday, August 16) of *Oz*, the Strand Theater, Oconomowoc, Wisconsin.

August 14, 1939, 12:10 p.m.: Judy and Mickey Rooney arrive in New York City, at Grand Central Terminal, to a crowd of over 10,000. (Newsreel footage survives, and some is on the 1999 *Oz* DVD.) They were later taken to their hotel, the Waldorf, for press interviews.

August 15, 1939, 8:30 p.m.: "Official" World Premiere of *The Wizard of Oz* at Grauman's Chinese Theater, Hollywood, California. (Judy was in New York, for the New York premiere two days later.)

August 16, 1939: Judy and Mickey Rooney Luncheon at the Waldorf in New York City to promote *Oz* and their appearance at the Capitol Theater, to open the next day. (This luncheon was also broadcast on radio.)

August 17, 1939: New York Premiere of *The Wizard of Oz*, with Judy and Mickey Rooney doing seven shows between screenings of the film, to a total of 37,000 customers for the day at The Capitol Theater, New York City. The first week of this engagement grossed $100,000. The schedule called for five shows a day—the Judy/Mickey show ran about 26 minutes—with seven screenings of *Oz* during the week; the weekend schedule was seven shows and nine screenings. Judy and Mickey worked from mid-morning, until midnight. Judy's songs in the show included: "The Lamp is Low"; "Comes Love"; "Good Morning"; God's Country" from *Babes in Arms*; and the show closed with "Oceans Apart," which Rooney cowrote (and which Judy would record during her next Decca recording session on October 16, 1939).

> *Variety* said of this engagement, "It's grade-A showmanship by both kids: they're young, fresh, and on the upbeat in the public's affection and imagination—a tousle-haired imp, and a cute, clean-cut girl with a smash singing voice and style."

The reviews for Judy's work in *Oz* were nearly complete raves.

> *The Hollywood Spectator*: "To me, the outstanding feature of the production is the astonishingly clever performance of Judy Garland, holding the picture together, being always its motivating feature, and so natural is she, so perfectly cast, one scarcely becomes conscious of her contribution to the whole. Praise is due this accomplished child: her performance strengthens my conviction that in a few years she will be recognized as one of the screens foremost emotional actresses."

> *The Los Angeles Evening News*: "Garland is sweet and sensitive, with an exceptionally good voice, and it is to her special credit that at the last she manages to touch the heart even in her unpredictable predicament."

> *The New York Daily News*: "4 STARS. Judy Garland is perfectly cast as Dorothy. She is as clever a little actress as she is a singer, and her special style of vocalizing is ideally adapted to the music of the picture."

> *The Hollywood Citizen-News*: "Judy Garland is rosy-cheeked, starry-eyed, and more alluring than a glamour girl."

> *The Daily Oklahoman*: "[Her] career, I think, will be dated by this picture. Her fine performance is going to win further big parts for her. [She is] sweet and thoroughly convincing [and] good use of her grand voice is made."

August 23, 1939: In addition to their shows at the Capitol, Judy and Mickey Rooney had a photo session for a *Daily News* color magazine cover.

August 27, 1939: In addition to their shows at the Capitol, Judy and Mickey made a fast visit to the World's Fair (newsreel footage still exists, and is excerpted in *The Ultimate Oz* documentary, included on the DVD.)

Late August 1939: (Radio) *The Fred Waring Show*, NBC (30 minutes). Broadcast from New York, this program was dedicated to Judy, who sang "Over the Rainbow."

August 30, 1939: Last day of appearances with Judy and Mickey. Rooney had to leave the Capitol engagement to go back to MGM for filming; Judy stayed on. Later that night, between shows, they made a special appearance at Madison Square Garden. (Newsreel footage still exists of them sitting in the audience for a short while after they had performed on stage. This is included in the documentary found on the 1999 *Oz* DVD, from Warner Home Video.)

Also on August 30, 1939: Loews, Inc. (MGM) issues Judy's work statement for the period from October 29, 1938 to October 28, 1939 per "option D" of her original contract (dated September 27, 1935). The "statement" guaranteed Judy forty weeks of work, at five hundred dollars per week, and covered nineteen-and-a-half weeks of work on *Oz* and eleven weeks of tests and production on *Babes in Arms*. The statement also provided for "casting office interviews," "idle time," and "layoffs."

August 31, 1939: Judy started a "new" show at the Capitol Theater, this time being paired with two *Oz* costars, Ray Bolger and Bert Lahr. (Judy added "FDR Jones" and "Blue Evening" to the show. Judy was paid $3,500 per week, earning $10,500 for the Capitol Theater engagement. Amazingly, she made more for this three-week stint than she had during the entire nineteen weeks and two days she spent making *Oz*, for which she received her MGM salary of $500 per week. Judy's MGM contract—signed in 1935 with preset raises—had started at $100 a week. Thus, her total income for the actual filming of *Oz* came to only $9,649.98. However, when she returned home, MGM would give her a "bonus" for the *Oz* tour of $10,600. Thus, the total amount Judy would make for starring in the most widely seen movie of all time, and doing all it's publicity, was only $30,749.98. She would never be paid royalties on any of her MGM movies. The final cost on *Oz* was $2,777,000, and it grossed $3,017,000 in its first release; it grossed an additional $1,564,000 on its first re-release in 1948–1949, and another $465,000 in 1954–1955 before it began its television airings in 1956.)

September 6, 1939: Judy and Company, and *Oz*, concluded their engagement at the Capitol in New York.

September 26, 1939: (Radio) *The Pepsodent Show Starring Bob Hope*, NBC (30 minutes), Los Angeles. Judy became a series "regular" on radio for the second time. (The first had been from February through June 1937, on *Jack Oakie's College* on CBS. Although she had also been a "semi-regular" on the MGM *Good News* program of 1938–1939, many of these performances may have been "lifted" from the soundtracks of her films.) As Bob Hope's "vocalist," Judy would make over 25 weekly appearances on this show through May 1940.

October 10, 1939: Hollywood Premiere of *Babes in Arms*, at Grauman's combined with the ceremony of Judy placing her hand and footprints in cement. (Judy was the 74th star to do so.) Judy inscribed her message "For Mr. Grauman/All Happiness." It was the "official" sign that Judy had "arrived", but there certainly were other signs as well: *Oz* and *Arms* would both place in the Top Ten for the year and Judy would place in the Top Ten exhibitors list for the year (Judy and Bette Davis were the only women to make the list). *Arms* began to play in the rest of the country in mid to late October 1939. (*Variety's* review appeared on September 20.) The total cost for *Babes in Arms* was only $745,341.03. (Judy's contract salary paid her only a total of $8,833 for her work on *Arms*.) The film would gross $3,324,819.

The best review was the *Hollywood Reporter's* assessment that "Judy Garland does Judy Garland, which is enough for any ticket buyer."

October 16, 1939: (Record) Decca Records session, Hollywood. Four songs were recorded this day in this order: "Oceans Apart," "Figaro"(from *Babes in Arms*), "Embraceable You," and her first recorded version of a song that would become associated with her in the "Concert Years" portion of her career, "Swanee."

The sign that a star has arrived: Judy (assisted by Mickey Rooney) is about to place her feet and hand prints in the forecourt of Grauman's Chinese Theater, on the night of the *Babes in Arms* premiere, October 10, 1939. (Courtesy of Photofest.)

(For unknown reasons, these tracks would not be released until the spring of 1940, when they showed up on two different volumes.)

October 17, 1939: (Radio) *The Pepsodent Show Starring Bob Hope*, NBC, Hollywood (30 minutes). Judy's weekly appearance (having missed the last two shows due to her work schedule).

This was a relatively "quiet" period professionally for Judy, from mid October 1939 to February 1940. Due to a delay in getting a suitable script ready for her next film—another Judy/Mickey pairing—there would only be Judy's weekly appearance on Bob Hope's radio show along with other misc. appearances. There were talks of Judy and Mickey starring in a film version of the Broadway musical *Good News* at MGM, but the movie wouldn't be made until 1947 when it starred June Allyson and Peter Lawford.

October 24, 1939: (Radio) *The Pepsodent Show Starring Bob Hope*, NBC, Hollywood (30 minutes). Judy's weekly appearance.

October 31, 1939: (Radio) *The Pepsodent Show Starring Bob Hope*, NBC, Hollywood (30 minutes). Judy's weekly appearance.

November 6, 1939: (Radio) *The Pepsodent Show Starring Bob Hope*, NBC, Hollywood (30 minutes). Judy's weekly appearance.

November 13, 1939: (Radio) *The Pepsodent Show Starring Bob Hope*, NBC, Hollywood (30 minutes). Judy's weekly appearance.

November 20, 1939: (Radio) *The Pepsodent Show Starring Bob Hope*, NBC, Hollywood (30 minutes). Judy's weekly appearance.

November 27, 1939: (Radio) *The Pepsodent Show Starring Bob Hope*, NBC, Hollywood (30 minutes). Judy's weekly appearance.

December 4, 1939: (Radio) *The Pepsodent Show Starring Bob Hope*, NBC, Hollywood (30 minutes). Judy's weekly appearance.

December 11, 1939: (Radio) *The Pepsodent Show Starring Bob Hope*, NBC, Hollywood (30 minutes). Judy's weekly appearance.

December 16, 1939: (Radio) *Arrowhead Springs Hotel Opening Broadcast*, CBS, (30 minutes). Palm Springs, California. Judy sang "Comes Love" at the show's conclusion. (This performance and the patter preceding it are available on the CD *All the Things You Are: Judy Garland on Radio, 1936–1944* on the Vintage Jazz Classics label released in 1993.)

December 18, 1939: (Radio) *The Pepsodent Show Starring Bob Hope*, NBC, Hollywood (30 minutes). Judy's weekly appearance.

December 25, 1939: (Radio) *The Pepsodent Show Starring Bob Hope*, NBC, Hollywood (30 minutes). Judy's weekly appearance. (She would not appear on the first show of 1940, on January 1. There was also a second broadcast this holiday: *Christmas with the Hardy Family*, which featured Judy singing "Silent Night." This performance was most likely taken from the MGM recording for her 1937 holiday short.)

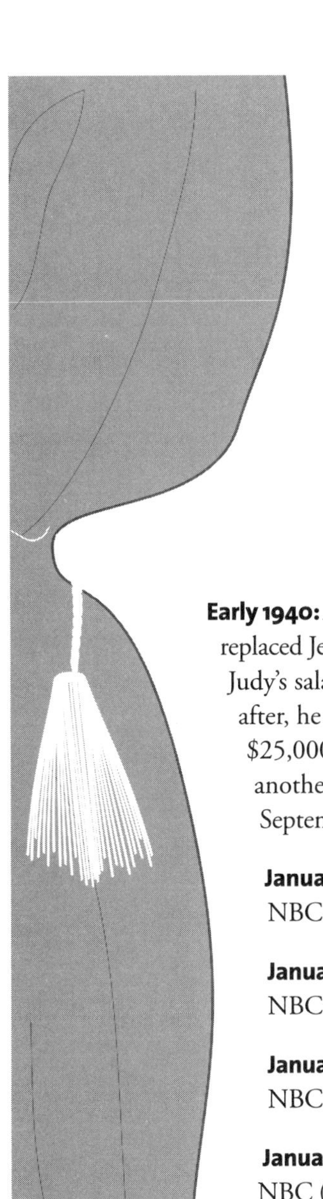

1940

Early 1940: A quick succession of agents took over Judy's affairs: Frank Orsatti replaced Jesse Martin (who had replaced Al Rosen.) Orsatti managed to get Judy's salary at MGM increased from $350 to $500 per week. Shortly after, he was replaced by Leland Hayward, who actually paid Orsatti $25,000 for the rights to manage Judy. Hayward started negotiating another new MGM contract for Judy, which would be signed in September 1940.

January 8, 1940: (Radio) *The Pepsodent Show Starring Bob Hope*, NBC (30 minutes). Judy's weekly appearance.

January 15, 1940: (Radio) *The Pepsodent Show Starring Bob Hope*, NBC (30 minutes). Judy's weekly appearance.

January 22, 1940: (Radio) *The Pepsodent Show Starring Bob Hope*, NBC (30 minutes). Judy's weekly appearance.

January 29, 1940: (Radio) *The Pepsodent Show Starring Bob Hope*, NBC (30 minutes). Judy's weekly appearance.

February 1940: Judy finally returned to the cameras for the first time since the end of July 1939, when she had finished *Babes in Arms* (a six month period of nonfilming at MGM that would only be surpassed by Judy's maternity leave to have Liza, which lasted approximately thirteen months). This period without filming meant that it would be nine months between the release of Judy's last film, *Babes in Arms* (October 1939), and her new film, *Andy Hardy Meets Debutante* (released in July 1940). This was a long length between movies for a movie star of this era. This well earned and needed "break" from an intense and often overlapping movie-making schedule was only due to Metro's lack of a suitable script.

February 6, 1940: (Radio) *The Pepsodent Show Starring Bob Hope*, NBC (30 minutes). Judy's weekly appearance.

February 13, 1940: (Radio) *The Pepsodent Show Starring Bob Hope*, NBC (30 minutes). Judy's weekly appearance. This week her song was a new one that would become a standard: "All The Things You Are." (This performance is available on the four–CD box set *Judy*, on the 32 Records label released October 13, 1998.)

February 20, 1940: (Radio) *The Pepsodent Show Starring Bob Hope*, NBC (30 minutes). Judy's weekly appearance.

February 27, 1940: (Radio) *The Pepsodent Show Starring Bob Hope*, NBC (30 minutes). Judy's weekly appearance.

February 29, 1940: Judy won her *only Academy Award* at the twelfth annual ceremony (Judy's first participation of any kind in an Oscar ceremony). She won "Best Performance by a Juvenile during the past year." (Judy would dub this Oscar her "Munchkin Award.") Though Judy would be nominated in 1955 for Best Actress for 1954s' *A Star Is Born* and in 1962 for Best Supporting Actress for 1961's *Judgment At Nuremberg*, she would not win those awards. *Oz* was nominated for five awards: Best Picture, Art Direction, Special Effects, Original Score, and Song, "Over The Rainbow". *Oz* won for Best Score and Song.

Spring 1940: During the same time Judy was filming *Andy Hardy Meets Debutante*, she recorded and filmed a song called "If We Forget You," for a Will Rogers Memorial Fund movie short. This film is on Judy's 1995 MGM laser disc set.

March 4, 1940: (Radio) *The Pepsodent Show Starring Bob Hope*, NBC (30 minutes). Judy's weekly appearance.

Early March, one week after Academy Awards, 1940: There was a plot to kidnap Judy by two male "fans": the police caught the young men before they could even proceed to Judy's home. This case—#7–3071— is the first of three FBI files on Judy. The second file—#9–7966—would be opened a year later after MGM received a questionable letter for Judy, and the third file—#87–99683, in the spring of 1968— involved two rings that Judy claimed had been stolen from her. Additional information on the third incident appears in this book under the following entries: March 6, 1968; April 4–5, 1968; April 8, 1968; and April 11, 1968.

Tuesday, March 11, 1940: (Radio) *The Pepsodent Show Starring Bob Hope*, NBC (30 minutes). Judy's weekly appearance.

March 14, 1940: MGM recording session for *Andy Hardy Meets Debutante*. Judy recorded "I'm Nobody's Baby," which she would also record for Decca Records on April 10, 1940, and would become a # 3 hit, and "Buds Won't Bud," which would be cut from the film before release; partial audio exists, but footage does not. (Judy would also record "Buds" for Decca during the April 10 session. An alternate version of "Baby" is on the two-CD Rhino *Collectors Gems* set, and the version heard in the movie is on the Rhino *Judy Garland in Hollywood* single CD.)

March 18, 1940: (Radio) *The Pepsodent Show Starring Bob Hope*, NBC (30 minutes). Judy's weekly appearance.

March 25, 1940: (Radio) *The Pepsodent Show Starring Bob Hope*, NBC (30 minutes). Judy's weekly appearance.

April 1, 1940: (Radio) *The Pepsodent Show Starring Bob Hope*, NBC (30 minutes). Judy's weekly appearance.

April 3, 1940: Judy started work on her next film, *Strike Up the Band* (while at the same time working on *Andy Hardy Meets Debutante*). On this day for *Band*: Called: 10 a.m.; dismissed: 2:15 p.m. Rehearsed "Nobody" number.

April 4, 1940: *Band* work. Called: 10 a.m.; dismissed: 3:45 p.m.; rehearsed "Our Love Affair" number.

April 8, 1940: (Radio) *The Pepsodent Show Starring Bob Hope*, NBC (30 minutes). Judy's weekly appearance. She sang "Say Si, Si" (the song exists in private collections).

April 10, 1940: (Record) Decca Records session, Hollywood. Judy recorded four songs in the following order: "(Can This Be) The End Of The Rainbow"; "Wearing Of The Green"; "I'm Nobody's Baby" (from *Andy Hardy Meets Debutante*); and "Buds Won't Bud" (which was cut from *Andy Hardy Meets Debutante*). "Baby" and "Buds" would be released as a 78 single—#3174—in June 1940 to coincide with the release in July of the *Debutante* film. "I'm Nobody's Baby" was actually meant to be the "B-side", or "flip-side" of the single; it would prove to be the real reason people bought the record, which made the single climb to # 3 on the charts. "Wearing Of The Green" would not be released until August—as the "B-side" of #3165. "Friendship," recorded during Judy's next session, five days later, would be the "A-side" of #3165. "End Of The Rainbow" would be the "A-side" of #3231, released in September 1940.

April 12, 1940: *Band* work. Called: 9 a.m.; dismissed: 4 p.m. MGM recording session—the first for *Strike Up the Band*. Judy recorded "Our Love Affair" with Mickey Rooney and "Nobody."

April 13, 1940: Judy was not needed for work on *Band* on this day.

April 15, 1940: This day is a prime example of the hectic work schedule Judy kept while she was at MGM (and throughout her entire career). During the day, Judy worked on *Band*: Called: 9 a.m.; dismissed: 6 p.m.; rehearsed "Gay Nineties" number. At night: (Record) The end studio time on a Decca Records session for Bing Crosby was utilized by Judy and Johnny Mercer for their recording of "Friendship." This was released as the "A-side" of #3165 in August ("Wearing Of The Green" from the April 10 session was the "B-side"). *Also* on April 15, 1940, Judy's weekly radio appearance on Bob Hope's radio show.

April 16, 1940: *Band* work. Called: 9 a.m.; dismissed: 3:20 p.m.; rehearsed "Gay Nineties" number.

April 17, 1940: *Band* work. Called: 9 a.m.; dismissed: 6 p.m.; rehearsed "Gay Nineties" number.

April 18, 1940: *Band* work. Called: 9 a.m.; dismissed: 6 p.m.; rehearsed "Gay Nineties" and also "Shoot tests Mickey Rooney and JG."

April 19, 1940: *Band* started filming. Called: 9:30 a.m.; dismissed: 5 p.m.; scene: Int. Library.

April 20, 1940: *Band* filming. Called: 9 a.m.; dismissed: 4:30 p.m.; scene: Int. Public Library.

April 22, 1940: *Band* filming. Called: 9 a.m.; dismissed: 4:40 p.m.; scene: Int. Library. At night: (Radio) *The Pepsodent Show Starring Bob Hope*, NBC (30 minutes). Judy's weekly appearance.

April 23, 1940: *Band* work. Called: 9 a.m.; dismissed: 5:50 p.m. MGM recording session for *Strike Up the Band*: Judy recorded the elaborate nineteen-minute production number "Nell of New Rochelle." This segment was shortened by a few moments when two of Judy's songs were cut from the sequence before release: "Curse Of An Aching Heart" and "While Strolling Through The Park One Day." The songs exist; film does not—only stills exist. The songs can be heard on the *Mickey and Judy* four–CD box set from Rhino Records, released in 1995.

April 24, 1940: *Band* work. Called: 9 a.m.; dismissed: 4:30 p.m. The day was spent doing publicity photos: "Gay Nineties" number photo gallery shoot.

April 25, 1940: *Band* filming. Called: 9 a.m.; dismissed: 4:30 p.m.; scenes: Prologue and Ext./Int. Delmonico's.

April 26, 1940: *Band* filming. Called: 9 a.m.; dismissed: 5:54 p.m.; scene: Int. Delmonico's.

April 27, 1940: *Band* filming. Called: 9 a.m.; dismissed: 4:15 p.m.; scene: Int. and Ext. Delmonico's.

April 29, 1940: *Band* filming. Called: 9 a.m.; dismissed: 4:20 p.m.; scenes: Ext. Delmonico's and Int. Backstage. That night: (Radio) *The Pepsodent Show Starring Bob Hope*, NBC (30 minutes). Judy's weekly appearance.

April 30, 1940: *Band* filming. Called: 8:30 a.m.; dismissed: 4:00 p.m.; scene: Int. Saloon.

May 1, 1940: *Band* filming. Called: 9 a.m.; dismissed: 4:30 p.m.; scenes: "Int. attic, Int. sawmill" (for "Gay 90s" Production Number.) (AD reports state: "2:05–2:56 JG in school.")

May 2, 1940: *Band* filming. Called: 10:30 a.m.; dismissed: 5:45 p.m.; scenes: Int. Sawmill and Int. Attic.

May 3, 1940: *Band* filming. Called: 9 a.m.; dismissed: 12:50 p.m.; scenes: Ext. Park and Ext. R.R. tracks. At 12:50 p.m., Judy went home ill.

May 4, 1940: *Band* filming. Called: 10:30 a.m.; dismissed: 5:10 p.m.; scenes: Ext. R.R. track and Int. attic. Judy went home ill at 5:10 p.m.

May 6, 1940 to May 14, 1940: Judy was excused from filming *Band* for work on *Andy Hardy Meets Debutante* retakes.

May 7, 1940: (Radio) *The Pepsodent Show Starring Bob Hope*, NBC (30 minutes). Judy's weekly appearance.

May 8, 1940: MGM recording session for *Strike Up the Band.* Judy recorded the "Finale."

May 10, 1940: MGM recording session for *Andy Hardy Meets Debutante*: "Alone" and "All I Do Is Dream Of You." ("Dream" would be cut before release; the song—mixed to stereo—exists on the two-CD Rhino set; footage does not exist, only stills remain.)

May 14, 1940: (Radio) *The Pepsodent Show Starring Bob Hope*, NBC (30 minutes). Judy's weekly appearance (and most likely her final appearance: the May 21 and May 28 shows were broadcast from Chicago and New York respectively, and thus kept Judy from appearing on these shows as she had to be in California for her movie work).

May 15, 1940: Judy had no call for *Band* work.

May 16, 1940: *Band* filming. Called: 9 a.m.; dismissed: 4:30 p.m.; scenes: Int. Gym and Ext. Carnival.

May 17, 1940: *Band* filming. Called: 9 a.m.; dismissed: 4:30 p.m.; scenes: Int. Judd Living Room and Int. Jim's bedroom.

May 18, 1940: *Band* filming. Called: 2:30 p.m.; dismissed: 10 p.m.; scenes: Int. Storeroom, Int. Judd Living room, and Ext. Holden Porch.

May 20, 1940: *Band* filming. Called: 9 a.m.; dismissed: 4:45 p.m.; scenes: Ext. Holden Porch and the Hospital.

May 21, 1940: *Band* filming. Called: 9 a.m.; dismissed: 4:32 p.m.; scenes: Ext. Holden Porch and Int. Class Room.

May 22, 1940: Judy was at home, ill, on this day.

May 23, 1940: *Band* filming. Called: 10:30 a.m.; dismissed: 6 p.m.; scenes: Int. Classroom and Locker Room.

May 24, 1940: *Band* filming. Called: 9 a.m.; dismissed: 1:55 p.m.; scene: Int. Gym.

May 25, 1940: *Band* filming. Called: 2:30 p.m.; dismissed: 10 p.m.; scenes: Morgan Home and Bar/Riverwood Street.

May 26, 1940: (Radio) *Red Cross War Fund Program*, CBS/NBC (60 minutes). Judy sang "Over the Rainbow."

May 27, 1940: *Band* filming. Called: 9 a.m.; dismissed: 4:30 p.m.; scene: Int. Holden Home.

May 28, 1940: *Band* filming. Called: 9 a.m.; dismissed: 4 p.m.; scenes: Int. Holden Home and Ext. Barbara's Car.

May 31, 1940: *Band* filming. Called: 9 a.m.; dismissed: 4:05 p.m.; scenes: Riverwood High School and Morgan Dining Room.

End of May 1940: Judy finished work on *Andy Hardy Meets Debutante*, which would be released on July 5, 1940.

June 1, 1940: *Band* filming. Called: 10 a.m.; dismissed: 5:30 p.m.; scene: Ext. R.R. Station.

June 3, 1940: *Band* filming. Judy reported to makeup at 7:37 a.m. Called: 9 a.m.; dismissed: 4:37 p.m.; scenes: Int. Holden Home and Int. Willy's Bedroom.

June 4, 1940: *Band* filming. Called: 10:30 a.m.; dismissed: 4:50 p.m.; scene: Int. Country Club.

June 5, 1940: *Band* filming. Called: 2:30 p.m.; dismissed: 10 p.m.; scenes: Country Club, Anteroom, and Bedroom.

June 6, 1940: *Band* filming. Called: 10 a.m.; dismissed: 4:30 p.m.; scenes: Int. Anteroom and Int. Hotel Room.

June 7, 1940: *Band* filming. Called: 10 a.m.; dismissed: 4:35 p.m.; scenes: Int. Backstage and Int. Radio theatre.

June 8, 1940: MGM recording session for *Strike Up the Band*: Judy recorded "Drummer Boy." Judy had a 10 a.m. call and was dismissed at 5 p.m.

June 10, 1940: Judy's eighteenth birthday. *Band* rehearsal. Called: 9 a.m.; dismissed: 5:10 p.m. Publicity photos of Judy and Mickey Rooney on top of a huge drum were shot for *Strike up the Band*. AD reports note that "Both Miss Garland and Mr. Rooney were shooting poster stills before reporting for rehearsal at 11 a.m." A still photograph also exists from this day of Judy and her mother with a birthday cake in Louis B. Mayer's office at MGM that is captioned "Judy's 18th Birthday." It is likely that this was Judy's 18th birthday "celebration." Judy's gift was her first car: MGM made certain they took publicity photographs of Judy posed with the car on the back lot at the studio.

June 11, 1940: Judy started production on her next film, *Little Nellie Kelly*, by shooting costume tests. (Producer Arthur Freed had bought the rights from George M. Cohen for $35,000.)

June 12, 1940: *Band* work: Called: 9 a.m.; dismissed: 5:45 p.m.; rehearsed "Drummer Boy" number.

June 13, 1940: *Band* filming. Called: 10 a.m.; dismissed: 10:30 a.m.; scenes shot were supposed to be Backstage and Int. Hospital Room, but the AD reports note that "When Rooney arrived on set at 9 a.m., his lower lip was in bad condition with a fever blister and unable to be photographed. After discussing situation it was decided to let Rooney rehearse with drum instructor to playback and company will move to stage #6 for shots backstage."

June 14, 1940 to June 17, 1940: Rooney still had fever blister and was unable to be photographed, so work was cancelled on *Band* those days. On June 17, Judy worked on tests for *Kelly* instead.

June 18, 1940: Rooney still couldn't be photographed, so the *Band* company rehearsed the "La Conga" number from 1:00–2:15 p.m.

June 19, 1940: *Band* filming. Called: 2 p.m.; dismissed: 11 p.m.; scene: "Drummer Boy" number and Int. Country Club.

June 20, 1940: *Band* filming. Called: 12 p.m.; dismissed: 1:43 a.m.; scene: Int. Country Club.

June 21, 1940: *Band* filming. Called: 1:45 p.m.; dismissed: 5:30 p.m.; scenes: Ext. Holden Home, Ext. School, and Int. Country Club.

June 22, 1940: Judy was not needed for *Band* filming.

June 24, 1940: *Band* work. Called: 11 a.m.; dismissed: 5:40 p.m.; rehearsed "La Conga" number.

June 25, 1940: *Band* work. Called: 10:30 a.m.; dismissed: 4 p.m.; rehearsed "La Conga" number.

June 26, 1940: *Band* work. Called: 10 a.m.; dismissed: 5:40 p.m.; rehearsed "La Conga" number as director selected camera setups for the "La Conga" shoot. Also this day, Judy graduated from University High School (presumably at night, after work on *Band* was done at 5:40 p.m.).

June 27, 1940: *Band* work: Called: 11 a.m.; dismissed: 4:30 p.m.; rehearsed "La Conga" in a.m.; recorded "La Conga" in p.m.

June 28, 1940: *Band* filming. Called: 9 a.m.; dismissed: 5:55 p.m.; scene: Int. Gym and "La Conga." Also, publicity shots were taken this day of Judy and Mickey for *Strike Up the Band* (wearing their "La Conga" number outfits).

June 29, 1940: *Band* filming. Called: 9 a.m.; dismissed: 5:59 p.m.; scene: Int. Gym ("La Conga").

July 1, 1940: *Band* filming. Called: 9 a.m.; dismissed: 11 p.m.; scene: Int. Gym ("La Conga").

July 2, 1940: *Band* filming. Called: 11 a.m.; dismissed: 6:10 p.m.; scene: Int. Gym ("La Conga").

July 3, 1940: *Band* filming. Called: 9 a.m.; dismissed: 11:10 p.m.; scene: Int. Gym ("La Conga").

July 5, 1940: *Band* work. Called: 1 p.m.; dismissed: 4:15 p.m.; rehearsed "Finale."

July 6, 1940: Judy did not work—she was ill with a sore throat.

July 8, 1940: *Band* work. Called: 10 a.m.; dismissed: 5:45 p.m.; rehearsed "Finale."

July 9, 1940: *Band* work. Called: 9 a.m.; dismissed: 5 p.m.; rehearsed "Finale."

July 10, 1940: *Band* work. Called: 11 a.m.; dismissed: 11:10 p.m.; Recorded "Finale."

July 11, 1940: Judy was not needed for work on *Band.*

July 12, 1940: *Band* filming. Called: 9 a.m.; dismissed: 5 p.m.; scene: Int. Radio Theatre—"Finale."

July 13, 1940: *Band* filming. Called: 1 p.m.; dismissed: 11:33 p.m.; scene: Int. Radio Theatre—"Finale."

July 15, 1940: *Band* filming. Called: 9 a.m.; dismissed: 7:20 p.m.; scene: Int. Radio Theatre—"Finale."

July 16, 1940: *Band* filming. Called: 3 p.m.; dismissed: 2:15 a.m.; scene: Int. Radio Theatre—"Finale."

July 19, 1940: *Band* filming. Called: 9 a.m.; dismissed: 12:15 p.m.; scenes: Int. Gym and "Gay Nineties" seq. retakes.

July 30, 1940: Wardrobe Test for *Little Nellie Kelly*. Time called: 1:00 p.m.; time dismissed: 6:55 p.m. Work that day involved coaching and Int. Noonans Cottage.

July 31, 1940: Filming on *Kelly*. Time called: 9 a.m.; dismissed: 5:02 p.m.; scene shot was Int. Noonan's Cottage.

August 1, 1940: Filming on *Kelly*. Called 9 a.m.; dismissed: 6 p.m.; scene shot: Int. Noonan's Cottage.

August 2, 1940: Filming on *Kelly*. Time called: 8:30 a.m.; dismissed: 5:45 p.m.; scenes filmed: Ext. Noonan's Cottage and Road. On this day, Judy's mother told MGM that her daughter could only work eight hours a day.

August 3, 1940: Filming on *Kelly*. Time called: 9 a.m.; dismissed: 6:02 p.m.; scenes filmed: Int. and Ext. Noonan's Cottage.

August 5, 1940: Filming on *Kelly*. Called: 9 a.m.; dismissed: 5:56 p.m.; scene filmed: Int. Noonan's Cottage, Int. St. Katherine's Vestry, and scene walking to cliff top.

August 6, 1940: Filming on *Kelly*. Called: 9 a.m.; dismissed: 6 p.m.; scene filmed: Ext. Cliff top.

August 7, 1940: Judy was ill, and did not work on *Kelly*.

August 8, 1940: Filming on *Kelly*. Called: 9 a.m.; dismissed: 6:02 p.m.; scenes filmed: Ext. Cliff top and Ext. Deck of Steamer.

August 9, 1940: Work on *Kelly*. Called: 11:30 a.m.; dismissed: 3:30 p.m. Wardrobe fitting and recording; Judy recorded "It's A Great Day For The Irish." (Almost twenty years later to the day—on August 8, 1960—Judy would record this song again, in London, for a two-album set of songs in stereo.)

August 10, 1940: *Band* retakes. Called: 7 p.m.; dismissed: 2:45 a.m.; scenes: Ext. Holden Home and Street. (Judy did no work on *Kelly* on this day.)

August 12, 1940: *Band* finished filming, with retakes: Called: 9 a.m.; dismissed: 6:15 p.m.; scenes: Ext. train, Int. Attic, and Int. Lower Floor. (Production notes for *Kelly* state that Judy was working with Busby "Berkeley Co." on *Strike Up the Band* postproduction.) *Band* cost $851,577.78, and would gross $3,472,059 upon release in September (two release dates have been noted: September 13 and September 30.) The following is a sampling of the reviews for Judy's work:

> *The New York Herald Tribune*: "While Rooney is just as effective and just as hammy as he ever was, Garland plays her part with considerably more integrity and sings with vitality."
>
> *Daily Variety*: "While all the young principals do themselves proud, Garland particularly achieves rank as one of the screen's great personalities. Here she is for the first time in full bloom and charm which is beyond childhood, as versatile in acting as she is excellent in song—a striking figure and a most oomphy one in the wild of abandon [of] 'The La Conga.'"

August 13, 1940: *Kelly* filming. Called: 9 a.m.; dismissed: 6:17 p.m.; scene filmed: Int. Kelly Flat.

August 14, 1940: *Kelly* filming. Called: 9 a.m.; dismissed: 5:12 p.m.; scene filmed: Int. Kelly Flat.

August 15, 1940: *Kelly* filming. Called: 9 a.m.; dismissed: 4:55 p.m.; scene filmed: Int. Federal Court Room.

August 16, 1940: *Kelly* filming. Called: 10 a.m.; dismissed: 5:35 p.m.; scene shot: Int. St Katherine's Hospital. This was the only death scene Judy would ever do in her entire career. (In the film, Judy played duel parts: both Nellie Kelly and Nellie's mother, who dies just after giving birth to Nellie. This moving scene was filmed on this day.)

August 17, 1940: *Kelly* filming. Called: 11 a.m.; dismissed: 6:04 p.m.; scene filmed: Int. Kelly Flat.

August 19, 1940: *Kelly* filming. Called: 9 a.m.; dismissed: 6:03 p.m.; scene filmed: Int. Kelly Flat.

August 20, 1940: *Kelly* filming. Called: 9 a.m.; dismissed: 4:45 p.m.; scene filmed: Ext. New York Parade, which included the song "It's A Great Day For The Irish." Judy had recorded the audio of the song on August 9.

August 21, 1940: Judy had an 8:30 a.m. call for work on *Kelly*. She worked only in the morning—filming the Ext. New York Parade scene. She was dismissed for lunch at 12:05 p.m. and "did not return to set. She took sick during the lunch hour," according to the AD reports.

August 22, 1940: *Kelly* filming. Called: 10 a.m.; dismissed: 3:25 p.m.; scenes filmed: Int. and Ext. Keevans Bar.

August 23, 1940: *Kelly* filming. Called: 9 a.m.; dismissed: 4:05 p.m.; scene filmed: Ext. St. Patrick's Day Parade.

August 24, 1940: *Kelly* filming. Called: 9 a.m.; dismissed: 5:32 p.m.; scene filmed: Ext. St. Patrick's Day Parade and Ext. 10th Ave.

August 26, 1940: *Kelly* filming. Called: 9 a.m.; dismissed: 5:57 p.m.; scene: Int. Kelly Flat.

August 27, 1940: *Kelly* filming. Called: 9 a.m.; dismissed: 6:02 p.m.; scene: Int. Kelly Flat.

August 28, 1940: *Kelly* filming. Called: 9 a.m.; dismissed: 5:54 p.m.; scene: Int. Kelly Flat (where she shows off her prom dress to her father, played by George Murphy.) Judy also shot publicity stills.

August 29, 1940: *Kelly* filming. Called: 9 a.m.; dismissed: 6:39 p.m.; scene: Int. Kelly Flat.

August 30, 1940: *Kelly* filming. Called: 9 a.m.; dismissed: 5:20 p.m.; scene: Ext. Excavation. Also on this day, Director Busby Berkeley gave a party for the cast and crew of *Strike Up the Band.*

August 31, 1940: *Kelly* filming. Called: 9 a.m.; dismissed: 5:32 p.m.; scene: Excavation Crosstown Bus. Also on this day, Judy shot publicity stills with Murphy for *Kelly.*

September 3, 1940: *Kelly* filming. Called: 9 a.m.; dismissed: 5:58 p.m.; scenes: Int. Kelly Apt. and Int. Hallway. AD notes that Judy "cries in scene today."

September 4, 1940: *Kelly* filming. Called: 9 a.m.; dismissed: 6:05 p.m.; scenes: Ext. Brownstone Front and Int. Kelly's Flat.

September 5, 1940: *Kelly* filming. Called: 9 a.m.; dismissed: 6:05 p.m.; scenes: Ext. Brownstone Front and Int. Kelly's Flat.

September 6, 1940: *Kelly* filming. Called: 9 a.m.; dismissed: 3:57 p.m.; scene: Ext. Street and Taxi.

September 7, 1940: *Kelly* work. Called: 10:30 a.m.; dismissed: 2:05 p.m.; "Rehearsed song and dance."

September 9, 1940: *Kelly* work. Called: 1 p.m.; dismissed: 3:20 p.m.; "Pre-Record and Rehearse Dance."

September 10, 1940: *Kelly* work. Called: 11 a.m.; dismissed: 6:32 p.m. "Rehearse Dance and record. . . . Note: Miss Garland was called to record at 11 a.m. and to be on stage at 4 p.m. to rehearse dance—She arrived on the stage at 4:40 p.m.—Miss Garland was with Mr. Freed." MGM recording session for *Little Nellie Kelly*: Judy recorded "Singing In The Rain"; "A Pretty Girl Milking Her Cow"; and "Danny Boy" ("Boy" would be cut from the film before release. The song is on the Rhino *Collector's Gems* set; the footage is not known to exist. One source lists the recording date for "Rain" and "Pretty Girl" as a day earlier, September 9).

September 11, 1940: *Kelly* filming. Called: 9 a.m.; dismissed: 6:11 p.m.; scene: Int. Astor Ballroom.

September 12, 1940: *Kelly* filming. Called: 9 a.m.; dismissed: 5:45 p.m.; scenes: Int. Astor Ballroom, Int. Astor Corr., and Telephone Booth.

September 13, 1940: Judy was out ill.

September 14, 1940: *Kelly* filming. Called: 9 a.m.; dismissed: 5:54 p.m.; scene: Int. Kelly's Apt.

September 16, 1940: *Kelly* filming. Called: 9 a.m.; dismissed: 5:55 p.m.; scene: Int. Kelly's Flat.

September 17, 1940: *Kelly* filming. Called: 9 a.m.; dismissed: 6:20 p.m.; scene: Int. Waldorf Ballroom. AD notes state: "3:55–4:36—Wait for Miss Garland to come back to set—She was dismissed from set at 3:37 p.m. to go to her dressing room—She wasn't feeling well and went to her room—the Nurse was sent to her room to care for her—returned to dressing room. On stage at 4:13 p.m.—she then had to put on wardrobe and get hair fixed."

September 18, 1940: *Kelly* filming. Called: 9 a.m.; dismissed: 6:31 p.m.; scene: Int. Waldorf Ballroom and Ext. terrace. AD notes state: "Miss Garland had to be at a Radio Broadcast and had to leave at 6:30 p.m." (What radio program Judy appeared on is not noted nor known.)

September 19, 1940: *Little Nellie Kelly* finished filming, but would require retakes on September 27. On this last day, Judy was called: 9 a.m.; dismissed: 8:25 p.m.; scenes: Ext. Hansom Cab, Ext. Cliff top, and Int. Kelly Flat.

September 24, 1940: (Radio) *Cavalcade of American Music*, ASCAP concert given at the Golden Gate International Exposition at Treasure Island. Judy sang "Over The Rainbow" accompanied by its composer Harold Arlen on piano (issued on CD as part of a four-CD set in late 1997 as *Carousel of American Music* by a small label based in California.)

September 25, 1940: Judy's new MGM contract was filed in Superior Court on this day. (For contracts, Judy was considered a minor until she turned twenty-one on June 10, 1943.) The new contract called for an immediate raise from $600 to $2,000 per week (Monday through Saturday), with options over seven years to bring her up to $3,000 per week. Thus, for seven years with at least forty weeks of work each year, MGM was willing to guarantee Judy a total salary of $680,000 for each of those seven years. (There would be another new contract in 1946.)

September 27, 1940: *Little Nellie Kelly* finished filming (with retakes). Judy had a 4 p.m. call and was dismissed at 5:09 p.m. The scene is noted as "Added scenes—Int. Kelly's Apt." The final cost for the movie was $655,300.28 and it would gross $2,046,000. It would preview in October and be released on November 22. The following are two reviews of Judy's work:

> *Variety*: "Miss Garland romps through the role of Nellie Kelly in grand style, emphasizing her stature as a top notch actress with plenty of wholesome charm and screen presence."

The Examiner: "A beauty; unsurpassable in her many talents and fresh young appeal."

October 1, 1940: After finishing her looping work for *Little Nellie Kelly*, Judy had her tonsils taken out at Cedars of Lebanon Hospital.

Early October 1940: Judy began rehearsals for her next film, *Ziegfeld Girl*.

October 11, 1940: *Little Nellie Kelly* previewed in Inglewood, California.

October 28, 1940: (Radio) *Lux Radio Theater*, CBS (60 minutes). Radio adaptation of *Strike Up the Band*, which had just been released in September. Judy and Mickey recreated their roles. (This program is available from Radio Spirits at 1-800-RADIO48 or from Radio Revisisted, on CD-R: Radiorev@aol.com.)

November 13, 1940: MGM recording session for *Ziegfeld Girl*. Judy recorded two versions (one "Comedic" and one "Balladic") of "I'm Always Chasing Rainbows" that were needed for the film.

(Around this time Judy wrote a private, personal book of poetry, which she would give to her mother and some friends. These poems were reprinted in Anne Edwards 1975 biography of Judy.)

November 28, 1940: "Judy shot publicity photos with costar Jackie Cooper on the set of *Ziegfeld Girl*." (Judy wore the costume she wears in the "Laugh? I Thought I'd Split My Sides" number.) *Also* on this day: (Radio) *Leo Is on the Air* holiday broadcast, "live" from "Santa Claus Lane" (Sunset Blvd., Los Angeles, California). Judy and Mickey Rooney spoke to people in the crowds, and Judy's warmth and humor and ability to connect with everyone is a joy to hear from this vibrant eighteen-year-old legend-in-the-making. (Available on the *Mickey and Judy* CD box set on Rhino Records.)

December 11, 1940: Publicity photos taken of Judy and costar Lana Turner on the set of *Ziegfeld Girl*. (Shots of Judy balancing her book and sitting on a piano, with Turner playing.)

December 18, 1940, 10:00 p.m. to 1:00 a.m.: (Record) Decca Records session: four songs recorded on this day in the following order: "I'm Always Chasing Rainbows" (from *Ziegfeld Girl*); "Our Love Affair" (from *Strike Up the Band*); "A Pretty Girl Milking Her Cow" (from *Little Nellie Kelly*); and "It's A Great Day For The Irish" (also from *Little Nellie Kelly*). All would be released in January 1941 ("Affair" and "Rainbows" were released on 78 single #3593—"A" and "B" sides respectively; and "Irish" and "Pretty Girl" on #3604, "A" and "B" sides).

December 22, 1940: MGM recording session for *Ziegfeld Girl*. "We Must Have Music" and reprise of "I'm Always Chasing Rainbows," both planned as the film's "Finale," although they would be cut and replaced by a new finale filmed in March 1941, a month before the movie opened. ("Music" footage was used as a short subject, using the same name, released in 1942, so we still have some of this "cut" song. Of the "Rainbow" reprise, only the audio exists and is on the Judy laser disc box set; the film is not known to exist.)

December 24, 1940: (Radio) *The Pepsodent Show Starring Bob Hope*, NBC (30 minutes). Judy sang "I'm Nobody's Baby" from *Andy Hardy Meets Debutante*; "It's A Great Day For The Irish" from *Little Nellie Kelly;* and "FDR Jones," which she would sing in an upcoming film *Babes on Broadway*.

December 30, 1940 and December 31, 1940: Judy filmed the "You Stepped Out Of A Dream" number (and publicity stills were shot on the set of her in costume for this song).

Judy's film successes in 1940 would again place her on the list of Top 10 Film Stars in 1941 (as they had in 1940, for her films released in 1939).

1941

January 1, 1941: (Radio) *Bundles for Britain*, NBC (60 Minutes). Judy sang "I Hear A Rhapsody."

January 1941: Filming continued (through March) on *Ziegfeld Girl*.

January 14, 1941: MGM recording session for *Ziegfeld Girl*. Judy recorded "Minnie From Trinidad," written for her by Roger Edens.

January 18, 1941: Judy filmed the "Minnie From Trinidad" number (and publicity photos were taken of her on the set in costume for this song).

January 26, 1941: (Radio) *Silver Theater*, CBS (30 Minutes). Judy's first straight, dramatic, nonsinging role, in the original radio play, *Love's New Sweet Song*. She wrote the story this show was based on, and her one number—"Love's New Sweet Song"— was a joint work of Judy's and her musical director, David Rose (who would soon become her first husband). (This program exists in private collections.)

February 22, 1941: (Radio/Personal Appearance) *Academy Awards*, all networks, Los Angeles, California. Judy sang "America (My Country Tis of Thee)." (This performance exists in private collections.)

February 25, 1941: (Personal Appearance) Greek Resistance Benefit, Los Angeles, California. Judy sang "Over The Rainbow" (with composer Harold Arlen at the piano) and "It's A Great Day For The Irish." (David Rose conducted the orchestra. Audio recording of this concert—including Judy's entire performance—is available on the two-CD set *Legends and Songwriters in Concert, 1941* from Original Cast Records, PO Box 496, Georgetown, CT. 06829.)

March 1941: *Ziegfeld Girl* finally completed filming, although a hastily assembled new Finale was filmed in March. The film was released on April 25, 1941. *Variety* called Judy: "A youthful but veteran trouper (who) carries the sympathetic end most capably and delivers her vocal assignments in great style."

March 15, 1941: (Radio) *Islam Temple Shrine Saint Patrick's Day Program*, NBC (60 Minutes), Los Angeles, California. Judy sang "Wearing of the Green" (which she had recorded on April 10, 1940 for Decca Records.)

April 1941: Judy started preproduction work on her next film, *Life Begins for Andy Hardy*, her last appearance in the *Andy Hardy* series. (This would film through July 1941.)

April 24, 1941: (Radio) *Young America Wants To Help*. Judy sang "Chin Up, Cheerio, Carry On" (which she would perform in an upcoming musical with Mickey Rooney).

May 19, 1941: MGM recording session for *Life Begins for Andy Hardy*. Judy recorded "America (My Country 'Tis of Thee)." (After Judy recorded and then filmed four songs for this movie, they were all cut before release for some unexplainable reason. The audio of all the songs still exist and are mixed to stereo on the *Golden Years* laser disc set, except for "America," which is presented in mono. No footage remains of any of these numbers.)

May 28, 1941: Judy and composer/conductor David Rose announced their engagement at Ciro's Restaurant in Hollywood. *The Hollywood Reporter* announced the engagement the next day. (Judy and David had been dating since spring 1940.) Their plan was to be married in September.

June 2, 1941: Invitations were sent out on this day, stating, "June 2, 1941. 1231 Stone Canyon Road. Miss Judy Garland requests the pleasure of your company at a tea and cocktail party. Sunday, 15 of June, 1 till 5 o'clock." Within this folded invitation was the printed "official" announcement of her first engagement.

June 4, 1941: MGM recording session for *Life Begins for Andy Hardy*: "Easy To Love"; "Abide With Me"; and "The Rosary." All of Judy's songs would be cut from this movie. (See May 19, 1941 for additional information. Judy sings only a brief a cappella version of "Happy Birthday" in the completed film. "Easy To Love" is also on the *Collector's Gems* CD set.)

Tuesday, June 10, 1941: Judy's nineteenth birthday.

June 12, 1941: Publicity photos were taken for *Life Begins for Andy Hardy* with Judy, Rooney, and Lewis Stone.

Sunday, June 15, 1941, 1 a.m. to 5 p.m.: Judy's engagement/birthday celebration, attended by over 600 guests. It was held on the grounds of Judy's home.

June 25, 1941: MGM recording session for *Life Begins for Andy Hardy*. Partial retake of "Easy To Love."

July 2, 1941: (Radio) "Millions For Defense" (*Treasury Hour*) CBS (60 minutes). Judy and Mickey Rooney performed a comedy sketch, which closed the first half, and sang "Strike Up The Band."

Judy with her first husband, David Rose, at their engagement party, June 15, 1941. A photo almost exactly like this one (with them sitting in the same position) hung on the wall of Judy's dressing room at MGM. (Courtesy of Photofest.)

July 9, 1941: Judy started production work on her next film for MGM: *Babes on Broadway* (while still filming the *Andy Hardy* movie). (Shirley Temple was recently signed by MGM and was also announced as one of the stars, although she does not appear in the film.) On this day Judy was called at 10:40 a.m., dismissed at 12:45 p.m., and rehearsed the "How About You?" song with Mickey Rooney.

July 10, 1941: *Babes on Broadway* work. Rehearsed "How About You?" Time called: 2 p.m.; time dismissed: 5:30 p.m.

July 11, 1941: Rehearsed "How About You?" Time called: 10 a.m.; time dismissed: 11:45 a.m.

July 12, 1941: Rehearsed "How About You?" Time called: 9:50 a.m.; time dismissed: 12:00 p.m.

July 14, 1941: *Babes on Broadway* starts filming. On this first day: scene: Int. Nick's Café. Time called: 11:30 a.m.; lunch: 12:45–1:45 p.m.; time dismissed: 6:05 p.m. (Wardrobe tests with Judy were also done this day.)

July 15, 1941: Judy was not needed for *Babes on Broadway.*

July 16, 1941: Time called: 2:30 p.m.; time dismissed: 3:15 p.m.; rehearsal. AD reports note that "Miss Garland was called on today to rehearse dance at 2:30 p.m.—At 2:45 was sent to Miss Monclair for a French lesson—At 3 p.m.; reported to Eddie Larkin to rehearse 'How About You?' routine; at 3:15 she said she had such a bad headache she could not continue—Went home."

July 17, 1941: Judy did wardrobe tests for *Babes on Broadway.* Time called: 2 p.m.; time dismissed: 4:30 p.m.

July 18, 1941: MGM recording session for *Babes on Broadway*: "How About You?" (which would be nominated for an Academy Award for Best Song.) Time called: 6:30 p.m.; time dismissed: 9:15 p.m.

July 19, 1941: Judy apparently did not report for work on *Babes on Broadway.* AD notes state that "Judy Garland was called for wardrobe fitting at 1:00 p.m. today and to come to rehearsal at 1:30 p.m. on stage 8. At 1:05 p.m. she arrived on lot; at 1:35 p.m.—when Miss Garland did not go to stage 8 for rehearsal—Her home was called and a message left for Miss Garland to call company on stage 4 when she arrived home—after not hearing from her by 6:30 p.m., Mr. Ryan called to give her call for Monday, and she had not yet arrived home."

July 20, 1941, 11 a.m. to 2:30 p.m.: (Record) Decca Records session, Hollywood, produced two songs: "The Birthday Of A King" and "The Star Of The East." (Both were released as a holiday single in December, as 78 #4050.)

July 21, 1941: *Babes on Broadway* filming. Scene: Int. Jonesy's Office. Time called: 3 p.m.; time dismissed: 5:20 p.m.

July 22, 1941: *Babes on Broadway* filming. Scenes: Int. Jonesy's Office and Ext. Roof Top. Time called: 9 a.m.; "11:30–11:42—Wait to have Miss Garlands skirt pressed—Was lying down in dressing room; lunch 12:55–1:55 p.m.; time dismissed: 6:15 p.m.

July 23, 1941, July 24, 1941, and July 25, 1941: Judy shot *Life Begins for Andy Hardy* retakes, and, thus, was not on the *Babes on Broadway* set. This was Judy's third and final appearance in the *Andy Hardy/Hardy Family* series—and certainly least satisfying or fulfilling, since all of her songs were deleted. The film would be released in August 1941.

July 26, 1941: The company of *Babes on Broadway* shut down for the day as Judy was ill and nothing could be shot that day without her.

July 27, 1941: Judy and David Rose went to Las Vegas with Judy's mother and stepfather.

July 28, 1941, at 1 a.m.: Judy and David Rose married. Judy wired the producer of *Babes on Broadway*. The Western Union telegram was sent at 2 a.m. to Arthur Freed, at 634 Stone Canyon Road, and reads: "Dear Mr. Freed, I am so very happy. Dave and I were married this AM. Please give me a little time and I will be back and finish the picture with one take on each scene. Love, Judy." MGM could not (or would not) hold up production on *Babes on Broadway*, so Mr. and Mrs. Rose headed back to California. (AD reports for *Babes on Broadway* on this day mention a "layoff due to Judy Garland.")

July 29, 1941: *Babes on Broadway* filming. Scenes: Ext. Roof Top and Int. Penny's Office. Time called: 9 a.m.; lunch 12:20–1:20 p.m.; time dismissed: 5:57 p.m.

July 30, 1941: *Babes on Broadway* filming. Scene: Int. Penny's Office and Int. Stone's Office. JG- Time called: 9 a.m.; lunch 12:50–1:50 p.m.; time dismissed: 5:55 p.m.

July 31, 1941: *Babes on Broadway* filming. Scenes: Int. Stone's Office. Time called: 9 a.m. Production AD notes state "9:00–9:15—Wait for JG to get into wardrobe, in her dressing room on stage—was ten minutes late in makeup department this morning—overslept; 10:35–10:45—Dr. Jones on set looking at Judy Garland's hand which she said she injured on a door in scene yesterday—She first complained of this when she arrived on stage today." Lunch 12:20–1:20 p.m.; time dismissed: 6:15 p.m.

August 1, 1941 and August 2, 1941: Judy was not on call for *Babes on Broadway* work.

August 4, 1941: *Babes on Broadway* filming. Scenes: Int. and Ext. Pitt-Astor. Time called: 2 p.m.; time dismissed: 4:30 p.m.

August 5, 1941 and August 6, 1941: Judy was out ill. (The *Babes on Broadway* company rehearsed "dance routine" on August 6.)

August 7, 1941: *Babes on Broadway* filming. Scene: Int. Pitt-Astor. Time called: 9 a.m. AD reports note "10:02–10:38—Judy Garland taking time to get in mood for scene. Necessary to cry in scene." Lunch: 12:15–1:15 p.m.; time dismissed: 5:50 p.m.

August 8, 1941: *Babes on Broadway* filming. Scene: Int. Old Duchess-Backstage; time called: 9 a.m.; lunch: 12:25–1:25 p.m.; time dismissed: 5:35 p.m.

August 9, 1941: *Babes on Broadway* filming. Scene: Int. Backstage (Old Duchess); time called: 9 a.m.; lunch: 12:40–1:40 p.m.; time dismissed: 4:15 p.m.

August 11, 1941: *Babes on Broadway* filming. Scene: Int. Morris Parlor ("How About You?" song). Also, recording at night—stage 1: Judy recorded "Bombshell from Brazil" with Mickey Rooney and the cast. Time called: 9 a.m.; lunch: 12:35–1:35 p.m.; time dismissed: 8:10 p.m.

August 12, 1941: *Babes on Broadway* filming. Scene: Int. Morris Parlor ("How About You?" song). Time called: 9:45 a.m. AD reports note: "10:08–10:16—wait for Judy Garland—late." Lunch: 12:30–1:30 p.m.; dismissed 6:10 p.m.

August 13, 1941: *Babes on Broadway* filming. Scene: Int. Morris Parlor ("How About You?" song). Time called: 9 a.m.; lunch 12:30–1:30 p.m.; time dismissed: 6 p.m.

August 14, 1941: *Babes on Broadway* filming. Scenes: Int. Dressing Room and Int. Morris Parlor ("How About You?" song). Time called: 3 p.m.; time dismissed: 6:40 p.m. AD reports note: "Judy was ill in the morning."

August 15, 1941: *Babes on Broadway* filming. Scenes: Int. Dressing Room and Corridor. Time called: 9 a.m. AD reports note: "9:00–9:20 a.m.—wait for Judy Garland to put on wardrobe & fix hair." lunch: 12:00–1:00 p.m. AD Reports note: "1:24–1:38—Dr. Jones on set to look at Judy Garland—complained of feeling badly with pains in neck and back. Dr. Jones said she probably had the starting of a cold but she was able to work." Dismissed: 3:55 p.m.

August 16, 1941: *Babes on Broadway* filming. Scenes: Int. Backstage (Old Duchess) and Carmen Miranda number. Time called: 9 a.m.; lunch: 1:30–2:30 p.m.

August 18, 1941: *Babes on Broadway* filming. Scene: Int. Old Duchess (Carmen Miranda). Time called: 9 a.m.; lunch: 12:30–1:30 p.m.; time dismissed: 3:30 p.m.

August 19, 1941: *Babes on Broadway* filming. Scene: Int. Old Duchess. Time called: 9 a.m.; time dismissed: 9:25 a.m. (No other information available.)

August 20, 1941: *Babes on Broadway* filming. Scenes: Ext. Stage Alley, Ext. Settlement House, and Ext. Morris Tenement. Time called: 1:30 p.m.; dinner: 5:15–6:15 p.m.; time dismissed: 9:05 p.m.

August 21, 1941: Judy was not needed for *Babes on Broadway* on this day.

August 22, 1941: *Babes on Broadway* work. Rehearsed "Hoe Down" number. Time called: 10 a.m.; lunch: 11:50–12:50 p.m.; dismissed: 4:10 p.m.

August 23, 1941: Judy was out ill this day.

August 25, 1941: Judy was out ill this day.

August 26, 1941: *Babes on Broadway* work. Rehearsed "Hoe Down" number. Time called: 10:45 a.m.; lunch: 12:25–1:25 p.m.; time dismissed: 3:00 p.m.

August 27, 1941: *Babes on Broadway* work. Rehearsed "Hoe Down" number. Time called 11:30 a.m.; lunch 12:10–1:10 p.m.; time dismissed: 3:20 p.m.

August 28, 1941: *Babes on Broadway* work. Rehearsed "Hoe Down" number. Time called: 10 a.m.; lunch: 12:05–1:05 p.m.; time dismissed: 4:20 p.m.

August 29, 1941: *Babes on Broadway* work: Rehearsed and MGM recording session for "Hoe Down." Time called: 10:30 a.m.; lunch 12:50–1:50 p.m.; time dismissed: 4:50 p.m.

August 30, 1941: *Babes on Broadway* filming. Scene: Int. Auditorium. Time called: 9:30 a.m.; lunch 12:30–1:30 p.m.; time dismissed: 3 p.m.

September 2, 1941: *Babes on Broadway* filming. Scene: Int. Gym ("Hoe Down" number). Time called: 10:30 a.m.; lunch: 1:00–2:00 p.m.; time dismissed: 6:03 p.m.

September 3, 1941: *Babes on Broadway* filming. Scene: Int. Auditorium ("Hoe Down"). Time called: 9 a.m.; lunch: 12:35–1:35 p.m.; time dismissed: 5:35 p.m.

September 4, 1941: Judy was out ill this day.

September 5, 1941: *Babes on Broadway* filming. Scene: Int. Auditorium ("Hoe Down"). Time called: 9 a.m.; lunch: 12:25–1:25 p.m.; time dismissed: 6:10 p.m.

September 6, 1941: *Babes on Broadway* filming. Scene: Int. Auditorium ("Hoe Down"). Time called: 9 a.m.; lunch: 12:30–1:30 p.m.; dismissed: 5:35 p.m.

September 7, 1941: (Radio) *The Chase and Sanborn Hour*, NBC (60 minutes). Judy sang "All The Things I Love" and "Daddy (I Want A Diamond Ring)" (with special lyrics). (Both songs from this show are on the out-of-print LP *Judy! Judy! Judy!* on the Star-Tone Label, #224.)

September 8, 1941: *Babes on Broadway* filming. Scene: Int. Auditorium–Sketch. Time called: 9 a.m.; lunch: 12:10–1:10 p.m.; time dismissed: 5:55 p.m.

September 9, 1941: *Babes on Broadway* filming. Scene: Int. Auditorium–Sketch. Time called: 9 a.m.; lunch: 12:25–1:25 p.m.; time dismissed: 5:50 p.m.

September 10, 1941: MGM recording session for *Babes on Broadway*. Judy recorded "Chin Up! Cheerio! Carry On!" Judy had a 12:30 p.m. call and was dismissed at 4:15 p.m.

September 11, 1941: *Babes on Broadway* work. Time called: 1:30 p.m. AD Reports note: "Call Cancelled on Stage 21 Int. Auditorium—Judy Garland ill with sore throat—However came in for poster still in p.m. (and publicity photos)—Company rehearsed Block Party." Time dismissed: 4 p.m.

September 12, 1941: *Babes on Broadway* filming. Scene: Ext. Street–Block Party. Time called: 9 a.m.; lunch: 12:30–1:30 p.m.; time dismissed: 5 p.m.

September 13, 1941: *Babes on Broadway* filming. Scene: Ext. Street (Block Party/"Chin Up, Cheerio, Carry On"). Time called: 9 a.m.; lunch: 12:30–1:30 p.m.; time dismissed: 6:50 p.m.

September 15, 1941: Judy was not needed for *Babes on Broadway* work on this day. (Keep in mind that any days not spent filming were most certainly spent doing publicity work, etc.)

September 16, 1941: *Babes on Broadway* work. Rehearsed Finale. Time called: 10 a.m.; lunch: 12:30–1:30 p.m.; time dismissed: 4:50 p.m.

September 17, 1941: *Babes on Broadway* work. Rehearsed Finale. Time called: 3 p.m.; time dismissed: 5:30 p.m.

September 18, 1941: Judy was not needed for *Babes on Broadway* work on this day.

September 19, 1941: *Babes on Broadway* work. Rehearsed Finale. Time called: 3 p.m.; time dismissed: 5:00 p.m.

September 20, 1941: *Babes on Broadway* work. Rehearsed Finale. Time called: 10 a.m.; lunch: 12:30–1:30 p.m.; time dismissed: 5:50 p.m.

September 22, 1941: *Babes on Broadway* work. Rehearsed Finale. Time called: 1 p.m.; time dismissed: 5:50 p.m.

September 23, 1941: *Babes on Broadway* work. Rehearsed Finale and MGM recording session for *Babes on Broadway*. Judy prerecorded "Minstrel Show Sequence" (which included her solo of "FDR Jones") and the *Babes on Broadway* finale, both with Mickey Rooney and the cast. Time called: 1 p.m.; lunch: 1:00–2:00 p.m.; time dismissed: 6:15 p.m.

September 24, 1941: *Babes on Broadway* work. Rehearsed Finale and prerecorded Finale. Time called: 10 a.m.; Judy arrived at 10:30 a.m.; time dismissed: 12:15 p.m.

September 25, 1941: *Babes on Broadway* work. Scene: Finale. Time called: 9 a.m.; lunch: 12:30–1:30 p.m.; time dismissed: 7 p.m.

September 26, 1941: Judy was out ill this day.

September 27, 1941: Judy was not needed for *Babes on Broadway* work on this day.

September 29, 1941: *Babes on Broadway* filming. Scene: Finale. Time called: 9 a.m.; lunch: 12:30–1:30 p.m.; time dismissed: 7 p.m.

September 30, 1941: *Babes on Broadway* filming. Scene: Finale. Time called: 9 a.m.; lunch: 12:30–1:30 p.m.; time dismissed: 5 p.m.

October 1, 1941: *Babes on Broadway* filming. Scene: Finale. Time called: 10 a.m.; lunch: 12:30–1:30 p.m.; time dismissed: 5:55 p.m.

October 2, 1941: *Babes on Broadway* filming. Scene: Finale. Time called: 10 a.m.; lunch: 12:05–1:05 p.m.; time dismissed: 6 p.m.

October 3, 1941: *Babes on Broadway* filming. Scene: Finale. Time called: 10 a.m.; lunch: 12:05–1:05 p.m.; time dismissed: 5:55 p.m.

October 4, 1941: Judy was out ill and *Babes on Broadway* could not film without her.

October 6, 1941: *Babes on Broadway* filming. Scene: Finale. Time called: 9 a.m.; lunch: 12:30–1:30 p.m.; time dismissed: 2:24 p.m.

October 7, 1941: *Babes on Broadway* work. Rehearsed Old Duchess Theatre Seq. 5–6. Time called: 10 a.m.; time dismissed: 3 p.m.

October 8, 1941: Judy was not needed for *Babes on Broadway* work on this day.

October 9, 1941: AD Reports for *Babes on Broadway* note: "Co. rehearsal cancelled at 11:14 a.m., account illness of Mr. Berkeley [the film's director]. JG—Call Cancelled."

October 10, 1941: MGM recording session for *Babes on Broadway*: Ghost Theater Sequence (including Judy's solos of "Mary's A Grand Old Name"; "I've Got Rings On My Fingers"; and "The Yankee Doodle Boy [Yankee Doodle Dandy]" with Mickey Rooney). Time called: 12:45 p.m.; time dismissed: 3:50 p.m.

October 11, 1941: *Babes on Broadway* filming. Scene: Int. Ghost Theatre. Judy in makeup at 7:36 a.m. Time called: 9 a.m.; lunch: 12:35–1:35 p.m.; dinner: 6:15–7:15 p.m.; time dismissed: 11:15 p.m.

October 12, 1941: (Radio) *Silver Theater*, CBS (30 Minutes). A play called *Eternally Yours* (Part 1; the second part would be performed the following week.)

October 13, 1941: *Babes on Broadway* filming. Scene: Int. Ghost Theatre. Time called: 9 a.m.; lunch: 2:43–3:43 p.m.; time dismissed: 7:25 p.m.

October 14, 1941: *Babes on Broadway* filming. Scene: Int. Ghost Theatre. Time called: 10 a.m.; lunch: 12:30–1:30 p.m.; time dismissed: 5:20 p.m.

October 15, 1941: *Babes on Broadway* finished filming (except for retakes done on November 6 and 7). Scenes: Int. Corridor, Int. Penny's office (retake), and Int. Ghost Theatre–Montage. Time called: 9 a.m. AD Reports note: "9:00–10:00 a.m.—Wait for Miss Garland. She called in this morning and said she was ill, but that she would be in later this AM. 10:00–10:17—Miss Garland on stage, fixing up in dressing room." Lunch: 12:20–1:20 p.m.; time dismissed: 4:52 p.m.

October 19, 1941: (Radio) *Silver Theater*, CBS (30 minutes). The second part of the play *Eternally Yours* (the first half had been broadcast the previous week).

October 24, 1941, 8 p.m. (to 12:15 a.m. on October 25, 1941): (Record) Decca Records session, Hollywood. Produced three cuts, in recording order: "How About You?" (from *Babes on Broadway*); "Blues In The Night"; and "FDR Jones" (also from *Babes on Broadway*). (The two *Babes* songs would be paired on 78 single # 4072 for a November release. "Blues" would also be released in November, on # 4081.)

November 3, 1941: (Radio) *Motion Picture Industry Community Chest Drive*, KFWB. Judy sang "Share a Little."

November 6, 1941: *Babes on Broadway* filming/retakes. Scenes: "Ext. Block Party, Int. Auditorium, Int. Penny's Office retakes, and Ext. Cellar." Time called: 1 p.m.; time dismissed: 5:20 p.m.

November 7, 1941: Retakes were done for *Babes on Broadway*, finishing the film. Scenes: Int. Corridor, Penny's Off., and Int. Auditorium. Time called: 9 a.m.; lunch: 12:35–1:35 p.m.; time dismissed: 3:25 p.m. The movie would be released in December, with the *Variety* review appearing on December 3. The film cost $955,300.37, and was an enormous success at the box office, grossing $3,859,000 in its initial engagements. The song "How About You?" would be nominated for Best Song at the Oscars, but would lose to "White Christmas." The following are two appraisals of Judy's work in the movie:

> *Time Magazine*: "Mickey Rooney, who would rather be caught dead than underplaying, has his hands full when he encounters bright-eyes Judy Garland. Miss Garland, now 19 and wise to her costar's propensity for stealing scenes, neatly takes the picture away from him. Rooney cannot sing, but Judy Garland can, and proves it pleasantly with sure-fire numbers."
>
> *Variety* (Billy Wilkerson, Editor): "Blurbs could never measure up to the performance of that ever surprising Judy. The shivers go up and down your spine in admiration."

November 9, 1941: (Radio) *Screen Guild Theater*, CBS (60 minutes). Judy and Mickey Rooney recreated their roles in a radio adaption of their 1939 film *Babes in Arms*. (This performance still exists in private collections.)

November 17, 1941: (Radio) *Lux Radio Theater*, CBS (60 minutes): *Merton of the Movies* with Judy and Mickey Rooney. (This entire performance is on the out-of-print LP *Merton of the Movies* on the Pelican label, #139.)

December 7, 1941: (Radio) *The Chase and Sanborn Hour*, NBC (60 minutes), broadcast from Fort Ord, near Monterey, California. It had been set up prior to the attack on Pearl Harbor, though it was frequently interrupted by news bulletins. Judy sang "Zing! Went The Strings of My Heart" and performed with Edgar Bergen and Charlie McCarthy. (This program is believed to still exist in private collections.) Also on this date, an incredible thing happened to Judy that no one has ever published before, and is not common knowledge: Judy was made an honorary Corporal. This is revealed in a copy of the *Esprit de Corps* newsletter for the First Medical Regiment at Fort Ord, California. Judy is on the cover of this extraordinarily rare newsletter receiving her stripes and citation. An abridged version of the article states:

> JUDY GARLAND JOINS REGIMENT—
>
> STAR MADE HONORARY CORPORAL IN H COMPANY
>
> Don't crowd, men. Stay in line. You can't all transfer to Company H at once. That's the sentiment around here when news leaked out that Judy Garland, lovely star of radio and screen, was given an honorary corporalcy in Company H of the 1st Medical Regiment.
>
> The minute Miss Garland came on the scene all eyes fastened on her. She was dressed in an attractive black and white outfit.
>
> Major Martin had Judy line up with a squad of men from Company H, and 1st Sergeant Marshall Hummel pinned corporal's stripes on each sleeve of Miss Garland's sweater. A corporal's warrant was then presented while a pair of identification tags were placed around her neck.

December 15, 1941: (Radio) *Motion Picture Industry Community Chest Drive*, KFWB. Broadcast from the Biltmore Bowl. Judy sang "Abe Lincoln Had Just One Country" (a new song by Jerome Kern). (This program is believed to still exist in private collections.)

December 23, 1941: (Radio) "Millions For Defense" (*Treasury Hour*), NBC (60 Minutes). Judy sang "Abe Lincoln Had Just One Country." (This recording exists in private collections.)

1942

Early 1942: Judy and David Rose were settled in their new home at 4020 Longridge in Sherman Oaks, California. The house once belonged to Jean Harlow, and was where Harlow's husband had unfortunately tried to commit suicide.

January 20, 1942: Judy signed an agreement on MGM letterhead to cover her appearance that day on a *Roy Shields Sustaining Program.* (Nothing is known about this radio show.)

January 21, 1942 to approximately February 9, 1942: (Personal Appearance tour for World War Two) Judy became one of (if not the) first Hollywood star to entertain the troops. She sang in five Midwestern training installations—including Fort Custer, Jefferson Barracks, Camp Robinson and Camp Wolters—over a three-week period. She did four shows a day, singing 12 songs each show. (Judy only ended the tour when she developed strep throat.)

Mid February (approximately February 13) 1942: Judy returned home to Los Angeles from Florida after a brief rest/long-delayed honeymoon of only a few days length.

February 14, 1942: Judy served as Matron of Honor at the wedding of actor Don Defore (best known as "Mr. B." from the 1950's television series "Hazel") to his fianceé Marion, which took place at the Chapman Park Chapel in Los Angeles, followed by a wedding breakfast at the Brown Derby.

February 1942: Judy extended her existing Decca Records recording contract, agreeing to record another 12 sides over the coming year (MGM continued to have approval on every aspect of her recordings).

February 19, 1942: Judy began work on her next film, *For Me and My Gal.* On this first day, Judy had a 1 p.m. call, and was dismissed at 4:45 p.m. The day was spent rehearsing a dance number.

February 20, 1942: *Gal* work. Time called: 1 p.m.; dismissed: 4:50 p.m. Rehearsed dance number.

February 21, 1942: AD reports for *Gal* note: "Cancelled Rehearsal Today Due to Fact Judy Garland did not want to rehearse."

February 23, 1942: *Gal* work. Time called: 1 p.m.; dismissed: 4:30 p.m. Rehearsed dance number.

February 24, 1942: *Gal* work. Time called: 1 p.m.; dismissed: 5 p.m. Rehearsed dance.

February 25, 1942 and February 26, 1942: Judy was ill and did not work on these days.

February 27, 1942: *Gal* work. Arrived: 1 p.m.; dismissed: 5:20 p.m. Makeup and hairdress tests.

February 28, 1942: *Gal* work. Time called: 1 p.m.; time dismissed: 5 p.m. Rehearsed dance.

Judy performing at one of the five Midwestern training installations she visited from January 21 to approximately February 9, 1942, making her one of the first to entertain the troups in World War II. Up through 1968, she would continue to do what she could to help lift the spirits of those fighting by visiting troops in hospitals, where she would sing, talk with them, and even make phone calls to their family members to let them know their loved one was alright. (Courtesy of Photofest.)

March 2, 1942: *Gal* work. Time called: 1 p.m.; dismissed: 4:30 p.m. Rehearsed dance routines.

March 3, 1942: Judy was out ill and did not work on this day.

March 4, 1942: *Gal* work. Time called: 1 p.m.; dismissed: 5 p.m. Rehearsed dance routine.

March 5, 1942: *Gal* work. Time called: 1 p.m.; dismissed: 4 p.m. Rehearsed dance routine.

March 6, 1942: *Gal* work. Time called: 1:30 p.m.; dismissed: 4 p.m. Rehearsed dance routine.

March 7, 1942: Judy was not needed for *Gal* work.

March 9, 1942: *Gal* work. Time called: 1:30 p.m.; dismissed: 4:30 p.m. Rehearsed dance routine.

March 10, 1942: Judy was not needed for *Gal* work.

March 11, 1942: *Gal* work. Time called: 11 a.m.; dismissed: 7:15 p.m. Sound and photo tests.

March 12, 1942: *Gal* work. Time called: 1 p.m.; dismissed: 5 p.m. Rehearsed dance routine.

March 13, 1942: *Gal* work. Time called: 1 p.m.; dismissed: 5 p.m. Rehearsed dance routine.

March 14, 1942: *Gal* work. Time called: 1 p.m.; time dismissed: 5:20 p.m. Rehearsed dance routine.

March 16, 1942: *Gal* work. Time called: 1:30 p.m.; time dismissed: 5 p.m. Rehearsed dance routine.

March 17, 1942: Judy was ill and did not work.

March 18, 1942: Time called: 10 a.m.; dismissed: 5:15 p.m. Rehearsed dance routine.

March 19, 1942: Judy was ill and did not work.

March 20, 1942: Time called: 1 p.m.; dismissed: 4:30 p.m. Rehearsed dance routine. Also, MGM recording session for *For Me and My Gal.* Judy recorded "The Doll Shop"/"Oh, You Beautiful Doll"/"Don't Leave Me Daddy" and "By The Beautiful Sea."

March 21, 1942: Time called: 11 a.m.; dismissed: 5 p.m. Rehearsed and prerecorded. MGM recording session for *For Me and My Gal.* Judy recorded "For Me And My Gal," a song she'd later develop into a concert-staple "sing-along" ("Sing it with me, please"), and "Ballin' The Jack"—both songs recorded with Gene Kelly, who was making his screen debut thanks to Judy's behind-the-scenes insistence.

March 23, 1942: Judy was ill and did not work.

March 24, 1942: Time called: 1 p.m.; dismissed: 2:45 p.m. MGM recording session for *Gal.* Judy recorded another song that would later become a staple at her concerts: "After You've Gone."

March 25, 1942: *Gal* work. Time called: 1 p.m.; dismissed: 5 p.m. Rehearsed dance routine.

March 26, 1942: *Gal* work. Time called: 1 p.m.; dismissed: 5 p.m. Rehearsed dance.

March 27, 1942: *Gal* work. Time called: 10:30 a.m.; dismissed: 5 p.m. Rehearsed. Also MGM recording session for *For Me and My Gal.* Judy recorded "Till We Meet Again"; "How 'Ya Gonna Keep 'Em Down On The Farm?"; "Where Do We Go From Here?"; and "For Me And My Gal" (Finale). (This ending would be replaced by a new one. The original song is available on the Rhino Records Soundtrack CD; footage is not known to exist of the original finale, only photographs exist.)

March 28, 1942: Judy was ill and did not work.

March 30, 1942: *Gal* work. Time called: 11 a.m.; dismissed: 4 p.m. Prerecorded "Doll Shop/Tramp Act."

March 31, 1942: Judy was ill and did not work.

April 1, 1942: *Gal* work. Time called: 10:30, dismissed: 4:15. Wardrobe tests and rehearsal.

April 2, 1942: *Gal* work. Time called: 3 p.m.; dismissed: 5:20 p.m. AD reports note: "Rehearsed w/boom."

Friday, April 3, 1942: *Gal* started filming. Time called: 10:30 a.m.; dismissed: 3:40 p.m. Scenes: Int. Backstage Dressing Room and Auditorium. Then at night, 8:30 p.m. to 11:30 p.m.: (Record) Decca Records session, Hollywood. Judy recorded four songs, in the following order: "The Last Call For Love"; "Poor You"; "On The Sunny Side of the Street"; and "Poor Little Rich Girl". ("You" and "Last Call" would be the "A" and "B" sides respectively on 78 #18320, released in June; "Sunny" and "Rich Girl" would be saved for a Judy *Souvenir* collection/album, released on May 20, 1943.)

April 4, 1942: *Gal* filming. Time called: 1 p.m.; dismissed: 6 p.m. Scene: Int. Bijou/Tramp Act/ Doll Shop.

April 6, 1942: *Gal* filming. Time called: 10 a.m.; dismissed: 6 p.m. Scene: Int. Bijou (Doll Shop).

April 7, 1942: *Gal* filming. Time called: 11 a.m.; dismissed: 4:15 p.m. Scene: Int. Bijou ("By the Sea").

April 8, 1942: *Gal* filming. Time called: 11 a.m.; dismissed: 5:30 p.m. Scene: Int. Bijou and Int. Dressing Room.

April 9, 1942: *Gal* filming. Time called: 10 a.m.; dismissed: 6:05 p.m. Scene: Int. Hicks Place. Judy also shot *Gal* publicity photos.

April 10, 1942: *Gal* filming. Time called: 10 a.m.; dismissed: 6:15 p.m. Scene: Int. Nick's Café.

April 11, 1942: *Gal* filming. Time called: 10:55 a.m.; time dismissed: 6:05 p.m. Scenes: Int. Hotel Lobby and Int. Jo's Room. Judy also shot *Gal* publicity photos.

April 13, 1942: Judy was ill and did not work.

April 14, 1942: Judy was on standby at home for *Gal* work, but was not called.

April 15, 1942: *Gal* filming. Time called: 11 a.m.; dismissed: 6:03 p.m. Scene: Int. Private Car.

April 16, 1942: *Gal* filming. Time called: 10 a.m.; dismissed: 6:15 p.m. Scenes: Int. Vestibule and Int. Jo's Room.

April 17, 1942: *Gal* filming. Time called: 10 a.m.; dismissed: 5:55 p.m. Scene: Int. Jo's and Harry's Dressing Room.

April 18, 1942: Judy was ill and left the studio at 9 a.m.

April 20, 1942: Judy was ill and did not work.

April 21, 1942: *Gal* filming. Time called: 10 a.m.; dismissed: 6:25 p.m. Scene: Int. Chicago Theatre.

April 22, 1942 through April 25, 1942: Judy was ill and did not work.

A rare candid shot of director Busby Berkeley watching George Murphy and Judy film a scene in *For Me and My Gal* (1942). (Courtesy of the Everett Collection.)

April 27, 1942: *Gal* filming. Time called: 10 a.m.; dismissed: 6:10 p.m. Scene: Int. Chicago Theater and Int. Jo's Hotel Room.

April 28, 1942: *Gal* filming. Time called: 2 p.m.; dismissed: 6:45 p.m. Scene: Ext. R.R. Station.

April 30, 1942: Judy was not needed for *Gal* filming.

May 1, 1942: *Gal* filming. Time called: 10 a.m.; dismissed: 5:55 p.m. Scenes: Int. Jo's Hotel Room and Int. Harry's Room.

May 2, 1942: *Gal* filming. Time called: 10 a.m.; dismissed: 5:55 p.m. Scenes: Int. Eve's Apt.

May 4, 1942: *Gal* filming. Time called: 11 a.m.; dismissed: 5:50 p.m. Scenes: Int. Eve's Apt. and Int. Palace Backstage.

May 5, 1942: Judy was ill and did not work.

May 6, 1942: *Gal* filming. Time called: 10 a.m.; dismissed: 5:20 p.m. Scene: Int. Palace Backstage.

May 7, 1942: *Gal* filming. Time called 10 a.m.; dismissed: 5:45 p.m. Scene: Int. Zeigfeld Roof.

May 8, 1942: *Gal* filming. Time called: 1:30 p.m.; dismissed: 6:50 p.m. Scene: Int. Zeigfeld Roof.

May 9, 1942: *Gal* filming. Time called: 10 a.m.; dismissed: 5:50 p.m. Scene: Int. Newark Dressing Room.

May 11, 1942: *Gal* filming. Time called: 10 a.m.; dismissed: 2:50 p.m. Scene: Int. Hotel Lobby and Elevator.

May 12, 1942: *Gal* filming. Time called: 10 a.m.; dismissed: 5:45 p.m. Scene: Int. Harry's Room.

May 13, 1942: *Gal* filming. Time called: 10 a.m.; dismissed: 5:58 p.m. Scene: Int. Jo's Hotel Room.

May 14, 1942: *Gal* filming. Time called: 10 a.m.; dismissed: 6:15 p.m. Scene: Int. Continental Hotel.

May 15, 1942: *Gal* filming. Time called: 10 a.m.; dismissed: 5 p.m. Scene: Int. Continental Hotel.

May 16, 1942: *Gal* filming. Time called: 10 a.m.; dismissed: 5:55 p.m. Scene: Int. Continental Corridor.

May 18, 1942: Judy was not needed for *Gal.*

May 19, 1942: *Gal* filming. Time called: 10:30 a.m.; dismissed: 5:15 p.m. Scene: Int. Palace.

May 20, 1942: *Gal* filming. Time called: 10 a.m.; dismissed: 6:25 p.m. Scene: Int. Palace (Finale).

May 21, 1942: *Gal* filming. Time called: 11 a.m.; dismissed; 5:50 p.m. Scenes: Int. Newark Palace and Ext. Palace.

May 22, 1942: Judy was not on call/not needed for *Gal.*

May 23, 1942: *Gal* filming. Time called: 10 a.m.; dismissed: 6:50 p.m. Scene: Int. Newark ("Ballin' the Jack" number).

May 25, 1942: Judy was ill and did not work.

May 26, 1942: *Gal* work. Time called: 10 a.m.; dismissed: 5 p.m. MGM recording session for *Gal*: "When You Wore A Tulip" and "YMCA Montage" (including Judy's "It's A Long Way To Tipperary," "Smiles," "Pack Up Your Troubles," and "Don't Bite The Hand That's Feeding You"). ("Smiles" would be shortened; "Don't Bite" would be cut. The complete versions of these songs are available on the Rhino Records CD soundtrack. The footage is not known to exist.)

May 27, 1942: *Gal* work. Time called: 12:50 p.m.; dismissed: 4:15 p.m. MGM recording session for *Gal*: Judy recorded "Three Cheers For The Yanks" (which would be cut from the film. The song is on the Rhino Records soundtrack CD; the footage is not known to exist).

May 28, 1942: *Gal* filming. Time called: 10 a.m.; dismissed: 5:30 p.m. Scene: Ext. French Square.

May 29, 1942: *Gal* filming. Time called: 10 a.m.; dismissed: 11 a.m. Scenes: Int. Cathedral, Int. YMCA, and Int. French Café. Also, time called: 1 p.m.; dismissed: 5:30 p.m. Scenes: Int. Theaters (stages and audiences).

June 1, 1942: *Gal* filming. Time called: 10 a.m.; dismissed: 12:00 p.m. Scenes: Int. R.R. Coach and Ext. Battlefield.

June 3, 1942: *Gal* work. Time called: 1 p.m.; dismissed: 5 p.m. "Synch to Loop" (dub) work.

June 4, 1942: *Gal* work. Time called: 2 p.m.; dismissed: 5 p.m. Shot publicity stills (including photos of Judy wearing her "When You Wore A Tulip" and "When Johnny Comes Marching Home Again" costumes).

June 10, 1942: Judy's twentieth birthday. (Husband David Rose gave Judy sables.)

June 11, 1942: Judy and David Rose drove in the afternoon to Lancaster, California, to attend the wedding of Judy's childhood friend. Judy volunteered to sing, and sang "Oh, Promise Me," accompanied by David on the piano.

Mid June 1942: Judy began preproduction for her next MGM film: *Presenting Lily Mars.*

June 21, 1942: (Radio) *The Chase and Sanborn Hour* (*Charlie McCarthy Show*), NBC (60 Minutes). Judy sang "I Never Knew (I Could Love Anybody Like I'm Loving You"). (The song is on *The Judy Garland Musical Scrapbook* LP on the Star-Tone Label, long out of print.) (The entire program is available from "Radio Spirits" at 1–800–RADIO-48.)

June 25, 1942: *Gal* work. Time called: 1:30 p.m.; dismissed: 5 p.m. MGM recording session for retakes: "When Johnny Comes Marching Home Again" and "For Me And My Gal" (reprise/New Finale). ("Smiles" is also noted as having been prerecorded on the AD Reports.)

June 26, 1942: *Gal* filming: Time called: 10 a.m. AD reports note: "JG called for 8 a.m. in makeup—10 a.m. on set—arrived in makeup at 9:35 a.m.—1hr 35 minutes late; At 9:40 a.m. in the makeup department, Judy Garland had an appendicitis attack and was taken to the studio hospital where Dr. Jones called her doctor and it was decided to give her heat treatment for 45 minutes at the end of which time she would be able to work." Dismissed: 10:40 p.m. Scene: Int. Palace Theatre.

June 27, 1942: *Gal* filming. Time called: 10 a.m.; dismissed: 6:05 p.m. Scenes: Int. Palace Theatre, Int. Hospital, Int. Chicago Dressing Room, and Ext. Theatre.

Mid to late July 1942: Preproduction work (Wardrobe/hair/makeup tests; dance/music rehearsals) continued on *Lily Mars.*

(Around this time, summer 1942, Judy's sister Jimmie had the lead in a musical review at the El Patio in Hollywood, and after one of the shows, Judy enjoyed an "Oh, Henry" candy bar on the curb outside the club while waiting for her car.)

July 26, 1942, 8:30 p.m. to 12:00 a.m.: (Record) Decca Records recording session, Hollywood. Judy recorded four songs in the following order: "For Me And My Gal" (with Gene Kelly, from their recently completed film of the same title); "When You Wore A Tulip (And I Wore A Big Red Rose)" (also with Gene and from *For Me and My Gal*); "That Old Black Magic"; and "I Never Knew (I Could Love Anybody Like I'm Loving You). (The two *Gal* songs were released in January 1943, on 78 single #18480; the other two would be released as a part of the second Judy *Collection*, on May 20, 1943.)

July 28, 1942: First MGM recording session with Judy for *Lily Mars.* Two songs recorded: "Tom, Tom, The Piper's Son" and "Every Little Movement."

July 29, 1942: *For Me and My Gal* finished filming, with re-takes. Time called: 10:30 a.m.; dismissed: 3:10 p.m. Scenes: Int. Draft Doctors Office, Int. Harry's N.Y. Hotel Room, Int. Jo's Hotel Room, Int. Theatre Stage, and Int. Eddie's Office. The total cost of the movie was $802,980.68, and it grossed $4,371,000 upon its release on November 20, 1942 (although engagements had actually started playing in New York City on October 21). This was the first time Judy had above-the-title solo billing in a movie, and her reviews were again raves. The following is a sampling.

> *The New York Herald Tribune*: "Miss Garland is someone to reckon with. Of all the youngsters who have graduated into mature roles in recent years, she has the surest command of her form of make believe. She turns in a warm, persuasive, and moving portrayal."
>
> *The Los Angeles Daily News*: "She has the faculty (wonderful for her but tough on an audience) of melting your heart. And in a sympathetic part, she's murder."
>
> *Daily Variety*: "She continues to gain impressiveness as a persuasive and skillful actress."
>
> *The Hollywood Reporter* (Billy Wilkerson, Editor; *front-page editorial!*): "It [*Gal*] would not attract such sales without Judy. Nor would audiences go out so satisfied if Judy was not in there punching as only she can punch out a hit performance."

August 1942 to September 1942: Production continued on *Lily Mars*.

September 18, 1942: MGM recording session for *Lily Mars*: Judy recorded "When I Look At You" (two versions: one "straight" ballad version, the other a "comedy" version. Both are performed in the film).

October 6, 1942: (Radio) *Lux Radio Theater*, CBS (60 minutes). Judy starred in the drama *Morning Glory*. Judy sang "I'll Remember April." (The program exists in private collections.)

October 16, 1942: The last "scheduled" MGM recording session for *Lily Mars*: "Paging Mr. Greenback" (This finale was scrapped before release, and a new, more spectacular ending was recorded and filmed only weeks before the film's premiere. The original finale's audio is available in stereo on the Rhino *Collectors' Gems* CD set; the footage is not known to exist; only stills remain.)

Early November 1942: *Presenting Lily Mars* finished filming, athough a new finale would be filmed in March 1943, only a few weeks before the film's release.

November 3, 1942: *Lily Mars* glamour portrait sitting at MGM.

November 30, 1942: Judy began preproduction on her next film (and the last starring vehicle for her and Mickey Rooney), *Girl Crazy*. On this first day, Judy and Mickey rehearsed. Time called: 10 a.m.; time dismissed: 4:45 p.m.

December 1, 1942: *Crazy* work. Called: 10 a.m.; dismissed: 4:45 p.m. Rehearsed number.

December 2, 1942: *Crazy* work. Called: 10 a.m.; dismissed: 4:45 p.m. Rehearsal.

December 3, 1942: Judy had no call/was not needed for *Crazy* work.

December 4, 1942: *Crazy* work. Called: 10 a.m.; dismissed: 3 p.m. Rehearsal.

December 5, 1942: *Crazy* work. Called: 10 a.m.; dismissed: Noon. Rehearsed number and test.

December 7, 1942: *Crazy* work. Called: 10 a.m.; dismissed: 3:30 p.m. Rehearsed number.

December 8, 1942: *Crazy* work. Called: 10 a.m.; dismissed: 4 p.m. Rehearsed: "Rhythm Number" and "Café Number."

December 9, 1942: *Crazy* work. Called: 3 p.m.; dismissed: 4:30 p.m. Rehearsed musical numbers.

December 10, 1942: *Crazy* work. Called: 10 a.m.; dismissed: Noon. Rehearsed "Rhythm" and "Café" Numbers.

December 11, 1942, December 12, 1942, December 14, 1942, and December 15, 1942: Judy had no call/was not needed for *Crazy* work.

December 16, 1942: *Crazy* work. Called: 1 p.m.; dismissed: 2 p.m. Rehearsed musical numbers.

December 17, 1942: Judy had no call/was not needed for *Crazy* work.

December 18, 1942: *Crazy* work. Called: 10 a.m.; dismissed: 2:30 p.m. Rehearsed musical numbers.

December 19, 1942: Judy was ill and did not work.

December 21, 1942: *Crazy* work. Called: 11 a.m., Arrived: 12:30 p.m.; dismissed: 3:30 p.m. Rehearsed "I Got Rhythm" number.

December 22, 1942: MGM recording session for Judy's special guest appearance in MGM's all-star *Thousands Cheer*. Judy recorded "The Joint Is Really Jumpin' Down At Carnegie Hall." (The film would be released on January 7, 1944. Judy, thus, had no call for any work on *Girl Crazy*.)

Judy never looked more breathtakingly beautiful than she did while filming *Presenting Lily Mars* in the fall of 1942. On November 3, 1942, as the majority of the film was being completed, Judy did an extensive publicity portrait session in the Gallery at MGM. Judy always wanted to look like Lana Turner—that's what she thought true beauty was. Here, she matches Turner's beauty—if not surpasses it. (Courtesy of Photofest.)

Lily Mars glamour portrait. (Courtesy of Photofest.)

Lily Mars glamour portrait. (Courtesy of Photofest.)

Lily Mars glamour portrait. (Courtesy of Photofest.)

Judy in her dressing room at MGM, preparing to film the original finale for *Lily Mars*. (Courtesy of Photofest.)

Judy filming the "Paging Mr. Greenback" production number, which was intended as the finale for *Presenting Lily Mars*. It would be replaced by a new, more lavish ending only weeks before the movie's release. (Courtesy of Photofest.)

December 23, 1942: Judy had no call for *Crazy* work. AD reports note: "Rehearsed for XMAS Show."

December 24, 1942: (Radio) Christmas Eve World War Two Entertainment Special, broadcast over CBS and NBC. (Judy had no call for any *Crazy* work.)

December 25, 1942: (Radio) *Elgin Christmas Day Canteen*, CBS (120 minutes). (Contents not confirmed, but it has been reported that "Judy had a dramatic spot with Bob Hope that lasted 10 minutes, 48 seconds.")

December 26, 1942: Judy had no call for any *Crazy* work. AD reports note: "Rehearsed Radio Show."

December 28, 1942: (Radio) *Lux Radio Theater*, CBS (60 minutes). Dramatic presentation of *A Star Is Born*, which Judy would bring to the screen as a musical in 1954. (This radio performance has been issued on LP, and now, on CD, on the Radiola Label.) Judy had no call for any *Crazy* work on this day; AD reports note: "With Radio Show."

December 29, 1942: *Crazy* work. Called: 10:15 a.m.; dismissed: 2:30 p.m. Rehearse and record. First MGM recording session for *Girl Crazy*. Judy recorded "I Got Rhythm."

December 30, 1942: *Crazy* work. Called for wardrobe at 9 a.m. Arrived there at 10 a.m.; dismissed: 3 p.m. Rehearsal.

December 31, 1942: *Crazy* work. Called: 9 a.m.; dismissed: 3:30 p.m. Fitting and rehearsal.

January 2, 1943: Wardrobe fittings and MGM recording session for *Girl Crazy*: "Bronco Busters" (which would be cut from the film, before it could be shot. The song exists, in stereo, on the *Mickey/Judy* box set and the single from the *Girl Crazy* Soundtrack CD, from Rhino Records). Additional takes for "I Got Rhythm" (original session was on December 29, 1942). Judy had an 11 a.m. call and was dismissed at 5:45 p.m.

Early to mid January 1943: Nine days were spent filming "I Got Rhythm" for *Girl Crazy* (four more than planned—thus, the film was immediately $60,000 over budget). Director Busby Berkeley made the number more elaborate and exhausting than originally conceived, which would wreak havoc on Judy's health later in the month.

January 4, 1943: *Girl Crazy* started filming. Called: 11 a.m.; dismissed: 5:58 p.m. Scene: Ext. Corral ("I Got Rhythm" number).

January 5, 1943: *Crazy* filming. Called: 10 a.m.; dismissed: 5:50 p.m. Scene: Ext. Corral ("Rhythm").

January 6, 1943: *Crazy* filming. Called: 10 a.m.; dismissed: 5:50 p.m. Scene: Ext. Corral ("Rhythm").

January 7, 1943: *Crazy* filming. Called: 1 p.m.; dismissed: 6 p.m. Scene: Ext. Corral ("Rhythm").

January 8, 1943: *Crazy* filming. Called: 10 a.m.; dismissed: 5:52 p.m. Scene: Ext. Corral ("Rhythm").

January 9, 1943: *Crazy* filming. Called: 1:30 p.m.; dismissed: 6 p.m. Scene: Ext. Corral ("Rhythm").

January 11, 1943: *Crazy* filming. Called: 1:30 p.m.; arrived: 3:10 p.m.; dismissed: 6 p.m. Scene: Ext. Corral ("Rhythm").

January 12, 1943: *Crazy* filming. Called: 10 a.m.; dismissed: 4 p.m. Scene: Ext. Corral ("Rhythm").

January 13, 1943: Judy was ill and did not work.

January 14, 1943: Called: 10 a.m.; dismissed: 6:50 p.m. Scene: Ext. Corral ("Rhythm" completed filming).

January 15, 1943: Judy was ill and did not work.

January 16, 1943 through January 21, 1943: Judy had no call/was not needed for *Crazy* work.

January 22, 1943: Judy was ill and did not work.

January 23, 1943: *Crazy* filming. Called: 3 p.m.; dismissed: 4:20 p.m.; working with Ballbusch Unit—Shot Rodeo Montage.

January 25, 1943 through January 30, 1943: Judy had rehearsals for the new *Lily Mars* finale, and thus had no call for *Crazy* work.

January 29, 1943: Judy's personal—and lifelong—family physician, Dr. Marcus Rabwin, ordered her not to dance for three weeks, and Ethel told MGM Judy was confined to bed. Judy was physically spent upon completion of the "Rhythm" number, her weight having dropped to 94 pounds; Berkeley had also been so cruel in his direction of Judy that he was replaced by Norman Taurog; Charles Walters would stage the songs.

February 1, 1943 through February 7, 1943: Judy had no call for *Crazy* work.

February 2, 1943: Announcement was made that Judy had separated from first husband David Rose.

February 8, 1943: *Crazy* filming. Called: 10 a.m.; dismissed: 4 p.m. Scene: Int. Western Dance Hall.

February 9, 1943: *Crazy* filming. Called: 11 a.m.; dismissed: 6 p.m. Scene: Int. Western Dance Hall.

February 10, 1943: *Crazy* filming. Called: 10 a.m.; dismissed: 6 p.m. Scene: Int. Western Dance Hall.

February 11, 1943: *Crazy* filming. Called: 10 a.m.; dismissed: 11:15 a.m. Scenes: Int. & Ext. Western Dance Hall and Int. Gov's Ballroom.

February 12, 1943: *Crazy* filming. Called: 9 a.m.; dismissed: 4:30 p.m. Scenes: Ext. Western Street.

February 13, 1943: Judy was ill and did not work.

February 15, 1943: *Crazy* filming. Called: 11 a.m.; dismissed: 5:40 p.m. Scene: Ext. Corral.

February 16, 1943: *Crazy* filming. Called: 2 p.m.; dismissed: 6 p.m. Scene: Ext. Western Street. Also, publicity stills were taken of Judy in her "I Got Rhythm" costume.

February 17, 1943 and February 18, 1943: Judy was ill and did not work.

February 19, 1943: *Crazy* filming. Called: 10 a.m.; dismissed: 5 p.m. Scene: Int. Dean's Office.

February 20, 1943, February 22, 1943 through March 3, 1943: Judy rehearsed the new, lavish *Lily Mars* finale.

March 4, 1943: MGM recording session for *Lily Mars*: "Broadway Rhythm" (as the ending for the new finale, "Where There's Music").

March 5, 1943: MGM recording session for *Lily Mars*: the rest of the "Where There's Music" Finale (which would be filmed later in March, then shortened before release. The entire routine can be heard on the Rhino *Collector's Gems* CD set, and additional takes are included on the *Golden Years At MGM* laser disc box set; the cut footage is not known to exist.)

March 6, 1943 to March 8, 1943: Additional work on *Lily Mars* finale.

March 9, 1943: *Lily Mars* finale was shooting—and on this day, Judy had a publicity portrait photo session in the studio Gallery wearing the gown she wears in the finale.

March 10, 1943 through March 16, 1943: *Lily Mars* finale finished shooting, completing the movie. *Presenting Lily Mars* would be released in late April 1943, with *Variety's* review appearing on April 27, and *The New York Times* on April 30. Judy perhaps never looked lovelier than she did in the fall of 1942 as she filmed *Lily Mars*, and certainly was never more beautiful on film. Here is an excerpt from one review.

> *The Motion Picture Herald*: "Judy grows better and better, and this picture registers a new high in performance and charm. She exhibits a dancing talent that is delightful in its grace and poise."

March 17, 1943: Judy resumed shooting on *Girl Crazy*. Called 10:33 a.m.; dismissed 4:26 p.m. Scene: Int. Post Office.

March 18, 1943 through March 20, 1943: Judy was ill and did not work.

March 22, 1943: *Crazy* filming. Called: 10:20 a.m.; dismissed: 4:30 p.m. Scene: Int. Post Office. AD reports note: "Company dismissed w/o completing shot to allow JG to leave for broadcast tonight." (Radio) *Screen Guild Players*, CBS (60 minutes). A radio adaptation of *For Me and My Gal* with Gene Kelly (and Dick Powell replacing George Murphy, apparently at the last moment; as of March 10, George Murphy was still slated to recreate his role, according to CBS press releases). (This program exists in private collections.)

March 23, 1943: *Crazy* filming. Called: 10 a.m.; dismissed: 6:10 p.m. Scenes: Int. Post Office and Int. Deans Office.

March 24, 1943: *Crazy* filming. Called: 10 a.m.; dismissed: 5:35 p.m. Scenes: Int. Dean's Office and Int. Governor's Office.

March 25, 1943: *Crazy* filming. Called: 10 a.m.; dismissed: 5:45 p.m. Scene: Int. Gov's Waiting Room and Office.

March 26, 1943: *Crazy* filming. Called: 10 a.m.; dismissed: 4:30 p.m. Scenes: Int. Governor's Office and Int. Ballroom.

March 27, 1943: *Crazy* filming. Called: 10:20 a.m.; dismissed: 11:25 a.m.; AD report notes: "Company dismissed without shooting because of illness of director and because JG's skirt did not fit."

March 28, 1943: (Radio) *Free World Theater*, NBC (30 minutes). Judy sang "The Wings Of Freedom (There'll Never Be Another England)."

March 29, 1943: *Crazy* work. Called: 11 a.m.; dismissed: 3:30 p.m. Wardrobe tests and MGM recording session for *Girl Crazy*: "But Not For Me."

March 30, 1943: *Crazy* filming. Called: 10:45 a.m.; dismissed: 5:10 p.m. Scene: Int. Dorm and Int. Dean's Home.

March 31, 1943: *Crazy* filming. Called: 10:35; dismissed: 5 p.m. Scene: Ext. Post Office and Ext. Campus (Judy as "Ginger," delivering the mail).

April 1, 1943: Judy was ill ("with bad throat" according to AD report notes) and did not work.

April 2, 1943: *Crazy* filming. Called: 10 a.m.; dismissed: 6 p.m. Scene: Ext. Capitol and Ext. Indian Rock.

April 3, 1943: Judy was ill and did not work.

April 5, 1943: *Crazy* filming. Called: 10:20 a.m.; dismissed: 5:55 p.m. Scene: Ext. Indian Rock.

April 6, 1943: *Crazy* filming. Called: 10:25 a.m.; dismissed: 5:50 p.m. Scene: Ext. Indian Rock. Then, that night: (Radio for World War Two) *Command Performance* #61. Judy sang "I Never Knew" and "Over The Rainbow" on this radio series for the troops fighting World War Two.

April 7, 1943: *Crazy* filming. Called: 10:22 a.m.; dismissed: 4:45 p.m. Scene: Ext. Indian Rock.

April 8, 1943: *Crazy* work. Judy was called at 10 a.m., but reported ill, so her call was postponed to 1:50 p.m.; dismissed: 4 p.m.; Rehearsed "Embraceable You" and "Bidin' My Time" numbers.

April 9, 1943: *Crazy* work. Called: 10 a.m.; arrived: 10:45 a.m.; dismissed: 5 p.m. Rehearsed "Embraceable You."

April 10, 1943: *Crazy* work. Called: 10:30 a.m.; arrived: 11:15 p.m.; dismissed: 4:30 p.m. Rehearsed "Embraceable You."

April 12, 1943: *Crazy* work. Called: 10 a.m.; dismissed: 4:15 p.m. Rehearsed "Embraceable You" and "Bidin' My Time."

April 13, 1943: Judy was ill and did not work.

April 14, 1943: *Crazy* work. Called: 10:30 a.m.; arrived: 10:50 a.m.; dismissed: 3:45 p.m. Rehearsed and recorded "Bidin' My Time."

April 15, 1943: *Crazy* work. Called: 1:30 p.m.; dismissed: 4:30 p.m. MGM recording session for *Girl Crazy*: "Embraceable You"; and a reprise of "Embraceable You" for the finale (though it would be cut before release, and replaced with the "I Got Rhythm" number—the deleted song is on the *Mickey/Judy* box set and from the *Girl Crazy* single-CD soundtrack from Rhino Records; the footage is not known to exist).

April 16, 1943: *Crazy* work. Called: 10 a.m.; arrived: 11 a.m.; dismissed at 11:45 a.m.; Camera rehearsal for "Embraceable You"; then a 4: 00 p.m. recording session to make a record for *Song Sheet*. (This must have been for World War Two. Judy signed an agreement on MGM letterhead on this date covering this session and stating that MGM would not be responsible for paying her for this performance. No information is known about this recording.)

April 17, 1943: Judy was ill and did not work.

April 19, 1943: *Crazy* filming. Called: 10 a.m.; dismissed: 5:30 p.m. Scene: Int. Assembly Hall. AD reports note: "10:00 a.m.: Makeup Phoned—they were having a little delay covering JG's eye cut; 10:10–10:40: Consultation with Mr. Freed and Dr. Jones as to whether to call shooting off due to possible head ache from moving around with swollen eye; Dr. Jones suggested Ice Packs of 10 minutes each between shooting shots. Mr. Freed decided to shoot only long shots today."

April 20, 1943: *Crazy* filming. Called: 10 a.m.; arrived: 10:25 p.m.; dismissed: 5:50 p.m. Scene: Int. Assembly Hall.

April 21, 1943: *Crazy* filming. Called: 10 a.m.; arrived: 10:30 a.m.; dismissed: 6 p.m. Scene: Int. Assembly Hall.

April 22, 1943: *Crazy* filming. Called: 10 a.m.; dismissed: 4:30 p.m. Scene: Int. Assembly Hall. Rehearsed "Bidin' My Time."

April 23, 1943: *Crazy* filming. Called: 10 a.m.; arrived: 10:25, dismissed: 4:50 p.m. Scene: Int. Assembly Hall.

April 24, 1943: *Crazy* filming. Called: 10 a.m.; dismissed: 5:50 p.m. Scene: Ext. Campfire. ("Bidin' My Time.")

April 26, 1943: *Crazy* filming. Called: 10 a.m.; arrived: 10:35 a.m.; dismissed: 5:40 p.m. Scene: Ext. Campfire. ("Bidin' My Time.")

April 27, 1943: *Crazy* filming. Called: 10 a.m.; dismissed: 5:50 p.m. Scene: Ext. Campfire. ("Bidin' My Time.")

April 28, 1943: *Crazy* work. Called: 1 p.m.; dismissed: 3:30 p.m. Rehearsal. Also, MGM prerecording session for *Girl Crazy*: "Could You Use Me?" with Mickey Rooney.

April 29, 1943 through May 1, 1943: Judy had no call/was not needed for *Crazy* work.

May 2, 1943: Judy left Los Angeles at 2 p.m. for Palm Springs location shooting of *Girl Crazy*.

May 3, 1943: Palm Springs locations scenes shot for *Girl Crazy*. Called: 9:30 a.m.; dismissed: 3:50 p.m. Scene: Ext. Dusty Road. Rehearsed "Could You Use Me?"

May 4, 1943: *Crazy* filming. Called: 9:30 a.m.; dismissed: 1:15 p.m. Scene: Ext. Dusty Road and Ext. Cliff.

May 5, 1943: Judy had no call/was not needed for *Crazy* work.

May 6, 1943: *Crazy* filming. Called: 11 a.m.; dismissed: 4:15 p.m. Scene: Ext. Roads.

May 7, 1943: *Crazy* filming. Called: 9 a.m.; dismissed: 4:45 p.m. Scene: Ext. Road to Station (Palm Springs Loc.).

May 8, 1943: *Crazy* filming. Called: 9 a.m.; dismissed: 3 p.m. Scene: Ext. Roads.

May 9, 1943: Judy had no call/was not needed for *Crazy* work.

May 10, 1943: *Crazy* filming. Called: 9 a.m.; dismissed: 4:25 p.m. Scene: Ext. Road to Station.

May 11, 1943: *Crazy* filming. Called: 8:30 a.m.; dismissed: 1:55 p.m. Scene: Ext. Roads (Palm Springs). *Girl Crazy* location work finished on this day, so Judy went home to Los Angeles. AD reports note: "Travel to LA Approx. 4hrs."

May 12, 1943: Judy was ill and did not work.

May 13, 1943: *Crazy* filming. Called: 10 a.m.; dismissed: 3 p.m. Scenes: Int. Gov's Office-Ext. Road.

May 14 and 15, 1943: Judy was ill and did not work.

May 17, 1943: *Crazy* filming. Called: 10 a.m.; arrived: 10:25 a.m.; dismissed: 5:50 p.m. Scenes: Ext. Station and Ext. Camp.

May 18, 1943: *Crazy* filming. Called: 10 a.m.; arrived: 10:10 a.m.; dismissed: 5:30 p.m. Scene: Ext. Dusty Road.

May 19, 1943: *Girl Crazy* finished filming (though Judy would do one additional, and brief, dubbing session for the film, on June 9.) Called: 10 a.m.; dismissed: 3:30 p.m. Scene: Ext. Road to Station.

June 7, 1943: The first of a chain of correspondence about a movie at MGM that Judy would never actually be assigned. Oscar Hammerstein wrote a letter on this date to producer Arthur Freed about Freed's recent discussion with Hammerstein and Richard Rodgers "regarding the Judy Garland picture you spoke to Dick and me about," which was *The Belle of New York*, to costar Fred Astaire.

June 9, 1943: MGM recording/post scoring session for *Girl Crazy*: Judy "hummed" (while Roger Edens was a "whistling" stand-in for Mickey Rooney) during this session for underscoring. (For the scene where Judy goes walking after her "birthday celebration.") The final cost for *Girl Crazy* was $1,410,850.85 ($322,935.30 over budget); the gross would top those of *Babes in Arms* and *Strike up the Band*, pulling in $3,771,000 (only *Babes on Broadway* grossed more: $3,859,000; though *Babes in Arms* most likely made a larger profit for MGM: $3,324,819, against an investment of only $745,341.03.) *Girl Crazy* was released November 26, 1943, following a June 17, 1943 preview at the Academy Theater in Inglewood. Here is a sampling of the reviews for Judy's work:

> *Variety*, 8-4-43: "Miss Garland is a nifty saleswoman of the numbers, right down to the overproduced 'I Got Rhythm' finale which was Busby Berkeley's special chore. Her 'Embraceable You' delivery is a standout; ditto 'Bidin' My Time' and 'But Not For Me.' She's also got two nice dancing sessions."
>
> *The New York Times*, 12-3-43: "Judy sings and acts like an earthbound angel. Miss Garland's songs, such as 'Bidin' My Time,' should soothe even the most savage beast; of all the child prodigies of Hollywood, Miss Garland has outgrown her adolescence most gracefully, and still sings a song with an appealing sincerity which is downright irresistible."
>
> *Time Magazine* 12-27-43: "As sung by cinemactress Judy Garland, 'Embraceable You' and 'Bidin' My Time' become hits all over again, and the new 'But Not For Me' sounds like another. Her presence is open, cheerful, warming. If she were not so profitably good at her own game, she could obviously be a dramatic cinema actress, with profit to all."
>
> *The Nation* (James Agee): "If, like me, you like Judy Garland: Miss Garland is a good strident vaudeville actor too, and has an apparent straightness and sweetness with which I sympathize. Judging by her frequent 'emotional' moments, I would very much like to see her in straight dramatic roles."

June 10, 1943: Judy's twenty-first birthday. Judy was now legally able to handle her own affairs as an adult. A custom-made comedy record was recorded and presented to Judy as a birthday present; meant to tell the "story" of Judy's life, the recording featured Danny Kaye, Phil Silvers, Keenan Wynn, producer/executive at MGM Dore Schary, Judy's MGM "assistant" Betty Asher, and Judy's sister Jimmie. (This recording still exists in private collections.)

Mid June 1943: Judy left Los Angeles for Philadelphia, where she would present her first "concert."

July 1, 1943: (Concert) Judy's first time "in concert," was at the Robin Hood Dell, in Philadelphia. 15,000 people jammed the amphitheater well past its 6,500 regular capacity; another 15,000 people sat on adjoining lawns, and in parking lots; another 5,000–10,000 people left when they could not get within listening distance. Following Andre Kostelanetz conducting several songs to start the concert, Judy's program (set by Roger Edens) was: a Gershwin Medley: "Someone To Watch Over Me"/"Do, Do, Do"/"Embraceable You"/"The Man I Love"/"Strike Up The Band"; a medley of film hits followed: "Over The Rainbow" (complete; then one chorus each, of:)/"For Me And My Gal"/"You Made Me Love You"/"It's A Great Day For The Irish"; "Our Love Affair"; "I'm Nobody's Baby"; and the closer: "The Joint Is Really Jumping." The encore was a reprise of "The Joint Is Really Jumping." Second and final encore: "But Not For Me." (By the end of the concert, crowds were swarming towards the stage "in a gigantic ocean wave," as they would do when Judy began the "Third Phase" of her career—after "The Vaudeville Years," and "The MGM Years"—there were, of course, "The Concert Years." Ironically, Judy would give her final U.S. Concert in Philadelphia also, 25 years later, on July 20, 1968, at JFK Stadium.) Here are two reviews for Judy's first concert:

> *Philadelphia Bulletin*: "A good little artist she is indeed . . . and her sense of rhythm and projection is simply amazing."
>
> (*Publication Unknown*): "Hundreds of people fought their way down the isles to get a nearer look; after the last number had been repeated, and the entire audience seemed to move forward as in a gigantic ocean wave, the lights were finally lowered to an accompaniment of quasi-hysterical cries and shrieks."

July 2, 1943 or July 3, 1943: Judy traveled from Philadelphia to New York, for:

July 4, 1943: (Radio) *The Pause That Refreshes On The Air*, (Sponsored by Coca-Cola), CBS (30 minutes). Judy sang "That Old Black Magic"; "Over The Rainbow"; and "This Is The Army Mr. Jones." (Andre Kostelanetz again conducted for Judy, as he had the July 1 concert. This program exists in private collections. "This Is The Army Mr. Jones" is on the out of print Star-Tone LP *The Judy Garland Musical Scrapbook, 1935–1949*.)

July 8, 1943 to early August 1943: (Personal Appearance/World War Two) Judy did her second Army-Camp tour for the troops (the first had been during January 1942 to February 1942, making her among the very first to entertain the troops). This new tour took her to USO camps in New York, New Jersey (including Fort Hancock), and Pennsylvania.

Mid August 1943: Shortly after returning home to LA, Judy was asked to join the Hollywood Bond Cavalcade/Third War Loan Campaign.

August 28, 1943: (Radio) *Command Performance* #81. Judy and Bing Crosby performed a comic song medley and then did a duet of "People Will Say We're In Love" from the new Broadway smash *Oklahoma!* (this song is on the 1977 LP *The Wit and Wonder of Judy Garland* on the DRG label); Judy also does a "Gershwin" medley similar to the one she sang in her Philly concert July 1. Judy's haunting "The Man I Love" from this show still exists in private collections.

September 8, 1943 through early to mid October 1943: (Personal Appearance/World War Two) Hollywood Bond Cavalcade opened in Washington, DC. The tour would hit fifteen other cities; ultimately raising over a billion dollars in bonds, and playing to over seven million people. In each city, there would be a two hour afternoon parade; mid-afternoon hotel press conference; and evening show. Although there were 12 other major stars along, including Fred Astaire, Lucille Ball, James Cagney, etc, Judy and Mickey Rooney had the final "star turn" spot of the show, before the finale with the entire cast.

Early to mid October 1943: Judy returned to Los Angeles from the tour, and began preliminary discussions/work on her next film: *Meet Me in St. Louis*.

November 2, 1943: (Record) Decca Records recording session, Hollywood: Judy recorded two songs from *Girl Crazy* in the following order: "But Not For Me" and "I Got Rhythm" (both would be released on Decca's *Original Cast Album* of 78s, on April 6, 1944).

November 3, 1943: Judy's first MGM recording session for *Meet Me in St. Louis*: "Boys And Girls Like You And Me" (this song had been cut from *Oklahoma!* and would suffer the same fate here; the song—in stereo—exists on the CD soundtrack from Rhino Records; footage is not known to exist, although MGM/UA Home Video put together a montage of stills to accompany the song on it's latest home video releases, and it is still on the most recent VHS edition from Warner Home Video.)

November 4, 1943: (Record) Decca Records recording session, Hollywood. Judy recorded three final songs for the Decca *Girl Crazy* "album." In recording order: "Embraceable You"; Could You Use Me?" (duet with Mickey Rooney); and "Bidin' My Time."

November 10, 1943: *St. Louis* work. Called: 1: 00, dismissed: 5:00 p.m. Wardrobe and makeup tests.

November 11, 1943: *St. Louis* work. Called: 11: 00, dismissed: 4:05 p.m.

November 12 and 13, 1943: Judy was ill and did not work.

November 15, 1943: *St. Louis* work. Called: 1 p.m.; dismissed: 3:40 p.m. Rehearsed "TheTrolley Song" and "Skip To My Lou" numbers.

November 16, 1943: *St. Louis* work. Called: 11:30, dismissed: 4:50 p.m. Rehearsed "Trolley" and "Skip To My Lou."

November 17, 1943: *St. Louis* work. Called: 11 a.m.; dismissed: 2: 20 p.m. Rehearsed "Trolley" and "Skip To My Lou."

November 18, 1943: *St. Louis* work. Called: 3:10 p.m.; dismissed: 5:00 p.m. Rehearsed "Trolley" and "Skip To My Lou."

November 19, 1943: *St. Louis* work. Called: 1 p.m.; dismissed: 3:40 p.m. Rehearsed "Trolley" and "Skip To My Lou."

November 20, 1943: Judy had no call/was not needed for *St. Louis* work.

November 22, 1943: *St. Louis* work. Called: 1 p.m.; dismissed: 4:00. Rehearsed "Trolley" and "Skip To My Lou."

November 23, 1943: *St. Louis* work. Called: 10 a.m.; arrived on set at 2 p.m.; dismissed: 4:20 p.m.; Dance rehearsals for "Trolley" and "Skip To My Lou."

November 24, 1943: Judy was ill and did not work.

November 25, 1943: *St. Louis* work. Called: 11:30, Came in at 1 p.m.; dismissed: 3:15. Dance rehearsal Only—"Trolly" and "Skip To My Lou."

November 27, 1943: Judy had no call/was not needed for *St. Louis* work.

November 29, 1943: *St. Louis* work. Called: 9 a.m.; arrived in Makeup as called but left Studio at 9 a.m.—came on set at 1 p.m.; dismissed: 6:10 p.m.; Wardrobe-Hair-Makeup tests (including Lon's party Sequence.)

November 30, 1943: *St. Louis* work. Called: 1 p.m.; arrived at 1:25 p.m.; dismissed: 3:45 p.m. Wardrobe-Hair-Makeup test /Pre record.

December 1, 1943: *St. Louis* work. Called: 4 p.m.; arrived at 4:30 p.m.; dismissed: 5:40 p.m. MGM rehearsal and recording session for *St. Louis*: Judy recorded "Meet Me In St. Louis, Louis." She also rehearsed "Trolley."

December 2, 1943: *St. Louis* work. Time Called: 1 p.m.; arrived at 1:45 p.m.; dismissed: 4 p.m.; Judy's first "public/professional" performance of another signature song: "The Trolley Song." After only one rehearsal, Judy completed the song in one continuous take—an additional take was completed for "insurance," though the first performance would be used. Upon completing the recording of "The Trolley Song," Judy then rehearsed "Skip To My Lou" with the chorus.

December 3, 1943: *St. Louis* work. Called: 1 p.m.; dismissed: 4:30 p.m. Rehearsed "Under the Bamboo Tree," and recorded "Skip To My Lou" and a portion of "Meet Me In St. Louis" (reprise).

December 4, 1943: *St. Louis* work. MGM recording session for *St. Louis*: Judy's first "public/professional" performance/recording of two more Garland Standards: "The Boy Next Door," and "Have Yourself A Merry Little Christmas."

December 6, 1943: *St. Louis* work. Called: 1 p.m.; dismissed: 5:30 p.m.; Camera and Dress Rehearsal of "Trolley."

December 7, 1943: *St. Louis* began filming. 10:00 a.m.; arrived 11:16 a.m.; dismissed: 4:30 p.m. Scene: Ext. Trolley Depot and Tests.

December 8, 1943: *St. Louis* filming. Called: 10 a.m.; dismissed: 5:55 p.m. Scene: Ext. Trolley Car.

December 9, 1943: Judy had no call/was not needed for *St. Louis* work.

December 10, 1943: *St. Louis* filming. Called: 10 a.m.; dismissed: 6 p.m. Scene: Int. and Ext. Trolley.

December 11, 1943: *St. Louis* filming. Called: 10 a.m.; dismissed: 5:30 p.m. Scene: Ext. Trolley Car and Ext. Treadmill of John Running.

December 12, 1943: (Radio) *Silver Theater*, CBS (30 minutes). Radio Drama *Ringside Table*, with Judy playing a singing star in a New York nightclub. Alan Ladd costarred as an FBI agent impersonating a playboy in order to follow a nightclub manager suspected of being an enemy agent. (This program exists in private collections.)

December 13, 1943: Judy was called for work on *St. Louis* and was there from 2:00–4:40 p.m.; but was not used.

December 14, 1943: *St. Louis* filming. Called: 10 a.m.; dismissed: 6 p.m. Scenes: Int. Trolley and Int. Smith Kitchen.

December 15, 1943: Called: 10 a.m.; dismissed: 6 p.m. Scenes: Int. Esther and Rose's Room and Int. Master Bedroom. Also this day: (Radio) *Christmas Program* on CBS, hosted by Robert Young; Judy was a guest, but there is no record of what her songs were. (No recording is believed to exist of this performance.)

December 16, 1943: Judy was ill and didn't work.

December 17, 1943: *St. Louis* work. Called: 1:00, dismissed: 2:15 p.m.; Prerecorded "Under The Bamboo Tree" (with Margaret O'Brien.)

December 18, 1943: At 8 a.m., Judy called the assistant director on *St. Louis*, Al Jennings, telling him she didn't feel well but that she would come to work, if a car picked her up. Jennings spoke with transportation and "arrangements were made to pick Miss Garland up in the company car." Upon arrival at the studio she called the stage and David Friedman and Jennings went to her dressing room, and called Dr. Jones, who came over and said she should return home. Judy "would not go without first speaking to Mr. Freed, which was accomplished, and at 10:30 a.m. I took her home in a studio car."

December 20, 1943: *St. Louis* filming. Called: 1 p.m.; dismissed: 5:35 p.m. Scenes: Int. Lower Floor and Kitchen.

December 21, 1943: *St. Louis* filming. Called: 10 a.m.; arrived: 10:25, dismissed: 5:10 p.m. Scene: Int. Lower Floor Smith Home.

December 22, 1943: Called: 10 a.m.; arrived: 10:22; dismissed: 6 p.m. Scenes: Ext. and Int. Foyer. Then, that night: (Record) Decca Records recording session, Hollywood. Judy recorded two songs in the following order: "No Love, No Nothin'"; and "A Journey To A Star" (released as 78 single # 18584, sides—A "No Love"; and B "Star"—on January 27, 1944.)

December 23, 1943: *St. Louis* filming. Called: 2:30, arrived: 3:20, dismissed: 3:45 p.m. Scene: Int. Kitchen.

December 24, 1943: *St. Louis* filming. Called: 9 a.m.; arrived: 9:45, dismissed: 12:15 p.m. Scene: Int. Living Room.

Judy reading over a script with comic legend Jack Benny, backstage at a radio show, circa 1943–1944. (Courtesy of Photofest.)

Saturday, December 25, 1943: (Radio) *Christmas Program*, CBS (120 minutes). (No other information is known about this program; nor is a recording known to exist.)

December 27, 1943 through December 31, 1943: Judy was ill and did not work. Production notes state she had been in the hospital on December 26, 1943 and December 27, 1943.

January 3, 1944: *St. Louis* filming. Called: 10 a.m.; dismissed: 5:50 p.m. Scene: Int. Master Bedroom/Upper Hall.

January 4, 1944: Judy was ill and did not work.

January 5, 1944: *St. Louis* filming. Called: 10 a.m.; dismissed: 6 p.m. Scene: Int. Living Room/Party Sequence ("Skip To My Lou" number).

January 6, 1944: *St. Louis* filming. Called: 10 a.m.; arrived: 10:25 p.m.; dismissed: 5:55 p.m. Scenes: Int. Hall and Living Room.

January 7, 1944: *St. Louis* filming. Called: 10 a.m.; arrived: 10:12 a.m.; dismissed: 5:55 p.m. Scenes: Int. Living Room and Hall.

January 8, 1944: AD reports note: "Judy Garland phoned at 8:25 that she was not well and could not be on the set ready to shoot until 11:30 instead of 10:00 (her call). Camera was set up and ready for 10:00 for same dance shot of which we made on take last night and which does not satisfy director. Mr. Freed (by phone at 9:50) requested Mr. Minnelli forget the dance shot and relight for closeup of song, which also includes Miss Garland. Eliminating the dance shot would partly compensate for the loss in shooting time due to Miss Garland's lateness. 12:30–12:50—Conference-Mr. Freed, Mr. Minnelli, and Miss Garland. Owing to Miss Garland's illness and failure to arrive on set until 12:30, company was unable to work before lunch." Dismissed at 5:40 p.m.

January 10, 1944: *St. Louis* filming. Called: 11 a.m.; dismissed: 5:40 p.m. Scenes: Int. Lower Hall and Stairs.

January 11, 1944: *St. Louis* filming. AD reports note: "Called: 10 a.m.; Wait for Miss Garland. Asst. Director phoned her home at 9:15. Said she had an earache and would be late. Arrived in studio 9:49. Came on stage at 10:30 madeup and hair dressed only." "1:50–2:25—Ready to light JG in closeup thru screen door. Miss Garland removed wig, makeup and wardrobe and slept thru lunch hour—Nurse called who put ice pack on head. Company waiting while Miss Garland getting ready." Dismissed: 5:20 p.m. Scenes: Int. Hall and Stairs, Ext. Porch, and Int. Kitchen.

January 12, 1944: Judy was ill and didn't work. According to AD reports filed by Dave Friedman: "At 11:20 last night Judy Garland phoned Al Jennings, assistant director, and said she was ill, she still had her headache, her eyes were beginning to swell, and that she would be unable to come in at all today. Mr. Jennings called me, and I notified Mr. Freed. Decision was made to let the crew come in and line, light, and rehearse the difficult boom shot we planned for today, going as far as we could without Miss Garland. As a result, company did not shoot today."

January 13, 1944: *St. Louis* filming. According to the AD reports, Judy had been due in wardrobe at 9 a.m. and on the set at 10 a.m.; at 9:10 a.m., a car was sent to bring Judy to the studio, as her eyes were bothering her, and she didn't want to drive, as she explained to the assistant director. The car returned with Judy at 9:45 a.m. At 9:50 a.m., Judy realized she could not find her "toothbridge": the portable "Caps" she wore on her front teeth to even them out and make them "Technicolor White." Judy's dentist, Dr. Pinkus, had a spare set; *St. Louis's* Unit Manager called the Transportation Department at MGM to get approval to send a car to get the caps. At 10 a.m. a car was sent to get them; returning at 10:40 a.m. with them. At 10:40 a.m. Judy arrived on the set; hair and makeup done, but in street clothes. For an hour, she and Tom Drake, as "The Boy Next Door," rehearsed the scene where they turn out the lights in the house. After Judy got into her costume, eleven takes of the scene were completed between 12:16 and 1:30 p.m. After an hour for lunch, rehearsals continued; two breaks were called: one for ten minutes when Judy retreated to be treated for a headache; another thirty minutes at a later point for an adjustment to Judy's costume. An additional seven takes were completed by 7:10 p.m., when production stopped for the day.

January 14, 1944: *St. Louis* filming. Called: 2 p.m.; dismissed: 6:10 p.m. Scenes: Int. Hall and Stairs & Living Room.

January 15, 1944: *St. Louis* filming. Called: 10 a.m.; dismissed: 5:58 p.m. Scenes: Int. Living Room and Upper Hall.

January 17, 1944: *St. Louis* filming. Called: 10 a.m.; arrived on stage at 10:22 a.m.; ready at 10:40, dismissed: 5:50 p.m. Scenes: Int. Little Girl's Bedroom and Int. Rose and Esther's room. That night: (Radio) *Let's Back the Attack*, with Glen Miller (the program exists in private collections).

January 18 and 19, 1944: Judy was ill and didn't work.

January 20, 1944: *St. Louis* filming. Called: 10 a.m.; arrived on set at 10:15 a.m.; ready at 10:25 a.m.; dismissed: 5:15 p.m. Scenes: Ext. Slope and trolley tracks and Int. Rose and Esther's bedroom.

January 21, 1944: *St. Louis* filming. Called: 10 a.m.; arrived on set at 10:27 a.m.; dismissed: 5:45 p.m. Scenes: Ext. Backyard, Int. Upper Hall and Grandpa's Room, and Int. Rose and Esther's room.

January 22, 1944: *St. Louis* filming. Called: 10 a.m.; arrived on set at 10:35 a.m.; dismissed: 5:55 p.m. Scene: Ext. Garden of Allaha.

January 24, 1944: *St. Louis* filming. Called: 10 a.m.; arrived on set at 10:36 a.m.; dismissed: 5:35 p.m. Scene: Ext. Site of Fairgrounds.

January 25, 1944: Called: 10 a.m.; arrived on set at 10:22 a.m.; dismissed: 12:00 p.m. AD reports note that: "Company will not shoot after lunch due to Miss Garland having her hair bleached at 2:00 p.m. for the ballroom sequence shooting tomorrow."

January 26, 1944: *St. Louis* filming. Called: 10 a.m.; ready on set at 10:47 a.m.; dismissed: 6:05 p.m. Scene: Int. Conservatory and Ballroom.

January 27, 1944: *St. Louis* filming. Called: 10 a.m.; arrived on stage at 10:24 a.m.; dismissed: 6 p.m. Scene: Int. Ballroom.

January 28, 1944: Judy was ill and didn't work.

January 29, 1944: *St. Louis* filming. Called: 10 a.m.; arrived on set 10:39 a.m.; dismissed: 6 p.m. Scene: Int. Ballroom and Conservatory.

January 31, 1944 though February 12, 1944: *St. Louis* couldn't film due to the absence of costar Margaret O'Brien. Judy still worked on two of those days.

February 3, 1944: From 2 p.m. to 3 p.m. Judy did "synch loops" (dubbing) work for *St. Louis*.

February 10, 1944: *St. Louis* work. Called: 1 p.m.; arrived on set at 3:15 p.m.; dismissed: 4:40 p.m. "Synch Loops" (dubbing work.)

February 14, 1944: *St. Louis* filming. Called: 1 p.m.; dismissed: 6 p.m. Scenes: Ext. Smith Home/Street and Int. Rose and Esther's Room.

February 15, 1944: *St. Louis* filming. Called: 11 a.m.; dismissed: 3:45 p.m. Scenes: Ext. Smith Home and Street.

February 16, 1944: Judy had a 10 a.m. call for "cover"—protection in case another scene or set wasn't able to be filmed—but was not needed for *St. Louis* on this day after all.

February 17, 1944: *St. Louis* filming. Called: 11:30 a.m.; dismissed: 6:15 p.m. Scenes: Ext. Smith home/street and Int. Living Room Hall/stairs.

February 18, 1944: *St. Louis* filming. Called: 7 p.m.; arrived on set 7:35 p.m.; dismissed: 9:20 p.m. Scenes: Ext. Smith Home and Street.

February 19, 1944: *St. Louis* filming. Called: 2 p.m.; arrived on set 2:52 p.m.; dismissed: 4:45 p.m. Scenes: Int. Living Room Hall and Stairs.

February 21, 1944: *St. Louis* filming. Called: 10 a.m.; arrived on set 10:35 a.m. AD reports note: "10:00–10:35—Wait for Miss Garland; called at 10 a.m.—in makeup; at 9: 25—before getting ready, she phoned stage that she could not make shot until she had her hair bleached for which she had appointment at 11:30. Mr Friedman told her hair would be OK in night lighting. Upon Garland phoning Mr. Freed for final decision, saying the shot might have to be retaken with her hair in its present condition, he instructed her to get made up and come to stage." Dismissed: 5:55 p.m. Scenes: Ext. Backyard, Int. Phone Booth, and Int. Living Room and Hall.

February 22, 1944: Judy was ill and didn't work.

February 23, 1944: *St. Louis* filming. Called: 10 a.m.; arrived on set 10:35 a.m.; dismissed: 6 p.m. Scene: Ext. Backyard—Winter.

February 24, 1944: *St. Louis* filming. Called: 10 a.m. AD reports note that "At 9:23 Miss Garland's mother phones: Judy was feeling ill but had left for studio anyway. 9:35 arrived thru gate. At 9:45 call came from her dressing room Miss Garland lying down ill and makeup not started. At 10:02 Mr. Freed and Mr. Friedman phoned from dressing room: Judy would be on set in twenty minutes—on set 10:50—getting dressed til10:58. Ready on set at 10:58." Dismissed: 5:45 p.m. Scenes: Ext. Backyard—Winter; Day and Night Sequences.

February 25, 1944: Judy was ill and didn't work.

February 26, 1944: *St. Louis* filming. Called: 10 a.m.; arrived on set 10:32 a.m.; dismissed: 6:20 p.m. Scene: Int. Children's Room & Ext. Window of Same ("Have Yourself A Merry Little Christmas").

February 28, 1944: *St. Louis* filming. Time Called: 10 a.m.; dismissed: 4:24 p.m. Scenes: Ext. Window Children's Room, Int. Upper Hall, and Int. Rose and Esther's room. After filming was completed for this day, Judy did a photo session for the movie's poster, along with other publicity shots, with costars Margaret O'Brien and Tom Drake until 6:00 p.m.

February 29, 1944: *St. Louis* filming. Time called: 10 a.m. AD reports note that "Garland phoned at 9:12—she had overslept; arrived thru gate at 9:25—at 10:30 we phoned her (in her dressing room)—said she had been delayed by conference with Mr. Freed; She arrived on stage at 10:45, and was ready at 10:50." Dismissed: 5:05 p.m. Scenes: Int. Esther and Rose's room, Int. Living Room, and Int. lower Hall.

March 1, 1944: AD reports for *St. Louis* note "At 5:05 last night, when company was finished shooting, Miss Garland told Al Jennings, assistant director, that she would be indisposed and unable to come in tomorrow. Due to Joan Carroll's illness, company is unable to shoot today and had planned to rehearse. Miss Garland being unavailable, rehearsal was cancelled and company is on layoff today."

March 2, 1944: *St. Louis* work. Called: 11 a.m.; arrived: 11:20 a.m.; dismissed: 4:45 p.m. Rehearsed dinner sequence and Halloween sequence.

March 3, 1944: *St. Louis* work. Called: 11 a.m.; arrived: 11:40 a.m.; dismissed: 3:15 p.m. Rehearsed Dinner sequence, Halloween sequence, and Xmas card game.

March 4, 1944: *St. Louis* work. Called: 12:30 p.m.; dismissed: 4:20 p.m. "Poster Art" (Photo portrait session for poster of *St. Louis*.)

Judy as "Esther Smith" in the classic *Meet Me in St. Louis*. This portrait was taken on the afternoon of March 4, 1944, during a session for publicity photos and poster art for the film. (Courtesy of Photofest.)

March 5, 1944: (Radio for World War Two) *Command Performance* #81. Judy sang "Embraceable You"; "The Man I Love"; and "People Will Say We're In Love" with Bing Crosby. (This program is believed to still exist in private collections. The duet with Crosby was released on the DRG LP, *The Wit and Wonder of Judy Garland*, issued circa 1977 and now out-of-print.) Also done apparently on this date were three additional *Command Performance* programs. # 91: Judy sang "Zing! Went The Strings Of My Heart" (this is also believed to still exist in private collections); #92: Judy bantered briefly with Bob Hope, then sang "Over The Rainbow." This performance was filmed, as well as recorded, and the footage can be found on the *Golden Years* laser disc from MGM/UA Home Video, released in 1995. And #106: Judy sang "No Love, No Nothin' "; "Embraceable You," with Frank Sinatra; and performed a "Desert Island" sketch with Sinatra (this program is also believed to still exist in private collections). Judy also made a series of appearances on the *Mail Call* programs for the troops; some of this material has been released on out-of-print LPs. A currently available CD from LaserLight/Delta Music features one of these programs with Judy where she sings "The Trolley Song"; "Can Do, Will Do"—a.k.a. "The Song Of The Seabees"—and "The Groaner, The Canary, And The Nose" (with Crosby and Jimmy Durante). Other songs that Judy sang on the *Mail Call* series included: "I Never Knew"; "The Joint Is Really Jumpin' Down At Carnegie Hall"; "Dear Mr. Gable: You Made Me Love You"; "The Dixieland Band"; and "Something To Remember You By" (with Crosby).

March 6, 1944: *St. Louis* filming. Called: 10 a.m.; ready at 10:17 a.m.; dismissed: 5:50 p.m. Scenes: Int. Esther and Rose's Room and Int. dining room.

March 7, 1944: *St. Louis* filming. Called: 10 a.m.; arrived at 10:20 a.m.; dismissed: 4 p.m. Scenes: Ext. Smith Home and Street.

March 8, 1944: *St. Louis* filming. Called: 10 a.m.; arrived at 10:40 a.m. (but not ready); dismissed: 5:40 p.m. Scene: Int. Dining Room.

March 9, 1944: Judy was ill and didn't work. She had been called for 3 p.m., but at 1:20 p.m. she called from her home saying that her sinus was bothering her so badly that she was worried she would miss an important night shoot the following day if she didn't rest.

March 10, 1944 and March 11, 1944: *St. Louis* filming. Time called: 10:30 a.m.; dismissed: 3:40 p.m. Scenes: Ext. Smith Home/Street and Halloween Street.

March 11, 1944 and March 12, 1944: AD reports for *St. Louis* only note that "Time Call Changed to 10:30 at her request. Dismissed: 2:30 a.m."

March 13, 1944: AD reports for *St. Louis* note that Judy was "Unable to work tonight on account of her own illness."

March 14, 1944: *St. Louis* filming. Time called: 10 p.m.; arrived at 10:24 p.m. (not ready); dismissed: 4:20 a.m. Scene: Ext. St Louis Street (Halloween).

March 15, 1944 through March 21, 1944: Judy was not on call/not needed for *St. Louis* work.

March 22, 1944: *St. Louis* filming. Called: 10:30 a.m.; ready at 10:45 a.m.; dismissed: 5 p.m. Scenes: Int. Living Room, Hall, and Dining Room.

March 23, 1944: *St. Louis* filming. Called: 10 a.m.; arrived at 10:12 a.m.; dismissed: 6 p.m. Scenes: Int. Lower Hall and Int. Dining Room.

March 24, 1944: *St. Louis* filming. Called: 10 a.m.; ready at 11 a.m.; dismissed: 4:30. Scenes: Ext. Smith House and Street.

March 25, 1944: *St. Louis* filming. Called: 10 a.m.; ready at 10:55 a.m.; dismissed: 5:50 p.m. Scene: Int. Dining Room.

March 27, 1944: *St. Louis* filming. Called: 11 a.m.; ready at 12:20 p.m.; dismissed: 5:40 p.m. Scene: Int. Dining Room.

March 28, 1944: *St. Louis* filming. Called: 10 a.m.; arrived at 10:15 a.m. (not ready); dismissed: 4:35 p.m. Scenes: Int. Dining Room and Ext. Halloween.

March 29, 1944: *St. Louis* filming. Called: 3:30 p.m.; dismissed: 5:50 p.m. Scenes: Int. living room and hall/stairs.

March 30, 1944: Called: 10 a.m.; ready at 11:08 a.m.; dismissed: 12:15 p.m. Judy went home ill.

April 1, 1944: *St. Louis* filming. Called: 10 a.m.; dismissed: 5:30 p.m. Scene: Ext. St. Louis Fair.

April 3, 1944: *St. Louis* filming. Called: 10 a.m.; ready: 10:25 a.m.; dismissed: 5:30 p.m. Scene: Ext. St Louis Fair.

April 4, 1944: *St. Louis* filming. Called: 10 a.m.; ready at 10:36 a.m.; dismissed: 5:40 p.m. Scenes: Int. Living Room, Stairs, and Hall. Judy also shot publicity photos for *St. Louis*.

April 5, 1944: *St. Louis* filming. Called: 7 p.m.; ready at 7:35 p.m.; dismissed: 12:00 midnight. Scenes: Ext. Smith House and Street.

April 7, 1944: *St. Louis* finished filming. Called: 10 a.m.; ready at 10:30 a.m.; dismissed: 4 p.m. Scene: Int. Smith Living Room.

April 10, 1944: Judy synched loops (dubbing) for *St. Louis* from her 10 a.m. call to 12:30 p.m. when she was dismissed. There would be one more day of dubbing/recording work, on May 26, 1944, to complete the film.

April 20, 1944, 8:30 p.m. to 11:30 p.m.: (Record) Decca Records recording session, Hollywood. The first of two sessions to record an "Original Cast Album" for *Meet Me in St. Louis*. Judy recorded three songs, in the following order: "The Boy Next Door"; "Boys And Girls Like You And Me"; and "Have Yourself A Merry Little Christmas."

April 21, 1944, 8:30 to 11:45 p.m.: (Record) Decca Records recording session, Hollywood. The second of two sessions to record an "Original Cast Album" for *Meet Me in St. Louis*. Judy recorded three songs in the following order: "The Trolley Song"; "Skip To My Lou"; and "Meet Me In St. Louis" (The "album" of 78s would be released on November 2, 1944 and would go to #2 on the new "Album" chart.)

April 28, 1944: (Radio) *GI Journal*, Number 41, with Judy and Bing Crosby. This was followed by *Mail Call* (#91) in May 1944 with Judy, Bing, and Jimmy Durante. All three performed "The Groaner, The Canary, and The Nose," available on the various LPs and Delta Music CDs of this material.

May 18, 1944: MGM Gallery Publicity Portrait sitting.

May 24, 1944: (Radio) *The Frank Sinatra Show*, CBS (30 minutes). Judy sang "Zing! Went The Strings Of My Heart" and "Embraceable You" (with Sinatra). (This program is believed to still exist in private collections.)

May 26, 1944: MGM postrecording session for *Meet Me in St. Louis*. Judy recorded the few lines of the song, "Over The Banister," completing her work in the film. What makes the movie all the more a miracle is the fact that nearly all actors playing major parts suffered illnesses or required some type of medical attention that closed the set for weeks at a time, including Margaret O'Brien, Mary Astor, Joan Carroll, etc. It's also amazing to consider that twenty-one-year-old Judy didn't want to play a seventeen-year-old (especially when she'd just played a nineteen-year-old in *Lily Mars*). She also didn't understand director Vincente Minnelli's unique and brilliant way of making movies, but she would ultimately grow to love him, and they started dating near the end of production. Judy had known Vincente since 1940, when he'd first arrived at MGM from his directing and designing days on Broadway and at Radio City Music Hall. (He contributed to the "fruit orchestra" sequence of Judy's *Strike up the Band*.) Another irony about *St. Louis* is that George Cukor had been wanted by Metro to direct the film, but after two months of work with the screenwriters on the script, he was drafted into the Army. Cukor would work with Judy ten years later as the director of her *A Star Is Born*. Along with Judy's performance, other benefits of *St. Louis* were its rich Technicolor hues (Judy's first full-length color appearance since "Oz") and her stunning beauty, thanks in part to her new makeup artist, Dottie Ponedel. Ponedel would work with Judy on all of her remaining Metro movies, becoming one of Judy's closest friends. The total final cost of *Meet Me in St. Louis* was $1,707,561.14. Upon its release in late November it would become Judy's biggest grossing film—bringing in $7,566,000 on its first release—as well as becoming MGM's second highest grossing film, after *Gone with the Wind*. (Keep in mind that MGM only released *Wind*; the Selznick Studios made it. Thus, *St. Louis* became the biggest hit to date made at and produced by MGM, in its twenty-year history.) "The Trolley Song" would be nominated for Best Song, losing to "Wishing On A Star." The film's success would also once again place Judy on the Top 10 List of Box Office Stars, as she had in 1940 and 1941. The following are three excerpts from reviews of Judy's work in *St. Louis*:

> *The New York Times*, 11-29-44: "Miss Garland is full of gay exuberance, and sings with a rich voice that grows riper and more expressive in each new film."
>
> *The Sunday Times* (British; critic Dilys Powell): "Miss Garland's talents as an actress are, I believe, of a much higher order than is generally recognized."
>
> *Variety*: "Miss Garland achieves true stature with her deeply understanding performance."

June 4, 1944: (Radio) *The Bakers of America Salute to The Armed Forces*, NBC (60 minutes). Judy sang "The Trolley Song" for the first time to the public; "Long Ago And Far Away"; and "The Way You Look Tonight" with Bing Crosby.

June 7, 1944: Judy filed for divorce from her first husband, David Rose.

June 10, 1944: Judy's twenty-second birthday. MGM gave a birthday party for her and for forty-six invited guests.

June 16, 1944: Judy started preproduction work on her next film for MGM, *The Clock*. This would be her first straight dramatic role, with no singing. On this first day of work, Judy did "silent wardrobe and hair test." She had a 3 p.m. call and was dismissed at 4:55 p.m.

June 25, 1944: (Radio) *The Chase and Sanborn Hour*, NBC (60 minutes). Judy introduced "The Boy Next Door" and also sang "Long Ago and Far Away."

June 25, 1944: (Radio for World War Two) *Command Performance*, #122. Judy sang "Dixieland Band"; "Something To Remember You By" with Bing Crosby; and performed in a comedy sketch with Bob Hope, Bing Crosby, and Frank Sinatra. (This show is available on CD on the LaserLight Label.)

June 27, 1944: A preview of *Meet Me in St. Louis*.

July 1944: (Radio) *Command Performance* (#129), with Judy, Bing Crosby, and the Andrews Sisters . The show featured "The All-Time Flop Parade"—Bing told Judy after she'd sung, "Thank you, Judy, that was really lousy." This was followed by "My Old Kentucky Home."

July 6, 1944: Rehearsals at MGM for Judy's next film: a guest appearance in the all-star film *Ziegfeld Follies*. Judy's production number was a comedic spoof on a glamorous movie queen called, "The Interview," a.k.a. "A Great Lady Gives an Interview," a.k.a. "Madame Crematon." (It is interesting to note that Judy had gone from playing a seventeen-year-old girl in her last film assignment at MGM—*St. Louis*—to portraying a sexy movie star in this film, only three months after *St. Louis* had been completed.) On this first day of work, Judy was called: 11:30 a.m.; dismissed: 4:30 p.m. Rehearsed scene: "Interview" number. "Miss Garland also fitted wardrobe for still picture," according to AD reports.

July 7, 1944: *Follies* work. Time called: 12:00 p.m.; dismissed: 3:00. Rehearsed scene: "Interview" number with Charles Walters and sixteen chorus boys in Rehearsal Hall A. AD reports also note that "Besides rehearsing, Miss Garland made still picture for oil painting." (This was a portrait used in "The Interview.")

July 9, 1944: *Follies* work. Rehearsal for scene: "Interview" number with Walters and men, Rehearsal Hall B.

July 10, 1944: *Follies* work. Time called: 3 p.m.; time dismissed: 6 p.m. Rehearsed scene: "Interview."

July 11, 1944: (Radio) *Everything for the Boys*, NBC (30 minutes). Judy talked with serviceman stationed in Honolulu and sang "There's A Tavern in the Town" (an "Autolight" singing commercial) with Dick Haymes. (The commercial is on *The Judy Garland Scrapbook* LP, Star-Tone ST 208. The musical director was Gordon Jenkins, who would record with Judy later in the 1940s and conduct for her during tours and albums in the 1950s.) This program must have been broadcast during the day, as Judy had a night call at MGM for work on *Follies*. Called: 7 p.m.; time dismissed: 10 p.m. Rehearsed scene: "Interview" number.

July 12, 1944: *Follies* work. Time called: 4 p.m.; dismissed: 10 p.m. Rehearsals.

July 13, 1944: *Follies* work. Time called: 4 p.m.; dismissed: 6 p.m. Rehearsed scene: "Interview."

July 14, 1944: *Follies* work. Called: 4 p.m.; dismissed: 9:30 p.m. Rehearsed scene: "Interview."

July 15, 1944: *Follies* work. Called: 1 p.m.; dismissed: 5:20. Rehearsed scene: "Interview" number.

July 17, 1944: *Follies* work. Called: 2 p.m.; dismissed: 5:05 p.m. MGM recording session for *Ziegfeld Follies*. Judy's number, "The Interview," was recorded.

July 18, 1944: *Follies* work. Time called: 9 a.m.; dismissed: 4 p.m. Rehearsed scene: "Interview."

July 19, 1944: *Follies* filming of Judy's scene: "Interview" number on Stage 21 (Vincente Minnelli, directed). Called: 9 a.m.; dismissed: 6:10 p.m.

July 20, 1944: *Follies* filming. Called: 9 a.m.; dismissed: 5:15 p.m.

July 21, 1944: *Follies* finished filming Judy's scene: "Interview" number. On this final day of filming, Judy had a 10 a.m. call and was dismissed at 5:45 p.m. The total cost of Judy's sequence was $57,334.85. The film had its first sneak preview on November 1, 1944, at the Westwood Village Theatre. With its new name *Ziegfeld Follies of 1946*, the movie had a road-show premiere in Boston on August 20, 1945 and finally went into wide release on April 8, 1946. Its total cost was $3,240,816.86, and it grossed over $5,344,000 in its initial run. The following are two excerpts from reviews of Judy's work:

> *The New York Times*: "A talent approaching Beatrice Lillie or Gertrude Lawrence."

> *Newsweek*: "An unexpected flair for occupational satire."

July 31, 1944: *Clock* work. "Silent photographic test," according to the AD reports. Called: 10 a.m.; dismissed at 3:30 p.m. That night, from 7 p.m. to 10:15 p.m.: (Record) Decca Records recording session, in Hollywood. Judy and Bing Crosby recorded (in order) "You've Got Me Where You Want Me," and

"Mine." ("Got Me" would not be released until April 19, 1945, as a "B-side"; "Mine" would also be a "B-side" and would not be released till January 20, 1947.)

August 1, 1944: *The Clock* started filming. Scenes: Magazine Stand, Ext. Tony's Shop, and Ext. Drug Store. Time called: 10 a.m.; time dismissed: 4:20 p.m.

August 2, 1944: *Clock* filming. Scenes: Ext. Arcade, Drug Store, Tony's Shop, and Int. Tony's Shop. Time called: 11:30 a.m.; time dismissed: 5:50 p.m.

August 3, 1944: *Clock* filming. Scene: Int. Drugstore and Int. Tony's Repair Shop. Time called: 10:30 a.m.; 12:05–1:05 lunch; 1:05–1:20—Judy arrived on the set; 1:20–1:40—Judy was getting into wardrobe; time dismissed: 5:10 p.m.

August 4, 1944: Judy was ill and didn't work. AD reports note: "JG reported sick: Miss Garland phoned Glazer last night after dinner that she was feeling a little ill and didn't think she'd be able to work today. Glazer phoned her mother's house before nine this morning and learned Miss Garland had spent a restless night with a temperature of 101, and they were waiting for a doctor to call. Company went ahead and made shots with [costar] Robert Walker as planned."

August 5, 1944: Judy was ill and didn't work.

August 7, 1944: *Clock* filming. Scenes: Ext. Station, Ext. Tony's Shop, and Ext. Top of Bus. Time called: 10 a.m.; time dismissed: 6:50 p.m.

August 8, 1944: *Clock* filming. Scenes: Ext. Top of Bus and Ext. Pond. Time called: 10 a.m.; "9:55–10:40— Waiting for Miss Garland—due 10:00; 10:40–10:45—Miss Garland arrived on set—getting into wardrobe." Time dismissed: 5:50 p.m.

August 9, 1944: Judy was ill; shooting was cancelled.

August 10, 1944: *Clock* filming. Scenes: Int. Living Room—Alice's Apt. Time called: 1 p.m.; time dismissed: 5:55 p.m.

August 11, 1944: *Clock* filming. Scene: Int. Living Room—Alice's Apt. Time called: 10 a.m.; time dismissed: 5:45 p.m.

August 12, 1944: *Clock* filming. Scene: Int. Living Room and Bedroom—Alice Apt. Time called: 10 a.m.; time dismissed: 3:20 p.m.

August 13, 1944: (Radio) *Your All-Time Hit Parade*, NBC (30 minutes). Judy sang "I May Be Wrong" and "Over The Rainbow" (both with the Tommy Dorsey Orchestra). (This version of "I May Be Wrong" is available on the CD *Judy Garland on Radio—All The Things You Are* on the Vintage Jazz Classics label; and her CD in the *American Legends* series from LaserLight/Delta Music. "Rainbow" is on the 1995 MGM laser disc set.)

August 14, 1944: *Clock* filming. Scene: Ext. Pond. Time called: 10 a.m.; time dismissed: 6:30 p.m.

August 15, 1944: *Clock* filming. Scene: Ext. Pond, Int. Museum-Int. Gallery-Rodin's Thinker; "scene where Joe pulls boy out of water—Alice-Policeman-Children and crowd." Time called: 10 a.m.; time dismissed: 6:05 p.m.

August 16, 1944: *Clock* filming. Scene: Int. Rodin's Thinker Room, Int. French Gallery, and 2nd Gallery. Time called: 10 a.m. "10:00–10:25—Waiting for Miss Garland—on set: [She was] in dressing room getting into wardrobe—finishing fixing hair, makeup, etc. 5:35–5:40—Discussing setup—set was decided upon and scene could have been shot by 6:30 but Miss Garland did not feel well and felt she could not work that late." Time dismissed: 5:50 p.m.

August 17, 1944: *Clock* filming. Scene: Int. French Gallery and Ext. Bus Stop. Time called: 10 a.m. "10:10–11:30—Waiting for Miss Garland—due 10:00, arrived in studio 9:35; on stage at 11:10 and getting into wardrobe, etc. in dressing room to 11:30. 2:35–3:00—Miss Garland not feeling well; rehearsed scene with Bob Walker to 2:50; looked at the process test scene on moviola until 3:00; Miss Garland and Bob Walker dismissed at 3:00 p.m."

August 18, 1944 and August 19, 1944: Judy was ill and didn't work. (Costar Robert Walker was out ill on these two days also.) On August 19, Judy did do a Broadcast: (Radio) *Command Performance* with Danny Kaye. (This performance exists in private collections.)

August 21, 1944: *Clock* filming. Scene: Ext. Bus Stop (process). Time called: 10 a.m.; time dismissed: 7 p.m.

August 22, 1944: *Clock* filming. Scene: Ext. Bus Stop & Street (process.) Time called: 11 a.m. "11:35–11:40—Rehearsing—using Miss Garland's stand-in; [Judy] arrived at studio 10:20, due at 11:00; [Was] on set at 11:55; 11:55–12:06—Rehearsing with Miss Garland." Dismissed: 5:45 p.m.

August 23, 1944: *Clock* filming. Scene: Ext. Street—Bus and Int. Egyptian Room and Crusaders Tomb. Time called: 10 a.m.; arrived at studio at 8:30 a.m., and from 10:15–10:26, she finished getting into wardrobe and fixing her hair, etc. Time dismissed: 5:40 p.m.

August 24, 1944: Director Fred Zimmerman was removed from *The Clock*, and replaced by Vincente Minnelli. Thus the company was on "layoff" on August 24 and 25. On August 26, Judy had "no call," was not needed for *Clock* work.

August 28, 1944: Judy and Robert Walker made *The Clock* poster stills for Publicity Dept. Time called: 12:45 p.m.; time arrived: 1:30 p.m., time dismissed: 4:30 p.m.

August 29, 1944 through August 31, 1944: Judy was not needed for any *Clock* work.

September 1, 1944: Filming resumed on *The Clock* under Minnelli's direction. Scenes: Int. Rodin's Thinker-Int. French Gallery. Time called: 10 a.m.; time arrived: 11:02 a.m. (Judy was in makeup at 8:55 a.m., but they had wrong fall for her hair, thus the delay; She arrived on the set at 10:53 a.m. and was ready for filming at 11:02 a.m.) Time dismissed: 6:40 p.m.

September 2, 1944: *Clock* filming. Scenes: Int. French Gallery, Int. Another Gallery, and Int. Egyptian Room. Time called: 10 a.m.; time arrived: 10:08 a.m.; time dismissed: 3:30 p.m. (Judy had to leave at 3:30 p.m. to keep a hair appointment.)

September 3, 1944: (Radio) *The Chase and Sanborn Hour*, NBC (60 minutes). Judy sang "I'm Glad There Is You" and "Swinging On A Star." (This program is not known to still exist.)

September 1944 to late November 1944: Production continued on *The Clock*. (Shortly after refilming began, Judy moved out of her rented home and into Minnelli's. Judy had been living in a small apartment after separating from Rose; later she rented Mary Martin's home on Ogden Drive in West Los Angeles while Mary was in New York. Finally, just before she moved in with Minnelli, Judy had moved back in with her mother, whose home was also on Ogden Drive.)

September 5, 1944: *Clock* filming. Scenes: Int. Egyptian Room-Int. Crusaders Tomb. Time called: 10 a.m.; time dismissed: 5:55 p.m.

September 6, 1944: *Clock* filming. Scenes: Int. Alice's Apt. and Int. Crusaders Tomb. Time called: 10 a.m.; time dismissed: 6:20 p.m.

September 7, 1944: *Clock* filming. Scene: Int. Alice's Apt. AD reports note that JG reported sick.

September 8, 1944: *Clock* filming. Scene: Int. Alice's Apt. Time called: 10 a.m. AD notes: "Miss Garland called for 10 a.m.—arrived 10:13—ready rehearsal; 10:13–10:30—Rehearsed for director; 10:42–10:48—Additional line and light after rehearsal; 10:42–10:48—wait for director to return from projection room—meanwhile finish makeup, hair and wardrobe for Miss Garland. Director back at 10:45; continued waiting for Miss Garland to be ready for shooting—ready at 10:48." Time dismissed: 6:15 p.m.

September 9, 1944: *Clock* filming. Scene: Int. Alice's Apt. Time called: 1:00 p.m. AD reports note: "note: original call for Miss Garland was 10:00 a.m. But (she was) ill in morning and unable to report on set until 1:00 p.m. At 9:25 Miss Garland informed asst. director that she was ill this morning. Will notify company later this morning at 11:00 if she will be able to report for shooting this afternoon. 11:30: Miss Garland phoned she would report to studio for shooting after lunch. Company continued to standby. 12:45–1:10—Wait for Miss Garland to finish makeup, hairdress. 1:10–1:50—Miss Garland on set. Rehearsals started for benefit of both dolly camera and Director. 2:05–2:35—Wait for Miss Garland and Brady to get into wardrobe—finish hairdress and final makeup touches; Scene of Alice alone in room—reflecting on date with soldier." Dismissed: 6:20 p.m.

September 11, 1944: *Clock* filming. Scenes: Int. Alice's Apt., Park Path, 15th Ave. at 79th—Int. Penn station." Time called: 10 a.m.; time dismissed: 4: 10 p.m.

September 12, 1944 through September 14, 1944: *The Clock* didn't film on these three days. AD reports note "Shooting cancelled due to illness of director."

September 15, 1944: *Clock* filming. Scene: Int. Penn Station. Time called: 11 a.m.; time dismissed: 5:45 p.m.

September 16, 1944: *Clock* filming. Scenes: Int. Penn Station (Lobby and Stairs.) Time called: 10 a.m.; time dismissed: 5:50 p.m.

September 18, 1944: *Clock* filming. Scene: Int. Penn Station Lobby. Time called: 10 a.m. Judy arrived on set at 10:30 a.m., and from 10:40 a.m. to 11:00 a.m. she was getting into her wardrobe. Time dismissed: 5:58 p.m.

September 19, 1944: *Clock* filming. Scene: Int. Penn Station Lobby and Gates (The scene where Judy and costar Robert Walker meet for the first time; when Judy trips over him and the heel of her shoe breaks off.) Time called: 1 p.m.; time dismissed: 5:50 p.m.

September 20, 1944: *Clock* filming. Scene: Int. Penn Station Gates and Ext. and Int. Tony's Repair Shop. Time called: 10 a.m.; time arrived: 10:25 a.m.; time dismissed: 6:00 p.m.

September 21, 1944: *Clock* filming. Scenes: Int. Tony's Repair Shop and Int. Magazine Stand. Time called: 10 a.m.; time dismissed: 6:05 p.m.

September 22, 1944: *Clock* filming. Scenes: Int. Magazine Stand, Ext. Station, and Ext. Top of Bus. Time called: 10 a.m. AD reports note that "Miss Garland phoned Al Shenberg early this morning that her tooth was troubling her, that she had an eleven o'clock appointment with the dentist and would not be able to come in until 1:30; company could not work without Miss Garland. [She] arrived on lot at 12:30; on stage 1:35; ready on set at 2:00 p.m." Time dismissed: 6 p.m.

September 23, 1944: *Clock* filming. Scenes: Ext. Top of Bus and Bus Stop. Time called: 10 a.m.; time arrived: 10:33 a.m. AD reports note that from: "2:43–2:57—Miss Garland discussing neuralgia pain with doctor/Fixing hair and makeup." Time dismissed: 6 p.m.

September 25, 1944: *Clock* filming. Scene: Ext. Bus Stop. Time called: 10 a.m.; time arrived: 10:14 a.m.; time dismissed: 6 p.m.

September 26, 1944: *Clock* filming. Scene: Int. Bus. Time called: 10 a.m.; time arrived on set: 10 a.m. AD reports note that from "1:30–2:12:Waiting for Miss Garland; Miss Garland knew that we had only one other shot to do this afternoon due to Robert Walkers illness. [She] arrived on stage at 1:57; ready at 2:12." Time dismissed: 3 p.m.

September 27, 1944: *Clock* filming. Scene: Int. and Ext. Bus-pro treadmill/Int. Hotel Astor Lobby. Time called: 10 a.m.; time arrived: 10:18 a.m.; time dismissed: 4:20 p.m.

September 28, 1944: *Clock* filming. Judy was on standby on *The Clock* set all day, until 6:05 p.m., but was not needed, and did not film any scenes.

September 29, 1944: *Clock* filming. Scenes: Ext. Telephone Booth and switchboard, Int. Astor revolving doors, and Int. small restaurant. Time called: 1 p.m.; time arrived: 1 p.m.; time dismissed: 6:05 p.m.

September 30, 1944: *Clock* filming. Scene: Int. Small Restaurant. (Scene with Judy and Robert Walker, piano player, and extras. Roger Edens played the piano player in this scene.) Time called: 10 a.m.; time arrived: 10:14 a.m.; time dismissed: 6:15 p.m.

October 2, 1944: *Clock* filming. Scene: Int. Small Restaurant. Time called: 10 a.m.; time arrived: 10:16 a.m.; time dismissed: 4 p.m.

October 3, 1944: *Clock* filming. Scenes: Ext. Al's House and Street and Ext. Riverside Park. Judy arrived at the studio at 8:40 a.m. and was on the set at 10:20 a.m. for her 10 a.m. call. AD reports note that from: "10:20–10:40—Rehearsing; 10:40–11:25—Line and Light (Miss Garland getting into wardrobe, fixing hair and makeup, etc.); 11:25–11:35—Miss Garland getting ready; 11:35–11:40—rehearsing; 11:40–11:46—Line and Light; 11:46–12:28—Shooting 11 takes; 12:28–12:30—stills (publicity stills shot on the set); dismissed at 12:30 (lunch was from 12:30–1:30 p.m.)."

October 4, 1944: *Clock* filming. Scene: Ext. Riverside Park. Time called: 10:30 a.m.; time arrived: 10:25 a.m., time dismissed: 6:55 p.m.

October 5, 1944: *Clock* filming. Scene: Ext. Riverside Park. Time called: 10:45 a.m.; time arrived: 10:45 a.m.; time dismissed: 6:32 p.m.

October 6, 1944: *Clock* filming. Scene: Ext. Riverside Park. Time called: 10 a.m.; time arrived: 10:07 a.m.; time dismissed: 5:55 p.m.

October 7, 1944: The scene for Int. U.S.O. was not shot that day, as the AD reports note: "Miss Garland arrived on lot at 9:15. At 9:30 she phoned Al Shenberg from dressing room saying she felt ill. Mr. Shenberg asked her to get madeup, etc., as we could finish the set before lunch or soon after. A little later, Miss Garland phoned again and said she really felt bad. Mr. Shenberg sent Dr. Jones to her. Dr. Jones reported that Miss Garland was running a temperature of 101 and sent her home."

October 8, 1944: "Hollywood Democratic Committee dinner to honor Harold L. Ickes," held at the Ambassador Hotel, Los Angeles. With Johnny Green at the piano, Judy sang a parody of "Over The Rainbow"; "Someone To Watch Over Me"; and the first known public performance of "The Trolley Song." (A recording of these songs exists in private collections.)

October 9, 1944: *Clock* filming. Scenes: Int. U.S.O., Riverside Park, and Int. Subway train. Time called: 10 a.m.; time arrived: 10:06 a.m.; time dismissed: 5:55 p.m.

October 10, 1944: Judy was ill and did not work on this day. No shooting was done on *The Clock*.

October 11, 1944: *Clock* filming. Scene: Int. Subway Platform at 42nd Street. Time called: 10 a.m.; time arrived: 10:15 a.m.; time dismissed: 5:40 p.m.

October 12, 1944: Judy was only on standby for *Clock* filming, and did not work on this day.

October 13, 1944: *Clock* filming. Scene: Int. Subway Platform-33rd St. ("train comes in—Alice goes through turnstile and up stairs"). Time called: 10 a.m.; time dismissed: 6:30 p.m.

October 14, 1944: *Clock* filming. Scene: Int. Subway Platform. Time called: 2 p.m.; time dismissed: 5:40 p.m.

October 16, 1944: *Clock* filming. Scene: Int. Dingy Restaurant. Time called: 10 a.m.; time dismissed: 6:05 p.m.

October 17, 1944: *Clock* filming. Scene: Int. Marriage License Bureau. Time called: 10 a.m.; time dismissed: 5:50 p.m.

October 18, 1944: *Clock* filming. Scene: Int. Lobby Medical Bldg. Time called: 10 a.m.; time dismissed: 5:50 p.m.

October 19, 1944: *Clock* filming. Scene: Int. Marriage License Bureau. Time called: 10 a.m.; time dismissed: 6 p.m.

October 20, 1944: *Clock* filming. Scene: Int. Laboratory and Corridor Outside. Time called: 10 a.m.; time dismissed: 6:15 p.m.

October 21, 1944: *Clock* filming. Scene: Int. Room 387 and Int. Marriage Chapel. Time called: 10 a.m.; time dismissed: 6:25 p.m.

October 23, 1944: *Clock* filming. Scene: Int. Marriage Chapel. Time called: 10 a.m.; time dismissed: 6:10 p.m.

October 24, 1944: *Clock* filming. Scene: Int. Marriage Chapel and Int. Church. Time called: 10 a.m.; time dismissed: 5:50 p.m.

October 25, 1944: *Clock* filming. Scene: Int. Church. Time called: 10 a.m.; time dismissed: 6:20 p.m.

October 26, 1944: *Clock* filming. Scene: Int. Hotel Bedroom. Time called: 10 a.m.; time dismissed: 6 p.m.

October 27, 1944: Judy was ill and did not work.

October 28, 1944: *Clock* filming. Scene: Int. Hotel Suite and Int. Taxi Cab. Time called: 10 a.m.; time dismissed: 6 p.m.

October 30, 1944: *Clock* filming. Scene: Ext. Riverside Drive and Street Corner. Time called: 10 a.m.; time dismissed: 12 p.m.

October 31, 1944: *Clock* filming. Scene: Ext. Restaurant, B'way and 41st, and Ext. Another Restaurant. Time called: 10 a.m. AD reports note that "Judy Garland phoned Harry Poppe last night that she would not be on the set until about 2:00 this afternoon as she would be at the hospital with her mother who is undergoing an operation. Arrived on set at 1:20." Time dismissed: 4:55 p.m.

November 1, 1944: *Clock* filming. Scene: Ext. Saint Faith Episcopal Church. Time called: 10 a.m.; time dismissed: 5:15 p.m.

November 2, 1944: *Clock* filming. Scene: Ext. Seal Pool. Time called: 10 a.m.; time dismissed: 6:05 p.m. AD reports note that: "[At] 6:05 Company dismissed without getting shot as Miss Garland looked too tired; cameraman changed key light, etc., but this did not help and it was decided inadvisable to photograph her."

The Clock costars Robert Walker and Judy, strolling along the back lot at MGM during production of this film, November 1944. (Courtesy of Photofest.)

November 3, 1944: *Clock* filming. Scene: Ext. Seal Pool. Time called: 10 a.m.; time dismissed: 12:15 p.m.

November 6, 1944: *Clock* filming. Scene: Ext. Street Riverside Drive/Int. Milk Truck. Judy arrived at MGM at 9:45 a.m., was on the set at 11:15 a.m., and was ready at 11:15 a.m. (for a 10 a.m. call). Time dismissed: 5:55 p.m. That night: (Radio) *Democratic National Committee*, CBS/NBC (60 minutes). Judy sang "You Gotta Get Out and Vote" (this song is on *The Judy Garland Musical Scrapbook*, Star-Tone, #ST 208).

November 7, 1944: *Clock* filming. Scene: Int. Milk Truck. Judy was on the lot at 8:55 a.m., on the set at 10:25 a.m. from makeup, and ready at 10:40 a.m. for a 10 a.m. call. Time dismissed: 6 p.m.

November 8, 1944: *Clock* filming. Scene: Int. Lunch Room. Time called: 10 a.m.; time dismissed: 6:05 p.m.

November 9, 1944: *Clock* filming. Scene: Int. Lunch Room and Int. Milk Truck. Judy arrived at 9 a.m. and was on the set and ready at 10:30 a.m. (from makeup) for a 10 a.m. call. Time dismissed: 5:50 p.m.

November 10, 1944: *Clock* filming. Scene: Int. Milk Truck. Judy arrived on the lot at 9 a.m.; and was the on set at 10:47 a.m. (from makeup) for a 10 a.m. call. Dismissed: 6:05 p.m.

November 11, 1944: Judy was ill and did not work.

November 13, 1944 through November 15, 1944: Judy was not on call/needed for *Clock* work.

November 16, 1944: *Clock* filming. Scene: Ext. NY Street-Flat Tire. Time called: 10 a.m.; time dismissed: 6 p.m.

November 17, 1944: *Clock* filming. Scene: Ext. NY Street. Time called: 10 a.m.; time dismissed: 5:55 p.m.

November 18, 1944: *Clock* filming. Scene: Int. Tenement Hall, Int. Fireside Circular Stairs, and Int. Al's Living Room. Time called: 10 a.m.; arrived on the set at 10:25 a.m.; time dismissed: 6:10 p.m.

November 20, 1944: *Clock* filming. Scene: Int. Al Henry Kitchen. Time called: 10 a.m.; arrived on the set at 10:33 a.m.; time dismissed: 7:15 p.m.

November 21, 1944: *The Clock* finished filming. Scene: Ext. Loading Platform. Time called: 6 p.m.; time dismissed: 10:30 p.m. The film's total cost was $1,324,000, and it grossed $2,783,000, and would win Judy raves upon its release on May 25, 1945, including the following two notices:

> *The Nation* (James Agee): "Proves for the first time beyond anybody's doubt that Judy Garland can be a very sensitive actress. In this film, Miss Garland can handle every emotion in sight, in any size and shape, and the audience along with it."
>
> *The New York Daily Mirror*: "To say she is superb is an understatement in two syllables. She need never sing or dance again."

November 22, 1944: World Premiere of *Meet Me in St. Louis* held in St. Louis.

November 24, 1944: Judy and Vincente Minnelli boarded a train from California to New York for the Premiere of *St. Louis* in New York, and, once in New York City, they announced their engagement. At this time, Judy was also on the cover of *Life* magazine; her first of two covers for the magazine. The second would be in September 1954 for *A Star Is Born*. (Judy was to be on a cover in June 1961, but Fidal Castro's Bay of Pigs replaced her at the last moment.)

November 27, 1944: New York City Premiere of *Meet Me in St. Louis*.

December 17, 1944: (Radio) *Philco Radio Hall of Fame*. Judy sang "The Trolley Song" and "Have Yourself A Merry Little Christmas" (both from the just released *Meet Me in St. Louis*) with the Paul Whiteman Orchestra. (Whitman had appeared in Judy's film *Strike Up the Band* in 1940. Judy had come back from New York to do the show. Both songs are on the *Judy Garland on Radio, 1936–1944* CD on the Vintage Jazz Classics label released in 1993.)

December 26, 1944: (Radio) *Everything for the Boys*, NBC (30 minutes). Judy spoke with serviceman from the Pacific. (This program is not known to still exist. Judy also did a Holiday Radio program as a Command Performance in which she sang "The Trolley Song" and "Come All Ye Faithful"—"Faithful" is on a Bob Hope, *Christmas Party*, CD from Vintage Jazz Classics.)

December 29, 1944: Judy began production on her next film, *The Harvey Girls*. (The movie had actually been planned since 1942 as a dramatic film with Lana Turner, and Judy had wanted to star in *Yolanda and the Thief* instead of *Harvey Girls*.) On this first day, Judy had a 10 a.m. call and was dismissed at 12:20 p.m. The first day was spent rehearsing the numbers "It's A Great Big World" and "On The Atchinson, Topeka And The Santa Fe."

December 30, 1944: Judy had no call/was not needed for work on *The Harvey Girls*.

1945

January 2, 1945: *Harvey Girls* work. Time called: 10 a.m.; dismissed: 2:45 p.m. Wardrobe fitting.

January 3, 1945: *Harvey Girls* work. Time called: 10:30 a.m.; time arrived on set: 12:20 p.m.; time dismissed: 5:30 p.m. Testing wardrobe and hair.

January 4, 1945: *Harvey Girls* work. Time called: 1:30 p.m.; time dismissed: 4:20 p.m. Wardrobe fitting.

January 5, 1945: *Harvey Girls* work. Time called: 1 p.m.; time arrived on set: 1:15; dismissed: 4:30 p.m. Recorded "It's A Great Big World."

January 6, 1945: *Harvey Girls* work. Time called: 2 p.m.; time dismissed: 4 p.m. Rehearsing "Atchinson, Topeka And Santa Fe." AD reports note that "after finishing rehearsal with Bob Alton at 3:00, [Judy] went over to rehearse with Kay Thompson." Kay was MGM's newest vocal arranger. She'd had a remarkable career in New York and would soon become a major influence on Judy's style—as well as on Judy's life. It should be noted, however, that as much as Thompson and Roger Edens did for Judy, they certainly should not be given *all* the credit—as they often have been. Judy Garland was a force to be reckoned with long before she stepped into Metro's world, and while Edens and Thompson gave her some polish, the true magic of her artistry came from herself and no one else.

January 8, 1945: *Harvey Girls* work. Time called: 10 a.m.; dismissed: 6:45 p.m. Rehearsed "Great Big World" and "Atchinson." Also, an MGM recording session for *The Harvey Girls*: "On The Atchison, Topeka, And The Santa Fe." The first public performance/recording of yet another Garland standard; this one would win the Oscar for Best Song.

January 9, 1945: *Harvey Girls* work. Time called: 10 a.m.; time dismissed: 4:45 p.m. Rehearsed "Great Big World"—Dress Rehearsal.

January 10, 1945: *Harvey Girls* work. A look at a not so great day in the life of a legend, courtesy of *Harvey Girls* production notes: "Judy had an 11:00 a.m. ready call to make wardrobe tests. She arrived at the studio at 10:45. At 12 noon she called Griffin—an assistant on the picture [*Harvey Girls*]—to say she couldn't be ready till after lunch. Lunch was at 12:30 and on return she still was not ready; she arrived on the set at 3:07 p.m. all made up but not in wardrobe; she came on set dressed at 3:25. At 4:00 she left the stage without making a test, for a conference with LB [Mayer] and did not return to the stage again."

January 11, 1945: *Harvey Girls* work. Another look at a day in the legend's life, via *Harvey Girls* production notes: "Judy Garland had a 10 a.m. makeup call to be ready on the set at 1 p.m. She arrived at the studio at 12:12 and came on the set at 1:48." Judy "tested changes," and was dismissed at 4:30 p.m.

January 12, 1945: The first day of *Harvey Girls* filming brings us another look at a day in the legend's life, via the production notes: "Last night Judy Garland was given a call for this morning, by the assistant: 8:00 in makeup; 10:10 ready on set. She told him she wouldn't be in until 8:30 as she didn't need more than an hour and a half for makeup. This morning she arrived at the studio at 9:25, onstage at 10:50, went into her dressing room and didn't come on the set until 11:25." On this first day of filming, the scenes were Ext. Balcony and Int. Dormitory, and Judy was dismissed at 6:12 p.m.

January 13, 1945: *Harvey Girls* filming. Time called: 10 a.m.; dismissed: 5 p.m. Scenes: Int. and Ext. Dormitory Balcony.

January 15, 1945: *Harvey Girls* filming. Time called: 10 a.m.; dismissed: 5:25 p.m. Scene: Int. Dormitory.

January 16, 1945: *Harvey Girls* filming. Time called: 10:30 a.m.; dismissed: 5 p.m.; Scene: Int. Dormitory. AD reports note: "After JG was dismissed from set she fitted wardrobe until 5:15 p.m."

January 17, 1945: *Harvey Girls* work. Time called: 1:30; dismissed: 3:15 p.m. Wardrobe fittings. That night: (Radio/Personal Appearance) *Esquire's 2nd Annual All-American Jazz Concert*, NBC (90 minutes). Broadcast from The Los Angeles Philharmonic Auditorium (2,800 people attended). Judy presented an award to Anita O'Day, who was in the "New Stars" category. (This program is believed to still exist in private collections.)

January 18, 1945: *Harvey Girls* work. Time called: 2:30 p.m.; time dismissed: 3:40 p.m. Rehearsal. After the rehearsal ended, MGM publicity portraits were taken at the studio Gallery (Shots of Judy sitting on a hay stack, in cowboy boots, jeans, and striped shirt.)

January 19, 1945: *Harvey Girls* work. Time called: 2:30 p.m.; time arrived: 3:00 p.m.; time dismissed: 3:30 p.m. Rehearsed "Atchinson." AD reports note that: "JG was to have a fitting at 1:15, then rehearse at 2:30; she called off the fitting and reported for rehearsal at 3:00 p.m."

January 20, 1945: *Harvey Girls* work. Time called: 10 a.m.; time arrived: 10:30 a.m.; time dismissed: 3:00 p.m. Rehearsed "Atchinson." That night: (Radio) *March of Dimes*, NBC/CBS (70 minutes). Judy sang "Love." (This program is not known to exist.)

January 22, 1945: *Harvey Girls* filming. Time called: 10 a.m.; time arrived: 10 a.m.; dismissed: 1:00 p.m.; Judy was on standby for scenes: Ext. Sandrock street, Ext. Alhambra, and Ext. Station.

January 23, 1945: *Harvey Girls* work. Time called: 1:30 p.m.; time dismissed: 2:30 p.m.. Warobe fittings and standby.

January 24, 1945: *Harvey Girls* work. Judy was on standby.

January 25, 1945: *Harvey Girls* filming. Time called: 10 a.m.; time arrived: 11:15 a.m.; time dismissed: 5:10 p.m. Scene: Int. Harvey House. That night the first preview of Judy's movie *The Clock* was held at the Academy Theater in Inglewood.

Friday, January 26, 1945: Another look at a day in the life of a legend via the *Harvey Girls* production notes: "Miss Garland called at 3:20 this morning to say that she was not feeling well and could not come to work today. We will try and shoot whatever we can without her." Judy must have been conserving her strength for an 8 p.m. to 11 p.m. Decca Records recording session in Hollywood. Produced one single, in recording order: "This Heart Of Mine," and "Love" (released as single #18660, with "Heart" being the "A-side," "Love" the "B-side," on March 22, 1945).

January 27, 1945: *Harvey Girls* filming. Time called: 10 a.m.; time arrived: 10:40 a.m.; dismissed: 2:45 p.m. Scene: Int. Harvey House and Training Montage.

January 29, 1945: *Harvey Girls* filming. Time called: 1:00 p.m.; time arrived on set: 2:00 p.m.; dismissed: 5:55 p.m. Scenes: Int. R. R. Engine and Train and Int. Dormitory.

Janaury 30, 1945: Judy had no call for *Harvey Girls* work. She did a (Radio) show for FDR's birthday and the March of Dimes.

January 31, 1945: *Harvey Girls* work. Judy had a 3 p.m. call for wardrobe fittings, but "didn't come in," according to AD reports.

February 1945: (Radio for World War Two) *Command Performance*, #134. Judy sang "I May Be Wrong, But I Think You're Wonderful" and performed in a sketch with Danny Kaye. (This performance exists in private collections.)

February 1, 1945: *Harvey Girls* work. Time called: 2:00 p.m.; time on set: 2:15 p.m.; dismissed: 3:15 p.m. Wardrobe fitting.

February 2, 1945: Judy had no call/was not needed for *Harvey Girls* work.

February 3, 1945: AD reports for *Harvey Girls* note that "Judy Garland's house was called this morning by Assistant Director to give her a 2:00 call for rehearsal. Her mother, who answered the phone, said that would be impossible as Judy had teeth pulled yesterday afternoon and last night at midnight and would not be able to come in."

February 5, 1945: *Harvey Girls* work. Time called: 10 a.m.; time arrived on set: 11:40 a.m.; time dismissed: 4:20 p.m. Wardrobe test.

February 6, 1945: Judy had no call/was not needed for *Harvey Girls* work.

February 7, 1945: *Harvey Girls* work. Time called: 10 a.m.; time arrived on set: 2:00 p.m.; time dismissed: 5 p.m. Rehearsed "Round and Round" and "Picnic" sequence numbers.

February 8, 1945: Judy had no call/was not needed for *Harvey Girls* work.

Friday, February 9, 1945: Another detailed look at the life of a legend, courtesy of *Harvey Girls* production notes: "At 4:30 p.m. yesterday, Thursday, the company called Miss Garland to give her Friday's shooting call. At this time Miss Garland advised the company that she could not work until possibly Monday due to having two teeth extracted and for which a bridge was being made. At 12:45 p.m. today, Friday, I telephoned Miss Garland at her studio dressing room to inquire if the situation was the same and she advised it was. Mr. Grady [an assistant] communicated with Miss Garland's dentist, Dr. Pinckus, and received the information that Miss Garland will receive the bridge on Saturday, wear it Saturday and Sunday and be in Dr. Pinckus's office on Monday morning for a checkup. Mr. Grady therefore advises Miss Garland should be ready at 1 p.m. on Monday for shooting purposes IF the dentist reports the bridge satisfactory. Under the present conditions it would not be wise for the company to plan a shooting day on Lot 3 on Monday, with a big crew and talent list, on the possibility of getting a couple hours work in the event Miss Garland is available. Inasmuch as we have nothing to shoot at this time without Miss Garland we must also avoid a shooting call for Saturday. We therefore plan on rehearsing musical numbers Saturday and Monday." The AD reports for this date state: "Judy Garland was given a 1:00 shooting call which she didn't accept on account of her teeth. The call was then changed to a 1:00 p.m. wardrobe fitting; she didn't come in for fittings."

February 10, 1945: *Harvey Girls* work. Time called: 2 p.m.; time arrived on set: 2 p.m.; time dismissed: 2:50 p.m.; AD reports note that "Company cannot shoot as Judy Garland does not accept call on account of her teeth; therefore Company is taking advantage of time to rehearse numbers."

February 12, 1945: *Harvey Girls* work. Time called: 2 p.m.; time arrived on set: 1:55 p.m.; dismissed: 4:50 p.m. Rehearsed "Round And Round" and "Hayride" numbers ("Hayride" would be cut from the film; The audio remains on the CD soundtrack from TCM Music/Rhino Records).

February 13, 1945: *Harvey Girls* filming. Time called: 10 a.m.; time arrived on set: 10:05 a.m.; dismissed: 3 p.m. Scene: Ext. R. R. Station.

February 14, 1945: *Harvey Girls* work. Time called: 2 p.m.; time arrived on set: 2:40; dismissed: 3 p.m. Rehearsed "Round and Round" and "Hayride."

February 15, 1945: *Harvey Girls* work. Fitting: time called: 1:00; time arrived on set: 2:10; time dismissed: 2:55 p.m.; Following fitting, there was a rehearsal with Kay Thompson. Time called: 2:30 p.m.; time arrived: 3:00 p.m.; dismissed: 4:00 p.m.

February 16, 1945: *Harvey Girls* work. Time called: 1:30 p.m.; time on sound stage: 1:30 p.m.; dismissed: 4:40 p.m. MGM recording session for *The Harvey Girls*. Judy recorded "My Intuition" (with costar John Hodiak; this song would be cut after filming, but it does exist and was in the 1994 *That's Entertainment 3* film and the 1995 Garland laser disc sets. The song is also scheduled to be on the spring 2002 release of the movie on DVD from Warner Home Video). Her solo "In The Valley (Where The Evening Sun Goes Down)" was also recorded on this date.

February 17, 1945: *Harvey Girls* work. Time called: 1 p.m.; time dismissed: 4:17 p.m. Recorded "In the Valley" (again); "Hayride"; and "March of the Doagies." (The first two songs would be cut from the film; both the audio and the footage from the two songs exist and are available on both the *That's Entertainment 3* and the *Judy: Golden Years At MGM* laser disc sets from MGM/UA. The first two songs are scheduled to be/should be included on the spring 2002 release of *The Harvey Girls* on DVD. The *Golden Years* CD also features a reprise of "Doagies." The songs are on *The Harvey Girls Soundtrack* CD from TCM Music/Rhino Records.)

February 19, 1945: *Harvey Girls* work. Time called: 1 p.m.; time arrived on set: 1:16 p.m.; dismissed: 5:45 p.m. MGM recording session for *The Harvey Girls*. Judy recorded "Swing Your Partner Round and Round," and "Hayride." (The latter would be cut from the film. The audio exists on laser disk, and on CD in stereo—see February 17 and February 19. Footage is not known to exist; only stills.)

February 20, 1945: *Harvey Girls* filming. Time called: 10 a.m.; time arrived on set: 10:22 p.m.; dismissed: 4:20 p.m. Scene: Int. Alhambra, and also Rehearsed "Hayride" and "Round and Round" numbers. Also, that night, Judy did (Radio) *Dick Tracy in B-Flat*. This musical spoof was an early practice in recording radio shows, as most were broadcast live. The show, recorded on this date in front of a studio audience, would be broadcast April 19, 1945 or April 29, 1945 (both dates have been noted). Judy played "Snowflake" and sang a brief parody of "Over The Rainbow" and "I'm Gonna Go For You." This program is available on CD from a small label, Hollywood Soundstage.

February 21, 1945: *Harvey Girls* filming. Time called: 10 a.m.; time arrived on set: 10:30 a.m.; dismissed: 5:10 p.m. Scene: Ext. R. R. Station.

February 22, 1945: *Harvey Girls* filming. Time called: 12 p.m.; time arrived: 12:20; dismissed: 3:50 p.m. Scene: Ext. R. R. Station.

February 23, 1945: *Harvey Girls* filming. Time called: 10 a.m.; arrived: 10:10; dismissed: 4:55. Scene: Ext. R. R. Station. AD reports note that from "4:48–4:55—Waiting for Miss Garland to come out of dressing room—she doesn't feel well. Note: Due to Miss Garland's disposition were unable to shoot last shot on lot 3."

February 24, 1945: *Harvey Girls* filming. Time called: 3 p.m.; arrived: 3 p.m.; dismissed: 6:10 p.m. Scene: Int. Alhambra.

February 26, 1945: *Harvey Girls* filming. Time called: 10 a.m.; time arrived on set: 10:33 a.m.; dismissed: 3:10 p.m. Scene: Int. Alhambra.

February 27, 1945: *Harvey Girls* filming. Time called: 10 a.m.—AD reports note, "Cancelled, went for hair checkup."

February 28, 1945: *Harvey Girls* filming. Time called: 3 p.m. AD reports note, "3:35–3:42: Mr. Sidney [the film's director, George Sidney] discussing scene with Judy Garland who, by the way, is still in slacks and hair not combed out, although she had a 3:00 ready call; she told Mr. Sidney that she was promised the scene would be rewritten and would rather not (shoot the scene) until then. Mr. Sidney then decided to do scene with her and Chill Wills on Ext. Alhambra; Chill Wills, who had no call, was phoned for. 3:45–4:29: Line and Light long shot with Garland and Wills; meantime, Sidney discussing scene above with Garland and Roger Edens; at 4:15 Miss Garland was sent to her dressing room to get ready for scene on Ext. Alhambra; Chill Wills Ready at 4:30; 4:29–4:47: Waiting for JG to get ready." Dismissed: 5:55 p.m.

March 1, 1945: *Harvey Girls* filming. Time called: 1 p.m.; time arrived on set: 1:10 p.m.; dismissed: 5:12 p.m. Scene: Int. Alhambra. AD reports note that from: "5:01–5:12—Time Lost in Discussion; Miss Garland told assistant director she was ill and would have to go to her room to lie down but might be back in 15 minutes; director decided to setup on an over shoulder shot of Susan and Em." That night, producer Arthur Freed's assistant Don Loper held a betrothal dinner for Judy and Vincente Minnelli.

March 2, 1945: Judy had no call, and was not needed for *Harvey Girls* work. Also, here is another detailed look at life with the legend via a *Harvey Girls* production note: "The company was informed by Evelyn Powers, Judy Garland's secretary, that as of this date use of her Webster phone number was to be discontinued and that a new address but no phone number would be supplied to us March 3rd. Our contact with Judy Garland from now on is to be through Evelyn Powers and a call bureau. This, of course, will be of inconvenience to the company and of greater inconvenience to Judy Garland should we ever wish to change a call to a later hour. She is aware of the latter possibilities."

March 3, 1945: Judy had no call/was not needed for work on *Harvey Girls*.

March 5, 1945: *Harvey Girls* filming. Time called: 10 a.m.; time arrived on set: 11:09 a.m.; dismissed: 5:50 p.m. Scene: Int. Alhambra.

March 6, 1945: *Harvey Girls* filming. Time called: 11 a.m.; time arrived on set: 11:28 a.m.; dismissed: 5 p.m. Scene: Int. Alhambra.

March 7, 1945: Time called: 12:30 p.m. AD reports note that there was a "Publicity Luncheon" on this day.

March 8, 1945: *Harvey Girls* filming. Time called: 11 a.m. AD reports note: "Judy Garland had a 11 a.m. call; she phoned from her dressing room at 10:50 and asked whether we needed her. Assistant director told her we would phone her when needed. At 11:15 Assistant Director phoned her and told her she would be needed for 1 p.m.; then changed it to 1:30 call; she was ready at 2:11." Dismissed at 6:05 p.m.

March 9, 1945: *Harvey Girls* filming. Scene: Int. Harvey House. Time called: 11 a.m.; arrived on set: 11:29 a.m.; AD reports note: From "4:50–5:15—Discovered Judy didn't like the way her hair was being fixed; her own hairdresser went home ill this morning and the substitute couldn't seem to hit the right note. It would take too long for Judy to get ready and as Judy had recordings to make right after six it was decided not to shoot any more tonight." Dismissed at 5:20 p.m. That night, from 8 p.m. to 11:15 p.m.: (Record) Decca Records recording session, Hollywood. Judy recorded two songs in the following order: "Connecticut" and "Yah-Ta-Ta, Yah-Ta-Ta (Talk, Talk, Talk)" (both with Bing Crosby). ("Yah" would be the "A-side" of single #23410, paired with "You Got Me Where You Want Me" as the "B-side," from the session of July 31, 1944; the single would be released on April 19, 1945. "Connecticut" would be the "A-side" of single #23804, with "Mine" from the July 31, 1944 session as the "B-side." The single would not be released until January 20, 1947.)

March 10, 1945: *Harvey Girls* filming. Time called: 10 a.m.; AD reports note that: "8:30–9:10: Judy's makeup woman (Dottie Ponedell) phoned from Judy's room that Judy wasn't feeling well and it would take her longer, she was still under the drier and would be late—she didn't know just how late." Time arrived on set: 4 p.m.; time dismissed: 5:45 p.m. Scene: "shot of Judy entering train."

March 12, 1945: *Harvey Girls* filming. Time called: 10 a.m.; arrived: 10:25 a.m.; dismissed: 5:10 p.m. Scene: Int. Rail Road Coach. That night, there was a preview of Judy's movie *Ziegfeld Follies*.

March 13, 1945: *Harvey Girls* filming. Time called: 10 a.m.; arrived: 10:35 a.m.; dismissed: 5:25 p.m. Scene: Int. R. R. Coach.

March 14, 1945: Judy was ill and did not work.

March 15, 1945: *Harvey Girls* filming. Time called: 10 a.m.; arrived: 10:35 a.m.; Time dismissed: 5:50 p.m. Scenes: Int. R. R. Coach and Int. Parlor.

March 16, 1945: *Harvey Girls* filming. Time called: 1 p.m.; dismissed: 5:30 p.m. Scene: Int. Harvey House Party.

March 17, 1945: *Harvey Girls* filming. Time called: 10 a.m.; arrived: 11:10 a.m.; dismissed: 12:30 p.m. Scene: Int. Harvey House.

March 19, 1945: *Harvey Girls* filming. Time called: 1 p.m.; dismissed: 4:30 p.m. Scene: Int. Harvey House Party.

March 20, 1945: *Harvey Girls* filming. Time called: 10 a.m.; arrived: 11:48 a.m. scene: Int. Harvey House Party ("Round and Round" number). AD reports note from "11:48–12:20 Rehearse w/JG although she said we could not shoot with her as her hair was done wrong and would have to be done over—it was decided to call lunch; 1:20–1:49—Rehearse w/Harvey Girls and stand-in while waiting for JG who was dissatisfied with her hair arrangement, which was done by other than her own hairdresser who is ill—Judy's hair had to be done all over; 1:49–2:55—Waiting for JG: she returned to the stage at 2:47, ready at 2:55." Dismissed at 6:40 p.m.

March 21, 1945: *Harvey Girls* filming. Time called: 10 a.m.; arrived: 10:50 a.m.; dismissed: 5:45 p.m. Scene: Int. Harvey House Party.

March 22, 1945: *Harvey Girls* filming. Time called: 10 a.m.; time arrived: 10:30 a.m.; dismissed: 5:10 p.m. (Judy went home ill).

March 23, 1945: *Harvey Girls* filming. Time called: 10 a.m.; arrived: 10:25 a.m.; dismissed: 5:10 p.m. Scene: Int. Harvey House Party.

March 24, 1945: Judy was ill and did not work.

March 26, 1945: *Harvey Girls* filming. Time called: 10 a.m.; time arrived: 10:33 a.m.; dismissed: 5:50 p.m. Scene: Int. Harvey House.

March 27, 1945: *Harvey Girls* filming. Wardrobe test and filmed Int. Harvey House ("March of the Doagies" number). Time called: 10 a.m. AD reports note: "10:20–10:22—Waiting for Judy—She meantime called Bob Alton and said she didn't like the steps in number; Note: JG due at 10 a.m.; called at 10:15 from her dressing room and said she wasn't feeling well and would like to rest as long as possible—she was told we would need her within a few minutes; 10:22–10:51—while waiting for Judy, Bob Alton rehearsed Garland's substitute and rest of cast in changed steps; 10:51–11:02—waiting for Judy; 11:02–11:14—Judy arrived but not dressed—rehearsed cast while Judy watched; 11:14–11:45—Rehearsed cast and Judy's substitute with camera moves in changed routine of number; 11:45–12:15—added lighting for changed routine; 12:15–1:15—Lunch; JG did not return from lunch until 2 p.m.—45 minutes late." Dismissed: 5 p.m.

March 28, 1945 and March 29, 1945: Judy was ill and did not work. (On March 28, she had arrived, but went home sick.)

March 30, 1945: *Harvey Girls* filming. Time called: 10 a.m.; arrived: 10:42 a.m.; dismissed: 4:30 p.m. Scene: Ext. Harvey House Ext. Alhambra.

March 31, 1945: *Harvey Girls* filming. Scene: Ext. Harvey House, Ext. Street, and Ext. Garden. Time called: 10 a.m. AD reports note that: "8:57–11:40—Waiting for Garland: due at 10 a.m.; at 9:15 she phoned that her makeup woman (Dottie Ponedell) was ill, that she didn't think that anyone else could make her up properly; Dave Friedman and cameraman went up to her room to see her and persuaded her to get made up by Bill Tuttle; she consented and arrived on Lot #3 madeup at 10:45 but not ready until 11:05—all dressed and madeup, but found that she has wrong hairdo: she had to be sent to dept. to have hair done over, and was ready on set at 1:18 p.m." Dismissed at 5:40 p.m.

April 2, 1945: *Harvey Girls* filming. Time called: 10 a.m.; arrived: 10:55 a.m.; dismissed: 3:25 p.m. Scenes: Ext. Train Platform and Int. Dormitory.

April 3, 1945: *Harvey Girls* filming. Time called: 7:30 p.m.; arrived: 7:50 p.m.; dismissed: 9:58 p.m. Scenes: Ext. Harvey House and Alhambra.

April 4, 1945: *Harvey Girls* filming. Time called: 7:30 p.m.; time dismissed: 3:10 a.m. Scene: Ext. Sandrock Street.

April 5, 1945: *Harvey Girls* filming. Time called: 7:30 p.m.; arrived: 7:50 p.m.; dismissed: 2:30 a.m. Scene: Ext. Sandrock Street. Judy twisted her ankle in a scene where she runs downhill.

April 6, 1945: *Harvey Girls* filming. Time called: 8 p.m.; dismissed: 2:15 a.m. Scene: Ext. Sandrock.

April 7, 1945: Judy had no call/was not needed for *Harvey Girls* work.

April 9, 1945: *Harvey Girls* filming. Time called: 10 a.m.; arrived: 10:40 a.m.; dismissed: 4:15 p.m. Scene: Int. Dormitory.

April 10, 1945: *Harvey Girls* filming. Time called: 10 a.m.; arrived: 10:15 a.m.; dismissed: 5:35 p.m. Scene: Ext. Desert—"My Intuition" number.

April 11, 1945: *Harvey Girls* filming. Time called: 10 a.m.; arrived: 10:23 a.m.; dismissed: 4:55 p.m. Scene: Ext. Desert—"My Intuition."

April 12, 1945: *Harvey Girls* filming. Time called: 10 a.m.; arrived: 10:57 a.m.; dismissed: 3:40 p.m. Scene: Ext. Desert—"My Intuition."

April 13, 1945: *Harvey Girls* filming. Time called: 10 a.m.; arrived: 11 a.m.; dismissed: 2:35 p.m. Scene: Ext. Desert—"My Intuition." AD reports note: "No satisfactory take, but Judy refused to do another take as horse frightened her by moving too fast (horse was very fractious): compelled to do another setup using double." (A double of Judy, not the horse.)

April 16, 1945: *Harvey Girls* filming. Time called: 10 a.m.; arrived: 10:45 a.m.; dismissed: 6:00 p.m. Scene: Int. Alhambra.

April 17, 1945: *Harvey Girls* filming. Time called: 10 a.m.; arrived: 10:35 a.m.; dismissed: 5:55 p.m. Scene: Int. Alhambra.

April 18, 1945: *Harvey Girls* filming. Scene filmed for *The Harvey Girls*: fight in the "bad girls saloon" with the "good girls" ("The Harvey Girls," of course.) Time called: 10 a.m.; arrived: 10:15 a.m.; dismissed: 5:35 p.m.

April 19, 1945: *Harvey Girls* filming. Another look at a day in a legend's life, through the MGM Memo: "Miss Garland had a 10:15 call to do loops (redubbing of dialogue) today. . . . At 8:45 a.m. she telephoned that she was all bruised up due to fight scenes of yesterday and didn't feel well enough to work today."

April 20, 1945: *Harvey Girls* filming. Time called: 10 a.m.; arrived: 10:40 a.m.; dismissed: 6:10 p.m. Scene: Ext. Picnic Grounds—"Doagies Number."

April 21, 1945: *Harvey Girls* filming. Time called: 10 a.m.; dismissed: 5:50 p.m. Scene: Ext. Picnic Grounds—"Doagies Number."

April 23, 1945: *Harvey Girls* filming. Time called: 10 a.m.; arrived: 10:20 a.m.; dismissed: 3:40 p.m.; Recorded and rehearsed Wedding Procession.

April 24, 1945: *Harvey Girls* filming. AD reports note that "At approximately 7:25 a.m. today, Judy Garland telephoned George Rhein, assistant director on above company [*Harvey Girls*], saying that she didn't feel well and didn't know whether she'd be in or not. Rhein telephoned me about it and I in turn telephoned Miss Garland, telling her that we had a crowd of people ordered for the day and would like to know definitely whether she would be in; she then said that she didn't feel well and would not be in today. Call on extras was then canceled and company had to go on layoff but utilized the day in rehearsing wedding scene, lining up shot for it and also rehearsed fight routine with stunt doubles in Harvey House."

April 25, 1945: *Harvey Girls* filming. Time called: 10 a.m.; arrived: 11:15 a.m.; dismissed: 5:30 p.m. Scenes: Ext. Picnic Ground and Int. Harvey House.

April 26, 1945 through May 2, 1945: Judy had no call/was not needed for any *Harvey Girls* work.

May 3, 1945: *Harvey Girls* filming. Time called: 1 p.m.; arrived: 1:30 p.m.; dismissed: 3:50 p.m. Scenes: Int. Harvey House and Ext. Harvey House.

May 4, 1945: *Harvey Girls* filming. Time called: 10 a.m.; arrived: 10:30 a.m.; dismissed: 6 p.m. Scene: Int. Alhambra House.

May 5, 1945: *Harvey Girls* filming. Time called: 10 a.m. Changed to 1:35 p.m. AD reports note: "JG had 10 a.m. call; at 10:15 she phoned that it would take her quite a while to get ready—she didn't feel well; at 10:55 assistant phoned her to relax as we wouldn't use her until after lunch. Arrived: 2:05. Dismissed: 5:05 p.m."

May 6, 1945: Judy had no call/was not needed for *Harvey Girls* work.

May 8, 1945: Judy had no call/was not needed for *Harvey Girls* work.

May 9, 1945: *Harvey Girls* filming. Time called: 8 p.m.; arrived: 8:45 p.m.; dismissed: 11:30 p.m. Scene: Ext. Sandrock.

May 10, 1945 through May 12, 1945: Judy had no call/was not needed for *Harvey Girls* work.

May 14, 1945: *Harvey Girls* filming. Time called: 11 a.m.; arrived: 11:10 a.m.; dismissed: 5:35 p.m. Scene: Int. Rail Road Coach. That night, from 8 p.m. to 11 p.m.: (Record) Decca Records recording session, Hollywood. First of two sessions to record a Decca *Harvey Girls* "original cast album": Judy recorded two songs, in the following order: "March Of The Doagies" (which would be cut from the released film) and "Swing Your Partner Round And Round." (The "album" of 78 singles would be released on November 1, 1945. "Doagies" would not be released until November 12, 1984, when it was included on the *From The Decca Vaults* LP.)

May 15, 1945: A *Harvey Girls* production note: "At 2:30 this morning Judy Garland called Griffin, second assistant on the picture, and told him she hadn't slept all night so far because she was making Decca records until 11:45 p.m. last night. She said that after she came home she wasn't able to sleep and knew that she wouldn't look good the next day, and since the scene was an important one she felt she better stay home today. . . . She called up as she knew we had people ordered and could cancel before it was too late. People were canceled on quarter checks and company was forced to lay off for the day as there are no scenes we could do without her." Judy was also conserving strength and voice for later that night, for a recording session from 8 p.m. to 11 p.m. (Record) Decca Records recording session, Hollywood. The second (of three) sessions to complete a *Harvey Girls* cast "album": Judy only recorded one song and she would actually *rerecord* her portion of the song in September, which would confirm the *Harvey Girls* movie production notes that she hadn't been feeling well. The song recorded this night was the elaborate "On The Atchison, Topeka And The Santa Fe" number.

May 16, 1945: *Harvey Girls* filming. Time called: 10 a.m.; arrived: 10:20 a.m.; dismissed: 5:45 p.m. Scene: Int. R. R. Coach.

May 17, 1945: *Harvey Girls* filming. Time called: 10 a.m.; arrived: 10:45 a.m.; dismissed: 6:20 p.m. Scene: Int. Rail Road Coach.

May 18 1945 through May 23, 1945: *Harvey Girls* filming. Judy had no call/was not needed for any *Harvey Girls* work.

May 24, 1945: From *The Harvey Girls* production notes: "Miss Garland had a 1 p.m. call today to do loops; at 12:45 she telephoned Ted Hoffman on stage 2A that she was hoarse and would not be able to record the loops today but that the hoarseness was breaking and she's be able to do them tomorrow. The loops were then set for 10 a.m. tomorrow."

May 25, 1945: Judy had no call/was not needed for any *Harvey Girls* work.

May 26, 1945: From *The Harvey Girls* production notes : "Judy Garland had a 10:30 a.m. call today to do loops; at 10:15 she telephoned that she was feeling ill and would not be able to do the loops."

May 28, 1945: Judy had no call/was not needed for any *Harvey Girls* work.

May 29, 1945: *Harvey Girls* filming. Time called: 10 a.m.; dismissed: 3:50 p.m. Scene: Ext. Train in Desert.

May 31, 1945: *Harvey Girls* filming. Time called: 10 a.m.; dismissed: 3:45 p.m. Scenes: Ext. Desert and train.

June 1, 1945: *Harvey Girls* filming. Time called: 10 a.m.; dismissed: 5:40 p.m. Scene: Ext. Desert.

June 2, 1945: *Harvey Girls* filming. Time called: 10 a.m.; dismissed: 5:56 p.m. Scene: Ext. Desert.

June 4, 1945: Last day of principal photography for *The Harvey Girls*. Time called: 10:30 a.m.; arrived: 10:30 a.m.; dismissed: 7:05 p.m. Scene: Ext. Picnic Grounds.

June 5, 1945: *Harvey Girls* work. Time called: 1:30 p.m.; dismissed: 5 p.m. Loops only. (Over-dubbing or postdubbing dialogue in scenes where sound wasn't properly recorded or where there was interference, etc.)

June 6, 1945: *Harvey Girls* work. Time called: 1 p.m.; dismissed: 5 p.m. Poster stills only.

June 10, 1945: Judy's twenty-third birthday.

June 11, 1945: Glamour publicity portrait sitting at MGM.

June 13, 1945: *Harvey Girls* work. Time called: 11 a.m.; arrived: 11:45 a.m.; dismissed: 12:20 p.m. Loops only.

June 14, 1945: *Harvey Girls* work. Time called: 10 a.m.; arrived: 10:15 a.m.; dismissed: 11:20 a.m. Loops only. This concluded Judy's work on *The Harvey Girls*. The movie would become another huge Garland success upon its release on January 18, 1946, grossing over $5,175,000 on an investment of $2,524,315.06. The following are excerpts from a few of the reviews Judy's work received:

The New York Times, 1-25-46: "Miss Garland, of course, is the center of most of the activity, and handles herself in a pleasing fashion."

Liberty: "It's a certainty that if Judy gets any more talented, she'll probably explode."

Movie Picture Daily: "(Judy displays a) sharpened demonstration of comic ability."

Hollywood Review: "You'll see some acting from her that will gain your respect for real talent."

(The movie is expected to be released on DVD in spring 2002 by Warner Home Video.)

June 15, 1945: Judy married Vincente Minnelli at her mother's home, with MGM's blessing: Louis B. Mayer, head of the studio, gave her away. The couple left that night on the Santa Fe Super Chief for their

Judy and her second husband, Vincente Minnelli, pose for a portrait either just before or just after their wedding, June 15, 1945. (Courtesy of Photofest.)

honeymoon in New York City. Their honeymoon/extended vacation included all the usual: clothes shopping, teas, parties, along with the New York City police spending hours finding Judy's pet poodle, and the announcement that she wanted to be on Broadway, and thus would not be renewing her MGM contract. Judy did not go on Broadway; just the thought of their "greatest asset" leaving them was enough to have studio executives spoil the newlyweds while they were in New York with expensive gifts, etc, and begin to start work on the renewal of her contract. Judy's honeymoon was interrupted for work.

July 7, 1945, 2:30 p.m. to 5:30 p.m.: (Record) Decca Records recording session, New York City. Judy recorded two songs in the following order : "On The Atchison, Topeka, And The Santa Fe" (from *The Harvey Girls*. This version was with The Merry Macs) and "If I Had You." ("Atchison" would be side "A," "If I Had You" would be the "B-side" of the 78 single, #23436, which was released September 9, 1945.) "Santa Fe" would reach #10 on the Billboard charts.

July 10, 1945, 2 p.m. to 5 p.m.: (Record) Decca Records recording session, New York City. Judy recorded two songs in the following order: "You'll Never Walk Alone" and "Smilin' Through." ("Smilin'" would be the "A-side" and "You'll Never Walk" the "B-side" of 78 single #23539, released April 15, 1946.)

July 12, 1945: *The Harvey Girls* was previewed in Inglewood.

July 27, 1945: A radio appearance in New York on *The Jerry Wayne Show* was postponed due to illness: it is possible that this illness was the first sign of "morning sickness," as, by now, Judy was pregnant. The radio program was rescheduled for August 10, 1945.

August 10, 1945: (Radio) *The Jerry Wayne Show*, CBS (30 minutes), broadcast from New York. Judy sang "If I Had You" (which she had just recorded on July 7 for Decca and would be released on September 9) and "Love" (which was also a "new" single, having been released March 22 on Decca; the recording date had been January 26). (Oddly, Judy sang the "B-sides" of both singles on this radio appearance, although it may have been because "On The Atchison, Topeka, And The Santa Fe" was already a hit and *Ziegeld Follies*, which featured the song "Love" would not be released until March, 1946. Judy did not sing "Love" in that film; it would become a Lena Horne standard. The program is not known to exist. A radio version of "Love" is on an out-of-print Star-Tone LP, although it is not known if it is this performance or the one from January 20, 1945.)

(No other professional work is known to have occurred during August 1945 while Judy and Vincente Minnelli concluded their honeymoon in New York.)

Early (first few days of) September 1945: Judy and Vincente Minnelli returned home to Los Angeles and began preliminary planning together for Judy's Guest Appearance in the film *Till the Clouds Roll By*. (Minnelli would once again direct his wife in her sequences.)

September 6, 1945: (Radio) *Command Performance* Program #190, with Bob Hope (the M. C), Bing Crosby, and Frank Sinatra. Judy auditions Sinatra and Crosby for her leading man in her next movie. (The entire show is a part of a 30-CD box set of radio shows called *Frank Sinatra and Friends: 60 Greatest Old-Time Radio Shows* from the label Radio Spirits: PO Box 2141, Schiller Park, Illinois 60176 or online at www. mediabay. com.)

September 7, 1945, 2 to 4:15 p.m.: (Record) Decca Records recording session, Hollywood; to complete *The Harvey Girls* "Cast Album." Judy cut two songs, in the following order: "It's A Great Big World"; then "In The Valley (Where The Evenin' Sun Goes Down.)" (One final *Harvey Girls* session would be done three days later).

September 10, 1945, 2 to 4:40 p.m.: (Record) Decca Records recording session, Hollywood; Final session to complete *The Harvey Girls* album: Judy cut one track: a retake of "On The Atchison, Topeka, And The Santa Fe." (The May 15, 1945 session's take had been deemed inferior; that had been a day

Judy had not felt well, and had not gone to work at MGM. The now completed *Harvey Girls* "album" of 78s, would be released November 1, 1945.)

October 2, 1945: First noted day of Judy's work on *Till the Clouds Roll By.* Called: 2:30 p.m.; dismissed: 4:30 p.m.; Judy prerecorded the song "Look For The Silver Lining."

October 3, 1945: Dance rehearsals with Bob Alton for *Clouds* were cancelled, when Judy was ill and did not work.

October 4, 1945: *Clouds* work. Called: 1 p.m.; arrived: 2 p.m.; dismissed: 3:30 p.m.; Wardrobe fitting only.

October 5, 1945: Rehearsals for *Till The Clouds Roll By* and that night: (Radio) *The Danny Kaye Show*, CBS (30 minutes). Judy and Frank Sinatra substituted for Danny Kaye, who was doing a USO tour. Judy sang "How Deep Is The Ocean?" and did a duet with Sinatra on "My Romance"; "Gotta Be This or That"; and a comedy sketch about the year 1995. Judy also plugged her upcoming *Harvey Girls* release. ("Ocean" is on the LP *Born In A Trunk, Superstar: 1945–1950* on AEI 2110. All three songs mentioned are on the LP *Frank Sinatra and Judy Garland* on the ZAFIRO label, #ZV 892. The LPs are, of course, out-of-print. The entire show is a part of a 30-CD box set of radio shows called *Frank Sinatra and Friends: 60 Greatest Old-Time Radio Shows*—See September 6, 1945 for ordering information.)

October 6, 1945: *Clouds* work. Called: 11 a.m.; dismissed: 3:10 p.m.; Rehearsal.

October 8, 1945: *Clouds* filming. Called: 10 a.m.; arrived: 10:25 a.m.; dismissed: 5:40 p.m. Scene: Int. Marilyn's dressing room.

October 9, 1945: *Clouds* work. Called: 1 p.m.; arrived: 1:15 p.m.; dismissed: 3:53 p.m.; MGM recording session for *Till The Clouds Roll By*: Judy recorded "Who?" (this number, which Judy found hysterical singing in her present condition, would be edited briefly, as would another song "Sunny"; "D'Ya Love Me?" would be deleted entirely: footage to "Sunny" is not known to have survived; a 1987 PBS *Minnelli On Minnelli* tribute by Liza to her father, available on video tape from MGM/UA, contains a part of the "D'Ya Love Me?" song, and the entire number—minus dialogue interwoven with the singing—is on a Laser Disc set from MGM/UA, *The Composer Collection*, released in December, 1996; The audio tracks of the cut songs can be found on the following CDs: the *That's Entertainment Part 3* Soundtrack CD, on Angel, contains the extended "Who?"; It is also included in the Rhino six-CD box set on all the *Entertainment* films; "D'Ya Love Me?" is found on *Cut* Volume 1, an LP from DRG, and is on the TCM/Rhino Records *Collector's Gems* CD set.)

October 10, 1945: *Clouds* filming. Called: 10 a.m.; arrived: 10:30 a.m.; dismissed: 5:45 p.m. Scene: Int. Orchestra of Theatre.

October 11, 1945: *Clouds* filming. Called: 10 a.m.; arrived: 10:18 a.m.; dismissed: 6 p.m. Scene: Int. Marilyn's Dressing Room.

October 12, 1945: *Clouds* filming. Called: 10 a.m.; arrived: 10:12 a.m.; dismissed: 2 p.m. Scenes: Int. Corridor and Stage.

October 13, 1945: *Clouds* work. Called: 1 p.m.; Rehearsed with Bob Alton, on dance routines for *Clouds*.

October 15, 1945: *Clouds* work. Called: 1:30 p.m.; dismissed: 2:30 p.m.; MGM recording session for *Till The Clouds Roll By*: Judy recorded "D'Ya Love Me" and "Sunny." (See October 9, 1945 for additional information.)

October 16, 1945: *Clouds* filming. Called: 10 a.m.; arrived: 10:45 a.m.; dismissed: 4:45 p.m. Scene: "Silver Lining" number.

October 17, 1945: *Clouds* work. Called: 1 p.m.; arrived: 2:15 p.m.; dismissed: 3:45 p.m.; Rehearsed "Who?"

October 18, 1945: *Clouds* work. Wardrobe Fitting 1:45–2:40 p.m. Rehearsed "Who?" from 2:40 p.m. to 3:25 p.m.

October 19, 1945: *Clouds* work. Rehearsed "Who?" 1:50–2:30 p.m.

October 20, 1945: Judy was out ill and did not work.

October 22, 1945: *Clouds* work. Called: 1 p.m.; arrived: 2 p.m.; dismissed: 3:30 p.m.; Camera and Dress Rehearsal for "Who?" number.

October 23, 1945: *Clouds* filming. Called: 10 a.m.; dismissed: 5:50 p.m. Scene: Int. Stairs set—"Who?" number.

October 24, 1945: *Clouds* filming. Called: 10 a.m.; dismised: 5:30 p.m. Scene: Int. Stairs—"Who?" number.

October 25, 1945: *Clouds* filming. Called: 10 a.m.; arrived: 10:50 a.m.; dismissed: 4:30 p.m. Scene: Int. Stairs—"Who?" number.

October 26, 1945: Judy was ill and did not work.

October 27, 1945: *Clouds* filming. Called: 10 a.m.; arrived: 10:52 a.m.; dismissed: 2:30 p.m. Scene: Int. Stairs—"Who?" number.

October 29, 1945: *Clouds* filming. Called: 10 a.m.; arrived: 10:47 a.m.; dismissed: 5:35 p.m. Scene: Int. Stairs Set—"Who?" number.

October 30, 1945: *Clouds* filming. Called: 10 a.m.; arrived: 10:55 a.m.; dismissed: 6:25 p.m. Scene: Int. Stairs Set—"Who?" number.

October 31, 1945: *Clouds* work. Called: 2:30 p.m.; arrived: 3:17 p.m.; dismissed: 3:45 p.m. Rehearsed "Sunny" number.

November 1, 1945: *Clouds* filming. Called: 10 a.m.; arrived: 11 a.m.; dismissed: 11:30 a.m. Judy went home ill at 11:30 a.m.

November 2, 1945: *Clouds* filming. Called: 3 p.m.; arrived: 4:54 p.m.; dismissed: 6:20 p.m. Scene: Int. Circus Set—"Sunny" number.

November 3, 1945: *Clouds* filming. Called: 10 a.m.; dismissed: 4:10 p.m. Scene: Int. Circus Set—"Sunny" number.

November 5, 1945: Judy had no call, and was not needed for *Clouds* work.

November 6, 1945: *Clouds* filming. Called: 1:30 p.m.; dismissed: 5:45 p.m. Scene: Int. Circus Set—"Sunny" and "D'Ya Love Me?" numbers.

November 7, 1945: Judy's last day of filming/work on *Till the Clouds Roll By.* Called: 10 a.m.; arrived: 10:30 a.m.; dismissed: 6:40 p.m.; Int. Stage—Circus set—"D'Ya Love Me?" number. Judy's songs in *Clouds* cost $467,305—20% of the film's $2,841,608 total cost. *Clouds* would gross over $6,724,000 upon its release on January 3, 1947, making it one of MGM's biggest hits of that year. It would also be one of the very first original motion picture soundtrack recordings released on records, of the actual performances heard in the movie. *Clouds* prerecording session material was remixed and edited for this first release from the new "MGM Records." All of Judy's remaining movies made for Metro would be released as soundtrack albums on 78s, and then eventually LPs. The score to *Clouds* was released on a Sony CD in the early 1990s, when that label released MGM soundtracks for a certain period of time. TCM/Rhino Records has yet to release the album, as much of the master material is either missing, has deteriorated, or the sound quality of the remaining material is not high. The movie itself is in the public domain and is on many low-budget/poor-quality VHS tapes and DVDs, as well as official VHS and Laser Discs from MGM/UA/Turner/Warner Brothers/Time-Warner. No word on DVD release yet from Warner Home Video. Here is an excerpt from one of Judy's reviews for *Clouds*:

> *Hollywood Revue*: "Judy Garland is the high point in an entertainment full of high points. It's the greatest work she has ever done. She is radiantly beautiful, winsomely appealing, and for 20 minutes the picture is all hers."

November 8, 1945: Judy officially went on "maternity leave" from MGM to await her baby's birth. She did three more radio shows in 1945—and would do one in January 1946 in her seventh month of pregnancy—but that would be her only work until July 1946, four months after giving birth, when she returned to work, via a radio appearance.

December 9, 1945: (Radio) *Jerome Kern Memorial*, CBS (60 minutes). Judy sang "Look For The Silver Lining" (which she had just filmed for *Till The Clouds Roll By*) and "They Wouldn't Believe Me" during the all-star finale. (Judy's parts from this program are available on the *All the Things You Are: Judy Garland on the Radio* CD from Vintage Jazz Classics.)

December 24, 1945: (Radio) *Command Performance*: Judy sang "Long Ago, And Far Away" and "It Came Upon A Midnight Clear." (This program is available on the CD *Bob Hope's Christmas Party* on the Vintage Jazz Classics label.)

December 25, 1945: (Radio) *Command Performance* Judy sang "Have Yourself A Merry Little Christmas."

1946

January 1946: Judy's MGM salary was raised $500: from $2,500, up to $3,000 a week. She was now making double the salary of other top stars (pretty good, considering she wasn't working at the moment, being on maternity leave.) She was still allowed to broadcast as a "free agent," keeping any fees she got, provided MGM was mentioned, or any MGM film "as we may designate." (Judy's current contract, signed in August 1940, was set to run until August 1947; She would sign a new one before her return to MGM after giving birth.)

(Vincente Minnelli's pink stucco house at 8850 Evanview Drive, overlooking Beverly Hills, was remodeled, enlarging the kitchen, Judy's dressing room, and, of course, adding a nursery, all at a cost of $70,000. During the renovation, the couple rented a house on Malibu Beach.)

January 3, 1946: *The Harvey Girls* was previewed in Chicago.

January 28, 1946: (Radio) *Lux Radio Theater*, CBS (60 minutes). The radio adaptation of Judy's 1945 hit *The Clock* (with John Hodiak, Judy's costar in *The Harvey Girls*, playing Robert Walker's role). (This performance exists in private collections. This was the last noted professional work that Judy did before she gave birth a month and a half later.)

Judy with her first born, Liza May Minnelli, 1946. (Courtesy of Photofest.)

March 12, 1946, 7:58 a.m.: Judy's first child, Liza May Minnelli, was born at Cedars of Lebanon Hospital, Los Angeles, weighing 6 pounds, 10 ounces.

July 17, 1946: (Radio) *The Bob Crosby Show*, CBS (30 minutes). Judy sang "I Got The Sun In The Morning" and "If I Had You." (This was Judy's first noted work since giving birth to Liza, four months earlier. This program is believed to exist in private collections.)

July 20, 1946: Concert at the Hollywood Bowl in honor of Jerome Kern. Judy sang her numbers from *Till The Clouds Roll By*, and also filled in for Lena Horne, singing Lena's numbers in *Clouds*: "Can't Help Loving That Man Of Mine," and "Why Was I Born?" (These performances are heard on an out-of-print Star-Tone LP *Judy Garland: Musical Scrapbook 1935–1949*.)

July 29, 1946: Agreement drawn on this date, between Judy and Loews, Inc. (MGM), stating that Judy is not to be paid any additional money for the August 6, 1946 AFRS Command Performance Radio Show.

August 6, 1946: (Radio) *AFRS Command Performance* (Program content unknown.)

September 11, 1946, 7:15 to 10:15 p.m.: (Record) Decca Records recording session, Hollywood. Judy recorded three songs in the following order: Recorded first were songs with singer Dick Haymes: "Aren't You Kind of Glad We Did?," then "For You, For Me, Forevermore"; Judy finished the session by recording "Changing My Tune." ("For You" would be the "A-side," and "Aren't You" the "B- side," of single #23687, released October 21, 1946. "Changing My Tune" would be the "A-side"—"B-side" unnoted; most likely an orchestral track—of single #23688, also released on October 21, 1946.)

September 14, 1946: (Radio) *Hollywood Star Time*, CBS (30 minutes). An original radio drama, *Holiday*. (This program is not known to exist.)

September 29, 1946: (Radio) *Command Performance* #241. Judy sang "I Got The Sun In The Morning," and did a "Movie Star" Sketch with Frank Sinatra and Phil Silvers. (This program exists in private collections. Around this time, *Command Performance* #246 was done, which featured a segment with Judy and Bing Crosby doing the Top Ten Worst songs of the day; this program still exists in private collections.)

October 1, 1946, 8 to 10:30 p.m.: (Record) Decca Records recording session, Hollywood. Judy recorded two songs in the following order: "Don't Tell Me That Story," then "There Is No Breeze (To Cool The Flame Of Love)." ("Breeze" would be the "A-side," "Story" the "B-side," of single # 23746, released December 2, 1946.)

November 6, 1946: Judy was due at MGM for a fitting for the movie she'd make upon her return following the birth of Liza: *The Pirate*, to be directed by Vincente Minnelli. Judy's secretary called in sick for her.

November 12, 1946: (Radio) *Philco Radio Time/The Bing Crosby Show*, ABC (30 minutes). Judy sang "Liza" (Bing noted that Liza turned eight months old this day), and, with Bing, "Wait Till The Sun Shines Nellie." (Bing was an innovator in radio, in that his shows were now being taped a couple of weeks in advance. This show aired November 27. This performance of "Liza" is on the four-CD box set *Judy*, released by 32 Records on October 13, 1998.)

November 21, 1946: (Radio) *Suspense*, CBS (30 minutes). Original Drama written and produced by William Spier, Judy's covocal arranger Kay Thomson's husband (Kay and William were also Liza's Godparents). (This had been available on a bootleg LP called *Drive-In* on Command Performance Records and is now on a CD-R from Radio Revisited at radiorev@aol.com.)

December 1, 1946: Rehearsal for a radio show, the next day.

Judy had, during the time of her pregnancy and recuperation, signed with new agents. In 1944, her agent Leland Hayward had sold his company to the Music Corporation of America—MCA—so that he could concentrate on backing Broadway shows. Her new agency, Berg-Allenberg, Inc., began by negotiating a new contract with MGM. Judy had actually told friends that when her current MGM pact expired in August 1947, she would not sign another long-term contract. Instead, she would free-lance, doing only one movie a year, and maybe a radio series. However, MGM offered numerous incentives to stay: she could continue to work with her husband; MGM would mount lavish productions starring Judy—along with a pledge that she need not make more than two films in one year, and one could be a "guest" appearance, though she would still get "top billing"; and Metro also stated Judy could continue to have Dottie Ponedell as her makeup artist, as long as Dottie would "be employed by the studio." Other terms of the agreement gave Judy the right to make "phonograph records" and radio appearances. With all of this, she agreed to a new 5-year contract. The financial rewards were of course also hard to pass on: A weekly salary of $5,619.23: nearly $1,000 a day for the 6-day work-week—with a guarantee of $300,000 a year—

$150,000 per film. Thus, the contract would be worth at least $1.5 million. Pretty incredible numbers for a 1946 movie star. The contract was typed on November 20, 1946, and Judy returned to MGM, after thirteen months.

December 2, 1946: Judy returned to MGM, to begin wardrobe tests, and rehearsals for *The Pirate*. (MGM had announced in August that she would star in the adaptation of the book her ex-lover, Tyrone Power, had given her called *Forever*, described by Metro as "a romantic drama with two songs." Other considerations had included another attempt at *Good News* with Judy and Mickey Rooney, though this would be filmed with June Allyson and Peter Lawford; and *Cimarron*, an *Oklahoma!* type "family saga," for her and Gene Kelly.)

This first day back at MGM was a short, easy day for her, as she also had a radio broadcast that evening: a sixty-minute radio adaptation of her 1944 film *Meet Me in St. Louis* for *Lux Radio Theater*, which featured Margaret O'Brien, Tom Drake, and all the film's hit songs. (This program still exists, and is available from "Radio Spirits, Inc." on cassette. Call 1-800-RADIO-48 to order, or e-mail radiorev@aol.com for a CD-R.)

December 5, 1946: Judy's mother called MGM to tell them her daughter was ill and couldn't work this day.

December 12, 1946: Wardrobe tests for *The Pirate*, including the wedding dress.

December 17, 1946: Judy's maid called MGM to tell them Judy couldn't make the wardrobe fitting scheduled for this day.

December 27, 1946: Judy's first MGM recording session for *The Pirate.* (Cole Porter had been paid $100,000 to write the score for Judy and Gene Kelly.) From 2 p.m. to 3:25 p.m., Judy recorded the song "Love of My Life." (An unused version from this session is on the Rhino Records *Collectors' Gems* set, in stereo.)

December 28, 1946: MGM recording session for *The Pirate,* from 1:10 to 5:20 p.m. Judy recorded "Mack The Black" (this would be rerecorded a year later, in December 1947). (This deleted version can be heard on the above-mentioned *Collectors' Gems* set.)

January 1947: Preproduction continued on *The Pirate.*

January 2, 1947: Judy's new five-year contract with MGM began on this date.

January 12, 1947: Judy did a radio show on this day according to production notes for *The Pirate.* No other information is known at this time.

January 21, 1947: Judy and Vincente Minnelli attend the premiere of *Till the Clouds Roll By* at the Egyptian Theater.

January 31, 1947: Judy was ill and did not work, canceling a wardrobe fitting session for *Pirate.*

February 3, 1947: *Pirate* work. Time called: 1 p.m.; dismissed: 5:20 p.m. Silent makeup and wardrobe tests (including the costume Judy was to have worn in the "Voodoo" number.) Also on this date, Judy signed an agreement (on MGM/Loew's stationary) to appear on a Bing Crosby radio show, saying she will be paid by Bing Crosby Enterprises. (See next entry below.)

February 4, 1947: (Radio) *Philco Radio Time/The Bing Crosby Show*, ABC (30 minutes). Judy taped a guest spot on Crosby's radio show, singing "I've Got You Under My Skin," and singing a duet with Crosby on "Connecticut" (which they had recorded in 1945), along with a comedy sketch, and "Tearbucket Jim." (These performances, along with the earlier November 12, 1946 show, and several others from the late 1940s, are on the CD *All The Clouds'll Roll Away* on JSP Records/England, # CD 702. "I've Got You Under My Skin" is also on the four-CD box set *Judy*, released by 32 Records on October 13, 1998. This show aired on February 19, 1947. Judy only did a couple of other radio shows and one recording session in 1947. The majority of her time this year was spent working at MGM.)

February 11, 1947: *Pirate* work. Time called: 3 p.m.; dismissed: 4:35 p.m. Rehearsed "Mack The Black."

February 12, 1947: *Pirate* work. Called: 3 p.m.; dismissed: 5 p.m. Rehearsed and recorded "Mack The Black."

February 13, 1947: *Pirate* work. Called: 3 p.m.; dismissed: 4:50 p.m. Rehearsed "Mack The Black."

February 14, 1947: *Pirate* work. Called: 2 p.m.; arrived: 4:30; dismissed: 5:10 p.m. Rehearsed "Mack The Black."

February 15, 1947: Judy had no call/was not needed for *Pirate* work.

February 17, 1947: First day of actual filming on *The Pirate*. Called: 9 a.m.; arrived: 9:14 a.m.; dismissed: 6 p.m. Scene: Int. Manuela's Pation.

February 18, 1947: *Pirate* filming. Called: 9 a.m.; arrived: 9:10 a.m.; dismissed: 5:45 p.m. Scenes: Ext. Pation and Int. Manuela's Bedroom.

February 19, 1947: *Pirate* filming. Called: 9:30, Dismissed: 6 p.m. Scene: Int. Manuela's Bedroom.

February 20, 1947: *Pirate* filming. Called: 9 a.m.; dismissed: 6:10 p.m. Scene: Int. Manuela's Bedroom. (Approximately February 20, 1947, Judy and Vincente Minnelli were photographed at Don Loper's latest fashion showing in Hollywood. The photo by Nat Dallinger was copyrighted by King Features Syndicate and ran in editions for the week ending February 27.)

February 21, 1947: *Pirate* filming. Called: 9 a.m.; arrived: 9:20 a.m.; dismissed: 6:30 p.m. Scenes: Int. Manuela's Bedroom (wedding dress) and Int. Hotel Bedroom.

February 22, 1947: AD reports for *Pirate* note that "Miss Garland was on her way to the studio, but had to return to her home as she was ill and nervously exhausted after spending a sleepless night."

February 24, 1947: Judy had no call/was not needed for *Pirate* work.

February 25, 1947: *Pirate* work. Called: 2 p.m.; dismissed: 4:40 p.m. Rehearsed "Voodoo."

February 26, 1947: *Pirate* work. Called: 2 p.m.; dismissed: 4:25 p.m. Rehearsed "Voodoo" number.

February 27 and 28, 1947: Judy was ill and did not work.

March 1, 1947: Judy had no call/was not needed for *Pirate* work.

March 3, 1947: *Pirate* work. Called: 2 p.m.; dismissed: 4:50 p.m. Rehearsed "Voodoo" number.

March 4, 1947: *Pirate* work. Called: 2 p.m.; dismissed: 4:35 p.m. Rehearsed "Voodoo" number.

March 5, 1947: *Pirate* work. Time called: 2 p.m.; dismissed: 5:25 p.m. Rehearsed "Voodoo" number.

March 6, 1947: *Pirate* work. Called: 11 a.m.; dismissed: 1:20 p.m. Rehearsed "Voodoo" number.

March 7, 1947: *Pirate* work. Called: 2 p.m.; dismissed: 4:15 p.m. Rehearsed "Voodoo" number.

March 8, 1947: Judy had no call/was not needed for *Pirate* work.

March 10, 1947: Judy was ill and did not work.

March 11, 1947: *Pirate* work. Called: 2 p.m.; dismissed: 4:30 p.m. Rehearsed "Voodoo" number. (Also on this date, Judy pulled out of singing "On The Atchison, Topeka, And The Santa Fe" at the Academy Awards due to the pressures of filming *The Pirate*. The number won for Best Song anyway.)

March 12, 1947: *Pirate* work. Called: 2 p.m.; dismissed: 4:30 p.m. Rehearsed "Voodoo."

March 13, 1947: *Pirate* work. Called: 2 p.m.; dismissed: 4 p.m. Rehearsed "Voodoo."

March 14, 1947 and March 15, 1947: Judy had no call/was not needed for *Pirate* work.

March 17, 1947: *Pirate* work. Called: 11 a.m.; arrived: 11:25 a.m.; dismissed: 1:25 p.m. Rehearsed "Voodoo."

March 18, 1947 through March 27, 1947: Judy had no call/was not needed for *Pirate* work.

March 28, 1947: *Pirate* work. Called: 10 a.m.; arrived: 10:53 a.m.; dismissed: 1:20 p.m. Orchestrate "Voodoo."

March 29, 1947 through April 5, 1947: Judy had no call/was not needed for *Pirate* work.

April 7, 1947: *Pirate* filming. Called: 11 a.m.; dismissed: 1:45 p.m. Scene: Ext. Port Sebastian Dock.

April 8, 1947: *Pirate* filming. Time called: 1 p.m.; dismissed: 3 p.m. Scene: Ext. Port Sebastian Dock.

April 9, 1947: *Pirate* filming. Called: 10:15 a.m.; dismissed: 3:30 p.m. Scene: Ext. Plaza.

April 10, 1947: *Pirate* work. Called: 12 p.m.; dismissed: 5 p.m. Rehearsed and prerecorded "Voodoo." (The number would be cut after filming. Footage is not known to exist; the song is on the Rhino Records *Golden Gems* CD set, in stereo.)

April 11, 1947: *Pirate* filming. Called: 3 p.m.; dismissed: 6:05 p.m. Scene: Ext. Plaza.

April 12, 1947: *Pirate* filming. Called: 11 a.m.; dismissed: 5:50 p.m. Scenes: Ext. and Int. Show Tent.

April 14, 1947: *Pirate* filming. Called: 10:30 a.m.; dismissed: 6 p.m. Scenes: Int. Dressing Room; Int. Show Tent.

April 15, 1947: *Pirate* filming. Called: 9:45 a.m.; dismissed: 6 p.m. Scene: Int. Show Tent—"Voodoo."

April 16, 1947: *Pirate* filming. Called: 9:45 a.m. AD reports note: "At 8:30 a.m. Miss Garland called Wally Worsley to say that she was in makeup dept. and that she was calling her doctor and would report to the set as soon as possible. Miss Garland on set 11:10 a.m.; Ready in Wardrobe to work at 11:32 a.m. Note: Miss Garland was taken ill during lunch and company was unable to continue 'Voodoo' number." Dismissed: 1:45 p.m. Scene: Int. Show tent—"Voodoo."

April 17, 1947 through April 21, 1947: Judy was ill and did not work.

Judy preparing to film a scene in "Port Sebastian," for *The Pirate*, April 1947. Her body makeup is applied or repaired, as is her hair, and Judy's slippers are exchanged for "Manuela's" shoes. (Courtesy of Photofest.)

April 22, 1947: *Pirate* filming. Called: 10:05 a.m.; dismissed: 5:25 p.m. Scenes: Int. Show tent and Int. Manuela Rec. Room. AD reports note that "Co. wrapped up at 5:25 p.m. as Miss Garland was too tired to continue."

April 23, 1947: *Pirate* filming. Called: 10:05 a.m.; arrived: 10:15 a.m.; dismissed: 5:45 p.m. Scene: Int. Manuela's Rec. Room.

April 24, 1947: *Pirate* filming. Called: 9:45 a.m.; dismissed: 6:05 p.m. Scene: Ext. Sea Wall.

April 25, 1947: *Pirate* filming. Time called: 9:45 a.m.; arrived: 10 a.m.; dismissed: 6:15 p.m. Scene: Int. Show Tent—"Voodoo."

April 26, 1947: *Pirate* filming. Called: 9:45 a.m.; dismissed: 5:25 p.m. Scene: Int. Manuela's Bedroom.

April 28, 1947: *Pirate* filming. Called: 9:45 a.m.; dismissed: 5:30 p.m. Scene: Int. Manuela's Bedroom and Hall.

April 29, 1947: *Pirate* filming. Called: 9:45 a.m.; dismissed: 4 p.m. Scene: Int. Reception Room.

April 30, 1947: *Pirate* filming. Called: 9:45 a.m.; arrived: 10:25 a.m.; dismissed: 5:20 p.m. Scene: Int. Reception Room.

May 1, 1947: *Pirate* filming. Called: 10:30 a.m.; dismissed: 2:10 p.m. Scene: Ext. Don Pedro's House.

May 2, 1947: Judy had no call/was not needed for *Pirate* work.

May 3, 1947: *Pirate* filming. Called: 3 p.m.; dismissed: 5:20 p.m. AD reports note that from "4:11–4:39: Present Birthday cake to Mr. Slezak [costar Walter Slezak who played the real Mack the Black Pirate/Mayor of the town]; serve cake and ice cream."

May 5, 1947: *Pirate* work. Called: 2 p.m.; dismissed: 3:30 p.m. Rehearsed.

Judy was always making the people around her laugh. Here her costars Walter Slezak and Gene Kelly share Judy's "wit and wonder" on the set of *The Pirate*, 1947. (Courtesy of Photofest.)

May 6 and 7, 1947: Judy was ill and did not work.

May 8, 1947: *Pirate* filming. Called: 9:45 a.m.; arrived: 11:35 a.m.; dismissed: 3:05 p.m. Scene: Int. Manuela's Bedroom. AD reports for the day note that from "11:44–12:00: Wait for Miss Garland, called for a 9:45 a.m. on set; 11:35 a.m.: changing into wardrobe and body makeup from 11:35 to noon. Note: Director arranged 1st setup so that only Miss Garland's dress showed in shot and off stage dialogue was read for her lines. 1:47–1:55—Wait for Miss Garland and Mr. Minnelli; 1:55–2:20—Mr. Minnelli changed setup: Shooting close cut of Mr. Slezak and Mr. Allen while waiting for Miss Garland who is in her dressing room waiting to talk to Mr. Freed. 2:46–3:05: wait for Miss Garland. 3:05—Finish. Note: Miss Garland is too ill to continue."

May 9, 1947 and May 10, 1947: Judy was ill and did not work.

May 12, 1947: *Pirate* filming. Called: 9:45 a.m.; dismissed: 6:20 p.m. Scene: Int. Manuela's Bedroom and Int. Sebastian Hotel Bedroom.

May 13, 1947: *Pirate* work. Called: 1 p.m.; dismissed: 3 p.m. Judy prerecorded "Love of my Life" and "You Can Do No Wrong."

May 14, 1947: *Pirate* filming. Called: 1 p.m.; arrived: 2:23 p.m. Scene: Ext. Plaza Calvados. AD reports note: "3:40 p.m.: Miss Garland too ill to continue—left set."

May 15, 1947: Judy was ill and did not work.

May 16, 1947: *Pirate* filming. Called: 9:45 a.m.; dismissed: 5:35 p.m.

May 17, 1947: *Pirate* filming. Called: 10 a.m.; arrived: 10:40 a.m. Scene: Int. Don Pedro's House. AD reports note: "1:15–1:52—Wait for Miss Garland; returned to stage after lunch at 1:49; Ready to shoot at 1:52 p.m. Note: At 1:15 p.m. Miss Garland told Mr. Shenberg in her dressing room that she had pains in her stomach and she was not well. She also said that was the reason she was late this morning, but that she would try and work out the day and that she would have to work slowly and take things easy in order to keep on her feet. 2:34–2:53: Wait for Miss Garland: resting in her dressing room. Dismissed at 6:20 p.m."

May 19, 1947: Judy was ill and did not work.

May 20, 1947 through May 24, 1947: Judy had no call/was not needed for *Pirate* work.

May 26, 1947: *Pirate* filming. Called: 9:45 a.m.; arrived: 10:15 a.m. Scene: Int. Don Pedro's. AD reports note: "3:45–4:07: Wait for Miss Garland. Note: At 3:40 Miss Garland asked to see Dr. Jones in her dressing room—she complained of a severe toothache and said she could not continue to work unless Dr. Jones gave her a pill to deaden the pain—Dr. Jones gave Miss Garland the pill and she was ready to work at 4:07." Dismissed at 5:30 p.m.

May 27, 1947: Judy was ill and did not work.

May 28, 1947: *Pirate* filming. Called: 9:45 a.m.; dismissed: 6 p.m. Scene: Int. Don Pedro's Salon.

May 29, 1947: *Pirate* filming. Called: 9:45 a.m.; arrived: 10 a.m.; dismissed: 5:55 p.m. Scene: Int. Don Pedro's Study.

May 30, 1947: Judy was ill and did not work.

May 31, 1947: *Pirate* filming. Called: 9:45 a.m. Scene: Int. Don Pedro's Salon. AD reports note: "4:35 p.m.: Miss Garland was too tired to Continue; Company dismissed."

June 2, 1947: *Pirate* filming. Called: 10:05 a.m.; dismissed: 5:40 p.m. Scene: Int. Don Pedro's Study.

June 3, 1947: *Pirate* filming. Called: 10:15 a.m.; dismissed: 5:50 p.m. Scene: Ext. Gallows.

June 4, 1947: *Pirate* filming. Called: 10:05 a.m.; dismissed: 5:20 p.m. Scene: Ext. Gallows.

June 5, 1947: *Pirate* filming. Called: 10:05 a.m.; dismissed: 5:25 p.m. Scene: Ext. Gallows.

June 6, 1947: *Pirate* filming. Called: 10:15 a.m.; dismissed: 6:05. Scene: Ext. Gallows.

June 7, 1947: *Pirate* filming. Called: 10:05 a.m.; dismissed: 5:55 p.m.

June 9, 1947: *Pirate* filming. Called: 9:45 a.m.; dismissed: 5:50 p.m. Scene: Ext. Gallows.

June 10, 1947: Judy's twenty-fifth birthday and filming on *The Pirate*. Called: 1:45 p.m.; dismissed: 4:20 p.m. Scene: Int. Don Pedro's Salon.

June 11, 1947: *Pirate* work. Called: 1 p.m.; dismissed: 4:55 p.m. Stills for poster were taken.

June 12, 1947 through June 21, 1947: Judy had no call/was not needed for *Pirate* work. (Gene Kelly was ill during this time and did not work.)

June 23, 1947: *Pirate* work. Called: 2 p.m.; arrived: 2:30 p.m.; dismissed: 5:05 p.m. Rehearsed "Be A Clown" number (another standard that Judy would introduce).

June 24, 1947: *Pirate* work. Called: 2 p.m.; dismissed: 4:30 p.m. Rehearsed "Be A Clown."

June 25, 1947: *Pirate* work. Called: 2 p.m.; dismissed: 5 p.m. Rehearsed "Be A Clown."

June 26, 1947: *Pirate* work. Called: 2 p.m.; dismissed: 4 p.m. Rehearsed "Be A Clown."

June 27, 1947: *Pirate* work. Called: 2:30 p.m.; dismissed: 4:45 p.m. Rehearsed "Be A Clown."

June 28, 1947: *Pirate* work. Called: 2 p.m.; dismissed: 4:50 p.m. Rehearsed "Be A Clown."

June 30, 1947 through July 3, 1947: Judy was ill and did not work.

July 5, 1947: Judy had no call/was not needed for *Pirate* work.

July 7, 1947: Judy was ill and did not work.

July 8, 1947 through July 10, 1947: Judy had no call/was not needed for *Pirate* work.

July 11, 1947 and July 12, 1947: Judy was ill and did not work.

July 14, 1947: *Pirate* work. Called: 1 p.m.; dismissed: 4:50 p.m. Recording session for *The Pirate*: "Be A Clown."

July 15, 1947: *Pirate* filming. Called: 1 p.m.; arrived: 2:45 p.m.; dismissed: 12:25 a.m. Filmed "Be A Clown" for *The Pirate*, completing thirty-three takes of five different camera setups.

July 16, 1947: Judy was ill and did not work.

July 17, 1947: Judy's last day of filming on *The Pirate* was a marathon day. Called: 9:45 a.m.; arrived: 10:35 a.m.; dismissed: 6:05 p.m. Judy finished "Be A Clown," along with retakes and pickups on five other scenes; changing wardrobe, hairstyle and makeup at least three times for more than twenty-five takes. (There would be additional retakes October 22 through December 19.)

Late July 1947: With Judy's work finished on *The Pirate*, she made a quiet, unpublicized suicide attempt and was admitted to Las Campanas, a California sanitarium, followed by a few weeks stay at the Austen Riggs Center in Stockbridge, Massachusetts. She arrived at Riggs on August 4, checking into the Red Lion Inn, where she stayed during her short, but intensive, treatment. She returned home to Los Angeles on August 20, 1947.

August 12, 1947: (Radio) *Show Time* #275. This hour adaptation differed from the December 2, 1946 *Lux Radio* broadcast in that all the supporting players were from the *Show Time* company. (This program, aired on this date, was obviously taped in advance as Judy was still in the Riggs Center in Massachusetts. The content of this radio program has not been verified and is not known to exist at this time.)

August 29, 1947: Judy saw a rough cut of *The Pirate* at MGM.

September 22, 1947: Judy began preproduction work for her next film: *Easter Parade* (Gene Kelly would be replaced by Fred Astaire after Kelly broke his ankle on October 13, 1947. Cyd Charise tore ligaments in her knee and was replaced by Ann Miller.) On this first day: Rehearsal of music. Time called: 2 p.m.; time dismissed: 4 p.m.

September 23, 1947: *Easter* work. Rehearsed music. Time called: 2 p.m.; time dismissed: 4 p.m.

September 25, 1947: *Easter* work. Rehearsed music. Time called: 1 p.m.; time dismissed: 3:45 p.m.

September 26, 1947: *Easter* work. Rehearsed "We're A Couple Of Swells" (another number that would become a Judy standard). Time called: 1 p.m.; time dismissed: 3:30 p.m.

September 27, 1947: Judy had no call/was not needed for *Easter* work.

September 29 and 30, 1947: Judy was ill and did not work.

October 1, 1947: *Easter* work. Rehearsed "Swells." Time called: 2 p.m.; time arrived: 2:15 p.m.; time dismissed: 4:30 p.m.

October 2, 1947: *Easter* work. Rehearsed "Swells." Time called: 1 p.m.; time dismissed: 4 p.m.

October 3, 1947: *Easter* work. Rehearsed "Swells." Time called: 1 p.m.; time arrived: 1:30 p.m.; time dismissed: 3:10 p.m.

October 4, 1947: *Easter* company was on "layoff."

October 6, 1947: *Easter* work. Rehearsed "Swells." Time called: 2 p.m.; time dismissed: 3:15 p.m.

October 7, 1947: *Easter* work. Rehearsed "Mr. Monotony" and "Swells." Time called: 12 p.m.; time dismissed: 3:45 p.m.

October 8, 1947: *Easter* work. Rehearsed "Mr. Monotony" and "Swells." Time called: 12 p.m.; time arrived: 12:15 p.m.; time dismissed: 3:30 p.m.

October 9, 1947: *Easter* work. Rehearse "A Couple Of Swells." Time called: 12 p.m.; time arrived: 12:25 p.m.; time dismissed: 2 p.m.

October 10, 1947: Judy's call for *Easter* was cancelled.

October 11, 1947: Judy had no call/was not needed for *Easter* work.

October 13, 1947: *Easter* work. Rehearsed "Mr. Monotony." Time called: 12 p.m.; time dismissed: 4 p.m. Also on this date, *Easter* costar Gene Kelly broke his ankle. On October 16 Fred Astaire took over his role, starting rehearsals that day.

October 14, 1947 and October 15, 1947: Judy had no call/was not needed for *Easter* work.

October 16, 1947: *Easter* work. Rehearsed "Mr. Monotony." Time called: 12 p.m.; time dismissed: 3 p.m.

October 17, 1947: Judy's call for *Easter* work was cancelled.

October 20, 1947: *Easter* work. Rehearsed "A Couple Of Swells." Time called: 2 p.m.; time arrived: 2:15 p.m.; time dismissed: 3:20 p.m.

October 21, 1947: Judy had no call/was not needed for *Easter* work.

October 22, 1947: Judy started refilming portions of *The Pirate* at MGM. (*Easter Parade* AD reports state she is "working with Minnelli company.") On this first day of *Pirate* retakes: Called: 10 a.m.; dismissed: 6 p.m. Scene: Int. Reception Room—Retakes.

October 23,1947 through October 25, 1947: Judy was ill and didn't work.

October 26, 1947: (Radio) *Hollywood Fights Back*. Judy and other stars protested against the House of un-American Activities Committee. (This program exists in private collections.)

October 27, 1947: *Pirate* retakes. Called: 10 a.m.; dismissed: 3:40 p.m. Scene: Retakes Int. Manuela's Pation.

October 28, 1947: *Easter* work. Rehearsed "A Couple Of Swells." Time called: 1:30 p.m.; time arrived: 1:45 p.m.; time dismissed: 3:50 p.m.

October 29, 1947: Rehearsed "Strut" and orchestrate "Mr. Monotony." Time called: 2:30 p.m.; time arrived: 2:45 p.m.; time dismissed: 4:10 p.m.

October 30, 1947: *Easter* work. Rehearse "Drum," "Strut," and "Mr. Monotony" numbers. Time called: 2 p.m.; time arrived: 2:15 p.m.; time dismissed: 4 p.m.

October 31 and November 1, 1947: Judy was ill and did not work.

November 3, 1947: *Easter* Wardrobe tests: Time called: 11 a.m.; time arrived: 11:40 a.m. Then *Easter* Rehearsal: Time called: 1 p.m.; time arrived: 1:10 p.m.; time dismissed: 4 p.m.

November 4, 1947: *Easter* work. Rehearsed "Mr. Monotony." Time called: 1:30 p.m.; time dismissed: 5:15 p.m.

November 5, 1947: *Easter* work. Rehearsed "Mr. Monotony." Time called: 1:30 p.m.; time dismissed: 3:35 p.m.

November 6, 1947: *Easter* work. Rehearsed "Fella With An Umbrella," "Couple Of Swells," and "Mr. Monotony." Time called: 2 p.m.; time dismissed: 4:45 p.m.

November 7, 1947: *Easter* work. Rehearsed "Fella With An Umbrella," "A Couple Of Swells," and "Ragtime Violin." Time called: 2 p.m.; time dismissed: 4:30 p.m. Also, that night, the second preview of *The Pirate* was held, in Inglewood.

November 8, 1947: *Easter* work. Rehearsed "A Couple Of Swells" and "Ragtime Violin." Time called: 10 a.m.; time dismissed: 3 p.m.

November 10, 1947: Judy had no call/was not needed for either *Easter* or *Pirate* work.

November 11, 1947: *Easter* work. Wardrobe and makeup test. Time called: 10 a.m.; time dismissed: 5:50 p.m.

November 12, 1947: *Easter* work. Time called: 2 p.m.; time dismissed: 5:55 p.m. Judy's first recording session for *Easter Parade* at MGM. Two solos were recorded: "I Want To Go Back To Michigan (Down On The Farm)" and a song especially written for Judy by Irving Berlin (who was supplying eight original songs and eight standards for a staggering $600,000 fee)—"Mr. Monotony," which would be cut before release. (The footage and song exist on the *Easter Parade* and *That's Entertainment 3 Deluxe* laser disc sets and on the Soundtrack CD from Rhino Records.)

November 13, 1947: (First performance/recording of another Garland standard) An MGM recording session for *Easter Parade*: "We're A Couple Of Swells" with Judy and Fred Astaire. Also, Judy rehearsed "It Only Happens When I Dance With You" and "A Fella With An Umbrella." Time called: 2:30 p.m.; time dismissed: 4:55 p.m. ("Swells" was written by Irving Berlin only after *Easter Parade* producer Arthur Freed didn't like Berlin's original song for this spot, which would later become a hit—"Let's Take an Old-Fashioned Walk.")

November 14, 1947: *Easter* work. Rehearsed "Mr. Monotony" and "Michigan" songs. Time called: 12 p.m.; time dismissed: 5 p.m.

November 15, 1947, 2:30 to 5 p.m.: (Record) Decca Records recording session, Hollywood. Judy's last session for Decca Records (and her last recording session for a label until five and a half years later, when she recorded four songs for Columbia on April 3, 1953). This final session for Decca resulted in three songs being recorded with only twin piano accompaniment. In recording order: "Nothing But You," followed by "I Wish I Were In Love Again," and then "Falling In Love With Love." "In Love With Love" was the very last song she would sing in front of a Decca microphone. ("I Wish I Were In Love Again" would be the "A-side" and "Nothing But You" the "B-side" of 78 single #24469, released July 14, 1948. "Falling In Love" would not be released until July 1992, as it was never marked on the session logs; it had simply been spontaneously recorded that day when there was still studio time left over after the two scheduled songs were completed.) All of the seventy-nine Judy Garland songs released by Decca Records, along with some alternate takes, can be found on the four-CD set *Judy Garland: The Complete Decca Masters (Plus)* issued by MCA Records in July 1994.

November 17, 1947: MGM recording session for *Easter Parade*. Judy recorded "Vaudeville Montage" with Fred Astaire (the medley included "I Love A Piano," "Snookey Ookums," and "When The Midnight Choo-Choo Leaves For Alabama.") Time called: 10 a.m.; time dismissed: 5:55 p.m.

November 18, 1947: *Pirate* retakes. Called: 9 a.m.; arrived: 10:07 a.m.; dismissed: 2:45 p.m. Scene: Retakes—Int. Manuela's bedroom. When this was completed: wardrobe test for *Easter Parade*: Judy was photographed wearing the dress she would wear for the scene in which Astaire tells her to walk ahead of him to see if she catches "the gentleman's eye." (One of Judy's most wonderfully comedic moments on film.) The above tests were shot upon completion of Minnelli *Pirate* retakes using Minnelli crews and equipment.

November 19, 1947: *Easter* work. Time called: 2 p.m.; time dismissed: 4 p.m. Rehearsed "Fella With An Umbrella" and "Mr. Monotony."

November 20, 1947: *Easter* work. Time called: 11 a.m.; time dismissed: 4:40 p.m. Rehearsed "Fella With An Umbrella" and "Mr. Monotony."

November 21, 1947 to Saturday, November 22, 1947: *Easter Parade* started filming. The "Mr. Monotony" number was filmed to the audio of Judy's November 12 recording. This solo was shot in a total of sixty-three takes over the two-day period. On November 21, Judy was in makeup at 7 a.m. for a 9 a.m. call, and was dismissed at 5:40 p.m. On November 22, she was in makeup at 7 a.m. for a 9 a.m. call, and was dismissed at 11:40 a.m. This electrifying sequence would be dropped from the film before release, although Judy would wear the same costume—the top half of a tuxedo—more than two years later for the song

"Get Happy" in the film *Summer Stock*. "Mr. Monotony" still exists; it was featured in abridged form in the 1994 theatrical release for *That's Entertainment 3*, as well as the home video versions. The deluxe laser disc set contains the complete number. A slightly different take is included on the restored *Easter Parade* laser disc, issued in 1992.

November 24, 1947: Judy was ill and did not work.

November 25, 1947: *Easter* work. Time called: 10 a.m.; time dismissed: 2:45 p.m. Rehearsal and fitting. Rehearse Int. Millinery Shop scene and "Fella With An Umbrella" song.

November 26, 1947: *Easter* work. Time called: 11 a.m.; time dismissed: 2:50 p.m. Rehearsed "Fella With An Umbrella" and "It Only Happens When I Dance With You." (This song was inspired by Irving Berlin's dancing with Judy. He quickly wrote down the title and handed it to Judy.)

November 28, 1947 and November 29, 1947. Judy had no calls/was not needed for work on either *Easter* or *Pirate*.

December 1, 1947: Judy had a call for *Pirate* retakes, but was ill and did not work.

December 2, 1947: *Pirate* work. Called: 11 a.m.; arrived: 11:40 a.m.; dismissed: 3:40 p.m. "Mack The Black" Rehearsal.

December 3, 1947: *Easter* filming. Time called for makeup: 7 a.m.; time on set: 9 a.m.; time dismissed: 5:35 p.m. Scene: Int. Globe Theater—"A Couple Of Swells" number.

December 4, 1947: *Easter* filming. Makeup: 7 a.m.; arrived on set: 9:05 a.m.; time dismissed: 4:35 p.m. Scene: Int. Globe Theater—"A Couple Of Swells."

December 5, 1947: *Easter* filming. Makeup: 7 a.m.; arrived on set: 9:17 a.m. Scene: Montage Medley: "I Love A Piano" and "Shooky Oukums." AD reports note: "9:50–12:00: Wait for Miss Garland; She left stage at 9:50 a.m. to see Dr. Jones. Left Dr. Jones office at 10:35 a.m. in studio car to see her own doctor; Miss Garland will call stage 5 after her doctor completes his examination; 12:00–1:00—Lunch: Note: Miss Garland called at 12:15 p.m. to say that she would be ready to work at 1:15 p.m.; 1:00–1:44—Wait for Miss Garland; on stage at 1:23—ready to work: 1:44 p.m." Time dismissed: 5:45 p.m.

December 6, 1947: *Easter* filming. Makeup: 7 a.m.; arrived on set: 9 a.m.; time dismissed: 2:45 p.m. Shoot Montage Medley ("Ragtime Violin.") Also, rehearsed "Everybody Step."

December 8, 1947: *Easter* filming. Makeup: 7 a.m.; time on set: 9:14 a.m.; time dismissed: 5:50 p.m. Scene: Int. Pastini's Café.

December 9, 1947: *Easter* filming. Makeup call: 7 a.m., Due on set: 9 a.m.; AD reports note: "Miss Garland was called for 9 a.m. today for Int. Pastini's Restaurant ['Michigan' Number.] Miss Garland called Wally Worsley at 1:30 a.m. this morning to say that she was exhausted and should be unable to work until after lunch today. Miss Garland called the set at 9:40 a.m. and said she would be in as soon as possible for shooting Int. Rehearsal Hall." Arrived on set: 1 p.m.; dismissed: 5:55 p.m.

December 10, 1947: *Easter* filming. Makeup: 7 a.m.; arrived on set: 9 a.m.; dismissed: 5:05 p.m. Scene: Int. Michaels and Int. Pastini's Café ("Michigan" number).

December 11, 1947: With Minnelli Company for *Pirate* retakes. Call: 1:30 p.m. AD reports note: "JG reported for recording at 1:30 p.m. She rehearsed until 3:30 p.m. when she said she felt as if she had temperature. Mr. Freed, who was on the set, asked to have the doctor called. Dr. Jones was summoned, but found no temp. However, advised that Miss Garland not work any longer today, and not tomorrow. Miss

Another legendary Judy number: filming "We're A Couple Of Swells" with Fred Astaire for the classic *Easter Parade*, on December 3 and 4, 1947. (Courtesy of Photofest.)

Garland was sent home with the understanding that we check with her tomorrow evening for further proceedings." Dismissed: 3:45 p.m.

December 12, 1947: Judy was ill and did not work.

December 13, 1947: Judy had no call/was not needed for either *Easter* or *Pirate* work.

December 15, 1947: *Pirate* work. Called: 2 p.m.; dismissed: 4:17 p.m. MGM recording session for *The Pirate*: Judy recorded a new, infinitely improved arrangement of "Mack The Black." (Test screenings in October and November had dictated revisions. Judy spent several days in November and December reshooting scenes for *The Pirate*—while at the same time working on *Easter Parade*. The original footage of "Mack The Black" is not known to exist; the audio is on the *Collectors' Gems* set from Rhino Records.)

December 16, 1947: *Pirate* work. Called: 10 a.m.; dismissed: 3 p.m. Rehearsed "Mack The Black."

December 17, 1947: *Pirate* retakes. Called: 8 a.m.; arrived: 9 a.m.; dismissed: 5:30 p.m. Scene: Int. Show Tent ("Mack The Black") retakes.

December 18, 1947: *Pirate* retakes. Time first called: 7 a.m. for makeup; on set: 9 a.m.; dismissed: 5:20 p.m. Scene: Int. Show Tent ("Mack The Black") retakes.

December 19, 1947: *Pirate* retakes. First called: 7 a.m. for makeup; due on set: 9 a.m.; arrived on set: 9:53 a.m.; dismissed: 11:45 a.m. Scene: Int. Manuela's Balcony. *The Pirate*, at last, finished filming. The total cost came to $3,768,496, more than half a million over budget. Although, upon it's release on June 11, 1948, it grossed very well—$2,956,000— it would be the only Garland MGM movie to lose money, due in part to its high cost and long production history, which dated back to the first drafts of the script in 1943.

December 20, 1947: *Easter* filming. Makeup: 7 a.m.; arrived on set: 9:16 a.m.; time dismissed: 5:25 p.m. Scene: Int. Amsterdam Theater Stage ("When The Midnight Choo-Choo Leaves For Alabama") and Int. Amsterdam Back Stage.

They cleaned up awfully nice: Judy and Fred Astaire work their movie magic for the "When The Midnight Choo-Choo Leaves For Alabama" number in *Easter Parade*, filmed December 20, 1947. (Courtesy of Photofest.)

December 22, 1947: *Easter* filming. Makeup: 7 a.m.; arrived on set: 9:25 a.m.; dismissed: 4:45 p.m.

December 23, 1947: *Easter* filming. Makeup: 7 a.m.; arrived on set: 9 a.m.; dismissed: 4:40 p.m. Scene: Ext. Drug Store and Ext. Alleyway—(Amsterdam Theater).

December 24, 1947 through December 27, 1947: Judy was ill and did not work.

December 29, 1947: *Easter* filming. Makeup: 7 a.m.; time on set: 9:52 a.m.; dismissed: 4:55 p.m. Scene: Int. Brevoort Restaurant with Peter Lawford.

December 30, 1947: *Easter* filming. Makeup: 7 a.m.; arrived on set: 9 a.m.; dismissed: 6 p.m. Scenes: Int. Dress Shop and Int. Hannah's Hotel Suite.

December 31, 1947: Judy was ill and did not work.

January 2, 1948: *Easter* filming. Makeup: 7 a.m.; arrived on set: 9:20 a.m.; dismissed: 6 p.m. (The scene where Judy and Fred Astaire plan their calendar, and Judy sees they'll be back in New York in time for the Easter Parade.)

January 3, 1948: *Easter* filming. Makeup: 7 a.m.; arrived on set: 9 a.m.; dismissed: 4:30 p.m. Scenes: Int. Hannah's Hotel Suite and Int. Don's Living Room.

January 5, 1948: *Easter* filming. Makeup: 7 a.m.; arrived on set: 9:35 a.m.; dismissed: 5:25 p.m. Scene: Int. Don's Living Room and Ext. Hannah's Dressing Room.

January 6, 1948: Judy was ill and did not work.

January 7, 1948: *Easter* work. Arrived: 1:30 p.m.; dismissed: 4:40 p.m. MGM recording session for *Easter Parade*. Judy recorded three songs: "A Fella With An Umbrella" (with Peter Lawford), her reprise of Astaire's "It Only Happens When I Dance With You," and "Better Luck Next Time."

January 8, 1948: *Easter* filming. Makeup: 7 a.m.; arrived on set: 9 a.m. Scene: Int. Don's Living Room. AD reports note: "1:15–1:43: Wait for Miss Garland and Mr. Astaire; detained at Mr. Mayer's party." Dismissed: 5:55 p.m.

January 9, 1948: *Easter* filming. Makeup: 7 a.m.; arrived on set: 9 a.m.; dismissed: 5:40 p.m. Scenes: Int. Don's Living Room and Int. Hannah's Dressing Room.

January 10, 1948: *Easter* filming. Makeup: 7 a.m.; arrived on set: 9 a.m.; dismissed: 5:05 p.m. Scenes: Int. Hannah's Dressing Room and Int. Pastini's.

January 12, 1948: *Easter* filming. Makeup: 7 a.m.; due on set: 9 a.m. AD reports note: "At 9:05 a.m. Miss Garland called Wally Worsley from her dressing room to say that she was not feeling well and that she had sent for her doctor. She said that she would report to set as soon as doctor completed examination. Miss Garland on stage at 10:19, changing into wardrobe. Ready at 10:44 a.m." Dismissed: 3 p.m.

Fred Astaire and Judy with the main musical mentor in Judy's life: Roger Edens. Edens was a constant in Judy's life for thirty years, coaching her and doing her special material from 1935 through 1965. He attended her closing night at the Palace on August 26, 1967. This photo was taken on the set of *Easter Parade*, January 2–5, 1948. (Courtesy of Photofest.)

January 13, 1948: Judy had no call and was not needed for *Easter* work.

January 14, 1948: *Easter* filming. Makeup: 7 a.m.; arrived on set: 9:29 a.m.; dismissed: 6:05 p.m. Scene: Int. Amsterdam Roof.

January 15, 1948: *Easter* filming. Makeup: 7 a.m.; arrived on set: 9 a.m.; dismissed: 4:30 p.m. Scene: Ext. Drugstore ("Fella With An Umbrella). (Twenty years later, on an August 1968 *Mike Douglas* show, Judy told the story of how the rain was making the red from the feather on her hat run into her face—until "they put Vaseline on it, and I thought that was kind of unattractive!")

January 16, 1948: *Easter* filming. Makeup: 7 a.m.; arrived on set: 9 a.m.; dismissed: 4:35 p.m. Scene: Ext. Drugstore ("Fella With An Umbrella").

January 17, 1948: *Easter* filming. Makeup: 7 a.m.; arrived on set: 9 a.m.; dismissed: 10:10 a.m. Scene: Ext. Drugstore ("Fella With An Umbrella"). Later that day: MGM recording session for *Easter Parade*. More takes of Judy's solo, "Better Luck Next Time." (This song would be trimmed, most likely before filming; the extended version is the best thing about the Soundtrack CD from TCM/Rhino Records.)

January 19, 1948: *Easter* work. Arrived: 10 a.m.; dismissed: 3 p.m. Rehearsed "Easter Parade."

January 20, 1948: *Easter* company layoff.

January 21, 1948: Judy had no call/was not needed for *Easter* work.

January 22, 1948: Judy was ill and did not work.

January 23, 1948: *Easter* filming. Makeup: 7 a.m.; time on set: 9 a.m.; dismissed: 3 p.m. Scene: Ext. 5th Ave. (First Easter Parade.)

January 24, 1948: Makeup: 7 a.m.; arrived on set: 9 a.m.; dismissed: 10:40 a.m. AD reports note: "Did not shoot on account of bad weather."

January 26, 1948: Judy's last recording session for *Easter Parade* at MGM: The title song, "Easter Parade," with Judy and Astaire. Arrived: 2:30 p.m.; dismissed: 4:45 p.m.

January 27, 1948: *Easter* filming. Makeup: 7 a.m.; arrived on set: 9 a.m.; dismissed: 5:30 p.m. Scenes: Ext. Michael's, Ext. 5th Ave., and Int. Vaudeville Theater.

January 28, 1948: *Easter* filming. Makeup: 7 a.m.; AD reports note: "Wally Worsley called Miss Garland in her dressing room at 8:55 a.m.; and she told him that she was not feeling very well and would be late in arriving on the set. Arrived on set: 10:07 a.m.; dismissed: 5:45 p.m." The scene, Flying Feathers, was shot where Judy and Fred perform for the first time as a team (very Ginger and Fred) and only get one curtain call.

January 29, 1948: Judy was ill and did not work.

January 30, 1948: *Easter* filming. Makeup: 7 a.m.; arrived on set: 9:23 a.m.; dismissed: 5:40 p.m. Scenes: Int. Vaudeville Theater Backstage and Int. Don's Apt.

January 31, 1948: *Easter* filming. Makeup: 7 a.m.; arrived on set: 9:10 a.m.; dismissed: 2 p.m. Scenes: Int. Don's Apt. ("Easter Parade") and Int. and Ext. Drug Store.

February 2, 1948: *Easter* work. Arrived: 10 a.m.; dismissed: 11:55 a.m. Sync to loops and taps (dubbing work.)

February 3, 1948: *Easter* work. Arrived: 2 p.m.; dismissed: 3:40 p.m. Sync to Loops.

February 4, 1948 and February 5, 1948: Judy had no call/was not needed for *Easter* work.

February 6, 1948: Judy was ill and did not work.

February 7, 1948: Judy had no call/was not needed for *Easter* work.

February 9, 1948: *Easter* filming. Makeup: 8 a.m.; arrived on set: 10:00 a.m.; dismissed: 2:35 p.m. Scenes: Ext. 5th Ave. (second "Easter Parade" song) and Int. Amsterdam Lobby. This completed filming on *Easter Parade*, except for retakes on March 12.

February 23, 1948: *Easter* work. Due on set: 1 p.m.; arrived: 1:50 p.m.; dismissed: 3:35 p.m. Sync to Loop. That day there was a preview of *The Pirate* at Loew's 72nd Street Theater in New York City.

February 28, 1948: A preview of *Easter Parade* at Westwood Village Theater.

March 2, 1948: A preview of *Easter Parade.*

March 10, 1948: *Easter* work. Arrived: 2 p.m.; dismissed: 3:25 p.m. Sync to Loops.

March 11, 1948: *Easter* work. Arrived: 2 p.m.; dismissed: 3:05 p.m. Rehearsed "Fella With An Umbrella."

March 12, 1948: *Easter* filming. Makeup: 7 a.m.; due on set: 9 a.m.; arrived on set: 9:25 a.m.; dismissed: 12:30 p.m. Retakes—Ext. Drugstore ("Umbrella" Number) and Int. Brevoort Restaurant. *Easter Parade* finished filming on this day. Final cost: $2,503,654—$191,280 under budget. The film would become Judy's second highest grossing film for a first release, an almost unheard of $6,083,000 gross when released at the end of June, with the official release on July 16, 1948. Only Judy's *Meet Me in St. Louis* grossed more during it's first release—$7,566,000. (Both films would be re-released in the 1950s—*Oz* was first re-released in 1948–1949.) The following are excepts from two reviews of Judy's *Easter* work:

> *The New York Tribune*: "Miss Garland has matured to a remarkable degree in *Easter Parade.* A handsome and knowing actress. Her latest film performance is altogether her best."
>
> *Hollywood Reporter*: "*Easter Parade* firmly establishes Judy as the screen's first lady of tempo and tunes. It's her picture, and it's to Astaire's everlasting credit that he let it be that way."

March 15, 1948: Judy cancelled photo portrait sittings for *Easter Parade.*

Mid March through early May 1948: Judy actually had two months vacation. (She was very thin and exhausted from filming *The Pirate* and *Easter Parade.*)

April 18, 1948: Judy and Vincente Minnelli attend a party at the Mocambo that Arthur Freed gave for Perry Como.

May 6, 1948: (Radio) *The Chesterfield Supper Club*, NBC. Judy sang three songs to promote the upcoming release of *Easter Parade*: "I Wish I Were In Michigan," "Fella With An Umbrella" (with Perry Como substituting for Peter Lawford), and "Easter Parade" with Fred Astaire. (This program is believed to exist in private collections. "Michigan" was released on the out-of-print bootleg LP *Drive-In* from *Command Performance* Records.)

May 17, 1948: Judy was ill and could not return to MGM as scheduled. Rescheduled for May 20.

May 20, 1948: Judy began work on her next film: playing herself in a guest appearance for the movie *Words and Music.* (MGM agreed to pay her $100,000 for two songs to be performed at a party sequence—this was the amount they had withheld from her for the delays they felt she caused during the filming of *The Pirate* the previous year.) On this first day: Called: 1:30 p.m.; arrived: 1:50 p.m.; dismissed: 2:30 p.m. Rehearsal of "I Wish I Were in Love Again" with Mickey Rooney—their last time together in a movie.

May 21, 1948 through May 27, 1948: Judy had no call/was not needed for *Words* work.

May 28, 1948: MGM recording session for *Words and Music.* Judy recorded "I Wish I Were In Love Again" with Mickey Rooney. Called: 3 p.m.; dismissed: 4:45 p.m.

(Around this time, Carlton Alsop became Judy's new manager.)

June 1, 1948: *Words* work. Called: 4 p.m.; dismissed: 5 p.m. Rehearsed "I Wish I Were In Love Again."

June 2, 1948: *Words* filming. Time called: 10 a.m.; due on set: 1 p.m.; AD note: "Was due in makeup at 10 a.m.; but arrived at 11:35 a.m." Arrived on set: 3:05 p.m.; dismissed: 4:10 p.m.

June 4, 1948 and June 5, 1948: Judy was ill and didn't work. AD reports for 6-5-48 includes note "Company Layoff due to JG."

June 7, 1948: Judy had no call/was not needed for *Words* work.

June 8, 1948: *Words* filming. Called: 7 a.m.; due on set: 9 a.m.; arrived: 9:10 a.m. Brief dialogue for the Party Scene in the afternoon, the "I Wish I Were In Love Again" number was completed with Mickey Rooney.

June 10, 1948: Judy's twenty-sixth birthday.

June 14, 1948: Rehearsals began for Judy's next film, *The Barkleys of Broadway*, with Fred Astaire. At this point, the film was called *You Made Me Love You*, recalling Judy's earlier—and first—movie song triumph. On this first day: rehearsal. Time first called: 10 a.m.; due on set: 10 a.m.; arrived on set: 10 a.m.; time dismissed: 5:30 p.m. (Judy had also been wanted for the starring role opposite Gene Kelly in *Take Me Out to the Ball Game* at this time. She had replaced Kathryn Grayson, but the role would ultimately be played by Esther Williams when filming started on July 28, 1948.)

June 15, 1948: *Barkleys* work. Rehearsal. Time first called: 1:30 p.m.; arrived on set: 1:30 p.m.; time dismissed: 5:15 p.m.

June 16, 1948: *Barkleys* work. Rehearsal. Time first called: 1:30 p.m.; arrived on set: 1:30 p.m.; time dismissed: 5:20 p.m.

June 17, 1948: *Barkleys* work. Rehearsal. Time first called: 1:30 p.m.; time arrived on set: 1:30 p.m.; time dismissed: 5:25 p.m.

June 18, 1948: *Barkleys* work. Rehearsal. Time first called: 1:30 p.m.; time arrived on set: 1:30 p.m.; time dismissed: 4:30 p.m.

June 19, 1948: Judy had no call/was not needed for *Barkleys* or *Words* work.

June 21, 1948 and June 22, 1948: Judy was ill and didn't work.

June 23, 1948: *Barkleys* work. Rehearsal. Time first called: 2 p.m.; due on set: 2 p.m.; arrived on set: 2:30 p.m.; dismissed: 5:30 p.m.

June 24, 1948: *Barkleys* work. Rehearsal. First call: 2 p.m.; due on set: 2 p.m.; arrived on set: 2 p.m.; time dismissed: 3:45 p.m.

June 25, 1948: Judy had no call/was not needed for *Barkleys* or *Words* work.

June 26, 1948: *Barkleys* work. Rehearsal. First call: 11 a.m.; arrived on set: 11 a.m.; time dismissed: 1 p.m.

June 28, 1948: *Barkleys* work. Rehearsal. Time first called: 2 p.m.; time dismissed: 5:30 p.m.

June 29, 1948: Judy had no call/was not needed for *Barkleys* or *Words* work.

June 30, 1948: Judy was ill. However, she must have been resting for a radio broadcast she had to make that evening (AD reports note that she "can't work and be on radio too"). (Radio) *The Tex and Jinx Show*, WNBC, Hollywood, California (30 minutes). To celebrate both Irving Berlin and the New York premiere/opening of *Easter Parade,* Judy and Fred Astaire sang "It Only Happens When I Dance With You," and Judy sang portions of both "Blue Skies" and "How Deep Is The Ocean?" (This program is not known to exist.)

July 1, 1948: *Barkleys* work. Time first called: 11 a.m.; time dismissed: 12:45 p.m. Wardrobe fittings only.

July 2, 1948 through July 6, 1948: Judy had no call/was not needed for *Barkleys* or *Words* work.

July 7, 1948, July 8, 1948, July 10, 1948, and July 12, 1948: Judy was ill and did not work.

July 12, 1948: At 3:30 p.m., *Barkleys* producer Arthur Freed had a phone conversation with Judy's personal physician, Dr. Schelman. The doctor told Freed he had given Judy medication to sleep, and that "her knowledge of having to report every morning would cause such a mental disturbance within her." Freed began to think about removing Judy from the film so she could rest.

July 13, 1948 through July 17, 1948: Judy had no call/was not needed for *Barkleys* or *Words* work.

July 18, 1948: MGM removed Judy from *Barkleys of Broadway* (despite having spent $23,077 for her work on the film) and replaced her with Ginger Rogers—who started work on July 19—and placed Judy on suspension.

(To gain additional rest, Judy's doctors advised her to rent a separate home from the one she was sharing with Vincente Minnelli; they had recently moved to a new home at 121 South Beverly Drive. She took her own one-year lease on a house at 10,000 Sunset Boulevard.)

July 19, 1948 to September 23, 1948: Judy rested, gained much-needed weight, and regained her health, once again withdrawing from her prescribed medications.

September 8, 1948: First preview of *Words and Music*—the audience demands that Judy do another number (her encore hadn't been filmed yet, but was about to be.)

September 10, 1948: Second preview of *Words and Music*.

Approximately September 23, 1948: (Radio) *Philco Radio Time*, ABC, Hollywood (30 minutes). This was Bing Crosby's latest radio series, which aired on October 6. (Since Bing "pioneered" taping shows for broadcast later, this show was most likely taped a couple of weeks earlier, probably just before Judy returned to MGM on September 24. The exact taping date information is not available.) Judy sang "Over The Rainbow" and two songs with Bing—"For Me And My Gal," and "Embraceable You." (These songs are on the *All the Clouds'll Roll Away* CD collection from England. It would be almost a full year to the day before Judy would perform on radio again; her filming schedule and health challenges took up most of her time.)

September 24, 1948: *Words* work. Time called: 10 a.m.; due on set: 10 a.m.; arrived: 11 a.m.; dismissed: 4:45 p.m. Wardrobe fitting, testing, and rehearsing "Johnny One Note."

September 27, 1948: *Words* work. Called: 1:30 p.m.; dismissed: 2:45 p.m. Rehearsed but didn't record "Johnny One Note."

September 28, 1948: *Words* work. Arrived: 10 a.m.; dismissed: 11:40 a.m. Rehearsed "Johnny One Note."

September 29, 1948: *Words* work. Due on set: 11 a.m.; arrived: 2 p.m.; dismissed: 3:15 p.m. Rehearsal and wardrobe fitting for "Johnny One Note."

September 30, 1948: *Words* work. Arrived: 11 a.m.; dismissed: 11:30 a.m. Recorded "Johnny One Note" in only thirty minutes. That evening, Judy did a radio broadcast: *Kraft Music Hall*, over NBC, in Hollywood (30 minutes). She sang the number she had recorded earlier that day at Metro, "Johnny One Note," a partial rendition of "Over The Rainbow," and, with Al Jolson, "Pretty Baby." (This is the only known recording to still exist of Judy and Jolson singing together. Most of Judy's segment of this broadcast can be heard on the *Judy Garland on Radio* LP or cassette, on the Radiola label. The tape is believed to still be in print. The "Rainbow" excerpt can be found on the four-CD box set *Judy*, from 32 Records, released on October 13, 1998.)

October 1, 1948: *Words* filming. Time first called: 7:30 a.m.; due on set: 9 a.m.; arrived: 9:35 a.m.; dismissed: 5:20 p.m. Shot "Johnny One Note" number, completing her *Words* work. Other songs that had been considered for this second solo: "You Took Advantage Of Me," "This Can't Be Love," "My Romance," "Ten Cents A Dance," "There's A Small Hotel," and "It Never Entered My Mind." The final cost of *Words and Music* was $2,799,970, and, upon its initial release on December 31, 1948, it would gross over $4,552,000. The following are two excerpts from reviews of her *Words* work:

> *Hollywood Reporter*: "Judy could sing 'I Wish I Were In Love Again' four or five times and still not wear out her welcome."
>
> *Daily Variety*: "Well worth seeing because of her great artistry."

October 11, 1948: Judy started rehearsals and preproduction work for her next film at MGM: *In the Good Old Summertime.*

November 1948: Filming started on *In the Good Old Summertime.*

November 16, 1948: MGM recording session for *In the Good Old Summertime*. Judy recorded "Merry Christmas," "Meet Me Tonight In Dreamland," "Put Your Arms Around Me, Honey," and "Last Night When We Were Young." These songs were each completed in three takes or less. ("Last Night" would be cut from the film before release: the footage has survived and is on the deluxe laser disc sets of *That's Entertainment 3* and *Judy Garland: The Golden Years at MGM* both from MGM/UA Home Video. The audio is on the Rhino Records homemade unit CD soundtrack of *Summer Stock/In the Good Old Summertime*, which is only available online at www.rhinohandmade.com or by calling 1–800–432-0020. The CD was pressed as a limited edition run of 6, 000 copies in the spring of 2001.)

November 17, 1948: Second and final MGM recording session for *In the Good Old Summertime*: Judy recorded "Play That Barbershop Chord," "I Don't Care," and "Finale/In The Good Old Summertime." ("Finale" would be cut, but is on the CD soundtrack.)

November 22, 1948: Filming started on *In the Good Old Summertime.*

November 1948 through December 1948: Filming continued on *In the Good Old Summertime.*

December 20, 1948: Photo of Judy in costume for the *Summertime* party scenes where she sings "Play That Barbershop Chord" and "I Don't Care."

December 23, 1948: Filming for *Summertime*: the scene where Judy's character, Veronica Fisher, is at home, not feeling well.

Judy did do one other radio appearance in the fall of 1948: *The Louella Parsons Show.* The exact date Judy did the show is not known, but this is the only noted time in Judy's career that she sang the entire opening verse of "Over The Rainbow"—"When all the world is a hopeless jumble. . . ." (Judy's performance exists in private collections.)

January 27, 1949: Judy completed filming of *In the Good Old Summertime* (only a couple of quick retakes would need to be done), finishing the film in only forty-five shooting days. Judy had been absent from the set for sixteen days due to illness, but the production finished filming five days early, thanks to her ability to complete her work so quickly. The film's cost: $1,576,635 (only $12,800 over budget.) It would gross more than double its cost—over $3,400,000—upon its release in August 1949. It remains one of Judy's finest performances, with her voice in its best mid-late 1940s' shape. Her shape was also at its mid-late 1940s' best, with Judy not being too thin for once, and appearing completely healthy. The following are excerpts from some reviews of Judy's *Summertime* work:

> *Time Magazine*, 7–18–49: "It's only claim to style is Judy Garland. In several spots, she manages to give the show the look and sparkle of a bang-up musical."
>
> *The New York Times*, 8–5–49: "Miss Garland is fresh as a daisy, and she sings a number of nostalgic songs in winning fashion. In fact, her amusing and freewheeling interpretation of 'I Don't Care' brought a burst of applause, which is not a common tribute in a movie house."
>
> *Newsweek*, 8–22–49: "Miss Garland's voice—as appealing as ever—this time plays second fiddle to one of her best straight comedy performances."
>
> *Film Digest*: "The little bundle of genius (scores) one of the most solid hits of her career."
>
> *The Hollywood Reporter*: "Great troupers come seldom in a theatrical generation, but when one does arrive, there is no mistaking that special magnetism that is their art. If there ever existed doubts that Judy Garland is one of the great screen personalities of the present celluloid era, the opportunity to alter the impression is offered in *In the Good Old Summertime.* It is her show from start to finish, as she turns in a performance whose acting elements are no less enchanting than the moments of high excitement she provides with her singing."

February 1949: Judy posed, along with other MGM stars, to celebrate MGM's Silver (Twenty-Fifth) Anniversary.

March 7, 1949: Judy started production on her next MGM film: *Annie Get Your Gun*. This first day was spent in wardrobe at 10 a.m. (Judy was on time) and then song rehearsal. She was dismissed at 2:40 p.m.

March 8, 1949: *Annie* work. Rehearsal (Hall A)—Rehearsal #1. JG—Due on set at 11 a.m.; arrived at 11:15; dismissed at 4:45 p.m. Rehearsed "Anything You Can Do, I Can Do Better" and "They Say Falling In Love Is Wonderful," both with costar Howard Keel.

March 9, 1949: *Annie* work. Rehearsal #2. JG—Due on set at 11:00 a.m.; arrived at 11:35 a.m.; lunch from 1:20 p.m.–2:20 p.m.; dismissed at 4:45 p.m. Rehearsed "Anything You Can Do," "They Say That Falling In Love Is Wonderful," and "You Can't Get A Man With A Gun."

March 10, 1949: *Annie* work. Rehearsal #3. JG—Due on set at 11 a.m. AD reports note: "Ms. Garland called Al Jennings at 10 a.m. saying that she was ill and would be unable to work until later in day—at this time she was given a call for 2 p.m." Arrived at 2 p.m.; dismissed at 4:20 p.m. Rehearsed "The Girl That I Marry," "Anything You Can Do," "They Say That Falling In Love Is Wonderful," and "You Can't Get A Man With A Gun."

March 11, 1949: *Annie* work. Rehearsal #4. JG—Arrived on set at 11:30 a.m.; lunch from 1:20 p.m.–2:20p.m.; dismissed at 5:15 p.m. Rehearsed "You Can't Get A Man With A Gun," "Anything You Can Do," "They Say That Falling In Love Is Wonderful," and "The Girl That I Marry."

March 15, 1949: *Annie* work. JG—Fit Wardrobe, 12:45 p.m.–2:00 p.m.; rehearsal 2 p.m.–5:30 p.m. Rehearsed "The Girl That I Marry," "Anything You Can Do," "You Can't Get A Man With A Gun," and "They Say That Falling In Love Is Wonderful."

March 16, 1949: *Annie* work. Rehearsal #7. JG—Fit Wardrobe, 12:45 p.m.–2:00 p.m.; rehearsal 2 p.m.–3:30 p.m. Rehearsed "You Can't Get A Man With A Gun," "Anything You Can Do" and "The Girl That I Marry."

March 17, 1949: *Annie* Wardrobe and makeup tests were cancelled—Judy was ill and did not work.

March 18, 1949 and March 19, 1949: Judy was ill and did not work. *Annie* company did not rehearse.

March 21, 1949: *Annie* work. Wardrobe and makeup tests/rehearsal #8. JG—Time first called 10 a.m.; due on set: 1 p.m.; arrived on set: 1 p.m.; time dismissed: 4:40 p.m. Rehearsed "Doin' What Comes Naturally."

March 22, 1949: *Annie* work. Rehearsal #9 and wardrobe fittings. JG—Fittings from 11 a.m.–12 p.m.; lunch from 12:20 p.m.–1:20 p.m.; rehearsal from 2 p.m.–3:20 p.m.

March 23, 1949: *Annie* work. Rehearsal #10. JG—Arrived on set: 11 a.m.; dismissed at 4 p.m. Rehearsed "There's No Business Like Show Business" and "Doing What Comes Naturally."

March 24, 1949: *Annie* work. Wardrobe and makeup tests. JG—Time first called 8:30 a.m.; AD reports note: "Miss Garland was in at 8:30 a.m. to have hair dyed; Lunch 11:30 a.m. to 12:30 p.m.; due on set: 1:15. Arrived at 1:15; due to illness of Frank Morgan, rehearsal was cancelled and Mr. Keel made comparative makeup test with Miss Garland from 2 p.m. to 2:30 p.m." Dismissed at 3:50 p.m.

March 25, 1949: MGM recording session, the first for *Annie Get Your Gun.* Judy recorded two songs: "Doin' What Comes Naturally" and "You Can't Get A Man With A Gun." Arrived on time at 1:30 p.m. and was dismissed at 3:15 p.m.

March 28, 1949: MGM recording session for *Annie Get Your Gun.* Judy recorded two songs: "They Say It's Wonderful" with Howard Keel and a reprise of Keel's "The Girl That I Marry." Judy arrived at 1:30 p.m. and was dismissed at 4:02 p.m.

March 29, 1949: *Annie* work. Shot silent makeup and hairdress tests. Time first called: 8 a.m.; due on set: 10 a.m.; arrived on set: 10 a.m.; dismissed at 11 a.m.

March 30, 1949: MGM recording session for *Annie Get Your Gun.* Judy recorded a song written especially for her by Irving Berlin, "Let's Go West Again," in only forty-five minutes. JG—First time called: 11:30; due on set: 1 p.m.; arrived on set: 1 p.m.; time dismissed: 1:45 p.m. (Also on this date, Judy and Vincente Minnelli announced their separation.)

March 31, 1949: MGM recording session for *Annie Get Your Gun.* Judy recorded two songs: "There's No Business Like Show Business" with Howard Keel, Frank Morgan (the Wizard from *The Wizard of Oz*), and Keenan Wynn; and her solo reprise of "Business." JG—First time called: 11 a.m.; due on set: 1 p.m.; arrived on set: 1 p.m.; time dismissed: 4 p.m.

April 1, 1949: MGM recording session for *Annie Get Your Gun*: Judy recorded two songs: "Anything You Can Do" with Howard Keel and "I've Got The Sun In The Morning." Judy arrived at 1:30 p.m. and was dismissed at 3:05 p.m.

April 2, 1949: *Annie* work. Tests—Stage #4. Silent wardrobe test, Judy Garland, J. Carrol Naish, Geraldine Wall. Hairdress test: Judy Garland. JG—First call: makeup, time first called: 8 a.m.; due on set: 10 a.m.; arrived on set: 10 a.m.; Lunch: 12:05 p.m.–1:05 p.m.; time dismissed: 2:25 p.m.

April 4, 1949 and April 5, 1949: Judy had no call/was not needed for *Annie* work.

April 6, 1949: Judy started filming *Annie Get Your Gun.* First up, the song "Doin' What Comes Naturally." Name of set: Ext. Wilson Hotel. JG—First call: Makeup, time first called: 8 a.m.; arrived in makeup at 9:25 a.m. AD reports note that "Miss Garland called cameraman on set at 9:40 a.m. to discuss her makeup after which time cameraman, Miss Garland and Mr. Freed looked at makeup test in projection room, cameraman returned to set at 10:05 a.m.; 10:05–11:25: Wait for Miss Garland on stage; 11:05 changing in wardrobe, and ready on set at 11:25 a.m.

11:25–12:07—Reh. with principles; set boom action

12:07–1:07—Lunch

1:13–1:17—Sew Miss Garland's jacket

1:17–1:29—Reh. with principles set boom action

1:36–1:39—Final makeup for principles

Time dismissed: 5:55 p.m.

April 7, 1949: *Annie* filming. Filming of the song "Doin' What Comes Naturally" was completed. Name of set: Ext. Wilson House. JG—First call: makeup at 7 a.m.; due on set: 9 a.m.; arrived on set: 9:30 a.m.

10:40–10:54—Wait for Miss Garland, putting on final wardrobe and makeup

10:54–11:08—Reh. with principles to playback

11:08–11:11—Add makeup for principles

11:11–11:35—Shoot 8 takes

11:35–11:42—Camera reload

11:42–11:44—Shoot 1 take

11:44- 12:10—Rehearse set boom action; continuation of number

Note: At 12 noon Miss Garland told Director she thought her toe was broken yesterday during rehearsal when she dropped a rifle on it. She left the lot at 12 noon to go and have her toe x-rayed.

12:10–1:10—Lunch

Miss Garland returned to set from x-rays at 1:55 p.m.

2:00–2:11—Rehearse set boom action with principals

2:11- 2:15—Rehearse Miss Garland for sync

2:15–2:19—Add lighting

2:19–2:23—Rehearse to playback, set boom action

2:23–2:25—Add lighting

2:25–2:31—Final makeup principals

2:31–2:35—Rehearse

2:35–2:47—Shoot 4 takes, and stills

2:47–3:54—Director laying out action of scene, set boom action (Children finish school from 3 p.m. to 4 p.m.)

3:54–4:07—L & L Ext. Wilson lawn

4:07–4:13—Shoot silent ward test Edward Arnold

4:13–4:25—Continue lighting Ext. Wilson Lawn

4:25–4:30—Wait for Carol Sue Sherwood: was hit in neck while playing, and went to hospital to have neck examined

4:30–4:51—Reh. action with principals

4:51–4:55—Final wardrobe and makeup for principals

4:55–4:59—Add lighting

4:59–5:01—Wait for director

5:01–5:04—Shoot 1 take

5:04–5:10—Camera reload

5:10–5:24—Shoot 5 takes

5:24–5:32—trim

5:32–5:45—Shoot 4 takes

5:45 Finish

April 8, 1949: *Annie* filming. Name of set: Ext. N.Y. Pier. JG—First call: makeup at 8 a.m. AD reports note: "Miss Garland who had a 10 a.m. call, ready on set and did not come thru the gates till 9:45 a.m."

Miss Garland on set 11:25 a.m.

11:25–11:53—Reh. set boom action with principals

11:53–12:18—Final wardrobe and makeup Miss Garland

12:18–12:30—Reh. with principals, add lighting

12:30–1:30—Lunch

1:30–2:07—Send main wardrobe to get new stockings for Miss Garland; meanwhile roll back canvas on top of set

2:07–2:16—Add lighting

2:16–2:25—Reh. set boom, action

2:25–2:27—Shoot 1 take

2:27–2:30—Add lighting

2:30–2:36—fix generator (blew out)

2:36–2:46—Shoot 4 takes

2:46–2:53—Fix dolly track, add lighting

2:53–2:56—Shoot 2 takes

2:56–3:00—Add lighting

3:00–3:05—Shoot 1 take and stills

3:05–3:17—Select setup

3:17–3:41—L & L boom dolly 2 shot

3:41–4:05—Reh. with principals, set boom action

4:05–4:13—Add lighting

4:13–4:19—Final makeup principals

4:19–4:42—Shoot 7 takes and stills

4:45 p.m.: Dismissed

April 9, 1949: *Annie* filming. Name of set: Int. Pullman Car. AD reports note: "At 8 a.m. Miss Garland called asst. director to say that she had a sore throat. Miss Garland called back at 8:15 a.m. and was given an 11 a.m. call ready on set (instead of 10 a.m. as previously called)."

11:44–11:58—Shoot 6 takes and stills

11:58–11:59—Record soundtrack

11:59–12:07—Rehearse with principals

12:07–12:09—Shoot set stills

12:09–12:17—L & L

12:17–12:25—Rehearse

12:25–12:42—Shoot 9 takes

12:42–12:45—Select setup

12:45–1:45—Lunch

1:45–1:50—Move out 2 pullman chairs

1:50–2:20—Reh. with principals

2:20–2:30—L & L

2:30–2:42—Rehearse set boom action

2:42–2:55—Add lighting

2:55–3:10—Reh. set B.G. action, set boom, action add lighting. Note: At 2:50 p.m., Miss Garland told Asst. Director that she was too ill to work and was going home. She left set at 3 p.m.

3:10—Company dismissed: had nothing to shoot without Miss Garland

April 11, 1949: Judy was ill and did not work.

April 12, 1949: *Annie* work. Rehearsal for Int. Pullman Car. Rehearsal Only. JG—Due on set: 9 a.m.; arrived on set: 9:18 a.m.; time dismissed: 11 a.m.; JG with Alton Unit until 12 p.m.

April 13, 1949: *Annie* filming. Name of set: Int. Pullman Car and U.S. Travel Montage. JG—First call: makeup, time first called: 7 a.m.; due on set: 9 a.m.; arrived on set: 8:59 a.m.; lunch: 12:00 p.m.–1:00 p.m.; time dismissed: 5:15 p.m.

April 14, 1949: *Annie* filming. Name of Set: U.S. Travel and European Montage Cuts—Reh. Int. Ferry. JG—First Call: makeup, time first called: 8 a.m.; arrived through gates at 8:05 a.m.; due on set: 9 a.m.; arrived on set at 8:25 a.m.; ready at 8:50 a.m., 10 minutes early; lunch: 12:00 p.m.–1:00 p.m.; time dismissed: 2:30 p.m.

April 15, 1949: *Annie* work. Judy worked with Roger Edens from 1:30 p.m.–2:30 p.m.

April 16, 1949: Judy had no call/was not needed for *Annie* work.

April 18, 1949: *Annie* work. Rehearsal for "I'm An Indian, Too" Number. JG with Alton Unit—Time first called: 2 p.m.; due on set: 2 p.m.; arrived on set: 1:50 p.m. (10 minutes early); time dismissed: 4:30 p.m.

April 19, 1949: *Annie* work. Rehearsal of "Indian" number. JG—with Alton Unit. Time first called: 2 p.m.; due on set: 2 p.m.; arrived on set: 2:35 p.m.; time dismissed: 4:30 p.m.

April 20, 1949: *Annie* work. Test wardrobe and makeup, Stage 4. JG—First call: Makeup, time first called: 10 a.m.; due on set: 11 a.m.; arrived on set: 11:30 a.m.; lunch: 12 p.m.–1 p.m.; time dismissed: 5:20 p.m.

April 21, 1949: *Annie* work. Rehearse "Indian" number. JG—Time first called: 2 p.m.; due on set: 2 p.m.; arrived on set: 1:50 p.m.; time dismissed: 3:20 p.m.

April 22, 1949: Judy had no call/was not needed for *Annie* work.

April 23, 1949: *Annie* filming. Scene: U.S. and European Montages. JG—First call: makeup, time first called: 8 a.m.; arrived in makeup at 7:50 a.m., 10 minutes early; due on set: 9 a.m.; arrived on set: 9:42 a.m. at Lot #3; ready at 9:57 a.m.; lunch: 12:00 p.m.–1:00 p.m.; time dismissed: 4:35 p.m.

April 25, 1949: MGM recording session for *Annie Get Your Gun*: Judy recorded the song "I'm An Indian, Too." Judy arrived on the set at 1:15 p.m. and finished recording the song in fifty-five minutes. She was dismissed at 2:10 p.m.

April 27, 1949: *Annie* filming. Filming began for "I'm An Indian, Too." JG—Time first called: 9 a.m.; due on set: 10:30 a.m.; arrived on set: 10:30 a.m.; lunch: 12:45 p.m.–1:45 p.m.; time dismissed: 5:30 p.m.

April 28, 1949: *Annie* filming. Scene: "Indian" number. JG—First call: makeup, time first called: 7:30 a.m.; due on set: 9 a.m.; arrived on set: 9 a.m.; lunch: 12:19–1:16 p.m. AD reports note: "3:18–3:25 p.m.: Wait for Miss Garland: had to leave stage." Time dismissed: 4:10 p.m.

April 29, 1949: *Annie* filming. Scene: "Indian" number. First call: makeup, time first called: 9:30 a.m.; due on set: 11 a.m.; arrived on set: 11 a.m.; time dismissed: 5:55 p.m.

April 30, 1949: Scene: *Annie* filming. "Indian" number. JG—First call: makeup, time first called: 8:30 a.m.; due on set: 10 a.m.; arrived on set: 10:05 a.m.; lunch: 12:25 p.m.–1:25 p.m.; time dismissed: 5:45 p.m.

May 2, 1949: *Annie* filming. Scene: "Indian" number. JG—First call: makeup, time first called: 7:30 a.m.; due on set: 9 a.m.; arrived on set: 9 a.m.; lunch: 11:58 a.m.–12:58 p.m. AD reports note "2:01–2:18—Wait for Miss Garland—went to her dressing room ill at 1:30 p.m.; doctor called and was to meet her there. Miss Garland on arrival at studio informed Asst. Director that she was indisposed and not feeling well, but that she would work until the number was completed and the dancing group would be finished after which time she would go home." Time dismissed: 2:40 p.m.—went home ill.

May 3, 1949: Judy was ill and did not work, according to AD reports, but it has been noted that on this date there was a serious blowup on the set of *Annie Get Your Gun* between Judy and her director Busby Berkeley—the same man who had caused her collapse early in 1943 on the set of *Girl Crazy*. It was also noted that on the first day of Judy working with Berkeley on *Annie*, the director was yelling at the crew when she arrived. Why this man—no matter how talented he may have been—was hired to guide Judy though another film (and one as important and as expensive as *Annie*) remains a mystery to this time.

May 4, 1949: *Annie* filming. Scene: U.S. and European montage—London, Italian, French Box (Int. Royal Box.) JG—First call: makeup, time first called: 7:30 a.m.; due on set: 9 a.m.; arrived on set: 9 a.m.; time dismissed: 11:50 a.m.—Judy went home ill and her director did not show up. Judy felt so badly about not being able to work the full day that she called the production manager Walter Strohm at 2:15 p.m. and asked that she not be paid for the day.

May 5, 1949: Busby Berkeley was replaced as director of *Annie Get Your Gun* by Charles Walters, who had directed Judy so successfully on *Easter Parade* in 1947–1948. (Walters can also be seen dancing with Judy during the final production number at the end of *Presenting Lily Mars*.) Judy spent three hours in Walter's office on this day, discussing *Annie* from 3:30 p.m. to 6:20 p.m. The rest of the company was on layoff.

May 6, 1949: Judy's 2 p.m. rehearsal call was cancelled at 11 a.m.

May 7, 1949: Judy had no call/was not needed for *Annie* work.

Sunday, May 8, 1949: *Annie* work. Rehearsed: "Doin' What Comes Naturally." JG—Time first called: 2 p.m.; due on set: 2 p.m.; arrived on set: 2 p.m.; time dismissed: 3:25 p.m.

May 10, 1949: A detailed look at a bad day in the life of a legend. 7:30 a.m.: Judy called the assistant director on *Annie* to tell him she had overslept, wasn't feeling well, had spent a very bad night, and didn't know if she would be able to come to the studio. However, after talking together for fifteen minutes, Judy said she was feeling better and would come to work, but would be a little late. 8:30 a.m.: Judy's makeup artist, Dorothy Ponedell, called the assistant director to again say that Judy would be in. 9:30 a.m.: Judy called the assistant director to say she would be in by 10 a.m. 10:10 a.m.: Judy checked through gate at MGM and went to her dressing room to be made up. 10:30 a.m.: Judy called to say she would be right down on the set. 11:18 a.m.: Judy arrived on the set made up, but not in her costume as she said she had a severe migraine headache and did not know whether or not she would be able to do the number ("I'm An Indian, Too"); but she rehearsed the dancing with Robert Alton, who was staging and filming the dance numbers. 11:55 a.m.: lunch break. 1:15 p.m.–1:30 pm: Just before returning to the set, Judy was handed a letter from L.K. Sidney, vice president of MGM, in her dressing room. The letter reprimanded Judy for being "responsible for substantial delays" on the film—Judy refused to accept the blame when she had been telling the studio all along that Berkeley was wrong for the film, with which MGM had finally agreed. Judy actually got the front office to apologize for the letter, but by the time she returned to the set, the company had already gone home—production shut down at 2:10 p.m. Later that afternoon: Judy was removed from *Annie Get Your Gun* and placed on suspension. The company was on layoff from May 11 through May 21, when the production was suspended, until Betty Hutton came on September 26 to take over *Annie*.

The footage Judy shot on the two songs she was working on before her dismissal—"Doin' What Comes Naturally" and "I'm An Indian, Too"—still exists and reveal her to be in excellent shape for the most part; especially on "Doin' What Comes Naturally," where she seems to be the only one who knows what she's doing. The film fragments—stops and starts—are known to exist in private collections and on out-of-print bootleg videotapes from All Star Video Corp and Video Images. They were to be included on the Warner Home Video DVD released in the fall of 2000, but the two songs were presented instead in a final, edited version. The quality on the DVD is breathtaking, especially for "Indian," since the original negatives still existed. The majority of both songs are also included in the "Director's Cut" version of *That's Entertainment Part 3* released on Home Video in November 1994. Judy's songs can be heard on three different CD sets. Two solos are found on the *That's Entertainment* Collection (and a single CD soundtrack on Angel Records), and the remaining Judy songs are on the *Collector's Gems* set—both available from Rhino Records. All of the *Annie* songs—including all of Judy's numbers—are included (many in stereo) on the original soundtrack CD released in the fall of 2000 by TCM/Rhino Records.

May 29, 1949: Judy entered Peter Brent Brigham Hospital in Boston to cure her dependency on prescribed medications.

June 6, 1949: Judy felt better enough, after only one week, to hold a press conference, during which she bravely announced her addiction to prescribed medications. She said she was "learning to sleep all over again."

June 10, 1949: Judy's twenty-seventh birthday was celebrated at the Ritz Carlton hotel in Boston with her manager Carlton Alsop and her daughter Liza.

June 14, 1949: Louella Parsons announced in her column that Judy would return to MGM in the movie *Summer Stock.*

July 4, 1949: Judy spent the Independence Day holiday with her manager's wife, actress Sylvia Sidney, in Cape Cod. Other summer outings included her first time singing "in four months," for over an hour, at a visit to a small theater company in Provincetown and a visit with Alsop's friends in Boston. Soon the hospital decided she could stay out on the Cape for a while, so she called for Liza and rented a cabin on the coast. Later she was allowed to move from the hospital to a hotel. During this period she also spent much time visiting and helping the children in the nearby children's hospital, where she later talked about how much they helped her ("just by taking my mind off my troubles for a while"). She also helped them. One young girl, who had never spoken the entire time she'd been in the hospital, uttered her first word, "Judy!" Judy missed her train back to California just so she could stay with the child and make sure the child would be okay. Judy had each of the nurses spend time with her and the child at the child's bed and to get the child to talk with the nurses before Judy would agree to leave her. Judy's manager, Carlton Alsop, confirmed this information to her biographer Gerald Frank.

Early to mid August 1949: Judy spent two weeks in Los Angeles to discuss *Summer Stock* (which was to have costarred Mickey Rooney, but Gene Kelly was grossing more at the box office at that time so he was assigned the role. The first name of Judy's character was also changed, from Judith, or Judy Falbury, to Jane).

Mid to late August 1949: Judy returned to Boston to spend her last two weeks at Brigham Hospital.

Early September 1949: Judy returned home to Los Angeles (she was now officially reunited with Vincente Minnelli).

Mid to late September 1949: (Radio) *The Bing Crosby Show*, CBS, Hollywood (30 minutes). (This show was most likely prerecorded mid to late September, as Crosby liked to tape his shows in advance; air date was October 5.) Judy sang "I Don't Care" to promote *In the Good Old Summertime* and performed a comedy skit about the early days of radio and the future of television with Crosby. The two dueted on "Ma, He's Making Eyes At Me" and "Maybe It's Because." (Most of Judy's portions—minus "Maybe It's Because"—can be heard on the 1974 Radiola LP and tape *Judy Garland On Radio* and on the 1990 JSP Records CD, from England, *All The Clouds'll Roll Away: Bing Crosby and Judy Garland.* There would be another full year before Judy returned to radio.)

First week of October 1949: Judy returned to MGM to begin rehearsals for *Summer Stock.*

October 5, 1949: Judy had food poisoning and didn't work on *Stock.*

October 13, 1949: MGM recording session, the first for *Summer Stock.* Judy recorded her first two songs in the film: "If You Feel Like Singing, Sing," and "(Howdy, Neighbor) Happy Harvest."

October 21, 1949: Judy was ill and did not work on *Stock.*

October 26, 1949: Judy was ill and did not work on *Stock.*

The legendary laughter of Judy Garland, shared with fellow MGM star Janet Leigh during a visit to the famed Mocambo, summer 1949. The photo is dated July 9, 1949, although Judy was not known to be in California from May 29,1949 until August 1949. (Courtesy of Photofest.)

October 27, 1949: MGM recording session for *Summer Stock*: "Friendly Star." (The recording date has also been noted as November 27.)

October 31, 1949: Judy received another "warning letter" from MGM because she had missed six out the first twenty days of preproduction. Later that afternoon, Judy spent ninety minutes with Louis B. Mayer and asked for a release from both *Summer Stock* and from her MGM contract—she wanted to maintain the health she had found during the summer in Boston. Sadly, Mayer talked her into staying and finishing the film, placing her health second, and the movie first.

November 1949: *Summer Stock* continued production with makeup tests, costume tests, and filming. (The opening song, "If You Feel Like Singing, Sing," was the first thing filmed.)

November 16, 1949: Wardrobe tests for *Summer Stock*.

December 1949: *Summer Stock* continued production.

December 19, 1949: Judy shot a scene in the kitchen with Marjorie Main and Gene Kelly in which she impersonates Kelly's character, Joe Ross, while dancing. There were also stills taken of Judy on the set with Kelly watching a scene being filmed.

1950

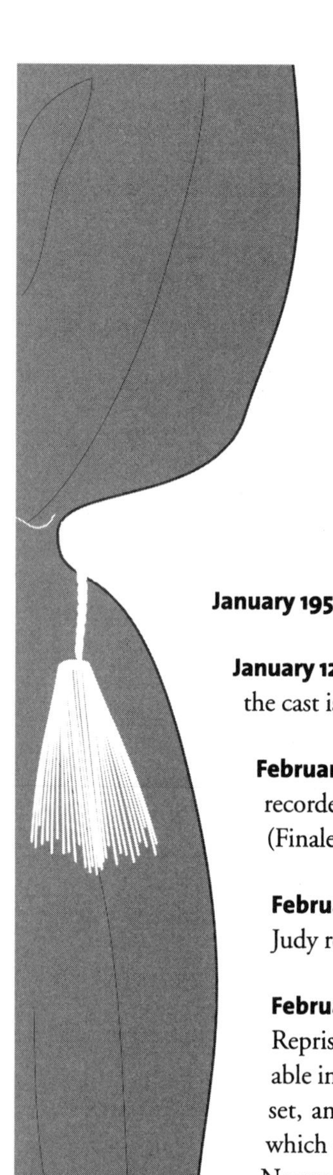

January 1950: *Summer Stock* continued production.

January 12, 1950: Judy filmed the rehearsal scene in *Summer Stock*, where the cast is seen rehearsing the number "All For You."

February 2, 1950: MGM recording session for *Summer Stock*: Judy recorded "All For You" and "(Howdy, Neighbor) Happy Harvest" (Finale), both with Gene Kelly.

February 3, 1950: MGM recording session for *Summer Stock*: Judy recorded "You Wonderful You" with Gene Kelly.

February 13, 1950: MGM recording session for *Summer Stock*: Reprise of "You Wonderful You" with Gene Kelly. (This is available in stereo on the MGM/UA *Golden Years At MGM* laser disc set, and also on the CD Soundtrack from Rhino Handmade, which contains the songs from *In the Good Old Summertime*. See November 16, 1948 for ordering information.)

Mid February 1950: Judy finished filming *Summer Stock*.

March 15, 1950: Judy returned to MGM and *Summer Stock* to record an additional solo, one that would become yet another song identified with Judy: "Get Happy."

Mid to late March 1950: "Get Happy" was filmed for *Summer Stock*, finishing the film (fifty filming days total). The final cost for the movie was $2,024,848—just $43,000 more than the original amount allotted. Upon its release in August 1950, the film would become a huge success, grossing 10% more than the initial receipts for Judy's last movie *In the Good Old Summertime*. *Stock* grossed over a million dollars in its first one hundred engagements alone, and also garnered Garland more raves for her work. Take for example, the following excerpts:

Judy filming another of the many numbers associated with her: "Get Happy" for *Summer Stock*, mid to late March 1950. (Courtesy of Photofest.)

Life: "The great song and dance actress makes this movie a personal triumph."

Time: "One of Hollywood's few triple-threat girls. Thanks to actress Garland's singing, dancing, and acting, the picture seems considerably better than it is. Though the show's only distinguished song is an old one, 'Get Happy,' her voice and showman-like delivery do wonders for the whole score."

The Los Angeles Times: "There can be no rivalry for the individuality she brings to a musical film."

The Rochester Democrat and Chronicle: "Hers is the genuinely satisfying performance of a seasoned, generously endowed trouper who instinctively knows what it's all about and who has a personality and an individuality of style which can't be replaced."

Los Angeles Herald-Examiner: "The mere flash of (her) name on the screen created excitement, but when the little star went into action Zounds!"

United Press (wire service report): "The Hollywood press gave Judy the kind of ovation that any big star dreams of."

(East Coast preview screening; source unknown): "(The preview audience) raised the roof with tremendous bursts of applause at every one of her numbers, certain proof that this young lady still holds the warmest spot in the hearts of millions."

Late April 1950: Judy rented a house in Carmel, California, where she planned to rest for six months; she was only there for less than three weeks when MGM called her back to the studio to replace a pregnant June Allyson in *Royal Wedding* with Fred Astaire.

May 11, 1950: Preview of *Summer Stock*.

May 23, 1950: Judy arrived at MGM for her first rehearsal of *Royal Wedding*. Called: 11 a.m.; dismissed 4:30 p.m.

May 24, 1950: *Wedding* work. Called: 11 a.m.; dismissed: 3:40 p.m. Rehearsal.

May 25, 1950: *Wedding* work. Called: 11 a.m.; dismissed: 4 p.m. Rehearsal.

May 26, 1950: *Wedding* work. Called: 11 a.m.; dismissed: 3:30 p.m. Rehearsal.

May 27, 1950: Judy had no call/was not needed for *Wedding* work.

May 28, 1950: *Wedding* work. Called: 11 a.m.; arrived: 2:25 p.m.; dismissed: 5:15 p.m. Rehearsal.

May 31, 1950: *Wedding* work. Called: 11 a.m.; dismissed: 12:30 p.m. Rehearsal.

June 1, 1950: *Wedding* work. Called: 10:30; arrived: 11 a.m.; dismissed: 3:55 p.m. Wardrobe fittings: 11 a.m. to 11:30 a.m., then rehearsed.

June 2, 1950: *Wedding* work. Called: 11 a.m.; arrived: 2:15 p.m.; dismissed: 5 p.m. Rehearsal.

June 3, 1950: Judy had no call/was not needed for *Wedding* work.

June 5, 1950: *Wedding* work. Called: 11 a.m.; arrived: 11:15 a.m.; dismissed: 12:20 p.m. Rehearsal.

June 6, 1950: *Wedding* work. Called: 10:30 a.m.; arrived: 11:15 a.m.; dismissed: 4:45 p.m. Rehearsal.

June 7, 1950: *Wedding* work. Called: 10:30 a.m.; arrived: 11 a.m.; dismissed: 5:35 p.m. Rehearsal.

June 8, 1950: *Wedding* work. Called: 10:30 a.m.; arrived: 11:15 p.m.; dismissed: 5:30 p.m. Fitted wardrobe from 11:15 a.m. to 11:40 a.m., then rehearsed to 5:30 p.m.

June 9, 1950: *Wedding* work. Called: 10:30 a.m.; arrived: 1:45 p.m.; dismissed: 4 p.m. Rehearsal. There was also a birthday party held for her on the set.

June 10, 1950: Judy's twenty-eighth birthday. She was not on call/needed for *Wedding* work.

June 12, 1950: *Wedding* work. Called: 10:30 a.m.; arrived: 2:05 p.m.; dismissed: 5 p.m. Rehearsal.

June 13, 1950: *Wedding* work. Called: 11:30 a.m.; dismissed: 5:45 p.m. Rehearsal.

June 14, 1950: *Wedding* work. Called: 1 p.m.; dismissed: 4:50 p.m. Wardrobe fitting and rehearsal.

June 15, 1950: *Wedding* work. Called: 2 p.m.; arrived: 2:50 p.m.; dismissed: 4:25 p.m. Rehearsal.

June 16, 1950: *Wedding* work. Called: 10 a.m.; dismissed: 5 p.m. Wardrobe and makeup tests and rehearsal. On this day, Judy appeared for wardrobe tests and looked beautiful in her Helen Rose creation, as those on the set reported. There does exist a wardrobe and makeup test still taken on this day of Judy with Fred Astaire for their "How Could You Believe Me When I Said I Loved You When You Know I've Been A Liar All My Life?" number (Scenes 70–74, in "London"). (Judy would later sing this on radio with Bing Crosby, and, in 1964, Liza Minnelli would sing it during her concerts with Judy at the London Palladium.) This was noted as Judy's fifteenth costume for *Wedding* (Astaire's sixteenth), and she does look lovely, if certainly different, due to the blond wig she's wearing. This would be the last time Judy worked on an MGM movie set.

June 17, 1950: Judy, awaking with a migraine, called at 11:25 a.m. to cancel her 1 p.m. afternoon rehearsal call, and then later that day was dropped from *Royal Wedding*—despite the $20,604 already spent on the film—and placed on suspension by MGM. (Judy had been due to start recording the score on Monday, June 19, which included the haunting ballad "Too Late Now." She would later sing this song on the first episode taped of her TV series in 1963. Shooting on *Royal Wedding* was to have started June 26.)

June 19, 1950: A distraught Judy attempted suicide at home. Although the slight scratch on her throat was superficial, the news made international headlines for days.

July 1950: Judy was seen frequently "out on the town" with Vincente.

Late July 1950: Judy spent some time relaxing at Frank Sinatra's Calneva Lodge, in Lake Tahoe. Afterwards, she and Liza went to Sun Valley, Idaho.

Early September 1950: Judy left Sun Valley for New York.

September 5, 1950: Judy attended a late-night showing of *Summer Stock* at the Capitol Theater in New York. When the audience spotted her after the screening, there was a gloriously supportive mob scene with cries of "We Love You, Judy!" This made all the papers the next day. While in New York, Judy attended the opening of the Broadway musical *Call Me Madam* with Ethel Merman. She also attended Edith Piaf's New York City opening in the fall of 1950, and photos were taken of them together, along with Ginger Rogers, Faye Emerson, and Sonja Henie, all of whom attended that first night.

September 18, 1950: Judy returned to Los Angeles. (Judy saw *Summer Stock* at the Egyptian Theater in Los Angeles, the first week it played there.)

September 20, 1950: (Radio) *The Bing Crosby Show*, CBS, (KNX Radio Studios), Hollywood (30 minutes). (This was the show's taping date—the broadcast date was October 11, 1950. Again, Crosby's shows were taped about two to three weeks or so in advance of air dates.) Judy sang "Get Happy" (promoting *Summer Stock*), and, with Crosby, sang "Sam's Song" and "Goodnight Irene" (Bob Hope joined in for this last song). (These three songs are on the previously mentioned *All the Clouds'll Roll Away* CD, from JSP Records, England, released in 1990.)

September 25, 1950: (Radio) *The Bing Crosby Show*, CBS, San Francisco, California (30 minutes). (This is the taping date; the date of broadcast was October 18; Crosby taped his shows in advance; at this point he was taping about three weeks in advance.) Judy sang "Friendly Star" (once again promoting *Summer Stock*) and dueted with Crosby on "Tzena, Tzena, Tzena" (These two songs are also on the JSP Records CD mentioned above).

September 29, 1950: Judy asked for, and was given, a release from her MGM contract on this date. MGM had actually been holding meetings since August 1 about keeping Judy at the studio (her fan mail had quadrupled—90 percent of it supportive, and *Summer Stock* was proving to be a hit), but Judy was granted her wish for freedom.

October 1950: Judy returned to New York for the baseball World Series and for business meetings with her new representative at the William Morris Agency, Abe Lastfogel. Despite meetings with Rodgers and Hammerstein about taking over Mary Martin's role in Broadway's *South Pacific*, and rumors of potential films and recordings, Lastfogel instead signed Judy for over a dozen radio broadcasts from November 1950 through March 1951—at $1,500 each. These shows would give her the chance to have direct contact with audiences in the studios, and also give her national exposure (without having to worry about dieting to remain slim for the cameras.) The first broadcast would be on November 5. (Rodgers and Hammerstein had also hoped to write a Broadway musical for Judy, who was also thinking of doing either a stage or film musical based on the 1936 Katherine Hepburn film *Alice Adams*. Judy had also been rumored to star with Ezio Penza in *Slightly Dishonorable*.)

November 5, 1950: (Radio) *The Theater Guild on the Air*, NBC, Los Angeles (60 minutes). The Booth Tarkington drama, *Alice Adams* aired (Judy played the title role). (This program is believed to still exist in private collections.)

Mid to late November 1950: (Radio) *The Bing Crosby Show*, CBS, Hollywood (30 minutes). (Taped a couple of weeks before the broadcast date of December 6—exact taping date unknown, but the probable date was November 15, as Crosby was taping about three weeks in advance at this time.) Judy sang "Rock-A-Bye Your Baby With A Dixie Melody," and, with Crosby, a new comedy version of "Rudolph, The Red-nosed Reindeer." (Both songs are on an unconfirmed out-of-print album called *Bing Crosby at the Music Hall*, on the AJAZZ label.)

First week of December 1950: Judy's legal—and final—separation from Vincente Minnelli was announced, and she moved from an apartment at 8850 Evansview in West Hollywood, into Marlene Dietrich's former apartment on Sweetzer Street, off Sunset Strip, also in West Hollywood. By this time, she was already dating Michael Sidney Luft—known as Sid Luft—a former test pilot turned producer. She and Luft had first met on the set of Judy's first MGM feature *Broadway Melody of 1938* back in 1937, when Luft was Eleanor Powell's assistant. They were reintroduced in New York City in September 1950, and soon began seeing each other.

December 25, 1950: (Radio) *Lux Radio Theater*, CBS, Hollywood (60 minutes). A radio version of *The Wizard of Oz*, with Judy recreating her role of Dorothy. Judy, of course, sang "Over The Rainbow," along with "We're Off To See The Wizard," and a reprise of "Rainbow." (This show is available on CD from Radiola Records.) Judy brought Liza to the studio that Christmas evening for the broadcast.

(Also, at some point this fall, Judy appeared on *The Bob Hope Show* on NBC Radio. She sang "The Third Man Theme" with Hope and Crosby. This performance is reportedly on an out of print bootleg LP.)

1951

January 1951: (Radio) *Hollywood Party*. Judy sang "Stars and Stripes Forever," "How Deep Is The Ocean," and "You're Just In Love" with Vic Damone. (This performance exists in private collections.)

January 9, 1951: (Radio) *Salute To Bing Crosby*, CBS, Hollywood (30 minutes). During this all-star salute to Crosby's twentieth anniversary in show business, Judy's "Rock-A-Bye Your Baby With A Dixie Melody" was played from an earlier broadcast. Judy also spoke a few lines of congratulations (which appeared to have been taped over the telephone). (This program exists in private collections.)

Approximately January 23, 1951: (Radio) *The Bing Crosby Show*, CBS, Hollywood (30 minutes). (Crosby taped his programs about two weeks in advance; the broadcast date was Wednesday, February 7.) Judy sang "You Made Me Love You" and, with Crosby, "Just The Way You Are." They also did a comedy skit that included the songs "In My Merry Oldsmobile"; "Hello, My Baby"; "Some Rainy Afternoon"; and "Walking My Baby Back Home. (All of these songs are on the CD *Judy Garland and Bing Crosby: When You're Smiling* from Parrot Productions, London, released in 1993.)

January 30, 1951: (Radio) *The Bob Hope Show*, NBC, Los Angeles (30 minutes). Judy sang "(I'm In Love With A) Wonderful Guy." (This program still exists in private collections.)

February 11, 1951: (Radio) *The Big Show*, NBC, Los Angeles (90 minutes). Judy sang "Get Happy"; "You And I" (with chorus); and "Let Me Call You Sweetheart" (with entire cast). (This performance exists in private collections.)

February 15, 1951: (Radio) *The Hallmark Playhouse*, CBS, Hollywood (30 minutes). An adaptation of the *Perrault's Fairy Tales* version of "Cinderella." Judy played a writer whose short stories are repeatedly rejected because they sound "too much like Cinderella." Judy sings "Wishing Will Make It So" and "Wishing Has Made It True." ("Wishing Will Make It So" can be found on the out-of-print bootleg CD *The Definitive Garland 1953–1965*, Pastel Productions, released in 1990. The rest of the program is believed to exist in private collections.)

Approximately February 23, 1951: (Radio) *The Bing Crosby Show*, CBS, Hollywood (30 minutes). (The broadcast date was Wednesday, March 7, 1951.) Judy sang "Mean To Me" and, with Crosby, "You're Just In Love." (These songs are on the CD *Judy Garland and Bing Crosby: When You're Smiling*, a British release from Parrot Productions.)

February 27, 1951: (TV) *The Red Cross Fund Program*, CBS, Hollywood (30 minutes). Ed Sullivan was master of ceremonies, for this all-star show; Judy's appearance had been taped. (This show has not been personally verified and is not known to still exist).

Approximately March 1, 1951: (Radio) *The Bing Crosby Show*, CBS, Hollywood (30 minutes). (This show's broadcast date was Wednesday, March 14, 1951.) Judy sang "When You're Smiling." (This version of the song is also on the previously mentioned Parrot Productions CD from London.)

Approximately March 8, 1951: (Radio) *The Bing Crosby Show*, CBS, Hollywood (30 minutes). (The broadcast date was Wednesday, March 21, 1951.) Judy sang "Carolina In The Morning" and, with Crosby, "How Could You Believe Me When I Said I Love You When You Know I've Been A Liar All My Life?" (These two performances are also included on the Parrot Productions CD mentioned above.)

Approximately March 14, 1951: (Radio) *The Bing Crosby Show*, CBS, Hollywood (30 minutes). (The broadcast date was Wednesday, March 28, 1951.) Judy sang "Rock-A-Bye Your Baby With A Dixie Melody," and, with Crosby, "Limehouse Blues," "April In Paris," "Isle Of Capri," and "The Story Of Sorrento." (All of these performances, except "The Story Of Sorrento," can be found on the Parrot Productions CD previously mentioned—this disc covers Judy's appearances on Crosby's shows from 1951–1952. At this time, Judy's secretary was Mrs. Jim Tully, Myrtle Tully.)

Late March 1951: (Radio) Version of *Easter Parade*. (No other information is known.)

March 23, 1951: Judy appeared in court for her divorce from Vincente Minnelli.

March 30, 1951: Judy sailed on the Ile de France, for . . .

April 5, 1951: Judy arrived in London, England, for . . .

April 7, 1951: Judy was in the audience at a theater that would have a special meaning for her in only two days . . .

April 9, 1951 to May 5, 1951: (Concert) The London Palladium, London, England. This was the start of Judy's legendary "Concert Years." (Most of Judy's appearances in the 1950s were actually more of a "Vaudeville" appearance or a "production" rather than strictly a two-act concert with Judy and musicians onstage with her—these would begin in 1960.) Judy's act at the Palladium consisted of a thirty-five minute set put together by Roger Edens and Oscar Levant—which she would do twice a night at 6:15 p.m. and 8:30 p.m., six nights a week. The eleven songs in her act: "At Long Last Here I Am"; "Judy's Olio" (a medley of some of her greatest MGM hits, "You Made Me Love You"/"For Me And My Gal"/ "The Boy Next Door"/"The Trolley Song"); "Get Happy"; "Love Is Sweeping The Country"; "Rock-A-Bye Your Baby With A Dixie Melody"; "Limehouse Blues"; "Just One Of Those Things"; "Embraceable You"; "But Not For Me"; "Easter Parade"; and "Over The Rainbow." (Judy was paid $20,000 a week—$80,000 total—infinitely more than the approximately $6,000 per week she was receiving from MGM by the time she left the studio. While in London on this trip, Judy stayed at the Dorchester Hotel. An audio tape of Judy's act at The London Palladium, recorded through the sound system, survives in private collections.) The reviews for Judy's work during this engagement were among the best of entire career, as you'll see from the following highlights:

The Evening Standard (Beverly Baxter): "The truth is that Miss Garland is now better than her material. This quality of vibrant sincerity opens up possibilities which probably she, herself, had failed to realize. She can command pathos without being maudlin. In fact, she is an artist. We saw a brave woman on Monday, but more than that we saw a woman who has emerged from the shadows and finds that the public likes her as she is, even more than what she was."

The Daily Telegraph: "She gave a more vital performance than anyone I have heard since Sophie Tucker, making me aware that what I have always thought to be a fortissimo was merely a forte. It was not only with her voice but with her whole personality that she filled the theatre."

The reviews were noticed in Hollywood. Judy was offered, or wanted for, starring roles in *Just for You* (with Bing Crosby), *Meet Me in New York* (a Sally Benson sequel to *Meet Me in St. Louis*), a biography of producer/songwriter Buddy De Sylva (to costar Crosby), a film version of *Kiss Me Kate* (the smash, Broadway musical), and *The USO Story* for RKO.

April 20, 1951: Judy was photographed dancing with Sid Luft in a west-end nightclub.

May 7, 1951: Judy went to Paris, France, by train with Luft, her secretary Myrtle Tully, and her makeup artist Dottie Ponedell, who had been with Judy at MGM since 1943 and *Meet Me in St. Louis*. By now Sid Luft had been officially engaged as Judy's personal manager at $500 a week.

Late May 1951 to early August 1951: Two-month tour of the provinces.

May 21, 1951 to May 27, 1951: (Concert) The Emire Theater, Glasgow.

May 28, 1951 to June 3, 1951: (Concert) Edinburgh (theater unknown).

June 4, 1951: Judy and Sid Luft took a quick overnight trip to Paris.

June 10, 1951: Judy's twenty-ninth birthday was spent traveling to Manchester, with Luft, where she would open the next night:

June 11, 1951 to June 17, 1951: (Concert) Palace Theater, Manchester, England.

June 18, 1951 to June 24, 1951: (Concert) The Empire Theater, Liverpool. (It has also been noted that Judy performed on Sunday, June 24, 1951, at the Blackpool Opera house.)

June 25, 1951: (Benefit) The London Palladium, London, England. "All-Star Midnight Matinee Benefit" for the family of the late comic Sid Field. Judy sang "Rock-A-Bye Your Baby" and "Over The Rainbow."

(Critic Kenneth Tynan): "She has only to open her throat, and send her voice, pleading and appealing, up to the roof, to leave no doubt that talent like hers is independent of age and appearance. The show had lasted 3½ hours before she came on, stood in a pale violet spot, and sang 'Rock-A-Bye Your Baby with a Dixie Melody.' The house rose to her in great crashing waves of applause, the kind for which the Palladium was built."

July 2, 1951 to July 8, 1951: (Concert) The Royal Theater, Dublin, England.

July 12, 1951 to July 18, 1951: (Concert) A week at the Hippodrome, Birmingham, England. (This was the last scheduled stop on Judy's tour, although she also appeared in Blackpool at a summer resort for one night, as well as appearing at a benefit one evening in Monte Carlo.)

August 7, 1951: Judy sailed home, for New York, on the Queen Elizabeth.

August 12, 1951: Judy arrived in New York, staying at the St. Regis Hotel.

August 13, 1951: This was the day Sid Luft had the idea, while walking down Broadway in New York City, for Judy to play the Palace Theater. The engagement—originally scheduled for four weeks, but ultimately extended to nineteen weeks—was announced on August 28, so you can see just how quickly the deal was put together. (Luft had also been thinking of a concert tour for Judy that would include Carnegie Hall, as well as the Winter Garden Theater on Broadway.)

Late August 1951 to early September 1951: (Radio) *The Milkman's Matinee*, New York City (local radio show). Judy talked about her upcoming Palace engagement. (This was shortly after the show was announced and just before she left for rehearsals in California.)

September 17, 1951 to the beginning of October 1951: Rehearsals for "Judy At The Palace," held at the Nico Charisse Studio, La Cienega Boulevard, Hollywood, California.

Mid to late September 1951: (Radio Interview) *The Louella Parsons Show*, syndicated. Judy discussed her Palace run (as well as the fact that she had just lost fifteen pounds and that MGM was "still home") and sang "Rock-A-Bye Your Baby." (The song was either taped at another date, or was lifted from another radio broadcast because the original tape—which still exists in private collections—merely pauses a second for the song to be inserted right before air time.)

September 30, 1951, 2 a.m.: An unfortunate minor car accident occurred. Luft had been driving, but Judy had run to the scene. No one was seriously hurt, but since Judy was involved, the incident received much press coverage. Later that day, however, . . . (Radio) *United Red Feather Campaign of America*, NBC, Los Angeles, Judy sang "You're Just In Love" with Bing Crosby. (This program is not known to exist.)

Early October 1951: Judy and company boarded the Super Chief train, from California to New York, for their final two weeks of rehearsal. (The first week was in an old rehearsal hall on Broadway; the second week, after the refurbishing of the Palace was completed, rehearsals were held at the Palace.)

October 16, 1951: (Concert/Vaudeville) *The Palace Theater, New York, New York*. Judy made her first appearance on the legendary stage, in an engagement that made Broadway history, and firmly established that seeing Judy Garland perform on stage would be one of the greatest experiences in a person's lifetime. No one should ever doubt the strength and courage it took for Judy to return to her roots, to reinvent herself from a movie star to a concert artist. The demand for tickets was so great that the scheduled four-week run would ultimately be extended to a record nineteen weeks. Judy's songs: "Call the Papers"; "On The Town"; "Judy At The Palace Medley" (which included the songs "Shine On Harvest Moon"/"Some Of These Days"/"My Man"/"I Don't Care") "Rock-A-Bye Your Baby"; "Love Is Sweeping The Country,"; "Judy's Olio" (the MGM hits "You Made Me Love You"/"For Me and My Gal"/"The Boy Next Door"/"The Trolley Song"); "Get Happy"; "We're A Couple Of Swells"; and "Over The Rainbow." (Later in the run, Judy would do at least a couple of encores. "Love Is Sweeping The Country," however, would be dropped.) The show also featured "Judy's Eight Boyfriends," who danced with her during the opening and "Get Happy" numbers and who filled the times when Judy would be changing her costumes. Judy occupied the second-act spot after intermission. Five variety acts filled the first half of this old-time Vaudeville show. The reviews were ecstatic, as you'll see from the following samples:

> *Life*: "*A Miracle*. Almost everyone in the theatre was crying and for days afterwards people around Broadway talked as if they had beheld a miracle. What they had beheld was Judy Garland making her debut at the old Palace, which was having a comeback to straight vaudeville. But the real comeback was Judy's. The girl with the voice meant equally for lullabies, love songs, and plain whooping and hollering, deserved the most overworked word in her profession—great."
>
> *Variety*: "Hers was a tour-de-force of no small caliber. The hep and sentimentally attuned first-nighters left the Palace in a burst of reflected stardust, for there is no disputing, at any time, that the ex-Metro songstress is simon-pure stellar quality. Miss Garland is a singer's singer. With her you hear every word and phrase. She's a great natural singer, who combines a high-powered little girl quality with a mature, authoritative approach that is undeniable."
>
> *The New York Times*, October 17: "Full of zip and electric energy, she gave plenty of evidence that she knows her way about the boards, and now that the big test is over, she should be able to settle down for a comfortable stay."
>
> *Holiday Magazine* (Clifton Fadiman): "*Where Lay the Magic?* Why did we grow silent, self-forgetting, our faces lit as with so many candles, our eyes glittering with unregarded tears? Why did we call her back again and again and again, not as if she had been giving a good performance, but as if she had been offering salvation. Some of the effect may be traceable to the extraneous drama of Judy's personal life. After a period of too highly publicized grief and failure and misfortune, this was her comeback. Of course we wanted her to be wonderful, as if her triumphs could somehow help to wipe out our own sorrows and weaknesses. But there was more to it than that. Much more. As we listened to her voice, with its unbelievable marriage of volume and control, as we watched her, in her tattered tramp costume, telling the most delicious jokes with arms, legs, head, and eyes, we forgot—and this is the acid test—who she was, and indeed who we were ourselves. As with all true clowns (for Judy Garland is as fine a clown as she is a singer) she seemed to be neither male nor female, young nor old, pretty nor plain. She had no 'glamour,' only magic. She was gaiety itself, yearning itself, fun itself. She expressed a few simple, common feelings so purely that they floated about in the dark theater, bodiless, as if detached from any specific personality. She wasn't being judged or enjoyed, not even watched or heard. She was only being *felt*, as one feels the quiet run of one's own blood, the shiver of the spine, Housman's prickle of the skin. And when, looking about eighteen inches high, sitting hunched over the stage apron with only a tiny spotlight pinpointing her elf face, she breathed the last phrases of 'Over The Rainbow' and cried out its universal, unanswerable query, 'Why Can't I?,' it was as though the bewildered hearts of all the people in the world had moved quietly together and become one, shaking in Judy's throat, and there breaking."

(Judy's act, minus "Love Is Sweeping The Country," can be heard on a recording made of her closing night at the Palace—See February 24, 1952, for more information.)

November 1951: Sid Luft arranged for Judy's film career/film offers to be handled by Charles K. Feldman, a leading film agent of that time. (Judy stayed with Feldman until 1960; his agency destroyed its Garland file in 1966, so we are not able to determine all of the film offers that came through his office.)

Judy recreating the "Get Happy" number onstage at the Palace, during her first record-breaking historic run at the famed theater, 1951–1952. The dancer you see on the right also appeared in the film version of the song; Judy was loyal to those she worked with, and they, in turn, loved to work with her. Most of her professional associations spanned many decades. (Courtesy of Photofest.)

November 11, 1951: The strain of doing thirteen shows a week was getting to Judy. She collapsed in the wings, after finishing part of her second show of the day; she had already done fifty-one shows in a row without a single day off; thus, Judy now took four days off.

November 16, 1951: Judy returned to the Palace Theater.

November 27, 1951: The seven theatrical unions of the AFL (American Federation of Labor) honored Judy with a testimonial luncheon.

Mid December 1951: Judy took a five day vacation just prior to the week of Christmas, when she resumed her shows at the Palace.

January 1952 to February 1952: Judy continued her appearances at the Palace Theater.

February 24, 1952: (Concert/Vaudeville) Judy ended her Palace engagement, having played there for a record-breaking nineteen weeks and given 184 performances, grossing nearly $800,000. (To satisfy the demand for tickets, Judy played 11 shows the last week, grossing $54,000 and breaking her own record at the box office. This last performance can be heard in its entirety on the out of print bootleg LP *Judy Garland 'Live' at the Palace: 2-A-Day* on the International Theatremusic [C.I.T.] label, #2001, and the performance has just been released on CD by the label Hollywood Soundstage. It is also currently available on a two-CD set that Sid Luft released in 1999 called *Judy Duets*. The first disc contains duets Judy performed with her guests from her television shows, and the second disc contains the Palace closing night 1952 in sparkling, glorious sound. Sadly, Sid cut out a talk between Judy and Lauritz Melchoir, the artist following her into the Palace; Sid added "After You've Gone," which Judy had sung on a different night; and Sid changed the order of the final songs, placing "Rainbow" after her encores. Judy's 1951–1952 Palace act can also be heard on the 1993 import, two-CD set, *Judy Garland in Concert—The Beginning and the End*, which is on the Legend label, #6011/6012. This version of her Palace act was recorded June 22, 1952 during her closing night of the "Palace Comeback Tour" at the Curran Theater in San Francisco.) Judy's closing night at the Palace was again raved about in reviews:

> *Variety*: "Speeches and three extra numbers didn't suffice. The crowd just didn't move, although most knew she had done three numbers more than her usual shows. There were requests from all over the house. It was one of the warmest tributes ever given a headliner in New York, one of the more memorable experiences in the history of the two-a-day."

Late February 1952: Just after closing at the Palace, Judy was paid tribute, in New York, by the theatrical unions.

Late February 1952 to early March 1952: Judy and Sid vacationed briefly in Palm Beach, Florida.

March 6, 1952: Judy's divorce from Vincente Minnelli became final while she was in Palm Beach. Judy was granted custody of Liza, with ample provisions made for Liza spending time with her father—this never seemed to be any issue between the parents and was handled splendidly. Judy and Vincente maintained a very friendly relationship, with Judy turning to him for advice on her first act before she left for England, etc., and they would even socialize on occasion throughout the rest of her life. Vincente certainly deserves credit for the influence he had on Judy's movie career, and for the sophistication and humor he sought for her on screen (as Liza would later say, her father really "got" her mother). At the same time, one wonders if Vincente influenced Judy's decision to renew her contract with MGM in 1946 when she was considering leaving after her contract expired in 1947 to return to "live" work, which better fit her desires and her body clock. Still, despite the ultimate failure of their union as husband and wife, their artistic union brought many riches to Judy's legacy, and their living legacy, Liza, continues to bring much to the world, both in her art and in her humanitarian efforts.

March 21, 1952: Judy and Sid Luft arrived in Nassau for the Bahamas Country Club Amateur Gold Cup Tournament.

March 30, 1952: Judy was awarded a special Antoinette Perry (Tony) Award, for the "important contribution to the revival of vaudeville" she made during her engagement at the Palace.

April 3, 1952: Judy returned to California and gave interviews for her next appearance. During one interview, she mentioned that she was wanted for a Broadway musical version of *Pygmalion*, which later became the legendary *My Fair Lady*.

April 21, 1952 to May 18, 1952: (Concert/Vaudeville) The Los Angeles Philharmonic, Los Angeles, California. This four-week engagement (which grossed $220,000) had sold out before opening day and was Judy's first major endeavor in California (other than the radio shows) since leaving MGM a year and a half earlier. The show was essentially the same that she had presented at the Palace Theater in New York. (Judy's salary was now $25,000 a week; she had been paid $15,000 weekly at the Palace.) The following are excerpts from two reviews for her work at the Philharmonic:

> *The Herald-Express*: "A night of nights for star and audience alike—the great big audience cried."
>
> *The Examiner*: "Some (in the audience) may have intended to be kind. Some may have not meant to be. As it turned out, they had no choice in the matter. Within ten minutes of Judy's arrival on-stage, the audience found itself taken on a trolley ride. Not since Jolson was in the prime of his reign have I heard a singer of popular songs split a house wide open as Judy repeatedly did last night."

Late April 1952 to early May 1952: (Radio) Judy recorded three more *Bing Crosby* radio shows, which aired on May 21, 1952; May 28, 1952; and June 4, 1952. Much of the material on these three shows had been songs sung earlier, on Crosby shows from March 1951. On the first of these three new shows, Judy sang "The Boy Next Door"; "When You're Smiling"; and, with Crosby, "Am I In Love?" and "When You Wore A Tulip." (The last song can be heard on the previously mentioned 1993 CD on the Parrot label, #PARCD 003, *Judy Garland and Bing Crosby: When You're Smiling*.) On the second show, Judy sang "Rock-a-Bye Your Baby"; "Carolina In The Morning"; and, with Crosby, "Noodlin' Rag"; "Isle Of Capri"; "April In Paris"; and "For Me And My Gal." (The last song from this broadcast is on the Parrot CD mentioned above.) On the third show, Judy sang "You Made Me Love You"; "Over The Rainbow"; and, with Crosby, "Hello, My Baby"; "In My Merry Oldsmobile"; "Walking My Baby Back

Home"; "In My Merry Oldsmobile" (Reprise); "You're Just In Love"; and "Sound Off," done as a commercial for Chesterfield cigarettes. ("Over The Rainbow" and "Merry Oldsmobile" from this show can be heard on the Parrot Records CD.)

May 26, 1952 to June 22, 1952: (Concert/Vaudeville) The Curran Theater, San Francisco, California. Judy's last engagement of the 1951–1952 Palace Theater show. (The final show on June 22 may be heard in its entirety on the double CD set released in 1993, *Judy Garland in Concert: The Beginning and the End*, which is on the Legend label, #CD 6011/6012.)

June 8, 1952, 6 p.m.: Judy and Sid Luft were married at a ranch that belonged to a friend of Luft's in the town of Hollister, ninety miles north of San Francisco. Judy and Sid drove back to San Francisco the next day to continue Judy's performances at the Curran Theater.

June 10, 1952: Judy's thirtieth birthday.

June 22, 1952: Judy concluded her engagement at the Curran Theater, San Francisco. (As previously mentioned, this closing night can be heard on the 1993 CD *Judy Garland in Concert: The Beginning and the End.*)

June 29, 1952: The Friars Club honored Judy at the Biltmore Bowl in Los Angeles. (Judy was only the second woman in the Friar's fifty-year history to be honored with a testimonial evening; Sophie Tucker had been the first.) Judy sang the "Judy At The Palace" medley and "Over The Rainbow" to end the festivities.

July 17, 1952: It was announced that Judy was pregnant once again.

July 19, 1952: Judy and Sid Luft hosted a party for 150 guests to celebrate Judy's thirtieth birthday, their marriage, Judy's impending motherhood, and their new and exciting deal:

August 1952: Judy's production company, Transcona, entered into a nine-film production deal with Warner Brothers (with three of the films starring Judy). The deal was announced on September 8. When the specifics for the first film were worked out in December 1952, it was agreed that Judy would be paid $100,000 for the first film, plus her production company would receive half of the film's profits. (Judy had been wanted for other films—former MGM head, Louis B. Mayer, was now developing independent movies and wanted Judy to star in his film version of the Broadway musical, *Paint Your Wagon*; George Jessel, of 20th Century Fox, wanted Judy for *Bloodhounds of Broadway*; and MGM had wanted Judy to star in the movie version of Broadway's *Brigadoon* [which was directed by Vincente Minnelli].)

October 30, 1952: (Radio) *The Bing Crosby Show/The General Electric Program*, CBS, Hollywood (30 minutes). Judy substituted for Bing Crosby, whose wife was ill. Judy sang "Alexander's Ragtime Band," "Wish You Were Here," "A Pretty Girl Milking Her Cow," "Carolina In The Morning," and "You Belong To Me." (The entire show, including commercials for the new General Electric kitchen appliances, can be heard on the second side of the LP *Judy Garland on Radio*, which is on the Radiola label, #MR 1040.)

November 21, 1952, 4:17 p.m.: Judy's second child, Lorna Luft, was born—weighing 6 pounds, 4 ounces—at St. John's Hospital, Los Angeles, California. (Lorna was nameless for four days while her parents debated over naming her Nora or Amanda before ultimately choosing Lorna.)

December 1, 1952: A letter dated this day, signed by Judy, hired California-based writer Cameron Shipp to write her biography based on material she would supply, for which he would be paid $25,000 total for a 90,000 word manuscript to be completed by August 25, 1953. The contract runs five pages and was arranged through the William Morris agency. Nothing ever became of this project.

December 25, 1952: Christmas Day. The Luft family boarded the Manhattan Limited for New York as guests of Jack Warner. Judy had agreed to sing, as a personal favor, for his daughter Barbara's coming-out party at the St. Regis Hotel in New York City early in January. While in New York, the Lufts stayed at the Waldorf.

December 31, 1952, New Year's Eve. Friends of Charlie Cushing gave a private party at the Sherry-Netherland Hotel in New York—guests included the Duke and Duchess of Windsor. Judy and the Duke harmonized at the piano.

1953

January 3, 1953: Judy sang at Jack Warner's daughter's "Coming-Out" Party, which was hosted by Elsa Maxwell, at the St. Regis Hotel in New York City.

January 5, 1953: Judy's mother, Ethel Gumm passed away in Santa Monica, California, early that morning. That night, Judy and Sid flew back home to California to make plans for the funeral. Although Judy was estranged from her mother at the time of Gumm's death, it hit Judy hard. Ethel had, in recent movie magazines, made a stir about how Judy was now earning vast sums of money and not sharing it with her mother. In truth, Judy had bought Ethel homes over the years, and a portion of her MGM salary had always gone to Ethel. While it's likely Ethel loved her daughter very much, Judy never felt that love, and, from all reports, that love was rarely expressed to Judy. A recent, startling revelation was the news that Ethel—and not MGM—had first introduced Judy to the horrors of chemical dependency by feeding Judy and Judy's two sisters pep pills by the time Judy was nine or ten. Author Gerald Clarke, in his haunting and moving biography of Judy, *Get Happy*, verified this discovery from sources who were close to Ethel in the late 1920s and early to mid 1930s—including Ann Miller. (Ann's mother was a confidant of Ethel's, and Ann's mother shared this information with Ann.) Judy would often speak out against her mother in interviews, and just knowing this one piece of information makes it much clearer why Judy felt as she did toward Ethel. However, add in other information, like Judy knew her mother had not wanted to give birth to her, and had, indeed, sought to have her aborted; as well as Ethel's presence among the people who forced Judy to abort her first pregnancy while she was married to David Rose; plus Ethel's treatment of Judy in general; and you come to realize that Judy Garland had every right to feel hostile toward her mother. Judy was even justified in calling Ethel Gumm "a stage mother—a mean one. . . . She would sort of stand in the wings and if I didn't feel well, if I was sick to my tummy, she'd say, 'You go out and sing or I'll wrap you around the bedpost and break you off short.' So I'd go out and sing."

January 7, 1953: Ethel Gumm was laid to rest.

February 16, 1953: (Radio) *Lux Radio Theater*, CBS, Hollywood, California (30 minutes). Judy played Liza Elliott in *Lady in the Dark* and sang "How Lovely To Be Me," "This Is New," "The Rights Of Womankind," and "My Ship." (This show can be heard on a bootleg LP on the Command Performance label that cut 10 minutes of the play and "This Is New"—the show is also on the Radio Yesteryear cassette *Voices of Hollywood* #30.) This was Judy's last major radio show, as the medium was changing thanks to the mainstream success television was having by this time.

March 1953: Judy signed with Mitch Miller of Columbia Records to record four songs for the label. In a separate deal, Columbia also signed an agreement to release the soundtrack album for Judy's next film. (Judy had reportedly signed with RCA/Victor in 1951, but that contract had been allowed to expire without any records being made.)

April 3, 1953: (Record) Judy had her first recording session for a record in five-and-a-half years (see November 15, 1947) when she cut all four songs contracted for Columbia Records in a three-hour session in a total of only thirty takes. The songs were "Send My Baby Back To Me" and "Without A Memory" (as Judy's first Columbia single, released on May 4, 1953); and "Go Home, Joe" and "Heartbroken" (released as the second single on June 29, 1953). (All four songs can be found on the recent CD *Judy Garland and Carol Channing: The Ladies of Show Biz* from Sony Music Special Products. "Heartbroken" was cowritten by Fred Ebb, who would later become Liza Minelli's main musical mentor from 1964 to the present.)

April 29, 1953: (Personal Appearance) "The Blue Grass Festival," Lexington, Kentucky. Judy headlined this new Derby Week event. Backed by Vaughn Monroe and His Orchestra, Judy concluded her set with my "My Old Kentucky Home," accompanied by a single violin, and received a standing ovation from the audience according to *Variety*. (While in Kentucky, Judy visited patients at the Shriner's Hospital in Lexington.)

Spring 1953 to summer 1953: These months were spent readying Judy's next movie, at Warner Brothers. Moss Hart was writing the script, Harold Arlen and Ira Gershwin were writing the songs, and the creative staff (including director George Cukor) and the talent for the production were hired. (The first idea for the film had been Sid Luft's, who had thought of it for Judy in September 1951. Judy had actually played the character she was to play in the film on a radio show on December 28, 1942. Shortly after that, she had gone to MGM head Louis B. Mayer about the possibility of her playing the part on screen. She was encouraged by Mayer, but was eventually turned down because the studio didn't think the part suitable for their "precious Judy." As mentioned earlier, the Warner Brothers deal was set orally in August 1952, the contract was announced on September 8, and the final contracts signed in December 1952.)

June 10, 1953: Judy's thirty-first birthday.

Summer or fall 1953: Sometime during the summer or fall of 1953, the Luft family moved into the home they would live in until the fall of 1960: their new, nineteen-room home at 144 South Mapleton Drive in Holmby Hills, near Beverly Hills, California.

August 18, 1953: Judy's first "official" day at Warner Brothers for her film "comeback," *A Star Is Born*. On this first day, Judy started at 2 p.m. and finished at 4 p.m. She rehearsed and laid out dance numbers.

August 20, 1953: *Star* work. Started: 11:40 a.m.; finished: 5:00 p.m. Rehearsal.

August 21, 1953: *Star* work. This day was a recording session spent at Stage 9. (*Star* would be released in stereophonic sound, thus the recording sessions were set for this method; although MGM had recorded

Judy in the recording studio for her return to records, April 3, 1953, for Columbia. During her recording career—which lasted from 1935 to 1969—Judy recorded for Decca, Columbia, Capitol, and ABC Records. Other labels that released her work during those years included MGM, Colpix, Warner Brothers, United Artists, EMI, and Juno. She also signed with RCA in 1951, although nothing was ever recorded for them. Judy had also announced her own label in 1966, but the label was never launched. Nor would she record for Blue Records/Juno, the last label she signed with on December 18, 1968, although they would release an album she knew was being culled from tapes recorded "live" in January 1969. (Courtesy of Photofest.)

Judy's sessions in stereo—using microphones placed at various angles—they did so only to achieve a full-bodied, balanced, but ultimately mono sound. Many of these MGM sessions would be remixed to stereo sound for various theatrical, audio, and video releases beginning in 1989, but this was Judy's first—and unfortunately last—movie musical to be released in stereophonic sound. Thus, Judy worked with one of the largest orchestras in her career.) Judy's first song recorded for *Star* on this day was "Here's What I'm Here For." (Unfortunately, not all of the original recording session tapes for *Star* have surfaced to date, and, as this song was cut from the original wide release of the film, the stereophonic film soundtrack for this number was probably destroyed along with the footage. The 1983 restoration used alternate footage and an "enhanced-for-stereo" soundtrack to recreate this song.)

August 22, 1953: Judy was not on call/needed for *Star* work. A late-night fire broke out in a rear portion of Judy's home; no one was hurt.

August 23, 1953: Recording session for *A Star Is Born*: "Gotta Have Me Go With You."

August 24, 1953 through August 26, 1953: Judy was not on call/needed for *Star* work.

August 27, 1953: *Star* work. Started: 2:30 p.m.; finished: 3:45 p.m. Prerecorded songs (no other information known).

August 28, 1953 through September 2, 1953: Judy was not on call/needed for *Star* work.

September 3, 1953: *Star* work. Started: 9:30 a.m.; finished: 5:00 p.m. Warner color tests (Photographic hair, makeup, and wardrobe).

September 4, 1953: Recording session for *A Star Is Born*: The first official performance of another Garland "standard": "The Man That Got Away." (The session went from 3:30 p.m. to 5:30 p.m., during which only four takes were needed to complete the number. One of these was an alternate, "sweet and low" version using a slightly lower key and a quieter interpretation: Judy would use this approach only once, nearly ten years later, when she sang the song on the fourth episode taped for her television series on July 23, 1963.)

September 5, 1953 through September 10, 1953: Judy was not on call/needed for *Star* work.

September 11, 1953: *Star* work. Started: 11 a.m.; finished: 5 p.m. Rehearsed and laid out dances. Recorded ("Lose That Long Face").

September 12, 1953: Judy was not on call/needed for *Star* work.

September 14, 1953: *Star* work. Started: 2 p.m.; finished: 5:45 p.m. Rehearsed and laid out dance numbers.

September 15, 1953: *Star* work. Started: 3 p.m.; finished: 6 p.m. Rehearsed and laid out dance numbers.

September 16, 1953 and September 17, 1953: Judy was not on call/needed for *Star* work.

September 18, 1953: *Star* work. Started: 11:15 a.m.; finished: 5:25 p.m. Worked on tests.

September 19, 1953 through September 23, 1953: Judy was not on call/needed for *Star* work.

September 24, 1953: *Star* work. Started: 8:30 a.m.; finished: 3:55 p.m. Test.

September 25, 1953 through September 29, 1953: Judy was not on call/needed for *Star* work.

September 30, 1953: *Star* work. Started: 10 a.m.; finished: 3:40 p.m. Makeup and hair test.

October 1 through October 3, 1953: Judy was not on call/needed for *Star* work.

October 5, 1953: *Star* work. Fitted wardrobe.

October 6, 1953: *Star* work. Started: 10 a.m.; finished: 3:45 p.m. Wardrobe tests.

October 7, 1953: *Star* work. Wardrobe fitting and meeting with Heindorf (musical director Ray Heindorf).

October 8, 1953: *Star* work. Started: 10:20 a.m.; finished: 5:15 p.m. Sound and photographic tests and wardrobe tests.

October 9, 1953: *Star* work. Started: 12:00 p.m.; finished: 12:50 p.m. Wardrobe test.

October 10, 1953: Judy was not on call/needed for *Star* work.

Monday, October 12, 1953 (Columbus Day): First day of filming for *A Star Is Born* at Warner Brothers, Burbank, California. Judy arrived at 7:30 a.m. to have her hair and makeup done; she reported to the set at 10:10 a.m. The first scene to be shot was Judy's character's first day on the soundstage—where she interrupts a take on a train set by allowing her face to enter the frame when only her arm is meant to appear. This scene was rehearsed until 11:20 a.m. and shot at 11:25 a.m. Five takes were needed as things kept happening during the first four. The final take lasted forty-four seconds (a minute and forty-nine seconds of film had been shot using nine separate camera setups, which covered one and a half pages of the script; approximately $25,000 had been spent). The entire scene was completed by 5:20 p.m., and the company was dismissed.

Tuesday, October 13, 1953: Judy's second day of filming for *A Star Is Born*. She was on the set at 10 a.m. to complete several short, silent shots for the sequence at her hotel late at night, trying to sleep while mulling over Norman Maine's offer to have a screen test. Her travel up the stairs to Danny's room was also shot (these were shot first, from 11:00 a.m. to the lunch break), as was Judy washing her hair, waiting for Maine to call her (shot from after lunch until 3:20 p.m. Judy wound up having her hair rewashed and reset eight times). After Judy's hairstyle and costume were changed, the first "outdoor" scene was completed—where Judy walks comically across a high catwalk, which was actually only nine feet from the ground, but shot to look higher up, as Judy ran towards actor Jack Carson. This was done in only two takes, and shooting for the day was finished at 4:30 p.m.

October 14, 1953: Judy's third day of filming *A Star Is Born*. This day was the film's first "location" shoot, which was at Robert's Drive-In at the corner of Sunset Boulevard and Cahuenga Street, in Hollywood, for the scene of Judy as a carhop. This scene was filmed in the morning, starting at 9 a.m., and required eight takes for the set-up shots and fourteen takes of Judy—medium shot—telling the customer the types of hamburgers they had that day (the numerous retakes were needed due to excessive background noises). After lunch, the company moved to 626 Spring Street, downtown Los Angeles, to the Bomba Club, where they filmed sequences of Judy unsuccessfully trying to get a singing job. (This scene would be edited before the film's first release in 1954.) The company was dismissed at 3:50 p.m.

October 15, 1953 to October 19, 1953: Judy was not needed for filming, and spent the four working days rehearsing dances for the film, shooting publicity stills, and having costumes fitted.

October 20, 1953: Filming of "The Man That Got Away." The song was shot utilizing two different systems: "CinemaScope," the new process, was the first version shot; this filming went from 2:30 p.m. to 5:00 p.m., by which time the standard Technicolor version had been relit and reblocked. The Technicolor filming at 5:00 p.m. required only three takes to complete the song (the first take was spoiled by the camera, the second by Judy bumping into a table, and the third take—filmed in one complete take for the whole number—was printed). The day had started at 10 a.m. and the company was dismissed at 6:15 p.m.

October 21, 1953: After viewing the two versions of "The Man That Got Away" at an 8:00 a.m. screening, it was agreed to start filming over using the CinemaScope process. (This would be the first Warner Brothers movie to be filmed in this exciting new widescreen process.)

October 27, 1953 to October 29, 1953: "The Man That Got Away" was reshot (this is the version seen in the final film). (The version done a week earlier, while filmed in CinemaScope, was deemed unsatisfactory. This take still exists and shows Judy in an unattractive brown dress—it is included in the DVD from Warner Home Video.) Twenty-seven takes were shot over these three days, all with Judy singing full blast and being heard over the playback of the recording that she was lip-synching to. Each of these three days found Judy on the set at 10 a.m. On October 27, she finished at 5:50 p.m.; on October 28, she finished at 4:45 p.m.; and on October 29, she finished at 6:15 p.m.

October 30, 1953: *Star* filming. Started: 10 a.m.; finished: 6 p.m. Scenes: Int. Publicity Offices and Libby's Office.

October 31, 1953: *Star* filming. Started: 10 a.m.; finished: 11 a.m. Scenes: Int. Publicity Offices and Libby's Office. Then: "record," from 1:30 p.m.–2 p.m.

November 2, 1953: *Star* filming. Started: 10 a.m.; finished: 5:50 p.m. Scene: Int. Tunnel Under Stage.

November 3, 1953: *Star* filming. Started: 10 a.m.; finished: 5:30 p.m. Scene: Int. Tunnel Under Stage and Int. Stage Dressing Room. Also: wardrobe tests and hair test of blonde wig.

November 4, 1953: *Star* filming. Started: 10 a.m.; finished: 5:05 p.m. Scenes: Ext. Rooming House and Hallway.

November 5, 1953: *Star* filming. Started: 10 a.m.; finished: 6 p.m. Scenes: Int. Proj. Room and Int. Danny's Room.

November 6, 1953: *Star* filming. Started: 10 a.m.; finished: 6:05 p.m. Scenes: Int. Danny's Room and Int. Nile's Proj. Room. Added Closeup.

November 7, 1953: *Star* filming. Started: 10 a.m.; finished: 3:25 p.m. Scenes: Ext. Cashier's Window, Ext. Walkway between bldgs., and Int. Esther's Room. AD reports note: "Company unable to continue shooting Exteriors as scheduled on account of Miss Garland being too exhausted to continue working."

November 9, 1953 through November 12, 1953: Judy was ill and did not work.

November 13, 1953: *Star* filming. Started: 10 a.m.; finished: 6:25 p.m. Scene: Int. Norman's Dressing Room (where James Mason performs his "makeover" on Judy).

November 14, 1953: *Star* filming. Started: 10 a.m.; finished: 5:45 p.m. Scene: Ext. Oleander Arms.

November 16, 1953: *Star* filming. Started: 10 a.m.; finished: 4:50 p.m. Scene: Ext. Rooming House and Roof.

November 17, 1953: *Star* filming. Started: 10 a.m.; finished: 5:30 p.m. Scenes: Ext. Rooming House and Street and Ext. Oleander Arms.

November 18, 1953: *Star* filming. Started: 10 a.m.; finished: 4:45 p.m. Scene: Ext. Oleander Arms.

November 19, 1953 through November 21, 1953: Judy was ill and did not work. (She had gotten sick from the outdoor location work done in cool weather while wearing summer clothes for the scenes at Oleander Arms.)

November 23, 1953: *Star* work. Started: 2 p.m.; finished: 5:30 p.m. Recorded "It's A New World" and "Tour de Force" a.k.a. "Somewhere There's A Someone." (AD notes that "Production 18 days behind schedule," but this was mostly due to the changeover to CinemaScope.)

November 24, 1953: *Star* filming. Started: 10 a.m.; finished: 5 p.m. Scenes: Ext. Makeup Dept. and Ext. Publicity Dept.

November 25, 1953: *Star* filming. Started: 10 a.m.; finished: 11:15 a.m. Scenes: Ext. Oleander Arms, Ext. Studio St. and Auto Gate, and Ext. Makeup Dept.

November 27, 1953: *Star* filming. Started: 10 a.m.; finished: 6:10 p.m. Scene: Int. Oliver Nile's Office—Prerecord dialogue.

November 28, 1953: *Star* filming. Started: 10 a.m.; finished: 5:50 p.m. Scene: Ext. Night Club Terrace and Routine with "Charlie."

November 30, 1953: *Star* filming. Started: 10 a.m.; finished: 5:20 p.m. Scene: Ext. Night Club Terrace and Int. Esther's Room, Rooming House.

December 1, 1953: *Star* filming. Started: 10 a.m.; finished: 5:15 p.m. Scene: Ext. Jail and Int. Sheriff's Office.

December 2, 1953: *Star* filming. Started: 10 a.m.; finished: 6:30 p.m. Scenes: Ext. Jail and Int. Sheriff's Office, and Int. Esther's Room, Oleander Arms.

December 3, 1953: *Star* filming. Started: 10 a.m.; finished: 5:35 p.m. Scene: Int. Television Commercial.

December 4, 1953: *Star* filming. Started: 10 a.m.; finished: 5:15 p.m. Scene: Int. Recording Stage—"Here's What I'm Here For."

December 5, 1953: *Star* filming. Started: 10 a.m.; finished: 5:30 p.m. Scene: Int. Recording Stage—"Here's What I'm Here For."

Judy on the set of *A Star Is Born*, December 8, 1953. (Courtesy of Photofest.)

Judy and costar James Mason between takes for the Academy Awards scene of *A Star Is Born,* filmed December 15–17, 1953. (Courtesy of Photofest.)

December 7, 1953: *Star* work. Prerecord: 11 a.m.–1 p.m.: "It's A New World," and then filming. Started: 1 p.m.; finished: 5:50 p.m. Scene: Int. Makeup Dept. and Int. Television Commercial (puppet show).

December 8, 1953: *Star* filming. Started: 10 a.m.; finished: 5 p.m. Scene: Int. Norman's Car. Also: "Color Test of wardrobe and color lights to be used at Shrine Auditorium."

December 9, 1953: *Star* filming. Started: 10 a.m.; finished: 6 p.m. Scene: Int. Motel Room.

December 10, 1953: *Star* filming. Started: 10 a.m.; finished: 5:10 p.m. Scene: Int. Motel Room.

December 11, 1953 and December 12, 1953: Judy was not on call/needed for *Star* work.

December 14, 1953: *Star* filming. Started: 10 a.m.; finished: 1:45 p.m. Scene: Int. Recording Stage—retakes and added scenes.

December 15, 1953: *Star* filming. Started: 10 a.m.; finished: 6 p.m. Scene: Int. Coconut Grove (Academy Award sequence).

December 16, 1953: *Star* filming. Started: 10 a.m.; finished: 5:40 p.m. Scene: Int. Coconut Grove (Academy Award sequence).

December 17, 1953: *Star* filming. Started: 10 a.m.; finished: 5:50 p.m. Scene: Int. Coconut Grove (Academy Award sequence).

December 18, 1953: *Star* AD reports state: "Held—wardrobe not ready."

December 19, 1953: *Star* filming. Started: 10 a.m.; finished: 4:10 p.m. Scene: Int. Malibu Home.

December 21, 1953 and December 22, 1953: Judy was ill and didn't work.

December 23, 1953: *Star* filming. Started: 10 a.m.; finished: 4:50 p.m. Scene: Int. Norman's Dressing Room—retakes.

December 24 and 26, 1953: Judy was not on call/needed for *Star* work.

December 28, 1953: *Star* work. Started: 11:30 a.m.; finished: 5:10 p.m. Rehearsal.

December 29, 1953: Judy was not on call/needed for *Star* work.

December 30, 1953: *Star* filming. Started: 10 a.m.; finished: 6:30 p.m. Scene: Int. Shrine Auditorium ("Gotta Have Me Go With You" number).

December 31, 1953: *Star* filming. Started: 11 a.m. Finished: 3 p.m. Scene: Int. Shrine Auditorium, Int. Preview Theatre Balcony, and Int. Box. (This included the completion of the "Gotta Have Me Go With You" number, which had shot a total of forty takes over the two days on the stage of the Shrine Auditorium in Los Angeles.)

Judy on the stage of the Shrine Auditorium for *A Star Is Born* filming, including the "Gotta Have Me Go With You" number, December 30, 1953—December 31, 1953; Costar Tommy Noonan can be seen on the left. Judy first worked at the Shrine when she was one of "The Gumm Sisters," and had played there as recently as 1952. (Courtesy of Photofest.)

1954

January 2, 1954: *Star* filming. Started: 10 a.m.; finished: 6:10 p.m. Scene: Int. Shrine Auditorium. ("This is Mrs. Norman Maine").

January 4, 1954: *Star* filming. Started: 10 a.m.; finished: 2:45 p.m. Scene: Int. Shrine Auditorium.

January 5, 1954: *Star* filming. Started: 10 a.m.; finished: 5:45 p.m. Scene: Int. Shrine Auditorium.

January 6, 1954 and January 7, 1954: Judy was not on call/needed for *Star* work.

January 8, 1954: *Star* work. Started: 4:15 p.m.; finished: 5:15 p.m. Wardrobe test.

January 9, 1954: *Star* filming. Started: 2:30 p.m.; finished: 5:25 p.m. Scene: Int. Malibu Home.

January 11, 1954: *Star* filming. Started: 5:30 p.m.; finished: 12:35 a.m. Scene: Ext. Theatre Lobby and St. (the "Sneak Preview," of Esther's first movie).

January 12, 1954: *Star* filming. Started: 2 p.m.; finished: 5:30 p.m. Scene: Int. Malibu Home.

January 13, 1954: *Star* filming. Started: 10 a.m.; finished: 5:50 p.m. Scene: Int. Malibu Home—Party Sequence. (The scene had been delayed from December 1953, when Judy was not happy with her gown for this scene: it's hard to imagine what the unflattering, form-fitting orange-colored dress seen in the movie was supposed to *replace*!)

January 14, 1954: *Star* filming. Started: 10 a.m.; finished: 5:50 p.m. Scene: Int. Night Court ("I'll be responsible for him").

January 15, 1954: *Star* filming. Started: 10 a.m.; finished: 4:10 p.m. Scene: Int. Night Court.

January 16, 1954: Judy was ill and did not work.

January 18, 1954: *Star* filming. Started: 10 a.m.; finished: 6:35 p.m. Scene: Int. Malibu Home.

January 19, 1954: *Star* filming. Started: 10 a.m.; finished: 5 p.m. Scene: Ext. Church.

January 20, 1954: *Star* filming. Started: 10 a.m.; finished: 7:10 p.m. Scene: Int. Malibu Home.

January 21, 1954: Judy was ill and did not work.

January 22, 1954: *Star* filming. Started: 10 a.m.; finished: 6:15 p.m. Scene: Int. Malibu Home.

January 23, 1954: *Star* filming. Started: 1:00 p.m.; finished: 6:10 p.m. Scenes: Ext. and Int. Malibu Home.

January 25, 1954: *Star* filming. Started: 11 a.m.; finished: 6:05 p.m. Scene: Int. Tunnel Under Stage.

January 26, 1954: *Star* filming. Started: 10 a.m.; finished: 5:55 p.m. Scenes: Int. Malibu Home, Ext. Malibu Home (retake), and Int. Courtroom (added close-up).

January 27, 1954: *Star* filming. Started: 2 p.m.; finished: 10 p.m. Scenes: Int. Sound Stage, Int. Nile's Car, and Ext. Jail.

January 28, 1954: *Star* work. Started: 11 a.m.; finished: 6:20 p.m. "Wild" wardrobe, hair and makeup tests for "Lose That Long Face" number; sound and photo tests; and rehearse "Tour De Force" (a.k.a. "Somewhere There's A Someone").

January 29, 1954: Judy was ill and did not work.

January 30, 1954: *Star* filming. Started: 10 a.m.; finished: 5:55 p.m. Scene: Int. dressing room.

February 1, 1954: *Star* filming. Started: 10 a.m.; finished: 5 p.m. Scene: Int. Malibu Home.

February 2, 1954: Judy was not on call/not needed for *Star* work.

February 3, 1954: *Star* filming. Started: 10 a.m.; finished: 3:30 p.m. Scene: Ext. Beach House. (Location shoot in Laguna, California, for a scene cut after the previews but before the premiere—the scene where Judy/Esther and James/Norman go to look at the beachfront property where their new home was going to be built. They have a picnic on the beach, where Judy sings a reprise of "It's A New World." This footage is not known to still exist.)

February 4, 1954: *Star* filming. Started: 11 a.m.; finished: 7 p.m. Scene: Int. Malibu Home (Tour De Force, a.k.a. "Somewhere There's A Someone"). This number had been rehearsed in the evenings during the month of January with Roger Edens—Judy's MGM musical mentor—devising much of the material. From production materials: "Camera and set ready at 10 a.m.; Judy Garland worked from 11:00 a.m. to 7:00 p.m. First shot (done) at 2:15. Six takes of start of number bars 1–16. Adjust lights for added business and light changes. Took bars 17–36 from 4:25 to 5:30 (Five takes). Shot bars 37–52 from 6:20 to 7:00 (Five takes.)" (Cukor had used a new technique for him—and perhaps for the movie industry—when he shot this number more like television, having two cameras running/filming at the exact same time instead of just one that would be moved to a new position after each angle was shot.)

February 5, 1954: *Star* filming. Started: 10 a.m.; finished: 6:15 p.m. Scene: Int. Malibu Home (Tour De Force, a.k.a. "Somewhere There's A Someone").

February 6, 1954: Judy was ill and did not work.

February 8, 1954: *Star* filming. Started: 10 a.m.; finished: 5:45 p.m. Scene: Int. Malibu House (Tour De Force, a.k.a. "Somewhere There's A Someone").

February 9, 1954: *Star* filming. Started: 10 a.m.; finished: 5:15 p.m. Scene: Int. Malibu Home (Tour De Force.)

February 10, 1954: *Star* AD reports note: "Miss Garland reported to stage at 10:10 a.m.—was ill and could not work and left stage at 12:10 p.m."

February 11, 1954: *Star* filming. Started: 10 a.m.; finished: 6:05 p.m. Scene: Int. Malibu Home.

February 12, 1954: *Star* filming. Started: 10 a.m.; finished: 6 p.m. Scene: Int. Malibu Home.

James Mason watches Judy film her "Big Fat Close-Up" in the "Somewhere There's A Someone" number for *A Star Is Born*, February 1954. This pose was recreated by Warner Brothers artists for the movie poster. (Courtesy of Photofest.)

February 13, 1954 through February 17, 1954: Judy was not on call/not needed for *Star* work.

February 18, 1954: *Star* filming. Started: 10 a.m.; finished: 5:25 p.m. Scenes: Added scenes: Int. Coconut Grove (Academy Award seq.). Retakes: Nightclub Terrace. Also: Postrecord Dialogue.

February 19, 1954: *Star* filming. Started: 10 a.m.; finished: 6:05 p.m. Scenes: Retakes: Int. Down Beat Club ("The Man That Got Away"). AD reports note: "6:05 p.m.: Miss Garland too tired to work; Production 41 days behind schedule."

February 20, 1954: *Star* filming. Started: 10 a.m.; finished: 6:15 p.m. Scenes: Int. Down Beat Club and Ext. Parking Lot.

February 22, 1954: Judy was ill and did not work.

February 23, 1954: *Star* AD reports note: "Miss Garland reported at studio at 10:05 a.m.: too ill to work, left lot at 12:15 p.m. The Company did not shoot; Production 43 Days Behind schedule."

February 24, 1954: *Star* filming. Started: 10 a.m.; finished: 5:40 p.m. Scene: Norman's Car.

February 25, 1954: *Star* filming. Started: 10 a.m.; finished: 6:15 p.m. Scenes: Retakes: Ext. Oleander Arms and Int. Esther's Room.

February 26, 1954: Judy was ill and did not work.

February 27, 1954: *Star* filming. Started: 10 a.m.; finished: 4:20 p.m. Scenes: Retakes: Int. Down Beat Club.

March 1, 1954: *Star* filming. Started: 1:40 p.m.; finished: 4:50 p.m. Prerecorded ("Lose That Long Face").

March 2, 1954: *Star* filming. Started: 11:20 a.m.; finished: 12:30 p.m. Rehearsed "Long Face."

March 3, 1954: *Star* AD reports include note: "Miss Garland ill—Unable to report today for rehearsal—Gloria Se Werd (Dance-in) going to Miss Garland's home to rehearse—8:00 p.m. to 10:30 p.m."

March 4, 1954: *Star* work. Started: 2:20 p.m.; finished: 4:00 p.m. Rehearsed "Long Face."

March 5, 1954: *Star* AD reports note: "Taking off to rest."

March 8, 1954: *Star* AD reports note: "Taking off to rest."

March 9, 1954: *Star* work. Started: 2 p.m.; finished: 5:15 p.m. Rehearsed "Long Face."

March 10, 1954: *Star* filming. Started: 10 a.m.; finished: 6 p.m. Shooting "Long Face."

March 11, 1954: *Star* filming. Started: 10 a.m.; finished: 6 p.m. Shooting "Long Face."

March 12, 1954: Judy was ill and did not work.

March 13, 1954: *Star* filming. Started: 11:20 a.m.; finished: 6 p.m. Shooting "Long Face."

March 15, 1954: *Star* filming. Started: 10 a.m.; finished: 5:45 p.m. Shooting "Long Face."

March 16, 1954: *Star* work. Started: 10:30; finished: 11:30 a.m. AD reports note: "Garland rehearsed on set 10:30 to 11:30 a.m.; She then went to her dressing room, saying she would rest for a while and have lunch and she would be made up and ready to shoot at 1:30 p.m. At 12:50 p.m. Garland drove off the lot. Mr. Luft said Miss Garland had gone to the doctor. At 2:30 p.m. Mr. Luft phoned that the doctor reported Garland could not work today, but that she should be able to work tomorrow. Mr. Luft added that the shooting call could be confirmed at 7:45 a.m. tomorrow."

March 17, 1954: Judy was ill and did not work.

March 25, 1954: A rough cut of *A Star Is Born* was screened for Judy et al. at Warner Brothers and was deemed a success.

Late March to early April 1954: Judy took a two-week vacation, for some much-needed rest; she also, at this time, quit taking her prescribed medications "cold turkey."

April 10, 1954: Judy returned to work on *A Star Is Born,* for "Lose That Long Face" rehearsals.

April 13, 1954: *Star* filming. Started: 4 p.m. Finished: 8:35 p.m. Retakes for scenes shot earlier for *A Star Is Born.* First up: Stan's Drive-In, at Sunset and Cahuenga, for Judy/Esther (the "Nut-Burger" scene).

April 14, 1954: *Star* filming. Started: 1 p.m.; finished: 5:50 p.m. Scenes: Added scenes Int. Esther's Room, and retakes Norman's Car.

April 15, 1954: *Star* filming. Started: 4:50 p.m.; finished: 5:50 p.m. AD reports note: "Miss Garland called for 10 a.m.—reported on set 4:50 p.m." Scene: Retake Ext. Pullman Car.

April 16, 1954: *Star* work. Started: 1:45 p.m.; finished: 2:45 p.m. Postrecord dialogue.

April 19, 1954 through April 23, 1954: Judy was ill and could not make postrecordings.

April 26, 1954: *Star* work. Started: 3:30 p.m.; finished: 5:10 p.m. Postrecord dialogue.

Late April 1954: Jack Warner, the head of Warner Brothers, gave the approval for the twelve-minute, $250,000 production number, "Born In A Trunk," for *A Star Is Born.*

May 3, 1954: *Star* work. Started: 2 p.m.; finished: 5 p.m. Rehearsed retakes of "Long Face."

May 4, 1954: *Star* work. Started: 2 p.m.; finished: 4:20 p.m. Dress rehearsal for retakes of "Long Face."

May 5, 1954: *Star* filming. Started: 10 a.m.; finished: 5:30 p.m. Shooting retakes of "Long Face." AD reports note: "Miss Garland very tired, shot called off, company dismissed at 5:35 p.m."

May 6, 1954: *Star* filming. Started: 10 a.m.; finished: 5:55 p.m. Shooting retakes of "Long Face."

May 1954: *Star* rehearsals for the "Born In A Trunk" sequence.

May 17, 1954: A screening of the incomplete *A Star Is Born* was held at Warner Brothers for some of the industry producers and directors who were working on the Warners lot at the time.

May 28, 1954: Judy began recording the songs and narration for the "Born In A Trunk" number.

June 7, 1954: Rehearsals for the "Born In A Trunk" number "officially" began.

June 10, 1954: Judy's thirty-second birthday.

June 14, 1954: *Star* work. Started: 2:15 p.m.; finished: 5:00 p.m. Prerecorded "Swanee" and "Black Bottom."

June 15, 1954: *Star* work. Started: 2 p.m.; finished: 4:45 p.m. Prerecorded "I'll Get By" and "You Took Advantage Of Me," then, more work. Started: 4:45 p.m.; finished: 5:30 p.m. Rehearsals for "Born In A Trunk."

June 16, 1954: *Star* work. Started: 2:25 p.m.; finished: 4:45 p.m. Prerecorded "When My Sugar Walks Down The Street" and "Peanut Vendor."

June 17, 1954: *Star* work. Started: 2:20 p.m.; finished: 5 p.m. Prerecorded (numbers recorded were not listed).

June 18, 1954: *Star* work. Started: 3:15 p.m.; finished: 4:30 p.m. Prerecorded narration for "Born In A Trunk."

June 19, 1954: Judy was not on call/not needed for *Star* work.

June 21, 1954: *Star* work. Started: 3:20 p.m.; finished: 5:15 p.m. Prerecorded (numbers recorded were not listed).

June 22, 1954: Judy was ill and did not work.

June 23, 1954: *Star* work. Wardrobe fitting at Western Costume.

June 24, 1954: *Star* work. Started: 2:30 p.m.; finished: 5:30 p.m. Rehearsed "Born In A Trunk."

June 25, 1954: *Star* work. Time Started: 2:00 p.m.; finished: 5:30 p.m. Rehearsed "Born In A Trunk."

June 26, 1954: Judy was not on call/not needed for *Star* work.

June 28, 1954: *Star* work. Wardrobe fitting at Western Costume.

June 29, 1954: *Star* work. Started: 12 p.m.; finished: 6:10 p.m. Dress rehearse and light set for "Swanee."

June 30, 1954: *Star* filming. Started: 8:10 a.m.; finished: 6 p.m. Shooting "Swanee."

July 1, 1954: *Star* filming. Started: 8 a.m.; finished: 5:25 p.m. Shooting "Swanee."

July 2, 1954: *Star* filming. Started: 9 a.m.; finished: 5 p.m. Scenes: Int. Stage and Backstage: "Born In A Trunk" and "Swanee."

July 3, 1954: *Star* filming. Started: 11:45 a.m.; finished: 4:15 p.m. Scenes: Int. Stage and Backstage: "Born In A Trunk" and "Swanee." AD reports note: "Garland resting 3:20–3:55 p.m.; Garland left stage—too tired to continue at 3:55 p.m."

July 6, 1954: *Star* filming. Started: 11:10 a.m.; finished: 5:45 p.m. Scenes: "Born In A Trunk" and "Swanee."

July 7, 1954: Judy was not on call/not needed for *Star* work.

July 8, 1954: *Star* filming. Started: 11 a.m.; finished: 5:45 p.m. Scene: "Born In A Trunk."

July 9, 1954: *Star* filming. Started: 12 p.m.; finished: 6:15 p.m. Scene: "Born In A Trunk."

July 10, 1954: *Star* filming. Started: 11 a.m.; finished: 4 p.m. Scene: "Born In A Trunk."

July 12, 1954: *Star* filming. Started: 5 p.m.; finished: 4:10 a.m. Scenes: Int. Stage and Backstage—"Born In A Trunk"—"Black Bottom." (Filming was switched to night, to better suit Judy's body-clock. Judy was still spending two hours a day, during the day, at Western Costume in Hollywood for fittings, since her new Irene Sharaff costumes were being made there.)

July 13, 1954: *Star* filming. Started: 6 p.m.; finished: 2 a.m. Scene: Ext. Stage Door and Sign (Rehearsal sequence), and Int. Stage and Backstage ("Born In A trunk"—"Black Bottom").

July 14, 1954: Judy was ill and did not work on *Star*.

July 15, 1954: *Star* work. Started: 4:40 p.m.; finished: 5:45 p.m. Prerecorded "Melancholy Baby."

July 16, 1954: *Star* filming. Started: 5 p.m.; finished: 1:40 a.m. Scene: "Born In A Trunk."

July 17, 1954: *Star* filming. Started: 7:50 p.m.; finished: 1:30 a.m. Scene: "Melancholy Baby" (Int. Third Nightclub).

July 19, 1954: *Star* filming. Started: 5 p.m.; finished: 12:55 a.m. Scene: Int. Third Nightclub—"Melancholy Baby."

July 20, 1954: Judy was not on call/not needed for *Star* work.

July 21, 1954: *Star* filming. Started: 5 p.m.; finished: 1:55 a.m. Scenes: Int. Elevator, Int. Hallway, and Int. First Agent's Office.

July 22, 1954: *Star* filming. Started: 5:30 p.m.; finished: 11:40 p.m. Scenes: Second and Third Agents' Offices.

July 23, 1954: Judy was ill and did not work.

July 24, 1954: *Star* work. Started: 4 p.m.; finished: 5:45 p.m. Rehearsal.

July 26, 1954: *Star* work. Rehearse 4:00 p.m.–5:00 p.m.; record: 5:00 p.m.–5:25 p.m. Rehearse: 5:25 p.m.–6:00 p.m.—"Born In A Trunk", Olio "Sugar" item, and "I'll Get By."

July 27, 1954: *Star* filming. Started: 7 p.m.; finished: 1:20 a.m. Scenes: Int. Backstage and Int. Stage.

July 28, 1954: *Star* filming. Started: 7 p.m.; finished: 2:45 a.m. Scenes: Int. Stage Olio; retake Second Nightclub. The last scenes shot were the retakes of the "Peanut Vendor" song, which was completed in five takes, ending the filming of *A Star Is Born* in the early morning hours of Thursday, July 29, 1954. The cast and crew celebrated with an onset "wrap party." Judy and Sid Luft had another reason to be celebrating: Judy was about three to four weeks pregnant, and the Lufts had just found out.

August 2, 1954: The first official "preview" of *A Star Is Born* was held in Huntington Park, California (a suburb of Los Angeles). The overwhelming response to the film was of people shouting to Judy, "Don't cut a single minute of it" (the rough cut of the film ran 196 minutes: 3 hours and 16 minutes).

August 3, 1954: The second "preview" of *A Star Is Born* was held at the Encino Theater on Ventura Blvd. Again the response was, in the words of Jack Warner in a telegram to Moss Hart, who wrote the screenplay, "tremendous."

Mid August 1954: Judy, Sid Luft, and Jack Warner had a three-week vacation in Europe.

September 4, 1954: Judy and Sid returned to New York from Europe, and left for Los Angeles immediately.

September 24, 1954: (Radio) *Bing Crosby 20th Anniversary Tribute*, NBC (90 minutes). On this all-star special, Judy sang "Swinging On A Star." (This was Judy's last "real" radio program; her few appearances that were to follow on this fading medium for new entertainment were interviews or performances that had been lifted from various recordings. This program is known to exist.)

September 29, 1954: The World Premiere of *A Star Is Born* was held at the Pantages Theater in Hollywood, California. This all-star event was telecast "live" as a half-hour special on NBC-TV. (This show has been available on videocassette from various small video companies, including Reel Images/Video Yesteryear. Its first "legitimate" release was in June 1997 from Sid Luft, and was on the videocassette *Judy Garland's Hollywood* released on the LaserLight/Delta Music Label. The special is also on the recent VHS and DVD releases of *A Star Is Born* from Warner Home Video, although the quality is better on the LaserLight VHS. NBC-TV's *The Tonight Show* devoted a segment of its show that night, from 11:45 p.m. to 11:59 p.m., to the premiere; Judy and Sid Luft were seen speaking with Jack Carson.) There was a party after the premiere at the Coconut Grove, and footage of this is on the recent DVD and VHS editions of the movie from Warner Home Video.

October 10, 1954: Ed Sullivan showed clips from *A Star Is Born* on his television show to promote the movie.

October 11, 1954: The New York premiere of *A Star Is Born* was another "event," and was again telecast as a "live" special over NBC-TV. At the same time, NBC Radio covered the premiere during the show *Best of All*, a sixty-minute show, during which Jinx Falkenburg interviewed Judy at the premiere. (The radio program is believed to still exist in private collections.) The premiere was actually held at two theaters: the Victoria and the Capitol. George Jessell was an emcee again (as he'd been in LA), and there was a dinner held afterwards at the Waldorf.

October 14, 1954: Contract drafted this date, signed by Judy, agreeing to pay her $1,000 plus five cents royalty for each copy sold of *The Judy Garland Album* songbook (published by New World Music and renamed *The Gershwin Songbook*), for use of her photo on the cover.

Mid October 1954: Judy attended the premieres of *A Star Is Born* in Chicago, staying at the Ambassador East Hotel.

A Star Is Born had one of the longest production periods in film history, and was also, at 196 minutes—3 hours and 16 minutes—the longest film since *Gone with the Wind*. Before its premiere, fifteen minutes were cut, including: Esther washing her hair at the boarding house; Norman Maine returning to the Shrine Auditorium to find the name of the orchestra with which Esther had been singing; Norman shooting a "pirate" movie; Esther and Norman on the beach planning their Malibu home; and the death of the mother—including the song "When My Sugar Walks Down The Street"—both from the "Born In A Trunk" sequence. The 181 minute version—3 hours and 1 minute—played until mid October 1954, when Harry Warner ordered cuts made so that the film could have more showings per day, and thus make more money. (The movie should have been presented in a "road-show" manner, with an intermission. This was the one area that Warner Brothers did not invest in wisely.) Therefore, twenty-seven minutes were cut from the film: Esther saying goodbye to the band; Maine being taken to location; Esther sitting in bungalow court and washing hair; Esther lying by the swimming pool; Maine on boat for location filming; Oliver Niles talking with Maine's director and Libby about Maine being sick; Esther at rooming house talking on phone about singing job; Esther singing Calypso commercial for shampoo outfit; Esther at burger drive-in talking in the phone booth with Danny and the scene with customer asking what's on the menu; Maine at Oleander Arms looking for Esther; Maine and Lucy Marlow hearing Esther's television commercial; Maine finding Esther on the roof of the rooming house; Esther and Maine driving to preview of Esther's picture; the recording session and song "Here's What I'm Here For," when Maine proposes to Esther; and "Lose That Long Face" song and reprise. All of these scenes, most in their entirety, were added back to the film—many using stills and alternate and/or stock footages—in its 1983 reconstruction, which premiered at Radio City Music Hall in New York City on July 7, 1983. (Except for a few moments of the scene were Maine talks with Esther after finding her on the roof of the rooming house—this scene would be shortened in the 1983 reconstruction.) Due to the adverse publicity from the cutting of the film, attendance started falling off about mid November 1954. *A Star Is Born* grossed $700,000 in its first week alone, at 17 theaters; as the shortened version began getting inferior reviews and press, business dropped off. *A Star Is Born* cost $5,019,770 before prints and advertising, etc., making it the second most expensive film ever made in Hollywood up to that time (1946's *Duel in the Sun* had cost about $205,000 more). *A Star Is Born* would gross $4,355,968 domestically, and another $1,556,000 overseas, for a total of $5,911,968 in its first run, and would be listed as the fourteenth highest grossing film of the year on *Variety's* list. The film would also be reissued every five years, in 1959, 1964, and in 1969, just after Judy Garland's passing. The 1983 reconstructed version would add to the film's total gross, along with *Star* sales in video, which began with the standard version's release on VHS in 1981. (The reconstructed version was released in 1984 and again in 1999 in a splendid new remastered version on VHS, laser disc, and then DVD, from Warner Home Video.) The film would also be sold to NBC-TV, where it would have its television premiere in November 1961. Regardless of its financial success, the film would become one of the best-loved films of all time, and, I feel, the finest, most artistically rich and lavish movie ever made. Read some of the critic's reviews and you'll see that many people felt the same:

> *Life Magazine*, 9–13–54: "The year's most worrisome movie has turned out to be one of its best. In it, one time teenage star Judy Garland, now thirty-two and out of movies for four years, not only makes a film comeback almost without precedent, but puts herself right in line for an oscar. . . . A brilliantly staged, scored, and photographed film . . . principal credit for the success of *A Star Is Born* goes to [the] imaginative, tireless, talented Judy."

> *The New York Times*, 10–12–54: "A remarkable range of entertainment is developed upon the screen. George Cukor gets performances from Miss Garland and Mr. Mason that make the heart flutter and bleed. . . . It is something to see, this *A Star Is Born*."

> *Time Magazine*, 10–25–54: "*Star* is a massive effort. Judy Garland gives what is just about the greatest one-woman show in modern movie history. She has never sung better: Her big, dark voice sobs, sighs, sulks, and socks them out like a cross between Tara's Harp and the late Bessie Smith. . . . Everybody's little sister, it would seem, has grown out of her braids and into a tiara. An expert vaudeville performance was to be expected from Judy; to find her a dramatic actress, as well, is the real surprise—although it should not be. A stunning comeback."

> *Newsweek*, 11–1–54: "*A Star Is Born* is best classified as a thrillingly personal triumph for Miss Garland . . . in more ways than one, the picture is hers."

The original theatrical poster—with extra copy at the top—for *A Star Is Born* (1954). (Courtesy of the Everett Collection.)

The Sunday Times (*London*, Dilys Powell): "There has been a great deal of talk about Judy Garland's comeback. This prompts me to say that, so far as I am concerned, Miss Garland never went away. The other day we had the chance of seeing her in an early piece, *Meet Me in St. Louis*. Ravishing there, in the new film she displays an extraordinary maturing of her talents. It is not only that her singing has a new strength and edge; nobody can do better with a song such as her 'The Man That Got Away;' and in a satire on what is known as a production number she shows a gift for parody that is brilliant. As an actress she has come a long way. Pathos she has always had; but today the pathos has deepened, and her acting has a nervous tension which, when I saw the film, held the audience silent and tear-stained."

Variety: "*A Star Is Born* is a socko candidate for anyone's must see list, scoring on all counts as fine entertainment. It is among the top musicals that have come from the Hollywood Studios. It is a big picture for big selling, and big box office should be the rule rather than the exception. The tremendous outlay of time and money is fully justified. It is to the great credit of Jack Warner that he kept his mind and purse strings open and thus kept the project going. For both Miss Garland and Warner, the racking months that went into the making of the film, will soon be forgotten in the joy of an artistic and box office smash."

Variety's Editor In Chief, Abel Green: "Boffola box office, period. It will not only mop up as a commercial entry (but) set a number of artistic standards. Fort Knox, move over."

Saturday Review of Literature: "It is a bountiful, beautiful film. . . . Miss Garland has the true star quality, that 'extra plus' that adds an indescribable poignancy and charm to everything she does. There is an ease and grace to her every movement, an originality and intensity in her gestures that go far beyond the merely skillful authority of the experienced actress. Her tremulous mouth, her voice always on the verge of tears, her large, brimming eyes can evoke any emotion at will. When she sings, it is with a felicity of phrasing, an inner awareness of both the rhythm and the meaning of her songs, that strikes straight to the heart."

Motion Picture: "1954's musical answer to *Gone with the Wind*. . . . There's no one in show business quite like Judy Garland. Her acting adds dimension to an already unbeatable story."

Musical Films (Douglas MacVay): "I consider it to be not only the greatest musical picture I have ever seen, but *the* greatest picture of any kind *I have ever seen*. . . . Above all, this film is a tragic masterpiece—especially due to the performances of James Mason and supremely, Judy Garland. She surpasses the lyric perfection of her playing in *Meet Me in St. Louis* and *The Pirate*, through an added, mature power of cathartic stature. Her combined singing and acting amount to the finest characterization I have ever encountered in the cinema; it is ultimately her picture, her monument, and it lights up the year 1954 like a colossal, flaming beacon."

Consumer Guide: "Judy's voice is certainly one of the enduring monuments of this century!"

The Times: "A monument that overshadows contemporary cinema!"

Films in Review: "As film entertainment, it has everything. *Star* is an almost perfect example of what Hollywood can do when a big budget is intelligently spent on a script everyone believes in [and] also an almost perfect example of the kind of entertainment for which Hollywood is unrivaled anywhere in the world. Miss Garland sings, dances, mimes, and acts almost every kind of role. What picture will ever again give her such scope?"

Judy spent the rest of 1954—from mid October through the end of the year—resting and waiting for the birth of her child, due in April 1955.

December 22, 1954: Contract signed by Judy drawn on this date, for a one-year deal with MCA for agency representation. (A year later, Judy would sign a five year deal with them.)

January 3, 1955: (Radio) *March of Dimes*, Los Angeles (no other information available at this time).

March 8, 1955: (television) *The Red Skelton Show*, CBS-TV, Hollywood, California. Judy was presented with *Look* magazine's Best Actress Award (for *A Star Is Born*) on this "live" broadcast. (Judy stood behind a podium to conceal her pregnancy while she delivered her acceptance speech. Judy also was voted Best Actress in *Film Daily's* poll and by *Box Office Publication*. She also won the Golden Globe Award. A film print of this appearance exists in private collections, and has also been released on a DVD collection of Red Skelton shows.)

March 28, 1955, 11 p.m.: Judy began showing signs of premature labor, and was rushed to Cedars of Lebanon Hospital.

March 29, 1955, 2:16 a.m.: Judy's third and last child—and only son—Joseph Wiley Luft, was born at Cedars of Lebanon Hospital, weighing 5 pounds, 8 ounces.

March 30, 1955: Judy was to be televised during the Academy Awards broadcast on NBC, as she was expected to win the Best Actress Award. After an entire television camera crew took over her hospital room to achieve the broadcast (which would make for one of her funniest stories during an episode of her television series in 1963), Judy was never seen, as the award went to Grace Kelly for *The Country Girl*. *A Star Is Born* was nominated for a total of six Academy Awards: Judy for Best Actress, James Mason for Best Actor, "The Man That Got Away" for Best Song, Best Score, Best Costume Design, and Best Art Direction. *Star* would not win any awards from the Academy. As Groucho Marx would wire Judy in an much-quoted telegram, her not getting the Oscar was "the biggest robbery since Brinx." The loss of the Oscar didn't stop film offers from coming. These offers included: *Carousel*, *South Pacific*, *The Three Faces of Eve*, *The Helen Morgan Story*; musicals of *Alice Adams*, *Saratoga Trunk*, *All About Eve*; and film biographies of Sophie Tucker, Laurette Taylor, Gertrude Lawrence, and Fanny Brice.

April 19, 1955: A "Seven City Tour" of *The Judy Garland Show* was announced by Sid Luft to begin on July 5, and was planned to be followed by a nationwide tour in the fall—an additional thirteen cities, to include stops at the Shrine Auditorium in Los Angeles and Orchestra Hall in Chicago. This tour was to be followed by a two-month engagement at the Winter Garden Theater in New York. (Jules Stein of MCA was now handling her live performances; Charles Feldman was still representing her for films.)

June 1955: Judy began rehearsals for the three-hour stage show/tour. (Melba Wedge was Judy's wardrobe mistress during this tour, and for an upcoming television special. June 10, 1955, Judy turned thirty-three.)

July 5, 1955: (Performance) *The Judy Garland Show*; San Diego (theater unknown). Judy's solos included: "Carolina In The Morning"; "While We're Young"; "Judy's 'Olio' of "You Made Me Love You"/"For Me And My Gal"/"The Boy Next Door"/"The Trolley Song"; "A Pretty Girl Milking Her Cow"; "The Man That Got Away"; "Rock-A-Bye Your Baby"; "A Couple Of Swells"; "Liza" and "Over The Rainbow." (Judy's guest stars on the tour included Frank Fontaine, The Hi-Lo's, The Jerry Gray Orchestra, and The Wiere Brothers—who joined Judy in the "Running Wild" first-act finale.) The July 13, 1955, review in *Variety* called Judy "dazzling," and said, "She has added a magnetic maturity to the old gamin quality."

July 9, 1955: (Performance) *The Judy Garland Show*, the Municipal Auditorium, Long Beach, California. The proceeds from this show went to the Exceptional Children's Foundation, to benefit retarded children. Judy's songs: "Let's Have A Party"; "The Man That Got Away"; "Carolina In The Morning"; "While We're Young"; "A Pretty Girl Milking Her Cow"; "Judy's 'Olio'"; "Zing! Went The Strings Of My Heart"; "Rock-A-Bye Your Baby"; "After You've Gone"; "A Couple Of Swells"; "Over The Rainbow"; "Liza"; and "Swanee." Frank Sinatra, Sammy Davis, Jr., Humphrey Bogart, and other celebrities attended the show and came on stage at the end. (A recording of this performance exists.)

After this date, the rest of the tour's stops—Eugene, Oregon; Portland, Oregon; Seattle, Washington; Vancouver, British Columbia; and Spokane, Washington—were all canceled, because Judy signed a contract with CBS-TV to make her "official" television debut, via her first special.

Mid July 1955: Judy began putting together, and then rehearsing, her special at CBS-TV in Hollywood.

August 1955: Judy signed a five-year recording contract with Capitol Records, where she would make her finest recordings. (She signed another long-term contract in the summer of 1960; she stayed with the label for ten years, until the spring of 1966.)

August 25, 1955: (Record) Judy's first recording session for Capitol Records at their Hollywood, California studios. She recorded "Pretty Girl Milking Her Cow," then "Rock-A-Bye Your Baby," "Over The Rainbow", and "After You've Gone," for her first "official" studio "album" (twelve-inch LP), *Miss Show Business*.

August 29, 1955: (Record) Judy recorded "Carolina In The Morning"; a medley of "You Made Me Love You"/"For Me And My Gal"/"The Boy Next Door"/"The Trolley Song"; "Judy At The Palace" medley; and "While We're Young" for the *Miss Show Business* LP; Capitol Records, Hollywood, California.

August 30, 1955: (Record) Judy recorded "On The Atchison, Topeka, And The Santa Fe" (this song was cut from the album before release, and the recording, to date, has not been found, and is not known to exist in any form) and "Danny Boy" for the *Miss Show Business* LP; Capitol Records, Hollywood, California.

September 1, 1955: (Record) Judy recorded "Happiness Is A Thing Called Joe" for the *Miss Show Business* LP; Capitol Records, Hollywood, California.

September 1, 1955 and September 2, 1955: Judy recorded "Danny Boy," finishing the *Miss Show Business* LP for Capitol Records. The album would be released on September 26, 1955, two days after Judy's television special for CBS aired; The album received rave reviews and spent seven weeks on the Top 40 List, peaking at number five on the charts. (It would be reissued on CD on June 28, 1989, though it would be out-of-print by the early 1990s and reissued on the *Miss Show Business/Judy* two-fer CD from Collectables Records in Spring 2002.) Judy's work was praised highly as in this review:

> *Variety*, October: "Even if this album weren't tied in with the recent Judy Garland CBS-TV special, it would be a socko item. Thrush is in top voice on this set, and shows a maturity and song selling savvy that makes her one of the standout belters in the business today. Capitol has taken a lot for granted with that *Miss Show Business* tag, but after hearing her belt those medleys of standards, you can't help but go along with it."

September 1955: Judy continued rehearsals for her television special.

September 24, 1955: (Television) Judy's first television special, *The Ford Star Jubilee,* (Premiere broadcast) CBS-TV, 90 minutes (9:30 p.m. to 11:00 p.m., Eastern Standard Time. Since the show came from Los Angeles, it was actually done from 6:30 p.m. to 8:00 p.m. Los Angeles time). Sponsored by Ford Motor Co, and broadcast "live" in color on the East Coast (the West Coast saw Kinescope) from CBS Studios, Hollywood, California. Judy's songs included: "You Made Me Love You" (Opener); "Swanee" (the audio was prerecorded); "Judy at the Palace Medley"; "It's de-Loveley"; "Get Happy" (the audio was prerecorded); "While We're Young"; "Judy's Olio Medley" ("Embraceable You"/"For Me and My Gal" (audio prerecorded)/"The Boy Next Door" (audio prerecorded)/"The Trolley Song" (audio prerecorded); "Rock-A-Bye Your Baby"; "A Couple Of Swells"; and "Over The Rainbow." ("The Man That Got Away" was cut from the rundown before airtime.) Judy won her time slot, drawing more people than any other special—40 million total—easily justifying the whopping $300,000 cost of the show; Judy had been paid $100,000 for the special. This was also one of the first specials to have what amounted to a "soundtrack album," since most of the songs on the Capitol *Miss Show Business* LP—released two days after the special aired—were the ones Judy had sung on television. (A black and white kinescope film print exists of Judy's segments and is available on videocassette released in 1997 by Bridgestone Multimedia, a company based in Chandler, Arizona.)

> *Variety* said: "When she was on camera, and particularly in the closing 30 minutes when it was her show, that old black magic and magnetism came through in all its treasured nuances. Nothing else mattered when she was on and her vibrant personality took hold of things. It didn't need color, nor for that matter, any production furbelows. Just the chance to go to work. First, atop a piano, in a sentimental mood, with 'While We're Young,' then into a whole medley of standards, and an unforgettable version of 'Rock-A-Bye Your Baby.'"

Judy's first television special earned Emmy Award nominations for Best Variety series and Best Female Singer (although *The Ed Sullivan Show* and Dinah Shore would win each award respectively).

Also on September 24, 1955: Judy's first fan club—outside of any that had been run for her by MGM—was started on this date by Al Poland, a young boy living in Indianapolis, Indiana. He finally placed a phone call to Judy at her home (with the help of several long distance operators) on December 31, 1955, and Judy's warm response was "a fan club for me?!" Within a few months, he'd begun printing the *Garland Gazette* fan journals, and his membership was quickly growing. When school demands created a time problem for him, he turned the running of the club over to its new president, Pat McMath, of Richmond, Indiana, in October 1956. McMath had, ironically, actually tried to start a fan club for Judy around 1949, but was politely turned down by Judy's manager Carlton Alsop, since he felt Judy's hold on the public was such that a club wasn't needed. McMath continued to have Judy's full blessing and cooperation (as Poland had), and her official fan club grew to a peak of about 500 due-paying members by the early to mid 1960s. The *Gazette* was often informative and enjoyable. However, Judy had not been too pleased with the way some of the fans had been abusing privileges, and, in the spring of 1963, she asked that the club be disbanded. McMath continued the club until the spring of 1966, and then, astoundingly, began a club and journal for Judy's current, but estranged, husband, Mark Herron (although this didn't last long). There were a few other fan journals running during the mid to

Judy and her third husband, Sid Luft (Michael Sidney Luft), on the set of her first television special, *Ford Star Jubilee*, September 1955. (Courtesy of Photofest.)

late 1960s, including *The Garland News*, an excellent account of Judy's activities by Max Preeo, Dana Dial, and others, and, finally, *Newsflash*, by Sonny Gallagher, another outstanding journal. All of these were ended within a short period after Judy's passing (if not before; *The Judy Garland Collector* was a fanzine that existed in the mid to late 1980s.) The one exception is the still running British club and publication *Rainbow Review*, which was begun by Lorna Smith in the spring of 1963 with Judy's blessings. The British club has a website for further information: www.judygarlandclub.org. I also publish a magazine that is devoted to the latest CDs, DVDs, videos, and other Judy events (past and present) called *Garlands For Judy: The Legend's Legacy*. (This zine was started in July 1995, when the late, great Sonny Gallagher decided to stop his outstanding *Beyond Rainbows*, which he'd published from 1990 to 1995.) For information on my tribute to Judy's work, visit www.GarlandsForJudy.com, send an SASE to me at PO Box 2743, New York, New York 10163–2743, or email me at Garlands63@aol.com

Mid December 1955: Judy signed a five-year contract with CBS-TV, calling for five yearly color specials from 1956 through 1960. The deal would pay Judy $83,333 for the first three shows, $90,000 for the fourth, and $95,000 for the fifth, a total salary of $434, 999.

December 22, 1955: Judy signed a five-year renewal contract with MCA Artists to act as her agents (which stated they would receive 10% commission on fees for work arranged for her).

December 26, 1955: (Television/Personal Appearance) *The Tonight Show*, NBC, Los Angeles, California, 90 minutes (from 11:30 p.m. to 1 a.m.). Judy was interviewed briefly through a mobile hookup at the premiere of *The Man with the Golden Arm* in Hollywood.

1956

January 1956: The concept for Judy's next television special was announced: a live, thirty-minute, all-music edition of *Judy Garland in Concert*, backed by Leonard Bernstein and the New York Philharmonic Orchestra. Unfortunately, just before rehearsals were to start, the plans fell through and a revamped format—using stylized sets and jazzy choreography—became the shape of the show. Rehearsals continued right up to the telecast, which was set for April 8.

February 4, 1956: Judy filed suit for divorce from Sid Luft for the first time, although the suit would be dropped the very next day.

March 19, 1956: (Record) Judy returned to Capitol Records for the first of four sessions to record her second studio album, *Judy*. Nelson Riddle arranged and conducted the orchestra for this LP, which would again feature songs that she would sing on her second television special. On this date, she recorded "Dirty Hands, Dirty Face," "April Showers," "I Feel A Song Comin' On," and "Maybe I'll Come Back"—Capitol Records studios; Hollywood, California.

March 26, 1956: (Record) Judy recorded "I'm Old Fashioned" (which would be dropped from the album before release, but was restored for the reissue on compact disc); "Memories Of You"; and "Just Imagine" for the *Judy* LP—Capitol Records studios; Hollywood, California.

March 27, 1956: (Record) Judy recorded "Lucky Day" for the *Judy* LP—Capitol Records studios; Hollywood, California.

March 31, 1956: (Record) Judy recorded: "Come Rain Or Come Shine"—this recording is perhaps her very best studio recording—followed by "Life Is Just A Bowl Of Cherries"; "Last Night When We Were Young"; and "Any Place I Hang My Hat Is Home" for the *Judy* LP—Capitol Records studios; Hollywood, California. This session completed the *Judy* album, which would be released on October 10, 1956, winning some of the best reviews of Judy's recording career, including the following:

> *The New Yorker*: "Judy Garland is at the top of her form. She comes across triumphantly. The arrangements by Nelson Riddle are all apt, as well as flattering to Miss Garland's voice. 'Come Rain Or Come Shine,' always an engaging song, becomes electrifying with Miss Garland, singing impulsively and altering the notes at will."

The album would stay in the Top 40 for five weeks, peaking at number seventeen. The CD version was issued on June 28, 1989, and contained a "bonus" track: "I'm Old Fashioned," which had been recorded on March 26, 1956 for the album, but cut before release; the CD was out-of-print by the early 1990s. In 2001 it was issued by EMI in England, along with the 1958 album *Judy in Love* on the same CD, a.k.a. a "two-fer"—two albums on one CD. The sound is fine, if not outstanding, as the album tapes at EMI in England were used instead of going back to the original session tapes, for the best sound possible. *Judy* is also on the *Miss Show Business/Judy* CD from Collectables Records, released in spring 2002.

April 8, 1956: (Television) *The General Electric Theatre*, CBS-TV, 30 minutes ("live"), Hollywood, California. Hosted by Ronald Reagan, this show featured Judy singing "I Feel A Song Comin' On"; "Maybe I'll Come Back"; "Last Night When We Were Young"; "Life Is Just A Bowl Of Cherries"; "Dirty Hands, Dirty Face"; "Come Rain Or Come Shine"; and "April Showers." The reviews were not very good for this somewhat bizarre, but interesting, show, although it placed in the Top 15 Highest Rated Shows for the week. Various small video labels have issued the show over the years, including "Video Images" in 1987—Box C-100, Sandy Hook, CT 06482—Release #384. As with the earlier *Miss Show Business* album, Judy's current Capitol output featured the songs sung on her television special. *Judy*, in fact, contains all the songs from the show, although the LP would not be released until six months later, on October 10, 1956.

Spring 1956: Judy signed a deal to make her Las Vegas debut with the New Frontier Hotel for a guaranteed $55,000 a week, the largest ever paid to a nightclub performer to that date. Judy immediately began planning and rehearsing the show, set to open on July 16. (On June 10, 1956, Judy was thirty-four.)

July 16, 1956 to August 19, 1956: (Performance-Concert) The New Frontier Hotel, Las Vegas. Judy's nightclub debut was so successful—7,000 people were turned away opening weekend—that a fifth week was added to the month originally planned, with Judy earning a total of $275,000 for the engagement. Judy did a total of seventy shows. The two-show-a-night act lasted sixty-eight minutes, and included two production numbers. The act consisted of "An Intro By Judy's Boyfriends"; "This Is A Party" (Judy with "Boyfriends"); "Judy's Olio"; "Come Rain Or Come Shine"; "This Is Our Spot" (Judy's "Boyfriends"); "Any Place I Hang My Hat Is Home" (production number with Judy and the Boys); "Pretty Girl Milking Her Cow"; "Happiness Is A Thing Called Joe"; "Rock-A-Bye Your Baby"; "This Is Our Spot" (reprise of "Boyfriends" number); "Lucky Day" (production number with Judy and the Boys); "We're A Couple Of Swells"; and "Over The Rainbow." (Often, Judy would encore with "Liza" and/or "After You've Gone" and/or "Swanee," during this period. An audio tape that was recorded through the sound system during the first show still survives.) The critics again raved, as you'll see from the following reviews:

> *Daily Variety*: "[She's] a singer's singer. Her style, her voice, and her delivery are the pride of her profession. There's no way to draw comparison between [her] and any of her contemporaries, male or female."
>
> *Variety*: "In an air of expectancy as electric as the opening of a promising new Broadway musical, one of the greatest modern-day singers caught fire last night in the first nitery engagement of her career. Not only is she tops in her field, but likely champ entertainer as long and as often as she desires to play the bistro circuit."

Judy was doing two shows each night, one at 7:30 p.m. and one at 12:30 a.m. Phyllis was Judy's secretary at this time. Black and white newsreel footage exists of Judy on stage alone and with Jerry Lewis on the night he helped her when she had laryngitis.

At this time, Judy was offered two film roles that she would eventually turn down—the lead in a remake of "Alice Adams," which RKO was preparing for her, and which she was talking about during the fall of 1956, and "All About Eve," for which Joanne Woodward would eventually win the Best Actress Oscar.

Late August 1956 to late September 1956: Judy prepared for her next engagement.

September 17, 1956: Judy returned to New York, for her next engagement.

September 22, 1956: Judy was interviewed and photographed at the Plaza hotel, where she was staying, to promote:

September 26, 1956: (Performance) *Judy Garland in Person*, the Palace Theatre, New York, New York. The originally scheduled four-week engagement was extended another four weeks, then on and on. After the first act—Vaudeville—Judy performed the second act. Judy's songs were basically the same as she had just done in Vegas, with a new opening of a medley arranged by Roger Edens: "New York, New York"/"Take Me Back To Manhattan"/"Give My Regards To Broadway"/"The Sidewalks of New York." Judy's closing (just before "Rainbow") was an elaborate version of the "Be A Clown" number from her movie *The Pirate*. The following are excerpts from reviews for Judy's second legendary run:

> *The New York Times* (Brooks Atkinson), 9–27–56: "Nothing really important seems to have happened since Judy Garland was last here five years ago. . . . As on her previous visit, she takes over the second half of the program with the songs she sings as though she were composing them on the spot. Her boyish grin, her pumping bows to the audience, and her breathless patter between songs complete the portrait of a wonderful singer who is also having a good time. It is all honest and hospitable . . . the songs begin so informally and gather such vocal warmth as she puts her heart into them, that you would swear she is improvising them. A song has not really been sung until Judy pulls herself together, and belts it through the theater."
>
> *The Herald-Tribune* (Walter Kerr): "It was perfect. [Her] barrel-house voice can bend the back walls into cyclotrons. The glorious steam-whistle that can shatter the chandeliers with a single, sustained note flung recklessly skyward, is in great shape."
>
> *Variety* (Editor-In-Chief Abel Green): "The prime song belter of our times . . . She makes a Brill building lyric sound like a Shakespeare sonnet. She could sing Toots Shor's menu and have 'em hungry for more. She takes command of the rostrum as none does."

(Liza made her first appearance on stage, at age 10, dancing, while Judy sang "Swanee," during the run of the show. Silent color clips shot from the audience remain in private collections; a few also appear in various television documentaries done on Judy.)

Judy onstage during her Las Vegas debut engagement at the New Frontier Hotel, July 16, 1956 to August 19, 1956. (Courtesy of Photofest.)

Onstage with "Judy's Boyfriends" at the 1956 New Frontier Hotel engagement in Las Vegas, performing the production number "Lucky Day." (Courtesy of Photofest.)

Fall 1956: Judy recorded a fifteen-minute radio appeal for the Muscular Dystrophy Association. Later, she also taped another fifteen-minute appeal for the March of Dimes and a five-minute spot for the Heart Fund.

November 3, 1956: Judy watched some of *The Wizard of Oz* during its television debut backstage in her Palace Theatre dressing room. Liza Minnelli and Bert Lahr (who played the Cowardly Lion in the movie) hosted the telecast.

December 17, 1956 to December 25, 1956: The stress of doing eight shows a week had gotten to Judy, who missed some shows at this time. She spent seven days in a hospital while the Palace closed down. (Judy returned on December 26, 1956.)

December 25, 1956: Judy spent Christmas in New York (still playing the Palace), attending a party given by the theatrical impresario, Gilbert Miller. (This is where Judy met the actor Dirk Bogarde; they would become great friends, and, five years later, costars.)

At some point this year (perhaps when she was at the Palace), Judy took another stab at writing poetry. The imagery spoke mainly of times both long ago and recent, involving beaches, shores, and the "splendid setting sun."

1957

January 4, 1957: During an interview from her closing days at the Palace, Judy said she planned to take her show to England, France, and Germany, and then return to England to film the movie of the book *Born In Wedlock.* (During this time, Judy's hairdresser at the Palace was Ernie Adler.)

January 8, 1957: (Performance-Concert) Judy completed her engagement at the Palace in New York: This engagement had lasted seventeen weeks, second only to her own 1951–1952 run of nineteen weeks. The show would have continued at the Palace, but Judy had to return to California for her next television special for CBS. After the show, there was a party backstage until 3 a.m. Judy sang "While We're Young" and, for Sid, "Eli, Eli." (The Lufts spent two weeks in New York City and then returned to California the latter part of January.)

January 10, 1957: *The New York Herald Tribune's* television writer, Marie Torre, printed some rude comments from certain CBS executives in her column on this day. There had apparently been friction between the network and Judy over a suitable script not being supplied for her next television special. As result of this column, Judy and CBS became involved in a lawsuit that would not be settled until early 1961. Judy made no television appearances during this time period. Torre also spent ten days in jail for refusing to name her sources. Since Torre was separated from her children while imprisoned, it brought further negative publicity to Judy through no fault of her own. (This also brought about a cancellation of a planned appearance by the Lufts on the *Person-to-Person* television series on April 15, 1957.)

February 6, 1957: (Record) Judy did the first of three sessions to record her third album for Capitol Records, *Alone*, a collection of blues and songs of solitude arranged and conducted by Gordon Jenkins. During this session, Judy recorded "Little Girl Blue"; "I Get The Blues When It Rains"; "How About Me?"; and "Me And My Shadow"—Capitol Records studios; Hollywood, California.

February 22, 1957: (Record) Judy recorded "Mean To Me"; "By Myself"; and "Blue Prelude" for *Alone*—Capitol Records studios; Hollywood, California.

March 6, 1957: (Record) Judy finished the *Alone* album by recording "Then You've Never Been Blue" (which would be cut from the LP before release, but would be restored for the CD version); "Just A Memory"; "Among My Souvenirs"; "Happy New Year"; and "I Gotta Right To Sing The Blues"—Capitol Records Studio; Hollywood, California. The album would be released on May 6, 1957, and would spend three weeks in the Top 40, going as high as number seventeen on the charts.

> *Variety*, October 1957: "This package marks a definite departure in the fashioning of Judy Garland for the market. And it should work out for big returns. Instead of the big-voiced, blasting-groove technique applied to her previous packages, she's now toned down to a tender and torchy mood that's tremendously effective. In addition to the Garland pipes, which seldom sounded better, credit Gordon Jenkin's arrangements and conducting for making it a socko set."

The CD version was released on June 28, 1989, but was out-of-print by the early 1990s.

March 1957 through April 1957: Judy rehearsed her new act for her next engagement:

May 1, 1957: (Performance) The Flamingo Hotel, Las Vegas, Nevada. Judy's ninety-minute act included the songs "Lucky Day"; "How About Me?" (which she had just recorded for her new album that would be released in five days); "Rock-A-Bye Your Baby"; "Mean To Me"; "By Myself"; "The Man That Got Away" (which was made a permanent part of her repertoire with this engagement after she had first included it in the act for the Palace show, the preceding fall); "Come Rain Or Come Shine"; "A Pretty Girl Milking Her Cow"; "A Couple Of Swells"; and "Over The Rainbow." The following are excerpts from two notices:

> *Variety*: "The strip headliners and the local VIPs were there, and they gave Miss Garland a standing ovation for her efforts. Her act is dramatic yet punctuated with down to earth casualness; it is nostalgic, yet holds its own in the freshness department. It is fulfilling in that it warmly presents—with intimacy—a living legend."
>
> *The Hollywood Reporter*: "To explain [her] artistry is like trying to take into parts a globule of mercury."

During this three-week engagement, eleven-year-old Liza sang "In Between" (on May 18) and "Swanee." Four-and-a-half-year-old Lorna sang "Jingle Bells"—which had been the first song Judy sang during her "official" stage debut, Christmas 1924.

May 21, 1957: Judy's engagement in Vegas concluded its three-week run.

May 30, 1957: (Performance) The Riviera Theatre, Detroit, Michigan. (Same act as Vegas.) One-week engagement.

June 1, 1957: Judy was carried out onstage for the second half of the show this night in Michigan because she had injured her ankle. (The show went on anyway.)

June 5, 1957: (Performance) Judy did her last scheduled show in Michigan.

June 10, 1957: (Performance) Dallas State Fair, Dallas, Texas. Judy's Vegas show continued its tour, playing here for two weeks (during which time she would be reunited with her sister, Jimmy, who lived in Dallas). The engagement went well, except for the Saturday, June 15, show, when, after singing four songs, Judy could not continue, a reaction to her friend, Robert Alton's—the MGM choreographer—death. (June 10, 1957 was also Judy's thirty-fifth birthday.) On Father's Day, Judy sang "Happiness Is A Thing Called Joe" for Joe, Lorna sang "Jingle Bells," and Liza sang "In Between."

June 23, 1957: (Performance) Judy played her last scheduled show in Dallas.

June 24, 1957: Judy flew home to California, for her next engagement.

June 25, 1957: (Performance) The Greek Theatre; Los Angeles, California. Judy's last stop on this nine-week tour, broke all house records at the box office, and was her first appearance in her hometown in five years.

> *The Mirror News*: "[The capacity audience was] mesmerized [by] her clear, full voice ringing on the soft summer evening air like a mockingbird serenading the moon."

> *The Hollywood Reporter*: "The terrific hand she got [on her entrance] was nothing compared to the way she proceeded to put the crowd in the palm of it."

In conjunction with this engagement, Barker Brothers store in downtown Los Angeles had a display of Judy memorabilia from the collection of "Judy's Number One Fan," Wayne Martin. The display was insured for $5,800.

July 7, 1957: (Performance) Judy did her last scheduled show for the two-week Greek Theatre engagement. There was a private party held for Judy after the show at the Little Gypsy on Sunset Blvd. Judy stayed at the party until 3:30 a.m.

July 8, 1957: The Lufts held a party at their home for the end of the tour. Judy sang "Lucky Day."

Summer 1957: Judy took this summer off, although she did do some light rehearsing for her next engagement, coming up in the fall, by working with musical arranger Buddy Bregman. (Judy did not have a secretary during this summer.) In August, the Lufts went to New York to deal with their CBS lawsuit. It was reported at the end of August that it looked as if the suit would be settled out of court (it was, but not until 1961, when both Judy and CBS would drop it).

Summer 1957: (Radio) Judy taped an interview at home for the NBC radio show *Nightline*, which aired on August 30, 1957, and featured four-year-old Lorna, who interrupted the interview at one point. (Audio of this portion of the program still exists in private collections.)

September 16, 1957: (Performance) Loew's Capitol Theatre; Washington, D.C. (week-long engagement).

> *Variety* said: "This is a different kind of theatrical engagement. It's a love affair between Judy Garland and the folks who are paying up to a $6.60 top this week, to hear her sing at the Capitol theatre here. Miss Garland makes a quick rapport with her audience, and you can feel the affection they have for her from the time she opens up with her big, deep voice."

(Color, silent home movie footage exists of this engagement, filmed in the audience at the Saturday matinee, when Judy brought Lorna and Joey up on stage. Judy sang "Rock-A-Bye" to Lorna—since she said, "Lorna likes the loud ones"—and "Happiness Is A Thing Called Joe" for Joe, with her son on her lap. The footage still exists.)

September 21, 1957: (Performance) Judy played her last show at Loew's (she had been scheduled to do a final show on September 22, but that show was canceled due to illness. Judy had the Asian Flu—which she'd developed the day before she left California for Washington, and now had a 103-degree temperature.)

September 26, 1957: (Performance) Mastbaum Theatre, Philadelphia, Pennsylvania (week-long engagement). (Judy was sporting a ponytail and wearing her hair out and long during this engagement. She also had a vocal coach with her.)

October 1, 1957: (Performance) Judy had twisted her ankle and, thus, did this show sitting down, but she strained her voice—due to a relapse of the flu and despite the efforts of her vocal coach. The final two shows of this engagement (the matinee and evening shows on October 2) were canceled.

October 4, 1957: Judy, Sid, Lorna, and Joe sailed on the United States ship, from New York to London, for Judy's next engagement. Judy also signed a contract on this date just before sailing, to perform at a large nightclub in Brooklyn, at a date still to be determined, in 1958, and received a $15,000 advance. The contract was through the Luft's latest corporation, "Gamma" Productions (for Garland and the role Judy was proudest of—"mama.") Judy was president of this production company, and Sid was vice president.

Thursday, October 9, 1957: The liner (ship) was delayed by fog, but Judy and company arrived in London at Waterloo Station at 4:30 a.m. and went to the Savoy, where they were staying during Judy's London engagement at the Savoy. That night there was a press reception for Judy at the Londonderry House from 6:00 p.m. to 8:30 p.m.

October 12, 1957: (Record) Judy recorded "It's So Lovely To Be Back Again In London" (written for her by Roger Edens) for Capitol-EMI Records to distribute to her opening night audience four days later. It just recently made its CD debut on the disc *Legends of the 20th Century: Judy Garland* from EMI, released in 1999.

October 16, 1957: Judy lunched with Aly Khan, but hardly touched her salmon. Judy then tried to rest, but couldn't, and left for the theater at 5 p.m., three hours before the show started, and more than four hours before she was due onstage, for (Performance) *The Judy Garland Show*, the Dominion Theatre, London, England. Judy opened a four-and-a-half-week engagement. This was her first engagement in London since she began "The Concert Years" portion of her career at the London Palladium in April 1951, six-and-a-half years earlier. ($180,000 was spent refurbishing the theatre for Judy's run, which had advance ticket sales of $100,000.) Judy's act (with her "Ten Boyfriends") played the second half of the show (proceeded by a First Act of various Vaudeville Acts, as was Judy's normal routine at his point, with Alan King closing the first half.) Judy's act included the new "Garland Overture," arranged by Buddy Bregman, who had started doing some work for her that summer/fall, and would do work on Judy's entire act in early 1958. (The Overture, which included "The Trolley Song," "The Man That Got Away," and her signature song, "Over The Rainbow," was so thrilling, that it would open all of her engagements for the rest of her life.) Judy's eighty-minute act included the songs "It's So Lovely To Be Back Again In London"; "I Feel A

The Luft Family (Joe, Judy, Lorna, and Sid) on October 4, 1957, the day they sailed from New York to London for Judy's engagement at the Dominion Theater. (Courtesy of Photofest.)

Song Comin' On"; the medley of "You Made Me Love You"/For Me And My Gal"/"The Trolley Song" ("The Boy Next Door" had been cut from this medley); "Come Rain Or Come Shine"; "The Man That Got Away"; "Rock-A-Bye Your Baby"; "Lucky Day"; "How About Me?"; "We're A Couple Of Swells"; and "Over The Rainbow." Her encores were "Me And My Shadow" and "Swanee." Gordon Jenkins was conducting for her once again. Judy's raves included the following:

> *The News Chronicle* (Elizabeth Frank): "All that is the essence of real star quality now holds the limelight at the Dominion Theatre. It was a wonderful experience to feel a London audience of 3,000 give themselves in a flood of affection and warmth and, I like to think, a certain pride, to the miraculous little waif, to whom they restored life and confidence six years ago. Judy is a great clown. That is why she can make you laugh and cry at the same time. The spotlight picked up the dirty little gamin's face, as she sang 'Over The Rainbow' squatting on the stage by the footlights, and we wondered at the strange guise in which genius can appear to us."
>
> Maurice Kim: "A mass hypnosis [as] patients succumb to the administration of a crushing telepathy. No vocal performer in living memory had poured so much into a session."
>
> *Variety*: "[Judy is] devastating [in a] brilliantly staged, irresistible production which leaves the audience screaming eagerly for more."

Lorna and Joe appeared onstage with their mother during one of the matinees. (Judy's assistant manager at this time was Bill Jones, and "Rikki" was her hairdresser—he had been with her when she'd toured the coast. He used to do her hair at her place, and then she'd go right on stage upon arriving at the theater. She reportedly would adopt this practice again frequently during her last engagement in London, at the Talk of the Town, in 1968–1969.) While in London, Judy visited the famous Winston's Club and attended the Tin Pan Alley Ball.

November 15, 1957: Judy was given a luncheon in her honor by the Variety Club of Great Britain, held at the Savoy where she was staying. (She attended with Alan King.)

November 16, 1957: (Performance) Judy played her last scheduled shows (an evening and a matinee) at the Dominion Theatre (delighting the audience by repeating "A Couple Of Swells").

November 18, 1957: (Personal Appearance) *The Royal Command Performance Variety Show*, The London Palladium, London, England. Judy sang three songs (instead of the two usually allotted each performer), "Rock-A-Bye Your Baby," "A Couple Of Swells" (after her "Boyfriends" had performed to give her time to change into her tramp costume), and "Over The Rainbow." (This show was broadcast over the radio. An audiotape of "Baby" and "Rainbow" exists in private collections.)

November 21, 1957: The Lufts left England that evening, arriving in New York a few days later, and went to Chicago for Thanksgiving. On Thanksgiving, Judy spoke with longtime fan Tom Cooper of Chicago, who had actually made his own home-movie version of *A Star Is Born.* (Cooper would eventually become close to the Lufts and to Liza, featuring her in one of his later home-movie epics.) Thanksgiving night, the Lufts caught a train to California, arriving home on November 30, 1957.

December 26, 1957: (Performance) The Flamingo, Las Vegas. Judy opened a scheduled three-week engagement, at $40,000 a week, introducing a new "My Fair Lady" medley and several numbers with dancer Bobby Van (including "You're Just In Love"). Other songs included "I Feel A Song Coming On" and "How About Me?"

Variety stated: "Miss Garland's preem audience found her in excellent voice and with a pleasing air of informality."

December 27, 1957 to December 30, 1957: Judy developed severe vocal problems and canceled four nights of shows.

December 31, 1957: Judy returned to the stage at the Flamingo. The New Year's Eve audience was rowdy, however, and the management continued to serve drinks during her show, which was not supposed to happen. After repeated attempts to quiet the crowd and do her show, Judy left the stage and canceled the rest of her engagement. Both parties sued, with Judy winning the case and being awarded $22,000.

1958

January 1, 1958: Judy flew home to California, from Las Vegas, after walking out of her Flamingo engagement, which was supposed to run through January 15. See December 31, 1957, for more information.

Late February *or* early March 1958: Judy hired Hollywood divorce attorney Jerry Geisler to begin divorce proceedings, although no immediate legal action would be taken. Judy withdrew $9,000 of a $25,000 bank loan Sid had secured, paid $5,000 to Geisler, gathered the children and their nurse, and then boarded a train to New York for her next engagement—the one for which she'd signed the contract on October 4, 1957. It would be her first opening night without Sid since she began her concert career in 1951. (During Liza's twelfth birthday, on March 12, Judy and her three children were en route to New York for Judy's next engagement.)

Mid March 1958: Shortly after arriving in New York, Judy had to make an appearance in the State Collector's office to arrange to pay over $8,000 in back taxes from her 1951 engagement at the Palace in New York. An agreement was made to take $3,000 a week out of Judy's $25,000 a week salary from her new engagement.

Thursday, March 20, 1958: (Performance) The Town and Country Club, Brooklyn, New York. Opening night of a three-and-a-half week engagement. The show was scheduled to start at 10:30 p.m. It started at 11:00 p.m. due to the delay caused by a huge, twenty-four-hour snowstorm. Judy's opening act—which included dancer/singer Bobby Van—ran for an hour, and then Judy came on at midnight for one hour. Judy's songs included (in the following running order): "Brooklyn" (special material); "Life Is Just A Bowl Of Cherries"; "How About Me?"; Judy's Olio: the medley of "You Made Me Love You"/"For Me And My Gal"/"The Trolley Song"; "When The Sun Comes Out"; "Mean To Me"; "After You've Gone"; "By Myself"; "I Guess I'll Have To Change My Plans" and "When You Wore A Tulip," both with Bobby Van; "Maybe I'll Come Back"; "Rock-A-Bye Your Baby"; "A Couple Of Swells" (with Bobby Van); "Over The Rainbow"; and "Swanee." *Variety* pronounced her a hit, filling the club to capacity (1,700 people in spite of opening during the middle of the snowstorm.) Judy's salary was $25,000 a week for this engagement; she'd been paid a $15,000 advance in cash when the contract was signed on October 4, 1957. (While performing at the Town and Country, Judy was staying in a beach house the club had rented for her in Neponsit on Long Island, about 20 miles away from the club. Judy had a male secretary and a maid with her backstage, on Friday, March 21.)

Sunday, March 30, 1958: (Performance) Judy managed to get through the first two songs of her act at the Town and Country this night, then announced she had been fired, and left the stage. (Judy had developed severe colitis shortly after opening, but had been somehow getting through her shows until this night, when the manager of the club fired her.)

Monday, March 31, 1958: Sid had followed his family to New York, and he and Judy reconciled. They held a press conference on this day at Judy's rented home in Neponsit, Rockaway, which was reported in the *Daily News* of April 1. It was reported Sid said $23,000 had been received from Ben Masik, the owner of the club, to which Judy interrupted with "what happened to the money?" Luft said "ask Uncle Sam." Sid also offered that Judy had "Federal and New York State tax liens totaling about $29,000."According to the reporter, "Luft also said that Judy had earned 'better than close to a million dollars within the last three years,' and again Judy asked 'what happened to it?' Sid answered 'you'll find out, dear.'"

Thursday, April 3, 1958: Judy had to make an appearance at the Supreme Court House in Jamaica, Queens, New York, to answer charges about her back tax payments now that her money from the Town and Country engagement would not be coming in. Joseph Brennan, an under-sheriff, served Judy with a warrant at her hotel suite, and he escorted her to the courthouse in the sheriff's squad car, but she was not under formal arrest. Judy's attorney Maurice Greenbaum said it had been "arranged for her to appear." Judy agreed to leave her jewelry and costumes as a lien, and to not leave the state until the money could be raised. The money—$8,673.00—was borrowed, and the lien was paid on Tuesday, April 8, 1958. (A separate check to cover court costs of $262.00 was also presented.)

Mid April 1958: The Lufts were back home in California, and officially reconciled.

May 11, 1958: (Performance) Minnesota State Centennial Celebration. Judy sang to a crowd of 20,000 people in her home state. Judy was the closing performer of the celebration. It was reported she performed with the thirty-two-piece Minneapolis Symphony Orchestra. Her songs were "At Long Last Here I Am" (her 1951 London Palladium opener, with reworked lyrics); the "Olio"; "Rock-A-Bye"; and "Rainbow." After the performance, Sid said he'd produce *Born in Wedlock* on Broadway in the fall—with an unknown starring in it—and then film it with Judy. This never happened.

May 19, 1958: (Record) Judy returned to Capitol Records, for the first of three sessions for her next album: *Judy in Love* (an album of "happy" songs to balance the sad ones found on her previous album *Alone*). The LP would be arranged and conducted by Nelson Riddle, and would be her first record or album to be recorded in stereo. (Although the songs for *A Star Is Born* were prerecorded in stereo, they could only be heard that way in movie theatres until a CD of *Star* songs was issued in 1988, in stereo, using the soundtrack of the film itself, not the tapes from the original sessions, which are not known to exist. As mentioned previously, Judy's songs at MGM were recorded in stereo, using multiangled microphones and tracks; these were mixed into mono sound for theaters. Starting in 1992, the existing multitrack recordings—which had been transferred from the film-stock originals to magnetic tape in the early 1960s—were remixed back to stereo and used for various video and theatrical releases.) On this day, Judy recorded "Day-In, Day-Out"; then "This Is It"; then "Zing! Went The Strings Of My Heart"—Capitol Records Studios, Hollywood, California.

May 26, 1958: (Record) Judy recorded "I Hadn't Anyone Till You"; then "More Than You Know"; then I'm Confessin'"; and then "I Can't Give You Anything But Love, Baby" for the *Judy in Love* LP—Capitol Records Studios; Hollywood, California. (June 10, 1958, was Judy's thirty-sixth birthday.)

June 17, 1958: (Record) Judy recorded: "Do It Again," "I Am Loved," "I Concentrate On You," and "Do I Love You?" completing the *Judy In Love* album. (The mono version would be released on November 3, 1958; the stereo version, which contains the exact same performances as the mono version—except for the ending of "Zing! Went The Strings of My Heart"—would not be released until February 16, 1959. The album—in stereo—made its CD debut in 2001 on an EMI British release. See March 31, 1956 for more information.)

> *High Fidelity* wrote: "A new recording by the charming Judy Garland that doesn't, for a wonder, include 'Over The Rainbow' or 'The Trolley Song.' For these omissions, much thanks. Here she tackles songs somewhat removed from her usual repertoire and gives them exuberant and exciting performances. Whether in 'Zing! Went The Strings Of My Heart' or 'Do It Again,' she still manages to suggest the wide-eyed wonder that endeared her to the public 20 years ago. Nelson Riddle is a considerate helpmate in the undertaking, and Capitol's handsome, warm sound makes this a must for Garland fans."

July 23, 1958: (Performance) The Coconut Grove; Hollywood, California. Judy opened a two-week stand, with no opening or supporting acts, just sixty minutes of songs, in a one-act presentation. (There was no intermission, nor a second act; this was a nightclub, however famed. Judy did only one show a night during the week, but agreed to do two shows nightly during the weekends.) Judy's songs included (after her now-standard "Overture"): "When You're Smiling" (the debut of this Roger Edens-arranged version, tailor-made to poke fun at Judy's recent weight-gain, and problems with the law in New York over the back taxes); "Day-In, Day-Out"; "I Can't Give You Anything But Love"; "Zing! Went The Strings Of My Heart"; "Purple People Eater"; Judy's Olio: the medley of "You Made Me Love You"/ "For Me And My Gal"/"The Trolley Song"; "Do It Again"; "When The Sun Comes Out"; "Rock-A-Bye Your Baby"; "Over The Rainbow"; "After You've Gone"; "Chicago"; "A Pretty Girl Milking Her Cow"; "Liza"; "Me And My Shadow"; and "Swanee."

> *Louella Parsons*: "In all the years I've been covering this town, I've never seen such a turnout of stars, nor have I felt under one roof such an outpouring of affection and love as greeted Judy, the home town girl, when she appeared at the top of the stairs in her cute 'lady tuxedo' garb. . . . What a show—what a night, with Judy giving back all that affection by singing her heart out. I think we all realized we were enjoying an event that has seldom been equaled and will hardly ever be topped."

> *The Hollywood Reporter*: "What words fit Niagara and the Grand Canyon, tornadoes and volcanos, sunsets and dawns, and Judy Garland at the top of her form? At the top of her gold-lined lungs, shoulders back, elbows out, fists clenched, [she] pelted our ears with the magic of that voice—an earthquake, a battering ram, a holocaust!"

> *Variety*: "On some notes, she opened at pianissimo and swelled to full fortissimo, a dramatic performance that few singers can match."

August 5, 1958: (Performance-Record) Judy's last performance at the Coconut Grove was recorded "live" by Capitol Records for an album—Judy's first "legitimate" and "legally released" "live" album. Unfortunately, by this time, Judy had developed laryngitis, and the album—a severely abridged version of her act—called *Garland at the Grove*, presents the strain in full clarity. The LP would be released in a mono version on February 2, 1959, and the stereo version two weeks later, on February 16, 1959. The album is out of print; two of the tracks not included on the LP—"Day In, Day Out" and "I Can't Give You Anything But Love"—were on Capitol's 1991 box set of three CDs called *Judy Garland: The One*

Twelve-year-old Liza with her beloved mama on Judy's opening night at the Coconut Grove, July 23, 1958. (Courtesy of Photofest.)

and Only. This set was deleted from Capitol's catalog in 1994. (In Capitol Records' files, they list reels "created August 5," not August 6. These also contain the song "Do It Again," scheduled to be on a two-CD Capitol set in spring 2002.)

September 1, 1958: Judy arrived in Chicago and gave a press conference that day for her next engagement.

September 4, 1958: (Performance) Orchestra Hall, Chicago, Illinois. Judy had the biggest advance sale in the Hall's history (an expensive $7.50 for the top priced ticket); 17,500 people came to see her, with another 6,000 people being turned away. Judy performed the exact same act she had at the Coconut Grove—see July 23, 1958 for song list—up through "Rainbow," then she added Roger Eden's arrangement of "Chicago" as her closing song (this was another number from the period that would stay in her concerts to the end of her career). Following this, she encored with "How About Me?"; "Swanee"; and "After You've Gone." This opening was a benefit for the Chicago Home for Girls. Nelson Riddle conducted the thirty-two-piece orchestra. Charles Walters did the staging, and Roger Edens, the special material and arranging. Comedian Alan King opened the first act, with Judy performing the second, along with a three-song stanza for Nelson Riddle and His Orchestra.

> *The Sun-Times* stated: "[Judy received] the kind of audience reaction usually reserved for the World Series. [The crowd] came running down the isles to shake the hands of *Miss Show Business*."

(An audiotape made through the sound system during this engagement survives in private collections, and is excerpted on an out-of-print LP released in 1973, called *Judy Garland in Concert: San Francisco*, on Mark 56 Records, produced by Sid Luft.)

September 9, 1958: (Performance) Judy played her seventh and final scheduled show for this engagement at Chicago Hall (there was a Saturday Matinee on September 6, at 2:30; all other shows were at 8:30 p.m.). The week's gross was $78,000, with $57,000 in advance sales.

October 1, 1958: (Performance) The Sands, Las Vegas. Judy continued with the same show (a one-act solo performance), for this two-week engagement. Her act was forty minutes and included twelve songs (in the following order): Overture; "When You're Smiling"; "Come Rain or Come Shine"; "I Can't Give You Anything But Love"; "Zing! Went The Strings Of My Heart"; "Purple People Eater"; "Judy's Olio"; "Do It Again"; "The Man That Got Away"; "Rock-A-Bye Your Baby"; "Rainbow"; and "Swanee."

> Critic Ralph Pearl wrote: "You sit there completely awed as your spine turns to jelly, and the roots of your thinning hair ache and stand straight up in the air. . . . She stands up there, no bigger than a fair-sized jockey, [and] every other singer seems to fade into quiet but definite obscurity. She has no equal! Of that you can be assured!"

Stars that attended Judy's show during this run included Shirley MacLaine, Gary Cooper, David Nivens, Debbie Reynolds, and Betty Hutton, who had replaced Judy in *Annie Get Your Gun* nine years earlier at MGM.

October 14, 1958: (Performance) Judy played her final scheduled show at the Sands. After the closing night show, Judy sang with Frank Sinatra and Dean Martin on the stage of the Sands, then flew home to California.

October 24, 1958: (Award Ceremony) The Hollywood Masquers Club dinner celebrated Judy, Los Angeles, California. Judy closed the show (following Sammy Davis, Jr. and emcee George Jessel), by singing "When You're Smiling"; "Rock-A-Bye Your Baby"; and "Over The Rainbow." (This performance exists in private collections.)

November 15, 1958: (Benefit) The San Bernardino Community Hospital. Judy was introduced by Sammy Davis, Jr. as "the world's greatest entertainer." Judy sang "When You're Smiling"; "Day In, Day Out"; "Judy's Olio"; "Rock-A-Bye"; "Rainbow"; and "Swanee."

December 1958: (Record) Judy learned the material for her next Capitol album, *The Letter*, which would tell the story of a an estranged relationship, through Judy's songs and John Ireland's narration. Composed by Gordon Jenkins, it is perhaps Judy's most ambitious recording.

December 8, 1958: *Hollywood Reporter* columnist Mike Connolly reported that Judy's forthcoming settlement with CBS was calling for a fifty-three-minute version of her "Born In A Trunk" number, to be sponsored by Chrysler. It never happened, possibly because Judy wanted three to six months of preparation time, and CBS was only offering five weeks of production time.

December 12, 1958: Judy dictated a letter to her secretary, Mr. George Feldsher (who would be with her through May 1959), thanking the president of the Garland fan club for the latest *Gazette* journals. At this time, Judy was reportedly taking some dance lessons at Gower Champion Studios in Los Angeles, and also attended Pat Brown's victory party and Sammy Davis, Jr.'s birthday party.

1959

January 1959: It was announced that due to popular response in art house engagements, *A Star Is Born* would be rereleased to a total of 500 theaters in April 1959, with a major PR campaign. The film would be reissued after five years, in 1964, and after ten years, in 1969, just after Judy's passing. There would be one final major reissue, in 1983–1984, of the restored *Star*.

January 15, 1959 and January 16, 1959: (Recording) Judy recorded *The Letter* album for Capitol Records.

> *Variety*, May: "This is a Gordon Jenkins production especially designed for disks and Judy Garland. A la his earlier work, *Manhattan Tower*, the platter presents a romantic story in song and narrative. The songs far outshine the narrative here and Miss Garland is in top form as she works her way through close to 10 Jenkins creations. The narrative is romantically handled by John Ireland. The Ralph Brewster Singers and Jenkins's orchestra help round out the overall socko musical package."
>
> *High Fidelity*, July: "Miss Garland is her usual, taut, emotional self."

The LP would be released May 4, 1959; it would be reissued as *Our Love Letter* on September 3, 1963; both versions have long been deleted from the Capitol catalog. The album has not appeared on CD to date.

January 30, 1959: (Personal Appearance) The Hollywood Masquers Club Salute to Jimmy McHugh, Los Angeles, California. Judy sang two songs, then tried to get through McHugh's "I'm In The Mood For Love," but she forgot the words; Jimmy couldn't remember his own lyrics, and the event's emcee, Milton Berle, supplied them.

Early to mid February 1959: Judy and Sid traveled by train to New York, then again by train from New York to Miami, which took 26 hours. (The whole trip took a week, from California to Miami; Judy was not fond of flying.) This was for Judy's next engagement:

February 17, 1959 to March 1, 1959: (Performance) The Fontainebleau Hotel, Miami, Florida. Judy's Miami cabaret debut was a sellout, capacity crowd of 800 in this somewhat intimate nightclub.

> *The Herald* (George Bourke): "[I was] a well-wishing doubtful Thomas at the start [and] a completely sold and devoted Boswell, eager to sing deserved praises, at the finish."

March 1959 to April 1959: Judy spent this time planning and rehearsing a new, full-scale production, the most spectacular that she would undertake for a tour (with a major destination in mind).

April 27, 1959 to May 3, 1959: (Performance) The Stanley Opera House, Baltimore, Maryland; a "try-out" engagement for Judy's new production. Judy grossed a "fine" $65,000 at the 2,800 seat house. She had a capacity crowd four of the six nights; the weakest nights were Tuesday—because of rain—and Friday, because the weekend tickets went up to a high price of $6.50, "a pretty high tag in these parts," according to one report. The reviews were raves, except there was some disappointment expressed over Judy lip-synching to a prerecorded taped vocal for "Born In A Trunk." The blocking was changed, so that Judy could sing the production number "live."

May 11, 1959 to May 17,1959: (Performance) *The Metropolitan Opera House*, New York, New York. Judy became the first female popular ("pop") singer (non-operatic), to play The Met (Sir Harry Lauder had performed there in 1927.) The run was a benefit for the Children's Asthma Research Institute and Hospital in Denver. The show grossed $190,000, an unheard of amount at that time. Also on May 11, Judy was given a citation by the Mayor of New York, Robert Wagner, for "distinguished and exceptional service," in her work and in her charitable work. (The only known copy of a professionally recorded audiotape of this show was sold at a 1978 auction by Sid Luft. The only known surviving tape is a tape of about 10 minutes worth of numbers—in fairly poor quality sound, not recorded through the sound system—including her Overture; "Almost Like Being In Love"/"This Can't Be Love"; "I'm In Love With A Wonderful Guy"; "The Man That Got Away"; and "When You're Smiling.")

> *The New Yorker* (Kenneth Tynan): "The engagement, which is now over, was limited; the pleasure it gave was not. When the voice pours out, as rich and as pleading as ever, we know where, and how moved, we are—in the presence of a star and embarrassed by tears."

> *The Journal-American*: "Her full, thrilling, throbbing voice welled up in the vast cathedral of vocal culture, filling every bit of space above the orchestra, the boxes, and family circle. Not even Maria Callas ever got a better reception."

Here is a rundown of Judy's show. Act One: Overture (not Judy's standard concert overture); "At The Opera" (which set up Judy's appearance amidst the chorus, who sang to her "You look like a singer: Are you a new Mimi from 'La Boheme?'" Judy responded: "My name is Ju-u-dy . . . but my children call me 'Mama' "). This led into "I Happen To Like New York"; "Almost Like Being In Love"/"This Can't Be Love" medley; "Wonderful Guy" (and reprise of "Guy"); John Bubbles's routine of "Me And My Shadow," joined by Judy, who copied his steps as his shadow, but didn't sing; Judy and John then danced to "When There's A Shine On Your Shoes"; Judy soloed on the "Shoe Shine Boy" dance routine (with the feet of the chorus seen behind her); then Alan King closed the first half. Act Two: Another Overture (again, not Judy's standard concert one); Judy solos on "When You're Smiling"; "The Man That Got Away"; selections from *The Letter* ("Ricky's"; "The Worst Kind Of Man" with dancers; "Red Balloon"; and "Come Back"); Bubbles and King performed together; then the complete "Born In A Trunk" production number from *A Star Is Born,* recreated with Judy and the entire cast of this vast production; a "Quick Change" with Bubbles; "We're A Couple Of Swells" with Judy and Alan King; Judy's "Olio"; "Over The Rainbow"; and "Rock-A-Bye Your Baby." The opening night party was at Sherry's (Judy wore the gown she wore while singing "Melancoly Baby" in *A Star Is Born.*) One of the chorus girls in the show was reported as saying that Judy "is always flattered and seems so pleased when we even stop to say hello to her."

June 1, 1959 to June 7, 1959: (Performance) The Chicago Opera House; Chicago, Illinois. This was the next stop on Judy's "Opera House" Tour. There were seven shows; the ticket prices ranged from $2.50 to a $10.00 top.

> Critic Richard Christiansen: "Something for which theatres were built—a constant outpouring of the best a performer has to give that makes an audience roar with excitement and sheer joy."

During an interview with the *Chicago Daily News*, Judy said, "I've been singing since I can remember. It's what I love and what I want to keep on doing."

June 10, 1959: Judy's thirty-seventh birthday.

July 1, 1959 to July 10, 1959: (Performance) The San Francisco War Memorial Opera House; San Francisco, California. Judy added a new, Roger Edens-arranged version of the song "San Francisco" as her final encore, which would stay in her act for the rest of her life. (Judy would, in fact, sing it during her very last concert.) While in San Francisco, a suit was filed against Judy's show by a group of ASCAP writers and publishers, claiming they weren't paid for the use of the songs "A Couple Of Swells"; "A Wonderful Guy"; and "This Can't Be Love." They were doing this because the venue didn't operate under a "blanket license" with ASCAP, as did other theaters. Sid Luft stated he had paid for the performing rights. Here's an excerpt from one of the reviews for this engagement:

> (Source unknown) : "[Garland] had her audience in a state akin to the fever that hypoed the Oklahoma land rush. If they had taken out their uppers, removed their toupees, and tossed same over the footlights, it wouldn't have surprised me."

Judy reportedly received $46,499 for the week's run.

July 11, 1959 to July 18, 1959: (Performance) The Shrine Auditorium, Los Angeles, California. Judy's "Opera House" tour ended here. On closing night, Liza attended with her father, Vincente Minnelli.

The Los Angeles Times: "(The Shrine) echoed and trembled with applause, stomping and shouts. The best of the (Garland) acts are all here."

Around this time (July 1959) it was reported that Judy and Sid were preparing a suit against Jack L. Warner for $14 million, representing their profits from *A Star Is Born,* with Luft also seeking an additional $300,000 of the profits for his services as the film's producer.

Late July 1959: The Lufts checked into a "Health Farm" in Hidden Valley, California, called Comanche Ranch, in an attempt to lose weight. (Due, in part, to the anticipated filming of *Born in Wedlock*—now called *Gaiety Girl*—since backers were in place. The film would never be made.)

October 18, 1959: (Performance) The Sahara Hotel, Las Vegas. One-week engagement—Judy filled in for Donald O'Connor, who was ill.

November 8, 1959: (Personal Appearance) Friar's Roast for Dean Martin, Los Angeles, California.

November 17, 1959: (Personal Appearance) A party by Elsa Maxwell, for Aly Khan, with Judy as Guest of Honor; Drake Hotel, New York, New York.

November 18, 1959: Judy entered Doctor's Hospital in New York City. She was near death. Her weight had gone to more than 180 pounds, and her liver was inflamed and more than four times its normal size. She began emergency treatment for hepatitis, but her condition was increasingly critical. Twenty quarts of fluids were slowly drained from her body. Judy began to recover, but was told, at the age of 37, that she would be a semi-invalid for the rest of her life, and could never be allowed to work again. Her doctors obviously did not know their patient, as nothing could keep Judy from singing for her audiences, and she was about to enter into the most successful period of her career.

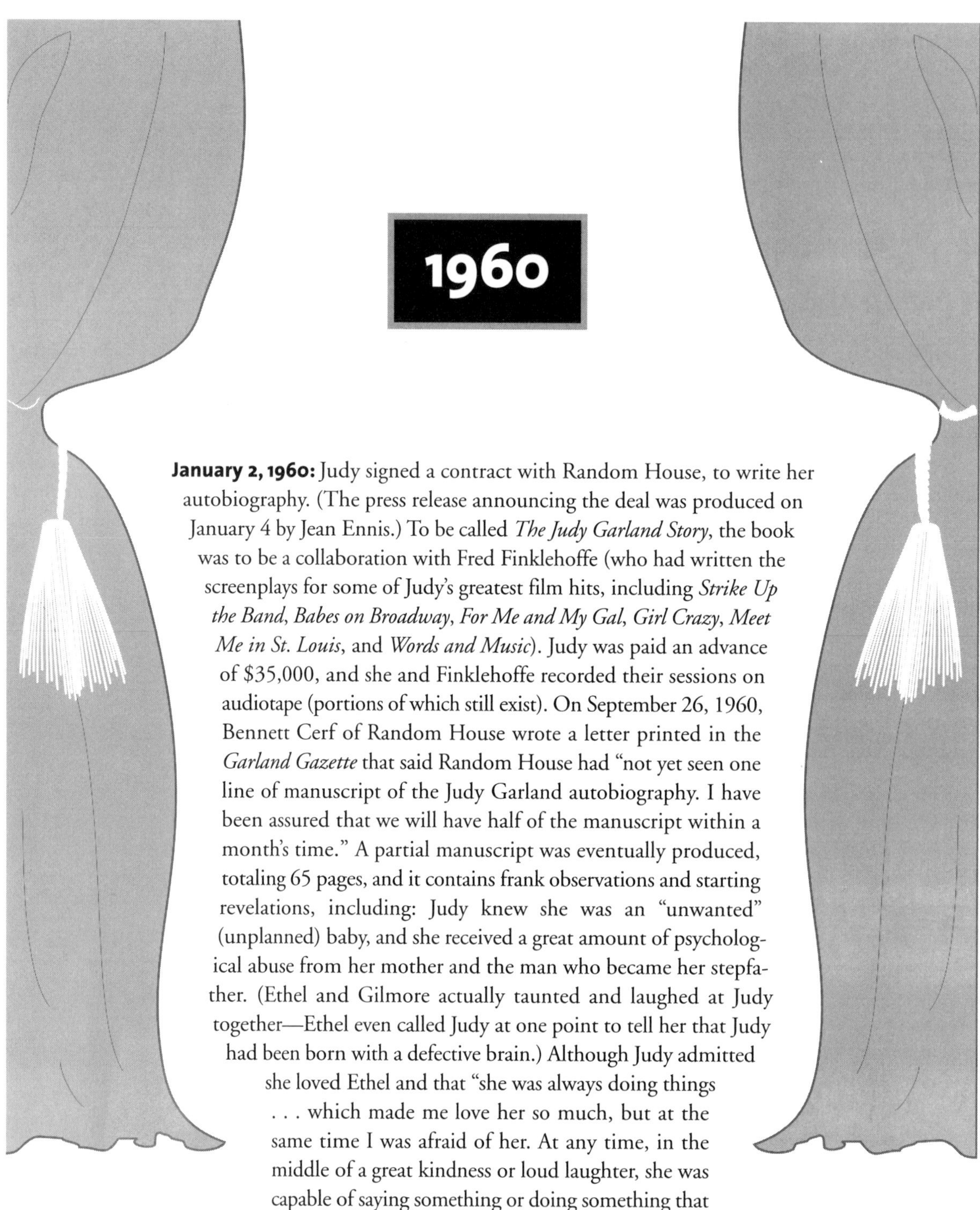

1960

January 2, 1960: Judy signed a contract with Random House, to write her autobiography. (The press release announcing the deal was produced on January 4 by Jean Ennis.) To be called *The Judy Garland Story*, the book was to be a collaboration with Fred Finklehoffe (who had written the screenplays for some of Judy's greatest film hits, including *Strike Up the Band, Babes on Broadway, For Me and My Gal, Girl Crazy, Meet Me in St. Louis*, and *Words and Music*). Judy was paid an advance of $35,000, and she and Finklehoffe recorded their sessions on audiotape (portions of which still exist). On September 26, 1960, Bennett Cerf of Random House wrote a letter printed in the *Garland Gazette* that said Random House had "not yet seen one line of manuscript of the Judy Garland autobiography. I have been assured that we will have half of the manuscript within a month's time." A partial manuscript was eventually produced, totaling 65 pages, and it contains frank observations and starting revelations, including: Judy knew she was an "unwanted" (unplanned) baby, and she received a great amount of psychological abuse from her mother and the man who became her stepfather. (Ethel and Gilmore actually taunted and laughed at Judy together—Ethel even called Judy at one point to tell her that Judy had been born with a defective brain.) Although Judy admitted she loved Ethel and that "she was always doing things . . . which made me love her so much, but at the same time I was afraid of her. At any time, in the middle of a great kindness or loud laughter, she was capable of saying something or doing something that would scare me to death." Judy also talked candidly about her attempts to rid herself of the medications she was on; the men at the studio who made advances on her, and most astonishingly, about the abortion she had when she was twenty. However, the book would not continue after a certain stage, as Judy felt too good and happy to look back.

January 5, 1960: Judy was released from Doctor's Hospital, and would return home to California to rest and fully recover. This period would be the most carefree time of her adult life, and she would actually be nearly free of any medications, except for a certain prescribed dose of Ritalin.

April 1960: (Film) Judy's first work after being released from the hospital was to record "The Far Away Part Of Town," a song for the soundtrack of the Columbia movie *Pepe*, to which Shirley Jones and Dan Dailey would dance. The song would be nominated for the Academy Award for Best Song. (The song was featured on the soundtrack album, on the Colpix label, #CPS 507; it can also be found on *The Definitive Judy Garland* CD issued in 1992 on the Pastel Label. Both have gone out-of-print. The CD soundtrack to *Pepe* has recently been released by Collector's Choice Music.)

June 8, 1960: (Record) Judy did the first of three sessions at Capitol Records in Hollywood for her next album *Judy: That's Entertainment!* At this session, she recorded, "How Long Has This Been Going On?"; "Yes"; and "It Never Was You."

June 9, 1960: (Record) The recording on the *Judy: That's Entertainment!* album continued at Capitol Records in Hollywood, with the songs "If I Love Again"; "Who Cares?"; "Puttin' On The Ritz"; "Just You, Just Me"; and "Down With Love."

June 10, 1960: Judy's thirty-eighth birthday.

June 17, 1960: (Record) Judy finished recording the *Judy: That's Entertainment!* album at Capitol Records in Hollywood, by doing the songs "That's Entertainment"; "Old Devil Moon"; "I've Confessed To The Breeze"; and "Alone Together." Judy also recorded the song, "Yes," for this album. The recording date has been noted as June 8, 1960, but the master number, 34026, is the highest number/last number listed in the logs for the album's sessions. Therefore, the song was most likely recorded on June 17. The following are excerpts from two reviews for the album.

> *Nottingham Evening Post* (John Mitchell): "She will always be welcome, for her voice will never lose its warmth or its power to hold an audience. . . . Yes, this is quite a triumph for Miss Garland—one that I hope will soon be repeated."
>
> *New Musical Express*: "Judy's qualities of heart and conviction speak loud and clear . . . a tour de force."

(The album would be released on October 31, 1960. It would be issued on CD in 1987, and then again in 1996.) "Yes" was deleted, but is being issued on the *I Could Go On Singing/Judy: That's Entertainment!* two-fer CD from Collectables Records in spring 2002.)

July 1960: (Personal Appearance) Judy sang at a Democratic fundraiser, sitting on the dais with John F. Kennedy and Adlai Stevenson. (Black and white newsreel footage exists.)

July 14, 1960: Judy flew to London, England (and would then go on to Rome) alone, overcoming a life-long fear of flying. She gave a press conference in London, upon her arrival, during which she said: "I've never been so happy in my life. My children—three of them—are well integrated. My marriage is just perfect. My voice is just great."

August 2, 1960: (Record) Judy arrived at 7 p.m. at EMI studios in London for the first of five sessions to complete a two-record set of both new songs and rerecordings of many Garland standards, all to be done in stereo. On this date she recorded: "Chicago"; "Do It Again"; "Lucky Day"; and finally "Stormy Weather."

August 3, 1960: (Record) Judy did the second of five sessions for her next (double) album, at EMI in London. On this date, she recorded, "I Happen To Like New York"; "Swanee"; "You'll Never Walk Alone"; and "Why Was I Born?"

August 4, 1960: (Record) Judy's double album continued recording at EMI in London (session three of five), with the following songs done on this date: "The Man That Got Away"; "Come Rain Or Come Shine"; "San Francisco"; and then "Over The Rainbow."

August 5, 1960: (Record) Judy continued recording songs for her two-LP set, with the fourth of five sessions at EMI in London. On this date she recorded the medley of "You Made Me Love You"/"For Me And My Gal"/"The Trolley Song"; then "You Go To My Head"; "Happiness Is A Thing Called Joe"; and finally "Rock-A-Bye Your Baby With A Dixie Melody."

August 8, 1960: (Record) Judy's two-record set concluded recording with its fifth and final session at EMI in London. On this date she recorded the "Judy At The Palace" medley; then "I Can't Give You Anything But Love"; "After You've Gone"; and "It's A Great Day For The Irish." (The album would not be released for quite some time, due to Judy singing much of the same material on a "live" album in the spring of 1961. Six of the tracks would be used to fill out a 1962 album *The Garland Touch*. All of the tracks would finally appear on a set released by the Capitol Record Club in 1972, when the two records would be called *Judy in London*—the same title would be used for a 1980 Capitol Records "Special Markets" release. The tracks would then be issued on CD as part of a Capitol Records box set on Judy in 1991, and on its own separate disc in 1992, which is still available, both of which are called *The London Sessions*. This album represents some of Judy's finest work—as does the previous *That's Entertainment* recording. Judy's rest during most of the first half of 1960 had restored her voice to its full force and power.)

August 28, 1960: (Concert) Judy's first two-act solo concert—which was actually the first known, two-act, solo, one-woman concert by a female pop vocalist—the London Palladium, London, England. Judy devised her own program of songs (saying in 1962, "I figured out my program myself on the inside of a pack of matches"), selected her clothes, and even helped design the lighting for this concert. She opened with "I Happen To Like This Town" ("I Happen To Like New York," with special lyrics about London) and closed her first act with "You'll Never Walk Alone," in tribute to Oscar Hammerstein, who had passed away five days before the concert. All the other songs would be the same as her concert program as presented on April 23, 1961—see that date for the program of songs.

> *The Record Mirror* (Isadore Green): "At the conclusion of every number there was an outburst of applause of tornado-like dimensions. At the end of an unforgettable performance, the reception was just as unforgettable. It was a standing ovation. People just went crazy with exhilaration. They stood-up and clapped and cheered and shouted at the top of their voices."
>
> Critic Jack Hutton: "Incredible, to see so many stars wallowing in unashamed admiration for another. Incredible to hear [her] magic set fire to the last chorus of some square old song and watch the audience burst at the seams and applaud bars before the end."
>
> Columnist Angus Hall: "[Judy is] the high priestess of pop."

September 4, 1960: (Concert) The London Palladium, London, England.

Around this time—either August 31 or September 7 (both dates have been noted) Judy was seen at the opening of Noel Coward's play *Waiting in the Wings*.

"We'll change you completely . . . Great big things out here: Spit curls, we used to call them in my day": so Judy later told the tale (at Carnegie Hall) of the elaborate hairstyle created for her by "this marvelous Parisian fellow who was just supposed to be the end, you know, and he came in and took one look at me, and was quite discouraged." Here Judy is seen with the spit curls intact, while in Paris, October 1960. (Courtesy of Photofest.)

October 5, 1960: (Concert) The Palais de Chaillot, Paris, France.

> *Variety*: "One of the first standing ovations for a singing artist since the war. Her kind of gifts broke the lingo barrier with ease."

The ticket prices ranged from $2.00 up to $10.00. There were a couple hundred empty seats during this concert, but two nights later the legendary hall was 100% sold out. While in Paris, the Duke and Duchess of Windsor gave Judy parties, and the Guinnesses gave her an after-show party in their penthouse.

October 7, 1960: (Concert) The Palais de Chaillot, Paris, France.

October 16, 1960: (Concert) The Leeds Odeon Theater, Leeds, England.

October 23, 1960: (Concert) The Birmingham Odeon Theater, Birmingham, England.

October 26, 1960: (Concert/Personal Appearance) A "Koncert For Kennedy" (John F. Kennedy), Wiesbaden, Germany.

October 28, 1960: (Concert) The Olympia Theater, Paris, France. (Portions of this show were allowed to be recorded for radio broadcast; these songs were released on the *Judy Garland: Paris* CD, from Europe 1 Records, in 1994.)

October 29, 1960: (Concert) The Olympia Theater, Paris, France.

November 5, 1960: Judy's scheduled concert at the Free Trade Hall in Manchester, England, was canceled when she, Sid, Fred Finklehoff and his wife, all came down with food poisoning; the concert was rescheduled for December 4. According to the November 14, 1960, issue of Billboard, Finklehoff was scripting the screenplay for *Born in Wedlock*, for filming in England "next year." (As mentioned previously, the movie would never be made.)

November 1960: Two concerts in Frankfurt.

November 15, 1960: (Concert) The De Montford Hall, Leister, England.

December 1, 1960: (Benefit/Personal Appearance) The Royal Variety Show; The London Palladium, London, England. Judy performed for thirty-five minutes, singing "When You're Smiling"; "Do It Again"; "Come Rain Or Come Shine"; "The Man That Got Away"; "San Francisco"; "Rock-A-Bye Your Baby"; "Judy's Olio"; "Over The Rainbow"; and "Swanee."

December 4, 1960: (Concert) The Free Trade Hall, Manchester, England (rescheduled from November 5.) Along with Judy's usual program, she and Liza sang "After You've Gone."

Friday, December 9, 1960: Judy arrived in Amsterdam for her concert there the following evening. While in Amsterdam, she stayed at the Doelen Hotel, and attended a party in her honor that night.

Saturday, December 10, 1960: (Concert/Radio) The Tuschinski Theater, Amsterdam, The Netherlands. This special "Midnight Concert" was broadcast "live." The broadcast of the complete concert was issued on a series of three LPs in the late 1970s and early 1980s, called *Judy Garland in Holland*, and in 1996

Judy onstage at the famed Olympia in Paris, October 28 and 29, 1960. Throughout her concert career, Judy appeared at the world's greatest theaters and concert halls, including the London Palladium, the Palace Theater, the Met, the Olympia, the Hollywood Bowl, and, of course, Carnegie Hall. (Courtesy of Photofest.)

on the two-CD set import *Judy Garland in Concert: Amsterdam*, on the Gold label. The only song missing from these releases is "Over The Rainbow."

Mid December 1960: Judy signed with Freddie Fields Associates to manage her career. The deal was announced in the December 21 issue of *Variety*, which also stated that Judy was signed to appear in the London production of the Broadway Musical, *The Unsinkable Molly Brown*. *Variety* also reported that Fields was talking with Broadway producer David Merrick about having Judy do a musical on Broadway; that Fields had acquired two film properties for her; and that she would be doing two television specials, in April and in October, one of which would be for the British company Granada. Also noted were concert dates in Copenhagen on January 19, 20, 22, 27 and 28, 1961—only one of these projects materialized (the film rights to *The Lonely Stage*, which had been a television drama about a famous star), although Judy would do a television special in America for CBS, in 1962.

December 25, 1960: Christmas was spent in London.

December 31, 1960: Judy and family returned to the States—for the first time since July—checking into the Carlyle Hotel in New York.

January 9, 1961: (Concert) The Deauville Hotel, Miami, Florida. This was an engagement Judy had needed to fill before she got ill at the end of 1959; she was paid $10,000 for the one performance. This same day all suits were dropped between Judy and CBS, with CBS having an option for her television services in the immediate future; they were looking for her to do a television special for the network in the fall of 1961.

At the same time Judy signed a management contract with Freddie Fields Associates, she also signed with Arthur P. Jacobs to handle her press relations; his chief assistant, John Springer, would work closely with Judy.

Judy and Fields—and his new partner, David Begelman—formed "Kingsrow Enterprises." Fields and Begelman would prove to be instrumental in rebuilding her career. Begelman was assigned to work exclusively with Judy. Their relationship would evolve, because, at this time, Judy separated from Sid Luft once again.

January 12, 1961: At the Carlyle Hotel—just before Judy moved into her new apartment that Field's personal assistant, Stevie Dumler, had found for her at the famed Dakota—she signed a contract for her "return" to movies in a supporting role in *Judgment at Nuremberg*, for which she received $50,000. At the press conference, Judy mentioned *The Lonely Stage*, and she also said she wanted to do *The Unsinkable Molly Brown* in London. Also at this time, she was reportedly working on a screenplay for a movie musical with Abby Mann, and had talked with Richard Rogers about writing the music. This project never materialized.

Late January 1961: Judy went to Sammy Davis, Jr.'s closing night at the Copacabana, and was introduced by Sammy. When the audience went crazy, Judy was coaxed into singing "Over The Rainbow."

February 12, 1961: (Concert) The Concord Hotel, the Catskills, New York.

February 21, 1961: (Concert) The State Fair Auditorium, Dallas, Texas. Judy's legendary 1961 Concert Tour "officially" started with this concert (which also saw an offstage reunion with her sister Jimmy, who lived in Dallas with her husband.)

February 23, 1961: (Concert) City Auditorium, Houston, Texas.

March 6, 1961: Hedda Hopper reported in her column that Judy was considering three plays, one with a score by Jerome Kern, for which Dorothy Fields was writing the lyrics. Another was the musical version

On the set of *Judgment at Nuremberg*, Judy gets into character of the German woman "Irene Hoffman," with help from director Stanley Kramer, in this rare rehearsal shot, March 1961. Judy's performance would earn her an Academy Award nomination. (Courtesy of the Everett Collection.)

of *Hold Back The Dawn*, and Roger Edens was supposedly writing the third play. None of these projects ever materialized.

March 8, 1961 through March 19, 1961: (Film) *Judgment at Nuremberg*. Judy spent eleven days at Universal Studios in Los Angeles filming her scenes. The movie was released in December and Judy's performance as Irene Hoffman would win her an Academy Award Nomination for Best Supporting Actress, which she would lose to Rita Moreno for her role in *West Side Story*.

March 1961: (Television) *Here's Hollywood* interview with Helen O'Connell, taped in Los Angeles, while Judy was filming *Judgment at Nuremberg*. The show would air on June 23. (A film print of Judy's interview exists.)

March 16, 1961: (Personal Appearance) The Hollywood Foreign Press Awards (Golden Globe Awards); Beverly Hilton Hotel, Los Angeles. Judy presented a Special Achievement Award to Stanley Kramer.

March 29, 1961: Judy and Sid reconciled at their son, Joe's, sixth birthday party.

Judy Garland and William Shatner in one of his first film roles, swearing in Judy as "Irene Hoffman," during filming of *Judgment at Nuremberg*, March 1961. Throughout her lifetime, Judy came into contact or worked with most of the major cultural icons of the twentieth century, including Al Jolson, Fanny Brice, Frank Sinatra, Gene Kelly, Fred Astaire, Barbra Streisand, and even Elvis Presley and The Beatles. (Courtesy of the Everett Collection.)

Easter 1961: Judy celebrated the holiday in Palm Beach.

April 6, 1961: (Concert) Kleinhans Music Hall, Buffalo, New York. Judy's 1961 concert tour resumed.

April 8, 1961: (Concert) Constitution Hall, Washington, D.C. (A few moments of silent home movie footage, in color, was shot at this concert, and still exists.)

April 9, 1961: Judy and Sid Luft attended a dinner party hosted by Robert and Ethel Kennedy at the White House.

April 11, 1961: (Concert) Municipal Auditorium, Birmingham.

April 13, 1961: (Concert) Municipal Auditorium, Atlanta, Georgia.

April 15, 1961: (Concert) Coliseum, Greensboro, North Carolina.

April 17, 1961: (Concert) Coliseum, Charlotte, North Carolina.

April 23, 1961: (Concert) Carnegie Hall, New York, New York. Judy's most legendary concert ever. Unworldly reviews, a topnotch performance, and the fastest selling, two-record set of the time, Capitol Record's *Judy at Carnegie Hall*, aided this nearly unanimous consensus. Released in July 1961, *Judy at Carnegie Hall* would spend 95 weeks on the charts—13 of those weeks at #1. It also collected a total of five Grammy Awards, including Best Solo Vocal Performance, Female, and Album of the Year—the first time an album by a female artist or a concert recording had won that coveted award. (It also won for Best Album Cover; Best Engineering Contribution, Popular Recording; and a special Artists and Repertoire Award, which was given to the set's producer, Andy Wiswell.) The album would be released on a single abridged version CD on April 23, 1987, and as a full-length concert, in January 1989, which also restored some dialogue. The concert was finally released in its entirety and in the proper order, exactly as it happened that evening, by DCC Compact Classics, on two twenty-four-karat gold discs in March 2000. On February 27, 2001, Capitol Records also issued the entire concert in a twenty-four-bit digitally remixed and remastered "Fortieth Anniversary" edition with additional photos and a remembrance by Judy's musical director/arranger/conductor, the genius Mort Lindsey. Lindsey did more for Judy than any other arranger/conductor with whom she worked (and he would work with her exclusively on all of her projects through May 1964, frequently in 1965–1966, and again on her two final U.S. television shows in December 1968). Here is the song list that Judy used for her 1960 and 1961 tour (changes made are noted during the particular performances; see the dates in summer and fall 1961): **Act One**: Judy: Overture: "The Trolley Song"/"Over the Rainbow"/"The Man That Got Away"; "When You're Smiling (The Whole World Smiles With You)"; Medley: "Almost Like Being In Love"/"This Can't Be Love"; "Do It Again"; "You Go To My Head"; "Alone Together"; "Who Cares (As Long As You Care For Me); "Puttin' On The Ritz"; "How Long Has This Been Going On?"; "Just You, Just Me"; "The Man That Got Away"; and "San Francisco." **Act Two**: "*More* Judy": "That's Entertainment!"; "I Can't Give You Anything But Love"; "Come Rain Or Come Shine"; "You're Nearer"; "A Foggy Day"; "If Love Were All"; "Zing! Went The Strings Of My Heart"; "Stormy Weather"; Medley: "You Made Me Love You"/"For Me And My Gal"/"The Trolley Song"; "Rock-A-Bye Your Baby With A Dixie Melody"; "Over The Rainbow"; "Swanee"; "After You've Gone"; and "Chicago." (That's a total of twenty-six songs—including the overture; twelve in the First Act, and fourteen in the Second Act.) Judy grossed $20,100.62 at the box office for this one concert at Carnegie, which had a top ticket price of $9.90. More than any monetary gain, however, was the fact that this evening—helped in large part by the album—would become not only the "live" performance most associated with Judy, but widely acknowledged as one of the greatest evenings

One of the greatest and most legendary performances of Judy's entire career: April 23, 1961, at Carnegie Hall in New York. The love in this photo (taken during the encores at the end of the concert) was captured on the recording made by Capitol Records, and is now available complete and uncut from the label on the *Judy at Carnegie Hall: Fortieth Anniversary Edition* CD set. (Courtesy of Photofest.)

in show business history. The following are excerpts from some of those who tried to explain what they experienced at Carnegie Hall that evening:

> *The New York Times's* Lewis Funke said, "The religious ritual of greeting, watching, and listening to Judy Garland took place last night at Carnegie Hall. [The concert] turned into something not too remote from a revival meeting. . . . What Billy Graham would have given for such a welcome from the faithful! [Judy was] always making her audience feel—as one listener remarked—'as if she's singing just to you.'"

Famed critic Judith Crist reported for the *New York Herald-Tribune* that "[Judy's] ingenuous warmth dominated the evening, but there is neither coyness or girly-girlishness in her approach. . . . Well, I can't give you anything but raves, Miss Garland."

The Los Angeles Times's Cecil Smith noted, "There was a winning simplicity to the show. . . . She did none of the routines she has leaned upon in recent years—there was no clown make-up, no tramp outfit. She stood up there and sang."

Bill Roberts reported for *The Houston Post* that "hundreds began crowding the aisles. Some of these creatures were actually in a transport of ecstasy and did not know what they were doing. They stared only at Judy with a fantastic light in their eyes."

The industry bible, *Variety*, said, "It's virtually impossible to remain casual and uninvolved when she's at work. . . . There was an ease and a self-assurance in her demeanor . . . the audience couldn't resist anything she did. . . . Capitol Records engineers were on hand to put *Judy At Carnegie* into the groove. Even pruned to the limitations of an LP's running time, it should be a socko platter."

The Long Island Daily Press's Burt Boyar said, "the condition in which Miss Garland left her audience is totally indescribable. Never before have I seen hundreds of people fill the aisles and move toward the stage where they stood in a mass with their hands outstretched, just trying to touch her. She might have been a great faith healer endowed with magical powers, so urgent was their need to get closer to her. The bravos roared from the back of the great concert hall like a massive tidal wave. When she had sung every song for which the orchestra had music, the people shouted 'Just stand there.' If she had remained there for an hour, they would have applauded that. If the building had caught fire, I think they'd have perished on the spot rather than leave her. . . . Within thirty seconds [of her entrance] the audience was on its feet greeting her with a standing ovation, the first of at least a dozen that were to follow. People were on their feet so often, it seemed a shame to have paid for seats. . . . God knows what has happened to her, but it should happen to everyone. She is completely relaxed, she danced around like a happy kid between and during her songs and her voice is rich and loaded with her unique Garland sound. . . . She is full of fun and absolutely lovable. When she bends back and pulls those big notes up from her toes—well, forget about it—there is no other woman in show business."

April 29, 1961: (Concert) The Academy of Music, Philadelphia, Pennsylvania.

May 2, 1961: (Concert) The Mosque Theater, Newark, New Jersey.

May 5, 1961: Hedda Hopper reported that Chuck Walters wanted to direct Judy in the movie version of *By the Beautiful Sea*, the Dorothy Fields musical. Judy would have played a Coney Island boarding house owner in the 1900s. (Shirley Booth played the part on stage.) This is yet another project that never happened.

May 6, 1961: (Concert) Civic Opera House, Chicago, Illinois. (Following the concert, there was a dinner party at midnight given for Judy at Cafe de Paris.)

May 8, 1961: (Concert) The Music Hall; Dallas, Texas.

May 10, 1961: (Concert) The San Houston Coliseum, Houston, Texas. (9,400 people attended the concert.)

May 11, 1961: Judy left Houston at 7 a.m. for her next concert:

May 12, 1961: (Concert) The Masonic Auditorium, Detroit, Michigan.

May 14, 1961: (Concert) The Music Hall, Cleveland, Ohio. Lorna and Joe shared this concert with their mother on Mother's Day.

May 21, 1961: (Concert) Carnegie Hall, New York, New York. Judy's return concert. (She sang "Swanee" twice; the second time with Liza. Silent, black-and-white home-movie footage was shot of this concert—including a brief bit of the mother-daughter duet—and still exists. June 10, 1961, was Judy's thirty-ninth birthday.)

June 30, 1961: Judy signed what would later become accepted as her Last Will and Testament, naming her children as equal beneficiaries, and David Begelman, Freddy Fields, and Allen Sussman as trustees in all areas. (At this time Judy was living at 1 Cornell Street in Mamaroneck in Scarsdale, New York.)

July 1, 1961: (Concert) Forest Hills Stadium (Tennis Club), Forest Hills (Queens), New York. Capacity audience of 14,672 attended this performance. Judy was staying at the Forest Hills Inn, where there was a party held after the concert, which she attended from 12:45 a.m. to 3:45 a.m.

July 3, 1961: (Concert) "Music at Newport" Jazz Festival, Rhode Island. This was a matinee; the show grossed $25,000. (While staying in Rhode Island, Judy stayed at Clift Manor.) Judy wore a new dress at this concert that she designed; it is the first known design she executed. She would design one of her last stage costumes, which she wore during her 1968–1969 concerts—including her very last concert—and on two television shows, *Mike Douglas* and *Sunday Night at the London Palladium.*

Summer 1961: Judy had rented a home for this summer, on Hyanisport, near the Kennedy compound, to which she and the children would return between social and professional engagements.

July 20, 1961: Judy attended a party held onstage at Carnegie Hall that Capitol Records gave to celebrate the release of the *Judy at Carnegie Hall* album. The following is an excerpt from one of the reviews that can sum up why it seems nearly every household had this album, even if it was the only Judy record they owned.

> *Melody Maker*: "I finally got around to getting myself the new Judy Garland album. The concert took place on April 23rd of this year, and from those who were there I gathered that this was a great night. I've always been a Judy Garland fan without getting to the fever stage, but brother, I am converted now. The album consists of two LPs without any inhibitions whatsoever. Let me confess I've never sat through such recorded emotion in my life."

July 30, 1961: (Concert) Forest Hills Stadium (Tennis Club), Forest Hills (Queens), New York. (Return engagement; this concert was postponed from the night before, due to rain.) "Just In Time" was added to her concert song list for the first time at this performance. At her hotel after the performance, Judy had dinner with Fields and Begelman until 2:45 a.m., out on the patio of the Forest Hills Inn, and sang "The Star Spangled Banner" and "My Country 'Tis Of Thee" to her managers at the table.

August 1, 1961: Judy wrote a letter to the president of her fan club, Pat McMath, who reprinted it in the *Garland Gazette*.

Judy was perhaps never more popular or profiled than in 1961, resulting in many publicity photo sittings, including this soulful portrait. (Courtesy of Photofest.)

"Dear Pat, Just a note to thank-you for your visit—and to thank-you again for your continued good wishes. I couldn't be more grateful . . . but then you must know that by now! Affectionate Regards, As Always, Judy."

August 4, 1961: (Concert) Convention Hall Ballroom, Atlantic City, New Jersey. (Judy stayed at the Claridge Hotel while she was in Atlantic City for this performance.)

August 9, 1961: A contract signed by Judy and drafted on this date for her Wednesday, September 20 concert in Denver. Her payment was $12,500; she would also receive 60% of the box office take once it got over $25,000.

Week of August 11, 1961: Judy went to Boston with her publicist John Springer, and with Kay Thompson, to attend the out-of-town opening of Noel Coward's new musical, *Sail Away*. Dorothy Kilgallen reported in her August 3rd column that Judy would record some of the songs from this show—but she would only record the title song a year later; see April 26, 1962. During this trip to see Coward's show, *Redbook* magazine recorded a backstage conversation between Judy and Noel, from which excerpts were published. An audiotape of these excerpts still exists.

August 23, 1961: Judy returned to New York this evening, with Lorna and Joe—Liza was in Massachusetts doing *Take Me Along*.

September 3, 1961: (Concert) Convention Hall Ballroom, Atlantic City, New Jersey. (Return engagement.)

September 13, 1961: (Concert) Civic Auditorium, San Francisco, California. 8,700 people attended, and the show grossed $45,000 at a $7.75, top price.

September 16, 1961: First, during the day, Judy attended a private screening of *Judgment at Nuremberg*, the first time she saw the movie. Then at night: (Concert) The Hollywood Bowl, Los Angeles, California. At this concert, Judy sang "Never Will I Marry" and "Oh, What A Little Moonlight Can Do," along with "Just In Time," keeping her Carnegie Hall program fresh for herself and her audience. 17,823 people—a sold-out, capacity crowd—refused to leave the concert during a heavy downpour of rain. The show grossed $72,412 that night, the Bowl's box-office record up to that time. (Judy had supper at Romanoff's after the performance.)

September 20, 1961: (Concert) The Coliseum, Denver, Colorado. A capacity crowd of 7,484 people attended, for a gross of $36,922; ticket prices ranged from $2.50 up to a $7.50 top.

September 29, 1961: (Concert) The Westchester Country Club, White Plains, New York.

October 1, 1961: (Concert) The Bushnell Auditorium, Hartford, Connecticut. (Liza attended this performance.)

October 7, 1961: (Concert) The Mosque Theater, Newark, New Jersey.

October 13, 1961: (Record) Due to the huge success of the Carnegie Hall album, Capitol Records had Judy record a single (the label only saw her as an album artist.) The 45 was two Broadway show tunes, "Comes Once In A Lifetime" backed with "Sweet Danger." This session was done in New York, with Mort Lindsey doing his usual brilliant job of arranging and conducting. The following is an excerpt from a review of the single:

> *New Musical Express*: "Judy Garland's latest Capitol waxing, and both numbers are from current Broadway musicals. . . . With Judy so hot on LPs at the moment, this single could easily be a big smash for her—something I would like to see, as there are not many artists of her caliber in the singles field."

Only the "A-side" ("Lifetime") has appeared on CD to date—on a Smithsonian tribute disc to Jule Styne. Both songs should be on a spring 2002 Capitol Records two-CD compilation.

October 17, 1961: (Concert) The War Memorial, Rochester, New York. After this performance, Judy played cards all night, then caught a 6 a.m. flight to Pittsburgh. She slept all day on October 18 upon her arrival.

October 19, 1961: (Concert) The Civic Auditorium, Pittsburgh, Pennsylvania.

October 21, 1961: (Concert) The Arena, Haddonfield, New Jersey.

October 27, 1961: (Concert) The Garden, Boston, Massachusetts. The Garden held 13,909 people; ticket prices ranged from $2.00 to a $6.00 top, and this performance was expected to gross $52,000.

October 29, 1961: (Concert) The Forum, Montreal, Canada.

November 1961: (Movie) Judy spent three weeks in Los Angeles recording the voice of the cat, "Mewsette," for the full-length musical cartoon-feature *Gay Purr-ee*, which included the new Harold Arlen and E. Y. Harburg songs written for Judy to sing. (Arlen and Harburg wrote the score to *The Wizard of Oz.*) Gene Kelly was rumored as wanted for the male cat lead that Robert Goulet ended up doing. Maurice Chevalier had originally been hoped to be the narrator. Judy was paid $50,000 and—in a rare gesture for the 1960s—10% of the gross. Warner Brothers released the movie in December 1962, during which Judy would make several promotional appearances. It made its television broadcast premiere on December 23, 1966. (In order to do the recording for the film, Judy did have to cancel a November 4 concert at the Civic Auditorium in San Francisco.) The movie's soundtrack LP was released by Warner Brothers Records, and has yet to be issued on CD.

November 20, 1961: (Concert) The Beverly Hilton Hotel, Los Angeles, California.

November 25, 1961: (Concert) Exhibition Hall, Miami Beach, Florida.

November 28, 1961: (Concert) The Stanley Theater, Jersey City, New Jersey.

December 3, 1961: (Concert) The O'Keefe Center, Toronto, Canada. The 3,211-seat hall was SRO (Standing Room Only). The following are excerpts from two reviews of this performance:

> [She] is the one star who never takes her ovations for granted, or the affection which greets her. Her discovery of it is as spontaneous as her singing is. The house vibrated with the wonderment at [her] limitless power. . . . [She] has one gift that came as a great surprise—she moves with grace and elegance. . . . Any cool investigation of the Garland mystique goes by the board after you find that unexpected moisture in your eyes. All you wonder at is how, in that great, big, crowded, noisy house, Judy Garland can find you out and sing directly to you.

A rare movie poster for *Gay Purr-ee*. Years before it became "in" to record a voice for an animated feature, Judy did just that in 1961. The photo of Judy in this poster is actually from October 1953, taken during the shooting of one of the discarded versions of the song "The Man That Got Away" for *A Star Is Born*. (Courtesy of Photofest.)

> *The Telegram*: "How do you record that the massive pile of the Center shook, that the air inside stirred and shuddered strangely, and that a host of citizens seemed supernaturally shocked with pleasure? How do you explain that it was due to the uncanny powers of one tiny woman singing songs? How do you measure miracles?"

December 5, 1961: (Concert) The O'Keefe Center, Toronto, Canada. Another SRO show.

December 9, 1961: (Concert) Armory, Washington, D.C. This was the final concert of Judy's legendary 1961 tour.

December 14, 1961: (Television) Judy taped an interview with Jack Linkletter for the show *Here's Hollywood* (it would be shown January 1962) in West Berlin, Germany, where she had arrived for the premiere of her new film.

December 15, 1961: (Premiere) World Premiere of Judy's *Judgment at Nuremberg*, in Berlin, Germany.

Late December: Judy spent some time in Rome before returning to the States to spend the holidays with Sid Luft and the children at their rented home at 1 Cornell Street in Scarsdale. Portions of an audiotape made of the Luft familiy's Christmas day are transcribed in Gerald Frank's 1975 biography, *Judy*. Judy also did some rehearsing in Scarsdale for a television special to be videotaped in early January 1962.

Also in December 1961: Judy was named "Show Business Personality Of The Year" for 1961. She also received "Female Vocalist Of The Year" and "Best Popular Album Of The Year" from *Show Business Illustrated* magazine. This was certainly proof that she had achieved amazing successes in all media: film, television, records, and theater/stage/concerts. Judy was perhaps more popular, more written about, and more loved than perhaps at any other time of her career—certainly on the same level as her success at the Palace in 1951 and her earlier movie box office days when she'd been at MGM. Although some may not agree with that assessment, it would seem that most people agree that Judy Garland hit the peak of her career in 1961 (and throughout the early 1960s). To think that little over a year before she stepped onto the stage of Carnegie Hall, she had nearly died, and here she was, supposedly free of her $375,000 worth of debt and at the peak of her powers, with more achievements ahead of her. Knowing what had happened to her at the end of 1959, no one can doubt the enormity of the woman's strength to have accomplished what she did in 1961.

January 2, 1962 through January 4, 1962: Rehearsals in Burbank, California, for Judy's new television special—her first in six years (some of the musical work had been mapped out the week before, while Judy was still in Scarsdale, New York). Also on January 4, Judy had a meeting with Stanley Kramer about her next movie, *A Child Is Waiting*, which would start filming later in the month.

January 5, 1962, January 8, 1962, and January 9, 1962: (Television) Videotaping of Judy's television special for CBS, *The Judy Garland Show* (originally called *Miss Show Business*), with guests Frank Sinatra and Dean Martin. (The show was actually videotaped at NBC in Hollywood, even though it was a CBS production.) Judy's songs included: "Just In Time"; "When You're Smiling"; "You Do Something To Me," with Sinatra and Martin; "The Man That Got Away"; "I Can't Give You Anything But Love, Baby"; "Let There Be Love" and "You're Nobody Till Somebody Loves You," with Sinatra and Martin; and the closing mini-concert segment (blocked and taped in front of a studio audience on January 9), "You Made Me Love You" and "The Trolley Song"; "Rock-A-Bye Your Baby"; "Swanee"; and "San Francisco." The Sinatra-Martin scenes and duets were videotaped January 5. On the evening of January 8, from 8:30 p.m. to 12:30 a.m., Judy videotaped "Man"; "Just In Time," and "Smiling" in front of a studio audience at NBC. Many of them returned the following evening for the taping of the final (concert) segment. During the blocking of "San Francisco," Judy sang "I never will forget Deanna Durbin" (instead of "Jeanette McDonald"). On this last night of taping, January 9, Judy worked until 1:30 a.m., and at 3 a.m. was signing autographs for her fans. The show won its time slot when broadcast on February 25, beating *Bonanza*; the special was also the second highest-rated show to air that season and was reported to be the highest-rated special in CBS history up to that date, drawing 49.5 of the television-viewing audience. The show was also nominated for four Emmy Awards, Best Program of the Year, Outstanding Variety or Music Program, Outstanding Performance in a Variety or Music Program, and Best Art Direction, although it did not win any. The following are excerpts from two reviews:

> *The Los Angeles Times*: "A beautiful hour [with] moments as memorable as any that television has ever given us."
>
> *TV Guide*: "Nobody can match her."

According to several reports, Judy was very active and aware when it came to how she should be photographed and lit. She often directed camera angles, etc., and, at one point, had lights adjusted when they were reflecting on her jacket; Judy would also watch the videotape after a segment had been shot to see how she looked. The show is available on video cassette—in a colorized version—from LaserLight Video on VHS and DVD, #82 017, from the same label, called *Frank Sinatra: Portrait of a Legend: The Man and his Music: Judy, Frank and Dean—The Legendary Concert.*

January 15, 1962 to mid April 1962: (Movie) Judy filmed a dramatic role in the Stanley Kramer film, *A Child Is Waiting*, costarring Burt Lancaster, for United Artists. The film was made at the Revue Studios in Hollywood, aside from a few shoots on location, and was released in January 1963.

> *The London Times* review said in part: "[Her] quiet performance is all the more effective for the fact that her well-known, well-loved mannerisms are kept in check. She has seldom been better."

February 26, 1962: Not only was Judy basking in the reviews and success of her television special, this was also the date that the Academy Award nominations were announced. As mentioned previously, Judy was nominated for Best Supporting Actress for her role in *Judgment at Nuremberg*; Rita Moreno won the award for her role in *West Side Story*. It was also reported on this day that CBS had signed Judy for two more television specials; Ethel Merman and Dean Martin were to appear on the first, and Judy would do another special for the network with different guests. (See January 30, 1963 through February 3, 1963 for information on the special; and see October 4, 1963 and December 13, 1963 for the times Judy worked with Merman.)

March 1962: (Award) Hollywood Foreign Press Awards (Golden Globes), Los Angeles. Judy was awarded the Cecil B. DeMille Award for outstanding contributions to entertainment throughout the world.

Part of the original "Rat Pack": Dean Martin, Judy, and Frank Sinatra during the videotaping of Judy's return-to-television special, January 5, 1962. Judy is wearing the outfit she wore during the first act of her Carnegie Hall concert and tour. (Courtesy of Photofest.)

A lovely portrait of Judy taken on the set of *A Child Is Waiting*, January 15–mid-April, 1962. Judy had a lifelong devotion to children and was vocal in her support of retarded children, saying "many of them have very high IQs. . . . they shouldn't just be shuttered away." (Courtesy of Photofest.)

April 6, 1962: Judy wrote her first of a series of notes/letters to David Begelman on this date, at 4 a.m. On Beverly Hills Hotel stationary, she wrote about having just returned from a poker game where no one introduced her to the one man she didn't know, and how lack of manners upset her. Still, Judy said she was so happy that she cared "about basic things—a little gentleness—a little warmth—and being able to give a little love whenever and wherever it's needed."

Mid April 1962: Judy finished filming *Child,* and flew directly into New York, checking into a hospital for a brief rest and complete checkup. She was released on April 23. However, she left the hospital on at least one day—April 18—to attend a rehearsal/taping session that Mort Lindsey was holding in a New York City recording studio with the orchestra he'd assembled for Judy's next album, which would be done the following week. Judy mostly listened, but did sing along (lightly, for the most part) and even recorded a vocal for "Something's Coming."

April 23, 1962: (Radio) *Make Believe Ballroom,* New York. On the first anniversary of the first *Judy at Carnegie Hall* concert, Judy reminisced on this live radio show, while selections from the album were played. (A tape of this show still exists in private collections.)

April 26, 1962: (Recording) A "live" recording session, starting at midnight, was held at Manhattan Center, for the Capitol album *Judy Takes Broadway.* Unfortunately, Judy was suffering from laryngitis, and the album would not be released (except for bootleg recordings) until 1989, when Capitol would release *Judy Garland Live* on June 28, 1989; the album would be out-of-print by the early 1990s. Judy's songs included: "Sail Away"; "Something's Coming"; "Just In Time"; "Some People"; "Never Will I Marry"; "Joey, Joey, Joey"; and "The Party's Over." She also attempted "Do What You Do" and "Why Can't I?"after the concert, when the audience had left. Her vocal condition prevented her from completing any takes on these two songs, and the partial takes have never been released. (Judy sang from midnight until 1:30 a.m. with the audience, and then until 4 a.m. without them.) At one point during the session, Liza came onstage and danced. Nineteen year-old Barbra Streisand—who had just opened in *I Can Get It For You Wholesale*—was in the audience. Also attending was Marilyn Monroe, who was photographed reaching out to Judy, Marilyn's favorite singer. Judy apologized to the audience for her vocal condition, saying, "I wanted to sing beautifully for you. But we'll get there, if you stay with me. You usually have—it's what's kept me alive."

April 28, 1962: Judy flew to London to start her next movie, *The Lonely Stage*—which would be changed to *I Could Go On Singing* before its release (when UA decided it should be obvious that Judy was singing on screen for the first time since *A Star Is Born.*) Judy created international headlines when she left with Lorna and Joe, after Sid had forbid her to take them with her to England ("Judy Flees Country" was one overly dramatic headline). Upon arriving in England, the film's PR man, Les Perkins, secured Judy and her three children in a secret address. To thank him, Judy, Liza and Lorna put on an "impromptu" show for him, which included the song "Food, Glorious, Food," from the musical *Oliver,* a big favorite of the family's. Judy had Lorna and Joe declared "wards of court," so Sid could not take them out of England.

While in England for the filming, Judy appeared at the opening night of Noel Coward's *Sail Away.*

May 1, 1962: Judy started rehearsals for *Singing* at the Shepperton Studios.

May 2, 1962: A ninety-minute press reception for *Singing* was held at the Dorchester with Judy and her costar Dirk Bogarde (back in August 1961, Hedda Hopper had reported that Laurence Oliver was being sought for the male lead, and later, Peter Sellers, before Bogarde was signed). During this press conference,

Judy mentioned she'd be rerecording the "quieter songs" for *Judy Takes Broadway* while in London. This session never happened. However, additional session tapes for this album were dated May 10, 1962 and included notes that "master sent to Andy Wiswell [Judy's record producer] 5-10-62 [via] overseas shipment." (Judy and Wiswell would be in England working on her next album—the soundtrack to a new movie.) Still, these tapes sent to Wiswell were derived from the April 18 rehearsal and the April 26 session.

Week of May 7, 1962: Judy recorded "Hello, Bluebird" in the studio in England, to which she would lip-synch the following week during filming of the number.

May 14, to July 13, 1962: *I Could Go On Singing* was filmed in England, starting with three days (May 14–16) for scenes at the London Palladium. The first day was spent filming the song "Hello, Bluebird."

"I Must Keep On Singing": Judy recording one of the songs for her last movie, *I Could Go On Singing*, in London, May–July 1962. (Courtesy of Photofest.)

Judy arrived at 8:30 a.m. for makeup and hair; rehearsals started at 11:30 p.m. Close-ups were shot first, and lunch was called at 1:30 p.m. Rehearsals continued in the afternoon on May 14; three takes were shot, but the camera faulted, so retakes were done later on. The audience was filmed on the second and third days at the Palladium. The title song was also filmed at the actual Palladium; "It Never Was You" was sung "live" on a set made to resemble the Palladium, as was "By Myself." On Friday, June 8, Judy shot studio retakes of the Canterbury Cathedral scene, and then celebrated her birthday with the cast, crew, her children, and Lorna Smith. June 10, 1962, was Judy's fortieth birthday. Judy also worked on the film's script with costar Dirk Bogarde; their highlight was the climatic eight-minute scene in the hospital, which was rehearsed for six hours, then filmed in one take. During an interview for *Inside Show Business* at the start of filming *Singing*, Judy said she'd learned "that everything passes. Friends go, and husbands and lovers. Even your children leave you, and you can't stop it. You just have to rely on you, yourself. I think I can . . . now."

May 22, 1962: Judy sent David Begelman a wire, originally written in pencil on 33 Hyde Park Gate stationary, that was received in New York on this date. It was a short, informal note expressing how she had just had dinner at Sir Harry's Bars and how she wanted to hear from him. It also said that she loved him. She signed it "Pussy Cat."

June 8, 1962: Judy sent David Begelman another wire, at 9:46 a.m. (It was on this day that she shot the studio retakes on the Cantebury scenes of *Singing* and had her birthday party on the set.) The wire was only a few words, in which she informed Begelman she was in need of his help, and that she wanted him to fly to England immediately.

July 4, 1962: Apparently Begelman did visit Judy, for she sent him another telegram, at 7:07 p.m. on this date, thanking him for flying over to see her, and apologizing for possibly upsetting him before he returned to the States.

There are several other letters that Judy wrote Begelman with no dates, but they are believed to be from this time period, in 1962, to 1963. They are not always easy to take, but are very revealing of how wonderfully emotional and romantic and loving Judy Garland was—even in times of distress:

> No date, one page, Savoy Hotel stationary: In black crayon, Judy wrote of what an exciting time it was for her family to return to England, and thanked Begelman for being "the tallest one."
>
> No date, one page, Savoy Hotel stationary: Judy gave Begelman presents with a note, and again mentioned her vast and loyal love to him.
>
> No date, one page, party-printed Memorandum sheet: Judy asked Begelman to wake her as she'd stopped an 8:00 call, and she asked that he relax, as others could handle all transactions that morning.
>
> No date, three pages, the Pittsburgh Hilton stationary (may have been October 19, 1961, when she played Pittsburgh): Judy wrote a moving letter to Begelman, shortly after they had been intimate, in which she realized that he was not capable of loving her, even though she felt he wanted to love her. She wrote that she had never thought she'd fall so completely in love with him, and that she would never love again. "As God is my judge—no one will ever receive my love, my mind—my body—my breathing again. I gave you all I had to give." She concluded the long letter by insisting he be proud that she loved him and that he had to be "quite a guy to have been so deeply loved and needed and wanted."

The next two are, apparently, suicide notes that Judy left. The first is to her children, the second to Begelman. Keep in mind that the 1975 Gerald Frank bio *Judy* also contained reproductions of suicide notes.

> No date, One page, torn into six pieces and taped back together: Judy wrote to her children that she hoped they would pardon what she'd done, but that she got "too tired." She assured them that she adored them, asked that they look after each other, and she thanked them for "the only true love I've ever gotten."
>
> In a similar vein, was Judy's suicide note to Begelman: No date, seven pages, written on sheets torn from an address book, in pencil. The first page is crossed out and appears unrelated to rest of note—this first page mentions Judy's desire to spend time with her children before they went back to school and to get them gifts for that occasion. Judy also mentioned a party to be held by Betty Comden, and thought to ask Liza along. Then came the actual note to Begelman, in which Judy mentions she was again, "tired," and "alone," that "I loved one man who could not love me." She asked that her children be protected and "don't think for 1 second I don't worship them." The note was concluded with the last lines from the famous song "I'm Old Fashioned": "I'm old fashioned, but I don't mind it. That's how I want to be, as long as you'll agree to stay old fashioned with me."
>
> And last, no date, the Plaza Hotel stationary, eight pages: Judy apologized for "the demands—the anguish—the hurt I've given you," and says she needed to not be in his life. "My only hope is to go away—someplace—and try, try in spite of my hideous weakness to create a dignity for myself. . . . I have to find a way somehow and somewhere—and I alone have to try to keep breathing. God willing I make it so that I can go on working and be a sane and deserving mother. My love for you was overwhelming—but I say it again—I've been terribly wrong in the harm my love brought you." Judy concluded by stating she would return to work for Begelmen, as her debts to her manager were "monumental."

If only Judy knew how much Begelman was in *her* debt. It should also be noted that Begelman was about to help Judy reach a new level of debt; she was soon to be destroyed financially.

July 13, 1962: Judy finished filming *I Could Go On Singing*. Coproducer Stuart Miller said in a mid-June statement that Judy had been on the set "every morning at 7:15, and doesn't leave until 6 p.m. We're rolling along so fast." In her column of August 3, 1962, Hedda Hopper had reported that the film had wrapped "last week," and that the final cost of the movie was $1.4 million. It would premiere in London on March 6, 1963, and then in the U.S. in May 1963. Judy received some of the best reviews of her career, as you'll see from the following excerpts:

> *Time*: "Her acting may be the best of her career."
>
> *The London Telegraph*: "She is the very best there is."
>
> *The Listener*: "Incandescent—an enchantress."

The movie, sadly, did not do very well, and, as its director Ronald Neame told me United Artists had told him, "Ronnie, it's as if someone put a sign up in front of the theater that said 'Warning: Quarantined.'" (*Singing* had its television premiere on December 21, 1967, from 9 p.m. to 11 p.m. on *The CBS Thursday Night Movies*.)

Mid July 1962 to mid August 1962: Judy stayed in London for court hearings in a custody battle with Sid Luft over Lorna and Joe. Finally, Judy's attorney David Jacobs had the children undeclared "wards of court," so they could return home.

Dirk Bogard and Judy between takes of the heartbreaking hospital scene, which was written by the two stars for *I Could Go On Singing*. This scene was shot in one continuous take, following hours of rehearsal. (Courtesy of Photofest.)

End of July 1962: Capitol Records released their new Judy LP *The Garland Touch*, which was actually a compilation of tracks from her 1960 London sessions, her 1961 single, and even two "repeat" songs from her 1958 album *Judy in Love*.

August 12, 1962: Judy flew home to Los Angeles, staying at the Beverly Hills Hotel. Shortly thereafter, she flew to Lake Tahoe in Nevada, where she filed for divorce again. While in Tahoe, she went on a fast, drinking nothing but two cups of tea all day; by mid September she had slimmed down to 100 pounds.

September 14, 1962: Judy's crash diet—while successful in returning her slim, trim self—brought a serious consequence: a sudden kidney attack. However, within forty-eight hours, Judy had checked herself out of the hospital and started her next engagement.

September 17, 1962: Letter from Begelman to Judy, handwritten on Hotel Sahara stationary. The letter talked about how he had arranged for Judy to get an additional $2,500 in cash from the Sahara for each week she played there. He said he had told the Sahara that the money was needed for additional security, but he told Judy that it would be going to her. She most likely never saw a dime of it.

September 18, 1962 to October 29, 1962: (Concert) The Sahara Hotel, Las Vegas, Nevada. Judy opened her four-week engagement (at $40,000 per week), which was extended for another two weeks, at an unheard of show time, 2:30 a.m.—and even at those hours, she packed them in. Mort Lindsey conducted a twenty-seven–piece orchestra. The show's running time was sixty-five minutes; Judy opened with "Hello Bluebird" and ended with "Chicago."

> *Variety* said: "[Garland is] more dramatically electric than ever, giving her stylized tones a vibrancy tour, as she sobs, shouts, caresses her songs."

During her opening night show, on September 18, Judy received a two-minute-and-eighteen-second standing ovation—and also a Gold Record from Capitol Records's president Glenn Wallichs for *Judy at Carnegie Hall.* They later posed together with the framed Gold Record backstage. (This is the only known engagement where Judy did *not* sing "Over The Rainbow.")

While at the Sahara, Judy wrote a long note to Donald O'Connor and his wife to thank them for having her over to their home and for "being what you are—Understanding, lovely, and true friends." Judy also mentioned wanting to do a concert she'd apparently been talking to Donald about, and concluded by telling Donald she was "in awe of [his] beautiful soul [and] great talent—as I have always been through the years."

End of September 1962: Judy was beginning to plan her next television special. She said the rumors that she wanted Jackie Gleason for the show were not true, but she did mention she'd love to work with Elvis Presley. Regrettably, the "guest star" fee of $50,000 was too low for "The King." Elvis, however, was known to play Judy's music on occasion, and in 1967, he had an encounter with Judy, while driving in his car—see May 7, 1967 for more information.

October 1962: (Record) Judy recorded the song "One More Lamb" for the United Nations Charity album *Three Billion Millionaires,* an all-star event that was released on United Artists Records. The song was recorded backstage at the Sahara, after her show, so her voice does sound slightly frayed and tired. (The orchestra and children's chorus that sing with her were recorded separately. The album is out of print; Judy's track can be found on *The Definitive Garland* CD, from Pastel Productions, 1990, which is also no longer available.)

Week of October 10, 1962: During the continuing Sahara engagement, nine year-old Lorna sang "Swanee"; seven-year-old Joey "hummed."

November 7, 1962: (Concert) Arie Crown Theatre, Chicago, Illinois. Judy gave her only real "concert" in 1962 on this night (with the Sahara engagement being more of a nightclub appearance, consisting of an hour show instead of a two-act concert). She was suffering from laryngitis, but in spite of this, she wowed the crowd.

November 8, 1962: Judy flew from Chicago to New York to see her throat doctor, without calling him first. It turns out he was in Las Vegas at that time, so Judy flew back to Chicago where she had to be the next day.

November 9, 1962: (Premiere) *Gay Purr-ee* had its "World Premiere" at the State Lake Theatre in Chicago. Judy also gave a press conference for the film, during which she mentioned, "I've finally learned who I am and how to enjoy life!" After the premiere, Judy had dinner at the Pump Room at Ambassador East Hotel where she was staying, and left there at 12:30 a.m. to attend Eddie Fisher's opening at the Villa Venice in suburban North-Brook. She sang with Fisher at a party after his show, then returned to the hotel with Fisher, at 3:45 a.m.

December 2, 1962: (Television) Judy taped an appearance on *The Jack Paar Program* at NBC-TV studios at Rockefeller Center in New York City (for airing on NBC on December 7). Here she enjoyed one of the best moments of her career, enchanting the audience and critics with her wit, voice, and appearance. It was so successful that it would lead to the biggest deal of her career, which would be signed at the end of the month. (The show survives on black and white film; it was available on a bootleg video from a company called "AllStar Video," released circa 1979–1980. Her November 19 contract for the Paar show stated she would be paid for first class round-trip transportation, and up to $2,500 for living expenses in New York, from November 28 through December 2.)

December 3, 1962 to December 5, 1962: Judy did promotional appearances for *Gay Purr-ee* at New York area theaters (a radio interview survives on tape, displaying Judy's humor while touring Queens, New York by bus on one of the days; the hysteria and her loyal following are also documented).

December 6, 1962: (Personal Appearance) Judy sang for President Kennedy at the White House in Washington, D.C. (Silent newsreel footage exists of her here, which includes her singing "The Trolley Song.")

December 28, 1962: Judy signed the biggest deal of her career (at the St. Moritz Hotel in New York)—a contract worth a total of $24 million with CBS, for her own weekly television series. The deal called for a $6 million outlay for the first season (giving Judy—not the network—the right to cancel after the first thirteen-week cycle; this was unheard of at the time), with additional options for up to four more years. Thus, the deal represented $24 million dollars total. (Her agents also stated that she could earn in the area of $4 million from syndication sales for the shows.)

December 31, 1962: A statement was typed with this date saying that Judy and Sid Luft were filing taxes together, but that each would be responsible for his or her own taxes, as though filing separately. This was signed "Judy Garland Luft."

January 1963: Judy began production meetings in New York, for both her television series and the "preview/pilot" special to be taped the first week in February.

January 18, 1963: (Personal Appearance) The White House, Washington, D.C. Inaugural Anniversary Salute to Kennedy and Johnson.

Another milestone in Judy's career: her December 7, 1962, appearance on *The Jack Paar Program* (taped in New York on December 2, 1962) was the first time the public saw Judy's incomparable wit—and her newly slim and curvy figure. Here Robert Goulet and Paar say goodnight to the audience. (Judy worked with Jack and Bobby three times each, and the electric sparks really flew between Garland and Goulet on-camera.) (Courtesy of Photofest.)

A scheduled January 24 concert at the Deauville Hotel in Miami, Florida, was canceled, due to rehearsals in New York for her television special.

January 30, 1963 to February 3, 1963: (Television) The videotaping of Judy's television special for CBS, *Judy Garland and Her Guests Phil Silvers and Robert Goulet*, in New York. The outing showcased Judy's comedic versatility in sketches that were the best she would ever get to do. She played such diverse characters as a Park Avenue matron; a lady wrestler; a terrible singer auditioning for a big Broadway producer; a thick New York–accented woman just attacked by a "masher" in Central Park; one of the "Three Musketeers"; a beatnik folk singer; an inept ballet dancer destroying "Swan Lake"; and even a fall-off-your-chair-funny spoof of . . . Judy Garland! Judy also sang three of her four solos from *I Could Go On Singing*, plugging her about-to-be-released movie by opening the show with "Hello, Bluebird," closing the show with the title song, and, her most effective musical moment of the show, an electrifying "By Myself." She also sang "Get Happy" and a medley of "Almost Like Being In Love"/"This Can't Be Love," which replaced "As Long As He Needs Me" in the lineup. The videotaping took place at a studio on 26th Street in New York City. At the first night's taping (of "Hello, Bluebird," Judy's three-solo segment of "Happy"; the "Love" medley; and "By Myself"), Roddy McDowell took photos of Judy. Famed photographer Milton Greene also shot photos during the tapings. Greene also did a portrait sitting with Judy, in which Goulet and Silvers participated. The "Manhattan" sequence with Judy and Silvers was taped the second night. The third night was devoted to the "Love Medley" with Goulet (Judy and Bob radiated much passion during this spot). They taped the segment again after some goofs over the lyrics, but the first version was the one chosen to air. The final two nights were devoted to taping the complex "I'm Following You" number, in which there was a multitude of costume changes. The special aired on Tuesday, March 19, 1963, from 8:30 p.m. to 9:30 p.m., and garnered great reviews for Garland. The following are excerpts from two of those reviews:

> *Variety*: "Taking her special last Tuesday as a sample of what may be in store when Judy Garland has her own weekly series on CBS-TV next fall, it's going to be welcome fair indeed. . . . Her singing last Tuesday projected over the footlights, with an immediacy and an impact that is rarely achieved in video. The series will have a star who is steeped in the know-how and who vocally is far from past her prime."
>
> *The Philadelphia Inquirer*: "Miss Garland, looking youthful, vibrant, and strikingly slender, opened strong, and closed the same way."

The show also was nominated for an Emmy award for Outstanding Music Program, but lost to *Julie and Carol at Carnegie Hall*. (The special is available on video cassette, in a legitimate release—although from a film print and not the original video master—from LaserLight/Delta Music, 1996.)

February 7, 1963: (Concert) Harrah's Resort; Lake Tahoe. Judy opened her scheduled three-week engagement of her mini-concert (one hour). Judy's song list (in order): "Hello, Bluebird"; "Almost Like Being In Love"/"This Can't Be Love"; " "Do It Again"; "Never Will I Marry"; "As Long As He Needs Me"; "Judy's Olio" ("You Made Me Love You"/"For Me And My Gal"/"The Trolley Song"); "By Myself"; "Rock-A-Bye Your Baby"; "San Francisco"; and Judy's debut performance of "As Long As He Needs Me" from the musical *Oliver*—a family favorite. (The song is not listed in the opening night rundown.) Mort Lindsey again conducted for Judy.

February 11, 1963: Judy canceled her show at Harrah's due to the flu.

February 12, 1963: (Concert) Judy returned to Harrah's.

February 13, 1963: Judy collapsed just before going on stage at Harrah's.

February 14, 1963: Judy was taken by ambulance to a hospital in Carson City in the morning. By afternoon, she paid a visit to the hospital administrator, saying she was fine, and returned to Lake Tahoe for a "quiet Valentine's Day party" with her children. The hospital had to hire extra help to handle the flood of calls that had poured in from her fans and the media.

February 15, 1963: Although Judy announced she was feeling better, the Sahara management allowed her out of her contract—she was suffering from complete exhaustion. Mickey Rooney was called in to replace her for the rest of the engagement. By this time, Judy had also reconciled with Sid Luft.

February 16, 1963: Judy stayed in Lake Tahoe an extra day, with Sid (who had been with her since February 13).

February 17, 1963: Judy and Sid went to Las Vegas for two days.

February 19, 1963: The Lufts went to San Francisco for a rest and what was reported as a "reconciliation/honeymoon." They stayed at the Fairmont Hotel, rooms 210, 212, and 214—the Bridal Suite.

February 22, 1963: Judy and Sid returned to the Fairmont at 6:30 p.m., to pack and "catch a train," Judy told a fan. From 8:25 p.m. to 8:30 p.m., they bought magazines in the hotel's newsstand, then left in a rented car at 8:30 p.m.

March 4, 1963: Judy flew to London, England. Due to arrive at 9:45 p.m. on the night of March 4, the plane was diverted to Manchester due to weather problems. Judy stayed the night (along with the rest of the plane—which was full of American press to cover the premiere of her movie. Judy and Mort Lindsey—who was with her for an appearance on March 10—would later talk about the flight on *The Merv Griffin Show* taped on December 19, 1968.)

March 5, 1963: Judy arrived in London by train, where there was a press conference that lasted about two hours for her and the movie at the Savoy (where she stayed during her trip).

March 6, 1963: (Premiere) The last "World Premiere" of a Judy Garland Movie. *I Could Go On Singing* was the new title United Artists had chosen for the movie only one month before it opened—they wanted it to be seen as a film in which Judy sang. The posters declared: "*It's Judy*! Lighting Up The Lonely Stage." The premiere—which was filmed by Ed Sullivan for Broadcast on his CBS show in April—was held at the Plaza Theater in London, England. (The footage of Judy arriving and of Judy with Sullivan still exists.)

March 10, 1963: (Television) *Sunday Night at the London Palladium*, a live British show. Judy sang the medley, "Almost Like Being In Love"/"This Can't Be Love"; "Smile"; "Comes Once In A Lifetime"; and "I Could Go On Singing." "Smile" and "I Could Go On Singing" would be broadcast on *The Ed Sullivan Show* on April 14, 1963. Judy gave such a moving performance of "Smile" that this rendition is one of the definitive moments of Judy's entire career. It would often be repeated on *Sullivan* and on other shows, including *60 Minutes* in 1975. (It can be seen on the abridged version of *The Concert Years* from LaserLight video.) Judy received the highest fee ever paid a performer on the show—3,000 pounds—and she donated it to Lady Hoare's Fund to Aid Thalidomide Children.

March 11, 1963: Judy flew back to New York, checking into the St. Regis Hotel.

March 12, 1963: Judy hosted a birthday party for Liza's seventeenth birthday.

March 14, 1963: Judy took an overdose of sleeping pills in her suite at the St. Regis. Her hairdresser and friend, Orval Paine found her in time, and a doctor treated her in her suite. The incident did, unfortunately, make Earl Wilson's column.

Judy onstage at the London Palladium, March 10, 1963, during the "live" *Sunday Night at the London Palladium* television program, portions of which would be rebroadcast on *The Ed Sullivan Show*, including yet another of Judy's definitive moments: the rendition of "Smile" from this show. The Palladium was Judy's British "home," as she started her concert career there, and she would make appearances on its stage in 1951, 1957, 1963, 1964, and 1969. (Courtesy of Photofest.)

The last two weeks in March 1963: Judy, Sid, Lorna, and Joe took a two-week vacation in the Caribbean.

April 2, 1963, late evening: The Lufts returned to New York, missing Liza's opening in the off-Broadway show, *Best Foot Forward*, supposedly due to missing a flight. Another theory is that Judy deliberately did not attend opening night so that she would not take the attention away from Liza.

April 3, 1963: Judy (and Sid, Lorna, and Joe) attended Liza's second night performance of *Best Foot Forward.*

April 1963: Judy continued preproduction meetings in New York for her television series.

"Happiness Is Just A Thing Called Joe": Joey and his mama share a loving moment, April 1963. (Courtesy of Photofest.)

April 1963: Judy and Liza attended Donald O'Connor's show at the Americana Hotel in New York; O'Connor brought them onstage, and the three performed together, "off the cuff," to the joy of the packed house.

May 1963: The production of Judy's television series was suddenly switched from New York to California, at CBS's Television City in Hollywood. Also around this time, Judy spent some time with artist Rene Bouchet, who did seven portraits of her, including one that graced the cover of TV Guide in October 1963 (the only time Judy would be on the cover of the magazine in her lifetime).

May 9, 1963: (Personal Appearance) Judy attended Danny Kaye's performance at the Ziegfeld Theater in New York, along with CBS affiliates and the president of the network, James Aubrey. (After the show, Aubrey, his daughter, Judy, and about seven other people went to an empty Italian bar where Judy proceeded to treat them to a private concert, which included "Over The Rainbow" sung directly to Aubrey's daughter.)

May 10, 1963: (Personal Appearance) Judy's "mini-concert" performance for the CBS television affiliates and executives, held at the Waldorf Astoria Hotel in New York. (She opened with a parody of the song "Call Me Irresponsible.")

Late May 1963: The Share Tenth Anniversary Party (the show business philanthropic organization's benefit for the Exceptional Children's Foundation), Los Angeles. Judy auctioned off her talents to the highest bidders. During the course of the evening, Judy sang "San Francisco"; "Shine On Harvest Moon" (as a duet with Sammy Davis, Jr.); "Up A Lazy River," in a medley with composer Johnny Mercer; and "For Me And My Gal" with Gene Kelly. Judy sat next to John Wayne during the show. She attended with Sid Luft.

June 3, 1963 (late evening/early morning of June 4): Judy took June Allyson, Aaron Spelling, and Aaron's wife, Carolyn Jones, from LaScala's restaurant in Beverly Hills, California, to Sid Luft's office down the street to watch Liza appear on NBC-TV's *The Tonight Show*, guest hosted by Arthur Godfrey. (Liza came on last, at 12:45 a.m.)

June 8, 1963: To celebrate Judy's forty-first birthday, the Lufts' eleventh wedding anniversary, their new Brentwood home, and the launch of Judy's television series, Judy and Sid gave a housewarming party at their new home at 129 South Rockingham Avenue, in the Brentwood section of West Los Angeles, just south of Sunset Blvd. (The home came complete with guest house and pool. See October 5, 1966 for a more detailed description.)

June 10, 1963: Judy's forty-first birthday.

Within days of their successful housewarming/anniversary party, the Luft's ironically separated for the final time.

June 18, 1963: Makeup, lighting, and camera tests at CBS for her series. (A large, $150,000 trailer-dressing room had been built for Judy.)

June 24, 1963: (Television) The first episode of *The Judy Garland Show* was videotaped at CBS Television City, Hollywood, from about 8:10 p.m. to 9:20 p.m. The audience included many stars: Lucille Ball, Jack Benny, Natalie Wood, Hedda Hopper, Louella Parsons, Agnes Morehead, Clint Eastwood, Dick Van Dyke, Carl Reiner, and Judy's costar in her 1943 *Presenting Lily Mars*, Van Heflin, among many others—including a lot of CBS stars, naturally. The guest for the first show was Mickey Rooney. Judy's songs included: "Keep Your Sunny Side Up"; "When The Sun Comes Out"; "Exactly Like You"; "I Believe In You"(with Jerry Van Dyke, who had been signed as a regular to be Judy's second banana); "You're So Right For Me" (with Rooney; this segment featured Judy and Mickey reminiscing about their days together at MGM); and for her "Born In A Trunk" segment that would close each episode, Judy sang: "Too Late Now"; "Who Cares?"; and "Old Man River"—one of her all-time greatest performances. Judy would add "Old Man River" to her concerts due to popular demand in 1967. Each show would end with Judy singing the closing theme "I Will Come Back."

> *The Los Angeles Times* actually reviewed the videotaping of the first show, at CBS Television City, June 24: "Judy, almost paper thin, stood on her spike heels, feet wide apart in that way of hers, rolled those wide, haunted eyes at the lights above, and sang her heart out. The audience was with her all the way. . . . Judy seemed so assured, so self-possessed, so happy in her work, that it sounds good for the shows."

At the dress rehearsal on June 23, Judy did sing "Two Ladies In The Shade Of The Banana Tree" during the "Born In A Trunk" segment, but by taping the following night, it had been dropped. This show would not air as the first episode; the telecast date would be December 8, 1963. The "Exactly Like You" song and sketch and the song, "I Believe In You," would be cut before broadcast date, and a new segment with Rooney was taped November 29, 1963. A new opening song would be taped, also, on October 11, 1963. The deleted segments still exist and were included on the DVD released by Pioneer Entertainment and Classic World Productions, Inc. and *The Judy Garland Show—Volume One*, released June 15, 1999. This show is also one of the shows on *The Judy Garland Show Collection* DVD box set, released November 2, 1999.

June 25, 1963 to July 3, 1963: *The Judy Garland Show* took a well-deserved break after several months of preproduction and the taping of the first episode. (In a June 27 article reprinted in the *Garland Gazette*, the television series director Bill Hobin said Judy was "always early—not late, as I'd been led to believe—for rehearsals and taping calls.")

This week from CBS was hardly a real "vacation" for Judy. Sid confronted Judy with news that her beloved manager David Begelman had allegedly "misappropriated" Judy's funds on several occasions, totaling anywhere from $200,00 to $300,000, with $78,967.20 already being documented. If this had been made public at the time, it would have affected the fate of her series, so Judy did not press charges against her managers. In fact, she ignored the matter completely. Judy's financial woes went beyond the debauchery of Begelman. Although Judy had supposedly paid off old debts by the end of 1961 and, supposedly, had money in the bank, all due to her tour and successes, bills were obviously not being paid by Begelman, who had been given power of attorney and complete control of Judy's money. In July 1963, Judy was sued by a London Hotel for a $3,000 long-distance telephone bill from the period she had been filming *I Could Go On Singing* (May 1962 to July 1962). There were also, supposedly, still some old IRS and other debts from the mid-to-late 1950s that had not been paid, would continue to grow, and would haunt Judy into the late 1960s.

July 4, 1963 to July 5, 1963: Rehearsals for "Episode Two" of *The Judy Garland Show* at CBS. (Some video pretaping was done on July 5 that was so successful it was used in the final aired version—the segment with guests Count Basie and Mel Torme where Judy sings "I've Got My Love To Keep Me Warm" and, with Torme, sang "April In Paris.")

July 6, 1963: Dress Rehearsal for *JGS*, "Episode Two," 7:30 p.m. to 9:00 p.m., held before a studio audience, on Judy's stage, #43. The dress rehearsals would be videotaped as well, starting with this episode, so that the "best" of the two performances could be edited together for the final "air" tape. (The entire "Born In A Trunk" segment on the air tape, came from this dress rehearsal taping.)

July 7, 1963: (Television) Final videotaping of *The Judy Garland Show* "Episode Two" at CBS's Television City, Studio 43, Hollywood. Judy's Guests: Count Basie, Mel Torme, and Judy Henske. Series Regular: Jerry Van Dyke. Judy's songs: "I Hear Music," "The Sweetest Sounds," and "Strike Up The Band" (with Count Basie and His Band); "Memories Of You" (with Basie on organ); "I've Got My Love To Keep Me Warm" (with Basie and His Band); "April In Paris" (with Basie and His Band and Mel Torme—these two songs had been videotaped on July 5); the "Born In A Trunk Segment": "A Cottage For Sale"; "Hey, Look Me Over"; and the closing theme: "I Will Come Back." (These last three songs were videotaped at the dress rehearsal the day before, July 6.) Judy also performed a dance to "Soul Bossa Nova," with some boy dancers—though successful and fun, it would be her first and only solo dance number in the series. The hour also featured scripted banter between Judy and Van Dyke, and also with Torme. This final taping was completed in record time, according to trade paper reports reprinted in the *Garland Gazette*—exactly eighty-four minutes. At this session, Judy and Van Dyke also taped a commercial for "Share A Child," a General Mills charitable endeavor to provide Christmas gifts to underprivileged children. It was shown during this episode, which aired on November 10, 1963, and still survives. There also exists about two minutes of video directly following the taping of Judy's dress rehearsal on July 6; Judy, Jerry, and producer George Schlatter bantering with the audience; Schlatter lifting Judy up briefly and carrying her offstage; Jerry thanking Count Basie; and the sounds of the audience leaving the studio. Almost all of this is on the DVD of *The Judy Garland Show—Volume Two* and on the *Collection* box set.

July 11, 1963 to July 14, 1963: General rehearsals for "Episode Three" of *The Judy Garland Show* (pre-recording was done on the evening of July 14).

July 12, 1963: A letter exists with this date, to franchise tax board, to request sixty additional days to audit Judy's taxes, due to a new business manager being assigned. This is signed "Judy Garland Luft."

July 15, 1963: Taping of the dress rehearsal for "Episode Three" of *The Judy Garland Show.*

July 16, 1963: Taping of "Episode Three" of *The Judy Garland Show* at CBS Television City, Studio 43, Hollywood, California. Guests: Liza Minnelli, the Brothers Castro, and Soupy Sales; Regular: Jerry Van Dyke. Judy's song's: "Liza" (tag includes a few bars of "My Heart Stood Still"); "Come Rain Or Come Shine"; "Together" (with Liza); Medley with Liza ("We Could Make Such Beautiful Music Together"/"The Best Is Yet To Come"/"Bye, Bye Baby"/"Bob White (Whatcha Gonna Swing Tonight)"; "As Long As He Needs Me" (in the "Born In A Trunk" spot); and, as a closer, Judy and Liza singing "Two Lost Souls" followed by "I Will Come Back," both performed in tramp costumes. (Judy also performed in a brief sketch with Soupy Sales.) The show aired on November 17, 1963. An outtake exists of Liza and Jerry Van Dyke talking, leading into his "Lone Ranger" sketch; There is also a brief "good-night" heard from Judy as the taping ends, although the cameras had not been turned back on after the final fade out, so you only hear it, you don't see her. This show is on *The Judy Garland Show—Volume One* DVD and the *Collection* box set.

July 19, 1963 to Sunday, July 21, 1963: Rehearsals for "Episode Four" of *JGS.*

July 22, 1963: Taping of the dress rehearsal for "Episode Four" of *JGS.*

July 23, 1963: Videotaping of "Episode Four" of *The Judy Garland Show* at CBS Television City, Stage 43, Hollywood, California. Guests: Lena Horne and Terry Thomas. Regular: Jerry Van Dyke. Judy's

Judy lovingly watches Liza onstage at Studio 43 at Televsion City in Hollywood, during rehearsals for show #3 of *The Judy Garland Show*, July 11–16, 1963. Note the two chorus members sitting behind Judy; the woman on the right can be seen on the Christmas episode. You can see the orchestra in the background, and you can also get a sense of just how small the studio was by the number of seats in the audience. (Courtesy of Photofest.)

songs: "Day In, Day Out" (with Lena Horne); "Judy Sings Lena; Lena Sings Judy" Medley (the greats sing each other's hits: "Honeysuckle Rose"—Judy, "Meet Me In St. Louis"—Lena, "Deed I Do"—Judy, "Zing! Went The Strings of My Heart"—Lena, "It's All Right With Me"—Judy, "The Trolley Song"—Judy and Lena, and "Love"—Judy and Lena); "Mad Dogs and Englishmen" with Lena, Terry, and Dancers; and in the "Born In A Trunk" closer: "The Man That Got Away"; followed by the standard "I Will Come Back" ending song. Judy also talked with Lena Horne during the intro to Terry Thomas's comedy monologue, and Judy appeared with Thomas during a new "Tea For Two" segment, during which they chatted, poured tea, and Judy sang "A Foggy Day" for Thomas. Judy also talked for the first time in the "Trunk" segment, telling about losing the Oscar for "A Star Is Born," which led into her singing "Man." (At one point, after singing with Lena, Judy said, "not bad for a couple of MGM

Judy singing "As Long As He Needs Me" from the musical *Oliver* (a family favorite) during the videotaping of the weekly "Born In A Trunk" sequence, for show #3 of *The Judy Garland Show*, July 16, 1963. The television series is the only existing professional audio-video material that remains of Judy at a physical and vocal peak during the concert years of her career, since location videotaping or filming of concerts in theaters was rarely done by networks in the 1950s and 1960s. *The Judy Garland Show* also represents the single finest overall work from Judy's entire career. It featured her singing scores of songs she never sang before or after the series—as well as many of her hits—and also has her performing with some of the greatest names in show business. (Courtesy of Photofest.)

rejects"; although this moment does not exist in reproduction—there are, however, outtakes from this show on the DVD.) This episode aired on October 13, 1963. This show is on *The Judy Garland Show—Volume Two* DVD and the *Collection* box set.

July 24, 1963: It was announced in this date's *Hollywood Reporter* (reprinted in the *Garland Gazette*) that Judy and her Kingsrow Enterprises company had just signed a new three-year pact with CMA (Creative

Management Associates/ Freddie Fields and David Begelman.) The same edition also had a blurb by John Bradford that "CMA's most unusual offer for Judy Garland comes from South Africa. . . . They just want seven days—and they'll pay for it with a bag of diamonds!" It should be noted that Judy also had a writer on the staff of her series by the name of . . . Johnny Bradford. During the time of the series, Guy McElwaine was Judy's press representative.

At some point during the summer, Judy participated in a Hollywood event meant to draw attention to an August 1963 Martin Luther King event in Washington, D.C. Judy was photographed with Eartha Kitt, Charlton Heston, and Marlon Brando. At about this same time, Judy also joined June Allyson, Carolyn Jones, and Liza in protesting the bombing of a church in Birmingham, Alabama, in which children were killed.

July 26, 1963 to Sunday, July 28, 1963: Rehearsals for "Episode Five" of *JGS*, CBS, Hollywood.

July 29, 1963: Taping of dress rehearsal for "Episode Five" of *JGS*, some of which would be used for the final air-tape, including the medley she would do with her main guest.

July 30, 1963: (Television) Videotaping of "Episode Five" of *The Judy Garland Show* at CBS Television City, Stage 43, Hollywood. Guests: Tony Bennett and Dick Shawn. Regular: Jerry Van Dyke. Judy's songs: "If Love Were All" (cut before broadcast, but still in existence); "Yes, Indeed" (with Bennett and Shawn); "Garland-Bennett Medley," during which Judy sang "Carolina In The Morning," "When The Midnight Choo-Choo Leaves For Alabama," and, with Bennett, "I Left My Heart In San Francisco"; "My Buddy" (with Shawn); and, in the "Born In A Trunk" closing spot: "Stormy Weather" (prefaced by a tale of a moth in her mouth during a show), and "I Will Come Back." Judy also taped a talk with Van Dyke before his duet with Shawn, but the talking was cut. A similar fate fell upon the "Tea For Two" segment, taped during the dress rehearsal on July 29, when its guest—Steve Allen—was such a success, he was signed as a "full-fledged" guest star for a later episode. This "Tea" segment still exists and is on the DVD of the show, as part of *JGS Collection* box set. This episode would air on December 15, 1963. (The July 30, 1963 edition of *Daily Variety*—reprinted in the Garland journal—had an article by Dave Kaufman about Judy's series and noted deals were being negotiated for appearances by Rock Hudson, Marlon Brando, Peter Sellers, Bing Crosby, James Garner, Charleton Heston, Gene Kelly, and Dean Martin. In the end, none of those stars would appear as guests on the series—although Martin was a guest on Judy's 1962 special.)

July 31, 1963: Judy and series producer George Schlatter flew to Las Vegas for two days of relaxation before flying back to Los Angeles for rehearsals for the next episode; this trip also gave them the chance to scout acts for the show.

August 2, 1963: An eventful day in the production of *The Judy Garland Show*. Just as Judy and George returned from their Vegas trip, and rehearsals had begun for "Episode Six," CBS executives declared they weren't happy with the first five shows taped, and fired the producer, writers, and choreographer. The director Bill Hobin stayed, as did the musical and scenic staffs. The current episode was canceled, and Judy would never get to work with the great Nat King Cole. The series took a three-week break for the new staff to assemble.

Early or mid August: Judy was at CBS in New York for meetings about the series.

August 26, 1963 to August 28, 1963: Judy entered Cedars of Lebanon Hospital in Los Angeles for her "routine annual check-up." Judy's patient number number was 63-11859.

August 30, 1963: Judy videotaped an interview with *Variety* columnist Army Archerd at CBS. This tape is not known to still exist.

September 5, 1963: Judy was awarded custody of Lorna and Joe in a court hearing.

September 6, 1963: Judy had another emotional, up-and-down meeting with Sid Luft after he had dinner with the kids at Judy's home; this encounter was detailed to biographer Gerald Frank by Luft.

September 7, 1963: Judy sent a telegram from her home in Brentwood to David Begelman at the Ritz Carlton, in which she briefly reminded him of her devotion, and the devotion that surrounded him.

Also on that first weekend of September 1963: Judy attended a social meeting with the Reverend Billy Graham at Debbie Reynold's Beverly Hills home.

September 9, 1963 to September 12, 1963: Rehearsals at CBS Television City for the new, "revamped" *JGS*.

September 13, 1963: The series was on a new schedule that would remain throughout its run. Every Friday: videotaping of the dress rehearsal (from 5:30 p.m. to 7 p.m.), then, one hour for dinner and another hour for notes and technical preparations (from 9 p.m. to 10:30 p.m.), then there was the final videotaping. This week was "Episode Six" of *The Judy Garland Show* at CBS Television City, Stage 43, Hollywood. On this first "revamped show" with the new team, Judy's guests were Steve Lawrence and June Allyson, and series regular Jerry Van Dyke. Judy's songs: "Life Is Just A Bowl Of Cherries" (opening); "Happiness Is A Thing Called Joe"; "Be My Guest" (with Lawrence); "Just Imagine" (with Allyson at the conclusion of their "Tea For Two" segment); "MGM Medley" (Judy sang "Cleopatterer" with Allyson; "Look For The Silver Lining"; and "Till The Clouds Roll By"/"Look For The Silver Lining" with Lawrence and Allyson). For the "Born In A Trunk" segment, Judy told a story about Jeanette McDonald filming "Naughty Marietta," then sang "San Francisco," followed by "I Will Come Back." Judy also spoke with Van Dyke—whoses character had changed from bumbling to obnoxious—and she taped a second "Tea For Two" segment with George Jessel, which would be inserted into "Episode Twelve"; during this "Tea," Judy sang a bit of the song "Bill." Judy, unfortunately, was suffering from laryngitis during this show, although she looks very lovely, healthy, and rested. (The dress rehearsal footage still exists and is on the DVD *JGS Collection* box set, along with the entire "Episode Six.") This episode would air Sunday, October 27, 1963. After the taping, Judy took her new executive producer Norman Jewison, Liza, her new writers, David Begelman, and others, to see Barbra Streisand's closing night (and last show)—the late show—at the Coconut Grove nightclub.

September 16, 1963 to September 19, 1963: Rehearsals for the next *JGS* episode at CBS, Television City.

September 20, 1963: Videotaping of both the dress rehearsal (5:30 p.m. to 7 p.m.) and the final performance (9:00 p.m. to 10:30 p.m.) of "Episode Seven" of *The Judy Garland Show* at CBS Television City, Stage 43, Hollywood. Judy's guest—for this episode, which was planned in advance to be the new "Premiere Telecast" episode—was Donald O'Connor along with series regular Jerry Van Dyke. Judy's songs: "Call Me Irresponsible" and "Keep Your Sunny Side Up" (Opener); "Be My Guest" and "Songs We're Famous For" Medley (with O'Connor—Judy sang "Be My Guest" with O'Connor, "If You Knew Susie," "My Mammy" with O'Connor, "Indian Love Call" with O'Connor, "Sweetheart" with O'Connor, and a reprise of "Be My Guest" with O'Connor); "Fly Me To The Moon"; "The World Is

Judy with her manager, David Begelman (on right), the man who was responsible for planning her big "comeback" in 1961 but who has also taken the blame from many biographers (and from Sid Luft) for having destroyed Judy financially. This photo was taken at the Coconut Grove, the evening of September 13, 1963, when Judy went to see Barbra Streisand's closing night there. The two singers would work together only three weeks later, on Judy's television series. (Courtesy of Photofest.)

Your Balloon" (with O'Connor and Van Dyke. This lavish production number, with the trio as clowns, was so elaborate that it was videotaped during the afternoon, before the taping of the dress rehearsal); "Vaudeville" Medley (with O'Connor—Judy sang "Yacka Hula Hickey Dula," "At The Moving-Picture Ball," and "The Old Soft Shoe," all with O'Connor). For the "Born In A Trunk" spot, Judy told the story about the stagehand caught in a curtain and sang "Chicago" followed by "Maybe I'll Come Back." Judy also bantered with Van Dyke, and taped two "Tea For Two" segments: one with O'Connor, which was aired, and one with Henry Fonda, which was never aired. The Fonda "Tea" is not known to exist—It's also possible that Fonda only posed for publicity photos on the set with Judy and a "Tea" segment was never actually taped. Judy's vocal condition had improved from the previous week, but was still slightly frayed. This "Premiere" episode aired Sunday, September 29, 1963, and is included on *The Judy Garland Show—Volume Five* DVD, released May 15, 2001.

Also on September 20, 1963: The earliest of over seventy checks from Judy's then-current checking account were issued on this date, and were later sold, through Sid Luft, by the Judy Garland Museum in Grand Rapids. All of the checks bear her actual, original signatures; no stamps were used to duplicate her signature. Judy's account was handled by her business manager, Edward Traubner & Co., Inc., located on Rodeo Drive in Beverly Hills. All of the checks cleared through City National Bank of Beverly Hills. The majority of the checks were used as a checking account for bills (staff, telephone, food, pharmacy, newspapers, etc.). A few were used to pay bills for her production company, Kingsrow Enterprises, although all funds were drawn from the same checking account. (There were possibly some errors made when the check numbers were typed onto the checks, as the check numbers don't always properly coincide with the date issued—this may be due to a stamp placed on the checks noting they cleared through Judy's account. These stamps often obsure the date the checks were issued.)

Check #216, to Fredrica (a fashion designer on 7th Avenue in New York) for $206.00.

September 23, 1963 to Thursday, September 26, 1963: Rehearsals at CBS Television City for the next *JGS*.

Also on September 23, 1963: The *Hollywood Reporter* (reprinted in the *Garland Gazette*), on this date, reported that writer Vernon Scott of the the UPI (United Press International) would be working on Judy's biography, but this did not come to fruition.

Check #205 was issued, payable to K. Omeara, with the address handwritten in, for $50.00. (This may have been a household staff member.)

September 27, 1963: Videotaping of both the dress rehearsal (from 5:30 p.m. to 7 p.m.) and the final performance (9:00 p.m. to 10:30 p.m.), for "Episode Eight" of *The Judy Garland Show* at CBS Television City, Stage 43, Hollywood. Guests: George Maharis, Jack Carter, The Dillards, and regular Jerry Van Dyke. Judy's songs: "Alexander's Ragtime Band" (opening); "Be My Guest" (with Maharis and Carter); "I Wish You Love" (the audio from the dress rehearsal rendition would surface on a 1991 Capitol Records box set); "Side By Side" with Maharis; "Country" Medley (with all guests—Judy sang: "Y'all Come," "Somebody Touched Me," and "Way In The Middle of The Air" with entire company; and reprise of "Y'all Come [Y'all Go]" with the entire company). During the "Born In A Trunk" segment, Judy told a story about a feather boa and sang "Swanee," followed by "Maybe I'll Come Back." Judy also taped a "Tea For Two" spot with baseball coach Leo Durocher. She also engaged in typical banter with Van Dyke, and the Dillards. Judy's temporary vocal problems had vanished, she was in great form, and looked breathtakingly beautiful. (The dress rehearsal footage still exists and is on the DVD of *The Judy Garland Show—Volume Four*, released in November 2000.) This episode aired on Sunday, October 20, 1963. After the taping, Judy went out to a nightclub with Maharis, Hunt Stromberg—a CBS executive—and the president of the network, James Aubrey. Stromberg and Aubrey had attended the taping, and Judy adlibbed "Hunt Stromberg, Jr. is a cousin of mine!" during "I Will Come Back."

Also on September 27, 1963: The following checks were issued and signed by Judy:

#205: K. Omeara (no other info available)

#206: James R. Cogan, M.D. (no other info available)

#211: Brentwood Pharmacy; $66.44

#212: So. Counties Gas Company in Santa Monica; $23.11

#213: Gavin Herbert Pharmacy; $80.86

#215: Joseph Magnin; (no other info available)

#219: Kobley/Stern Inc.; (no other info available)

#220: Rush Sales/Service; $14.00

#221: Alvena Tomin (possibly member of household staff); $83.15

#223: Colony House Liquors; $788.34

#224: Akira Ohno; $166.57

#23(?—Number not clear): Lionel Doman (Judy's butler); $145.53

#231: Hettie J. Chapman (Lorna and Joe's Governess); (amount not available)

#232: Mattie J. Oliver (household staff); (amount not available)

#233: Cloretha B. Gland (household staff); $122.43

#234: Lionel Doman (Judy's butler); (amount not available)

September 29, 1963, 9:00 to 10:00 p.m.: *The Premiere Broadcast of The Judy Garland Show* was a great critical success. The following is an example:

> *The New York Herald-Tribune*, 9-30-63: "When Judy Garland was front and center last night, singing her heart out, all was right in the world, and all was right in the world of entertainment. And all was right with *The Judy Garland Show*, which started the young veteran off on still another triumph in show business. . . . Never looking better, Miss Garland worked a wizard's spell in her big variety numbers, and was sparkling and magnetic. . . . For dark and vivacious beauty, for grand voice and style, and for expert showmanship and simple human appeal, there's no one to compare with Miss Garland."

More importantly, the show was a smash in the ratings also, winning its time slot with a 35.9 Nielson rating and a 44.0 share, beating *Bonanza*, which had a 24.7 Nielson rating and a 30.3 share. Sadly, since the Nielson families watching *The Judy Garland Show* actually saw one of the blandest and weakest shows taped to date, they didn't return the following week, and the ratings would begin to sink.

September 30, 1963 to Thursday, October 3, 1963: Rehearsals at CBS Television City for the next *JGS*.

Also on September 30: Check #239 was issued, to Brentwood Pharmacy, for $480.91. A number 720-315-888-1 appears on it.

October 2, 1963: A recording session is listed as being held at Capitol Records in Hollywood to attempt to get completed takes for Judy's in-limbo album *Judy Takes Broadway*. However, the single reel of tape only contained orchestra tracks of "Do What You Do," "76 Trombones," and "Why Can't I?" with no vocal track. Judy can be heard very faintly in the background, so perhaps she decided not to record that day, especially if she were conserving her voice for the videotaping of her next television show two days later. This tape was noted as being a "dub (original in England)," and thus, it's possible that it was derived from a session in England, or mixed from other takes made in April 1962. The master numbers are the exact same for the three songs from this session as they are from the April 1962 sessions, so it is entirely possible that a session was not actually held on this date.

On October 3, 1963: The following checks were issued:

#240: Kermit E. Osserman, M.D.; (no other info available)

#242: Myron Prinzmetal, M.D.; (no other info available)

#244: Little Poppy Cleaners; (no other info available)

#246: Lionel Doman (Judy's butler); $120.47

#249: Cloretha B. Gland (household staff); $102.64

#250: Mattie J. Oliver (household staff, no address); $81.70

October 4, 1963: Videotaping of both the dress rehearsal (5:30 p.m. to 7 p.m.) and the final performance (9:00 p.m. to 10:30 p.m.) of "Episode Nine" of *The Judy Garland Show* at CBS Television City, Stage 43, Hollywood. Judy's guests were Barbra Streisand and the Smothers Brothers, with regular Jerry Van Dyke. Judy's songs included: "Comes Once In A Lifetime" (opener); "Be My Guest" (with Streisand, Smothers Brothers, and Van Dyke); "Just In Time"; "Get Happy" and "Happy Days Are Here Again" (with Streisand); "Happy Harvest" (Streisand comes in at final line); and "Hooray For Love" Medley (with Streisand—Judy sang "Hooray For Love" with Streisand, "After You've Gone," "S'Wonderful," "How About You?" with Streisand, "You And The Night And The Music," and "It All Depends On You" with Streisand). In the "Born In A Trunk" spot, Judy sang the medley of "You Made Me Love You"/"For Me And My Gal"/"The Trolley Song," followed by the "I Will Come Back" closer. Judy also performed scripted banter with Van Dyke and a splendid "Tea For Two" chat segment with Streisand, during which Ethel Merman joined them for some talking, and a belting of "There's No Business Like Show Business." This show was deemed so successful by CBS chairman and founder William Paley and the network president James Aubrey, that it was ordered to air that coming Sunday, only two days later, October 6, 1963. This show is available on the DVD of *The Judy Garland Show—Volume Five*, released May 15, 2001. This was the only time Judy and Barbra worked together, but Judy would always declare herself a Streisand fan. (See January 4, 1969 for more information.) Barbra would call Judy "the greatest actress and the greatest singer. My heart went out to her. She was generous, very generous. She touched me so deeply. I was twenty-one and she was forty-one. She was extraordinary, and God, I thought she was great! I'd never heard her until a year before that. I didn't know her—even though she was so famous—except for *The Wizard of Oz*, and then one day I happened to walk into a studio on 40th Street where they were recording her 'live,' and I thought 'holy mackerel-this woman is fantastic.' So it was a great thrill to work with her. We had this instant soul connection. One of the greatest singers who ever lived. Miraculous. Soulful. Divine."

Also on October 4: The following three checks were issued:

#243: Don Loper (designer in Beverly Hills); $775.00

#245: Harrahs, Nevada (Casino; Judy had been to Vegas 7/31–8/2/63); $700.00

#247: Crosskey/Yvonne Flowers; $10.40

October 7, 1963 to October 10, 1963: Rehearsals for the next *JGS* at CBS Television City.

Also on October 9: The following check was issued:

Check # 253 was issued, payable to "Cash" in the amount of $100.00.

October 11, 1963: Videotaping of both the dress rehearsal (from 5:30 p.m. to 7 p.m.) and the final performance (from 9 p.m. to 10:30 p.m.) of "Episode Ten" of *The Judy Garland Show*, at CBS Television City, Stage 43, Hollywood. Judy's guests were Ray Bolger and Jane Powell, and series regular Jerry Van Dyke; this was his final show—he was fired from the series. Judy's songs included: "A Lot Of Livin' To Do"; "Be My Guest" (with Bolger, Powell, and Van Dyke); "That's All"; "One For My Baby" (Comedy version with Van Dyke and Company); "Romantic Duets" Medley (with Powell and Van Dyke—Judy sang: "Romantic Duets" with Powell; lip-synched "I Remember It Well" and "Will You Remember? (Sweetheart)" with Van Dyke; then the three ended the medley by singing "All Aboard For Movieland"); "If I Only Had A Brain" and "We're Off To See The Wizard" with Bolger during the "Tea For Two" segment; and "The Jitterbug" (with Bolger, Powell, and dancers). For the "Born In A Trunk" spot, Judy sang "When Your Lover Has Gone," "Some People," and, the closer, "Maybe I'll Come Back." (The new opening for the Mickey Rooney episode, "Episode One," was taped this day also: "I Feel A Song Comin' On." "That's All" and "One For My Baby" would be cut from this episode and inserted into "Episode Five"—with Tony Bennett as a guest, taped July 30—to replaced the "Tea For Two" segment with Steve Allen.) This show is available on *The Judy Garland Show Collection* DVD box set. The broadcast date would not be until Sunday, March 1, 1964.

Also on October 10, 1963: A check was issued to: Bergdorf Goodman, 754 Fifth Ave., New York, N.Y., for $105.99.

October 11, 1963: The following checks were issued:

#255: Hettia J. Chapman; $98.62

#256: Cloretha B. Gland (household staff); $106.40

#259: Mart Pharmacy; (no other info available)

#260: Wil Wrights Ice Cream; $34.49

"The Three Belters": Barbra Streisand, Ethel Merman, and Judy, during the videotaping of "There's No Business Like Show Business," for show #9 of *The Judy Garland Show*, October 4, 1963. (Courtesy of Photofest.)

#261: Helms Bakeries; $20.44

#263: Humphrey Bakery; (no other info available)

#265: *Los Angeles Times* Dealer (newspaper); $7.50

#266: William Goodley, DDS (dentist); $25.00

#267: General Telephone Company; (no other info available)

#268: Gavin Herbert Pharmacy; $20.54

#269: Ed Gemar Farms; $81.63

#271: Hospi/Video (possibly a television rental fee for when Judy had been in Cedars of Lebanon Hospital for her annual check-up on 8/26–8/28/63); $4.00

#271 (also marked #271): Brentwood Pharmacy; (no other info available)

#272: Pacific Telephone; $2.14 (The numbers 274-6681-35033 appear on this check: it's possible that the phone number 274-6681 belonged to a line in Judy's home—most likely for a staff member, as that cost is rather low.)

#278: Internal Revenue Service; (no other info available)

#280: Wayne Jones (household staff); $417.83

#2(unclear): Brentwood Pharmacy; $283.12

(# ???): Santa Glen Drug Co. Inc., 10401 Santa Monica Blvd., W. Los Angeles 25 Calif., $40.25

October 14, 1963: CBS decided they wanted Judy to continue the production of her series for another thirteen episodes (for a total of twenty-six programs), to be followed by six reruns (although Judy's contract with CBS gave her the call on whether or not to continue. CBS would not air any reruns though).

October 14, 1963 to Thursday, October 17, 1963: Rehearsals at CBS Television City for the next episode of *The Judy Garland Show.*

Also on October 14: A check was issued to: Hotel Sahara, Las Vegas, Nevada; for $1,783.72

October 15, 1963: The following checks were issued:

#279(?): Kevin L. Enright (household staff member; no address on check); $439.49

#281: Pritkin, Finkel, & Co. (Beverly Hills; possibly a legal bill); $1,070.00

(# ???): Petticoat Lane, 11236 Wilshire Blvd., West L.A. Calif.; $135.20

October 18, 1963: Videotaping of both the dress rehearsal (from 5:30 to 7 p.m.) and the final performance (from 9 p.m. to 10:30 p.m.) of "Episode Eleven" of *The Judy Garland Show* at CBS Television City, Stage 43, Hollywood. Judy's Guests were Steve Allen and Mel Torme. Judy's songs included: "This Could Be The Start Of Something Big" (opener); "Be My Guest" (with Allen and Torme—Judy sang "We're From Old Metro" to the tune of "Are You From Dixie?"); "Here's That Rainy Day"; "Sophie" Medley (with Allen—Judy sang "I Love You Today" and "When I'm In Love" with Allen, and soloed on "I'll Show Them All"); "The Party's Over" (with Torme); "Songwriter" Medley (with Allen and Torme—Judy sang: "Ain't Misbehavin'," "Way Back Home," "Mean To Me," "Tip Toe Through The Tulips," "My Heart Stood Still," and "Let's Do It," with Allen and Torme). In the "Trunk" spot, Judy sang "Island In The West Indies," "Through The Years," and "Maybe I'll

Come Back." (Judy had privately stated "Through The Years" was her favorite song; her performance here is among the finest of her career.) Judy also taped a "Tea For Two" segment with actress Jayne Meadows, Steve Allen's wife. This show was conceived as the first show to air in the New Year, so it was televised on Sunday, January 5, 1964.

Also on October 18: The following checks were issued:

#283: Hettia J. Chapman (Lorna and Joe's nanny); $96.22

#284: Lionel Doman (Judy's butler); $120.47

#285: Cloretha B. Gland (household staff); (no other info available)

#287: Cash; (no other info available)

#288: Cash; $75.00

#29(?) (Number not clear): Cloretha B. Gland (household staff); $106.40

October 19, 1963 to October 27, 1963: Judy spent a week in New York for meetings with CBS about the series, and for interviews to promote the show.

On October 21: A check was issued to: Mel Burns Ford, 2000 Long Beach Blvd., Long Beach, Calif., for $163.88 (payment for Judy's cars.)

October 28, 1963 to October 31, 1963: Rehearsals for the next episode of *The Judy Garland Show* at CBS Television City. (Audio prerecordings were made on October 31 to achieve superb sound because Capitol Records was planning a series of albums from the series, though only one LP would materialize.)

Also on October 28: The following checks were issued:

#294: General Telephone Co, Santa Monica; $79.33

#297: Fred Harvey (Electrician in West Los Angeles; I spoke to Harvey's son, who said his dad repaired toasters and things of that nature, for all the stars); $27.88

#299: Executive Office Interiors; $192.40

#301: State Wide Carpet Service; (no other info available)

#302: Mrs. Lynn S. Blackburn (possible household staff); $85.00

#303: Robert W. Bidle; (no other info available)

#304: AFTRA (Dues for American Federation of Television and Radio Artists); $54.00

#305: New York Department Of Labor, Albany; $17.37

#306: Wayne Jones (household staff; no address); $371.40

#307: Kevin Enright (household staff; no address); $371.40 (same amount paid to Wayne Jones)

#308: Lionel C. Doman (Judy's butler); $173.09

#309: Hettia J. Chapman (Lorna and Joey's nanny); $98.62

#310: Cloretha B. Gland (household staff); $134.46

#335: CMA; $1,177.47 (a Kingsrow check)

Date not known: check #367: City National Bank (Judy's bank in Los Angeles); (no other info available)

October 30, 1963: A check was issued to household staff member Cloretha B. Gland, for $500.00 (the large amount may, perhaps, have been for a birthday gift.)

November 1, 1963: Videotaping of both the dress rehearsal (from 5 to 7:30 p.m.), and the final performance (9 to 10:30 p.m.) of Show #12 of "*The Judy Garland Show,*" at CBS Television City, Stage 43, Hollywood. Judy's Guests were Vic Damone and Zine Bethume. Judy's songs included: "From This Moment On" (opener; the audio had been prerecorded on October 31 to which Judy would lip-synch); "Be My Guest" (with Damone and Bethume); "Moon River"; "Getting To Know You" (with Bethume); "Porgy and Bess" Medley (with Damone; again, this medley was also prerecorded on October 31—Judy sang "Summertime," "It Ain't Necessarily So," "I Got Plenty O' Nuttin'," and "Bess, You Is My Woman Now" with Damone); "All-Purpose Holiday" Medley (with Damone, Bethume and Company—Judy sang "Auld Lang Syne," "Deck The Halls" with Damone and Bethume, "Easter Parade" with Damone and Bethume, "Dear Old Donegal" with Damone and Bethume, "Brother, Can You Spare A Dime?" "Yankee Doodle Boy" and "You're A Grand Old Flag" with Damone and Bethume, "Happy Birthday To You" with Damone and Bethume, "Me And My Shadow," "M-O-T-H-E-R" with Damone and Bethume, and "Seasons Greetings" with Damone and Bethume). In the "Born In A Trunk" spot, Judy sang "Smile" and "Rock-A-Bye Your Baby With A Dixie Melody," followed by the closer "Maybe I'll Come Back." (Also taped was the very last "Tea For Two," with Carl Reiner. The "Tea For Two" segment taped during "Episode Six", the Lawrence/Allyson show, on September 13, was inserted into the air-tape of this program, which was quickly edited to air only two days after taping, on Sunday, November 3, 1963. The *Chicago American* paper on this date had a blurb in Bill Irwin's column, reprinted in a Garland club journal: "Judy said she's going to Hong Kong when she gets a vacation respite from television. She may also do a concert in Japan." (She would go to Hong Kong, but not Japan, after the television series.)

Also on November 1, 1963: Checks were issued to: Western Union, 741 S. Flower St., L.A. 17 Calif, for: $18.19, and to: Mitchell Silverburg Knupp, 6399 Wilshire Blvd., L.A., Calif.: $130.44.

November 4, 1963 to November 7, 1963: Rehearsals for the next episode of *The Judy Garland Show* at CBS Television City.

November 8, 1963: Videotaping of both the dress rehearsal (from 5:30 to 7 p.m.), and the final performance (from 9 p.m. to 10:30) of "Episode Thirteen" of *The Judy Garland Show* at CBS Television City, Stage 43, Hollywood. Judy's Guests were Peggy Lee and Jack Carter. Judy's songs: "It's A Good Day" (opener; the audio had been recorded November 7 for Judy to lip-synch to); "Never Will I Marry" (also prerecorded on the 7); "I Love Bein' Here With You" (with Lee; this incorporated quick bits of other songs, of which Judy sang "It's A Good Day"; and both "Under The Bamboo Tree" and "Witch Doctor" with Lee); "Broadway" Medley (with Carter—Judy sang "They Say It's Wonderful" as Ethel Merman, "I'm Gonna Wash That Man Right Out Of My Hair" as Mary Martin, "Wouldn't It Be Lovely?" as Julie Andrews, then "Too Close For Comfort" and "Mr. Wonderful" with Carter); "I Like Men" Medley (with Lee—Judy sang: "I Like Men" with Lee, "You Make Me Feel So Young," "Tess's Torch Song" with Lee, "It's So Nice To Have A Man Around The House" with Lee, "Charlie, My Boy," "Big Bad Bill [Is Sweet William Now]" with Lee, and "Bill Bailey" with Lee). For "Born In A Trunk," Judy sang "How About Me?" and "When You're Smiling," followed by her closer "Maybe I'll Come Back." This episode used the final "Tea For Two" with Carl Reiner, that was taped with "Episode Twelve" on November 1; "Episode Thirteen" aired on December 1, 1963.

November 9, 1963 to November 17, 1963: A one-week break in production so a new team could be assembled for *The Judy Garland Show*. (A November 14, CBS *Judy Garland Show* personnel sheet lists Judy's secretary as Doris Steele of Hollywood.)

November 15, 1963: A check was issued to: Elizabeth Arden, 3 East 54th St., New York, N.Y., for $25.39.

November 18, 1963 to November 24, 1963: Preproduction work with the new *Judy Garland Show* team.

Also on November 18, 1963: A check was issued to: Barrington Hardware, 145 S. Barrington Ave., L.A. 45 Calif., for $28.23.

November 22, 1963: President Kennedy's assassination devastated Judy, who immediately went to console Pat Kennedy. Judy also canceled a Capitol Records session to complete or rerecord the aborted 1962 *Judy Takes Broadway* album.

Also on November 22, 1963: A check was issued to: Will Wrights, 8252 Santa Monica Blvd., L.A. 46 California, for $16.10.

November 25, 1963 to November 29, 1963: Rehearsals at CBS for the next episode of *The Judy Garland Show*. Judy had wanted to do a one hour concert of patriotic songs to lift the spirits of the country, and was turned down by CBS, who didn't want any tributes of any kind on any of their shows.

November 29, 1963: Videotaping of a new comedy/musical sketch with Judy and Mickey Rooney at CBS Television City, Studio 43, Hollywood, to take the place of a deleted Rooney/Van Dyke sketch that featured Judy ("Exactly Like You.") This new sketch was a takeoff on the old Mickey/Judy "Let's Put On A Show" musicals, and featured Judy singing: "Where Or When" with Rooney; "How About You?" with Rooney; "But Not For Me"; "Fascinating Rhythm" with Rooney; "Gods Country" with Rooney; "Could You Use Me?" with Rooney; "Our Love Affair" with Rooney; and "How About You?" reprise with Rooney.

Also on November 29: The following checks were issued:

#392: Lyn S. Blackburn (possible household staff); $120.00

#393: Aaron Brothers & Co.; $28.08

#396: Alvena Tomin (staff; has address on check); $501.02

#399: Bonwit Teller (fashion designer/shop); $187.20

#402: Mattie J. Oliver (household Staff); (no other info available)

#403: Hettie J. Chapman (Lorna and Joe's Nanny Governess); (no other info available)

#404: Kevin L. Enhigh(I) (staff member; no address); $297.12

#405: Wayne Jones (staff); (no other info available)

#406: Cash; (no other info available)

#408: Grace Eddinger, RN (Registered Nurse); $50.00

#410: *Herald Examiner* (newspaper); $7.50

#412: Pritkin Finkel Co; $1,075.00

#413: Flowers By Jacoue; $26.00

#415: Macs Fine Spirits (Beverly Hills); $223.52

November 30, 1963: First, an afternoon audio prerecording of a "Football Medley," with a team of little boys (which had Judy singing "Buckle Down, Winsocki," "You Gotta Be A Football Hero," and "Jamboree Jones"); then the dress rehearsal taping (from 5:30 p.m. to 7 p.m.) and the taping of the final performance (from 9 p.m. to 10:30) of "Episode Thirteen" of *The Judy Garland Show*. Judy's guests were Bobby Darrin and Bob Newhart. Judy's songs included: "Football Medley" (cut before airing; The footage still exists); "Sing, Sing, Sing" with Darrin and Newhart; "More"; "Train" Medley (with Darrin—Judy sang "Sentimental Journey" with Darrin, "Goin' Home Train," "On The Atchison, Topeka And The Santa Fe," "River, Stay Away From My Door," "Bye, Bye, Blackbird," "Beyond The Blue Horizon," "I've Been Working On The Railroad" with Darrin, and "Lonesome Road" with Darrin). The "Born In A Trunk" segment had Judy singing "Do It Again" and "Get Me To The Church On Time," followed by the "Maybe I'll Come Back" closer. Judy also taped a wonderfully funny sketch with Bob Newheart about a couple watching *The Judy Garland Show*. Video of the song "Jamboree Jones" exists in two takes. "Episode Fourteen" would air as the final show of 1963, on Sunday, December 29, 1963.

December 2, 1963 to December 5, 1963: Rehearsals for the next *Judy Garland Show* at CBS Television City.

Also on December 2: Check # 418 was issued for Judy's business manager Edward Traubner & Co., Inc., for $2,500 (possibly his monthly fee; Of course his office issued the check as well as being the payee). A check was also issued to: May Co., 801 S. Broadway, Los Angeles, Calif., for $19.27.

December 3: The following checks were issued:

#417: CMA (Creative Management Agency; Judy's agents); $625.63

#418: Edward Traubner & Co (Judy's business manager); (no other info available)

#419: Credit Bureau Of The Greater East Bay, Oakland, California (possibly payment[s] for Judy's mortgage on her home in Brentwood); $3,430.11

December 6, 1963: Videotaping of the both the dress rehearsal (from 5:30 to 7 p.m.), and the final performance (from 9 p.m. to 10:30 p.m.) of "Episode Fifteen"of *The Judy Garland Show*, at CBS Television City, Stage 43, Hollywood. This episode is known as "The Judy Garland *Christmas* Show"—Judy's guests were Jack Jones, Mel Torme, and Judy's children—Liza Minnelli, Lorna Luft, and Joe Luft—and Liza's beau Tracy Everitt (who was a dancer on the series.) Judy sang: "Have Yourself A Merry Little Christmas"; "Consider Yourself" with Lorna and Joe; then reprised with Liza, Lorna and Joe; "Little Drops Of Rain"; "Holiday" Medley with Minnelli and Jones (Judy sang "Jingle Bells" and "Sleigh Reigh" with Minnelli and Jones, then "Winter Wonderland, and a reprise of "Jingle Bells" with Minnelli and Jones); "The Christmas Song" with Mel Torme; "Traditional Carol" Medley with All (Judy sang "What Child Is This?" and "Deck The Halls" with All); "Over The Rainbow" was the closer, sung to Lorna and Joe (Judy also did a spirited high-kicking dance with a group of Santas, to "Rudolph, The Red Nose Reindeer"). The "Christmas Show" was Judy's favorite episode of the series; it is currently available on video cassette from the remastered two-inch "air" tape, complete with commercials, from LaserLight. A CD of highlights from this show is available also on the label. Classic World Productions, Inc. has a VHS available drawn from the original tape, which includes three takes of a Holiday Greeting Judy taped after the show—this is the version on *The Judy Garland Show—Volume Three: The Christmas Show* DVD, released in 1999.

Also on December 6: Check #420 was issued to Judy's butler, Lionel Doman: $120.47.

December 9, 1963 to December 12, 1963: Rehearsals for the next *Judy Garland Show* at CBS Television City.

Also on December 9: A check was issued to: General Telephone Co., P.O. Box 1114, Santa Monica, Calif., for: $235.11.

December 11: A check was issued to: Screen Actors Guild, 7750 Sunset Blvd., L.A., California 90046, for: $185.00.

December 13, 1963: Videotaping of both the dress rehearsal (from 5:30 p.m. to 7 p.m.) and the final performance (from 9 p.m. to 10:30 p.m.) of "Episode Sixteen" of *The Judy Garland Show* at CBS Television City, Stage 43, Hollywood. Judy's guests were Ethel Merman, Shelly Berman, and Peter Gennaro. Judy sang: "Everybody's Doin' It" and "Let's Do It" (opener, with Merman, Berman, and Gennaro); "Shenandoah"; "Makin' Whoopee" (with Gennaro, then joined by Berman); "Merman Medley" (all sung with Merman: "Friendship," "Let's Be Buddies," "You're The Top," "You're Just In Love," "It's De-Lovely," and "Together"). "Born In A Trunk" consisted of "A Pretty Girl Milking Her Cow," "Puttin' On The Ritz," and the electrifying "Battle Hymm Of The Republic", one of the highlights of Judy's career and of television history, which she sang in tribute to John F. Kennedy. Judy also videotaped an unaired comedy sketch with Berman, in which she played a pushy newspaper reporter who "interviews" Berman about working with Judy Garland; this sketch still exists and is on the DVD box set, along with the rest of "Episode Sixteen." This episode aired on January 12, 1964.

December 16, 1963 to December 19, 1963: Rehearsals for the next *Judy Garland Show*.

December 17, 1963: A check was issued to: Kevin L. Enright (household staff), for $259.98.

December 19, 1963: An afternoon videotaping session for a new segment for the Bobby Darrin episode ("Episode Fourteen"; taped November 30), as that show's "Football" medley was cut. The new segment

Four of the greats who guested on *The Judy Garland Show*: Liza Minnelli (top left), Lena Horne (top right), Ethel Merman (bottom left), and Barbra Streisand (bottom right). (Courtesy of Photofest.)

was a "mini concert" of "Hello, Bluebird," "If Love Were All," and "Zing! Went The Strings Of My Heart." Later that evening, Judy prerecorded a medley, which Capitol Records planned on releasing in April, though that album never materialized.

December 20, 1963: Videotaping of both the dress rehearsal (from 5:30 p.m. to 7 p.m.) and the final performance (from 9 p.m. to 10:30 p.m.) of "Episode Seventeen" of *The Judy Garland Show* at CBS Television City, Stage 43, Hollywood. Judy's guests were Vic Damone, Chita Rivera, Louis Nye, and Ken Murray. Judy sang: "They Can't Take That Away From Me" (opener); "I Believe In You" (with Rivera, and Nye); "By Myself" (for which Judy received a standing ovation from the audience. This footage of the audience was actually inserted into "Battle Hymm" from "Episode Sixteen," because the cameras never turned onto the audience standing at the end of that song. The "By Myself" standing ovation still exists on video and is on the DVD Collection, at the conclusion of "By Myself"); "West Side Story" Medley (with Damone—Judy sang "Something's Coming," and "Somewhere" and "Tonight" with Damone. The audio had been recorded the night before, on December 19). In "Born In A Trunk," Judy sang "Better Luck Next Time," and "Almost Like Being In Love"/"This Can't Be Love" medley, followed by the last performance of "Maybe I'll Come Back" as the closer. Judy also videotaped a segment with Ken Murray and his "Hollywood Home Movies," a new segment for the show that showed Murray's silent film clips while Judy commented. On this first outing, a clip of Judy was shown playing tennis, circa 1939; This show is on the DVD *Collection* box set. The episode aired Sunday, January 19, 1964.

December 23, 1963 to January 10, 1964: *The Judy Garland Show* was on a three-week "Holiday" break (but would tape two "back-to-back" episodes in the same week upon its return).

December 26, 1963: Checks were issued to: Abbey Rents, 11841 Wilshire Blvd., Los Angeles, Calif., for $27.80; and to: Aaron Brothers Co., 960 W. La Brea Ave., L.A., Calif., for $46.75.

January 1, 1964 to January 10, 1964: Judy's television series was on a "Holiday Season" break, that had started on December 23; the series would tape two episodes "back-to-back" within the same week, upon its return to work.

Apparently, Judy spent some time the first week of January in New York, as Suzy's gossip column of Saturday, January 11, mentioned in the *Garland Gazette*. Suzy stated that Judy was "the mystery guest" at Eleanor Lambert's fashion show at the Waldorf, "looking like a chic angel in Roy Aghayan's fire-engine red dinner suit with sable cuffs and a pink beaded blouse."

Also around this time, Judy switched law firms; her affairs were to be handled by Hollywood attorney Greg Bautzer, who Judy dated briefly about this time. He was still representing her in 1965, and billing her a $3,500 monthly retainer fee.

At this time, Judy hand-wrote a list of songs she wanted to sing on upcoming episodes of her television series. Some were ones she wanted to repeat, and others were songs she had never sang before. I will note which ones she did repeat, or perform, and which ones she never sang on the series or elsewhere, professionally: The heading is *January Music/Garland Music*.

Let Me Be Different (never sang, ever)

Quiet Nights (never sang, ever; Diahann Carroll would sing as a solo on "Episode Twenty-One")

Something Cool (Judy attempted this song on the final show, "Episode Twenty-Six," but would not complete it)

Play, Orchestra, Play (never sang on series; Judy had sung it in 1937; See 5-18-37)

Cottage For Sale (Judy sang it once, on "Episode Two")

4 Blank Walls and 1 Dirty Window Blues (never sang, ever)

How We Know (W. Robson) (never sang, ever)

Glory Of Love (sang only as part of a Steve Allen and Mel Torne Medley; "Episode Eleven")

Boulevard Of Dreams (never sang, ever)

I Believe In You (sang twice on series: cut from air-tape of "Episode One"; sung on "Episode Seventeen")

Too Close For Comfort (Sang on "Episode Thirteen", as duet with Jack Carter)

Witchcraft (Judy was scheduled to have sung on "Episode Two", but the song was cut before airing, and was probably never even videotaped.)

I Walk With Music (never sang, ever; Judy wrote name of songwriter and publisher)

One Morning In May (never sang, ever; again Judy wrote songs credits)

Skylark (never sang, ever; again Judy wrote songs credits)

Basie Band Background

Sweetest Sounds I Ever Heard/Strike Up The Band (Sang on "Episode Two"; and on 7-20-68)

Why? (Judy may have meant the song "Why Can't I?" which she sang on "Episode Twenty-Five")

Memories Of You (Sang on "Episode Two"; never repeated)

April In Paris (Sang on "Episode Two", as a duet with Torme; sang with Crosby: 3/51); and in parts 10/60)

Don't Rain On My Parade (Sang with Liza at London Palladium concerts, 11/64)

Travelin Life (Never sang: Liza sang it on her first LP in 1964; and at 11/64 concerts)

Sometimes I'm Happy (never sang, ever)

Great Day (Sang on "Episode Twenty-One")

You And The Night And The Music (Sang with Streisand on "Episode Nine"; with Liza 11/64)

Life Is Just A Bowl Of Cherries (Sang on "Episode Twenty-Five"; recorded for Capitol on 3-31-56)

Ten Cents A Dance (never sang, ever; was considered for *Words and Music* movie)

Guess I'll Have To Change My Plans (never sang, ever)

Old Man River (Sang on Series twice: "Episode One" and "Episode Twenty-Five"; and in concerts in 1967)

Old Folks (never sang, ever)

How About Me? ("Berlin" handwritten by Judy; Sang on "Episode Thirteen"; recorded 2-6-57)

January 11, 1964 to January 13, 1964: Rehearsals for the next *Judy Garland Show* episode.

January 14, 1964: Videotaping of both the dress rehearsal (from 5:30 p.m. to 7 p.m.), and the final performance (from 9 p.m. to 10:30 p.m.), of "Episode Eighteen" of *The Judy Garland Show*, at CBS Television City, Stage 43, Hollywood. Judy's guests were Martha Raye, Peter Lawford, Rich Little, and Ken Murray. Judy sang: "76 Trombones" (opener); "I'm Old Fashioned" (as part of a sketch with Lawford); "Glen Miller" Medley (with Raye—Judy sang "I've Heard That Song Before" with Raye, "Moonlight Cocktail" with Raye, "Pennsylvania 6-5000" with Raye, "Elmer's Tune" with Raye, "At Last," and "St. Louis Blues" with Raye; the dress rehearsal performance of this segment was used); "Hit Parade 1964" Medley (with Raye and Lawford—Judy sang "The Boy Next Door" [Rock Version] and "That Wonderful Year" with Raye and Lawford). In "Born In A Trunk," Judy sang "All Alone" and "Oh, Lord, I'm On My Way." (Judy dropped the first song she was to sing—"Just You, Just Me"—on camera, by saying "Let's not do the fast one"; she also exited the stage while the orchestra played "Maybe I'll Come Back"; this entire segment was actually taped at a later, unknown, date.) Judy also taped a segment where impressionist Rich Little sang "The Man That Got Away" as different famous stars. She taped another segment of "Ken Murray and His Hollywood Home Movies." This episode aired on Sunday, January 26, 1964, following the annual broadcast of *The Wizard of Oz*, and is on the DVD *Collection* box set, along with outtakes.

January 15, 1964 to Thursday, January 16, 1964: Rehearsals for the next *Judy Garland Show.*

January 17, 1964: Videotaping of both the dress rehearsal (from 5:30 p.m. to 7 p.m.), and the final performance (from 9 p.m. to 10:30 p.m.) of "Episode Nineteen" of *The Judy Garland Show* at CBS Television City, Stage 43, Hollywood. Judy's guests were Louis Jourdan, The Kirby Stone Four, and Ken Murray. Judy sang: "San Francisco" (opener); "Whispering" with The Kirby Stone Four; a brief bit of "Luie" to introduce Louis Jourdan; "Paris Is A Lonely Town" followed by a "comedy version" of "Smoke

Gets In Your Eyes" where Judy's lavish suite is destroyed by smoke, but mostly by the firemen; "Children's Songs" Medley (with Jourdan—Judy sings "Popeye The Sailor Man," "Give A Little Whistle" with Jourdan, "When You Wish Upon A Star" with Jourdan, "Zip-a-Dee Doo-Dah" with Jourdan, and "Some Day My Prince Will Come"). "Born In A Trunk" had Judy singing "What'll I Do?" and repeating "Battle Hymn Of The Republic." Judy also taped another segment with "Ken Murray and His Hollywood Home Movies," as well as an introduction to the "Glen Miller Medley" dress rehearsal performance for the previous episode, taped that Tuesday, January 14. This episode aired on February 2, 1964, and is on *The Judy Garland Show—Volume Four* DVD, released in November 2000.

January 20, 1964 to January 21, 1964 (Announced on January 22, 1964): CBS allowed Judy to announce the cancellation of her series, saying (in an open letter to James Aubrey, that was reprinted) she was ending the series as she needed to "give my children the time and attention that they need." Everyone knew the real story—CBS was never really behind her show and the ratings had toppled from that high of the first episode aired on September 29 (a 44 share) to a low (28 share; compared to *Bonanza* at a 38 share) by late October, to an even lower 66 out of 80 shows. The critics, fans, and stars raced to her defense, including Lucille Ball, who said "I was furious when Judy Garland was given lines like 'I'm a little old lady,' and someone talking about 'the next Judy Garland.' I bet she's glad her series is over. She's the best."

January 24, 1964: A 2 p.m. rehearsal, followed by a 6 p.m. to 7:30 p.m. dress rehearsal taping, and the final taping from 9:30 p.m. to 11 p.m., of the next *Judy Garland Show*, "Episode Twenty," called *Judy Garland in Concert*, from CBS Television City, Studio 43, Hollywood. Judy's concert consisted of an "Overture" followed by her songs: "Swing Low, Sweet Chariot"/"He's Got The Whole World In His Hands" (medley); "World War One" Medley ("When Johnny Comes Marching Home," "There's A Long, Long Trail A-Winding," "Keep The Home Fires Burning," "Give My Regards To Broadway," "Boy Of Mine," "Oh, How I Hate To Get Up In The Morning," and "Over There"); "That's Entertainment"; "Make Someone Happy"; "Liza"; "Happiness Is A Thing Called Joe"; "Lorna's Song"; "Rock-A-Bye Your Baby"; "A Couple Of Swells"; and "America The Beautiful." The show aired on February 9, garnering raves, including the following excerpt:

> *The New York Times*: "After five months of trial and error in which the show has been subjected to various and ill-fated formulas, CBS is going to let Miss Garland do what she does best—sing. . . . Miss Garland did her first solo performance of the season, singing songs with which she has been identified for years. Seemingly a simple format, the show still contained certain production techniques used to instill excitement for the audience. In the center of a huge stage was this little girl, everybody's Judy, singing her heart out for her public. . . .
>
> The next day, many people who had known mostly disappointment in watching the Garland show were commenting about the delightful change. No wonder CBS is going to put that same little girl back on that great big stage alone three Sunday evenings. It could be that the Garland show will register the highest rating of the season."

(The ratings *did* rebound due to the concert shows—back up into the 30s; any other show improving that much would have been rewarded with a renewal! This is one of the five shows that has not yet been released in "the series of the series" from Pioneer Entertainment and Classic World Productions, Inc., although "America The Beautiful" is on the special DVD to benefit the American Red Cross: *The Judy Garland Show—Songs For America*, released on October 30, 2001.)

Also on January 24, 1964: Check issued to: Mel Burns Ford, 2000 Long Beach Blvd., Long Beach, Calif. for: $163.88.

January 25, 1964 to January 30, 1964: Rehearsals for the next *Judy Garland Show* at CBS.

January 29, 1964: Judy signed check # 221 on her Kingsrow Enterprises, Inc., checking account: $245.48 payable to L.F. Houser, Plumbing Service, PO Box 18, Beverly Hills, California. The check cleared through her account at the City National Bank of Beverly Hills, on February 4, 1964; and also a check to: Kevin L. Entwright, household staff, for $259.98.

January 30, 1964: A check was issued to Clorethea Gland, household staff, $96.37.

January 31, 1964: Videotaping of the dress rehearsal (of the segments with guests) from 2 p.m. to 3:30 p.m.; their final performance from 5:30 p.m. to 6:30 p.m.; from 6:30 p.m. to 8:30 p.m. the stage would be set for Judy's "Mini-Concert"—the first half of the hour; from 8:30 p.m. to 10 p.m., the audio and camera set-ups would be tested; at 10 p.m. Judy's Mini-Concert would be taped. This was "Episode Twenty-One" of *The Judy Garland Show* from CBS Television City, Stage 43, Hollywood. Judy's Guests were Diahann Carroll and Mel Torme. Judy sang: a brief bit of "Stranger In Town" to introduce Mel Torme; Judy and Mel sang "The Trolley Song"; Judy and Diahann Carroll sang a "Richard Rodgers /Harold Arlen" medley—Judy sang "Let's Call The Whole Thing Off" (with special lyrics; sung with Carroll); "It's Only A Paper Moon"; "That Old Black Magic"; "Ill Wind"; "Hit The Road To Dreamland"; "Stormy Weather" with Carroll; "Take The Long Way Home" with Carroll; "Any Place I Hang My Home." For the Mini-Concert taping: Judy sang "Hey, Look Me Over"; "Smile"; "I Can't Give You Anything But Love"; "After You've Gone"; "Alone Together"; and "Come Rain Or Come Shine." For "Born In A Trunk," she sang "Don't Ever Leave Me." Judy also taped the last "Ken Murray and His Hollywood Home Movie" segment. This show aired on Sunday, February 16, 1964, and is included on the DVD *Collection* box set.

February 1, 1964 to February 9, 1964: *The Judy Garland Show* took a one-week break, with Judy flying immediately to Manhattan with Lorna and Joe. During that week, Judy attended a Liza performance of *The Fantasticks,* with Elliot Gould, at the Mineola Playhouse in Long Island, New York, and Judy made a personal appearance at an Eleanor Lambert fashion show. Unfortunately, she also slipped in her suite at the Sherry-Netherland Hotel on Saturday, February 8, suffering a mild concussion, and spent the night at Mt. Sinai Hospital, where she was accompanied by her physician, Dr. Kermit Osterman, but was released the following day. Judy took Lorna and Joe to CBS headquarters in New York to watch the first *Concert* show on February 9, which followed The Beatles on *Ed Sullivan.*

February 4, 1964: The following checks were issued:

#547: Wayne Jones (staff; no address); $148.56

#549: Lionel Doman (Judy's butler); $120.47

#550: Cloretha B. Gland (household staff); $96.37

(# ???): Harry E Dietrich, M.D., 153 S. Lasky Dr., Beverly Hills, Calif, for $40.00; Issued on 2-5-64.

February 10, 1964 to February 13, 1964: Rehearsals of the next *Judy Garland Show* at CBS.

February 14, 1964: Videotaping of "Episode Twenty-Two" of *The Judy Garland Show* at CBS Television City, Stage 43, in Hollywood. Judy's guest was Jack Jones. Judy sang (in the opening

"Mini-Concert"): "Swanee"; "Almost Like Being In Love" and "This Can't Be Love"; "Just In Time"; "A Foggy Day"; "If Love Were All"; "Just You, Just Me"; "Last Night When We Were Young"; and "Judy At The Palace"; with Jones, Judy sang a "Jeanette McDonald-Nelson Eddy" medley (during which Judy sang "San Francisco" with Jones, "Will You Remember?" with Jones, "I'll See You Again" with Jones, "Lover Come Back To Me," and "The Donkey Serenade" with Jones). For "Born In A Trunk," Judy sang "When The Sun Comes Out." The last "Ken Murray and his Hollywood Home Movies" segment taped on January 31 with "Episode Twenty-One," was inserted into this episode. Judy also taped another song, "Great Day," for the "Trunk" spot of "Episode Twenty-One." This show, "Episode Twenty-Two," aired on Sunday, February 23, 1964, and is included in the *Collection* box set.

Also on February 14, 1964: A letter was drafted to Frank Rohner of CBS, from Judy, demanding that the episode scheduled for that Sunday's broadcast (2-16-64) be switched from the Ray Bolger/Jane Powell episode ("Episode Ten"), to the Diahann Carrol/Mel Torme episode ("Episode Twenty-One"). Judy stated she would pay all the additional costs involved in making the switch. (She obviously wanted to continue the momentum of the concert episodes, as the first concert episode had aired the previous Sunday, 2-9-64, and had made such a huge hit in the press.)

February 17, 1964 to February 20, 1964: Rehearsals for the next two episodes of *The Judy Garland Show*, as tapings would occur back-to-back once again, only two days apart.

February 21, 1964: Videotaping of another *Judy Garland in Concert* episode of *The Judy Garland Show*, "Episode Twenty-Three," at CBS Television City, Stage 43, Hollywood, this one being "Songs From The Movies." Judy sang: "Once In A Lifetime" and "I Feel A Song Coming On" (medley); "If I Had A Talking Picture Of You" and "Toot, Toot, Tootsie" (medley); "Dirty Hands, Dirty Face"; "Love Of My Life"; "The Boy Next Door"; "On The Atchison, Topeka, And The Santa Fe"; "Alexander's Rag Time Band"; "You're Nearer"; "Steppin' Out With My Baby"; "I'm Always Chasing Rainbows"; "The Man That Got Away"; "Be A Clown"; and a reprise of "Once In A Lifetime." (This episode aired on March 8, 1964, and is one of five episodes that has not yet been released on DVD.)

February 23, 1964: Videotaping of "Episode Twenty-Four" (only two days after the taping of "Episode Twenty-Three") of *The Judy Garland Show* at CBS Television City, Stage 43, Hollywood. Judy's guest for this "Semi-Concert" was Vic Damone. Judy sang: "Lucky Day"; "Sweet Danger"; "Do I Love You?"; "I Love You"; "When Your Lover Has Gone"; "Down With Love"; "Old Devil Moon"; "Never Will I Marry"; "Any Place I Hang My Hat Is Home"; "Chicago"; a "Kismet" Medley (with Damone, Judy dueted on "He's In Love" and "This Is My Beloved"). In the "Born In A Trunk" spot, Judy sang a haunting "Lost In The Stars," another of her greatest performances. (Additional takes of both "Lost In The Stars" and "This Is My Beloved" exist: in the latter, after Judy blows the next to last note, she bows to Damone, hits the floor, turns on her side and starts pounding the stage while laughing; This is included on the DVD.) This episode aired on March 15, 1964, and is on *The Judy Garland Show—Volume Four* DVD.

February 24, 1964 to February 28, 1964: Judy had a week off from the taping of her series.

February 25, 1964: A check was issued to: General Telephone Co., P.O. Box 1303, Santa Monica, California, for: $335.61.

March 2, 1964 to March 5, 1964: Rehearsals for the next *Judy Garland Show*.

Also on March 2, 1964: A check was issued to Cloretha B. Gland, household staff, for $96.37.

Near the end of the television series, Judy shares laughter, love, and a box of chocolates (a gift from the crew) during the Valentine's Day videotaping of show #22, February 14, 1964. (Courtesy of Photofest.)

March 5, 1964: Judy had to make a court appearance at the Santa Monica courthouse against Sid Luft, for custody hearings over Lorna and Joe.

March 6, 1964: Videotaping of "Episode Twenty-Five" of *The Judy Garland Show* at CBS Television City, Stage 43, Hollywood. Another "Semi-Concert" Show, with guest Robert Cole and His Trio. Judy sang: "Sail Away"; "Comes Once In A Lifetime"; "I Am Loved"; "Life Is Just A Bowl Of Cherries"; "Why Can't I?"; "I Gotta Right To Sing The Blues"; "Joey, Joey, Joey"; "Love"; "By Myself"; "Get Happy"; "As Long As He Needs Me"; "Poor Butterfly" (with Cole). In the "Trunk" spot: "Old Man River." ("By Myself" would be dropped and inserted into "Episode Twenty-Six.") This episode aired on March 22, 1964, and is on *The Judy Garland Show—Volume Four* DVD.

March 6, 1964: Judy signed check #263 of her Kingsrow Enterprises, Inc. account, c/o Edward Traubner & Co., Inc, 132 South Rodeo Drive, Beverly Hills. The check—for $79.70, made payable to Don The Pool Man, 15952 Ventura Blvd, Encino, California—cleared through her account # 1222 1606 001044741 with City National Bank of Beverly Hills, on April 3; Another check was also issued on March 6, to: Kevin Entwright, household staff, for $229.03.

March 9, 1964 to March 12, 1964: Rehearsals for *The Judy Garland Show.* (Also on 3-9-64, a check was issued to: Mel Burns Ford, 2000 Long Beach Blvd., Long Beach, Calif., for $163.88. Obviously for Judy's cars.)

March 13, 1964: Videotaping of the last episode of *The Judy Garland Show* "Episode Twenty-Six," at CBS Television City, Stage 43, Hollywood. Taping of the next-to-closing song began first, at 8 p.m. to about 8:20 p.m., with Judy completing two takes and a pickup of a new song "Where Is The Clown?" which was sung by an off-camera chorus, while Judy, in clown makeup and costume, pantomimed the song. At about 10 p.m., Judy appeared in front of the assembled audience for the first time, and taped the closing number while still in the clown outfit, a song called "Here's To Us" from the Broadway musical "Little Me" (various trade items appeared around this time that Judy would have loved to do the movie version if it were ever made). The performance remains one of Judy's definitive performances, as she created some of the lyrics for the song, especially her "Here's to us, for letting me do what I'll do to the end of my days." Judy so loved the song, she considered singing it at her concerts; it would also be played at her funeral. About 1:00 a.m. in the morning (of Saturday, March 14), Judy appeared in her gown, to tape the concert, with about fifty faithful fans in the audience. Judy sang: "After You've Gone"; "The Nearness Of You"; "Time After Time"; "That Old Feeling"; "Carolina In The Morning"; "When You're Smiling"; "Almost Like Being In Love"/"This Can't Be Love" (medley); "Suppertime"; and "The Last Dance." Most songs required several takes, either due to Judy, or technical problems; this, and breaks, meant that these nine songs took about three hours to complete, then Judy left the stage about 4 a.m. Earlier, at around 2 a.m. or 3 a.m., Tony Bennett was seen entering the artists entrance at CBS, according to the *Garland Gazette* so he must have gone to help Judy get through the ordeal of the final taping. From about 5:45 a.m. to exactly 5:54 a.m., Judy videotaped three spoken intros to the song "Something Cool," and then attempted the song itself, but faltered midway after getting less than two minutes into the song, and walked off the stage. (All of this footage—including "Where Is The Clown?"; "Here's To Us"; and "Something Cool"; as well as other takes of some of the concert songs—still exists, as does a quick glimpse of Judy in her clown outfit as the marker is hit for "Where Is The Clown?"—Judy is seen touching up her clown makeup, and then turns her head and coughs. "Episode Twenty-Six" is one of the five shows that has not been released yet on DVD.)

March 16, 1964: A check was issued to: Barrington Hardware, 145 S. Barrington Ave., L.A. 45 Calif. for $102.71; and a check to City National Bank —Judy's bank in California—for $682.66.

Approximately Tuesday, March 17, 1964: Judy and producer Bill Colleran viewed the tapes of the last episode and realized another session would have to be scheduled to complete the hour.

Also on March 17, 1964: A check was issued to the Savoy Hilton, New York, New York, for $137.33.

March 18, 1964: Judy was rushed to Cedars of Lebanon Hospital, suffering from an attack of appendicitis according to her physician, Dr. Lee Siegel.

Also on March 18, 1964: Checks were issued to: CMA Ltd., 9465 Wilshire Blvd., Beverly Hills, Calif., for $46.50, and one for "Cash," in the amount of $250.00.

March 20, 1964: Judy left the hospital to fly to San Francisco for a few days rest, with her musical advisor Robert Cole. On Wednesday, March 25, according to information from Garland fan journals, she attended the opening there of a musical called "Firefly," which she was apparently interested in purchasing.

March 26, 1964: Judy returned to Stage 43 at CBS, directly from San Francisco, to videotape the twelve-minute production number of "Born In A Trunk" from *A Star Is Born*, and also to tape another song to air as the last song on the final episode. Judy arrived at CBS at 5:20 p.m. (forty minutes early); a rehearsal with the band was from 8 p.m. to 9 p.m.; the taping scheduled from 9:30 p.m. to 10:30 p.m. Unfortunately, the twelve minutes of surviving videotape show Judy trying to get through the routine, with only the first few minutes of the number usable. The final airing of *The Judy Garland Show* on Sunday, March 29, 1964, would use the thirty minutes/nine songs from March 13; five songs from "Episode Twenty-Two," taped February 14 (Jack Jones); and one song—"By Myself"—(deleted from "Episode Twenty-Five" due to time restraints), to fill out the hour. A special honor for Judy, despite the ending of the show, was being voted Best Female Vocalist in the fifteenth annual nationwide poll of television critics and editors, along with an Emmy nomination. Judy's television series earned four Emmy nominations in all: Outstanding Variety Program (which *The Danny Kaye Show* won), Judy *and* her guest Barbra Streisand, individually, for Outstanding Performance in a Variety or Music Program or Series (which they both lost to Danny Kaye), and Best Art Direction. With the television series now over, so were Judy's chances of a regular routine and life with her children in one home, instead of having to be out on the road, "singing for her supper in the throngs." In many ways, the television series was the ideal job for Judy, as it combined all the elements of her two main venues of work: her "live" concerts—since she would be performing in front of a studio audience—and her film work, since the shows were being done on a "preserved" medium. Sadly, despite being promised that she would make $20 million or more from the series, and certainly around $4 million for syndication sales, Judy never saw a penny for all the hopes and dreams she put into the series. The real payoff would come after her passing, as the series is the only audio-video work that captures her at a vocal and physical peak during the concert years portion of her career, and thus becomes the most important—as well as being the finest—work from her entire career. It is ensuring that people will not think of her only as an old movie star, but as a major force on stage, in her best format, and in her best "role"—herself.

March 30, 1964: Judy's latest album was released by Capitol Records. *Just For Openers* contains 12 solos from tapes recorded through the sound system—in mono, not stereo—at CBS during the tapings of *The Judy Garland Show*. Though future "Television Series Soundtrack" LPs were planned (thus the title), including one with material from the shows with Vic Damone (who was also under contract to Capitol Records), this would be the only legitimate album from a major label to use material from Judy's series, during her lifetime. (Also on this date: checks were issued to: Paul Gastelum, 12620 Short Ave., L.A., Calif., for $65.00, and to: General Telephone Co., P.O. Box 1303, Santa Monica, Calif., for $270.78.)

April 1964: (Personal Appearance) The Chalk Garden (Hollywood Museum benefit fashion show), at Universal Studios, Hollywood.

April 1964: Judy spent some time recording some thoughts on a tape recorder at home, for possible use in a book. Meant as perhaps an introduction to the autobiography she planned, Judy is in wonderful spirits as she insists "I am funny. . . . I can't take myself seriously, because if I did I would have died a long time ago, and I have no intention of dying. . . . When my number's up, I want a new one, and I have no intention of 'checking out'; and this (tape) machine won't get me either. . . . I have a rather good intellect; I have a good sense of humor. But it's high time to cut the comedy, and high time to stop the trolley ride, because I, Judy Garland, am gonna talk. And everybody better just sit on the bench and watch the ballgame." Another tape exists of Judy talking with her "Number One Fan," Wayne Martin, at this time. Not much information is gleamed from the tape, as this conversation—that Wayne taped—was brief; he had called simply to congratulate Judy on her Emmy nomination. Later conversations recorded by Wayne are more revealing, and often fascinating.

April 7, 1964: A check was issued to: Southern Pacific Railroad, for $65.95.

April 10, 1964: Checks were issued to: Lionel Doman (Judy's butler) for $115.64, and to Palisade Travel Bureau, 15235 Sunset Blvd., Pacific Palisades, Calif., for $213.90.

April 13, 1964: The following checks were issued:

#681: Wayne Jones (household staff); (no other info available)

#683: Lionel Doman (Judy's butler); $120.47, and one dated 4-10-64 to Doman: $115.64

#329 (Kingsrow): Orval Paine (Judy's hairdresser); $645.00

April 17, 1964: A Kingsrow Enterprises check was drawn on this date from a different bank account: Chase Manhattan Bank at 410 Park Avenue. The check number is not filled in: it is made payable to Kingsrow for $20,000.

April 21, 1964: Check #694 was issued to Mattie U. Oliver (household staff) for $96.37.

April 24, 1964: Hedda Hopper's column announced that "Judy Garland says she will do *The Owl and The Pussycat*, a straight drama without songs, on the stage in London and New York. It will be backed by the *Hamlet* financier, Alexander Cohen, with Ray Stark producing. Judy still plans to keep her three singing dates in Australia the middle of May." Judy never would do this play; Streisand would do the film.

May 2, 1964: Judy left for a week vacation in Hawaii, with her new escort, actor Mark Herron.

May 11, 1964: Judy arrived in Sydney, and gave several interviews at a large press conference/reception for her. A few of the interviews remain on film, and they reveal a calm, warm, funny, and aware Judy.

May 13, 1964: (Concert) Judy's first work, only six weeks after the series, was this concert at the 10,000 seat Sydney Stadium in Sydney, Australia. It was a huge success. (She was to be paid $52,000 total for this concert and the next two concerts in Australia.)

Judy with her favorite male singer, Tony Bennett, circa 1963–1964. They worked together on many occasions, both planned and impromptu performances, and on an epiosde of *The Judy Garland Show*. Tony always mentioned the great fun he had around Judy, and that comes through in this photograph. (Courtesy of Photofest.)

> *Variety* reported: "At Wednesday's premiere concert, Miss Garland won the greatest audience ovation in the history of Australian show-biz. She had the audience in the palm of her hand from the moment she stepped on the rostrum."
>
> *Sydney Sun Herald*: "The Beatles may come and go, but the past week belongs to Judy. The little figure under the lights conquered all."

May 16, 1964: (Concert) Sydney Stadium, Sydney, Australia. Judy's second concert was an even greater hit than the first, three nights before. An audiotape recorded in the audience still survives, with about sixty-eight minutes of Judy's two-act concert. The songs on the tape are: "When You're Smiling"; "Almost Like Being In Love" and "This Can't Be Love"; "Do It Again"; "Judy's Olio"; "Love Of My Life" (the only known concert performance of this song from *The Pirate*, although Judy had recently performed it on "Episode Twenty-Three" of her television series); "The Man That Got Away"; "San Francisco"; "That's Entertainment"; "Swanee"; "Make Someone Happy"; "Just In Time"; "As Long As He Needs Me"; "By Myself"; "Rock-A-Bye"; "Chicago"; and "Over The Rainbow." At the end of the concert, a promoter insulted Judy by calling her a "freak" singer because of what she had done to her audience. He meant it as a compliment, but Judy slapped his face after asking him to repeat what he had said, and everything began to unravel.

May 19, 1964: Judy traveled by train—a twelve-hour trip from Sydney to Melbourne—for her next concert. (Black and white newsreel footage exists of her arrival, looking exhausted. Judy did not give any interviews to the press before her concert.)

May 20, 1964: (Concert) Festival Hall, Melbourne, Australia. Judy had been an hour late to the show, and was fighting vocal problems—and members of the audience. Judy only managed to get through about half the show, when she fled the stage. The cruel and outright vicious reviews would come to haunt her.

May 21, 1964: Judy and Herron fled Melbourne, returning to Sydney, aboard an 8 p.m. flight.

May 22, 1964: Judy and Herron flew from Sydney to Hong Kong on an 11 p.m. flight, checking into the Mandarin Hotel.

May 27, 1964: This was the only day Judy left her hotel—to consult a doctor.

May 28, 1964: Typhoon Viola struck Hong Kong, and the twenty-second floor of the Mandarin Hotel—where Judy and Herron were staying—swayed and shook. At some point very late that night or in the very early morning hours of Friday, May 29, 1964, Judy took an overdose of pills; was found by Herron, and rushed, through the typhoon, three blocks to a small Catholic hospital, called Canossa Hospital; Judy's stomach was pumped—damaging her vocal cords with the tubes—and she was in a coma for 15 hours. At one point a valve actually broke on her oxygen tent; until it was fixed, Judy hadn't moved; therefore, a nurse left the room saying Judy had died; this news traveled throughout the world, although the information was, thankfully, incorrect. (It actually was reported on the radio that Judy had died, although it was corrected before being printed in newspapers.) Judy did survive—barely. Among other ailments, Judy had pleurisy in both lungs, and her throat, and her heart was damaged. Due to the tubes damaging her vocal chords, she was told not to sing for a year. Most people were (and are) unaware that her vocal cords were damaged—to say nothing of her heart and lungs, amongst other damages. What Judy Garland was to give to the world the last five years of her life is perhaps even more astounding when considering the state of her physical condition.

May 30, 1964: Judy's doctor, Lee Siegel, flew from California to Hong Kong to treat Judy. Her road manager/CMA agent Karl Brent accompanied Siegel.

June 1, 1964: Judy left the hospital, saying, "I am still very weak. I am going to take a long rest." Dr. Lee Siegel agreed that Judy could rest in her hotel. Siegel said she was suffering from pleurisy.

June 4, 1964: Dr. Siegel was called to Judy's hotel room, because she was running a fever.

June 5, 1964: Judy returned to the Catholic Canossa hospital for x-rays, and told the press she would be leaving Hong Kong "in about ten days," and taking "an ocean voyage. I want to travel all over the world."

Early June 1964: Little more than a week after her overdose, Judy saw Peter Allen perform for the first time, as part of "The Allen Brothers" act, at the Starlight Room in Hong Kong. Judy sang that night. (Her doctors, once again, obviously did not know their patient; nothing could keep Judy from singing since the time she was two, and nothing ever would. Still, one wonders if she was doing further damage to her vocal cords by singing only a week after they had been damaged.)

June 10, 1964: Judy's forty-second birthday was celebrated in a small private party in her Hong Kong hotel room.

June 11, 1964: Judy and Herron made the rounds of the local nightclubs in Hong Kong. At one, the President Hotel (where they watched "The Maori Hi-Five"), the band played "Happy Birthday" to Judy. While there, she and Herron announced that they were married. Judy supposedly said, "We've been married five days now. I'm very happy." While there, she sang "Over The Rainbow."

Mid to late June 1964: Judy and Herron continued their travels:

On June 12, 1964 they were in the Mandarin, aboard the President Roosevelt ocean liner, which had left Hong Kong for Tokyo on that day, where they were reportedly "married" by a Buddhist priest (even though Judy's divorce from Luft would not be final until late 1965.) Another version had Judy telling reporters on June 12 that she and Herron had been married that day in their hotel suite in a traditional Chinese ceremony, and that they had also been married on Saturday, June 6, on the Norwegian freighter "Bodo."

A letter dated June 15 is signed by Judy. Typed on hotel stationary—The Mandarin, Connaught Road Central, Hong Kong, Telephone: 29211, Cables: Mandarin Hong Kong. Obviously meant to be sent out to her fans, the letter says:

> My dear Friend,
>
> Thank you very much for your kind message which gave me so much happiness that I have now completely recovered from my bout with pneumonia.
>
> Naturally, your message helped so much, and the gracious letters, cards and cables from all over the world were a great inspiration to me.
>
> Best Wishes, and God bless you.
>
> (Signed) Judy Garland.

Upon leaving Hong Kong, Judy told reporters that her illness there had been brought on from overwork: "I'll never overwork again. I'll remember this my whole life." (If only that had been true.)

June 16, 1964: Judy landed in Yokohama.

June 17, 1964: Judy's attorney Howard Schwab announced that Judy had merely received a blessing by a Buddhist priest, and that had started the rumor that she had been married.

June 25, 1964: Judy left Tokyo by plane for Denmark, where she arrived in Copenhagen on June 26, after a stopover in Anchorage, Alaska (where she told the press "I am very happy—We are very happy!"). (A photo exists of Judy on June 26 at the airport in Copenhagen.) Judy only stayed in Copenhagen overnight, at the Royal Hotel. Judy and Herron then traveled to London.

June 30, 1964: Judy and Herron arrived in London, renting a large house in the Boltons. Around this time, Judy attended a screening of either *Meet Me in St. Louis* or *Words and Music*—depending on which report you read—in a London theater one Friday afternoon. Judy and Herron were also seen at this time in various nightclubs. At one spot, the pianist played "Over The Rainbow" as she entered, and she sang it, saying "Now, I can't pass that up, can I?"

July 7, 1964: *The Hollywood Reporter* carried an item that Judy had fired Freddie Fields and David Begelman as her managers, via a letter, and put Karl Brent in charge of her career. Apparently this was to be temporary—if true at all—for although Karl Brent may have handled Judy on a day-to-day basis, Fields and Begelman, through CMA, continued to represent Judy into 1966.

July 20, 1964: Judy cut her wrists while attempting to open a trunk, and was taken to St. Stephens Hospital.

July 23, 1964: Judy made a spectacular "comeback" at the "Night Of 100 Stars" benefit at the London Palladium. Though Judy was set to only take a bow, after three ovations and demands from the audience that she sing, Judy performed both "Over The Rainbow," and "Swanee." Although the bill included such greats as The Beatles, Judy received the greatest reception by far, both from the audience and the critics all of whom agreed she had stolen the night, as the following report indicates:

> Stars today have become devalued and it is tempting to dismiss them as merely a product of their publicity. So it is salutary to be reminded that a star is a star, with an inexplicable magic which more than justifies the fame and the ballyhoo. . . . Tears were in many eyes at what appeared to be a personal triumph over adversity, while Miss Garland's magnificent voice fully deserved the cheers which eclipsed any that had gone before in this genuinely starry show. This was an exceptional occasion which everyone present will remember forever.

July 31, 1964: Judy and Mark Herron flew to Rome for a brief trip.

August 3, 1964: Judy and Mark returned to London.

August 5, 1964 to August 6, 1964: (Recording) Judy did her last recording session, ever, for records: Lionel Bart's *Maggie May* for Capitol/EMI Records, in London. Judy recorded four songs: "Maggie May"; "It's Yourself"; "There's Only One Union"; and "The Land Of Promises." On the first session of August 5, set for 9 p.m., Judy arrived at 9:15 p.m., and did a run through of the two songs to be done that night ("The Land Of Promises" and "It's Yourself"). Then came the set "tea break" time. Finally, from 10 p.m. to 11 p.m., Judy recorded both songs. (Requiring only four takes of each song.) The EP—Extended Play—recording was never officially released in the United States, but two of the songs have appeared on two EMI CD releases from England, *Legends of the 20th Century* (from 1999, includes "Maggie May") and *The Best of Judy Garland* (from 1995, which includes "Maggie May" and "It's Yourself"—"Yourself" is in stereo; "Maggie" in mono). "In The Land Of Promises" is on *The Definitive Judy Garland* bootleg CD that is now out of print. "There's Only One Union" has never appeared on CD, but all four songs were on a 1982 EMI LP, *Con Plumas Judy Garland.*

August 1964: Judy was seen at the opening of Marlene Dietrich's show at the Queens Theater (which would result in an amusing tale about her arrival on a later *Jack Paar Program*). (At around this time, August 1964, Judy's secretary was Miss Rene J. Kaiser; Rene's bosses were Judy and Karl Brent, her Judy's "personal manager." Judy and Brent each had their own office—along with a file room and a reception room. "Kingsrow Enterprises" was located at the Kirkeby Center, 10889 Wilshire Blvd, Suite 265, Los Angeles, California 90024. That office had opened circa spring of 1964, and it is believed it stayed open for approximately two years.)

August 20, 1964: Judy attended the premiere of the show *Maggie May* in Liverpool.

Mid to late August 1964: Judy decided she wanted to share the bill with Liza Minnelli at the London Palladium. Liza originally said no, but Judy announced it anyway, in October, and the show sold out in one afternoon, and a second show was planned. Judy made a tape recording of ideas for the concerts, including the lyrics to be sung to the tune of "Hello, Dolly": "Liza—'Hello, Mama, well, Hello, Mama; May I say that name tonight cause I'm so proud.' / Judy—'Oh, by all means daughter, but it seems, daughter, a bit too formal cause we're gonna sing so loud.'" Judy also thought of some sketches, including one where Liza would play a young reporter who was interviewing an older movie star. None of these ideas would be used in the concert, except for some special lyrics for "Hello, Dolly," which differ from the words Judy mentioned.

September 2, 1964: Judy was photographed attending—and spontaneously taking part in the finale of—the revue *We're Only Joking*, at Danny LaRue's Club in London. (She would apparently come to see the show again in mid to late September.)

September 10, 1964: Liza arrived in London, to spend a week with Judy and Mark. At this time, the British papers were reporting that Judy and Liza would do a television special together in London later that year, and that Judy and Mark were to costar in a television comedy called *It's Better in the Dark* for ABC-TV, to be filmed in London. Neither of these projects would materialize—although mother and daughter's concert would be taped by British Television.

September 14, 1964: Judy was photographed and interviewed by the British press, at home in London.

September 16, 1964: (Personal Appearance) Judy attended the opening—as Guest Of Honor—of a new gay club in London, with Mark Herron.

September 18, 1964: (Personal Appearance) Judy and Mark Herron gave a lecture about American cinema and the theater at the All Saint's Church "84" Club for young people.

September 23, 1964: (Personal Appearance) Judy attended the London premiere of *Maggie May*. Immediately following the opening night party, Judy felt a pain in her stomach as she and Herron were getting into their car, and she was rushed to a nursing home.

September 24, 1964: X-Rays were being taken all day; appendicitis was suspected. Judy's doctor, Phillip Lebon, said, "Miss Garland is suffering from an acute abdominal condition. At present there is no danger."

September 25, 1964: Judy was released from the nursing home: "The first thing I did when I got home was to bake myself a chicken pie, just to settle in again. I guess people get the impression I'm seriously ill every time I go into a hospital, but all I had was a good old fashioned tummy ache," she explained to the *Daily Express*. While Judy was hospitalized, ABC-TV in London announced that she had "quit" the play she planned to do with Mark Herron.

October 10, 1964: Press interview at home in London (photo exists of Judy at home on this date), to officially announce the concert "Judy and Liza at the London Palladium" on November 8. This sold out before it could be officially advertised, so a second date was set for November 15.

October 12, 1964: Press interview at home in London. (Photos were taken by Associated Newspapers Ltd. in London)

October 26, 1964: Liza arrived in London to begin rehearsals for the concert with Judy at the London Palladium.

October 27, 1964: Judy greeted Peter Allen and his stage partner Chris as they arrived in London—black and white silent newsreel footage still exists of this first meeting between Liza and Peter. Later that evening, Judy attended the opening night of *Hay Fever* at the National Theater in London. There had also been, on this day, the second and final day of a court hearing where Sid Luft was granted increased visitation rights after he had brought out unflattering tales of Judy that were then made public. Though Judy told the press at the airport "In spite of everything that was said back there, I am a very good mother," her unhappiness can be heard in existing tapes made at this time, where she expresses her anger at Luft, and where Mark Herron comes on at one point to defend her.

October 28, 1964: Sid Luft, Lorna, and Joe had to appear at a Santa Monica courthouse for a hearing on the custody case. That evening Judy attended the second performance of *Giselle* at the Covent Garden in London.

October 29, 1964: The second "Judy and Liza at the London Palladium" concert was announced for November 15.

Also on October 29, 1964: A letter from Herbert Schwab, her attorney in Los Angeles, indicated that she had "the following matters on hand":

1) Depositions, LUFT vs. LUFT

2) Deposition, MEL TORME vs. JUDY GARLAND

3) Delinquent federal income taxes

4) Furniture appraisal re Kingsrow

5) Preparation of a new will

6) Possibility of forming a Litchenstein corporation to avoid certain tax liabilities

Legal cases then pending included: (10):

LUFT vs. CREATIVE MANAGEMENT ASSOCIATES, INC.

BRADFORD vs. KINGSROW & JUDY GARLAND

TORME vs. KINGSROW & JUDY GARLAND

GARY SMITH vs. KINGSROW

DAN DAILEY vs. KINGSROW & JUDY GARLAND

SULTAN & WORTH vs. KINGSROW & JUDY GARLAND

GARBER vs. KINGSROW & JUDY GARLAND

OSCAR STEINBERG vs. JUDY GARLAND

HARRY ZEEVER vs. JUDY GARLAND & SID LUFT

CLOSED CREDIT CORPORATION vs. JUDY GARLAND and MILTON HOLLAND

Alan Sussman law firm, $70,000 indebtedness, settled ultimately for $15,000.

A legal bill for $55,815 for 1,273 hours of service.

November 1, 1964: (Personal Appearance/Benefit) Judy presented a $8,500 check on behalf of the Damon Runyon Cancer Fund, from the Fund's treasurer, Walter Winchell, to Dr. Henrik Kacser of Edinburgh University, for research.

November 3, 1964: Judy attended the opening night of *High Spirits* in London.

November 4, 1964: Logs exist that show a master for the song "Joey, Joey" was recorded on this date. Since Judy performed this song in concert on November 8, 1964, it's possible that it was also recorded in the studio on November 4. The recording is being sought after and may be included on a two-CD set of the complete *Judy Garland and Liza Minnelli "Live" at the London Palladium* I am working on with Capitol, currently scheduled for an April 2002 release. (This version of "Joey, Joey" is actually from 1962.)

November 6, 1964 and November 7, 1964: Rehearsals at EMI studios in London, for the Judy/Liza Palladium concert. (The music had only just arrived from the U.S. the previous Tuesday, November 3.)

November 8, 1964: (After a four-hour afternoon orchestra/rehearsal call, which had Judy singing from 2:30 p.m. to after 6 p.m.): (Concert) "Judy Garland and Liza Minnelli At the London Palladium." This was a fifty-song concert! Judy's fifteen solos included: "Once In A Lifetime"; "Maggie May"; "As Long As He Needs Me"; "Just In Time"; "It's Yourself"; "Smile"; "Never Will I Marry"; "What Now, My Love?"; "The Music That Makes Me Dance"; "Joey, Joey, Joey"; "Make Someone Happy"; "The Man That Got Away"; "Rock-A-Bye Your Baby"; "San Francisco"; and "Over The Rainbow." Judy and Liza had over 20 duets, including two medleys from the series that Judy and Barbara had done, along with

"Hello, Dolly"; "There Is A Brotherhood Of Man"/"When The Saints Go Marching In"; "Battle Hymn Of The Republic"; and "He's Got The Whole World In His Hand." Although Judy's voice was worn by the four-hour afternoon rehearsal, the reviews were still ecstatic.

> *The Daily Mail*, November 9: "History was made last night at the Palladium, when Judy Garland and her daughter Liza Minnelli sang together for the first time on any stage. History was made too, by a frenzied mob of fans who gave Judy the ovation of a lifetime. . . . To talk about Judy Garland rationally is about as difficult as describing magic. Apart from still being the greatest of them all, through every routine it was apparent that she also is an accomplished actress. And if, to the very critical, the voice is no longer always what it used to be, she still has that elusive 'star quality,' which makes her the most-loved performer in the world today."

(The concert was recorded by Capitol Records, who would also record the second concert. After the concert, Judy attended the reception in the Monte Carlo Suite at the Mayfair Hotel, from 12:10 a.m. to 2 a.m.)

November 15, 1964: (Concert) Judy and Liza at the London Palladium. This concert had been scheduled due to the overwhelming demand for tickets of the first concert on November 8. This second concert was also enthusiastically reviewed.

> *The Viewer* (Ian Brown): "Down the aisles ran the so-called unemotional British—balding, middle-aged men in dinner jackets and long-haired youths jostling to get to Judy's outstretched hands—and to kiss them. A fantastic sight to climax a fantastic night."

Capitol Records recorded this night as well; although only one Liza solo was taken from this night for the two-record set. Other surviving outtakes are in the Capitol vaults—some of which can be heard on the 1991 Capitol box set *The One And Only*, now out-of-print. Also, ITV British Television taped this second concert, although the telecast five weeks later was only 55 minutes of the 130-minute concert; the remaining footage does not present Judy at her best, due in large part to the way the film was transferred from British broadcast standards to American standards. (The surviving fifty-five minute television show was released officially for the first time by LaserLight/Delta Music, in 1997, as *Judy Garland "Live" At The London Palladium with Special Guest Liza Minnelli*. After leaving the theater at 4 a.m.—the show had been at midnight—Judy, Herron, and Liza went to Danny LaRue's nightclub.)

November 21, 1964: (Television) Judy was seen briefly on British television, sitting in the audience of the show *Juke Box Jury*, where a panel votes on new records: Liza was a member of the panel.

November 23, 1964: Judy and Liza rerecorded some vocal tracks in a studio in England for the *Judy Garland and Liza Minnelli "Live" at the London Palladium* album that Capitol was anxious to release. They both sang over the orchestra tracks that had been made mostly from the second concert, so no musicians were present during this session. Judy dubbed new vocals to "Just Once In A Lifetime" (one take); "His Is The Only Music That Makes Me Dance" (two takes); and, with Liza, new versions of "Hello, Dolly" (one take); "Don't Rain On My Parade" (three takes); "San Francisco" (three takes); and "Chicago" (two takes; this song used the orchestra tracks from the first concert). (Liza also dubbed new versions of her "Mama" tribute, and "Who's Sorry Now?") Part of the reason for recording these new takes is that much of the second concert audiotapes were ruined by a buzzing sound that bled through from some of the television cameras that were videotaping the show that night. For all this effort, the only thing that would be used from this session on the album was the ending of "Hello, Dolly," that occurs after the dialogue between Judy and Liza and the audience. In spite of the two-album set being poorly edited—and quite short—the LP would hit number 19 on the charts in the fall of 1965, following its release on July 25, 1965.

November 25, 1964: (Television) *The Jack Paar Program*, NBC. Judy taped this guest appearance at the Prince Charles Theater, Fielding's Music Hall, London, England, with sixty-five members of her British fan club in the audience, for the 8:45 p.m. taping (which followed a rehearsal with Judy and the orchestra at about 7 p.m.). Judy was interviewed by Paar, and sang "Never Will I Marry" and "What Now, My Love?" One of the funny tales that didn't make the final air-tape, was about the time Judy's Chinese assistant, Snowy, took a phone call from Tallulah Bankhead, and the message to Judy read: "*Mr.* Lullah Bankhead called, and *he* was so rude, and hung-up." Unfortunately, Judy was not in top form, appearing somewhat medicated in her delivery—although incredibly funny—and the airing on December 11, 1964, had the opposite effect of the Carnegie Hall concert and album. Thus, many people were actually turned off of Judy Garland. It was something that would happen frequently when she appeared on television during her last few years. It was becoming increasingly difficult to find her in good voice, appearing in good form, and looking lovely all at the same time, as writer Randy Henderson talked about in his outstanding Emmy Magazine article on Judy's television work. The show did get at least one good review.

> *Journal American*: "Judy is visual, emotion evoking. You don't hear her only with the ears. She soaks in through your pores."

(Backstage after the taping of this Paar show, Judy confessed that she hated the song "Stardust." This was apparently also the day that Peter Allen proposed to Liza at the Polynesian restaurant at the Hilton Hotel; just before the Paar show. This might help explain Judy's below-par *Paar* performance; there certainly would have been major celebrating over Liza's engagement.)

November 26, 1964: Judy gave interviews on this day to announce Liza's engagement to Peter Allen. During a 2 a.m. interview in London, just after the Paar taping, for columnist Mike Connally, Judy mentioned she was thinking of possibly staying in London, to do the movie version of the unsuccessful Judy Holiday stage drama *Laurette*, which was about the late actress Laurette Taylor. This was a project that never transpired. Mark Herron also stated during the forty-five minute conversation with Connally that he was, "giving up his acting career to become director and mentor to Judy." Later that day Judy went to the airport to see Liza off, who was returning to New York.

November 29, 1964: Judy attended the British Fan Club meeting at the Russell Hotel in northern London, from 3 p.m. to 7 p.m. While there, Judy watched a screening of *Gay Purr-ee*, which apparently had never played London before, and was making its debut at the Judy fan club meeting. Judy mentioned her favorite films were *Meet Me in. St. Louis*, *The Clock*, and *For Me and My Gal*—"Even though it is so corny!" She also said some rerecording was done at EMI studios for the Palladium concert album because the television cameras had affected the sound at times (see November 23, 1964, for more information on that session.) When the print of *The Harvey Girls* jumped some frames, Judy announced "This film must have been made by *Warner Brothers*!" . . . . She also said later that "we always *had* to have *red* hair in color films. It took forever." Before leaving, Judy sang "Make Someone Happy," and, with the Allen Brothers, "I Wish You Love." Judy then said: "Goodbye and God Bless you all. I Thank You so much. I couldn't have imagined a sweeter or nicer thing than today, and I'm terribly and eternally grateful." (An audiotape of these songs still exist in private collections.) While pulling away in the car—after being interviewed by the *TV Times*—Judy smiled as she made her "big fat close-up" pose from *A Star Is Born*.

November 30, 1964 or December 1, 1964: Judy and Mark Herron flew to Athens, for a six-day holiday in the sun, before returning to London.

Early December 1964: Upon returning to London, Judy and Herron attended the show *The Royal Hunt of the Sea* at the National Theater.

December 17, 1964: Judy, Herron, and the Allen Brothers attended *Beyond the Fringe* at the Mayfair theater, London, in row E. (Judy said she had seen it "three times, and I always laugh at it!")

December 19, 1964: Judy returned to the States—for the first time since May 2, 1964—on a 6:30 p.m. flight for New York, staying at the Regency Hotel on Park Avenue and 61st Street. Just before boarding, Judy told reporters in London that she would be doing another Jack Paar television show and appearing at Harrah's in Lake Tahoe; neither of these engagements would occur, though she would do one final guest appearance on a Paar show in 1967. Upon arrival at Kennedy Airport, Judy, Mark, and Peter and Chris, were met by Liza. Upon her arrival in New York, Judy was interviewed by Harrison Carrol of the *Los Angeles Examiner*, and said she hadn't decided whether to leave California to live in New York. She also said she would be opening at Harrah's, Lake Tahoe in February, and might also do concerts in San Francisco, Mexico City, and Honolulu. Louella Parsons had it in her column that Judy would do an "open" recording session at Carnegie Hall before returning to California. None of these projects would come to fruition. Lawrence Eisenberg was handling Judy's press relations starting at this time (he first met Judy at the airport on this day), through 1966, although by the fall of 1965, her main publicist in California was Tom Green.

While staying at the Regency Hotel in New York City, Judy hand wrote a letter (not dated) on hotel stationary, to a New Jersey based fan, Bill Fielding. Bill had apparently been sick during that holiday season, and Judy basically was being wonderful enough to send cheer his way, along with love to this mom. She concluded with a PS: "I'm sure we'll meet someday. God Bless."

While in New York City, fan Wayne Martin taped another phone call he made to Judy, to wish her a Merry Christmas. Judy sounds terribly depressed, as she said Sid "has kidnapped the children." (Sid spent Christmas with his children, telling reporters it had been the first Christmas he'd been able to spend with them in years, most likely since the holidays of 1961, in Scarsdale, New York.)

December 29, 1964: Judy was reunited at last with Lorna and Joe, who were finally allowed to fly in from California, for a delayed holiday celebration with their mother. "None of our presents have been opened yet," Judy told reporters at the airport. "We've been waiting for them. . . . We're going to do the town, go to shows, go shopping, all the things you want to do at this time of year."

December 31, 1964: (Benefit/Personal Appearance) The Actor's Studio Benefit (Lorna and Joe attended with Judy and Herron; Shelly Winters was among the other celebrities there).

January 6, 1965: (Personal Appearance) *Cue* Magazine Awards, New York. (Les Crane showed a film clip of Judy talking with Sammy Davis, Jr. on his television show the following evening. Footage is not known to exist.)

January 11, 1965: Judy's financial situation was so bad, that on this date she borrowed $25,000 from the Bank of America National Trust and Savings Association in Hollywood, with the understanding that she repay it by March 5. The mailing address for Judy was "c/o Beutzer, Irwin & Schwab, 190 North Cannon Drive, Beverly Hills, Ca 90210"; Greg Beutzer was Judy's attorney, to whom she was still paying a $3,500 monthly retainer.

January 12, 1965: Judy arrived back in Los Angeles (for the first time since May 2, 1964). (An audio recording still exists of television report of Lorna and Joe meeting her plane, which was late due to fog.) It had been announced around this time, that Judy would do four concerts in South Africa in either the spring, or June, or July; one each in Durban, Johannesburg, Cape Town, and Port Elizabeth. Morton Gould was Judy's requested pianist, along with a twenty-seven-piece orchestra. Judy's salary for the concerts was said to be "colossal . . . the highest price paid in South Africa," and later revealed to be $110,000 for the four concerts, or $27,500 each. Tickets were to have a $20 top price, unheard of in 1965. Judy never would perform in South Africa, though. (About this time, Judy and Mark Herron were seen with Denise and Vincente Minnelli at the Daisy, a nightclub in Hollywood.)

January 19, 1965: Judy gave statements regarding her financial affairs to Sid Luft's attorney, in his Los Angeles office.

January 27, 1965: Judy's secretary, S. A. Wagner, sent a letter to Pat McMath, who was heading Judy's American fan club, to thank her for the January *Garland Gazette*. The letter was on Kingsrow Enterprises stationary, with the address of Kirkeby Center, Suite 265, 10889 Wilshire Blvd, Los Angeles, CA 90024.

February 2, 1965: (Television) *On Broadway Tonight*, CBS, New York. Judy taped an appearance on this variety series. Judy arrived at the CBS studio (which had once been a Broadway theater), Studio 50, at 4 p.m. in her limousine with her manager Karl Brent, Mark Herron, and her maid Snowy, along with her chauffeur. Liza was also at the studio, along with Peter Allen and his stage partner Chris. Sammy Davis, Jr. and Peter Lawford also stopped in from Studio 52 where they were doing a show. Judy sailed through both the rehearsal and the dress rehearsal with flying colors, only making two suggestions/requests during the former, about not turning her back on the audience at one point, and also being allowed to get closer to the audience. For the show, Judy sang "When You're Smiling"; "Almost Like Being In Love"/"This Can't Be Love"; "I Wish You Love" (with The Allen Brothers); "The Music That Makes Me Dance"; and "Rock-A-Bye Your Baby."

> *New York Daily News*, February 6: (Headline) "Garland In Great Form On *Broadway Tonight* Show": "For a short time last night our television screen lit up like a Broadway marquee, and all too briefly the pulse and excitement of real show business was there. Judy Garland was back! One could only wish when the curtain went down that Judy was back on television. No matter how uneven her CBS show was, there were moments of magic in it that no one else can produce."

This was Judy's first television appearance taped in the US—and her first on CBS—since the end of her television series; the producer Irving Mansfield told Earl Wilson he received 27,000 requests for the 1,100 available seats to the taping. This show aired three days later, on Friday, February 5, 1965. It was also rumored that Judy received $7,500 for the appearance. (The appearance does exist, in a black and white film version.)

Around this time it was announced that Judy had been signed by the Palace Hotel in St. Moritz, Switzerland, to appear at a "gala evening" on February 27, at $15,000 for the one concert. This would not occur, however, as they refused to pay for Judy's musicians to play. Also at this time, Judy's lawyers were successful in stopping an unauthorized biography by Charles Samuels, called *Judy*, from being published by Putnam. The book, set to sell for $4.95, was to have been released the end of February 1965, then rumored again for June 30, 1965. In early June, Putnam sent out postcards to people who had advance-ordered the book, saying it would not be published, and money would be refunded.

February 6, 1965: Judy flew to Toronto from New York (where she had been staying in Miriam Hopkin's town house), for her next engagement, staying at the King Edward Sheraton Hotel, suite # 844.

February 7, 1965: Judy gave a press conference in Toronto, saying "My ambition is to be a good cook, a good mother, do a good show, and have some fun." Her favorite film was mentioned as *Oz*; her favorite singers were mentioned as Tony Bennett and Peggy Lee. (Judy had dinner that evening with Mark, and Peter and Chris, in the hotel's Victoria Room, from 9:15 p.m. to 10:05 p.m.)

February 8, 1965: (Concert) The O'Keefe Center; Toronto, Canada. (Judy's first concert engagement with The Allen Brothers, for this week-long engagement.) Judy was actually filling in for Nat King Cole, who had originally been booked for this week, but had canceled due to illness. The Allen Brothers opened the evening at 8:40 p.m., with thirty minutes (doing the songs: "Don't Rain On My Parade"; "You're Nobody Till Somebody Loves You"; "They Call The Wind Mariah"; "Hello, Dolly!"; "Raspberries, Strawberries"; "LaBomba"; "Cotton Fields"; "Waltzing Matilda"; "The Kangaroo Twist"; "Never Will I Marry"; and "Together.") Next came Nipsy Russell, who did his comedy routine for twenty minutes, then closed the first act with a ten-minute dance routine. After a twenty-minute intermission, Judy's overture was played at 10:02 p.m.; Mort Lindsey was conducting at this engagement. Judy's songs were: "When You're Smiling"; "Almost Like Being In Love"/"This Can't Be Love"; "The Music That Makes Me Dance"; "Smile"; "Swing Low, Sweet Chariot"/"He's Got The Whole World In His Hands"; "I Wish You Love" (with the Allen Brothers, who then sang "Don't Let The Rain Come Down" and "Toreador" while Judy changed; she came on during "Toreador" and danced with Peter); "Joey, Joey, Joey"; "You Made Me Love You"/"For Me And My Gal"/"The Trolley Song"; "By Myself"; "Rock-A-Bye Your Baby"; "Swanee"; "Chicago" and "Over The Rainbow." Judy was having some off-and-on vocal problems this show, fighting the flu.

February 9, 1965: (Concert) The O'Keefe Center, Toronto. Judy changed her program somewhat this night, opening with "Swing Low, Sweet Chariot"/"He's Got The Whole World In His Hands"; then "When You're Smiling"; "Almost Like Being In Love"/"This Can't Be Love"; "The Music That Makes Me Dance"; added the song "Just In Time"; "You Made Me Love You"/"For Me and My Gal"/"The Trolley Song"; "Smile"; "Make Someone Happy" (added); "By Myself"; "The Man That Got Away" (added); "Rock-A-Bye Your Baby"; and "Chicago" (Judy did not sing "Swanee" or "Rainbow" this performance, as she was obviously fighting a cold.)

February 10, 1965: Judy canceled both the matinee and evening shows, following the advice of Dr. L.A. Kane, due to a severe cold and laryngitis.

February 11, 1965: Judy returned to the O'Keefe Center, for her concert, arriving at 7 p.m. She began her portion of the show at 9:50 p.m., and her program was now in a set order for the remaining shows: "Sweet Chariot"/"Whole World"; "Smiling"; "Love" Medley; "Smile"; "Just In Time"; "You Made Me Love You" Medley; "Make Someone Happy"; "By Myself"; "Rock-A-Bye"; "Chicago"; "Man That Got Away"; and "Rainbow." (The day of rest had helped her throat a great deal, and she was in the best voice of all the shows that week.)

February 13, 1965: Judy played her final scheduled two shows—matinee and evening—in Toronto, to great success. Liza had flown in to see the final show that evening. (Judy and Mark returned to their hotel at 1:15 am on February 14.) Judy's show at the O'Keefe Center had grossed $98,000 for the six shows. The theater held 3,200 people, at a $6.00 top price. The potential had been $126,000 for eight shows; Judy was at SRO capacity for the six shows she did. She had been paid a flat fee, plus a percentage. (An audiotape, recorded in the audience, still exists of one of the shows.)

February 14, 1965: Judy and Mark Herron visited Niagara Falls for this Valentine's Day, via car, dined at the Seagram Tower, and headed back to Toronto immediately after dinner—then they returned to New York.

February 20, 1965 and February 21, 1965: Judy appeared in Manhattan Supreme Court, to testify in a suit brought against her by her former television series producer Gary Smith, for $12,000, in a "breach of contract": Judy's company Kingsrow countersued for $50,000 charging he "did not supply proper services." Judy told Justice I. L. Levy, "I didn't agree with his choice of material," and revealed that Smith had hired the Smothers Brothers at $7,500 for a second appearance, and Dan Dailey and Betty Grable at $5,000, yet they were not used because they did not fit into the production. Judy won; Smith's case was thrown out of court.

Late February 1965: Judy, Liza, and Mark Herron attended the premiere of Columbia Picture's *Lord Jim.* (Photo exists of Judy and Liza at the post-premiere party.)

Late February 1965 to March 1965: It was reported that Judy was reading the script of Ray Stark's film *This Property Is Condemned* to be directed by John Huston. Judy was wanted to play Natalie Wood's mother. Ruth Gordon wound up with the role. . . . Dean Martin also said he wanted Judy for his first NBC-TV series show of the 1965–1966 season. This also did not occur. . . . Westinghouse Broadcasting announced they wanted the *Judy and Liza at the Palladium* videotape for distribution in the U.S.

March 3, 1965: Judy and Mark Herron flew to Miami for Judy's next engagement.

March 10, 1965: Judy signed to play Jean Harlow's mother in the Electronovision version of *Harlow.* This was announced on March 11, in Hedda Hopper's column, and on March 12 elsewhere. Full-page ads with Judy's name appeared in the trade magazines; there were to be three weeks of rehearsal, with shooting set to start on March 31, and the film set to open in 1,200 theaters on May 12. (This production would be shot and edited on videotape, then transferred to film.)

March 11, 1965 to March 20, 1965: (Concert) The Fountainbleau Hotel; Miami, Florida. Judy was in incredible voice, as these excerpts from some of the reviews state:

> *The Miami Herald,* March 13: "Judy Garland is belting out the best show she's ever given on Miami beach. . . . She sang a full hour of tunes, some with her own trademark—others as new as today's hit parade. And she delivered each as though there was only today and tomorrow. . . . her voice danced."
>
> *Miami Beach Daily Sun* (Frank Meyer), March 12: (Headline) "She Had Them In Her Hands": "Miss Garland, a fantastic showman, was a mature Judy Garland last night. There is a lot of the little girl quality remaining, but this is a better performer than we have ever seen in her. She doesn't overdo the play on emotions, but she has the timing down to perfection. Miss Garland knows when to move, how long to wait off-stage while the audience tries to rush

her back for more, how long to pause between numbers for ultimate effect; which numbers to sing in sequence, building to her closing songs, which all were worth waiting for. In short, there is beneath the wonderful performance, a knowledge that everything will go right. While some performers have trouble staying in one key, Miss Garland switches keys with ease—at one time making four key changes in two sentences. She uses her musicianship for the ultimate effect. If you can get in, go see Judy Garland. Judy's back, and may she be around a long, long time."

(Judy had appeared at the Fountainbleau in January 1959.) During a press conference at her hotel for this engagement, Judy said "I'm kind of a pratt fall comedian, actually. I enjoy being able to laugh. I have three beautiful children. I'm a good cook. Life has been very good to me. There's nothing tragic about my life. I enjoy it. And I'm grateful for what I have. I'd just like to be happy. To be relaxed. To be myself. A woman. I have great respect for an audience. They pay their money. They take time away from things they have to do at home. I'd like to do a play. A straight play. I've never done a play before. That way I could settle down in one place—*If* people come to see it!" Roger Edens had flown in from California to rehearse and go over arrangements with Judy, most likely for the medley he was putting together for Judy to sing at the Oscars on April 5. Mort Lindsey was conducting for her in Miami. Liza came in from New York on March 12—her nineteenth birthday—to see her mother . . . and to see her fiance, of course, as the Allen Brothers were still opening for Judy. Judy's act was basically the same as the previous month's engagement in Toronto, with the addition of "What Now My Love?" which always stopped the show. Judy didn't have the orchestration with her the previous month in Toronto.

March 20, 1965: After finishing her last show at the Fountainbleau, Judy rushed to the Eden Roc Hotel to substitute for Debbie Reynolds, who had collapsed, and could not go on . . . and Judy was thought of as "unreliable?!"

March 21, 1965: Judy flew back home to Los Angeles, to begin work on *Harlow*, being met at the airport by Joe and Lorna, members of the cast, and producer Bill Sargent. Apparently Judy was driven right to the studio, where a publicity shot was taken of her and a cast member reading the trade paper ad announcing the film, with Judy's name prominently featured, and then rehearsals were started. But things were not going well.

March 22, 1965: On only her second day on the set, Judy withdrew from the cast of this quickie production of *Harlow* a week before the movie was due to start filming, March 31, because of "prior commitments." She was replaced by Eleanor Parker, who *also* left the film, and was in-turn replaced by Ginger Rodgers, who had replaced Judy previously, in 1948 on *The Barkley's of Broadway*. The film's producer told *Variety* that Judy had withdrawn due to "billing problems." A spokesman for Judy said her decision was based on a "commitment conflict," that she had never signed a contract for the film, that her ability to do the film had rested on her "ability to juggle other commitments," and that she needed "lengthy rehearsal for her appearance at the Oscar Awards." Judy had apparently told Carol Lynley—who was to play her daughter, Jean Harlow—"Honey, I'm not drunk, I'm not on drugs, and I'm telling you this is a piece of junk, and I'm getting out!"

March 30, 1965: Judy gave a birthday party at the Beverly Hills Hotel for son Joey's 10th birthday, and for Peter Lawford's son Chris, who also turned 10 on the same day (Chris would star on the ABC-TV soap *All My Children* in 1995.) Judy then took them to a movie.

Monday, April 5, 1965: (Television) *The Academy Awards*, ABC-TV, Los Angeles, California. Introduced by Gene Kelly, Judy sang a lengthy 12-song medley in tribute to Cole Porter, arranged by Roger Edens.

March 21, 1965: Actor Barry Sullivan, Lorna, Judy, and Joe look at the poster planned to advertise Judy's role as Jean Harlow's mother in the Electrovision version of *Harlow*. (You can see Judy's name in the ad if you look closely.) There was another version being released at around the same time, with Angela Lansbury playing Harlow's mom, and the producers of Judy's version were planning on having their film hit theaters first, on May 12. (Note that Lorna is wearing the same top she wore for the cover of *Look* magazine, shot in December 1961; This is also the same top that Judy would wear on March 6, 1967, for her interview with Barbra Walters for *The Today Show*.) (Courtesy of Photofest.)

(This would be the last work Edens would do for Judy, aside from one additional brief arrangement of a "My Kind of Town, Houston Is"/"Houston" medley for her December 17, 1965 concert in Houston. The man who had played for Judy at her MGM audition, and helped Judy grow into her "style" at the studio, passed away in July 1970.) Judy received cheers from the celebrity crowd (her performance still exists on a black and white film print of the show.)

April 9, 1965: Judy, Mark Herron, Lorna, Joe, and a female assistant to Judy, Snowy, (Judy had brought her back from Hong Kong with her) left California for a week's vacation together in Honolulu, renting a small cottage on Diamond Head Road.

April 14, 1965: Judy's cottage on Diamond Head Road caught fire at about 3:40 p.m. A neighbor, Mrs. Rosalie Barlow, called the fire department at 3:59 p.m. The fire was small and soon extinguished at 4:08 p.m.by the firemen, with assistance from Judy, who was photographed in a blue, two-piece bathing suit and broad-brimmed straw hat. Damage was estimated at $2,000 to the cottage, $1,000 in clothes, a $300 jade ring, and $400 in cash. Defective wiring was blamed. Judy didn't talk to the press, but Lorna and Joe did, and photos were taken of Lorna sweeping the debris, before Judy called her back into the cottage.

April 16, 1965: The publisher of *The Garland News*, Max Preeo, spoke with Mark Herron on the phone. Herron said he and Judy were "very impressed with them. We thought they were very nice." At some point during that day or the next, Max dropped off the latest issues, leaving them with Lorna, as Judy and Mark weren't home at the moment.

April 19, 1965: Judy, Mark Herron, and Judy's aide Snowy arrived at the airport at 1:55 p.m., to fly into New York—Lorna and Joey had flown home to California the previous day, Sunday, in order to be back for school.

April 21, 1965: Judy flew from New York into Charlotte, North Carolina, for her next concert, and was immediately taken to a 6:30 p.m. press conference at the Red Carpet Motor Inn. Among her comments: "I think it would be very nice to be a housewife, especially with all that equipment they have"; "My happiest times are when I'm cooking and when I'm with my children. Lots of times when I'm on stage, too. And I do like to travel."; "Mark Herron, who programs my shows, is always making me learn new songs from new shows. I just can't sit on 'Over The Rainbow' all my life." When asked what she'd be singing at the concert: "Why, 'Hush, Hush, Sweet Charlotte,' of course!"

April 22, 1965: (Concert) The Coliseum; Charlotte, North Carolina. (Judy was, unfortunately, in poor voice.) (She had appeared at the Coliseum during her 1961 tour.) This appearance was actually a "fund-raiser" for the Democratic Party, although the ads had ticket buyers—who paid a $10 top—make their checks payable to "An Evening With Judy Garland." (The concert—set to start at 8:45—began at 9:20 p.m. The Allen Brothers opened for Judy; After the 30-piece orchestra played her overture, Judy sang: "He's Got The Whole World In His Hands"; "When You're Smiling"; "Music That Makes Me Dance"; "Almost Like Being In Love"/"This Can't be Love"; "Just In Time"; "What Now My Love?"; "You Made Me Love You"/"For Me and My Gal"/"The Trolley Song"; "By Myself" and "Over The Rainbow." Judy's concert was a short one, 40 minutes, ending at 10:20 p.m., although it had apparently already been announced that the concert would only be an hour long, anyway—the Allen Brothers opened the show for Judy, doing about 20 minutes, so the total time of the show was an hour.

April 23, 1965 to May 3, 1965: Judy returned to New York on April 23, catching a 2:35 flight, and then spent several days rehearsing some new songs for her next concert. Judy and Mark also went to some film premieres in New York, including *Ship of Fools*. In a phone interview on May 3, with Ann Masters of the *Chicago American*, Judy said she would be doing "some new albums, at least one of them will be with Liza." These never materialized.

May 4, 1965: Judy flew to Chicago for her next concert.

May 5, 1965: Judy gave a press conference in the Astor Tower, for her concert on May 7. (She later moved to the penthouse apartment at the Ambassador East. One of the press interviews was a television show that was filmed and shown on May 11, called *Lee Phillip's Chicago*, a local CBS-TV show, in which he interviewed Judy. This is not known to still exist.)

May 7, 1965: (Concert) The Arie Crown Theater; Chicago, Illinois. (Judy was again plagued by vocal troubles, although she received good reviews.) The concert was scheduled for 10 p.m., and top price was $10. Judy's songs included: "My Kind Of Town, Chicago Is"; "He's Got The Whole World In His Hands"; "When You're Smiling"; "Almost Like Being In Love"/"This Can't Be Love"; "Do It Again"; "What Now My Love?"; "San Francisco"; (Intermission); "That's Entertainment"; "The Man That Got Away"; "Zing! Went The Strings Of My Heart"; "Just In Time"; "You Made Me Love You"/ "For Me And My Gal"/"The Trolley Song"; "Rock-A-Bye Your Baby"; "Chicago"; and "Over The Rainbow." The Allen Brothers did 18 minutes as an opening; Judy was on for an hour total. (An audiotape of this concert, recorded from the audience, does still exist.) Judy reportedly was paid $29,000 for this concert. (Judy and Mark arrived back at the Ambassador East hotel at 3:10 a.m., on the morning of May 8.)

May 8, 1965, late afternoon/early evening: Judy filmed an interview on Chicago's *Kup Show*. During her 35 minutes on the 2½ hour show, she revealed that MGM would not even *sell* her a 16MM print of *The Wizard of Oz*. Upon leaving the television station, Judy then arrived at O'Hare airport at 7:10 p.m., spent some time with a few fans, before boarding the 7:30 flight at 7:25, with Mark, her maid Snowy, and Karl Brent—who was acting now, according to Mark Herron on this day, as Judy's secretary. The plane arrived at 10:20 p.m. in New York, where Judy was greeted by more fans.

May 11, 1965: Judy attended daughter Liza's Broadway debut, in the musical *Flora, The Red Menace*, and the party afterwards at Ruby Foo's—next door to the Alvin theater on West 52nd Street, where *Flora* played. At the party, mother and daughter did a duet on the songs "Swanee" and "Together," and also apparently attempted to do "Don't Rain On My Parade."

Also at this time, while in New York, Judy attended a party for dancer Rudolph Nureyev, at Andy Warhol's the "Factory," along with Montgomery Cliff and Tennesee Williams.

May 12, 1965: Judy and Mark returned home to California.

May 17, 1965: (Personal Appearance) Judy danced "a wild watusi" at the birthday party of her "road manager" Karl Brent, at the Daisy Club in Hollywood, according to Harrison Carrol's column on May 18.

May 19, 1965: Judy was granted a California divorce from Sid Luft, with her final testimony in court, in California. The final papers, making it official, would go through in September.

Judy at this time was reportedly in talks with ABC-TV about a series of specials from key cities around the world. CBS was—according to rumor—planning on rerunning Judy's television series in the daytime for the 1965–1966 season. Neither of these deals ever became reality. Judy was also at this time satirized in Mad Magazine.

Late May 1965: Judy flew into New York with Mark, to see Liza again in *Flora*. At this time it was announced that Judy had signed a two-year contract with the Sahara Hotel Corporation, to appear in Las Vegas a total of two months over the next two-year period.

May 25, 1965: Judy arrived in Cincinnati for her next concert, staying at the Vernon Manor Hotel, and giving the usual press conference.

May 26, 1965: Judy visited the Playboy Club this evening, while in Cincinnati. (Judy began feeling ill after leaving the club.)

May 27, 1965: Judy was reportedly feeling "worse" this day, according to her publicist, Guy McElwaine.

May 28, 1965: Judy's personal physician in New York, Dr. Kermit, was flown in to attend to Judy.

May 29, 1965: (Concert) Cincinnati Gardens, Cincinnati. Judy completed the first act in fine vocal form, but had to cancel the second half when her doctor announced—with Judy on-stage—that she could not continue, as she had a virus infection and a temperature of 102. Judy had reportedly been paid $20,000 for the concert, according to one report: a $5,000 advance, then the remaining $15,000 apparently an hour before the concert; another report had Judy earning a guaranteed $40,000 against 60% of the gross; 4,500 people had paid from $3.75 to $7.50. Judy's songs in the 32-minute first half, were: "He's Got The Whole World In His Hands"; "When You're Smiling"; "Almost Like Being In Love"/"This Can't Be Love"; "What Now My Love?" (standing ovation); "Do It Again"; and "San Francisco," all backed by a 30-piece orchestra.

May 30, 1965: Judy and Mark flew home to Los Angeles, and Judy checked into UCLA Medical Center, where she withdrew from the medication she had been taking.

June 2, 1965: *Variety* noted that Judy had supposedly bought a number of songs, to get into the publishing business, according to her attorney Herb Schwab, who was drawing up articles for incorporation. She was also forming a talent management firm, to include the first-signed Allen Brothers. All this—including just-purchased Louisiana oil wells—were to come under the aegis of "Judy Garland Enterprises." Sadly, except for managing the Allen Brothers career for a short time, none of the other transactions are known to have actually occurred.

Early June 1965: (Personal Appearance) Judy and Mark Herron attended Jack Jones's opening night at the Coconut Grove in Los Angeles (shortly after her release from UCLA.) Also at this time, Judy taped an interview for *The World of Showbusiness* program, which was broadcast on the Armed Forces Radio and Television Service overseas. This audiotape is not known to exist, but newsreel footage of the Jones opening does.

June 10, 1965: Peter Lawford hosted a birthday party for Judy, on her forty-third birthday.

June 12, 1965: Judy suffered an allergic reaction to a prescribed medication, and was rushed back to UCLA.

June 15, 1965: Judy was released in the morning from UCLA and immediately flew to Las Vegas on a TWA jet for her next engagement that night.

Judy with Mark Herron at the Coconut Grove for Jack Jones's opening, early June 1965. Judy would marry Herron on November 14, 1965. (Note actresses Jane Wyman and Ursella Andress in the background.) Judy is wearing the "poppy" dress she wore on show #21 of her television series. (Courtesy of Photofest.)

June 15, 1965 to June 28, 1965: (Concert) The Thunderbird Hotel; Las Vegas, Nevada. Judy's two-week engagement (with the show starting at 10:30 p.m., and backed by the Allen Brothers and a 31-piece orchestra under the direction of Nick Perito) out-drew every other hotel on the strip, and garnered, again, outstanding reviews—including the following two, excerpted here:

> *The Sun*: (Headline) "First Nighters Go Wild Over Judy: Wins Standing Cheers": "(She) is the most exciting performer in the entire history of show business."
>
> *Variety*: "In the distinctive tones hoped for, she socked across [her opening song]. It was as if she had hit a home run with the bases loaded."

This success occurred even though, on the afternoon of the opening, she had suffered convulsions from a newly prescribed medication. Opening night's filled-to-capacity house of 900 people gave her several standing ovations. Due to arriving right from UCLA, Judy hadn't been able to rehearse on the opening day. An audiotape recorded in the audience during this engagement, of a portion of Judy's performance, still exists, and reveals a strong-voiced, in-control Garland. Judy's songs for this engagement: "He's Got The Whole World In His Hands"; "When You're Smiling"; "Almost Like Being In Love"/"This Can't Be Love"; "Smile"; "Just In Time"; "What Now My Love?"; "You Made Me Love You"/"For Me And My Gal"/"The Trolley Song"; "Rock-A-Bye Your Baby"; "By Myself"; "Chicago"; "The Man That Got Away"; and "Over The Rainbow." While in Las Vegas, Judy called into a radio show hosted by Jack Wagner, to tape a promo/interview spot about the London Palladium album with Liza; this recording still exists, and is planned on being included as a bonus track on Capitol's spring 2002 release of the two-CD set of the complete *Judy Garland and Liza Minnelli "Live" at the London Palladium*. It was reported that Capitol had recorded Judy at the Thunderbird, though this most likely did not actually occur, as tapes have never surfaced, and there are no files in Capitol's archives about any remote sessions being done.

June 16, 1965: A lien was placed on Judy's Thunderbird salary, due to a judgment awarded attorney William Morse, who had represented Judy in her fall 1962 divorce action against Sid Luft. Judy supposedly had stopped payment on a $3,000 check she had given Morse, who had been awarded that sum, plus an additional $1,000 in attorney's fees back on June 19, 1963.

June 23, 1965: It was reported that Judy had been treated in her dressing room by her doctor and that oxygen had been dispatched for her, but was ultimately not used. Indigestion was later reported as the cause of the incident. Judy did not miss any of her shows in Vegas.

June 28, 1965: Judy completed her run in Las Vegas.

June 29, 1965: Judy flew home to Los Angeles.

June 30 or July 1, 1965: It was reported in *The Herald Examiner*, July 2, that Judy had slept through a fire alarm, when smoke came out of an air conditioner in her home. She was not harmed.

July 5, 1965 to July 8, 1965: Rehearsals in Hollywood for Judy's next television appearance.

July 9, 1965: (Television) *The Andy Williams Show* videotaping, at NBC Television Studios, in Burbank, California. Judy sang: "On A Wonderful Day Like Today" (opening; with Williams); "Get Happy" (a new Pop/Rock/Jazz version; with male chorus); and a Medley with Williams, during which Judy sang "Why Don't We Do This More Often?" with Williams; "On The Atchison, Topeka, And The Santa Fe"

Judy poses on her lawn in a portrait session at her Brentwood home in the summer of 1965. (Courtesy of Photofest.)

with Williams; a bit of "Over The Rainbow" (which included part of the opening verse, which she only sang a couple of times); "Rock-A-Bye Your Baby" with Williams; "You Made Me Love You"; "The Trolley Song" with Williams and Company; and reprise of "Why Don't We Do This More Often?" with Williams. (Judy also performed a pantomime comedy sketch with Williams, which may have been from the dress rehearsal, as the final taping was stopped when they had the wrong camera on Judy; there may have also been another sketch taped with Williams, as a posed photo still exists that shows Judy and Williams in Matador outfits! This could have been done as a gag, or for a publicity photo only. No audiotape or videotape of the sketch is known to have surfaced.) Judy looked fairly well, and seemed in reasonably good spirits, but is in only fair voice, and appears slightly sluggish and slurry. (The episode aired on September 20, 1965 on NBC. The color videotape of the show still exists in William's archives, and the comedy pantomime sketch with Andy was included on a recent VHS and DVD *The Best of Andy Williams*.) This "Guest Appearance" started a television season, 1965-1966, of guest spots by Judy on the top Variety Shows. This was part of a game plan to have Judy do six or seven such spots a year at about $50,000 a shot, for about $250,000 total; and to do about another six weeks or so of concert appearances, making about another $250,000 a year. This way, she would only work about three to four months per year, only half of that time touring—the rest of the year would be spent at home in California, "guest-starring," and recording, etc. This way she would not have too demanding a schedule, yet still earn a half-million or so per year, assuring her a comfortable, if not overwhelmingly lavish, lifestyle—assuming that someone would simply make sure her bills were paid, since Judy herself cared little for material possessions, and actually rarely spent vast sums of money. Besides the fact that Judy's money always seemed to be spent *for* her, by spring 1966, she would have nothing to show for all her recent hard work; Old debts—including the IRS—kept eating away at any current income, and a videotaping in late March/early April 1966, would effectively end her primetime network television career.

July 15, 1965: Judy flew to New York, for her next concert, staying at the Regency Hotel, and late that night had an interview with Leonard Harris of *The New York World-Telegram and Sun*, in her suite at the Regency, during which she said "I guess singing is a good outlet and if you can get paid for doing it, you're damned lucky."

July 16, 1965: (Television) *The Les Crane Show* (Syndicated.) Judy was heard in a phone interview. That evening, Judy took Lorna and Joe to see Liza in *Flora* on Broadway, then later they went to the club "Arthur."

July 17, 1965: (Concert) The Forest Hills Stadium; Forest Hills, New York. According to *Variety*, Judy broke a record, for longest standing ovation: *Thirty Minutes* at the conclusion of Judy's 20-song, 90-minute concert (which grossed $55,000), in front of 10,000 people. The reviews were raves, including these, excerpted here:

> *The New York Times*, 7-19: "That fascinating phenomenon of modern show business, the long and widely publicized love affair between Judy Garland and her following, was on full display Saturday night. . . . [The audience] was quick to respond to that potent fervor that Miss Garland packs into her delivery. . . . This audience also appreciated her wondrous sense of showmanship, with calculated pause, imitation dance steps, and hand gestures that were not merely the nervous mannerisms of many television performers."
>
> *Billboard*, 7-31: "She simply is one of the rare artists who can transfix an audience by sheer personal magnetism."
>
> *Variety*: "Trim, confident, and buoyant, she could have gotten away with 'The Internationale' sung in Russian."

(The audiotape of the show exists; and shows Judy in fairly strong voice.) Mort Lindsey conducted the 30-piece orchestra. Judy told some fans backstage that she was going to record a studio version of "What Now, My Love" "*next week*"; this never did happen. Judy's songs at this concert: "He's Got The Whole World In His Hands"; "Almost Like Being In Love"/"This Can't Be Love"; "Do It Again"; "Just In Time"; "When You're Smiling"; "Smile"; "What Now My Love?"; "San Francisco" (Intermission); "That's Entertainment"; "The Man That Got Away"; "Zing! Went The Strings Of My Heart"; "As Long As He Needs Me"; "You Made Me Love You"/"For Me and My Gal"/"The Trolley Song"; "By Myself"; "Rock-A-Bye Your Baby"; "Chicago"; and "Over The Rainbow." After the concert, Judy, Liza, Lorna, Joe, and Mark Herron went to the nightclub "Arthur" (for the second night in a row), where Joe played the drums. This made Earl Wilson's column on Monday, July 19. (Judy and Mark Herron got back to their hotel, the Regency, at 4 a.m. on Sunday morning July 18, after the concert, and "Arthur"; the next morning, Monday, the 19, they arrived at the hotel at 3 a.m.)

A Sheila Graham item in the papers said that Judy's divorce would be official on September 19, and that she would immediately marry Herron; and that she would earn $750,000 this year from concerts, records, and Vegas; that she had invested $20,000 in 10 oil wells in Louisiana, and that eight were winners, and she would thus receive $20,000 a year for the next 25 years, from the wells. Apparently none of this was true. Also in the "not-to-be" category: the report that Judy would record a new album for Capitol Records, between early October and mid November 1965.

August 12, 1965: Judy and Mark vacationed in Northern California, near San Francisco. On this date, it was reported that Judy had stopped at a private home in Yankee Point, to ask directions to the Hillsdale Inn.

August 16, 1965: About 2 pm, Judy stopped into the Hillsdale Inn's coffee shop, where waitress Kathy Van Eaton blurted "Judy, I won't tell anyone you're here," to which Judy replied: "Bring me a hamburger and you can tell the world!"

August 18, 1965 and August 19, 1965: (Personal Appearance) Judy sang at the Basin Street West nightclub in San Francisco, when she came, two nights in a row, to hear Duke Ellington.

Late August 1965: (Television) *The Gypsy Rose Lee Show* (Syndicated). Videotaped in San Francisco. Judy chatted with the performer whose life was the basis of the show *Gypsy*. (A brief, one-minute black-and-white film clip of Judy from the show still exists, from a promotional reel put together to promote Rose's show; audiotape of entire show exists. The show aired on August 30, 1965.)

August 25, 1965: Press conference, lasting two hours, for Judy's next engagement, revealed that she thought The Beatles—who were appearing the same night at the Cow Palace—were "great guys. Awfully nice young gentlemen. They're very intelligent. They *own* Liverpool now, don't they?" And "When I do a performance, when it is over, I'm a wreck, and I sleep until about 4 p.m. the next day!" When asked about her large homosexual following, Judy snapped: "I couldn't care less. I sing to *people*!" Judy also announced a concert in Houston in December, and that it would be recorded. The concert was done, but no tapes have turned up, to date, in Capitol Record's vaults.

August 28, 1965: Judy called a reporter with the *San Francisco Examiner*, at 3:30 p.m., for an interview. In talking about what can happen to her onstage, Judy said: "You can expect *anything*!"

August 31, 1965 to September 5, 1965: (Concert) The Circle Star Theater; San Carlos, California. This was Judy's first appearance in "the round," and the turning stage made her voice a bit unsteady on opening night, but she was in fine form for the rest of the engagement. Judy's songs: "He's Got The Whole World In His Hands"; "Almost Like Being In Love"/"This Can't Be Love"; "You Made Me Love You"/"For Me And My Gal"/"The Trolley Song"; "What Now My Love?"; "Just In Time"; "By Myself"; "San Francisco"; "Over The Rainbow"; and "Rock-A-Bye Your Baby." Lorna and Joe joined their mother onstage at several of the performances; on September 4 and 5, Lorna sang "Zing! Went The Strings Of My Heart," and Joe played the drums. *Daily Variety* reported that Judy brought in $105,000 for the eight sold-out performances, $15,302 for opening night. On the last evening in San Carlos, it was rumored that some over-eager fans knocked Judy down accidentally, and she hit her knees, and had been taped-up, and was in pain; but a member of a Judy fan club stated that she was there with only five other people and that Judy was fine.

September 6, 1965: Judy took an early morning flight from San Francisco airport, returning home to Los Angeles, amid rumors she was recording an album for Capitol, and that she had made reference to concerts in Texas in October—neither of which transpired.

September 13, 1965: (Concert) The Greek Theater, Los Angeles, California. Judy received raves for her opening of a scheduled weeklong engagement, with one feeling she was even better than when she had been at the Greek in 1957. Judy's songs included: "He's Got The Whole World In His Hands"; "As Long As He Needs Me"; "Joey, Joey, Joey"; "Smile"; "Make Someone Happy"; "If Love Were All"; "Rock-A-Bye Your Baby"; "Chicago"; "By Myself"; "San Francisco"; "What Now, My Love?"; "The Party's Over"; and "Over The Rainbow"; Mort Lindsey conducted the 33-piece orchestra, 13 of which were strings. Judy was guaranteed $35,000 for the week, plus 65% of the gross above $70,000; there was an advance sale of $40,000. (A few selections from this show still exist, on an audiotape recorded through the sound system.)

September 14, 1965: Judy tripped over her dog and broke her arm. She did her second show at the Greek anyway (although in great pain), with the help of Mickey Rooney, Martha Raye, and Johnny Mathis. (This show also exists, on a tape made through the sound system.) Judy only sang five songs: "He's Got The Whole World In His Hands"; "Just In Time"; "San Francisco"; "Together" (with Martha Raye); and "Over The Rainbow."

September 15, 1965: The rest of Judy's engagement at the Greek Theater was canceled, due to the pain she was in from her broken arm. (She was supposedly admitted to a hospital in Hollywood on this day, as she had torn all the ligaments in her forearm, and had broken her arm in two places.)

Mid September: It was rumored that Judy had finished recording an album for Capitol and that she would appear on a Steve Lawrence television show, a second *Andy Williams* television show, film a cameo for the movie *The Long and the Short of It*, according to *The Hollywood Reporter*, and that Martin and Blane were writing a musical version of *The Member of the Wedding* for Lorna to play on Broadway, with 17 tunes already finished. None of these projects ever actually came into being.

October 2, 1965: Judy first did a dress rehearsal at CBS Television City, for a television show the next day; And that night, she and Mark attended the Thalian's *Cloak and Dagger* show.

October 3, 1965: (Television) *The Ed Sullivan Show*, CBS, broadcast "live" from Television City, Hollywood. Judy sang: "Come Rain Or Come Shine"; "By Myself"; and "Rock-A-Bye Your Baby." This was Judy's only "real" appearance on the famed Variety series, as her April 1963 appearance consisted of clips from a March 10, 1963 appearance on a London variety show. (This 1965 Sullivan appearance was rerun on August 7, 1966; the show still exists on color videotape.) Judy was in great form, and in pretty good shape vocally. Reviews were excellent. At the dress rehearsal on Saturday, October 2, she had sung "Never Will I Marry": by the next day it had been replaced by "Rock-A-Bye." Judy's cast was put back on her arm right after the show.

October 13, 1965 to October 14, 1965: Rehearsals in Hollywood, starting at 10 a.m., for Judy's next television Guest Appearance. Judy arrived early for the two days of rehearsals and also for the day of taping. On Wednesday evening, October 13, Judy and Mark attended Judith Anderson's *Medea* opening at the Valley Music Theater, and Judy was photographed with Anderson after the show.

October 15, 1965: (Television) *The Hollywood Palace*, ABC-TV, videotaping at the Hollywood Palace Theater. Judy was "Guest Hostess" for this episode, and sang: "Just Once In A Lifetime" (opener); "West Side Story" Medley with Vic Damone (during which Judy sang "Something's Coming," and "Somewhere," and "Tonight," both with Damone); "A Couple Of Swells"; "I Loved Him"; "The Palace Medley" ("Shine On Harvest Moon"/"Some Of These Days"/"My Man"/"I Don't Care") "A Couple Of Swells" and "I Loved Him" were videotaped last, after a two-and-a-half hour break. Judy was in fine form, and fine voice, and looked lovely, making this one of Judy's more completely successful television appearances of the mid to late 1960s. (The show was broadcast on November 13, 1965, and rerun on September 3, 1966. The color videotape of the show still exists.)

Late October 1965: (Personal Appearance) Judy joined Tony Bennett on stage in Las Vegas, during his nightclub act, and according to *Daily Variety*, said to Tony, "Don't encourage me, or I'll sing 30 or 40 songs!"

November 6, 1965: (Personal Appearance) Judy sang a few songs during a party for Princess Margaret and her husband Lord Snowden, at the Bistro in Beverly Hills, California. According to Earl Wilson, she sang "what the Princess wanted me to sing": "I Left My Heart In San Francisco," "Chicago," and "The Man That Got Away."

November 14, 1965: Judy was married to actor Mark Herron, her fourth husband, in Las Vegas, at 1:30 a.m., at the Little Church of the West, by Dr. David Howe of the Church Of Religious Science. Her publicist, Guy McElwaine, was best man, and his wife, actress Pamela Austin, matron of honor. *The Los Angeles Herald-Examiner* stated that after the wedding ceremony, the party, including Eddie Fisher, moved on to catch Don Rickles's show. Rickles gave the newlyweds a terrific ribbing. The party went on until 7 a.m. Apparently the decision to fly to Vegas was so sudden, that jeweler Marvin Hime had to go to Judy's home at 3 p.m. Saturday, November 13, to fit them for their wedding rings. Judy and Mark honeymooned for a week in San Francisco and Carmel.

November 23, 1965: (Personal Appearance) Judy attended Liza's opening night at the Coconut Grove, with Mark, and Lorna and Joe.

November 29, 1965: Judy had dinner at the Sahara Hotel in Las Vegas, at 10:15 p.m., with Mark, as well as Snowy, and Alton Huckins (her maid and hairdresser, respectively.)

November 30, 1965 to December 13, 1965: (Concert) The Sahara Hotel, Las Vegas. Judy was paid $50,000 per week for this two-week engagement.

> *The Sun* (Paul Rice) wrote of her opening: "(Judy's appearance) may well have been the most fabulous night in show business . . . and I've never been much of a fan."

Backed by the 30-piece Louis Basil orchestra, Judy's songs were: "He's Got The Whole World In His Hands"; "Almost Like Being In Love"/"This Can't Be Love"; "As Long As He Needs Me"; "Just In Time"; "What Now My Love?"; "Joey, Joey"; "The Man That Got Away" (or, on some nights "Stormy Weather"); "Do It Again"; "By Myself"; "Rock-A-Bye Your Baby"; "San Francisco"; "Swanee"; "You Made Me Love You/For Me and My Gal/The Trolley Song"; "Chicago"; and "Over The Rainbow." On Friday, December 10, Judy and Lorna sang "Hello, Lorna!" and "Jamboree Jones"; On Saturday, December 11, Judy and Lorna sang "Hello, Lorna!" and "Bob White." On closing night, December 13, Judy also sang "Liza," in tribute to the next headliner at the Sahara, who was opening on Christmas Day. It was reported at this time that Judy and Mark would spend the Holidays in England, and then return to New York in the middle of January, for another *Ed Sullivan* show. These two events never occurred. (Attending Judy's opening performance on November 30 were her manager Freddie Fields and her publicist Guy McElwaine.)

December 14, 1965: Judy arrived in Houston, at 7 a.m. (having boarded a plane directly after her final show in Vegas), for her next concert, giving an interview in her police-escorted limo, to a reporter from the *Houston Chronicle*. Judy couldn't understand why she couldn't have slept in Vegas and taken a flight to Houston later in the day, and joked "just get her there, and make sure she sings!" She said she was ordering a large breakfast, and then sleeping all day.

December 15, 1965: Judy's Houston press conference, at the Shamrock Hotel's Grecian Room (set for 3:30 p.m.; Judy arrived at 4:30 p.m.) The day of Judy's concert (Friday, December 17) was declared "Judy Garland Day!" in Houston. "I like Harold Arlen and Jerome Kern songs," was Judy's response to her favorite music. After the conference, Judy, Mark, and her producer for the concert, Stan Irwin, went to dinner at the Red Lion.

December 17, 1965: (Concert) The Astrodome; Houston. Judy was the first artist to play the Astrodome, and was paid $43,000 for the one show. Diana Ross and The Supremes were her opening act. The dome seated 48,000, with another 12,000 seats added for this show; ticket prices ranged from $1.00 to $7.50. Judy's songs: "He's Got The Whole World In His Hands"; "Just In Time"; "My Kind Of Town, Houston Is"/"Houston" (arranged by Roger Edens: the very last work he would do for Judy); "As Long As He Needs Me"; "Joey, Joey, Joey"; "Do It Again"; "What Now My Love?"; "By Myself"; "Rock-A-Bye Your Baby"; "San Francisco"; "Chicago"; and "Over The Rainbow." Judy came on at 10 p.m., and her program ran 40 minutes; Mort Lindsey conducted. It was in Maxine's column in the *Houston Chronicle* of December 9, that Roddy McDowall would be at this concert, shooting photos for *Life* magazine, and that *Look* magazine would be there as well. These photos are not known to exist, if they were actually taken.

December 18, 1965: Judy, Mark, Shep Fields (brother of Freddie Fields, Judy's manager), and Snowy, caught a 5:00 p.m. flight out of Houston, arriving home in Los Angeles at 4:45 p.m., L.A. time.

December 24, 1965: Judy, Mark, and the kids spent Christmas Eve at home in Brentwood.

December 25, 1965: Judy, Mark, and the kids flew to Liza's opening at the Sahara Hotel in Las Vegas, where Judy had just played. Judy developed a minor ear boil, and had to be driven back home to Los Angeles in her limo, while Mark flew home with Lorna and Joe, after taking them to see *Hello, Dolly* at the Riviera.

December 31, 1965: Judy and Mark attended a New Year's Eve party given by Pamela Mason.

An outfit called Publimetrix measured the amount of publicity that stars received during the year: Following Sinatra, Julie Andrews, Bob Hope, and Elizabeth Taylor, Judy was ranked the fifth most highly publicized star of 1965. (Judy was followed by Dorothy Malone, Richard Burton, Marlon Brando, Patricia Neal, and Rex Harrison.)

1966

January 9, 1966: Judy watched *The Wizard of Oz* on television, supposedly for the first time all the way through: "Always before," she told the *Louisiana Baton Rouge Morning Advocate's* Dick Kleiner, "I'd spend most of the show trying to keep the children from crying. I'd tell them 'Don't worry, kids, those munchkins are only little boys, they won't hurt you.' I think it's too scary for kids."

January 14, 1966: (Personal Appearance) Judy and Mark attended Phyllis Diller's opening at the Coconut Grove in Los Angeles.

January 17 or 18, 1966: Judy reportedly had the flu, according to Mike Connelly's column on January 19.

Mid to late January 1966: (Personal Appearance) Judy and Mark attended Omar Sharif's party at "Whiskey a Go Go" in Hollywood, during which they danced a "wild Watusi," according to columnist Harrison Carroll.

January 27, 1966: *The Hollywood Reporter* announced Judy's next television guest shots, stating the aforementioned career plan to "limit her television guest appearances to six a year."

Late January 1966: (Personal Appearance) Judy and Mark attended the University of Southern California's honoring of Gregory Peck, Lucille Ball, and producer Hal Wallis, according to columnist Dorothy Manners.

End of January 1966: Judy and Mark flew to Florida, for her next engagement.

February 1, 1966: Judy attended Arthur Godfrey's closing night at another room in the Diplomat, in Hollywood, Florida, the night before she opened in the main room. She was then seen clowning and singing on stage at the Tack Room of the Diplomat with Kay Stevens and Linda Bennett.

February 2, 1966 to February 10, 1966: (Concert) The Diplomat Hotel, Hollywood, Florida. Judy reportedly filled in for Robert Goulet, and was held over an additional day, on February 10. The room Judy played carried a $7.50 dinner charge, or a $10.00 beverage minimum. Show time was 10 p.m. nightly. Judy's opening act was comic Pat Henry. Her portion of the show ran 45 minutes, and she was backed by the 26-piece Van Smith Orchestra. Her songs included: "He's Got The Whole World In His Hands"; "Almost Like Being In Love"/"This Can't Be Love"; "Just In Time"; "Joey, Joey"; "Do It Again"; "Rainbow"; "Rock-A-Bye"; "Chicago" and "San Francisco." Here are excerpts from a couple of reviews for Judy's work:

> *The Hollywood, Florida Sun-Tattler*, February 4 (Pat Mascola): (Headline) "Judy Lifts Them Off The Seats": "Judy Garland electrified her opening night audience at the Diplomat hotel, with enough current to lift them off their seats for the first standing ovation seen this year along the strip. Judy was never in better voice, and never better composed . . . Miss Garland is, without question, the queen of phrasing, and can get more out of the lyrics of a song than most pros. . . . She can do no wrong. Just being on stage generates excitement."

> *The Miami News* (Herb Kelly), February 4: (Headline) "Judy Garland's Rainbow Glows In The Diplomat"; "Judy is singing in the Diplomat's big Cafe Crystal and it's a very good room for her. She's not so far away that she looks like a pygmy standing in front of a 26-piece orchestra. We're close to her and that's the way we want it. . . . Requests are shouted from all corners of the nightclub, and she meets as many of them as she can."

While in Florida, on Friday, February 4, there were actually rumors circulating that Judy had died—she laughed them off as she was playing golf that day before doing her show that night.

February 12, 1966: (Personal Appearance) Children's Hospital, Miami, Florida.

February 14, 1966: Judy flew to New York, for her next television appearance, staying at the Plaza, where she met singer Lana Cantrell, when Liza brought her to Judy's suite. Cantrell had known Peter Allen for years, as they both were from Sydney, Australia.

February 15, 1966: Mike Connolly's column in the Hollywood Reporter on this date announced that Judy had been signed to do a dramatic role on an upcoming "Chrysler Theater." (He also revealed that Lorna and Joey had signed with a talent agency, under the names "Lorna Herron," and "Joe Wiley.") Judy never did an appearance for the "Chrysler Theater." Judy and Mark attended one of Liza's first shows at the Perisian Room of the Plaza Hotel shortly after their arrival in New York. Not certain of the exact date; Liza opened on February 9, and *The Hollywood Reporter* of February 16 stated that Judy was at Liza's second night, which would not have been possible, as Judy performed in Miami for the Children's Hospital Benefit, on February 12.

February 16, 1966 to February 19, 1966: Rehearsals for:

February 20, 1966: (Television) *The Kraft Music Hall*, NBC-TV, videotaped in color at NBC Studios in Brooklyn, New York, from 7:30 to 9 p.m. This show was hosted by Perry Como; Bill Cosby was a guest. Judy sang: "If You Feel Like Singing, Sing"/"It's A Grand Night For Singing" (with Como and chorus); "What Now, My Love?"; "Just In Time"; "In My Baby's Loving Arms" (with Como); "Medley: Rock-A-Bye Your Baby"/"Over The Rainbow"/"The Man That Got Away" (with Cosby); "Bye, Bye, Blues"/"For Me And My Gal" (with Como); and "Side By Side" (with Como). (Carol Burnett was in the audience at the taping.) The show aired on February 28, 1966. (A black and white film print still exists of the show; the original color videotape is thought lost.) An interesting backstage quip—while waiting for the taping of her solo "What Now My Love?" to be videotaped, Judy, wearing a gown that was engulfed in feathers, folded her hands under her arms, clucked like a chicken, and said if she had to wait any longer to start, she would "lay an egg in this dress!" This was Judy's finest television performance of the mid to late 1960s, and the critics obviously agreed, as you'll see from these excerpts.

> *Oakland Tribune* (Bob MacKenzie), March 1: (Headline) "Moddy For Judy": "We Judy Garland fans, a high-strung breed, have one characteristic in common: we worry. When Judy is scheduled for a television appearance, we're thinking: will she look o.k? Will her weight be down? Will she wear something flattering? Will her voice be in shape? (The Garland voice is a fragile instrument, and has its good days and its bad days). At times, this solicitous anxiety reaches neurotic proportions. Members of the Garland congregation have been known to write angry letters to television directors when Judy isn't photographed at a flattering angle. All these fraternal jitters were put to rest last night when Judy appeared on Perry Como's special on NBC. She sounded fine and looked marvelous. Clad in a crazy cluster of black feathers, she was in good voice and was no more a bundle of nerves than was necessary to bring her

own special drama to a ballad. [Como's] moments with Judy had a nice chumminess. All in all, it was worth the seeing, and it stopped our worrying until next time."

Cleveland Press, March 1: "Cheers For Judy" (Headline); "Miss Garland, heftier, looked downright handsome and healthy. She was in better voice, too."

The New York Daily News, March 1: "Como Comments" (Headline); "The Judy-Perry duet was cozy Como at his best—and Judy at hers."

Pasadena Star News, March 2: "Miss Garland's numbers were gay and off-hand. The hour, which sometimes moves very slowly, zipped by."

The Philadelphia Inquirer, March 2: "Miss Garland, introduced as 'my little friend, Liza's mother,' was in good form . . . and scored in a 'singing' medley, in musical answers to Bill Cosby's clue-seeking questions, and in other ditties, alone and with her harmonious host."

February 23, 1966 to February 26, 1966: Rehearsals for Judy's next television appearance. (At some point this week, Judy and Mark attended the premiere of Tennessee Williams Broadway play *Slapstick Tragedy*.)

February 26, 1966, 12:30 a.m.: Judy and Mark, along with Sammy Davis, Jr., turned up at Liza's 12:30 show at the Persian Room at the Plaza (Liza introduced Judy to the audience.)

February 27, 1966: (Television) *The Sammy Davis, Jr. Show* was videotaped in color at NBC Studios in Brooklyn, New York. Judy sang: "When You're Smiling"; "The Man That Got Away"; "Give My Regards To Broadway"; and a medley of some of her greatest hits with Davis (performed in Tramp costumes): "A Couple Of Swells"/"The Lady Is A Tramp"/"How About You?"/"Bidin My Time"/"For Me and My Gal"/"Meet Me In St. Louis"/"Ding-Dong The Witch Is Dead"/"A New World"/"Johnny One Note"/"I Got Rhythm"/"Get Happy"/"On The Atchison,Topeka, And The Santa Fe"/"Could You Use Me?"/"I Wish I Were In Love Again"/"Treat Me Rough"/"If I Only Had A Brain"/"A Couple Of Swells." At the end of the show, Davis asked her to return the very next week. This show was telecast on NBC-TV, on March 18, 1966. (The only known surviving copy of this show—a black and white Kinescope film print—was thought lost or stolen, until discovered by this author at the Museum of Broadcasting, in 1995.) A look at Judy's sense of humor: when there was a delay due to a camera problem, Sammy sang "Day In, Day Out" for the studio audience, while Judy played the bongos in the orchestra.

March 2, 1966 to March 5, 1966: Rehearsals for Judy's next television appearance:

March 6, 1966: (Television) *The Sammy Davis, Jr. Show* was videotaped in color, at NBC Studios in Brooklyn. Judy sang: "Almost Like Being In Love"/"This Can't Be Love"; "If Love Were All" (sung at the piano with Mort Lindsey), and "Love" (the last two songs were cut before airing, although an audiotape recorded through the sound system still exists); and a Medley with Davis, consisting of: "Let Us Entertain You"/"Alexander's Ragtime Band"/"April Showers"/"Look For The Silver Lining"/"Keep Your Sunny Side Up"/"Life Upon The Wicked Stage"/"Rock-A-Bye Your Baby"/"Smile"/"Terpsicory"/"Song And Dance Men"/"Grand Old Flag"/"Toot Toot Tootsie"/"Carolina In The Morning"/"California Here I Come"/"Swanee"/"Born In A Trunk."

The New York News (Kay Gardella), March 26: "Davis And Garland Score" (Headline); "Judy Garland went all out on Sammy Davis, Jr's NBC-TV hour, sparkling in a medley of trusty favorites with her host. And while we're enthusiastic, we'll add that there's nobody in our book, besides the late Al Jolson, who can do as much justice to standbys like 'Swanee,' and 'April Showers,' as Judy did last night."

This show aired on NBC-TV on March 25, 1966. (Judy was in good form, but was suffering from laryngitis. A black-and-white film print survives; not the color videotape, unfortunately.)

March 6, 1966: (Television) *The Soupy Sales Show*, a never-aired special was videotaping across the hall from *The Sammy Davis, Jr. Show*—Judy made a brief walk-on. The show's "running-gag" was that Judy was to be Soupy's guest, but her flight was delayed, so Soupy had Ernest Borgnine (of all people) "play" Judy and read her lines and sing and dance some of Judy's greatest hits on a lighted runway, with Soupy. At the end of this medley, while Ernest (as "Judy") was taking his bows, he was handed roses, as the real Judy walked onto the stage, waved to the audience, and asked Ernest what he was doing with her roses—"Those are *my* roses!" When Soupy said her plane was late, Judy said "That's no reason to do my *spot*!" kissed Soupy, snatched her roses, as she waved to the audience while walking off the stage. Judy wears the same knee-length white gown outlined with black fur that she wears on her solo spot of the second *Sammy* show taped this day. This appearance was never talked about, though is wonderfully funny, and the color videotape still exists.

March 7, 1966: Judy flew home to Los Angeles, set to tape an appearance on *The Andy Williams Show* on March 11, for airing on April 4.

March 8, 1966: A look at a not so great day in the life of a legend: First, Judy's laryngitis forced her to cancel, on this day, a scheduled return to *The Andy Williams Show* in Los Angeles, that would have been taped on March 11, and aired on April 4; she would have received Williams top guest star fee of $7,500. Then, a sheriff's attachment was placed on her Rockingham home. Though the repossession of the home would be avoided, Judy's financial affairs were at an all-time low. By June 1966: her assets—only $12,163.29; her liabilities—$122,001.08, which included 120 creditors; this amount does not include the $400,000 she owed the IRS. Judy rehired her business manager from the mid 1950s, Morgan Maree, Jr., who worked out a monthly expenses list for Judy: $600.00 for automobiles; $700.00 for her house payment (mortgage); $3,000.00 for monthly staff salaries; $3,718 monthly retainer for Bautzer, Erwin, and Schwab (Judy's law firm); $833.33 for Maree's monthly fee (Judy's business manager); $1,283.88 for Guy McElwaine and Associates, public relations; and $3,000.00 for Sid Luft (as part of the divorce settlement).

Approximately March 16, 1966 to March 23, 1966: Judy and Mark flew to Acapulco for a week, to help Judy get over her flu in time for her next television appearance. (In the March 19, 1966 issue of *Billboard*, the magazine printed the result of a poll of 2,300 college students from 44 colleges and universities, and the students had ranked Judy as 19th on their list of favorite singers.)

March 27, 1966 to March 31, 1966: Rehearsals in Los Angeles, for her next television appearance:

April 1, 1966: (Television) *The Hollywood Palace* was videotaped in color for ABC-TV. Judy was the hostess, and her songs taped this day, included: "What The World Needs Now Is Love" and "Mr. And Mrs. Clown" (with Van Johnson). ("What the World" needed about four takes before Judy got the lyrics to the new song correct and got a tape of a performance she thought good enough.) Apparently the intros to the guest acts were "pretaped" in advance, before the final taping in front of the studio audience. There still exists a color videotape of the 10 a.m. orchestra call run through—Judy had apparently slept in her trailer overnight; She was found as the rehearsal was ready to start, and just ran out of her trailer, with no makeup, and her hair all askew, and barely awake; and yet, as always, somehow still magical. To then view the final taping, done only hours later, is a startling experience. The show does not reveal Judy in the best shape either vocally, or in spirits; a decision was made to tape her closing songs—"Comes Once In A Lifetime" and "By Myself"—two days later to give her a chance to present herself in better form. While Judy might have been grateful for this, she was, at the time, facing both a crumbling marriage and financial condition, along with the just-received news that Capitol Records was not renewing her recording contract, after nearly 11 years with the label. In a horrible "April Fool's" display, she, in a rage, tore-up her dressing room. This action blacklisted her from any future variety series television work.

April 3, 1966: (Television) *The Hollywood Palace* videotaped Judy's closing segment, containing the songs "Comes Once In A Lifetime" and "By Myself." This would be the last time Judy would tape a song for primetime, network broadcasting. (This now completed *Hollywood Palace* show would air on May 7, 1966, on ABC-TV; the color videotape still exists, along with the mentioned dress rehearsal tape of Judy's opening song "What The World Needs Now Is Love.")

April 12, 1966: Judy—escorted by her *A Star Is Born* director, George Cukor—arrived 45 minutes early to attend the opening of her husband Mark Herron's appearance in Noel Coward's *Private Lives*, at the Ivar Theater in Hollywood, in which Herron played opposite Kathie Browne. (Judy sat in the front row, with Cukor, singer Marti Stevens, and actress Hermione Gingold.) Judy and Cukor gave a cocktail buffet at Martoni's after the show, where Judy sang "Play Orchestra Play" and "Someday I'll Find You" with Stevens, and then Judy soloed—wrapping up the party at 4 a.m.—with "The Party's Over."

April 15, 1966: Judy and Herron separated, and Herron moved out of Judy's Brentwood home on this date (although Judy later gave the date as April 25); apparently, part of what fueled the separation was the knowledge that Herron would have been responsible for half of all of Judy's liabilities if they remained together any longer.

As Judy separated from Mark Herron—announced officially on May 4 by Judy's attorney Herbert Schwab as a "trial separation," with Judy saying she was still going to name her new company 'Marland Music,' after Mark and herself—and as the IRS and other creditors were ready to seize any monies she made, she refused to work, and began the longest period of professional inactivity of her entire life and career.

May 10, 1966: (Personal Appearance) Judy sat ringside at Tony Bennett's Los Angeles opening (where she delighted in his singing of "The Trolley Song"), and later spent time with Tony—and her new escort Tom Green (her publicist's assistant, whom she first met in September 1965) at Eddie Fisher's, where they "talked the biz until dawn."

May 14, 1966: Judy flew to New York, for:

May 15, 1966: (Personal Appearance/Benefit) Tribute to Judy Holiday/Cancer Benefit for The American Medical Center in Denver; held at the Americana Hotel in New York City. Judy sang: "When You're Smiling"; "Rock-A-Bye Your Baby"; "Just In Time"; "The Party's Over"; and encored with: "You Made Me Love You"/"For Me And My Gal"/"The Trolley Song" and then "Over The Rainbow." Among the stars appearing with Judy, who posed for photos with her: Alan King, and Betty Comden and Aldolph Green.

May 16, 1966: Though Judy had said she'd perform at the March of Dimes salute to Ed Sullivan at the Hilton in New York, she decided to return home to Los Angeles.

Mid May 1966 to mid June 1966: An extremely quiet time for Judy; the only reports of any activity were of her appearing at various nightclubs and supper clubs.

June 10, 1966: Judy celebrated her forty-fourth birthday at the Captain's Table with escort Richard Grant (they had also been seen at the Beverly Hilton's Escoffier Room), but Harrison Carroll reported in his June 14 column that Judy told him "Richard is just one of my associates in my music publishing firm. I'm very excited about this new project." Unfortunately, this was another project that never materialized.

Mid June 1966: Judy reportedly phoned Bennet Cerf, president of Random House, about another attempt at writing her autobiography, according to columnist Mike Connolly. This report was most likely true, as Judy often gave reports to Connolly; she did need the money that a book advance would give; and tapes were made around this time, summer and/or fall, of Judy talking about her life with Tom Green.

Week of June 25, 1966: Judy was reportedly signing a new recording contract with a new label called Weatherby Records, headed by Candy Weatherby Mossler. Dorothy Manners had mentioned in her column that Judy had "broken off musical relations" with Capitol Records.

Early summer 1966: (Concert) The Sahara Hotel Casbah Room, Las Vegas (This was a last-minute substitution for an ailing Martha Raye.)

July 1966: Sid Luft approached Judy with the idea to form a new production company, "Group Five." This would be finalized nearly a year later, in May/June 1967.

Early August 1966: Judy officially had a new personal publicist and an escort—when Tom Green left Guy McElwaine, where he had been working on Judy's publicity since September 1965, to now work on his own for Judy, at a reported $500 a week.

August 3, 1966: Mark Herron sued Judy for separate maintenance. He stated he had not filed for divorce because he hoped reconciliation was still possible.

August 7, 1966: Judy issued the following statement regarding Herron: "His public and private behavior, which has been distasteful and untenable, makes any reconciliation impossible."

August 14, 1966: Judy and Tom Green flew to Mexico City for her next appearance, arriving at 4:40 p.m. They left the plane at 5 p.m., and headed for the Maria Isabel Hotel, where they occupied the Marco Polo suite. The evening was spent there with the impresarios who were presenting her. Judy dined on only a bacon-lettuce-and-tomato sandwich, and retired after 11 p.m.

August 15, 1966: Judy woke at 11:00 a.m., having a "frugal" breakfast of a glass of tomato juice with vodka, water, and soda, along with two fried eggs. At 12 noon she spent some time on the balcony, then napped. As a "preview" before the press conference at 2 p.m., Tom Green told reporters that Judy would be in Mexico City for 12 days, and that on September 9, she would open at Caesar's Palace in Las Vegas, for which she would be paid $70,000. This engagement would not take place, however. Judy arrived at the press reception about 4 p.m., and told the press she had left Capitol Records and was forming her own label, hoping she would sign Eddie Fisher—whom she expected at her Saturday performance, along with Lorna and Joe—as well as other singers, to the label. (*Billboard Magazine*, in its August 27 issue, carried an item from this time that Judy was in Mexico City, in which she states that she owned 50% of the new record label, for which her first album would be released in four months, that the songs would be new, and that the album had not yet been "taped," although most of the songs selected. Judy candidly admitted "I didn't leave Capitol—they fired me. But I'm glad it happened: now I can record for my own company." However, the deal would never actually come to anything; no album would ever be recorded or released for this label; Capitol at this time began to license tracks from Judy's albums to the label Pickwick, who released a compilation album called *I Feel A Song Coming On*, in 1966. Sears in turn issued this LP as *By Myself* in 1967. Capitol would also issue a six-LP set *The Magic of Judy Garland* in June 1968.) At the Mexico City press conference, it was also revealed that Judy would sing "The Party's Over" in Spanish, and that she wanted to learn Mexican songs before she left. That evening was spent touring the city, where Judy bought everything that several children on the street were selling, and assigned members of her entourage to look after them while she was there.

August 16, 1966: Judy continued touring Mexico City, and had a Mexican guitarist, Manolo Medina, to her suite to play songs. (Also on this date: Herron changed his plea and sued for divorce.)

August 17, 1966: (Concert) The El Patio Nightclub; Mexico City. Judy made her Mexican singing debut, opening a scheduled two-week run—12 days, 14 performances—for a large cash payment at the end of every show (so it could not be traced by IRS): $17,500 a week, a guaranteed $35,000: Judy expected to emerge with a net of $20,750, after expenses. Judy sang over 21 songs with a 50-piece orchestra, in a 90-minute performance, even though her contract (arranged by the Leonard Artists Agency) stated she need do only a 30-minute show. Here are three of the raves she received for this first show:

> *Exito*, August 21: "Glorious, extraordinary, electrifying, and magnetic was the triumphant presentation of the great star of world cinema, Judy Garland, the formidable show woman. . . . In my 20 years of reviewing performances of the greats of show business I have never before experienced the strange emotion of seeing a spontaneous and adoring ovation with which the Mexican public received the little giant, Judy. . . . Her early artistic capabilities were smothered by the motion picture studios, the factories of cement and fiction. She has a large and devoted audience, and during an act that included more than 20 songs, one was not able to say less than that she was a great artist. When she finished her performance, the tempest of emotional applause continued until her diminutive figure was lost in a crowd of men, women and children that stood and threw flowers at her. She shook hands with the throng, and there was a lot of hugging and kissing. After the admirable act, we were all in her dressing room for more than an hour, and everyone agreed that she treated us with courtesy. I and my colleagues were enthusiastic and impressed by the personal attention given by the extraordinary Judy. When one has lived all this, it is small wonder that she suffered from laryngitis on Thursday night. She went on the second night, refusing to heed the advice of her doctor, the very professional artist presented herself in order to fulfill her contract with the public, and no one was able to say less than what a great woman and artist she was."

> *El Heraldo*, August 19: "Judy Garland Triumphs" (Headline): "Judy Garland triumphed spectacularly in her debut in Mexico Wednesday night in El Patio. When she appeared on the scene the people stomped their feet and received her with an ovation. . . . An artist of the soul and the heart, physically fragile but strong in spirit, Judy electrified the audience."

> *Cine Mundial*: "An Impact And a Debut Of The Celebrated Star of Hollywood" (Headline): "How can we describe an act such as that of Judy, celebrity among celebrities? Indisputably, Judy is all a star, a star of immortal fame that will never disappear for centuries and centuries in the site that she now occupies. There are those who make adverse comments about Miss Garland as a person, but these are bad opinions, as she has demonstrated her professional art. She is an example of professional art. We owe her our respect." (It should be noted Judy gave this tremendous performance on her opening night, just after she was made aware of Herron's filing of divorce papers, shortly before her show.)

August 18, 1966: Judy did her second show in Mexico City, in spite of fighting laryngitis.

August 19, 1966: Judy's laryngitis worsened, and having barely struggled through the concert the night before on August 18, she decided to cancel the rest of the engagement, before this evening's scheduled performance (of course it meant that she left with nothing after expenses). According to Jackie Cooper in the 1975 book *Rainbow*, Judy stayed on in Mexico for several days, alone, and not in the best shape emotionally; although Tom Green was with Judy in Mexico, and they actually left the following day.

August 20, 1966: Judy and Tom Green left Mexico City to return home to Los Angeles, taking an evening flight.

September 1, 1966: It was announced that Judy had left CMA (Creative Management Agency), the firm that her agents Freddie Fields and David Begelman had started, shortly after signing Judy in December 1960, nearly six years earlier.

Early September 1966: Judy took Lorna and Joe to Disneyland, according to columnist Mike Connolly (this was covered in the February 1967 issue of *Movie Mirror Magazine*).

Mid September 1966: Judy was seen dining in San Francisco, according to the *Santa Monica Independent* of September 15.

Mid September 1966: Judy signed a deal with Bernard Glassman and Pathe News (a.k.a. Pathe Pictures) of North Miami, Florida to handle the distribution of her 26-episode television series, and her 1962 and 1963 specials. Judy was paid a $35,000 advance, and Sid Luft received $5,000 according to trade paper reports. The deal was announced in the *Hollywood Reporter* on September 19, 1966. The shows would begin airing in Australia in November 1966, and in Los Angeles in January 1967, before being pulled, due to legal problems: Apparently Judy's production company—Kingsrow Enterprises, Inc.—had not secured permission from the guest stars for additional airings after the original broadcast, although they would eventually all be obtained. Additional lawsuits would be filed between Judy and Luft and Glassman; Glassman sued for $97,877, the amount he stated he had paid out in expenses. A series of LPs of Judy solos from the television series were released immediately after her passing by Radiant Records, who were in turn sued by Tucker Records. In 1974, Glassman used the masters for a deluxe two-LP set *Judy Garland: Concert* with booklet and photos, sold exclusively at Woolworth/Woolcos, and in 1983–1984, Audio Fidelity Records released two double-LP sets, including "Star Eyes," which included a dress rehearsal take of "Here's That Rainy Day." Even though Luft would at last legally obtain full rights to the series and the 1962 and 1963 specials in 1980, the original two-inch tapes sat in Glassman's garage in Florida. They were then transferred to a basement in the home of a relative of Glassman's in New Jersey, and finally returned to Luft in 1994, at which time they were transferred to a D-2 digital format. Although a moment or two wound up on the MGM's Fiftieth Anniversary home video edition of *Meet Me in St. Louis*, the recovered masters were not used until 1997 when Luft signed a deal with Classic World Productions for all rights to the series, except theatrical, as Luft had entered into a deal for a film with Oliver Stone. CWP in turn sold all broadcast, video and audio rights—except for DVD—to 32 Records, who began to release the material via a compilation CD/video box set called *Judy*, which I coproduced, on October 13, 1998. (The label would ultimately release the material back to CWP, retaining only the audio rights.) Starting in June 1999, Pioneer Entertainment began releasing DVDs using the original two-inch videotapes (which were transferred onto Digi-Beta tapes, and then digitally restored and remastered.) To date, all but five of the twenty-six episodes of *The Judy Garland Show* have been released on DVD, with "the series of the series" of "The Show That Got Away" continuing from Pioneer and Classic World Productions.

September 21, 1966: Judy went to the Buddy Rich Orchestra opening, along with Tony Bennett, Eddie Fisher, and Lainie Kazan (and reportedly made several "return visits," being accompanied by Tony Bennett on one of the reappearances).

September 29, 1966: Judy dismissed her Los Angeles attorney Dwain Clark, and hired Godfrey Isaac, according to the *Los Angeles Herald Examiner* of September 30.

At the end of September, Judy fired Mrs. Chapman, Lorna and Joe's governess. She had been with them for the past three years, from the time Judy moved back to California and bought the house in Brentwood, at the start of production on her series in May 1963. Lorna was nearly 14, Joe was 11, at the time Mrs. Chapman left. The decision may also have been financial.

October 1, 1966: Judy officiated at the opening of the "Yellow Brick Road," an art gallery, outdoor cafe, and unusual gift shop, located on La Cienega Blvd., in Los Angeles. Judy cut the ribbon, while standing on a tiny bridge, which was on top of a painted yellow brick road that ran over the entire length of the place. Judy also autographed a yellow brick.

October 2, 1966: Judy told Mike Carroll (in his October 3 column) that "I'd like to rest my voice for six months, and do something else—see a lot of my kids, and maybe write my book."

October 1966: Judy attended Jack Carter's Coconut Grove opening, with old friend John Carlyle. (She was also seen there at a slightly later date.)

Fall 1966: Judy spent much time in front of the tape recorder at home, with Tom Green interviewing her about her childhood, and in private sessions where she would rant and rave about MGM, CBS, and, especially, her managers David Begelman and Freddie Fields and their CMA agency, for, she said, stealing her money. (At this point Judy was $100,000 in debt, and owed another $400,000 to the IRS) Much of the taping—done at the urgency of Swifty Lazar, who wanted to get some cash for Judy through a book deal for her autobiography—is quite horrifying as Judy wails about what had been done to her.

October 5, 1966: Judy spent six hours at her home with fans Nancy Baar and Lynda Wells, who reported the proceedings in a fan publication called *Judy*, published by Eva Rieckmann (who was actually . . . Nancy Baar!) Arriving at 5 p.m., Nancy and Lynda were wondering how to get in through the electric wrought iron gates, when they spotted Lorna, who contacted the house via the intercom, and the gate swung silently open. The piece then describes Judy's Rockingham Avenue home (two of Judy's neighbors at this time, included Phyllis Diller, who lived up the street, on the same side as Judy and Pat O'Brien, who lived across the street from Judy). Nancy and Lynda drove their car from "the winding driveway, past the palms, birdbath pool in front of the one story dwelling, and pulled up near the garage with its basketball backboard mounted high on the front. The house has so much glass it resembles a fishbowl." (They mention a "handsome young chap by the name of Walter Pearson, who was then handling business matters at the house for Judy." This may have actually been Tom Green, or simply Judy's "house boy"; Judy's final "house boy" would be James Sutherland who worked there from January 1967 to June 1967.) Judy had just awakened when they arrived, and still "had to shower, eat and dress in her room," so they stayed in the living room, which they described as:

"Extremely comfortable, light and airy, the room is done in pale champagne beige, white, and Emerald Green. There is a fireplace similar to the one used on Judy's Christmas Show. Two small green couches are set before it, with a large round, green table between them. There is a dark baby grand piano, a bar area in one corner, several small single lamp tables, and a long curved sofa. Behind the sofa, a white shelf has been built, level with the back of the sofa. On it are lamps, a white telephone, and photographs in frames of various sizes: John F. Kennedy; a postcard sized reproduction given her by Nancy of a picture which appeared in a national magazine in the spring of 1960; a 1955 photo of Liza and her poodle; another 1955 shot of Liza cradling newborn Joe in her lap; Lorna touching Joe as he lay in his bassinet; Judy, Johnny Luft, Lorna, Liza, and Joe on the lawn of their Mapleton Drive home in 1956; Judy and Lorna on the set of *A Star Is Born*; Judy, Queen Elizabeth, and others after Judy sang for her in 1957; Liza at a party in 1958; and Judy with baby Liza in 1946. On a small lamp table stands a color portrait of Judy sitting on a box in tramp garb, from her 1955 "Ford Star Jubilee" special. About the room there are surprisingly few mementos of her career. Few pictures are hung: four or five contemporary oils, among them a semi-profile portrait of the mistress of the house. In the bar area are a few photographs of Judy, one of them a uniquely lit profile of Judy holding Lorna, taken onstage circa 1956/1957, and a standing 5x7 color print of the Sahara Hotel shot which appeared in issue number one of *Judy*. Also in this grouping, on the wall, is the certificate dated May 11, 1959, from Mayor Robert Wagner of New York, honoring her for the benefit performances she gave at the Met. On the piano stand four framed 11x14 photos: a 1954 shot of Judy; Lorna and Joe, 1965; Lorna, 1965; and Maurice Chevalier, with an inscription beginning to fade with age."

As Judy's "breakfast" tray was being removed, Lorna took Nancy and Lynda "out to the little courtyard which is surrounded by one end of the kitchen, laundry room, children's room, and back of the garage. Here we found the headquarters of the two family dogs: "Tippy," a Heinz dog—57 Varieties—and his son, "Sam," who resembles an Irish Setter—his mom was one." They describe Lorna and Joe's shared room as such: "The sleeping area is set apart from the study and television area by a 3/4 screen. On the wall above their beds is a huge portrait of Judy in her pink 'Meet Me In St. Louis' costume, done from the album cover." Judy's den/study is only described in terms of having a bizarre letter she received after she played the benefit to Judy Holiday on May 15 of that year (The letter expressed regret at Judy *not* being able to attend, and then mentioned her as one of the performers), along with a 5x7 pastel sketch of Judy holding a bunny, for the last episode of her series, which was broadcast on Easter Sunday 1964. Soon Lionel ("the only round-the-clock servant in the house") told them Judy was "dressed and ready to receive us." Judy was described as "slim, elfin and quite beautiful, and wore little makeup. Her hair was wet from her shower, and she wore black slacks, a pale gray sweater, pearl earrings, pearl necklace with the jade clasp, her jade and diamond ring, seamed hose, and black slippers which soon disappeared." While smoking Salems in her "little red holder," Judy enthralled her audience with many funny tales. As far as "news" was concerned, Judy mentioned that she was going to "name names" the following evening (October 6), during an interview for the *Ladies Home Journal.* "I've made $5 million in the past five years, and I don't have a penny of it. It seems incredible, and it is, that's why I'm doing this." As Judy kissed Lorna and Joe goodbye on their way off to dinner with their Dad, who was taking them to "Hamburger Hamlet," Judy mentioned that she would be seeing her lawyers at the house at 11 p.m. the night Nancy and Lynda were there—"Laugh now, let's have fun now, business later." Judy played several demos and tapes of songs that Capitol never released, including "When Your Lover Has Gone," which was most likely from her television series, as she was not known to have recorded it—A fascinating, fun evening at home with a legend.

October 11, 1966: Judy joined forces with Sid Luft in a $3 million dollar suit against CMA, Fields, and Begelman, filed on this date, charging that they "deliberately and systematically misused their position of trust so as to cheat, embezzle, extort, defraud, and withhold" monies from her. The suit also alleged that they "did not honestly or fully account to her for all monies received on her behalf and did not pay to her the amounts to which she was entitled." Judy stated it was the intention of the defendants to "take advantage" of her, "well-knowing" that she "was a star of major standing in the entertainment world and not knowledgeable about financial or money matters and that she was relying wholly upon them and their integrity."

Late October 1966: Judy sang at Rock Hudson's lounging party for Lauren Bacall, at the end of Bacall's vacation from *Cactus Flower*.

Around this time, Judy had apparently agreed to appear at the World Music Festival in Rio, although this did not work out. During this period, Judy was seen out quite frequently with Tom Green in the Los Angeles area, and she attended parties for Pat Kennedy Lawford and Princess Margaret. She also attended Cardinal Cushing of Boston's annual Benefit for crippled and retarded children, singing "Over The Rainbow." Also at this time, Judy was being sued by Mel Torme *again*, this time for back pay of $30,000; Judy herself had actually just finally collected some back pay from CBS for her 1963–1964 series. It was reported in one of the Los Angeles papers that Judy had just walked out of the Polo Lounge in the Beverly Hills Hotel, when she found out that Jacqueline Susann had walked in. Susann had authored *Valley of the Dolls*, the best-seller that contained a character reported to be molded on Judy. Judy's sister Jimmie, and her husband Johnny, were spoofing this book in their nightclub act at Dallas's Adolphus Hotel.

November 3, 1966: Judy gave statements about the legal case against CMA.

November 20, 1966: (Personal Appearance) Judy appeared at the Friars Club tribute in Los Angeles for George Jessell, and won the greatest cheer, with her line: "George, you knew me when I was nine years old: You should have *married* me!"

December 3, 1966: Judy amended her plea from divorce to annulment, as she said the marriage to Herron was never consummated.

December 1966: Judy spent the holidays in Lowell, Massachusetts with Tom Green and he introduced her to his family; stopping en route in Chicago (and possibly Detroit, reportedly), on the way to Lowell (they traveled by train). In Chicago, they were seen at the Pump Room at the Ambassador East Hotel. Judy attended midnight mass on Christmas Eve with Green and his family—which would be written about in a beautiful local newspaper article "Judy at Midnight Mass," which ran on December 28: Judy was so pleased with the article, that on December 30, she called the writer, Jim Droney, who had a call-in show on radio station WCAP in Merrimack Valley, and spoke to him on the air. No tape is known to exist of this "impromptu" radio appearance. Judy also invited Droney to a New Year's Eve party (that he was unable to attend). The holidays were climaxed with the announcement that Tom Green had given her an engagement ring. Tom's brother-in-law, Jerry, taught Judy how to run a *snowplower* at this time. Judy became so good at it, and bonded so well with Jerry, that he began calling Judy "Murphy," or "Murph"—"Murph the Snowplower!"

1967

January 6, 1967 to January 10, 1967: Judy left Lowell, Massachusetts (where she'd spent the holidays with Tom Green and his family), and she and Green spent these four days at his alma matter, Dartmouth College, in Hanover, New Hampshire. (Green was class of 1960.) Judy spent their Monday night shooting pool with the students on the Alpha Theta campus. The Dartmouth student paper of January 11 quoted Judy as saying "Dartmouth is the most beautiful campus I have ever seen. I'd love to live in Hanover."

January 11, 1967: Judy and Tom Green arrived in New York, staying at the Waldorf-Astoria. Most of their time was reportedly taken up with "business meetings."

January 14, 1967: Judy and Tom Green changed hotels, moving six blocks uptown to the Drake.

January 16, 1967: Judy, Tom Green and his sister and brother-in-law, the Gerald Coughlins, attended that evening's performance of *Mame* at the Winter Garden Theater, sitting in the front row. (Judy wore the pink sequined gown from the television series, "Episode Twenty-Five"; also seen on the 1964 *Jack Paar Show*.) They visited with Angela Lansbury backstage after the show (and thus irritated the theatre's coat checkroom, as their wraps were waiting to be picked up.)

January 18, 1967: Judy and Tom Green dined out with Liza and Peter Allen in New York City.

January 19, 1967: Judy and Tom Green dined at the Hickory House in New York City, and then went further on West 52nd Street, to Jilly's, where Judy sang with Bobby Cole and his trio, who were appearing there.

January 20, 1967: Judy and Tom Green dined at the Italian restaurant, La Scala. During the following several evenings, Judy and Green were seen at various nightspots, including many returns to Jilly's.

January 26, 1967: Judy and Tom Green attended a party, and then went to the midnight show at the Copacabana to see Jack E. Leonard and Lana Cantrell.

January 30, 1967: Judy and Tom Green again saw *Mame* at the Winter Garden Theater (this was Judy's second time seeing the show, and Tom's third), attending with Liza and Peter Allen. Judy went backstage prior to the start of the show and said she wanted to watch the show from the wings, but the stage manager thought she would be injured, so she returned to her seat. Soon after the second act started, they all left, as Judy had suddenly been hit with indigestion.

January 31, 1967: Judy and Tom Green flew back to Los Angeles, along with Liza, who was about to videotape her second "Hollywood Palace" show.

Early to mid February 1967: Sid Luft hired agent John F. Dugan to negotiate with 20th Century Fox who wanted Judy for a featured role in their adaptation of the best seller *Valley of the Dolls*. In February, Dugan wrote Judy that he had set the deal: $75,000 for eight weeks of work; then $25,000 each week if she would be needed longer. (The earliest mention of this in the press was in Jack Bradford's column in *The Hollywood Reporter* of February 14.)

February 25, 1967: An endorsed check for $1,890, and a file cabinet key were reportedly taken from Judy's home, between the hours of 11:00 a.m. and 3 p.m., as she told the police on February 26.

February 27, 1967: Judy stopped by friends of her sometimes-escort John Carlyle. Tucker Fleming and Charles Williamson were having their home on Norma Place remodeled, with a suite designed just for Judy, who would call it "her room."

February 29, 1967: Judy left Los Angeles for New York.

March 1, 1967, 12:21 a.m.: Judy arrived in New York on TWA Flight #8, with son Joe; Lorna was flying in later with Sid; Liza and her best friend Pam Rhinehart met Judy's plane, and Judy's limo took them all back to the St. Regis Hotel.

Judy with Tom Green at the Coconut Grove early in 1967. Green was her publicist from September 1965 through August 1967 and was also her on-again/off-again fiance. This is the first known photograph of Judy with Tom published in a Garland book. (Courtesy of Photofest.)

March 2, 1967 11 a.m.: Press Conference held at the Versailles Room of the St. Regis Hotel in New York, to officially announce Judy's participation—playing fictional Broadway musical comedy legend "Helen Lawson"—in *Valley of The Dolls*. (Audiotapes and color sound newsreel footage of the conference still exist.) Among Judy's quotes: "Let's face it: the role calls for an old pro over 40. That's for me. It's for sure I am no longer Dorothy in *The Wizard of Oz*. . . . And let's cut out the talk about tragedy in my life: There has been a lot of tragedy, but there have been a lot of marvelous parts too, which people forget. . . . Everybody gets upset if I'm happy. People don't know how to pencil me in any other way than miserable. . . . The part of Helen Lawson is no more me than the part in *Judgment at Nuremburg*. It doesn't pertain to me. . . . *Dolls* is an important picture" and Judy said her part was "challenging." The author of *Dolls*, Jacqueline Susann, sat next to Judy, and said Judy would bring a "very warm and sympathetic understanding to the role." Judy also mentioned she'd love to do a film with Bette Davis about Aimee Semple McPherson and her close association with her mother, though nothing would become of this. After the press conference, Judy went to Liza's final fitting at Annemarie Gardin's, the designer of her wedding gown.

March 3, 1967: Liza married Peter Allen in New York, at Stevie (and Richard) Friedberg's, her manager's, apartment. Judy was escorted by Vincente Minnelli. (Sid Luft was there as well, with Lorna and Joe.) The ceremony was from 6:30 p.m. to 7 p.m.; the reception followed immediately, at Liza's business manager's apartment, Marty Bregman, who lived across town, through Central Park. Judy mingled with the others, including Yul Brynner, Tony Bennett, Elizabeth Ashley, Diahann Carroll, Gwen Verdon and Bob Fosse, Phil Silvers, Jule Styne, John Kander, and ironically, both Freddie Fields and David Begelman of CMA (with Begelman on crutches.) Judy left a little after 9 p.m.

March 5, 1967: (Television) *What's My Line?* CBS-TV. Judy was the "Mystery Guest" on this "live" show from New York, during which she mentioned *Valley of the Dolls*. Bennett Cerf guessed correctly when he said "that voice could belong to only one woman in the world, and that is Judy Garland!" (A black and white film print exists of Judy's appearance.)

March 6, 1967: (Television) Judy filmed an interview with Barbara Walters for NBC-TV's morning program *The Today Show*, with Lorna and Joe participating, at her suite in the St. Regis Hotel. The final, edited 25 minute piece still exists, in color, and reveals a wonderfully warm, candid Judy (there are also a few seconds of extra "trim" footage on either side of several of the edits on the original existing film.) Although fighting the first signs of a flu affected her speaking voice, she looks lovely, and is wearing a blue outfit of Lorna's that Lorna can be seen wearing in the December 1961 photos taken at home in Scarsdale for the March 1962 issue of *Look* magazine.

March 9, 1967: Judy did at least two interviews on this last day in New York. The first was an afternoon session with a woman reporter who said people believe Judy "hits the bottle," to which Judy replied "What does that mean, actually *smacking* a bottle?!" The evening session started at 7 p.m. with John Gruen of the *New York World Journal Tribune*, which appeared on April 2. During this interview, Judy revealed "I'm happiest when I'm working, and when I work I give a lot. . . . My job is entertaining. Fortunately, I'm mad about an audience. I really, truly appreciate anyone taking time out and spending money to hear me sing. And believe me, I love singing for them. No matter how many people hurt me, when that orchestra starts playing, I *sing!*" Also on March 9, *Daily Variety* announced that Judy had signed with a new agent: Johnny Dugan of Johnny Dugan Enterprises. Dugan had been with MCA at the same time Judy was with them, under Freddie Fields. He had also just put together the deal with Fox for Judy's services on *Dolls*.

March 10, 1967, 5:30 a.m.: Judy met her future husband, Mickey Deans, for the first time, when he delivered some Ritalin pills to her at the St. Regis, as she hadn't slept, and needed to be "up" to catch a plane to fly to California to report for work on *Valley of the Dolls*. Deans had the pills, and Judy was able to catch her plane, flying home to Los Angeles with Lorna and Joe and Sid Luft.

March 12, 1967: An article appeared in the *Chicago "American"* newspaper, about Judy apparently consulting a vocal coach in Beverly Hills, Randy Herron—no relation to Mark Herron, Judy's former husband. Roger Dettmer, the writer of the article, states Judy talked about doing the movie version of *Mame*; not being able to read music; her tax problems; "the Brentwood house she rattles around in"; and she sang, including new songs: "the score of *Mame* virtually complete, and "Roar Of The Greasepaint" as well as a couple that Liza had recorded, though Judy would soon stop, saying "Liza's the big singer in the family now. . . . I couldn't begin to do them as well as she does."

March 27, 1967: Judy reported to work at 20th Century Fox for *Valley of the Dolls* to do wardrobe tests, hair and make-up tests, and to prerecord her solo "I'll Plant My Own Tree." On a still existing audiotape of a phone conversation Judy's life-long "Number One Fan" Wayne Martin recorded at this time, Judy told Martin that she wasn't thrilled by the song, didn't want to sing it, and was having troubles with Fox over it, as she wanted to sing "Get Off Looking Good," written by Bobby Cole. ("Get Off" exists on an audiotape of a November 3,1967 concert at Seaton Hall.) Judy does not sound enthusiastic—understandably—about her participation in the film, and as Martin tries to reach her on the phone, he is repeatedly told that Judy—at home on her days off from the studio during this preproduction time—was sleeping until 3 or 4 in the afternoon, which was her usual time to awaken, as she rarely got to sleep before 7 or 8 a.m. when her body-clock could work at its preferred concert-work function.

April 8, 1967: (Personal Appearance/Benefit) The City of Beverly Hills tribute dinner honoring Marcella Rabwin at the Beverly Hilton Hotel. Judy sang "Make Someone Happy," and from the audience, sitting next to Marcella, "Over The Rainbow."

April 11, 1967: Judy was granted her divorce from Mark Herron; audiotape of television newscasts with Judy talking to reporters in the courthouse, still exist; Judy also at last made "Judy Garland" her legal name: until that point she had been Frances Ethel Gumm Rose Minnelli Luft Herron.

Early April 1967: Judy had apparently wanted Roger Edens to score her songs for *Dolls*, according to Jack Bradford's column in *The Hollywood Reporter* of April 11; on April 14, he reported Judy said Fox should be "grateful" they had Edens, as she didn't like any of the songs written for her by Andre and Dory Previn; on April 17, he reported that Judy had finally agreed to sing "I'll Plant My Own Tree" by the Previns. (An early prerecording of "Tree" still exists, revealing Judy in only fair voice.)

Mid April 1967: Judy finally started actual filming on *Valley of the Dolls*. Things did not go smoothly: On the first day, Judy came in around 7:30–8:30; Had her hair and makeup done; but by 11 a.m. everyone was still waiting for her to come out of her dressing room; after lunch, Judy was still not ready to work. On the second day, it was more of the same, with Judy not coming out of the dressing room; On the third day she could not find the caps for her front teeth, and most of the day was spent with friend John Carlyle, dashing around to a dentist to get new ones done: it was 3 p.m. before Judy was on the set and made-up to her satisfaction; Still, no takes could be successfully completed of her opening scene in the Broadway dressing room of her character Helen Lawson (although there are surviving photographs; footage shot this day is *rumored* to still exist.) This continued for almost a week, with not one foot of film completed satisfactorily.

April 27, 1967: Judy was fired from *Valley of the Dolls*, although Fox announced she had "resigned for personal reasons," which Judy denied, saying "I have not withdrawn. I was up at six this morning to go

A wardrobe test still for one of the four costumes Judy was to wear in the film *Valley of the Dolls,* April 14, 1967. (Courtesy of Photofest.)

to work. It's a shocking thing. Why? That's what I want to know. Why?" There have been conflicting reports about the real reasons why Judy didn't make *Dolls*, ranging from Judy seeing nude scenes being filmed; Liza finally convincing her that the film was not right for her; Judy at last reading the script just prior to the first day of filming; to Jacqueline Susann convincing Judy that the part was not right for her; to Judy's house assistant, Jim Sutherland insisting that Judy had wanted out when Fox was dragging their heals on rewrites that Judy demanded—not only for her character, but *especially* for that of Neely O'Hara, the character Judy was *now*, finally, convinced *was* based on *her*! Judy was also trying for a "softer" approach to Lawson, which the director, Mark Robson, did not understand, and he was "tough" on her, according to reports from the set; to Judy feeling she was being exploited for publicity purposes; to Judy much later saying the whole thing was "sort of a mutual agreement"; etc. Whatever the real reason (or reasons), the film was not worthy of Judy's still considerable and legendary talents. Oddly enough, Fox was quite generous to someone they had fired: letting her keep the sequined pants suit (which she would soon make her standard concert costume), and paying her half of the $75,000 salary. Of the $37,500, $3,700 went to Judy's agent; $23,500 to the government; and $10,000 to Judy. The press would have much to say about Judy leaving *Dolls*, and Judy would have conflicting things to say about it in future interviews, as her feelings evolved:

> "I had recorded the song. I had the beautiful clothes. On Monday, the day before I was fired, I had a heart flutter on the set. I was tired. I hadn't been sleeping. But it really was just indigestion. They called the studio doctor to the set. . . . I have not withdrawn. How dare they say I've withdrawn?! They simply didn't call me to go to work. It was a good part, with wonderful songs, and beautiful clothes. I was thrown out—and I don't like it. It's a shocking thing. Why? That's what I want to know. Why? . . . I found the part difficult because the woman I was to play was coarse and shouting all the time. I was brought up to be polite and not raise my voice—except in song. . . . It was a terrible part. I played a dirty old lady. My first line was 'Who the hell are you?' . . . I was fired. I'm undependable. Independable? Which is it? Anyway, I'm irresponsible. Isn't that the story about me? I'm 102 years old and it's been the same story about me almost from the beginning." Tom Green offered "You know, the first day we got to the *Dolls* set they were shooting a nude scene. A nude scene! Right then, at that very first moment, I knew it wasn't the kind of film for Judy, not the kind of thing for America's Sweetheart! I mean, there's a long reputation here. She just can't be a glittering bitch in a Hollywood film. America wouldn't accept it." Judy also said: "Hollywood is cruel and not wise now. When they made fine pictures it was hard work but fun. Now they make dirty pictures. . . . The part was not right for me. . . . I didn't give them complications. They had a lot of other complications, in that they were shooting for the foreign market at the same time. It was a political thing, and I always get caught in the switches. *The Wizard of Oz* took a year and a half to make—nobody ever brings that out. I think they were a bit untidy. I think it was Daryl Zanuck's son trying to be like Louis B. Mayer. . . . I can't use tough language on the screen. People who saw me in *The Wizard of Oz* don't want to see me that way. I only took the part for the money, and to be honest, I just wasn't any good at it. . . . I didn't like the role. I thought I could do it, but I couldn't—I couldn't force myself to use that kind of language. And I don't think it's too important. I think the fact that I grossed $110,000 in Boston is more important than that bloody movie!"

(A story has circulated that when Judy was fired, she called Howard Hughes over to her home in Brentwood, and when he got there, she told him she wanted him to buy her 20th Century Fox so she would own *Valley of the Dolls* and could then fire everyone. Such was Judy's incredible sense of humor. Although it wouldn't have been a bad idea to at least hit Howard up for a spare million—forget the studio!)

May 7, 1967: (Television) Judy's last primetime network television appearance, *A Funny Thing Happened on the Way to Hollywood*, an NBC-TV/Jack Paar special, was videotaped in color, at NBC's Rockefeller

Center, Studio 6B, in New York City. Escorted by Sid Luft and Tom Green, Judy arrived around 6:20 p.m.; the taping started at 8 p.m. There were several stories that Judy told that were cut from the final air tape: The story of Elvis pulling up in his car, only the week before, to tell her he was a fan, but ignoring Paar who was in Judy's car with her; A "recreation" of her dance down the yellow brick road; And the time she was to sing "God Bless America" on stage with a model who was made up as the Statue Of Liberty, who, on the day of the performance, got "plastered," and fell flat on her face, as Judy was trying to sing the song. The special aired on May 15, 1967. (A black-and-white film print still exists, showing Judy in funny form, and clear, but not looking or sounding well.)

Also at this time while in New York: Judy was staying at the Gotham Hotel, in a two-bedroom, drawing-room suite, which was paid for by the *Ladies Home Journal*, as Judy had agreed to write an exclusive piece for them, and to do a fashion sitting with designer Bill Smith. The August 1967 issue would only feature one color photograph of Judy that was neither very clear, nor flattering, and the piece was written with Tom Green. Another writer that Judy came into contact with during this trip was Sanford Dody, who had worked on Bette Davis's recent book. Though Dody had only one session with Judy, it turned out to be a long evening, going until 7 a.m. or so the following morning, with Judy getting fresher and more alert by the hour, and he fading fast. Though nothing would come of their working together, the evening would make for a fascinating chapter of his book *Giving Up the Ghost* published in 1980.

May 1967: Sid Luft sold Judy's house for her, for $130,000 (much less than it was worth, according to Gerald Frank): many thousands went to back taxes, stemming from the late 1950s; Judy was left with $15,000. There exists an audiotape of Judy expressing her feelings about losing her home, during which she is accompanied by someone playing the piano, with the effect being closer to a song, or at least a poem. She also sings a haunting, a cappella version of "My Man's Gone Now." This was the last home Judy owned; she lived in hotels in 1967 to 1968, while on the road much of that time, and also rented a townhouse in New York City in 1967. She did rent an apartment in Boston in the fall of 1968 for a few months, and would settle in London not long before her passing. But this was her last true home that she owned and shared with her family. The new owners gave Judy some extra time so she could stay in Brentwood up until the time she left to go on tour on June 9, 1967.

Approximately May 23, 1967: Judy was back in Los Angeles and in the Cedars of Lebanon hospital for a check-up, which was first reported on May 24, in Jack Bradford's column.

May 24, 1967: Judy spoke to Harrison Carroll, who ran a piece in his column the next day, how Judy was fine, that she was just in Cedars for a check-up, would be out in a couple of days, and was preparing a tour with Liza, Lorna, Joe, and Peter Allen, which would also "eventually windup as a television special." (She would tour, and although Liza and Peter would occasionally join her on stage, only Lorna and Joe were "officially" part of the family "act." There would also not be any television special, unfortunately.)

May 31, 1967: Fan Wayne Martin called Judy at the hospital (the conversation was recorded by Martin, and still exists).

June 1, 1967: Judy returned home from the hospital, and on this day, it was announced in Harrison Carroll's column that Judy would marry Tom Green, sometime in August, "at Dartmouth University, which is Tom's alma mater."

June 4, 1967: The world got a glimpse of Judy as she would have looked in *Valley of the Dolls* when *Parade Magazine*—a Sunday newspaper supplement—ran a costume test photo of Judy in the white gown she was to wear for her song "I'll Plant My Own Tree."

June 8, 1967: Judy was packing for her trip east, sounding ecstatically happy during a phone call, taped by fan Wayne Martin. (The tape still exists.) On this date Judy also signed a fake check from a phony gag check book that a fan had printed up for her usage, for the account of "Judy Garland" at an address of "Legend Lane" in "Gale, Kansas." Drawn on "The Bank of Oz on the Yellow Brick Road." This check is paid to the order of "*My Dear John Condon,*" for "*1,000,000 One Million Dollars in Love and Respect.*" Condon was Judy's hairdresser. This was also the day Judy signed a contract with "*Group Five,*" which she thought was a new production company where the "Five" would be herself, Sid, and the three children. The "Five" in reality were Sid, Ray Filiberti—a rich "business man" with a police record—and three of Filiberti's "associates." While the "Group Five" contract presented Judy and Sid as employees—to protect them against the IRS—it offered Judy no security, and in fact her contract would be used as collateral by Filiberti, and turned over to people Judy had never heard of at some point during 1968. In the meantime, the deal paid Judy $1,200 for each concert, then $1,500 for each concert after the tenth concert, plus *all* of her living expenses: household, hotel, medical, entertainment, clothes, cars, transportation, aides—everything a star could need. It was arranged that the IRS would take $300 from her $1,500 "Group Five" nightly concert salary.

June 9, 1967: Judy left for her trip East, along with Tom Green. It was the last time she would ever be in a real home that she would own. (Phyllis Diller is believed to own the home now, although the exterior has been changed a great deal since the time Judy owned it from 1963–1967.)

June 10, 1967: Judy and Tom got off the train at Chicago, having dinner at the Pump Room at the Ambassador East Hotel, to celebrate her forty-fifth birthday. The conditions were not quite fitting for a birthday celebration, though. First, the train had air-conditioning trouble, so the temperature climbed to 92 degrees. Then, their arrival in Chicago coincided with a rainstorm, which caused a power failure to the front elevators in the hotel, so Judy had to use the service elevator. Then, the kitchen was flooded in the hotel, so Judy and Tom had their meal prepared at their table. Judy soon decided to take an evening flight to New York, instead of continuing by train. She returned to her suite by the back elevator, but had to walk down fifteen flights of stairs when even that elevator wouldn't work on her way out. In the meantime, her driver had been sent to get her luggage off the train, and as the twenty-three pieces filled the entire back area of the limousine, Judy and Tom rode up front with her driver to the airport.

June 11, 1967: Judy and Tom Green arrived in New York.

June 13, 1967 to June 18, 1967: (Concert) The Westbury Music Fair; Westbury, New York. This engagement kicked-off Judy's last lengthy tour, and was Judy's first time on stage in nearly a year, since the August 1966 engagement in Mexico City. (A still existing audiotape from this engagement shows Judy in fair voice, but fine form, and performing with Liza, in a show that was much different than the concert that would shortly evolve.) Here are excerpts from some of the reviews:

> *The New York Post*: "And then she did her third number, 'Almost Like Being In Love.' Second chorus, she waited, leaned back, hit it, socked it, let it ride. It was all there, it mounted, it sailed. There were those listening who were torn with shudders, with tears, but mostly there were hundreds and hundreds on their feet, shouting—shouting love—the place was in an uproar. It was frequently in uproar . . . Judy, as is her custom, gave it her all. Up there on stage and screen she is one of the greatest talents of this lifetime, and her own lifetime has seen her incredibly reborn, again and again. I shall be holding my breath, hoping she can use some of it, hoping for one more notch of the incredible."

A publicity photograph for ABC Records' new recording artist, to promote her last professionally recorded album, *Judy Garland: At Home at the Palace*, released on August 15, 1967. The photo was one of many taken during the time Judy was working at the Westbury Music Fair, June 13–18, 1967. She wore the jeweled pantsuit throughout her 1967–1969 concerts, including her last run at the Palace (it was one of the costumes she was to wear in *Valley of the Dolls*). (Courtesy of Photofest.)

The Long Island Press: "When Judy Garland walked down the aisle to the stage of the Westbury Music Fair last night, the entire audience was on its feet. Their salute to her filled the air with electricity generated by love [and] admiration. . . . 'Judy, we worship you!' shouted one young man over and over again. 'We love you, Judy' was heard all over the huge circular theater . . . the bravos filled the air. People wept and screamed. Some actually jumped up and down in excitement as they showed their love for a Judy Garland now slim in a sequined, mod pants suit, her hair somewhat gray, and her spirit indomitable. . . . Dragged on stage by her mother, Liza sang and received an ovation all her own. Liza's husband Peter Allen also sang with Judy . . . Judy clowns and sings wistful tunes. She is always the Judy Garland who has overcome. For that, audiences love her with a fervor this reviewer has never seen demonstrated in a theater, as it was at her opening last night. The evening belongs to Judy Garland, and triumph is a small word for her performance. See her, if you can still get tickets."

The Hollywood Reporter (Radie Harris), June 14: "Judy Garland opened here last night in the first engagement of a 3-week tour through the East, to a capacity audience of 2,700 who greeted her with enthusiastic cheers and gave her a standing ovation. . . . Her appearance at Westbury certainly gave the lie to critics who have said she was not up to the ardors of such performances. She never looked and sang better."

The Valley Stream New York Maileader, June 15: "She was a beautiful woman to watch. Her eyes sparkling more radiantly than her jeweled slack suit, she dominated the stage for an hour, belting her songs out one after the other, as though she would never tire. What special magic is it she's got? . . . I think Miss Garland represents for us the ability—the audacity, perhaps—to survive . . . she sings, and she survives, and she triumphs. . . . As you sit and watch, you become aware that each song, each note, comes from some deep reservoir inside, from which she gives too freely, too impulsively, caring not at all about the cost of such generosity. Never mind. Better minds than mine have groped for definitions of Judy Garland's magnetism. It's some show at Westbury, and you'll have to see it to believe it."

The New York Times, June 15: "'The old Garland throb still thrills.' . . . The audience that circled the round, white stage of the Westbury Music Fair last evening came to cheer Judy Garland, to adore her, to be overwhelmed by her. . . . She came running down an aisle, behind a flying wedge of burly young men, and burst into the gleaming light of the stage. The anticipatory cheers turned into a billowing ovation. She basked in it, a slight, slim figure in spangled paisley jacket and pants. . . . Then she reached back for one of her old climaxes, belting and familiar—and she found it—all of it. It came through in an electrifying burst of power that brought the audience to its feet once more. 'We love you, Judy!' someone shouted. 'I love you, too,' she called back, her eyes big round pools, her lips forming the vowels with such sincerity. It was an evening of mutual adulation. . . . When she opened up to belt out an ending, she never missed. The old Garland zing was still there! At the end, after she sang 'Over The Rainbow,' sitting in a small, soft spotlight, the audience rose and cheered and clapped as though it would never let her go. As the orchestra played it over and over, someone threw a single red rose and she managed to catch it. She waved armfuls of kisses, and then made her way slowly around the perimeter of the stage, reaching out to the audience, touching, shaking hands, even offering a kiss here and there. . . . 'We saw her!' a girl cried ecstatically to a group of her friends. 'We really saw her. And I touched her!' 'You touched her?!' exclaimed a young man. 'Are you kidding? I touched her hand!"

The Springfield Mass. Union (Richard Hammerich): "Her impact on the audience is electric, magical, indefinable, and probably unexplainable. One thing is sure. She puts out all of her-

> self in tremendous physical effort in an obvious attempt to perform for her listeners. She doesn't hold back. She forces her voice to levels far beyond a judicious vocalist should if she cares about protecting its future quality. She sings every song as if it were her last. And members of the audience in Westbury were standing and applauding and shouting in the midst of nearly every song. This vast muscular effort takes its toll. But it is easily the most identifiable quality of her performance that attracts the emotional response of the audience."

One of the typically hysterical quips Judy made during this run, centered on her still getting used to the revolving stage, as this was only her second engagement "in the round": "I don't know why they don't let *you* revolve around *me*!" (While in Westbury, Judy stayed at the Island Inn. The opening-night party was held at the John Peel Restaurant. One of Judy's quotes from backstage, during an interview: "Lorna sings better than Liza and I put together." This engagement at Westbury grossed a huge $70,000 from only six performances, at a $6.50 top; Judy's take from this gross was a straight $25,000 plus a percentage of another $23,000, for a total of $48,000 that she received; Or rather that "her" production company "Group Five" took for her!)

June 26, 1967 to July 1, 1967: (Concert) The Storrowtown Music Circus; Springfield, Mass. Here are excerpts from two of the reviews:

> *Springfield News* (Sam Hoffman), June 27: "How can one explain Judy Garland's tremendous showing? Was it strictly a nostalgic yearning that brought the crowd out? Then how does one explain a very large attendance of young people? They certainly don't remember Judy as we older folks do. Whatever it is, Miss Garland has a certain magic on stage—a real pro—that makes her a living legend in show business. 'An evening with Judy Garland' is truly an entertainment experience and one that should not be missed by anyone."

> *Pittsfield Mass. Berkshire Eagle* (James A. Lynch), June 27: "Her voice has the same electric pulsations it did when she was riding the crest of her palace comeback in the 1950s. . . . Her face is almost the same, some added lines, but surprisingly youthful and glowing."

After the opening, at the press reception/party held at the Old Storrowton Tavern, Judy told a reporter "People are my life." Judy also revealed that she would love to do a Broadway musical on the life of Laurette Taylor: "It's something I would like to do and I hope I get a chance to do it."

July 10, 1967 to July 15, 1967: (Concert) The Camden County Music Fair; Camdem/Haddonfield, New Jersey. Judy's wit was definitely evident during this engagement: As she stopped to take a sip of water, someone in the audience yelled out: "Drink hearty, Judy"; Judy repeated it slowly, as if trying to decide if was meant as a compliment, or as an insult: "Drink hearty . . . drink hearty . . . Nope, I don't know him. Only Hearty I know is *Andy* Hardy!" Here are some excerpts of reviews from the July 10 opening:

> *The Philadelphia Inquirer* (Samuel L. Singer), July 11: "Judy Garland is a phenomenon. She could run for president. Judging from the hysterical greeting of her fans at the Camden County Music Fair, she'd make it easily. . . . No such greeting has been accorded any other entertainer within memory. . . . Judy is an eyeful in multi-colored, spangled slacks and coat. Her dark hair, flecked with gray, is in a becoming Sasoon haircut. She looks and sounds a bit older, but the characteristic throaty singing is as strong as ever."

> *The Woodbury Daily Times*: "Looking slim and healthy and using the good sense to show her hair in its natural gray, Miss Garland sported her famous sequined paisley pants suit. . . . This entertainer can do no wrong! . . . Even at 45, the Garland magic endures. But what is the

> magic? The Garland magic lies in the rarest of talents: the star's ability to pour all of her great vitality into her songs and 'project' that vitality over the footlights into the hearts of her audience. This is no simple achievement. Very few entertainers can 'give' themselves to their audiences like Judy Garland does, and that is why the public has tried to repay her and has rewarded her with fame for 'lo these 30 years."
>
> *Trenton Evening Times* (Dana Stevenson), July 11: "Her rhythm is perfect; her small right foot keeps time as body and voice combine to make each song important and her very own. . . . The entire show was aided by a large orchestra, and when Miss Garland sang, a quartet of violins was added."
>
> *The Cherry Hill Suburban* (Carole Butcher), July 20: "Judy Garland has stood with the greats of all time as far as singers go. Many have claimed that's strictly in the past, she's losing her voice, and she'll never be able to captivate an audience the way she used to. Judy Garland still stands with the greats of all time as far as singers go. She can still belt out a song the way she did 10 years ago."
>
> *The National Observer*, (Daniel Greene), July 31: "Here in Haddonfield, [Judy's voice] is big and throbbing and clear as a trumpet. She ends with a punch you can feel in the last row."
>
> *Philadelphia Temple News*, July 19: "Garland's Voice Still Magic magic" (Headline): "She had regained the vocal power which eluded her in recent months, and the quality of her voice was gratifying to hear. . . . One cannot comprehend what Judy Garland has until he sees and hears her and her fans, or returns home with hands red from clapping for a woman he never thought he would enjoy listening to."

Judy personally mapped-out an arrangement of the song "Singing In The Rain," for Lorna to sing, starting at this venue (Judy had sung this in the movie *Little Nellie Kelly* back in 1940). Judy's notes were very musically detailed, mentioning tempos (including rufalto) and key changes. She is very exact, and it's a wonderful testament to her musicianship. The opening night party was held at Henry's in Cherry Hill. To the press, along with introducing her hairdresser Frank Buscarello, she revealed:

> "Rock-and-roll music is just too much noise. I don't know anything about it, and I don't know how to sing it. . . . [Am I] tired of 'Over The Rainbow?' Listen, it's like getting tired of breathing. The whole premise of the song is a question. A quest. At the end, it isn't 'Well, I've found my world and I am a success and you and I will be together.' The lyric is having little bluebirds 'fly over the rainbow. Why, oh why, can't I?' It represents everyone's wondering why things can't be a little better. . . . Audiences have kept me alive since I was 30 months old. I enjoy them as much as they enjoy being entertained by me. I come alive on a stage. I lose every pain. I don't feel a damn thing but happiness. When I get out there, I'm myself; when I'm off, I sometimes play somebody else. . . . Audiences and I have a private love affair going. Maybe it's that simple."

July 20, 1967: Judy started rehearsals at Nola Studios on West 57th Street in New York City for her next engagement (and mentioned to *The New York Times*, that she had recently watched a print of her *A Star Is Born* at Sid Luft's house! Judy had often run a 16MM print of the 55-minute BBC-TV special of *Judy and Liza at the London Palladium* at her home). (Around this time, Judy's driver was Dominick Piervinanzi, who was then thirty-six, a father of four, who drove Judy when she was in New York City through the end of 1968, and said "she accepted me as a person—not as a chauffeur. . . . She was a good person to me.")

July 29, 1967: Judy was telephoned by Lorna Smith, the president of her London fan club, who called Judy at her New York City hotel, to wish her the best of luck on her impending opening. Judy said she was in the midst of rehearsal, but that she'd have to bring the show over to the Palladium, and her "beloved London."

July 31, 1967 to August 26, 1967: (Concert) The Palace Theater, New York, New York. Judy's third and final legendary engagement at the Palace, this time featuring Lorna and Joe. On opening night, Judy

Judy meets and greets her loyal fans after one of her performances during her final engagement at the Palace, July–August 1967. She usually left through the front of the theater and would make her entrance onstage by walking through the theater to the stage. Judy loved her audiences as much—if not more—than they loved her, and that shows in this photo. (Note the rave reviews and the photos taken at Westbury in the background. Judy's Palace conductor, Bobby Cole, is just behind her right shoulder.) (Courtesy of Photofest.)

gave Lorna flowers with a handwritten card that wished her success and the advice that fear was all right, and to be present, and to "do it!" Judy had also handwritten a list of items she wanted in her dressing room at the Palace: Piano, Bar, television, Radio, food supply for ice box, liquor, small tables, record player, Chandelier, small book and record table, porcelain, hot plate, plumes, false flowers, and crystal. She also wanted the outer room to resemble a tiny, lovely, happy parlor. The reviews were incredible, as you'll see from these excerpts:

> *The New York Post* (Jerry Tallmer): "An aging critic, shuddering happily with tears coursing down his cheeks as talent and the times are once again, beyond belief, reborn. Judy, for the thousand and first time, has come all the way back."
>
> *The Daily News* (Lee Silver): "Right now, Judy is up—way up . . . [the] one thing that came through, despite the audience's roar of cultish adulation, is that she is as great a performer as they think she is. . . . She looked slim, lovely and vibrant. . . . Her voice was richer, stronger and truer than ever. And time, instead of taking its toll, has given an even greater authority to her stage presence, and a more dramatic quality to her vocal control."
>
> *The New York Times* (Vincent Canby): "That magnetic talent is alive once again in New York, and so is one of the most remarkable personalities of the contemporary entertainment scene. . . . Miss Garland was in fine fettle last night . . . most importantly, the shape of the Garland personality—wry and resilient—is intact, whether she is wrestling with a microphone cord that looks like the loch ness monster, or calming an overly exuberant balcony clique, that is behaving like a group of elderly Beatles fans. . . . An evening of spectacular showmanship."
>
> *New York Park East* (Mort Lawrence), August 3: " 'Judy Garland At Home At The Palace' is a dramatic demonstration that genius can conquer everything, that talent will out, and that Judy Garland is still the reigning queen at the Palace."
>
> *UPI Roto Service* (Stephen E. Rubin): "Judy Garland is that rare talent that can turn a normally sedate group into a pack of howling, loving enthusiasts. . . . It's not the kind of shrieking that accompanies the Beatles. The Garland hysteria, and it is hysteria, is based on, among other things, genuine admiration and affection. And when love flows from one side of the footlights back across the other side, it's wonderful. . . . Maybe [the audience] loves her all the more for being the Judy that she is and not the Judy they first loved."
>
> *Boston Herald Traveler* (Ken Mayer), August 31: "Those who witnessed her closing night at New York's Palace Theater will never again see the outpouring of human emotion that greeted Judy's farewell down the aisles as her worshipers reached out to touch their idol. Those who heard the thunder that shook the theatre as she thanked the audience from the stage, will never hear its equal. . . . For this column, or any other for that matter, to capsule Garland within its confines is an insult to a legend. You don't write about Judy Garland, you merely announce her coming. Greatness makes its presence felt; to describe it only dulls its luster."
>
> *Providence, R. I. Journal* (Leroy F. Aarons), September 10: "How can (people) talk about the 'weakness' of Judy Garland? Audiences must see this: their hysterical reaction . . . is a tribute to human endurance—both hers and theirs. The Judy Garland show is *a celebration of survival.*"

Judy signed a recording contract with ABC Records, who recorded her first three nights. The single LP—*Judy Garland: At Home at the Palace—Opening Night*—would be released quickly, on August 15;

it appeared on the charts on September 16, for the first of three weeks, peaking at #174. Only the first side of the album was recorded on the opening night—the second side was drawn from either the second or third nights, as the label recorded the first three nights. The original tapes are not known to still exist—only the final album master does. (Judy's recording contract was through "Group Five," and was care of her attorny, Melvin Altman at 10 East 40th Street in New York City. Judy signed the contract and she wrote her social security as 569-18-8964.) Here is an excerpt from two reviews of the record:

> *Billboard*: "A memorable disk. . . . Miss Garland sparkles . . . a must for all Judy fans."

> *Baltimore Morning Sun* (Bob Stuart): "A recording of the warm humanity and the inimitable gifts of one of America's most exciting musical personalities. It proves 100 million Americans have not been wrong in holding her dear to their hearts."

Judy personally netted a salary of $227,602, of the $303,470 gross of the run. $64,730 was made at the box office the first week; $75,952 the second; $79,861 the third, and $82,927 the closing week. Top ticket price was $9.90. The opening night party was held at El Morocco, where Judy was escorted by John Carlyle. One of Judy's most telling statements, as recorded by *Time* magazine was: "Everything I want is right here." On August 24, two nights before closing, Judy's voice was feeling strained, so she took a cortisone spray, and while it helped her vocal cords, she had an allergic reaction to it, and her face swelled up slightly. Still, she was wonderfully insightful to reporter Leroy F. Aarons of *The Providence R .I. Journal*:

> "We've all settled down and realized that I'm an entertainer. I think that thing about 'Will she come out?' 'Will she appear?' 'Will she be all right?,' is gone. People feel 'well, of course she'll be all right, of course she'll be here.' Because they've seen me around too many years and they finally feel a little more secure. I never have *wanted* to miss *any* show. . . . I usually *did* appear. . . . It took me a while to grow up, too, and live up to the audience . . . the audience has always been much more mature than I. . . . I just feel that I'm so happy to be entertaining and there's no pressure. It's a heck of a great feeling to get up on stage and know that no one is against you in the audience. . . . I don't think the public had any ill feelings. I haven't really had any empty theaters to work in. And I haven't gone on and been told to get off. I've entertained them and they've entertained me and that's about the ball game. The complexities that people have fit me into are the complexities of themselves. . . . I think I've been cruelly used. But the audience didn't take it seriously. The audience always came, even though they were told by people who maybe make a profit from newspapers and magazines, that I was unreliable. The audience never believed that. The audience didn't let me down. They always had belief in me, and I in them."

When asked if she was now a happy person, she answered without hesitation "Completely happy . . . completely happy." When asked what she saw for the Judy Garland of five years in the future: "Even better than today. Just fun. Fun, enjoyment, peace of mind, happiness, and entertainment." To another reporter, Stephen Rubin of *UPI*, she had more to say:

> "I'd like to explain myself a little. So much of the past that has been written about me, has been so completely, just 'authored': Not even correct. . . . I think that the nicest thing to say is that I enjoy my work, that I'm a very happy woman, a very healthy woman, and that I look forward to my shows every night, and am having a marvelous life. I've had press agents that I've paid, to whom I've said 'Why don't they put that in a magazine?' And they've said 'No, they're not interested in that. That's not news. You have to do something terrible.' I don't believe you do. I think it might be awfully smashing news for people to find out that I'm a very contented, healthy, happy woman."

Judy works her magic from the stage of the Palace, during her third and final engagement at the famed venue, July 31–August 26, 1967. (Courtesy of the Everett Collection.)

To Johna Blinn of *The Baltimore Maryland Evening Sun*, Judy shared:

> "My children are my champions. . . . I guess my best role is having children. Being a successful mother is simply liking your children. I never had to read Dr. Spock to know how to make friends with them. Each one is very different, but all three are full of sunshine, and humor, and that's very gratifying. I'm busy looking for a new apartment in New York these days, one with a good kitchen. I've got to get back for the children to start school. Lorna and I take turns in the kitchen. I'm a very good cook. I probably cook *better* than I sing! When both my daughters and I get into the kitchen, it's like one of those Pillsbury bake-off things! Lorna's very good with pastries, and now that Liza's married, she's terrific. She even cooks up whole Christmas dinners. Joey's role is getting in there and stealing chocolate cake and cookies. I didn't really know how to cook until about 12 years ago, although I've always been interested in it. My mother was a hell of a cook, but when we kids came into the kitchen she'd shove us out saying, 'Never mind.' She never seemed to want us to be successful in the kitchen, so I sorta sneaked around and learned a little. I can now cook for 36 people, *and I'm prouder of that than anything else I do!*"

For her voice, Judy said:

> "I can't eat certain foods at all. And I can't eat at least three hours before show time, or for several hours afterwards. And I don't dare get too tired or too angry or excited. *It's like being in training!* If your equipment gets out of whack, you're out of luck. But what's really important is to drink liquids only at room temperature before and during performances. Hot liquids cause swelling in the throat. Only drink tepid water or wine. Tea with honey is terrible for singers. They finally found that out a few years ago, confirming the facts in the medical journals that hot drinks only multiply problems for singers."

Judy also shared her recipe for Shepherd's Pie: "It's beautiful. It comes out looking like a birthday cake, all fluffy and delicious." Judy also taped a lengthy interview backstage in her dressing room with Martin Block of the National Guard Radio Network, which was aired over a few different installments. The surviving recordings prove Judy sounded truly as happy and together as the above press interviews presented. Judy laughed, talked about everything from meeting John Dillinger just before he was shot, to the stage being her preferred medium to work in. The next-to-last night at the Palace had Liza coming on stage, to chat, then she danced, while Judy sang "Chicago." The next night, closing night, Liza came up on stage to sing "Cabaret" accompanied by Peter Allen, and again danced to Judy's singing "Chicago." In the audience for this last performance at the theater that had established Judy as the premiere concert artist 16 years earlier, were two of Judy's biggest musical influences: her favorite composer, Harold Arlen, who of course had composed "Rainbow" and "The Man That Got Away"; and her MGM mentor, Roger Edens, who had perhaps a bigger influence on her style than anyone else. Judy's deal for the Palace engagement gave her 75% of the gross, but this huge amount of $227,602 from 27 consecutive evenings of devastating work, was in vain from a financial stance: Judy's net was seized by federal tax agents on closing night, due to back taxes she owed. Another judgment she was facing was a Federal Court attachment of almost $98,000 from Bernard Glassman's suit for selling the rights to the television series to his Pathe Pictures when the complete clearances for most of the shows hadn't been taken care of at that point. (An audiotape recorded from the audience during closing night, still exists, showing Judy in wonderful form, and good voice. There are also many moments of silent, color, home movie footage shot from the audience during this engagement.)

Also at this time, Group Five rented a brownstone on 8 East 63rd Street, a few doors off 5th Avenue, around the corner from Central Park, where she stayed through early 1968. It belonged to a Dr. Murray

Banks, and from all reports was uniquely decorated. One example of this would be the antique lamps on either side of Judy's bed: the lamps had been made from military helmets which had long red horsehair flowing down from the top, to the base of the lamp. Judy one day gave "the hairy, beastie *dust collectors*" haircuts!

August 29, 1967: Tom Green announced that Judy had called-off their engagement. They had apparently separated shortly after her opening at the Palace. In a long and often moving piece, Tom still gallantly proclaimed: "Judy Garland is probably the finest, kindest, most morally responsible person I have ever met. Her only outstanding fault to my knowledge has been listening to the wrong people and taking their advice, which has often resulted in great personal loneliness and unhappiness."

August 30, 1967: Judy arrived in Boston this evening, taking the Merchant's Limited train from New York with Lorna and Joe, and going right to a press conference for her next appearance, during which she stated: "It's wonderful how different my three kids are. Liza and Joey are the most like me—outgoing, affectionate, want to be liked. But Lorna! I call her the 'cruise director.' Mind like a whip, a born comedian and independent! Liza and Joey go to people, instinctively. Lorna sits and lets people come to her. And they do!"

August 31, 1967: (Concert) The Boston Commons; Boston, Mass. Judy played to her largest single concert audience: 108,000. The now famous concert producer/promoter Ron Delsner produced this concert. He had a special 24-foot runway made for Judy. There was a 26-piece orchestra, and a jazz trio, accompanying Judy. Near the end of the concert, the mayor of Boston reached up to Judy and handed her a silver bowl in honor of the occasion, saying "Judy, we've taken you into our hearts; I think that is the sentiment of all of us. God bless you." Here are excerpts from two reviews:

> *Boston Morning Globe* (Ernie Santosuosso), September 1: "It was as if her voice had come out of the long years past. It was as biting crisp as burnished brass. At times it was a quasi-echo of Dorothy, from *The Wizard of Oz*. Her pipes [were] as awesome as those in the Mormon Tabernacle. . . . The Garland voice is a powerfully dramatic instrument."
>
> *Boston Evening Globe* (Gloria Negri), September 1: "*Earth Mother. Soul Sister. Living Legend. Judy Garland is all these things to people.*"

(Color footage, synched-with-sound, exists of this concert, and was used on *The Concert Years* PBS special in 1985; a shorter clip is found on the abridged version of this show, available on videocassette on the LaserLight label. An audio recording made in the audience also still exists.)

September 1, 1967: (Personal Appearance) VA Hospital, Boston, Mass. Judy personally visited about 80 veterans. She sang a few verses of "Over The Rainbow" to them, and then did a brief concert in the motion picture room of the hospital, during which about 50 people were present, as she sang "Just In Time," dueted with her conductor Bobby Cole on "Bye, Bye Blackbird," and concluded with "Over The Rainbow."

September 4, 1967, Labor Day: Judy visited Paragon Park—an amusement park in Nantasket Beach, near Boston; she went with son Joe, and two assistants, Vern Alves, Pamela Perry, and also her hairdresser, Frank Buscarello—who had been with her throughout her tour. Judy ate cotton candy, hot dogs, and rode everything in the park, including dozens of rides on the roller coaster; her group also won many stuffed animal trophies, which filled the trunk of their limousine; photos exist of Judy and Joe in the park. Afterwards, they had dinner at the Galant Fox, then went to the Blue Bunny nightclub where Joe was hypnotized by Sam Vine and made to tap dance.

September 5, 1967: Judy returned to New York for a couple days rest before continuing her tour, and gave an interview to Glenna Syse of *The Chicago Sun Times*:

> "Adoring audiences like I do, to have them give back that sort of affection, suddenly I feel it's absolutely marvelous to be Judy Garland. I'm so proud to give people even just a moment of fun, to take their minds off their worries. Frightened? I used to be frightened on stage until I finally realized the only time I have an enormous amount of fun is when I'm on the stage. . . . All I know is whether I sing to 8 people, or 108,000, I do sing to each person. I believe what I'm singing, and we have an electric current going back and forth. They call out lovely things like 'We love you, Judy!' They wrap me up in cotton batting. They don't want anything to happen to me. They want me to know they love me and I want them to know I love them. Everything changed about 12 weeks ago. If you ask me why, it's because I got a job. I went back to work. They had missed hearing me and I had missed them, too. My career has had its ups and downs like a roller coaster. And I am hoping . . . I am hoping . . . it will stay on top."

September 7, 1967: Judy, Lorna, Joe, and Sid arrived in Maryland, with their luggage lost, and late, arriving for her 8:30 p.m. press conference at 9:15, held at the Madison Hotel, to promote her next engagement. Judy seemed interested in the idea of doing a play or movie about Edith Piaf, and spoke about writing her autobiography: "I must do it, they tell me. Someday I will. I don't know where to start. I have taped some things, and made notes, but when I hear them and look at them I get embarrassed." After the conference, Judy and Sid drove out to "see where I'm going to work." For a phone interview done at this time for an upcoming engagement, the Chicago News on September 9 reported Judy said: "I finally got wise to myself and realized that it's a wonderful thing to have the approval of so many people. I'm not frightened anymore; I can't wait to get on the stage, and everyone feels that. I've never been more satisfied in my life. On the stage is where I'm happiest, and now I can relax."

September 8, 1967 and September 9, 1967: (Concert) The Merriweather Post Pavilion; Columbia, Maryland. Judy played to capacity audiences in this 3,000-seat theater. *Variety* stated she grossed $45,000 for the two nights. Judy said at one point to the audience: "You know I wouldn't leave you. I'd die first, and I'm not going to die. When my number's up, I want a new one."

September 10, 1967: (Personal Appearance) Bethesda Naval Hospital; Bethesda, Maryland.

September 11, 1967: Judy returned to New York for a couple of days rest before the next stop on her tour.

September 12, 1967: Judy canceled her plans to take the 20th Century Train to Chicago for her next appearance, and decided to fly from New York.

September 13, 1967: Judy arrived in Chicago, checking into the Ambassador West hotel about midnight on this morning. Judy appeared at the 11:30 a.m. press conference an hour late, while her "theatrical press agent," Bill Doll, kept the reporters together. (Apparently Doll had taken Tom Green's place on the "Group Five" payroll.) Sid Luft announced during the wait that Judy "had made a television commitment for the New Year, and would (also) appear in concert with the Washington Symphony Orchestra with Arthur Fiedler conducting." Unfortunately, these two projects never did materialize. During the reception, Judy said: "I think there's really a certain time in your life when it's too much of a hassle to have fears. You mature. You say, 'What good is fear going to do me?' Now life seems to be sort of a steady upgrade. I'm enjoying it. I think my children have helped a great deal."

September 14, 1967 to September 16, 1967: (Concert) The Civic Opera House, Chicago. Judy's songs on September 15 included: "I Feel A Song Coming On"; "Almost Like Being In Love"/"This Can't Be

Love"; "Just In Time"; "How Insensitive"; "Judy's Olio Medley"; "What Now My Love?"; "Me And My Shadow"; "Bob White"; "Jamboree Jones" (both with Lorna); "Together" (with Lorna and Joe); "Old Man River"; "That's Entertainment"; "I Loved Him"; "Rock-A-Bye Your Baby"; "Chicago"; "Swanee"; and "Over The Rainbow." On September 16, she substituted "The Last Dance" with Bobby Cole instead of "I Loved Him"; "Bye, Bye Blackbird" with the kids *and* Sid, instead of "Together"; and added "San Francisco" after "Rainbow." Here is an excerpt from a review:

> *Chicago News* (Michaela Williams), September 15: "Judy Garland keeps being reincarnated, but somehow manages to come back every time as herself. . . . So, Judy, carry on. Give the lie to mortality. *If anybody can live forever, it's going to be you.*"

(Existing audiotapes made in the audience reveal Judy in fine form.) Judy was backed by a 25-piece orchestra, conducted by Bobby Cole. Tickets in Chicago went to an amazing $12.50 top price.

September 17, 1967: (Personal Appearance) The Great Lakes Naval Training Hospital; Chicago.

While in Chicago, Judy filmed an interview for Irving Kupcinet's local television show: a ten-minute excerpt, on color film, still exists today. Among the things Judy talked about was that she enjoyed "any phase of entertainment work. I prefer the stage." When asked about a recent *Time* magazine article that wrote about her audience consisting of homosexuals, Judy said "That's just ridiculous: I have little children who come to see me from seeing *The Wizard of Oz*, then people my age . . . for years I've been mistreated, but I'll be damned if I'll have my audience treated badly."

September 19, 1967: (Concert) The Public Auditorium; Cleveland. Also on this date, a 10-minute interview with Judy appeared on *The Dorothy Fuldhelm Show* on Cincinnati television. It is not known to still exist.

September 27, 1967: (Concert) The Kiel Auditorium; St. Louis. A review that brilliantly identifies a part of Judy's magic and appeal was in the *St. Louis Globe-Democrat* (John Brod Peters), October 10:

> "Judy Garland's secret is that she knows how to provoke and foster involvement. . . . She tears herself open—she's basically a sweet waif wanting love. . . . She says what others dare not say for fear of embarrassment, for fear of being hurt: 'I Love You. I want you to like me, to love me. I need your love.' The pleading of this button-eyed waif of a celebrity—pleading to you and me—is utterly irresistible and she's saying openly and boldly what the rest of us all our lives only say indirectly—when we say it at all. . . . The experience of a Judy Garland performance may not turn everyone into a true believer, but it cannot fail to leave one utterly moved."

September 29, 1967: (Concert) Cobo Hall; Detroit.

> *Detroit Free Press* (Shirley Eder), October 2: "Judy, do you realize how much love there is for you in this world? Bask in it, bake in it, and blossom in it, and please be happy in it!"

After the concert, there was a small party in Judy's suite at the Pontchartrain hotel. One of the guests was Jimmy Nederlander, who managed the Palace Theater in New York, and many other theaters. Judy asked him if she could come back to the Palace next year, and he said she could come back anytime she wanted to, and was "welcome to play any and every Nederlander theater in the country—and there are plenty!" Judy joked that when she saw "the size of that Cobo Arena, I felt I should have made my entrance dribbling a basketball." Judy had also mentioned her move around the time of the Palace engagement, from the St. Moritz Hotel to the rented townhouse on East 63rd Street: "I love the service in hotels, but who can afford to live like that with a family these days?" (Shirley Eder reported in the *Detroit Free Press* of October 2, that "Judy and her older daughter, Liza, have become very close again, after a slight rift for a while.")

October 1, 1967 and October 2, 1967: (Concert) Clowes Hall; Indianapolis.

> *Star*, October 2: "Now she has new depth of feeling and variety of tone color that give her a more dramatic quality to supplement her wonderful exuberance. She has a voice like an organ. . . . When she cuts loose with a crescendo, it makes people want to stand up and cheer."

Variety reported Judy grossed $33,940 against a possible $36,000, with attendance at a total of 4,050, out of a potential 4,400. Ticket prices were at a $10 top, which was Judy's standard top ticket price, a very high price for that era. By early 1968, her top price would sometimes hit $15!

October 7, 1967: (Concert) Veterans Memorial Auditorium, Columbus, Ohio. Judy had arrived at Union Terminal at 8:30 a.m. that morning, admitting as she went into the press conference, that she hadn't slept well on the train, and this can be heard in the discs that were recorded, made from tapes in the audience, that have recently surfaced. Judy is in fairly strong form, but only fair voice.

October 8, 1967: Judy returned to New York.

Around this time Judy hand wrote notes to remind her to talk with Sid about upcoming appearances and her finances, etc., including her upcoming concert at Seton Hall, in New Jersey.

Another Judy note is on a paper pad that is preprinted with the words: "*Murmil Associates, Inc., Eight East Sixty-Third Street, N.Y. 10021.*" This was the address of the townhouse Judy was renting from Dr. Banks, who could have been "Murmil Associates, Inc." On this pad, Judy again wrote to ask Sid about Seton Hall, and also about when her first night was at Madison Square Garden. She also wanted to know about what she had earned so far, and asked about "Difallco."

On another sheet (no preprinted header) Judy hand wrote song titles she wanted to sing:

Last Dance

At Last (our love has come along)

Last Night When We Were Young

Through The Years

she concluded by mentioning that she should make a request of Harold Arlen (but she doesn't say what she wanted from the man who wrote "Rainbow.")

October 11, 1967: Judy took a flight to London, for a brief vacation, but as soon as she arrived, she turned around and came right back to New York, due to a disagreement with the wife of Raymond Filiberti, the owner of the production company she was working for, "Group Five." The round trip took 19 hours, 15 of them spent in the air. She arrived back in New York's Kennedy airport, at 2:45 p.m. on October 11. Judy told the waiting press "I'll see him, he's my boss. But I'll be darned if I'll see her. She's about nine feet tall, and I wouldn't dare."

October 16, 1967: (Personal Appearance) Judy sang at a party after an ASCAP salute thrown by *Cue* magazine, at Lincoln Center's Philharmonic Hall. The October 18 edition of *Variety* reported that Judy gave an "an informal, sentimental song session. . . . She was among friends and she sang their songs with ease and fine effect." Judy also sang "Over The Rainbow" *with* its composer, Harold Arlen. Walter Winchell ran a lovely bit on this night, in his column on October 22. (See photo below.)

Judy may have traveled to California for a brief trip, on October 17, or so, as press coverage of her arrival at the next concert stop, stated that she had been late "en route from California."

October 20, 1967 and October 21, 1967: (Concert) Bushnell Auditorium; Hartford, CT. Judy arrived late from California—according to press from Hartford papers—checking into the Hartford Hilton at 2:30 a.m., the morning of her first concert, October 20. There had been a press conference sched-

Judy in bliss, singing. With her conductor Bobby Cole at a party after an ASCAP salute in New York, October 16, 1967. Note the suitcase just behind her: shades of her 1962 joke about her 1961 tour: "I'd hit the theater and sing, then get out. . . . before they caught us!" Judy apparently left for a brief trip to California just after this appearance. (Courtesy of the Everett Collection.)

uled for Thursday evening, October 19, which she, Sid, and the children missed. One reporter who waited for them was Allen M. Widem of the *Hartford Times*, who got a few scoops—that there was "constant talk of a television series, but at the moment nothing offered seems to smack of the Judy Garland individualistic approach. She's still open to suggestions, however." This might explain the sudden and quick trip to California: for business meetings about doing yet *another* television series, which seems incredible considering the ratings failure of the one she did, and the fact that she was blacklisted from all primetime television variety series work, after the April 1, 1966 "Hollywood Palace" debacle. However, the Palace Theater engagement and tour had established yet another "comeback" for Judy, so it's possible that there were some offers; it could just as easily have been talk for benefit of the press. At this time, Judy also said she'd "love" to do the movie version of the Broadway musical *Mame*, saying she didn't believe anyone was signed yet, "and the field's still wide open. The role's the kind that contains a tremendous excitement to me as a performer." The morning of the first show, October 20, found Judy starting a six-hour rehearsal with Bobby Cole and the 26-piece orchestra at 11 a.m., only 8½ hours after her arrival—keep in mind that Judy didn't fall asleep usually till seven or eight in the morning.

November 3, 1967 and November 4, 1967: (Concert) Seton Hall; South Orange, New Jersey. (Audiotapes recorded in the audience still exist from November 3.)

November 11, 1967: (Personal Appearance) Judy sang at the TaySachs dinner honoring Tony Bennett as "Man Of The Year," held at the Waldorf in New York. Earl Wilson's column of November 13 stated she sang "with him, and to him."

November 15, 1967: (Personal Appearance) Judy sang informally at a party following a Lincoln Center ASCAP tribute in New York.

November 21, 1967: Lorna's 15th birthday was celebrated at Trader Vic's in New York.

November 30, 1967 to December 16, 1967: (Concert) Caesar's Palace; Las Vegas. (The December 4 performance was canceled due to death of Bert Lahr.) Judy did one show a night only, at a special time: midnight. A reminder that in the fall of 1962, she had played the Sahara in Vegas at 2:30 a.m. Judy could draw an audience anytime, proved by the fact that there was often an over-flow of 200 people that would stay outside the Circus Maximus room where Judy was playing, to at least *hear* the show. Judy's humor was of course evident: When a squeal came from the sound system, Judy said "and that may be the best note you hear all night!" There was apparently at least one evening where Judy was in such great form, that she did a two-and-a-half hour concert, featuring some songs seldom sung in her concerts, including "Joey, Joey." Judy's show consisted of: "I Feel A Song Coming On"; "Almost Like Being In Love"/"This Can't Be Love"; "Just In Time"; "How Insensitive"; "By Myself"; "Old Man River"; "That's Entertainment"; "What Now My Love?"; "For Once In My Life"—her first time singing this song, which would stay a part of all her subsequent concerts—"Rock-A-Bye Your Baby"; "Swanee"; and "Over The Rainbow." Perhaps one of the reasons for Judy's extra exuberance came from her reunion with Tom Green, reported in Harrison Carroll's column of December 13. Tom had flown out to Vegas from Boston, arriving on December 1, the day after Judy's opening. (Audiotapes were recorded through the sound system on at least two nights, and they still exist.)

December 21, 1967: The television premiere of Judy's *I Could Go On Singing* movie, on "The CBS Thursday Night Movies."

December 22, 1967: Evening rehearsal for Judy's next engagement:

December 25, 1967 to December 31, 1967: (Concert) The New Felt Forum, Madison Square Garden, New York. On opening night, Judy brought Tony Bennett on stage, who sang a Christmas song. (Mort Lindsey conducted the orchestra. Color, silent film footage, and an audiotape from opening night—revealing Judy in only fair voice, but reasonably strong form, both made in the audience by fans—still exist.) Judy only played Christmas through December 27; on December 28 she canceled the remaining shows due to laryngitis. This engagement grossed $75,000 in the first three shows, and would have grossed another $75,000 for the three canceled shows.

There exists many handwritten notes Judy made throughout 1967 and beyond, as reminders to herself. One of the most haunting, and one that shows that Judy was more aware and intelligent than people give her credit for, is one written on Capel, Macdonald & Co, Cappel Building's in Dayton, Ohio, "Executive Reminder of THINGS TO DO" pad; Judy made a list of the people who could "control" her medication. She lists the amount that she should take each day as sixteen of the green capsules and four Seconal pills at night. Dr. Lester Coleman was listed as "controller," but the people on this list could take his place when he was not available, which proves that Judy knew she needed to be careful with her medication. The list of names included Sid Luft, Ray Filiberti (the head of "Group 5"), Mel Altonen, Tom Green, Nick Potter, Lorna Luft, Gene Palumbo (Judy's conductor), Barry Leighton, Delores Cole (wife of Judy's other 1967 conductor, Bobby Cole), and Vern Alves (Sid's longtime assistant, dating back to the 1950s).

Other notes from this time show that Judy was also keeping an eye on the business side of her work. Judy lamented the fact that she was not one of the heads of "Group 5," but that she would be. She also wanted to see all contracts for her concerts before they were signed, and wanted monthly meetings with her current financial advisor, Israel Katz, so she would know what was going on with her money.

On yet another note, Judy recapped how "Group 5" came to be: it was first talked about in July 1966, then became reality in May 1967. She also noted that Filiberti loaned Luft $10,000, and that she owed nearly $20,000 to him, but she wasn't certain, since that sentence had several question marks next to it. Judy also again lamented the fact that contracts and checks were being signed without her knowledge.

* * * * *

For a forty-five-year-old "unreliable," Judy Garland had achieved some incredible feats in 1967—even for her. The return to the concert stage in her first lengthy tour since 1961, saw a staggering eighty concerts performed—with only four shows being canceled—in a tour that grossed nearly a million dollars, as well as winning her superior reviews, a Billboard-charting album, and a new generation of fans. On the downside, Judy had lost the last home she would ever own, and was signed to a contract with certain "questionable" business associates, which would create a multitude of problems in the coming year, 1968.

1968

January 5, 1968: Judy called Tony Bennett in terror, as she thought Sid had sent someone to hurt her or Lorna and Joe (even though she knew Sid had gone to California, and Ray Filiberti had stopped by Judy's apartment that day to say he was going out of town for a while on business.) Tony in turn called Frank Sinatra, and Jilly in Florida, who, in minutes, had four detectives and two policemen at Judy's apartment. Judy later wrote that Tony and Frank had been calling her each day and each evening (as had Jilly also, apparently.) Judy was touched that they "have offered—on their own—to love and protect my children and myself from the agony of the fear that is all around us."

January 1968: Judy met with the producers and director—and Jerry Herman—of the Broadway Musical smash *Mame*, about replacing Angela Lansbury, who was leaving the show in the spring. Herman later reported that Judy sang the entire score, and that while the "money men" agreed she would have first call at the film version, they thought she was too "unreliable" to be able to do the show.

January 1968: Depressed over not getting *Mame*, Judy went to see Liza's engagement in a New York Hotel/Nightclub, and got up to bow, and proceeded to steal the show when Liza invited her up on-stage, with the crowd screaming for Judy to sing, again, and again (which, she did, of course).

Late January 1968: Judy and the kids left the East 63rd townhouse of Dr. Murray Banks, as Judy was "bored" with it and checked into the Hotel Stanhope, then the St. Moritz.

Judy and Tom Green did not marry in August 1967: they split that month, and reconciled early December 1967, soon announcing they would marry in May 1968.

Another note on the "*Things To Do*" pad from around this same time had Judy inquiring about her upcoming concert in Baltimore with Tony Bennett. She was apparently thinking of not working for "Group Five" any longer, and wondered how this would work with the deal she had made with the IRS to pay her back taxes, that had been arranged by Israel Katz and Jerry London. Judy also questioned whether it was all right to use two different attorneys for two different cases.

February 18, 1968: (Concert) The Civic Center; Baltimore, MD. Judy was suffering from food poisoning, and the concert—a shared bill with Tony Bennett—was not completed; an audiotape recorded through the sound system proves that Judy was in horrific shape; it's amazing she was allowed to go on. This had one of the highest ticket prices to see Judy: from $5, up to an unheard of $15 top! The show grossed $27,093.85—9,990 people had to sadly see Judy when she was perhaps at her all-time worst on stage.

February 25, 1968: (Concert) Philharmonic Hall, Lincoln Center; New York, New York. Judy was in good form only a week after the disastrous Baltimore engagement. (Audiotape recorded in the audience, still exists, in private collections.)

March 18, 1968: Judy slipped in her tub at the St. Moritz, injured her left shoulder and collarbone and was hospitalized, and prescribed Demerol for the pain. Since there was no money to pay the hospital bill, Tom Green took both the diamond and jade ring she had bought in Hong Kong, and a diamond and cultured pearl ring she also owned, and pawned them for $1,000 at the Provident Loan Society, at Park Avenue and 25th Street. Judy was admitted to St. Claire's Hospital at 415 West 51st Street at 3:30 p.m. Her doctor was Bernard Mintz, and even with her AFTRA Insurance, a $100.00 deposit was requested, which Sid Luft was to bring in.

March 30, 1968: Joey's thirteenth birthday was celebrated at the Tin Lizzie restaurant in New York City. A color snapshot exists of Judy with Tom Green at the party.

April 3, 1968: Judy filed a report with the West 54th Street police station—near the St. Moritz—and said two rings vanished March 19. She said they were last seen on St. Patrick's Day, March 17, and on

March 18 she had spent one day at St. Claire's Hospital for "a day of rest," and when she returned on March 19, she noticed they were gone. Judy had obviously forgotten that Tom had pawned them so her hospital and hotel bills could be paid, per her instructions.

April 4, 1968: Judy actually called the FBI about Tom Green, accusing him of stealing her rings. The FBI File Number is 87-99683.

April 5, at 6 a.m., Tom Green wrote a long, moving letter to Sid Luft, in which he explained about Judy calling the FBI. The letter touches on a multitude of topics. Tom mentioned recently completing the books for the period ending March 31, and found that he had spent a total of $48,756.74 to that date, on Judy. He mentioned pawning $3,000 worth of his family's jewelry in order to get a $350 loan for food for her and the kids the last spring. Green concluded by stating

> "I always only wanted to help her . . . because goddam it, in spite of her whatever the hell nonsense it is, I do love her very much."

April 6, 1968: (Benefit) The Plaza Hotel; New York, New York. Clad in her white pantsuit (and shoeless), Judy sang five songs: "I Feel A Song Coming On"; "How Insensitive"; "Just In Time"; "What Now, My Love?" and "For Once In My Life." Then Judy sang "Over The Rainbow" sitting in the middle of the ballroom, surrounded by about 50 people.

Approximately April 8, 1968: Judy had Tom Green arrested for stealing her two rings, which were valued at $110,000.

April 11, 1968: Judy appeared in night court to press the charges against Tom Green. A photo of Judy talking with detectives appears in Christopher Finch's 1975 book *Rainbow*. The charges would later be dropped against Green, and they would resume their friendship. (A cover for a note pad exists from this time period, a Cappel MacDonald and Company—"Creators of Merchandise Prize Incentive Campaigns Sales Promotion Plans . . . Plans"—"Business Improves where incentives are used" pad of "*Executive Reminder of Things to Do.*" On this Judy wrote that she planned to have Green incarcerated, and he *was* jailed briefly as a result of Judy's charges.) Judy and Green continued to socialize, and were photographed when they attended the opening of a new restaurant together, mid April to mid May 1968.

Early May 1968, 2 a.m. New York City time, (11 p.m. Los Angeles time); Just after Easter 1968 : Another phone conversation that Wayne Martin taped between himself and Judy—with Lorna coming on the line at one point—reveals that Judy was in terrible shape financially, and could "use a buck." Reaching her at the St. Moritz Hotel, Martin spoke of putting together some ideas for a photo book using his famed *Garlandia* collection, with Judy writing the captions, although nothing further would come of the project. Apparently an earlier book project had recently been considered at the EP Dutton publishing house. Just how bad Judy's finances were became quite clear only a couple of weeks later.

May 16, 1968: After spending the day with Mickey Dean's roommate, Charlie Cochran, at their apartment in the East 80s in Manhattan, Judy and Charlie went back to the St. Moritz Hotel to find Judy locked out of her two-room suite, as she owed them $1,800 (reportedly just for one week, which seems incredibly high for that time, and is probably not correct.) Judy was under the correct impression that "Group Five" were to be paying her hotel bill, which they obviously had not done, although Sid later told a reporter that he had personally been paying her bill until the previous week, and had

"I think I'll miss you most of all": Judy poses with Ray Bolger following his opening at the Empire Room of the Plaza Hotel, New York, in spring 1968. This would be the last time "Dorothy" and the "Scarecrow" would cross paths, although she would work briefly with the "Wicked Witch," Margaret Hamilton, on December 23, 1968. (Courtesy of Photofest.)

even left spending money for her at the hotel. The next week or so Judy stayed at Cochran's apartment, while, somehow something was done about the bill, although some of Judy's possessions remained confiscated. (This incident was reported in Earl Wilson's column of May 18, 1968.) Also on May 16, 1968, Judy and "Group Five" reportedly filed a suit in New York State's Supreme Court against Madison Square Garden, in the amount of $251,500, for failure to provide Judy with a microphone and proper lighting. As a result, she was "rendered sick, lame, and disabled, and compelled to seek medical assistance."

May 17, 1968: Luft and Filiberti, who were really "Group 5," sold Judy's contract—as security, in exchange for a loan of $18,750—to two businessmen, Leon Greenspan and Howard Harper; The latter's real name was Harker, and he, like Filiberti, had a police record, a long one, and had been found guilty by the state of New Jersey, on various dates, of disorderly conduct and of strong-armed threats. For the payment of one dollar, Greenspan and Harper got the exclusive use of Judy's services for the next year, along with both the screenplay of the still unmade *Born in Wedlock* from 1956, *and* "certain coal deposits located in the countries of Grundy, Sequatchie, Bledsoe, and Cumberland in the State of Tennessee." The $18,750 loan to Luft and Filiberti had to be repaid within 90 days, which was August 17, 1968. The final and official signing-over of her contract was not completed until October 28, 1968, when Harper, and Greenspan—Greenspan had acted as his own Notary Public on the Assignment agreement—filed a Summons and Complaint against Group Five and Raymond Filiberti, in the Supreme Court of Westchester County. A copy of the May 17, 1968, assignment still exists, minus the signatures, and was reprinted in Anne Edwards's 1975 biography, *Judy Garland*.

May 23, 1968: (Personal Appearance) After arriving in Boston and checking into a suite at the Sheraton Plaza, Judy went that afternoon with Lorna and Joe to visit the crippled and paraplegic at the Chelsea Naval Hospital.

May 24, 1968: (Concert) The Back Bay Theater; Boston, Massachusetts. Judy was in strong spirits, and fairly good voice, for this nonstop two-hour plus performance (an audiotape recorded from the audience, still exists, in private collections). Tickets for this concert had just gone on sale April 29, 1968 and were priced from $4 to a $7 top. This was a 5,000 seat converted movie house, and Judy was the last artist to play there.

May 25, 1968: Judy, at 7 p.m. that evening, canceled her scheduled second night at the Back Bay Theater. She said she was fine, just that she had nothing left to give that night, having drained herself over the last two days.

Later on her pad with the preprinted header "*Executive Reminder of Things to Do*," Judy wrote that she was stopped from appearing by the managers of the theater and Sid.

Another note on the "*Things to Do*" pad from around this same time again shows Judy's concern with the handling of her finances, that she wanted cash given to her in an easier way then what was currently being done, and that she would take care of her own medication.

On another note, Judy wrote a reminder that she had to record again, and often! She also lamented the fact that she had been told she would definitely star in *Mame*, and that from this point on, nothing could be planned for her without her being present at the time. She concluded the note by saying Sid had finally told her he was the head of "Group Five."

On another note, Judy stated that she had to wait for some cash that was being wired that day for the kids and herself, and that she hoped to have a meeting with an attorney that day.

On the last note from this period, Judy talked about the lawsuit from Bernard Glassman that had placed a lien on her income from the Madison Square Garden engagement of Christmas week 1967 and that she was insisting on the return of the tapes of her television series.

Early June 1968: Sid Luft signed Wesley M. Fuller, Professor of Music at Clark University in Boston, to be Judy's "Sole Artistic Advisor," at $350.00 a month. Fuller, whom Gerald Frank called "a quiet, divorced man in his 30s, with a small daughter," in his 1975 biography, *Judy*, met Judy when he sent her a note after the canceled Boston show, saying he "could understand how an artist could find it impossible to appear." Judy and Fuller were supposedly involved romantically for a brief period, as Judy spoke about being "Mrs. Wesley Fuller," according to Gerald Frank. Judy stayed in Boston through mid June 1968.

June 8, 1968: Group Five exercised their first of "one-year options," extending Judy's contract with them, for an additional year. (On June 10, 1968, Judy turned forty-six.)

June 15, 1968: Judy attended the opening of the Garden State Arts Center in Holmdel, New Jersey. She would be the first artist to play the semi-outdoor theater, starting on June 25.

June 24, 1968: (Television) *The Tonight Show*, NBC-TV, videotaped at NBC's studios in Rockefeller Center, New York City. Judy was interviewed by Johnny Carson, but did not sing. She was quite funny, seemed in good spirits, and looked lovely (the color videotape still exists) and plugged her next engagement, which opened the following night:

June 25, 1968 to June 29, 1968: (Concert) The Garden State Arts Center; Holmdel, New Jersey. Judy was the first artist to play this new $10 million dollar indoor/outdoor theater. On the afternoon of the opening, she had someone hastily write an arrangement of Barbra Striesand's "Free Again": She sang it once that afternoon, then said "I'll never sing it as good as she does," and never sang it again! Opening night, Judy was in fine shape, and gave a strong performance, verified by this excerpt of a review:

> *The Evening News* (Johnathan Kwinty): "Judy still has it . . . those who came cheered, clapped, rushed the stage, filled the aisles, tossed presents, and confetti to her, reached out a hundred hands along the stage apron to touch hers and generally behaved as an audience will for Judy Garland and perhaps no one else. . . . Miss Garland stayed on stage an hour and 35 minutes and sang 19 songs. Her voice has lost nothing with the years. She still can control that slowly pulsating vibrato so breathtakingly she well be suspending the rhythm of waves breaking against the shore. . . . She still can sing the words to those trite old songs as if any one of them could break her heart, and she can make an audience believe it. . . . She is a master of every pose and piece of stage business. She sits by the piano, she sits on the stage, she struts across the apron, and with each new movement she brings down the house. Each is a test of the audience's adoration, and they never fail her. She is like a poker player who calls all the bets, and always has the cards. People constantly call out from the audience things like 'you still look good;' 'you're great Judy;' dozens of song requests; and 'we love you Judy!' She is always ready to receive it with a comic retort or mime. She can do it all, and keep singing! . . . She can blast out songs like 'What Now, My Love?' and 'Rock-A-Bye,' without ever leaving the same vocal register that can torch 'The Man That Got Away.'"

After the concert, she sent author Gerald Frank, with whom she had been working on yet another attempt at an autobiography, running from her dressing room with: "You not only *wrote The Boston Strangler*, you *are* 'The Boston Strangler!'" The next day, Wednesday, June 26, she gave an "up" interview to *The Asbury Park Press*, at her hotel, the Berkeley Carteret:

Asbury Park Press: How do you like singing outdoors?

Judy Garland: I don't mind it, but I don't like it in the summer. The bugs, you know. They fly into my mouth.

APP: What do you do in that case?

JG: You park the bug like this. [She tucks her tongue into one cheek.]

APP: How's your autobiography coming?

JG: It's been quite a packed-in life. It will take years.

APP: Would you choose show business if you had your life to live over again?

JG: No! It's a brutish business.

APP: Why do you attract a cult-like following?

JG: Maybe I'm some kind of female Billy Graham.

APP: Are you going swimming here?

JG: I'm afraid of water. I'm also afraid of flying.

APP: How do you get around?

JG: Dogsled!

APP: Who are your favorite singers?

JG: Tony Bennet, Peggy Lee, and Liza Minnelli!

APP: Your favorite food?

JG: Chicken, any way but fried, and Ice Cream Cones. They never let me eat them at MGM.

Judy also mentioned a "possible" return to the Palace that fall 1968, but she never played there again. Later that day, on June 26, she insisted that Sid Luft pay her daily salary of $1,200 (after taxes) for each performance, by 4 p.m., before every show: An agreement on this day, written by Sid Luft on hotel stationary—reprinted in the 1975 Anne Edwards book—states that her salary would be paid to her by John Larson of the Garden State Art Center, if "Mr. Luft is not available." Judy's salary was to be paid to Wes Fuller, her musical advisor, and current romantic interest, or to Gene Palumbo, Judy's conductor, if Fuller was not available; or, then, as a final option, directly to "Miss Garland." For the concerts of June 26 and June 27, Judy was ill and in poor voice; on June 28, her performance was powerful. On closing night, June 29, she was 35 minutes late in taking the stage; after 25 minutes, during her third song, at 10:50 p.m., Judy fell asleep on stage, and had to be helped from the stage, and taken away by ambulance to the nearby Monmonth Medical Center. Judy was carried off the stage on a stretcher, in full-view of the audience, still clutching the microphone! She then, apparently, went from the Monmonth Medical Center, to New York, where a Dr. Udall Salmon placed her in the LeRoy Hospital.

Early to mid July 1968: Judy went through a withdrawal program at the Peter Brent Brigham Hospital in Boston. By the time of her next engagement, Judy would be medication-free, and in incredible shape.

July 16, 1968: Judy went to Philadelphia, Pennsylvania for her next engagement, checking into the Warwick Hotel with daughter Lorna. Judy gave several press interviews in her hotel suite, and photos show her with Lorna, looking at a copy of Liza's newest album, *Liza Minnelli*. Judy also again mentioned "possibly" playing the Palace that fall, although it did not happen.

July 19, 1968: Judy rehearsed at the venue of her next concert, singing four songs with Count Basie's group, including "Stormy Weather." Judy's powers still must have been a force of nature, since shortly after she sang that song, there was a sudden storm, and the concert was postponed to the next evening, due to rain.

July 20, 1968: (Concert) J.F.K. Stadium; Philadelphia, Pennsylvania. *Judy's last concert in the United States.* Over 20,000 fans were treated to one of the finest performances of Judy's career. Healthy, happy and medication-free, Judy was in strong voice and fine form, going immediately from one song to the next. Judy's songs: "For Once In My Life"; "Almost Like Being In Love"/"This Can't Be Love"; "Just In Time"; "How Insensitive"; "What Now My Love?"; "That's Entertainment"; "Do I Love You?"; "The Man That Got Away"; "Rock-A-Bye Your Baby"; "By Myself"; "Make Someone Happy"; "The Man I Love"; Medley of "I Hear Music"/"The Sweetest Sounds"/"Strike Up The Band" with Count Basie; "For Once In My Life" (reprise); and "Over The Rainbow." The critics raved, and here are excerpts from two of them:

> *The Philadelphia Inquirer* (Samuel L. Singer), July 21: "Garland Sings To 20,000 In Stadium" (Headline): "A warmly affectionate Judy Garland was her old self at the Philadelphia Music Festival on Saturday night, which means that she held the audience in the palm of her hand from her first entrance. The crowd of 20,000 at John F. Kennedy Stadium gave her a standing ovation on her entrance and an ovation at the close of her program. . . . Her voice had that distinctive throb and resonance, and she sang with her practiced ease . . . audience was always affirmative. It was a love affair from first to last."
>
> *South Philadelphia Chronicle* (Tom Cardella), July 25: "It was a beautiful love affair in this ugly football stadium. . . . Close by, there was a young man dressed in hippie attire, and he was shouting 'Judy, I love you.' On this magical night, he was speaking for many of us."

Ironically, Judy's first concert—in July 1943—had been in Philadelphia, and now her last, her final U.S. concert, 25 years later, was also taking place in my hometown, the "City of Brotherly Love." (A bootleg LP, on the Paragon label, was released in the late 1970s. This album was slightly abridged. The full concert does still exist in private collections, in a tape apparently made through the sound system. There have also been rumors about this concert being videotaped by WHYY-TV, Channel 12, the local Public Broadcasting Station in Philadelphia. The rumors may stem from the giant projection screen used at the stadium to show Judy, but no videotapes have surfaced to date.) Wesley Fuller escorted Judy to the concert. After the performance, Gene Palumbo mentioned the possibility of a fall concert in White Plains, New York, but this did not transpire.

July 31, 1968 through August 7, 1968: A short trip to Los Angeles. On July 31, Judy called her friend John Carlyle on the Coast. She was coming in for a brief visit to see Joe, and collect some music she needed. John picked her up at Los Angeles airport, and was surprised to see she had only brought along one small suitcase, a Bloomingale's shopping bag with an extra dress, and her purse. That night she had dinner with Joe and John. The next day or so, she moved from John's apartment, to another on Norma Place—John's friends, Tucker Fleming and Charles Williamson, who had a suite/guestroom designed with Judy in mind—See February 27, 1967 for more information. During the day, Judy swam in their pool and read in their library, where she found she was listed in the new Random House Dictionary! On the night of Tuesday, August 6, along with Tuck and Chuck, Judy and Joe Luft went to the Factory discotheque, where mother and son danced for possibly the first, and certainly the final time, in public. It would be the last time she would see her son. The next evening, Wednesday, August 7, 1968, at about 8:30 p.m., Judy suddenly decided that she was leaving on a 10:30 p.m. flight to go back to Boston, which she had chosen as her new "hometown." It would be the last time she would ever be in Los Angeles. The next night she had been scheduled to take son Joe to see Tony Bennett open at the Coconut Grove. The rush to leave may have been a call to help "surprise" an old friend who was cohosting a television show back East.

August 9, 1968: (Television) *The Mike Douglas Show* was videotaped in color, at KWY-TV Studios, Channel 3, in Philadelphia, Pennsylvania. This syndicated talk show was cohosted on this date by Judy's long-time friend Peter Lawford. Judy appeared (after an hour delay backstage: the only time the show was held in its history) wearing her red pants and cape outfit with feathers that she had designed (and that she would wear at her final concert). Although her face was still slightly puffy from her medication-withdrawal, and she did not appear to have had either her hair or makeup professionally done, she was in superb form and voice, winning cheers for her opening numbers "For Once In My Life" (perhaps the definitive version) and "How Insensitive." After engaging in talk with Douglas and Lawford, she was persuaded to sing "Over The Rainbow." It would be only the third—and the final—time she would sing her theme song in full on television. Judy stayed while the ventriloquist Willie Tyler performed with his puppet "Lester"—Judy's legendary laugh can be heard throughout his routine. As the show closed, she also did a duet with Lawford on "Blue Skies." Judy's most successful television appearance of the late 1960s would air in most markets on Friday, August 16, although it was broadcast in Philadelphia on Monday, August 12, 1968. (Color videotape exists of Judy's solos and interview section, and audiotape of the other portions, in private collections. The original videotape is not believed to be in Mike Douglas's possession, but is rumored to be sitting in the apartment of a long-time fan, where it is certain to be deteriorating as it is not being stored in a proper facility meant to house videotape masters.)

August 16, 1968: Judy had dinner with her attorney Ben Freeman, his wife Pearl, Tom Green, and Ken Mayer at the Parker House in Boston. Mayer asked her to consider appearing at a benefit two days later:

Sunday, August 18, 1968: (Personal Appearance/Benefit) Rockingham Park, Boston. The Cardinal's Annual Kennedy Memorial Hospital Show. (It is not known exactly what Judy sang.)

Judy had spent much of the summer socializing with Wes Fuller and her new attorney, Benjamin S. Freeman, of Boston, Massachusetts, whom she had found through the Boston Bar Association, or possibly the Yellow Pages, as she would later tell John Meyer. Judy hit it off so well with Freeman, and especially his wife Pearl, that she moved into their home in Brighton, Massachusetts. Previously she had been a houseguest of Wes Fuller and his parents. Judy also socialized again with Tom Green, and with Ken Mayer, a newspaperman who had been confidential secretary to Edmund McNamara, Boston's Chief of Police. Judy told Mayer one evening while dining that she had pawned a ring that morning because she had so little cash, yet she had a hired limousine and chauffeur waiting outside the restaurant to take her to a nightclub after dinner, saying that "once you're a star, you live like a star."

At this time it was reported that Mickey Rooney wanted to do a nightclub review with Judy, and had placed an advertisement in *Daily Variety* asking Judy or Sid Luft to contact him; nothing came of this.

September 1968: (Advertisement) Judy posed for famed photographer Richard Avedon in New York, to be the third star in the "What Becomes A Legend Most?" series of ads for Blackglama Mink. As was the custom, Judy was not paid for the ad: she was flown-in from Boston, and her hotel expenses were paid. The stars were allowed to keep the fur they wore; Judy took hers directly from the shoot, not leaving it behind to be lined. The ad ran in the *New York Times* on Sunday, November 24, 1968, and the December issues of *Vogue* and *Harpers Bazaar*. (A sheet of photo proofs from this session were sold in a New York City auction house in the early 1990s. Included in the lot was a contract for Judy's December 1968 *Tonight Show* appearance. Some alternate shots from this session, shot by famed photographer Richard Avedor, exist in private collections.)

Around this time, while still in New York, Judy apparently contacted members of her family, for the first time in a number of years, looking for a photograph of her father. No one had a photo.

September 7, 1968: Judy simultaneously signed a statement releasing CMA from any claims she had previously made against them in her October 11, 1966, and March 15, 1967, lawsuits (her new attorney, Benjamin S. Freeman, of Boston, Massachusetts had arranged the papers on Judy's behalf), and she signed a new, three-year management contract with them. Judy held a press conference in Boston to announce the signing of the pact. CMA announced that she would be "enjoying life for the first time": there would be "fewer concerts, but more movies and some television." It was also reported that Judy was interested in "the lead role of a proposed film drama," and that "professional plans should be formulated within a few weeks." Perhaps this could have been a film about the life of Edith Piaf, as there had been brief talks about Judy doing this, with George Cukor as her director. The real reason for Judy dropping her suit and resigning with Fields and Begelman, was so she could receive the $8,000 in back royalties that CMA were holding for her. Judy desperately needed the money, which she used to rent an apartment for herself in Boston, Massachusetts, at 790 Boylston Street—the Prudential Center Apartments, a complex of three high-rise buildings, the Boylston, the Gloucester, and Judy's building, the Fairfield. Judy rented apartment #12J, which had three and a half rooms, a living room, kitchen, bedroom, and bath. There was also a 24-hour doorman service, and downstairs featured a cavernous, multilevel garage, and a shopping mall that featured a grocery market, cleaners, travel agency, liquor shop, etc. Judy's rent was $265.00 per month. Also, there is a possibility that Judy thought that in resigning with Fields and Begelman, they might be able to transform her career to new heights as they had done earlier in the decade—despite what she may have felt about them as human beings. At this time, Judy was also supposedly reunited with Tom Green, and no longer with Wesley Fuller.

Judy spent most of September—except for the New York City Blackglama photo shoot—in her new apartment in Boston. In early October 1968, a young actor named Michael Taft (a.k.a. John Tefft) allegedly told a reporter he would marry Judy within a week, in Greenwich, Connecticut. A retraction was printed when Judy said she'd never even heard of Tefft. In early October, Judy returned to New York, and saw *George M* at the Palace Theater in New York, in October. A photo of her backstage visiting the show's star, Joel Grey, was published on October 20, 1968, in the New Jersey Journal newspaper, and in an issue of *MovieLand* magazine (a noted date of the photo has been mentioned as October 3, 1968). Around this time, Judy was invited to attend the opening of the show *Hair*, in Munich, but she told columnist Earl Wilson the IRS "prevented" her from leaving the country, as they must have feared she'd never return. There were rumors of additional Judy concerts in the U.S: November 30, in Pittsburgh, and the Stanley Theater in Jersey City, New Jersey announced in early November that Judy would be one of 14 artists in a series of 14 concerts, and that she would appear "probably in late December 1968, or during January 1969." Neither of these concerts, nor any others, happened at this time. Not surprisingly, mere weeks after re-signing Judy amidst much hoopla and talk of much upcoming film, television, and concert work, CMA in New York was reported to have "no concrete plans for Judy Garland."

Also during this time, Judy did an interview from "the 14th floor of a celebrated New York hotel," to talk about Tony Bennett for the 40-page supplement "20 Years With Tony" for the November 30 issue of Billboard magazine. Keep in mind as you read Judy's thoughts on Tony that she could have been talking about herself :

> "I remember the first time I heard Tony sing on a record, years ago. I thought: *That Sound!* He isn't copying *anyone*! His sound gets into your ear and into your heart. I know a lot of singers who sing very well, but they sound like a trombone, because they don't pay attention to the lyrics. But Tony's feeling for a lyric sometimes will make his voice tremble just a tiny bit, and it's from pure masculine emotion. I adore that man. I adore his talent and I adore him as a person. There's more to it than that. He's an entertainer. I've always thought of Tony Bennett as a thoroughly professional entertainer, and entertainers are born to do just that—to entertain. He's giving to his audiences. He lives for music. He comes onto a stage and he's happy, because he wants to give. He lets the audience know that he's gone through many of the things they've gone through. I think he's the epitome of what entertainers were put on earth for. He was born to take people's troubles away, even for an hour. He loves doing it. He's a giver. Each audience has different people in it, but he never gets bored. He'll give over and over again, no matter how many shows. I'd like to see nothing but goodness for Tony all his life, because he deserves that. I'd like to see him respected and acclaimed for the great artist he is. You see, an artist has to *trust*, because if he didn't trust whoever is managing or advising him he would be so suspicious all the time that he wouldn't have time to learn a new song. The world's a mess, and the entertainers should be revered now more than at any other time. We go out onto the stage and sing, or dance, or juggle, to entertain people. The entertainer should have nothing but respect paid to him—through money, through honesty, and through sheer reverence. We've worked hard. Most people think an entertainer of any caliber is automatically a millionaire. They don't know about what comes off the top—the taxes, paying for the orchestra, and all the other expenses. Entertainers are so vulnerable to trouble; they can be robbed blind while they're still on stage, which is a good trick. 'The show must go on!'—I'm sure it was someone holding the money who made that one up! And yet, Tony has none of the show business toughness or hardness you come to expect. He's unable to be hard. He's vulnerable—but masculine. I've never seen him lose his temper, but I hope he does, now and then. He is a Tony Bennett, and there isn't any resemblance to anyone else. There's just one, and everybody had better appreciate him. Nobody knows what makes him tick. I don't, but I like, whatever it is. He doesn't ask for anything more than to give. He really does give his heart to an audience, and of course they give him their hearts in return. Tony Bennett is the finest male entertainer in the world today!"

October 24, 1968: Judy met songwriter John Meyer, about 8 p.m., at the Carnegie Hall apartment of the late Richard Striker, on West 58th Street in New York City, where Judy had been staying. This was after meeting with an IRS rep, Mr. Wong, earlier that day. Judy, John, and Jenny Wheeler (whom Judy introduced as her secretary, but who had been a member of her fan club two years earlier) had dinner at the Buena Mesa, a Spanish restaurant on 28th and Lexington.

October 25, 1968, 2 to 5 a.m.: (Personal Appearance) Judy sang four songs for the crowd at the Improvisation nightclub on West 44th Street. At 5:30 a.m., Judy and Jenny became houseguests of John Meyer at his parent's apartment at Park Avenue and 84th Street. Meyer played Judy the 1935 *Shell Chateau* radio shows he had on tape from when she appeared on the show at age thirteen; Judy listened "intently, and warmly." A short while later, they became lovers, according to Meyer.

October 26, 1968, a little after 1 a.m.: (Personal Appearance) Judy and John Meyer arrived at "Three": a nightclub on 72nd Street and Second Avenue, run by singer /actress Mary McCarty, who had known Judy since they worked together in the Vitaphone film short *Bubbles*, in December 1929. Meyer had arranged a little "business deal" for Judy: She would sing over the weekend at Mary's club for $100 a night. Mary McCarty later said that Judy was thrilled about having some money of her own in her pocket: "Oh, Mary, do you realize I can buy stockings with this—that no one can take any part of it—it's all mine?" With Meyer playing for her, Judy sang six songs: "Zing! Went The Strings Of My Heart"; "The Man That Got Away"; "Here's To Us"; "Melancholy Baby"; the debut of a Meyer original that Judy would adopt, called "I'd Like To Hate Myself In The Morning"; and "Over The Rainbow." They left just before 4 a.m., after many ovations and cheers from the crowd, and the praises afterwards. Mary said Judy told her "If you only knew how good it makes me feel, what this kind of love means to me."

October 27, 1968, a little after 1 a.m. to just before 4 a.m.: (Personal Appearance) Judy's second performance at the nightclub "Three"; followed by dinner with John Meyer at P.J. Clarke's, which was interrupted by Jake LaMotta, the former middleweight champ, later immortalized by Robert De Niro in the 1980 classic film *Raging Bull.* Judy also had to deal with drunken patrons.

October 28, 1968: (Personal Appearance) Judy sang a few numbers at Jilly's nightclub in New York City, with John Meyer, in the early morning hours. Then, on their way to go dancing, around 4 a.m., Meyer proposed marriage to Judy, and she accepted.

October 29, 1968: In the early morning hours, Judy, John Meyer, his friend Larry Lowenstein, and Jenny, drove in Lowenstein's mustang, to his studio apartment on the sixth floor of a high rise called the Sea Verge, because it overlooked the ocean on the New Jersey Shore. Later that afternoon, Judy's foot was treated by a Dr. Lester Barnett at the Monmouth Clinic; the day ended with Judy and John having a massive food fight at dinner, practically destroying Larry's apartment.

October 30, 1968: Judy slipped on the parquet floor of Lowenstein's apartment, and knocked her face on the edge of the coffee table, resulting in a bruise above her left eye; later she spoke to Vincente Minnelli, as she was looking for Liza, so that she and Meyer could stay in her apartment: after calling everywhere, including Arthur Freed at MGM, Liza could not be found.

October 31, 1968: Judy, Meyer, and Jenny Wheeler, drove back to New York City, to Meyer's parent's apartment on Park Avenue, very late that night.

November 1, 1968: Judy met with Harold Arlen, Jay Blackton (musical director), and Henry Guettel (production supervisor for Lincoln Center), at Meyer's parent's apartment, from 3 to 6 p.m., to set songs and keys for Judy's appearance at a tribute to Arlen at Lincoln Center. Before leaving, Judy sang "Last Night When We Were Young" with Arlen playing his song on the piano.

November 2, 1968: (Personal Appearance) Judy again sang at the "Three" nightclub. Afterwards, Judy, Meyer, and Mary McCarty sang around Stan Freeman's player piano: a tape exists of this, featuring Judy singing "Hello, Bluebird" and "I've Confessed To The Breeze." Judy also did an accurate, though comedic and deadly impression of Marlene Dietrich singing "Falling In Love Again." Upon arriving home at the Meyer's apartment, they found a clipboard of notes that Marlene had left in the lobby (she lived in the same Park Avenue building as John's parents), and Judy made some wonderfully funny comments on them, digging at Marlene. Later that day, Tom Green dropped off an envelope summing up his personal and professional relationship with Judy from 1966–1968, along with plans that various people had come up with, for—a chain of "Judy Boutiques" to feature a line of Judy sportswear and cosmetics; a "Judy Coloring Songbook"; a Judy Nightclub; and a movie with a cameo part with the screenplay enclosed, with or without a song. There was also a total of Green's expenses in support of Judy: $58,815.62—which had increased $10,000 from his $48,756.74 estimate of April 5, 1968—along with a copy of a legal summons, instituting suit by Green, against Judy, for the monies owed him. The suit would never be filed.

November 3, 1968: (Personal Appearance) Another early-morning appearance at the "Three" nightclub with John Meyer. This was followed by a business meeting at the Candy Store, a gay bar where Judy and John met with the money men who Green had mentioned wanted to have Judy lend her name and prestige—and an occasional appearance—to a nightclub, which these "gentlemen" would run, with the location to be on East 63rd Street in New York City. Judy would be paid a $5,000 advance in cash, under the table, and receive a percentage of the room's gross, also off the record. Ultimately, these "gentlemen" were not deemed to be suitable business associates, when they stated they could "make" Mr. Green stop "bothering her"; it was the end of Judy's career in the nightclub business.

November 4, 1968: (Business Meeting) Judy met with independent booker Ken Roberts, to arrange concert dates. Although several smaller houses (which Judy preferred to "stadiums, and art centers and bowls") were discussed (including the Academy of Music in Philadelphia; The Kleinhaus in Buffalo; and Symphony Hall in Boston), as well as length of engagement (one-nighters, up to a weekend's worth, per venue), and Judy's take (a guarantee of $5,000 per performance), there would ultimately be no concerts booked by Mr. Roberts. Ironically, Judy had just resigned with CMA, but refused to turn to them to book her concerts.

November 5, 1968: (Business Meeting) At 2 p.m. Judy met with Mr. Wong and Mr. Rosen of the IRS, to continue negotiations in repayment of back taxes. Judy signed forms giving power of attorney to her new "business managers"—John Meyer, and his accountant Aaron Schecter; and a statement that Sid Luft had collected all monies from the sale of Kingsrow Enterprises' automobile and office equipment, etc. Late that afternoon, Judy met with Meyer's publishers, Bob Colby and Ettore Sratta, who were forming their new record company, Blue Records, and they wanted to sign Judy. She sang Meyer's "Hate Myself" and "It's All For You." By the end of the afternoon, it was agreed that Judy would receive a recording contract with Blue Records. Upon signing, she would receive a $2,500 cash advance, nondeclarable; and the first two songs for Judy's debut on the label would be "Hate Myself" and "It's All For You."

November 6, 1968: (Business Meeting) Jay Blackton, the musical director for the Arlen tribute Judy was to do, arrived at the Meyer's apartment, along with Jim Tyler, his orchestrator, to set what would be needed for the musical arrangements; this took two hours. Later, Judy and John dined at Orsini's, one of Manhattan's top restaurants, to celebrate the $2,000 worth of free arrangements they'd be getting from the Arlen tribute.

November 7, 1968: Judy's foot had not been healing properly from a prior injury, so Meyer decided she had to be in the hospital. The Leroy, at 40 East 61st Street, was the only one Judy felt comfortable in, and the Leroy's Dr. Harold E. Klinger checked Judy into room 1103; this was mentioned in Leonard Lyon's column in *The New York Post*, on Tuesday, November 12: "Judy Garland has her meals sent up from Voisin while she's recovering from a minor foot injury at the Leroy hospital."

November 11, 1968: An article appeared on this date in *The New York Times*, in which Judy's doctor, Dr. Klinger, said that she had "blood poisoning," but was in "adequate condition." An ulcer on her heel caused the condition.

November 13, 1968: Mickey Rooney called from California, talking to Judy in the hospital at 5 p.m. He told her to come to California to open the "Mickey and Judy Schools of Musical Comedy" for kids. Despite his sending Judy a plane ticket, and telling her everything would be taken care of, Judy did not want to leave New York.

November 16, 1968: While still at the Leroy hospital, Judy was visited by Gene, her hairdresser with Bendel's in New York City, to give Judy's hair a cut and a touch-up. The gray streaks were gone, and Judy's hair was "the color of charcoal." Judy was then granted a leave from the hospital to have dinner with Meyer and his parents; Meyer picked her up at 7 p.m., and that evening, just before they dined: Judy recreated the dance she did to "Lose That Long Face," which had been cut from *A Star Is Born*. (This, despite her injured foot.)

November 17, 1968: (Performance/Tribute/Benefit) ASCAP Salute To Harold Arlen, Vincent Youmans, and Noel Coward; Lincoln Center; New York, New York. Tickets were $100.00 and $150.00, and the show grossed $220,000. Since this was a "performance" day, Meyer allowed Judy to sleep at the apartment, after she could not fall asleep at the hospital; she finally started to relax at 6:30 a.m., waking at noon, taking four Ritalin. Judy and John left the apartment at 2:40 p.m., stopping at the hospital to pick up Judy's gown; the drug store for an Ace bandage for her heel; and at a delicatessen for a bottle of grapefruit juice to go with the vodka they'd brought. They arrived at Lincoln Center at 3:20 p.m.; From approximately 3:30 to 5 p.m., Judy rehearsed her four songs with the orchestra. During the rehearsal, just after the introduction to "The Man That Got Away" had been played, Judy cracked: "Can you imagine if they played that, and *Florence Henderson* came out!" From 5 to 6 p.m., they traveled to and waited for, Judy's dressing room in Philharmonic Hall. (They were driven by a production assistant, as Judy and John had kept the $250 given them for expenses, like hiring a limousine.) By 6 p.m. they were in the dressing room, where Judy and Gene, her hairdresser, used the bathroom for "a quick set and comb out." When Judy came out of the bathroom, she coughed twice, and complained of losing her voice, so John called Dr. Klinger, who prescribed a throat spray, a cocaine derivative, to freeze her vocal cords temporarily, which would be delivered by the pharmacy; about 7:30, Judy's hair was finished, and Richard Rodgers showed up to say hello, and wound up warming up Judy, as he played, and she sang "Boys And Girls Like You And Me" (in the key of "G"), "Why Can't I?" and "With A Song In My Heart." Show time: After Judy's Overture, she swung out from behind a flat to the gasp of the audience, as her participation in the show had not been announced. Judy sang: "The Man That Got Away"; "It's A New World"; "Get Happy"; and with Harold Arlen at the piano: "Over The Rainbow." Backstage, Judy was visited by Arlen and Rodgers, and Gloria Vanderbilt, etc. (An audiotape of Judy's performance, recorded in the audience, still exists in private collections.)

November 18, 1968, 12:30 a.m.: Judy, John, his mother, her escort, and Irv Squires—Judy's assigned agent from CMA, who suddenly turned up—all went to celebrate Judy's performance at PJ Clark's in Manhattan. Judy tore into Squires about CMA not getting her any work, with John calming her down by saying they'd talk to David Begelman, and get it straightened out. Later that day, Meyer did pay a visit to Begelman's office, where it was determined that the quickest way to get Judy cash would be to book concerts for her, which would be difficult, as a promoter/producer named "Marelli" was holding all of Judy's orchestrations since she supposedly canceled a concert she was to do for him. Marelli wanted Judy to do the concert, plus pay him $25,000—with $5,000 down—and 2% of her gross earnings for the next year. Let alone the fact that this was blackmail, Judy Garland did not have $5,000. ("Marelli" was most likely Anthony DeFalco.)

November 19, 1968: Judy was released from the hospital, and she and John Meyer caught the 3:30 p.m. American Airlines flight to Boston, where Judy had her apartment; by 7 p.m. they were filling Judy's prescriptions; then home to Judy's large apartment complex in Boston: see September 7, 1968, for complete information on Judy's apartment. Later that evening, Judy, John, and his friend Marvin, who worked for the Boston Symphony, had dinner at Amalfi restaurant.

November 20, 1968: Judy and John unpacked—resulting in $32.85 of dry cleaning being picked up from the downstairs cleaners. In the mid afternoon, Anne Bryant, a 19-year old student at the Berklee College of Music that Judy had befriended, came over to take down "sketches" of seven more songs from which orchestrations would be made for Judy—so that Judy would not need to pay to get her orchestrations back, and would be able to work again.

November 21, 1968: At 2:30 p.m., Judy and John went shopping at Jordon Marsh, buying $108.69 worth of items for the kitchen. About 4:15 p.m., Judy went downstairs looking for the cocktail lounge, where some people gathered around her. Eventually, she and Meyer were in the South Seas lounge. About 10 p.m. they were dining at the Half Shell, a seafood house, where they met a married couple, Jim and Lois, and their friend Dick.

November 22, 1968, early a.m.: (Personal Appearance) After cavorting at a Turkish belly-dancing room called the Casbah, Judy, John, and their new friends, wound up at an after-hours bar called Napoleon, where Judy sang "I'd Like To Hate Myself In The Morning" and "It's All For You." They left at 4:30 a.m. Several hours later, at 7 p.m. that evening, John Meyer called Harold Arlen in New York, and asked him for $1,100 to pay Judy's recent hospital bill at the Leroy in New York City, where she had just been for her foot. Judy was sitting there listening with John. Arlen said to send him the bill, and he would take care of it.

November 23, 1968: A quiet day, spent mostly going through boxes and boxes of the recent fan mail forwarded to Judy from CMA; reprints of some of the mail exists, falling into three categories: "well wishers and fans"; "people asking for things/requests"; and "kooks."

November 24, 1968: (Business Meeting) Over the phone, Judy spoke with a London, England booking agent, Harold Davidson, whom she told she wanted to work in London. He was certain he could get her a top figure at one of London's leading nightclubs, and that he would call her back in a few days. Judy also called Sid Luft in California, to try to get help in getting her orchestrations back. Sid told her to forget Marelli, that he could never get the orchestrations, which he claimed "Group Five" had paid $14,000 for (or to get back.) The conversation really went nowhere.

November 25, 1968: Judy and John went to the movies, to see *The Boston Strangler*; a nearby couple had been looking at them during the movie, and the man, Vinnie Toscano, had a restaurant up the street, the "Beef and Ale House." Judy and John joined them there after the movie.

November 26, 1968: About 2:30 in the morning, Judy decided she wanted to spend the night in a hotel in Cambridge; after checking into the wrong hotel, Judy and John finally found the Charter House

Motel, about 6 a.m. At about 9:20 am, Judy slipped and struck her head sharply on the edge of a marble coffee table; a Dr. Brecher arrived to bandage Judy's bleeding head. At 2:30 p.m., a waitress at the Beef and Ale, Margret, came by to bring Judy to her (Margret's) apartment so that John could get back to Boston for some things, which he did late that night.

November 28, 1968: Judy saw John Meyer's going back to Boston to get some things and sleep for a day, as abandonment, so she and John broke up this morning, Thanksgiving morning, and Judy spent Thanksgiving alone . . . her last Thanksgiving.

November 29, 1968: About 5:30 p.m., Judy called John at his folks apartment, wondering why he had walked out on her; he said she had thrown him out; the conversation really went nowhere, and Judy kept calling, forcing John and his sister out of the apartment.

November 30, 1968: By 5 a.m. Judy had apparently lost control, banging her head against the wall so hard that her downstairs neighbor called the police, the police soon called doctors, and by 8 a.m. Judy was in Peter Brent Brighman Hospital. At 10 p.m. John called the hospital, room 131, and reconciled with Judy.

December 2, 1968: (Personal Appearance) After setting Judy's new recording contract with his attorney, John Meyer caught the 5:30 flight from New York City to Boston. After a brief, intimate reunion between Judy and John, in Judy's hospital room, they joined with their friend Annie (who was making new orchestrations for Judy) in singing Christmas carols to some of the patients in Peter Brent Brigham Hospital, including "God Rest Ye Merry Gentlemen," which Judy started. There also exists from this date, a receipt from Lord & Taylor, 12/2/68 : $15.97 total (pink receipt) Boston, Mass (Picked-up by John Meyer as soon as he got into Boston to go see Judy in the hospital); Paid by BC (Bank Card). (There were three or four items here, including a new hat):

$9.00

$5.00 (2 at $2.50 each, I believe)

$1.50

.47 (tax)

$15.97 Total

December 3, 1968: Judy was allowed out of the hospital for dinner; John Meyer picked her up at 7 p.m. and they dined at Anthony's Pier Four.

December 4, 1968: Judy was released from the hospital. Late that afternoon/early evening John Meyer visited with Jenny Wheeler who was close to mononucleosis, and was going down South, for a long rest. About 7:30 pm, Judy managed to get Ken Darrell of the Furniture Company of America to deliver a Baldwin spinet to her apartment. Judy started singing, Ken had his girlfriend over, and by 9:30 p.m. they were having a party, which ended about 1:00 a.m.

December 5, 1968: (Business) John Meyer confirmed three New York City–based television talk shows for Judy: Dick Cavett, Johnny Carson, and Merv Griffin. Judy also spoke with her long-time conductor Mort Lindsey (1961–1966), calling him at his Long Island, New York home to tell him she'd be taping Merv's show (for which he was the musical director) on December 19, and that he had to do the arrangement of "Hate Myself In The Morning" for her. Later that afternoon, Harold Davidson, the London booking agent they had spoken to on Sunday, November 24, called: It had taken him only a week and a half to arrange and confirm Judy's booking: She was all set to open on December 30, at the Talk of the Town nightclub in London's Leicester Square, at 2,500 pounds a week, which translated to $7,000 a week for four weeks. Davidson was mailing the contract that night to Judy, and also arranged rooms at the Ritz hotel. Later that evening, Judy, John, and their friends Annie and Marvin were playing the piano and singing; When it got to be 12:30 a.m., Judy's downstair's neighbor called the police again, who came and knocked on Judy's door. The officers were of course no match for Judy Garland, who practically had them in tears when she sang "Over The Rainbow" for them.

December 6, 1968: Judy and John went to the movies, seeing *Funny Girl* with Barbra Streisand, and Judy again fell asleep; the reason for her dozing off in movie theatres was revealed to Meyer when they got home: Judy wanted to be up there singing or acting . . . as she should have been.

December 7, 1968: A quiet day at home in Boston; Judy cooked John a casserole for dinner: baked beans, sausages, and brussel sprouts.

December 8, 1968: About 1:30 a.m., Judy fell asleep. By 4:10 a.m. she was awake and it was clear she wanted attention, resenting John's sleep; this resulted in a confrontation: Judy was telling John that she thought it was too late, that she always drove people away, and that he should save himself, and leave now. He insisted he could help make things different for her. A short time later, Judy was saying her prayers in front of him, which became Meyer's "Prayer" song (a.k.a. "God Bless Johnny") which she would sing on Dick Cavett's television show, less than a week later.

December 9, 1968: The manager of Judy's apartment building, Donald Sisk, called to tell Judy she was being evicted because of the noise; she would have to be out by December 15; her security deposit would be refunded. At 2:30 that afternoon, a girl named Bunny Carnazzo, who was 16, arrived to help them sort through Judy's things, and to pack. Most of Judy's furniture was leased, and some of it was Ben Freeman's, Judy's attorney.

December 10, 1968: Before leaving Boston for New York, John Meyer confirmed that: the Bellaire Storage Company in Beverly Hills, California, who were holding all of Judy's furniture and other possessions, would need $1,200 in back storage costs, and Sid Luft's signature before they could release anything; and CMA had sent Judy's AGVA (American Guild of Variety Artists) contracts for the "Talk of the Town"—odd, considering that Judy and John had arranged the engagement, and that they were so down on CMA. At 6 p.m., their driver Joe Bazarian from Arleen's Bridal Service arrived in a 1968 Cadillac limousine, to take Judy, John, and a ton of Judy's things, back to New York, making 30 trips to load the car. They stopped at a Holiday Inn on the thruway for a brief stop, where a lady saw Judy, had her "pinch" her and sign an autograph. They stopped for dinner at the Stonehenge, in Ridgefield, Connecticut. After dinner, they found a piano upstairs, and Judy sang her three Meyer songs—"Hate Myself," "It's All For You," and "After The Holidays"—for Joe, their driver, then again for the staff. At 11:30 p.m., they were stopped by a Mrs. Stockli, the wife of the owner and chef; she asked them to stop, and also said there were no rooms for them to stay the night . . . obviously *not* a Garland fan.

December 11, 1968: Arriving at the St. Regis hotel at 1:45 a.m., Judy and John discovered that there was no reservation, or message for them; when they tried the Americana at 53rd Street and 7th Avenue, there was a reservation, but when they saw Judy they asked for a cash deposit, given her credit history. They wound-up going back to John's parent's apartment at 84th and Park Avenue, finishing unloading everything at 4 am; that afternoon was spent speaking to producer Bob Shanks of the *Griffin* show (an audiotape was made of the conversation and still exists) and Mort Lindsey, about the botched hotel arrangements; 45 minutes later they met with Len Friedlander, from the "Cavett" show, to discuss what Judy wanted to do on the show. Judy told some stories, and sang "Prayer" for the first time.

December 12, 1968: While Meyer met with his lawyer David Grossberg to finalize Judy's new recording contract, Annie took Judy to her dentist, Dr. Pact on West 57th street, as a chipped tooth in the middle of her uppers was turning brown. While in the lobby, Judy met Sid Luft briefly, who was having root canal work done at another dentist in the same building. It was the last time Judy and Sid were to see each other. Meyer met Sid in his dentist's office, and arranged to have a drink with him at 6:30 that night, at the King Cole bar in the St. Regis hotel. At their meeting, Sid admitted that he had the orchestrations, that they were "safe with me." He also said if Judy could pay the storage costs for the last year and a half, she could have the furniture. Meyer left Luft to meet Judy at the Hilton hotel where Merv Griffin had arranged for a two-room suite; He also had flowers sent over, had a piano moved in; and even $250 in cash, with a note saying "just some mad money."

December 13, 1968: (Television) *The Dick Cavett Show*, videotaped in color at ABC-TV Studios in New York City (broadcast on Monday, December 16, 1968, in the morning). (An existing videotape, of poor quality, is in black and white.) Judy was wonderfully funny, entertaining, and sharp, aware, and "there"; however, she did not look her best, as the actor Lee Marvin was late ("Good! It wasn't *me* for a change!" Judy said during the show, to the hysterical laughter of the audience), causing Judy to come on before him, instead of closing the show; therefore, her makeup and especially her hair, were not satisfactorily completed—as she says on the show "If I came out looking well, it's simply because of my *good spirit*!" Judy also sang bits of two songs written by a Peter A. Follo: "You Lousy Jippy-Jippy Japs" and "Uncle Sam Is Going To Build An Army," accompanied by John Meyer at the piano. Judy also sang Meyer's "Prayer" (Bobby Rosengarten's orchestration had been written and copied in 24 hours) in only fair voice. ("I might as well *crack* my way through it" as Judy says.) One of her most enjoyable, and funniest outings, with Cavett and Judy zinging one-liners back and forth. Think *Neil Simon* at his best.

December 14, 1968: At 2 a.m., Judy was finally hungry, wanting some chili from PJ Clark's, which arrived cold at 3:20 a.m. Judy then decided she wanted to go to the nightclub "Arthur's," which by now was managed by Mickey Deans—who had first met Judy on the morning of March 10, 1967, when he delivered the medication she needed to get herself together to fly to work on *Valley of the Dolls*. Deans sent a car, and 15 minutes later they were in a Cadillac limousine, which dropped them off at the club, at East 54th street. They stayed at the club awhile; then Judy and John left with Deans, went food shopping at Smiler's, and then on to Dean's apartment on East 88th Street. Judy and John left at 8 a.m., returning to the Hilton. Awakening at 6:30 p.m., John found Judy was still asleep, where she would remain, while Meyer went to a party, where he realized he was sick: he had the Hong Kong flu.

December 17, 1968: (Television) *The Tonight Show* (with Johnny Carson), videotaped in color at NBC-TV in New York City (aired that evening.) Judy talked with Johnny, announcing her gig in London, which she unfortunately gave as *The Town and Country* and not *The Talk of The Town*. Judy also sang John Meyer's "It's All For You" and "Til After The Holidays." Judy stayed for the next guest: a football player with whom she proceeded to playfully flirt. (A color videotape of Judy's segment only still exists, which shows her looking lovely, but away from Meyer's caring and watchful eye, she appears to be slightly medicated in her speaking, and vocally only slightly warmed up from her *Cavett* stint, although, as always, she gets you in the gut with her delivery of pure emotional devastation.) This is the *last* television appearance by Judy known to *still* exist.

December 18, 1968: Judy signed her new recording contract with Bob Colby and his *Blue Records*—only after he went to the bank to cash her advance check of $2,500.

December 19, 1968: (Television) *The Merv Griffin Show*; videotaped in color in New York City. (The syndicated show would air in most markets on Thursday, January 2, 1969.) Judy chatted with Griffin, Mort Lindsey, and Arthur Treacher. To an ovation from the audience, Judy walked out and sang Meyer's "I'd Like To Hate Myself In The Morning," and later sang an impromptu solo rendition of "Have Yourself A Merry Little Christmas, " and then "The Trolley Song" with all the guests. Merv also asked Judy if she wanted to "take over" for him while he was on vacation the following week (this was after Judy brought up the idea herself, of course.) Judy looked lovely, and was in fairly good voice, and spirits—despite telling Merv she had a 102 temperature; unfortunately, this show is not known to exist; only silent color footage shot from television, and an audio recording of the show, are known to remain. Merv has since stated that the tapes are no longer in his vaults, since the material from this time was erased after his series went to CBS in 1969. After the taping, John Meyer went to the Hilton, where Judy told him she was now engaged to Mickey Deans, which apparently just happened earlier that evening at Merv's Christmas party, directly after the taping, held at Arthur's, where Deans was night manager. Apparently John Springer, who had been Judy's publicist at the time of her Carnegie Hall tour in 1961, was there this evening, and told Earl Wilson to come over to the club. The announcement appeared in Earl Wilson's column in *The New York Post*, a few days later.

December 23, 1968: (Television) *The Merv Griffin Show*; videotaped in color in New York City; Syndicated (aired in most markets on January 6.) This was Judy's last television appearance in the United States. Judy was the *Guest Hostess* (filling in for Merv, who was on vacation; this had been announced during the taping of Judy's guest appearance on December 19.) Judy's guests were: Margaret Hamilton (the Wicked Witch from *The Wizard of Oz* . . . who did not take her broom home after her brief appearance, but rather the New York Subway: a New York-based fan explained to this author that he left the taping with Hamilton after her early, brief appearance); the Ohio Express (a rock group); comic Marty Brill; comedian Moms Mabley (who had Judy falling down with laughter); Judy's old friend and MGM costar Van Johnson; and critic Rex Reed, who praised Judy, and criticized the Oscars for not giving her the award for *A Star Is Born*—"Let the Princess keep it" was Judy's reply. Judy also sang "If You Were The Only Girl In The World" with Arthur Treacher, and soloed on "Just In Time." This was the most successful of all the four recent television appearances: Judy looked lovely and was in fine voice, form, and spirits, and proved to be a charming and relaxed hostess; as stated above, unfortunately, Merv Griffin says the videotapes no longer exist; all that is left is an audiotape, some color stills, and some silent color clips filmed off the television during the broadcast. After the taping, John Meyer again went to the Hilton, and played Mickey Deans some of the arrangements on a couple of the songs Deans would need to know for the London engagement. Also later that night—or one night the last week in December—Judy and Deans attended a nightclub performance of a Hollywood girl singer at the Plaza's Persian Room, with Judy wearing a wide-brimmed black hat trimmed with coq feathers, apparently one of her own creation.

December 26, 1968: (Rehearsal) Judy had Stan Freeman and John Meyer over to rehearse at the Hilton, where she chose Stan's "I Belong To London" (written overnight) as her opener, over John's "I'm Back In Business." John still stayed and played "London," as well as "Who?"; "The Darktown Strutter's Ball"; and "It's A New World." Also: in this date's edition of *Variety*, it was reported that a new book on Judy had just been finished, and was making the rounds of the publishing houses through the project's agent, Dick Irving Hyland. The writers were Sid Luft with Leo Guild, and the title was *Good Girl, Bad Girl*. It was never published.

December 27, 1968: Judy, Deans, and his best friend Charlie Cochran, flew to London, after having John Meyer, Cochran, and Bobby Cole over to say goodbye. Cole went over the complicated arrange-

Judy with her fifth and final husband, Mickey Deans (real name Michael DeVinko), thirty-five, just after they arrived in London on December 28, 1968. They would marry there on March 15, 1969. (Courtesy of Photofest.)

ment of "What Now, My Love?" that he'd conducted for Judy at the Palace in the summer of 1967. (Judy would never again sing "What Now, My Love?" most likely since the arrangement could not be easily or quickly duplicated.) Judy and Deans's Pan-Am flight left Kennedy Airport at 8:30 p.m.

December 28, 1968: As Judy and Deans landed in London at 7:30 a.m., they were served with a writ at Heathrow Airport—with a UPI photographer catching it on film; color newsreel footage exists of this moment also. The writ was served by a private detective, Keith Cockerton, who was working for the lawfirm, Lawford and Company, who were representing Greenspan & Harper. The writ was to prevent Judy from appearing in London, as the two "businessmen"—Howard Harper and Leon J. Greenspan—to whom Luft had assigned Judy's "Group Five" contract to in May 1968, when he was unable to repay a loan from these men—were now insisting that Judy could only work for them. Lawford and Company had in fact warned the Talk of the Town management, via a letter on December 24, that closed with:

> We must ask you to undertake *not* to engage Miss Garland as arranged. Failing such an undertaking from you before 10 a.m., Friday, December 27, we shall apply to the Vacation Judge for an injunction restraining you and Miss Garland in the show *Fine Feathers*, or any other show without our client's prior consent. To protect our client's position we have already taken an appointment with the Vacation Judge Mr. Justice Magarry—for 2:15 pm on Friday, 27 December. For the same reason we are immediately issuing a writ which we will endeavor to serve on you later today. Your's faithfully, Lawford & Co.

When Judy said through her London attorney, Stanley Waldman, that she had no knowledge of the assignment, the British judge, Judge Magarry, threw the case out of court, making Harper and Greenspan accountable for the court costs: about $2,600 at that time.

December 29, 1968: Judy rehearsed at the Talk of the Town.

December 30, 1968: (Concert) The Talk of the Town cabaret; London, England. (This was, of course, proceeded by the court victory of this day, only five hours before the show, allowing Judy to appear.) Judy supposedly went through some physical exercises, and a yoga headstand to relax before opening night, then took a long bath and a shower, before her hairdresser came to start her hair; the Talk of the Town's resident makeup artist, Vivian Martyne, was waiting for Judy when she arrived at the club that night. Judy opened her now already extended engagement (from four weeks to five weeks, earning about $7,000 each week), walking out at 11:15 p.m.—only fifteen minutes late—to a star-studded audience (Zsa Zsa Gabor, Ginger Rogers, David Frost, Danny LaRue, and Johnny Ray, among others.) Judy's songs included: "I Belong To London"; "Get Happy"; "The Man That Got Away"; "I'd Like To Hate Myself In The Morning"; "For Once In My Life"; "You Made Me Love You"/"For Me And My Gal"/"The Trolley Song"; "Just In Time"; San Francisco"; "Rock-A-Bye Your Baby"; "Over The Rainbow"; and "Chicago." These were all the orchestrations that Judy had, and had just been made to replace the ones being held "ransom." Judy also brought Danny LaRue up on stage with her at one point. This first night, Judy quipped " I haven't learned a new song since Andy Hardy met Deanna Durbin," and "I've been through a lot. People ask 'is she going to appear? Is she dead?' Well, I'm here and you couldn't keep me away." For this opening, Judy wore the now legendary bronze, sequined pant suit design for *Valley of the Dolls*, and worn for her Palace Theater and other concert engagements in 1967. Ginger Rogers writes in her autobiography that she could tell that Judy didn't look well, and that she wanted to have lunch with her alone, the next day, to find out what was going on—to see if she could help. Deans refused to "let" Judy, telling her backstage in a strict tone, in front of Rogers, that "You won't have time, Judy!" On a lighter note, the new editor of her London-based fan magazine *Rainbow Review*, Ken Sephton, says that Judy told him "I hope you will write something nice about me." When Ken mentioned he had only missed one of her films, *Listen, Darling*, Judy told him "Everyone should have missed that one!" (A nonprofessionally recorded album taped during this engagement—by a small tape recorder in the audience—was released in the early fall of 1969: *Judy. London. 1969*, by Juno Records, the new name of Bob Colby's label. "Over The Rainbow" from this LP is on the *Judy* box set from 32 Records. During an interview in March 1969, Judy mentioned the album being compiled by Deans, so she was obviously aware of it. Rex Reed would be nominated for a Grammy Award for the liner notes. There is also a tape existing in private collections made with the same recorder, but featuring a few songs taped on different evenings than the ones used on the LP.) Judy's reviews were mostly raptuous, as you can see from these excerpts:

> *The Stage*: "There are few artists who create an emotionalism—almost amounting to hysteria—minutes before they actually set foot onstage. Of these, probably the greatest is Judy."

> *The Financial Times*: "[Judy is] the Maria Callas of popular music. Her voice still holds its tremendous charge of suppressed excitement."

Clive Hirschhorn, journalist: "[Judy's] splendid performance [had] a capacity audience yelling for more. [And] who can blame them? When she is on form, there is no star in the world today more exciting to watch, or more thrilling to listen to."

(James Green; paper unknown): "Judy Wows 'Em With Songs To Remember" (Headline): "Predictably, the nervy and restless Miss Garland, so slim and boyish at 46 that she might have been Peter Pan, turned in a raw emotion-packed powerhouse performance. . . . She has personality plus . . . Judy still has punch. She has the star-quality, magnetism and confidence. . . . She is what the business is about. She may no longer be the little girl crying for the rainbow, the voice may waver, and the notes come harder, show business may eat its young, but the former Frances Ethel Gumm retains most of the magic given her by *The Wizard of Oz.*"

Variety (Rich), 1-8-69 (Judy's *last review* from the Show Business *Bible*): "Those looking to Judy Garland for an impeccable, stop-watch-timed, disciplined nightspot act clearly don't know what the gal is all about. The act has too many errors to satisfy the purists. But those who are not abashed by genuine nostalgia and who can recognize and rise to the peculiar alchemy that makes a woman a personality as well as a performer will have a very good time at her 5-week London cabaret debut. And there's a profitable SRO crowd every night to prove it. Those who are sniffy are mainly so in the cloakrooms and on the way home. The majority are embraced by Miss Garland's warmth, ebullience, and affable way of bringing enthusiasts into the act. At the show I caught she made her entry 45 minutes late. Not exactly professional behavior, and she paid for it by facing an at first sticky audience. They applauded Burt Rhodes and the orchestra playing an overture of Garland hits [first time any Talk Of The Town topper has received such a come-on bouquet] but then tended to sit on their mitts. But by the time she had sung "I Belong To London" for starters, "Get Happy" and "The Man That Got Away," all was forgiven. "Just In Time" came just in time and lit the act, as, at the star's invitation, 50 or so fans invaded the stage, sat on it, and made it a party. Miss Garland doesn't bother much about new songs. They're for the new little telly-birds. She plies her trade with a small batch of old trusties, which she can sing sideways, backwards, and upside-down, and, when in the mood, is quite likely to do so. Clad in a silverish trouser suit, she looks pretty chipper. The torso's fined down and the happy smile's still there. The voice tends to rasp and croak too often but it's still vibrant and a peppy belter. She also moves, not particularly gracefully, but with the deft verve and energy of a pro. Her songs are interspread with overlong, but quite funny gagging in which she chats up folk in the ringside seats and which she appears largely to ad-lib. After 'You Made Me Love You,' 'For Me And My Gal,' 'The Trolley Song,' and 'Rock-A-Bye Your Baby,' Miss Garland wound her 45-minutes act with the obligatory 'Over The Rainbow.' . . . Make no mistake, the Garland magic, warmth, and heart are as irresistible as ever. Nagging question is how long can Judy Garland keep it up? How long does she want to? Audience affection and goodwill are there, but there can be a limit to how long folks will watch a well loved champ gamble with her talent. Meanwhile, Judy Garland's alive and well, living in London and doing very nicely for Bernard Delfont at 'Talk Of The Town,' where she's admirably backed by Burt Rhodes and the resident orchestra, having brought no special musicians with her."

The press agent for Talk of the Town stated that out of 18 national press reviews of Judy's opening night, seven were raves, three were very good, two were good, and six were critical.

1969

January 1, 1969 to January 31, 1969: (Concert) Judy continued her performances at the Talk of the Town nightclub in London, England.

January 4, 1969: (Personal Appearance) The National Film Theater; London, England. During this informal appearance between the first and second showings of *A Star Is Born*, Judy took questions from the audience. Judy was wonderfully funny, and in answering one question, very supportive of Barbra Streisand: "She is a *star*, she makes a *sound*, she has a *look*. No one will be able to really deny the fact that Barbra Streisand is a great talent. . . . There doesn't have to be a comparison. She has her way of singing, I have mine. There's enough room for all of us." Judy also said she hoped to do more recording work, and stay in London for awhile. She did say that MGM "still doesn't trust me," and wouldn't consider her for their planned musical biography picture on Irving Berlin, "Say It With Music"—although there were reports of Judy starring in the film, as early as 1963, up until her passing; Arthur Freed was to produce, and Vincente Minnelli was to direct. Judy spoke twice at the theater: after the first screening, and again before the second. (For these talks, Judy wore her Blackglama mink over a pink mini dress. An audiotape, recorded in the audience, exists in private collections.) After her show that night at the Talk of the Town, Judy brought friends back to the National Film Theater, for a private, late-night showing of *A Star Is Born*.

January 9, 1969: Judy and Deans were married in a secret ceremony in a chapel, St. Marylebone Parish, by the Reverend Peter Delaney; a larger, public affair would be held at a later date; it is also doubtful that this private ceremony was legal, for according to Judy's California attorney, Godfrey Isaacs, the final divorce papers on Judy's marriage to Mark Herron had not been picked up. Judy was happy and well, and the shows apparently went very well for ten days or so after the exchange of vows: "I love him," she told columnist Arthur Helliwell, "and loving him means I no longer have to love the lights and the applause."

January 19, 1969: (Television) *Sunday Night at the London Palladium* ("*Live*" British Television.) Subbing for an ailing Lena Horne, Judy sang (following her full overture): "For Once In My Life"; "Get Happy"; and "I Belong To London." Judy arrived at the Palladium 10 minutes before she went on, and was not directed about any staging. (Surviving black and white footage of Judy taking her bows shows her looking lovely; though too slim, and wearing an unbecoming outfit, which she had designed herself: the ensemble she wore for her JFK Stadium concert and *Mike Douglas Show* outing the previous summer.) Her voice was in fairly good shape, and she seems in good spirits on the surviving audiotape—unfortunately the entire videotape or film is not known to exist. This was Judy's last appearance at the London Palladium, and also her very last appearance for television.

January 20, 1969: Judy was reported as being nearly an hour late for her show at the Talk of the Town.

January 21, 1969: Judy and Deans went to see Johnnie Ray in his cabaret act at Caesar's Palace in Luton, England. Judy was brought onstage by Ray, and they sang together. By the time Judy got to Talk of the Town for her show, she was fighting the flu, and had a fever; her doctor advised her to cancel the show, but she went on anyway.

January 22, 1969: Though Judy was scheduled to appear "Evenings At Eleven-Thirty" at the Talk of the Town, (in mid January the show time had been changed from 11 p.m. to 11:30 p.m.), Judy and Deans did not pull up in their rented Rolls-Royce Silver Cloud with chauffeur, until 12:40 a.m., although it had been agreed that Judy could make up at her hotel (the Ritz), and go directly on-stage from her car. (Judy's overture would be started as the car pulled up to the stage door.) After the overture, and Judy's first three songs ("I Belong To London," "Get Happy," and "The Man That Got Away"), she brought John Meyer on stage before singing his song "I'd Like To Hate Myself In The Morning (and Raise A Little Hell Tonight"). As Meyer was dancing around Judy during the second chorus (at her insistence), he noticed a thread lose on her sleeve, and began to pull it, unraveling the sleeve of Judy's white sequin pants outfit. A short while later, John and Deans were watching the show from the wings, where John suggested Judy should start bringing Deans onstage for the song "For Once In My Life." Though meant sarcastically, considering that Deans had replaced John in Judy's life, this was a practice Judy would quickly adopt. After the show, John went back to the Ritz with Judy and Deans about 4 a.m., where he found out that there was a chance that Judy might not do the recording session in London for the new contract she had signed last month in New York, on December 18, 1968, with Bob Colby's Blue Records, for which she received a $2,500 advance. The session had been set for February 4, but now it looked like Judy might be going to New York to film a television commercial with Mickey Rooney for TWA Airlines. (CMA had just called about two days before about the commercial, though the contracts had not been signed, and Judy would never do a television commercial.) To wrap up the evening, Judy had John play "It's All For You" (though her singing was interrupted by Deans doing an impersonation of a noisy waiter trying to serve food while Judy was singing).

January 23, 1969: Judy did not arrive at the Talk of the Town until 12:50 a.m., an hour and 20 minutes late. Even at that, she did not go directly onstage; Judy was still suffering badly from a bout with the flu, and according to author Anne Edwards, Deans demanded that Judy go on, as the club's makeup artist, Miss Martyne, repaired her makeup through her tears. Burt Rhodes, the resident musical director, did not start Judy's overture until 1:05 a.m. Unfortunately, nothing had been explained to the audience, and when Judy didn't say anything after her first song, the noise and hostility from certain parts of the audience grew, and during her second song, "Get Happy," a cigarette pack (Senior Service brand) was thrown onstage, followed by rude shouting, and more cigarette packs. A red-haired man managed to get onto the stage and grabbed Judy's microphone; this was followed by a glass being thrown, and shattering onto the stage, only three feet from where Judy was standing. Judy decided finally that she could not control these obnoxious people, and walked off. Her doctor, John Traherne, announced she had been ill all week, but had been still making a valiant effort to appear. Apparently backstage, while upset that no announcement had been made about her lateness, Judy was still in good spirits. It was decided that she should have the weekend off, and return on Monday, January 27, for her final week. Andrew Lloyd Webber was in the audience at this performance on January 23, and it inspired him to write "Don't Cry For Me Argentina" for his show *Evita*.

January 27, 1969: Judy started her final week at the Talk of the Town. John Meyer rented a portable Nagra reel tape recorder—which used five-inch reels—and a multidirectional Sehheiser microphone, and recorded Judy's performance that night. Judy, Deans, and Meyer were up at the Ritz hotel listening to the tape till 4 in the morning. Judy and Deans agreed to pay the $10 a day—three guineas—to keep the machine in order to get more performances on tape. (These tapes, including the ones Meyer made, would ultimately become the *Judy. London. 1969* LP on Juno Records, released in the fall 1969; Rex Reed would be nominated for a Grammy Award for the liner notes he wrote for this album. After the show on January 27, photos were taken of Judy and Deans backstage hugging.)

January 28, 1969: Judy again brought John Meyer up onstage when she sang "I'd Like To Hate Myself In The Morning" (a tape of this song as a duet from this evening still exists in private collections).

January 30, 1969: (Business Meeting) At 5:30 p.m., Bob Colby and Hector (Ettore) Sratta, along with John Meyer, met at the Ritz, in Judy's hotel suite, to determine with Deans what was going to happen about the recording session set for February 4. Despite the studio being booked, and musicians hired (along with Johnny Spence, as arranger, who had worked with Tom Jones and Engelbert Humperdinck), it was decided that after five weeks of singing, Judy would sound better after a month of rest. (Deans also said he decided to not accept the offer of the commercial, as Judy wanted to go to the Virgin Islands.)

February 1, 1969: Judy played her last scheduled performance at the Talk of the Town in London, completing the five-week engagement. Backstage after the show, Judy told reporter Michael Dove that she and Mickey planned to settle in London and "take over a club and run it and will make it a thriving business." When asked if she would sing at the club, Judy said "of course." The nightclub Judy and Deans were to buy was in the west-end, in the Haymarket area, a side street off Picadilly Circus; Mickey to act as general manager, and Judy to sing whenever she wished. This never happened. Judy also told fans after that last show in London, that she *would* be going to New York City briefly to tape a television commercial with Mickey Rooney; Rooney would soon after tape a commercial for Braniff Airlines—with Rex Reed. While signing a fan's magazine cover before leaving the club, she said about that photo of herself, as she covered first her eyes, and then her mouth on the photo, with her hand: "See? The mouth smiles . . . but the eyes do not." Judy left the club at 2 a.m.

Early February 1969: Judy and Deans moved from the Ritz hotel, to a small mews cottage at # 4 Cadogan Lane in the Belgravia district/Chelsea, in London. The tiny home consisted of six small rooms; the front door led directly into the living room, which was next to a small bathroom, followed by a dining room and kitchen; the master bedroom upstairs was directly above the living room; also upstairs were two small bedrooms, one for Judy's dressing room, the other as Dean's den; a large bathroom was across the master bedroom, through the hall.

February 9, 1969: Judy sang a duet with Johnnie Ray at Caesar's Palace in Luton, England, where he was performing. Judy had just seen his show there on Tuesday, January 21. Ray held up a sweater from the stage that Judy had washed—and it had shrunk to the size of a child's television shirt. While leaving the club, Judy said she hoped to catch Ray's act yet again "later in the week."

February 11, 1969: Judy's divorce from Mark Herron was at last final: her attorney, Godfrey Issac, wired Judy: "final judgment Herron versus Herron entered February 11, 1969, in judgment book 6308, page 11, and signed by court Judge William E. MacFadden. Court will not send wire, but entry may be verified by telephone directly to Los Angeles county superior court clerk. Best regards—Godfrey Isaac."

February 1969 through mid March 1969: The day was spent fixing the rented mews home; seeing plays; shopping; but staying home much of the time; she made a new friend in Emil Abdelnour and to a lesser extent his partner John Francis: they owned the beauty salon at the corner of her street; Judy would see Abdelnour daily: they discussed history, politics, and religion: he would name a passage from the bible, and Judy would repeat it from memory; particularly loving the Psalms and Corinthians; they discussed the poets Shelly and Keats, as Judy had memorized many of Shelly's poems, favoring "The Skylark," which she would repeat often; Judy also spoke about the Kennedys; she was reading a book about Hearst, and asked if Abdelnour had ever read a book by Taylor Caldwell called *Dynasty of Death*.

Early March 1969: Judy had received an offer from a New York firm to start a chain of approximately 500 first and second-run theaters throughout the United States to be called Judy Garland Cinemas. The theaters would be small, about 350 seats, and Judy would only have to make promotional appearances and interviews, and be at openings. She would receive cash against a percentage of the venture's profits. Deans flew to New York immediately to start negotiations (although this project never materialized, sometime later, there were a number of Jerry Lewis Cinemas, but they quickly folded). Deans's deciding to go off to New York and leave Judy in London resulted in an argument: Johnnie Ray's manager, in his book, states that Deans was verbally abusive to Judy at this point, and had even reached out to strike her, but was stopped by Ray. When Deans got back from his short, 10-day trip, Judy and Deans reconciled.

March 15, 1969: Judy and Deans were legally married at the Chelsea Registry Office, at noon, by M. A. Laurence; then drove to St. Marylebone Parish Church for a "service of prayer and dedication" by their friend the Reverend Peter Delaney. This was followed by the reception at Quaglino's in London's West End, where Judy and Deans danced to the band's "Over The Rainbow"; they later sang "You Made Me Love You" together. Judy's headdress was made from her own design, by John Francis of her neighborhood beauty salon. There is much newsreel film footage that exists of Judy, Deans, and best man Johnnie Ray at all three locations, both in sound, and silent; black and white and color; including one black and white sound newsreel clip of Judy being interviewed at the reception, where she says it was "a lovely day, a perfect day." The reporter asked how long she knew her husband she answered "I've known my husband as long as he's known me; about three years now." When asked what she wanted now, Judy laughed "to be happy!" While Judy looked extremely frail, she seemed to be in great spirits, alert and aware. During an interview that appeared the next day in the London Sunday Express, Judy said "I've reached a point in my life where the most precious thing is compassion." Judy and Deans left for a brief honeymoon on Majorca, before switching to Paris, staying at the Georges 5 Hotel. They then moved on to fulfill engagements for four concerts for which Judy had just signed a contract, which would pay her $10,000 total, though Judy was to receive 50% of the box office take. The initial offer had apparently come in January, when the producer came to see Judy at the Talk of the Town.

March 18, 1969: Judy arrived in Stockholm, staying at the Apolonia Hotel. While on this tour, Judy's dresser would be Bridget Johansson, who had just divorced Ingemar Johansson, the former heavyweight champion of the world.

March 19, 1969: (Concert) Stockholm (theater unknown). (The performance followed that day's rehearsal with the orchestra.) Judy was doing this short tour with Johnnie Ray, who would open for her, then Judy would do the second half. The concert was a triumph, with Judy getting a standing ovation that lasted 10 minutes. The critics were equally impressed, as you'll see from these notices:

> *Dagene Myheter* (Not certain if name of critic, or name of newspaper), March 20: "At last we got the opportunity to hear Judy Garland in Sweden. She arrived happy, charming, concentrated, and relaxed, all at the same time. The audience loved her, and the evening might have turned out to be really fabulous if the loudspeakers had done what they were supposed to do. They didn't—the sound was very bad and there was no balance at all between the soloist and the orchestra. . . . Judy Garland is a great artist. She made her entrance in her poppy red dress with ostrich feathers and matching trousers. When she finished the concert, the audience went wild. . . . When Judy sang 'For Once In My Life,' she did it with great intensity. The only trouble was the loudspeakers. Sometimes they made a strange sound that Judy could scarcely be blamed for. Her vitality is of such a type that she can easily balance a 30-man orchestra, but under the circumstances we lost the fine detail in a compact and loud orchestra sound. All who know her recordings know the rhythmic subtleties she makes when she, for instance, begins a

song a fraction of a second late on the strong piece of the bar. We were not able to hear such detail in this concert and it was so good when a couple of times she sang only with the piano. It was great to see how she changed mood from song to song, and also the way she used the stage. You could pick your favorite Garland song, because she did all of them in her special and great way. I think most of us were most thrilled by her 'Somewhere Over The Rainbow.' She sat on the floor in a pink spotlight and sang it softly and beautifully."

Expressen (Critic and date unknown): "Judy Garland gave her first concert in Sweden and there were no breakdowns or trouble—just sunshine and happiness. Of course she was fabulous. She sounded exactly as she has for the last 30 years—full of warmth, intensity, and drama, and it is certain that we felt her stage magnetism and her ability to handle an audience. She worked for 55 minutes and sang 12 songs, most of them well known. When she came to take applause for the last time, it was like when Sweden wins a football game."

Deans apparently caught unauthorized professional recording equipment in the audio booth, and opened up the audio levels, ruining the recording.

March 21, 1969: The concert in Gothenburg was canceled, when, in trying to get some rest, Judy took too many sleeping pills, though she quickly recovered and went on to the next stop on the tour.

March 22, 1969: Judy and Deans had dinner with a Captain Christiansen, in Demark.

March 23, 1969: (Concert/Film) The King Kroner Club in Malmo. (Another report has the venue as the Kronprinsen.) Along with the concert, Deans and the concert promoter, Arne Stivell and his Music Artists of Europe company, agreed to film this concert as part of a documentary, to be called *A Day in the Life of Judy Garland*, with Deans to be a coproducer, along with Stivell. (Apparently a recording—made in mono, instead of recording in stereo—was made of this concert also, although the audio portion of the film would be dubbed with the sound from Judy's next concert, apparently because her voice was in stronger shape. The only audio that would remain of Judy from this concert in the final film is "Til The Clouds Rolly By" with Johnnie Ray.)

March 24, 1969: Judy arrived in Copenhagen for the tour's last concert, staying at the King Frederick Hotel, rooms 511 and 512. A lot of work was done this day, filming Judy and Mickey, as they walked about the city, etc. Judy also met the press in her suite. That evening at 10 p.m., Judy and Deans had a piano brought to their suite, which cost them "500 kronor," though they apparently didn't stay long to play it, as Judy was also reportedly at a "delightful, sweet little club" this night, the "Badstuestraede 10," till 6:20 a.m. on March 25.

March 25, 1969: (Concert) The Falkoner Centret; Copenhagen. The closing concert of this short tour with Johnny Ray, and *the last concert of Judy's career*. Judy's songs included: (Overture); "Get Happy"; "Just In Time"; "The Man That Got Away"; "I'd Like To Hate Myself In The Morning"; "For Once In My Life"; "Till The Clouds Roll By" (with Johnnie Ray); "Judy's Olio"; "Rock-A-Bye Your Baby"; "Chicago"; "San Francisco"; and "Over The Rainbow." The twenty-nine–piece orchestra was conducted by Tony Osborne. The 1,100-seat theater was sold out, at a record 125 kroner each—about $18. Only one other artist, Maria Callas, had been able to command that price, though most of the great contemporary artists had performed at the Falkoner Centret since it opened in 1959. It was reported in the Ekstrabladet paper of March 26, that "punctually at 4 p.m., Judy Garland began to apply her make-up for her performance," and that after the concert finished at 10 p.m., the filming of the documentary would continue until dawn, at which time it would be finished. The audio portion of this concert can

Judy onstage at the Falkoner Center in Copenhagen, March 25, 1969, for the last concert of her career. (Courtesy of Photofest.)

be heard on a CD: *Judy Garland in Concert—The Beginning and the End* on the Legend label; Released in 1993, this two-CD set contains Judy's Closing Night of "The Palace" Tour, from San Fransico, June 22, 1952 on the first CD; and this Copenhagen concert on the second disc; the duet of "Till The Clouds Roll By" with Ray, is actually from the March 23 concert in Malmo.

The film *A Day in the Life of Judy Garland* immediately disappeared with Arne Stivell and his Music Artists of Europe outfit after this last concert. Legal action had to be taken to prevent the film from being shown; it has also been rumored that footage was shot of Judy nude in her bathroom with hidden cameras, though none of this footage has ever been known to have ever been seen by anyone. In 1970, a thirty-three-minute version of what was shot, turned up on British television as *The Last Performance*. It features color film of the March 23 Malmo concert with the audio dubbed in—carelessly—from the final concert of March 25 in Copenhagen; while the black and white footage of Judy offstage shows her doing various activities such as walking around with Deans, or singing around a piano with Ray, getting her makeup on, etc. It often horrifying to see, as Judy appears painfully thin and old beyond her forty-six years; the concert footage onstage in color, and with Judy made up, and under the lights, is much easier to take on the eye, and the heart. Despite her appearance, Judy does seem to be in control, and aware, and in great spirits, both on and off-stage. Her final concert was warmly, indeed enthusiastically received, and Judy's voice was still amazingly able to send chills through its listener's spines, maintaining its vibrancy, and in fact sounding stronger than it did earlier in 1969, and even in better shape than on many occasions in 1967 and 1968. *The Last Performance* had not been heard of since 1970—except for circulating among Garland fans—until March 1995, when the syndicated television show *Entertainment Tonight* featured clips from the film, as its main "Inside Story," as the recently uncovered film was about to be auctioned-off by a London auction house. Apparently Arne Stivel had left it in his will to someone who was now selling it. It is believed that the auction never took place, as Judy's daughter Lorna Luft was having the attorney of Judy's estate stop the sale, as Judy's original contract gave her 25% ownership of the film, with Deans owning 25% and Stivell the other 50%. This film is certainly not for consumption by the general public.

What *should* be seen are these reviews from Copenhagen: Longtime Judy fan Sonny Gallagher spent a great deal of time and money, just after Judy's passing, to obtain the reviews and have them translated—since they represent the last notices of Judy Garland's career. They are reprinted here—extensively—for the first time outside of Sonny's journal and assorted lines elsewhere:

> *Ktuelt* (Knud Voeler), March 26: "Judy With All Her Personality" (Headline): "She was herself. Her distinctive personality was intact . . . Judy Garland's talent, vigorous as before. Her microphone technique is dazzling, her mode of delivery strong and glowing, her personal charm indisputable. She was dressed in a simple fire-red but not gaudy pants suit without an elaborate hairdo: She was just herself—without anything not belonging to her type. She flung her hit songs into the microphone in a way that produced dramatic and brilliant effects, or she chatted quietly and intimately, apparently aware, a little awkwardly, uncertain, but at the same time witty, warm, and winning all hearts. There were the old standbys—'Just In Time,' 'Somewhere Over The Rainbow,' 'San Francisco.' The applause was long and persistent."
>
> *Politiken* (Herbert Steinthal), March 27: "Judy Garland's Triumph" (Headline): "How was she then? Before Judy Garland's long-awaited first appearance in Copenhagen the air was thick with rumors that the star was no longer a star, that she had lost not only her voice but also that she could no longer even get through her program at all. And so she stood suddenly there on Falkoner Centret's enormous stage and disproved all the rumors in the world. After

only a few minutes she held the entire hall in the palm of her hand . . . the little woman who immediately filled the air with electricity. She was slim and gracious in her red pants suit under a flowing feather-trimmed robe. The great brown eyes sparkled in the little gamin face. Chatting, while ruffled her hair with small, quick movements, relaxed and nonchalant in manner, concentrating on her show program—that is Judy Garland as we know her from her films. 'Get Happy'—there is nothing here to indicate for even one instant any sign of collapse. Her voice is, in truth, under control and bright with infectious vitality. It strikes sparks in 'Chicago' and 'San Francisco.' The latter, which Judy Garland began with a comical vignette reminiscing of Jeanette MacDonald, simply got one's heart to beat with local patriotism. Humor bubbled in 'Rock-A-Bye Your Baby With A Dixie Melody' and in the impudent verses about the girl who dreams of doing something really wicked in 'I'd Like To Hate Myself In The Morning' ["I haven't learned a new song since, well, the original Vikings!," explained Judy]. Enthusiasm was so great that a spectator in the back of the hall shouted at the top of his lungs—"I love you." We all agreed. . . . [She] sang with poignant warmth and intensity. For 50 minutes we enjoyed the rhythmic finesse of Judy Garland's songs. Time after time Tony Osborne's 29 man orchestra played her signature melody but it seemed that she didn't want to sing it. After a large number of curtain calls she finally gave in to the deepest wish of the audience. She sat herself down on the stage floor and began to sing 'Somewhere Over The Rainbow.' It was as though she sang it for the first time, with fervent innocence and sweetness. It was so lovely that tears came to one's eyes. All the spectators arose and cheered Judy Garland. She had a great triumph."

Kristeligt Dagblad (H.M.), March 27: "At the close of the Judy Garland concert Tuesday evening in Falkoner Centret, an attendant came forward with a wreath of flowers shaped in the likeness of the famous rainbow that Garland sings about in 'Somewhere Over The Rainbow.' The familiar melody was played again and again during the evening. The big star of the 40's and 50's ('Easter Parade, 'A Star Is Born,' 'Meet Me In St. Louis") was a huge success. Rumor had it that Garland's health was precarious, but between the routine numbers (which, it seemed, were gone through very rapidly) there were moments of great entertainment."

Se Og Hor (A. U.), April 4: "Enthusiasm for Judy—Tumultuous Meeting With Judy Garland At Falkoner Center—She Sang Herself To a Victory At Frederiksberg" (Headline): "Seldom have expectation and skepticism been so great as in the last week in Falkoner Centret in Frederiksberg. For the first time Judy Garland stood on a Danish stage—and already with her first song the frail ex-film star swept away all skepticism. She more than repaid the expectations, so much so that the enthusiastic audience at the conclusion of the performance stood and rhythmically applauded the little great artist as an accompaniment to her familiar melody 'Somewhere Over The Rainbow.' Many well-known names from the worlds of theater and music enjoyed this first meeting with Miss Garland. Judy Garland was so grateful for her success that she, obviously touched, quietly asked about the possibility of another concert in 'wonderful Copenhagen.'"

Information (Pim), March 26: "Still Going Strong" (Headline): "It has not always been encouraging news that has been received of Judy Garland's health in the last few years and it was therefore comforting yesterday evening to ascertain that the unforgettable musical star of 'Easter Parade,' 'A Star Is Born, and 'Meet Me In St. Louis' is still in fine form and full of the old vitality. Her concert in Falkoner Centret was an enormous success and there was a contagious mutual good will between performer and public. Judy Garland has all of her old register intact. This was obvious whenever she let go in star numbers such as 'The Man That Got

Away' or held herself to the more tranquil, such as the introduction of 'Just In Time.' Her talk is still characterized by a remarkable blending of a little strength and a little helplessness: of an enormous skill that, as it were, is on the verge of snapping. The professional certainty is impressive, held down to the very suitable small talk between numbers. More than a trace of exhibitionism forms a part of her nervous strain—a style of naked emotion—and accentuated somewhat tastelessly when a newly acquired husband is brought up into the spotlight, for no particular reason. But Judy Garland's shining personality and artistic vitality are so strong that one must bow and accept the painful. It was good to see her on top and herself again."

Frederiksberg Bladet (Virtus Schade) March 27: "It Was There Anyway—Judy Garland's Success At Falkoner Centret It Is a Question of Radiance" (Headline): "A type of radiance, a stage presence. There is something that comes through that makes people enthusiastic. The audience at Falkoner Centret normally belong to the city's happiest, but this time they went wild. People streamed down the side aisles to applaud as near to the star as possible. The sounds of applause began after the first line in each song. These were a collection of old chestnuts, a collection of rehearsed gestures used time and time again on other stages and in other connections. In any event, they achieved their purpose—one felt part of a cult ceremony. The public seeks a star, an idol, and if one has neither the age nor the temperament to admire the Beatles, Judy Garland can fill the need. She is obviously fashioned of the stuff from which stars are made. . . . One immediately likes her and hopes that the evening will go well for her. And because we all hope so the evening does go off well. . . . One sees how a star like this is reborn each time, taking form for each spectator's eyes, and that is suspenseful."

Berlinske Tidende (Svend Kragh-Jacobsen), March 26: "A Star In Her Full Radiance—Judy Garland, at Falkoner Centret, showed Herself to be One of the Truly Great Personalities of Show Business" (Headline and sub-headline): "We found her last evening to be an enchanting entertainer, an exquisite artist in her field. Her confidence, her well-planned effects reveal a skillful competency; added to this is the radiant personality so uniquely hers. . . . So there she stood youthful against the large stage, slim as a boy, with a boy's long thin arms—in constant movement. The long slim legs, tight harem-pants, and the trailing robe bordered with large ostrich feathers—the whole costume in bright cerise, extremely low-necked. She wore only a little costume jewelry—a buckle, a brooch, and a necklace, and above their glitter rose the gamin head with the short-clipped, elegant hair-do, the black hair tight about her head. There was something infinitely fragile about her—almost touchingly in the first few minutes, as she, with a type of curtsy, advanced to the center of the stage and at once began 'Forget Your Troubles, Come On Get Happy.' Clear, thin tones, but therefore keen, compelling. They grow warmer and suddenly the full tones pour forth. This is her trick—in the nature of a coup. And out of this delicate little body emerges a surprising sound, surprising in its strength, in its power to fill the spacious hall, in its ability to sound at the same time both vulgar and elegant. We were caught up and held spell-bound for the three-quarters of an hour in which she sang, spoke, strolled, and coquetted through her numbers. We knew them all, and the audience gave her the cue for one after the other. The song above all others was 'For Once In My Life.' She has finally captured happiness. The tomboy became completely feminine here: a woman of impressive temperament in her certainty that, for once at least, she really owned something, had something to call her own. Naturally, she brought out here her broken life, her good and bad luck, and this gave added color and depth to her rendition. Here one listened and was truly thrilled. . . . There were naturally the songs from films, of which she has a great store. For example, 'San Francisco,' where she 'never will forget Jeanette MacDonald,' as humorously stated in the introductory stanzas. Judy Garland gave the well-known popular song her full

> tone and made it her own. She also gave a dazzling rendition of 'Chicago,' using her warm and witty coquetterie to bring, as she is impressively able to do, new luster to an old matter. The love songs were never sickly sentimental. 'Just In Time' had the characteristic glow the song calls for, and 'I'd Like To Hate Myself In The Morning' received all the color of its text in the tuneful gaiety that she is so well able to give. The delight of he audience increased with each number. In between she made small talk—and abandoned elegance a little in order to stimulate further cheers from the gentlemen in the hall. She left about 10 o'clock but as the thunderous applause continued, came back in again. She seemed greatly amused by the Danish specialty of clapping in time. Humming her familiar theme song, she sank to the floor and then sang 'Over The Rainbow.' A star was not only born, but reborn before our eyes. A star with personal sweetness, with a style distinctly her own that allows her to shift from the somewhat surprising boyish attitude to a convincing and strongly erotic femininity. Our experience with Judy Garland served to reinforce the fact that she is one of the truly great in show business. She became a captivating experience face-to-face."

March 26, 1969: (Interview) Judy gave her last known interview—with Hans Vangkilde, for Radio Denmark. Vangkilde recorded her in her hotel suite. The surviving portions of the interview that exist in private collections (along with some moments that were spliced onto the soundtrack of *The Last Performance* film) reveal Judy to be in excellent form and spirits the day after her final concert triumph. She sounds happy, but also very reflective. Among her comments:

> You don't always keep on top. No one does. My career, my life, has been a roller coaster. I've either been an enormous success or just a down-and-out failure, which is silly. Everybody always asks me, "How does it feel to make a comeback?" I don't know where I've been. I haven't been away, I've been working all the time.

Judy apparently spent that evening with Vangkilde at his home, as Deans had to attend to business with the film, in Stockholm; when Deans was telephoned at Judy's request, at his hotel, the Strand, Vangkilde claimed to Anne Edwards he was "incoherent, possibly drunk," and Vangkilde was not certain "he understood how serious Judy's condition appeared," as she had been crying, and seemed depressed, worrying that Deans had left her, that the hotel bill was unpaid, and Deans had only left her with $50.00.

Thursday, March 27, 1969: Judy and Deans flew to Torremolinos, on the Costa del Sol in Spain, for a long weekend. Deans apparently felt the sun was better for Judy than a hospital, but it is doubtful that this "long weekend" did any good: upon arrival, Judy took to her bed in the hotel, but the first night she slipped in the bathroom, bruising herself slightly. The next morning she fell asleep on the floor of the bathroom, with Deans having to break the door down. The day after that, they moved into a suite when it became available. The local doctor changed her medication from Ritalin to a milder medication, Longacton, and suggested that she be moved to a hospital—Deans again insisted he could help her more in the hotel. After "a few days" she seemed "considerably improved: she was in good spirits, eating, and determined to get well, her sense of humor returned." Deans then released the chauffeured car and rented a Fiat, taking Judy for a drive along the coast, which "seemed therapeutic." That night, however, "a change came over her": Judy was talking to herself and "irrational." Deans's only thought was to get her back to London, not to a hospital. He made a plane reservation, called their public-relations man Matthew West in London to arrange to have a car meet them at Heathrow Airport, and to have the mews cottage ready. The B.E.A. Caravelle plane with Judy and Deans landed at Gatwick Airport instead of at Heathrow; it was 3 a.m., and Deans only had a handful of Spanish coins and two $500 travelers' checks. He finally got "a bill changed," and hired a car and driver who drove them back home. Judy's doctor, John Traherne, came over immediately. The doctor wasn't sure what was wrong and feared possible brain damage, thinking she might not fully recover. He gave her tranquilizers. Judy woke up the next morning "bright and alert" with "no recollection" of the last 24 hours. After seeing her again, Dr. Traherne suggested that Judy had suffered the trauma of withdrawal: the abrupt discontinuance of Ritalin and the change to Longacton, which was milder. Though Judy seemed recovered, a nurse was hired to stay at the mews cottage.

April 3, 1969: Deans and his lawyer George Eldridge went to court to keep *A Day in the Life of Judy Garland* in London; the film was allowed to return to Sweden. So Deans and Eldridge flew to Sweden immediately, on the same flight as Arne Stivell. In Sweden, a copyright law was found that made it a criminal offense to show any of the disputed film footage there. When Deans returned home to London, he found that Judy's representative in France had booked her at the Olympia Theater in Paris for May 8. Deans says he then made unreasonable demands deliberately to cancel the concert; surviving notes seemingly based the cancellation on illness, as it was rescheduled for May 19, then that date was also canceled, on May 15. Other concerts contemplated at this time were for dates in Italy, Spain, Switzerland, and South Africa, although none of them happened.

April 6, 1969 to April 14, 1969: Judy and Deans took the train with Matthew West and his partner Brian Southcombe, to the latter couple's cottage in Hazelmare/West Sussex, an hour's ride from Waterloo (an hour and a half from London) to spend the weekend. The cottage was two stories high, fair-sized, with a big country kitchen that had its own huge hearth. Judy's upstairs bedroom overlooked the garden. Judy spent the weekend sitting in the sun, resting, eating tiny amounts, and sleeping a good deal. When Monday arrived and Deans had to return to London, she had been making such favorable progress that she agreed to remain at the cottage for the week, with Deans returning every evening. Judy, at one point, actually spent three hours reorganizing the kitchen, where she spent a lot of time. On cooler days she'd sit in the kitchen reading before the fire. She listened to the radio; sang; made notes for lyrics; and spent time reading: that week she was "devouring" *Citizen Hearst.* Nights were spent watching old movies on television, with Judy turning down the sound and ad-libbing her own dialogue for all the characters. When the week was up, they drove back to the mews cottage. Anne Edwards states in her 1975 biography that it was this weekend that Judy and Deans had spent the disastrous weekend in Spain, and that is was actually 10 days before he brought her back home. Apparently more certain is a Friday, April 12, 1969, Swedish newspaper *Ekstabladet*, that stated the *Day in the Life of* film would not be delivered to Arne Stivell from the London lab where it was processed, as it contained footage of Judy in the nude. Stivell is quoted as saying, "One agrees that the film contains pictures of Judy Garland in the nude and that the film shows her in an intoxicated condition, but she knew all along that she was being filmed according to the terms of the contract." Judy and Deans lost the initial London court case, and would be responsible for court costs, but on April 22, her attorneys wrote her a letter informing her that her performances were covered by the Swedish law of copyright, and it appeared as though the film could not be shown.

Mid April to mid May 1969: Judy spent the time resting in the mews cottage with Deans.

May 21, 1969: Judy and Deans flew to New York. They returned to London on May 29. They then flew back to New York the following week, and stayed until June 17, 1969. These trips were for meetings on the Judy Garland Cinema Mini-theatres, and they stayed at the apartment of the great jazz singer/pianist/arranger Charlie Cochran, on Lexington Avenue and 88th (Mickey had lived there with Charlie before moving to London with Judy). During this time in New York, Judy also saw Liza, who told biographer Gerald Frank that Judy resembled a calm, middle-aged housewife, asking Liza if she had ever tried Teflon ware, and not at all seeming like mama or "Judy Garland." Judy also saw Peter Allen, who took her to a nightclub called "Aux Puces." Judy wore a straw hat with flowers in it, and a

One of the last photographs of Judy Garland known to exist. Taken at London's Heathrow Airport on May 21, 1969, exactly one month before her passing. (Courtesy of Photofest.)

white sweater. She left them behind at the club, where the hatcheck girl, Laura, found them, and kept them at the club until it closed in 1971. After leaving the club, Peter Allen sang his song "Simon" for Judy—the first and only time Judy would hear her son-in-law sing an original Allen composition. (Also, during this time in New York, Judy was apparently on tranquilizers "rather than uppers and downers," according to Deans; at one point, Gerald Frank's biography states that Deans called his New York physician, who took Judy off her usual sleeping pill Seconal, and put her on Thorazine instead.) Other activities that trip included: a clothes shopping trip to "Revelation," escorted by friend Bob Jorgen, Deans's old roommate, where she added extravagantly to her new "mod" wardrobe, encouraged by Deans. After the shopping, Bob took her to a florist shop, where the florist refused any money, saying "you've brought too much happiness to the world": Deans claimed Judy was so touched that she wrote lyrics for a song "Words From A Flower Vendor," which she apparently hoped Deans would set to music; the lyrics are not known to have surfaced. Bob Jorgen also took Judy to lunch at Maxwell's Plum, one day; one night was spent at the Apartment, a nightclub on Second Avenue, where Charlie Cochran was entertaining. During this time Deans also took Judy into New Jersey, where he showed her the various nightclubs where he had started, playing a bit of "Over The Rainbow" for her at one place. Deans also took her and Bob Jorgen to meet Deans's parents, Mr. and Mrs. Mary DeVinko, who lived in a one-story red bungalow in Garfield, New Jersey.

June 10, 1969: Judy's forty-seventh—and last—birthday was spent in bed at Charlie Cochran's apartment. Harold Arlen had found out Judy was in New York, and sent her flowers. That day, she called her friend John Carlye. John said that Judy asked him to "let me come to California," where she often stayed with John, or his friends Tucker Fleming and Charles Williamson. John then kidded Judy that she was a "married lady now—I can't ask you. I would, you know I would." Gerald Clarke states in his biography that her releationship with Deans "was showing such strain." When John mentioned that his cat named after Judy was ill and not expected to live much longer, Judy had him put the cat near the receiver, where he heard Judy sing for the last time, softly, and tenderly, "Ju-dy . . . Ju-dy darling, get well, darling, for John and me, please get well. . . ." Also on her birthday, NBC-TV's *The Today Show* aired a Birthday Tribute to Judy.

June 15, 1969: (Personal Appearance) The Half Note nightclub; Greenwich Village, New York City. Anita O'Day was appearing there (Day was apparently now also staying with Judy and Deans at Charlie Cochran's apartment). Judy, Deans, and Cochran went to see her this night. Judy, wearing a black dress and huge picture hat, was invited onstage by O'Day, and sang "Day In, Day Out" and "Over The Rainbow." Then Anita and Judy sang "April Showers." This is the last time Judy sang on stage. An audiotape exists of a "jamming session" done either just before this appearance, or just after: Judy can be heard singing "I Love A Piano," a cappella, after O'Day is heard yelling "Play the piano!" Judy—heard in the background behind O'Day's voice—sounds lovely, bright and in strong, fine voice. Slightly less successful is her later attempt at a new song for her: the standard "When Sonny Gets Blue." Judy was not very familiar with the words, and is prompted on many of the lyrics by Cochran. Her voice sounds slightly tired, not helped by being unfamiliar with both the words, and the melody for the most part. Still, the amazing Garland instincts are there, and she makes it a haunting performance. This is the last recording known to exist of Judy Garland.

June 17, 1969: Judy and Deans flew back to London. Something she took with her was the first real Judy book that had just been published—*Judy: The Films and Career of Judy Garland*, a warm look at her great body of work, mainly concentrating on her films. (The deal for the Judy Garland Cinema had fallen through. In the early 1970s a chain of Jerry Lewis Cinemas opened, and failed immediately.) Bob Jorgen took them to New York's Kennedy Airport, and according to Gerald Clarke, after saying his good-byes, Jorgen called Mickey back to say "take very good care of her, because she's dying." On the plane, apparently Judy had agreed to Dean's proposal of their own *Day in the Life of* film, and a concert, for which she had handwritten a list of songs:

Orch Arrangments

Georgia Rose

Georgia On My Mind

Second Hand Rose

San Francisco Bay

You Came A Long Way From St. Louis

Before The Parade Passes By (Segue)

Second Hand Rose

Into Orchestra and

I Love A Parade

Good new songs

Open 1. Someone Needs Me

2. Who Am I?

(Segue into)

At Last I Have Someone Who Needs Me

(above-definite!)

Newley's This Dream

Get Lindsey's Orch of Here's To Us

When they arrived home at the mews cottage, Judy's friend, and head of the London fan club, Lorna Smith, who had dressed her at the Talk of the Town in January, came over to help unpack. Judy also spoke on the phone with Brian Glanvill, a London fan, who called Judy at the suggestion of their mutual friend, the designer Beatrice "Bumble" Dawson. Dawson thought Brian might work for Judy as an assistant. Brian says Judy told him he should come over to see her soon, and he sent her flowers to thank her, until he would be able to meet with her. They would never meet.

June 18, 1969: (Personal Appearance) Judy made her final public appearance: She was picked up at 9 p.m. by her neighbors Gina Dangerfield, and Richard Harris, and taken to Bromley, nearby, to Dangerfield's friend's—singer Jackie Trent and her husband, orchestra leader Tony Hatch's—"grand opening" of a new men's apparel shop that Trent and Hatch owned. Judy was in good spirits and didn't mind that the shop was extremely crowded; she was "gay and talkative."

June 19, 1969: Judy stayed home, engrossed in the book *Nicholas and Alexandra*. She also made a piece of molding from a tube of ready-mixed plaster that Deans had brought home; Deans then painted it gold and heated it in the kitchen until it was hard; he finally placed it by her bedside, in a Tiffany box that had held pearls Tony Bennett had given her the last Christmas.

June 20, 1969: Judy's publicist Matthew West came over to her mews cottage for lunch. Judy told him she wanted to go back to work. Judy told him she wanted to go back to work. There had apparently been talk of doing both the album for Blue Records *and* a television special, both to be done in London, in July 1969. Matthew has also mentioned to me that Judy was again making concert plans to return to the Olympia in Paris. It was hoped that Lorna and Joe would come over to London in July—then in August, they'd all fly back to the States, to spend the rest of the summer at Jerry Herman's summer home in Fire Island. Looking at her skinny arms, she announced to West that she would have to put some weight on and build up her strength. With Judy in a light and fun mood, the two of them had a lunch of doughnuts and milk. That day, Deans says he saw Judy write in her red leather-bound "Ye Olde Bitch Book"—he later found the last page still intact. It had the name "Sid" written on it, along with a comment that a friend had sent her a clip from a New York paper. Sid was apparently having a legal hassle over a hotel bill that Group Five did not pay. (This must have stemmed from a June 16 Monmouth County New Jersey Courthouse hearing when Luft had to answer bad check charges. Luft also accused Wesley Fuller of blackmail.) Judy wrote "Joey and Lorna" on this page, underlining their names, apparently afraid of any adverse publicity affecting them. Anne Edwards says the Reverend Peter Delaney called to tell her about it.

Edwards says that later Judy called Lorna in California, and the call seemed to make Judy feel much better.

Later that evening, Judy and Deans went to a dinner party celebrating the Reverend Peter Delaney's birthday. Judy appeared to be enjoying herself, but they didn't stay at the dinner party long.

June 21, 1969: Judy had a difficult time sleeping that night (from June 20 to June 21), even with barbiturates. (Anne Edwards—who worked with Mickey Deans on the first draft of his book on Judy—claims Judy had taken a heavy dosage of Nembutal.) She was very restless and still awake when the postman came at 8 in the morning. She went down to collect the mail but didn't bother to read it. Judy wrote Deans a note, as he was asleep, leaving it on the television set. The note talked only about where Judy had placed their mail, that she was going to have some food, and, after that, she was going to bed.

Saturday, June 21, 1969, was spent as a quiet day at home. Deans said they listened to their favorite records, and he played the piano for Judy, taping "some of her favorite numbers. I still have the tapes, and I can feel, when I listen to them, the intensity of Judy listening as I played them for her. Her voice comes through clearly: 'Great-groovy-brilliant, darling. . . .'" (These tapes are not known to have surfaced. According to one fan's written report, Deans was apparently big on taping Judy, for he had been known to be "taping candid conversations between Judy and others at private parties.") Deans says he was suffering from a sore throat this day, and that Dr. Traherne had sent over some penicillin tablets for him. They had planned, with Matthew West, to see Danny LaRue's closing night, but decided that Matthew should go on his own. Later in the day, Philip Roberge, a 29-year old American friend of Deans, who was said in the *Daily Sketch* to be a "close friend," and someone who assisted Deans in his "recording and show business deals" (who Deans said "has a theatrical agency"), "dropped by." As, by then, Judy "felt a little ill too," Deans says Phillip offered to fix dinner; Judy claimed she had eaten earlier, which is doubtful if she wasn't feeling well, and hadn't slept well the night before; She excused herself, and went upstairs to bed. Deans says Phillip "broiled hamburgers, and they ate as they watched the television documentary *The Royal Family*. He left before midnight, and I went to our bedroom. Judy was still awake"

Deans said he didn't think it would be wise to sleep in the same bed, as his throat was very sore. Judy apparently pointed to her own throat, and laughed, with Deans getting into bed with her. Deans does not mention that Matthew West had called from the theater during intermission and had spoken with Judy. Matthews has said that Judy and Deans were going back with him to his country home the following day (where Judy had stayed the first week in April). Matthew would be the last person to talk with Judy Garland, and he told me during an interview that Judy "was not panicky. She had a lot to live for—including three great big reasons to live: Liza, Lorna, and Joe. She sounded happy and serene, and rather mellow."

In David Shipman's controversial and often-questioned biography *Judy Garland: The Secret Life of an American Legend*, published in the States in 1993, Shipman claims that after the television documentary, "Deans and Garland began another of their interminable quarrels, during which Garland ran screaming into the street, waking neighbors. Deans left the house. . . . Sonia Roy, wife of the dance band leader, Harry Roy, later claimed that she was visited by Garland on the evening of June 21. Garland told the Roys that she intended to kill herself. The Roys tried to talk her out of it, and believed they had succeeded. . . . When Deans returned, he thought Garland was sleeping. A transatlantic telephone call at 10:40 a.m. London time woke him." Deans makes no mention of any of Shipman's statements, although, again, much of what Shipman wrote has been deemed controversial and unsubstantial by those that were around Judy at the time.

There have been unsubstantiated rumors among Garland fans that Deans was one for taking late night walks without Judy, in a park near their mews cottage, and that Deans had only *just* returned home at the time of the phone call at 10:40 a.m. (Although Matthew West told me that Judy told him that Deans was home, upstairs in bed with a sore throat. It was noted that in the summer of 1980 when Deans overdosed—though not lethally—he was reported by the press at that time to have been living over a garage in a Hamptons, New York home with a young male lover, and that he is currently believed to be running a gay bar in Dayton, Ohio. *The New York Post* reported in November 1995 that he was seen in a New York City Greenwich Village gay bar, Julius, "sporting gold chains, and a pot belly.") There have also been questioned raised about the strength of the medication Judy was taking during that week, including unfounded rumors that she may not have known she was taking medication that was double the strength of her normal dosage. According to a news-wire service report, reprinted in the July 11, 1969, issue of *Life Magazine*, there had been medication (barbiturates), "prescribed on Thursday, June 19, 1969, 25 tablets, found half empty, and on Saturday, June 21, a bottle of 100—found unopened."

Although a clear and precise picture has yet to be painted of her final hours, at some time during the very early morning hours of June 22, 1969, sometime between 2:30–4:40 a.m., Judy Garland did pass away. Deans had been awakened at 10:40 a.m. London time by Charlie Cockran and John Carlyle calling from California, where it was 2:40 a.m. Deans says he didn't see Judy on her side of the bed, went knocking on the locked bathroom door, then came back to tell Charlie he'd call him back. He climbed out of the window of the dressing room, walked over the roof, and peered through the window of the bathroom, where he saw Judy sitting on the toilet with her arms on her lap, and her head resting on her arms. As he picked her up, Deans knew she had passed away, put her back gently in the same position, then ran downstairs to call the police and an ambulance. The police said Judy had been dead for "several hours," and the coroner later stated "six to eight hours."

Judy's body was taken to Westminster Hospital, where on Wednesday, June 25, it was announced by the pathologist Dr. Derek Pocock, that Judy had died from "an accidental death by an incautious overdose of barbiturates." Apparently there were the equivalent of ten one-and-a-half-grain Seconal sleeping tablets in her system, and no food! The Death Certificate, completed by the coroner Gavin Thurston, as Application # 496418; QDX 083932; Entry # 20, of the Chelsea district, states the Cause of Death as "Barbiturate poisoning; incautious self-overdose; accidental," and lists the medication as Quinalbarbitone. The certificate also lists her residence address: 4 Cadogan Lane; her maiden surname as "Gumm"; her occupation as "Entertainer" and "wife of Michael DeVinko, an Artiste's manager." Dean's real name is Michael DeVinko. The certificate is signed by P.A. Burton, Deputy Registar. Of course, Judy's general health had deteriorated to a remarkable degree, which anyone looking at her would be able to see, yet no one demanded that she be in a hospital until she was healthier and heavier (though of course, *making* Judy do anything she didn't want to do was a whole other matter). Apparently, Judy's autopsy shows that all of her systems—including her liver—had completely shutdown, that she was totally dehydrated, and that eating had become painful, as nothing could pass properly through her system. Even in the end, Judy was a walking miracle, as she kept on going—years after any normal mortal would have not been able to—in order to share her gifts with her audiences.

Judy's funeral on Friday, June 27, 1969, was legendary, as over 22,000 people came to pay their last respects.

Though Judy's legacy started immediately afterwards—with the Stonewall riots in the early morning hours of Saturday, June 28, 1969, being attributed to her passing by many who were there that night—Judy's real legacy has grown in the last thirty-plus years, to the point where she is perhaps just as loved today as she was in her lifetime.

It is hoped that "the Legend's Legacy," as I like to call it, is quite obvious to you from having read all of these pages. The legacy is not the problems she faced, but the fact that she kept overcoming them in order to create the real legacy she has left the world: 40 films; 60 television shows; over 12 albums and 100 single recordings; hundreds of radios shows; and well over 1,500 concert, nightclub, vaudeville, military, charitable, and personal appearances—the greatest body of work any performer ever accomplished—all of which continue to touch, move, and inspire countless millions of people, and new generations, with the soaring artistry and soul of the single greatest talent the world has ever known, or ever will know—Judy Garland.

"GOODNIGHT . . . I LOVE YOU VERY MUCH! GOOD NIGHT . . . GOD BLESS." Despite all the loves of her life, her greatest love affair was with her audience. No one gave more to audiences than Judy Garland. The Legend's Legacy of talent, heart, strength, and most of all soul, continues to this day. (Courtesy of Photofest.)

Appendix A

The "*After-Life*" Career Highlights

Fall 1969: The album Judy reportedly knew was taped at her last London engagement, and that her last husband Mickey Deans was editing, was released by the label she signed to record for, now called Juno Records. The LP, *Judy. London. 1969* would receive a Grammy Award nomination for Best Liner Notes—Rex Reed. The label Radiant released seven LPs and/or cassettes of solos from Judy's television series, although they would be sued by a rival label, Tucker Records, who claimed they had the rights to the material.

1970: First major reissue of recordings, when Decca Records released *Judy Garland: Collectors Items 1936–1945*, a two-record set of singles she recorded for the label, of songs that were not generally associated with her.

1972: A 60-minute television documentary is done for the British series *Omnibus*, which features clips of Judy's movies, along with interviews with Liza, ex-husband Mark Herron, Mickey Rooney, Peter Lawford, and others. (Liza and Herron were often edited out in versions shown after the original airing.)

1973: Capitol Records released a single, "abridged" LP of "highlights" from the two-record set *Judy Garland and Liza Minnelli "Live" at the London Palladium* just after Liza Minnelli won the Academy Award for *Cabaret.*

May 1974: The theatrical feature film *That's Entertainment*—a celebration of the MGM Musical—was released. It became the sixth highest grossing film of the year, and its two-LP soundtrack was a huge success on the charts. These both feature excerpts of many Metro highlights of Judy's work there from 1935–1950, and Judy seemingly was "discovered" again by a whole new generation (including this author). Also that year, an episode of Judy's television series—the "Americana" Concert—was rebroadcast in many markets, and one of the finest—and first—books on Judy was released: Al Diorio's *Little Girl Lost* was the first biography to offer detailed lists of Judy's movies, television shows, and recordings.

1975: Judy becomes the "darling" of the book publishing industry, as no less than three major books are released this year. First out of the gate (February, I believe) was Anne Edwards *Judy Garland* (often poorly executed, but comes to life in the coverage of Judy's final months), followed by Christopher Finch's *Rainbow* (released early spring, I believe; full of glossy, stunning, black and white photos, the book has been praised and proclaimed a favorite by many; I find it a bit scattered, and uneven, as it skips over Judy's concert years, but occasionally illuminating, and obviously written by an author with talent), and finally, in May, came *Judy*, a massive tome (639 pages) by famed author Gerald Frank. Liza called it: "The next best thing to being there," as it had the full cooperation of Judy's family: her three children, and other relatives; four of the five husbands; and scores of Judy's friends and coworkers. A brilliant, alive, "you are there" epic, chock full of information. Also that year, in August, the CBS television show *60 Minutes* did a lengthy profile on Judy, interviewing the three children, Sid Luft, and several of her associates. It would prove to be a favorite of Mike Wallace, who narrated the piece. In fact, it would be repeated on Christmas Day, 1977 (although slightly edited.)

Summer 1976: *That's Entertainment Part 2* is released to movie theatres, and once again, it—and its soundtrack LP on MGM Records—features many excerpts of Judy's MGM work.

1978: Two of Judy's Capitol Records LPs are reissued (although the label cuts a song from each): 1957's *Alone*, and 1960's *That's Entertainment*. Also in November of that year, NBC-TV broadcast a two-hour made-for-television movie about seven early years in Judy's life, from 1932 through *Oz* in 1939. *Rainbow* (based on Finch's 1975 book), was highly promoted and rated, and received raves for the direction by Jackie Cooper (Judy's first "Hollywood" boyfriend in 1936). But pans were given to its star, Andrea McArdle (Broadway's "Annie"), for giving no life to her role as one of the most vital performers in history. (It continues to be rebroadcast on late night television or on certain cable channels, like Lifetime. At one point it was available on videocassette from a small label that actually specialized in "X" rated "adult" films.)

1979: Another Judy album is reissued by Capitol Records: 1964's *Just For Openers* (compilation of songs from 1963–1964 television series), again as an "abridged" LP with a track cut.

1980: Judy's unreleased 1960 two-record set recorded in London is finally released to stores as *Judy in London*. Also that year: the first home video releases of Judy's work hit the stores. Most of them are "bootleg" copies of television shows and out-takes of *Annie Get Your Gun*, but one is the first legitimate release: MGM/CBS Home Video issues *The Wizard of Oz* in November, 1980, at the price normally charged then: $59.95.

1981: More home video releases: *Meet Me in St. Louis* (speeded-up slightly, to fit on a shorter length tape) and *The Pirate* from MGM/CBS Home Video, and *A Star Is Born* from Warner Brothers. (This film is also speeded-up to fit the 2½ hour movie on a 2-hour tape. It's amazing to see how far companies have come in restoring and remastering their video releases.)

1982: Pioneer Artists releases the first Judy LaserDisc, by presenting a Sid Luft-produced compilation, *Judy Garland in Concert.* (It was reissued in 1990, in Digital Sound, but has since been discontinued.)

1983: One of the best years of Judy's "afterlife" career!: Her *A Star Is Born* is restored by Warner Brothers to its nearly complete 181-minute running time (only a few moments are not found/restored), and a new print—in stereo—is lauded at gala Re-Premieres in New York at Radio City Music Hall, on July 7, and in Los Angeles, and other key cities a short time after. The media frenzy—including Judy on the *cover* of the prestigious *American Film* magazine—gets the film a nation-wide art-house release.

January 1984: The restored *A Star Is Born* is released in a deluxe two-tape box, with notes by Sid Luft, and also becomes available on LaserDisc.

1985: Another "afterlife" milestone. The PBS-TV documentary *The Concert Years* is presented as part of the network's *Great Performances* series. Hosted by daughter Lorna Luft, this clip-filled tribute wins raves in the media, and the amount of pledge dollars it brings into PBS, makes it one of the greatest successes in their history, along with winning a multitude of new fans for Judy.

1986: Judy's first *compact disc* is released: *America's Treasure*, produced by Sid Luft, features tracks from Judy's 1960 London sessions, along with added applause and dialogue from her series, made it seem as a concert. (The disc is re-issued in 1995 by DCC Compact Classics.)

1987: Capitol Records jumped on the digital bandwagon, by releasing two Judy CDs that year: An *abridged Judy At Carnegie Hall* in April (which so outraged the public, that Capitol made plans to re-issue the complete two-record set), and the complete *Judy! That's Entertainment* disc in the fall.

1989: (January 17) Capitol Records finally released its two-CD set of the all the songs from the *Judy at Carnegie Hall* album (and even restores some of Judy's dialogue and stories.) The set apparently does well enough to inspire the label to release four more CDs in June: 1955's *Miss Show Business* ; 1956's *Judy*; 1957's *Alone* ; and a *never*-Legitimately-*released* "live" recording session from 1962, known as *Judy Takes Broadway* but *needlessly* retitled *Judy Garland "Live."* Also this year, the fiftieth anniversary of *The Wizard of Oz* movie garnered much worldwide press; and a remastered video and laser which sold in the millions.

1991: The first week of December saw the release of Capitol Record's three-CD box set: *Judy Garland: The One and Only.* The set received much press, rave reviews, and brisk sales (75,000 units, according to *USA Today*, although a recent SoundScan report shows that figure as 17,094).

1994: In May, MGM released *That's Entertainment Part 3* to select theatres, winning Judy additional raves for her MGM work (*USA Today* called her "the *heartbeat* of the film!"). In July, MCA Records released *The Complete Decca Masters, Plus*, a four-CD box which contains *all* 79 Judy singles released by Decca from 1936–1947, along with several alternate versions. It sells incredibly well, reportedly between 15,000–20,000 units. Other CD releases that year: a 1960 *Paris* concert, and the soundtrack to *That's Entertainment.* Liza mentions the twenty-fifth anniversary of her mother's passing, at the June "Gay Pride" rally, to which she is welcomed by a million people chanting "Judy! Judy! Judy! Judy!" over and over again!

1995: A banner year: Over *thirty* CDs and a dozen *video* releases that year! Among the highlights: Rhino Records issuing MGM Soundtracks (Judy's various sets sell over 108,000 copies) and MGM/UA Home Video releases in March in a much ballyhooed five-laser-disc box set *The Golden Years at MGM.* I started my *Garlands for Judy: The Legend's Legacy* tribute magazine. For more information, visit www.garlandsforjudy.com or e-mail me at Garlands63@aol.com or send a self-addressed-stamped-envelope to me at PO Box 2743, New York, NY 10164-2743. (Email is preferred.)

1996: More Rhino Records releases, including the ultimate two-CD set: *Collector's Gems from the MGM Films*, a breathtaking anthology released October 1, that includes rare outtakes—including *Annie Get Your Gun* songs—many mixed to true *stereo* for the first time.

1998: The ultimate Judy CD box set was released on October 13 by the label 32 Records. Called *Judy*, the box set covers the 40 years of surviving Judy material (from 1929, at age 7, to 1969, including one of her last performances) on four CDs (of which two focus on her legendary television series), along with a videotape of highlights from the television series, and 100-page color book with essays and thoughts by Will Friedwald, Camille Paglia, Aretha Franklin, Mort Lindsey, and this author, who also coproduced the box set along with Grammy-winner Joel Dorn and his son, Adam Dorn. Nine months in the making, *Judy* is a must for any Judy fan, either new or a long-time fan, mainly because it is the only audio release to span the length of Judy's entire career. Also, on November 6, Warner Brothers reissued *Oz* to 1,800 theaters in a digitally remastered version.

1999: Pioneer Entertainment and Classic World Productions, Inc. began releasing DVDs of *The Judy Garland Show* on June 15 (*Volume One*), followed up with *Volumes Two* and *Three* (the Christmas Show), and a DVD box set *The Judy Garland Show Collection*. The best book on the making of *Oz* was published: *The Wizardry of Oz* by Jay Scarfone and William Stillman. Warner Home Video releases *The Wizard of Oz* in a restored VHS and deluxe DVD with hours of extras, and also issues *A Star Is Born* in a newly remastered digital transfer on VHS and laser disc (the DVD would finally come in the fall of 2000.) Liza Minnelli sings "The Trolley Song" with Judy from the soundtrack of *Meet Me in St. Louis*, during her *Minnelli On Minnelli* show at the Palace Theater in New York City, where Judy played three of her most famous engagements, including her 1951 and 1967 "comebacks." (Liza's show would be recorded at the Palace, and released on Angel Records in February, 2000. The CD includes her duet.)

2000: *The Judy Garland Show—Volume Four* is released, as is the New York Times bestselling book *Get Happy: The Life of Judy Garland* by Gerald Clarke, a powerful, devastating and illuminating look at the legend. Warner Home Video at last issued the movie *Annie Get Your Gun* on DVD and VHS, including much of the material from the two songs Judy shot for the movie. Turner Classic Movies Music/Rhino Records released the soundtrack to *Annie*, with all of the Garland-cast songs following the Betty Hutton tunes as well. DCC Compact Classics issues *Judy at Carnegie Hall* complete and uncut in a direct transfer from the original tapes, on two 24-karat Gold CDs.

2001: Capitol Records issues *Judy at Carnegie Hall: Fortieth Anniversary Edition* in a 24-bit digitally remixed and remastered deluxe edition that also presents the entire concert exactly as it happened, from the original three-track remote session tapes, along with new photos shot by Milton Greene, and thoughts from Mort Lindsey and yours truly. The CD debuted at Number 26 on the Billboard Pop Catalog Charts, and Number 20 on their Internet charts. Judy scores on television in early 2001: E! presents a two-hour highly rated and critically acclaimed look at her life on their *E! True Hollywood Story* series, and the four-hour miniseries *Life with Judy Garland: Me and My Shadows* based on Lorna Luft's 1998 book airs on ABC-TV over two nights, with the first night becoming the fourth highest rated show of the week, and drawing 20.3 million viewers. A host of Emmy Award nominations follow, with five wins, including Judy Davis for Best Acress and Tammy Blanchard for Best Supporting Actress for their brilliant work. *The Judy Garland Show* DVDs continue, including *Volume Five* with Barbra

Streisand, *Just Judy*—a collection of some great solo moments from the series, and *Songs For America* with all profits going to benefit the American Red Cross.

2002: Capitol is also planning to release a two-CD compilation of hits and rarities (initially sold through television); Collectables Records is issuing two "two-fers" of *Miss Show Business/Judy* and *I Could Go On Singing/Judy: That's Entertainment!*; Uncle Jim's/S&P Records will release a "two-fer" CD of *Alone/Judy in Love*; and Hip-o Records/Universal is releasing the ultimate CD of duets, solos, and outtakes from Judy's television series—*The Judy Garland Show: The Show that Got Away*; and Warner Home Video is planning on releasing a remastered *The Harvey Girls* with many extras on DVD in the first part of 2002. Look for many more projects this year in honor of Judy's eightieth birthday in June 2002, and know that there will be many more in the years to come. Remember that "The Legend's Legacy" is forever.

Appendix B

Judy's Last Will and Testament

I, JUDY GARLAND LUFT, do hereby make, publish and declare this to be my Last Will and Testament.

FIRST: I hereby revoke all former Wills and Codicils by me made.

SECOND: I direct my Executor, hereinafter named, to pay all of my just debts, funeral expenses and testamentary charges as soon after my death as can conveniently be done.

THIRD: I desire that my body be cremated and my remains disposed of as my Executor, in his sole discretion, shall decide.

FOURTH: I direct that all estate, succession, legacy, inheritance or transfer taxes however designated that shall become payable by reason of my death with respect to all property comprising my gross estate for death tax purposes, whether or not such property passes under this Will, shall be paid from my residuary estate as part of the expenses of the administration thereof, with no right of reimbursement from any recipient of any such property.

FIFTH: I hereby give and bequeath all of my right, title and interest in and to all literary, dramatic and musical works, compositions and arrangements, and any and all other works, including any written work of any form, nature and description relating thereto, composed, created, adapted, or arranged by me or for me, including any such works or compositions which may be written or composed after my demise in which I would have had any right, title or interest had I been alive, together with all participation rights, or any disposition of any nature or otherwise, to my Literary Trustees, hereinafter named,

IN TRUST, NEVER-THELESS, for the following use and purpose:

a) I direct my Literary Trustees to pay the income of said literary trust in equal shares to my Residual Trustees hereinafter named which said income is to then be paid into the trust funds hereinafter set forth for the benefit of my children.

b) I make no provision for distribution of corpus of the above literary trust because it is contemplated that, upon the expiration of all copy-rights, domestic and foreign, of said property, there will be no corpus susceptible to distribution. It is my express intention that my Literary Trustees to be authorized, in their sole discretion, to sell, lease, license and otherwise and in every manner dispose of any literary, dramatic, musical works which constitute all or part of the literary trust herein established, and that the moneys received from any and all such disposition including absolute and outright sale of such properties, be deemed income of said literary trust and distributed by the Literary Trustees pursuant to the provisions hereof.

SIXTH: All of my estate, real, personal and otherwise, of which I shall die seized or possessed, or to which I shall be in any way entitled, or over which I shall possess any (line not reprinted clearly) including Trustees, hereinafter named, IN TRUST NEVERTHELESS, for the following use and purpose:

a) to divide the principal of the trust into as many equal parts as shall equal the number of my children surviving; and

b) my Residual Trustees shall set apart and hold one (1) equal part as a trust fund for the benefit of each of my children and shall collect the income therefrom and apply so much of the net income therefrom, and any of the accumulated income, to the support, education and maintenance of the child for whom such trust fund shall have been set apart, as my Trustees shall see fit; and shall accumulate, invest and reinvest the balance of said income until such child shall attain the age of twenty-one (21) years, at which time all accumulations of net income shall be paid to such child; and thereafter shall pay the entire net income to such child until such child shall attain the age of twenty-five (25) years, at which time Two Hundred Fifty Thousand ($250,000) Dollars of the principal of the trust fund shall be paid over to such child; and thereafter shall continue to pay the entire net income annually from the balance of the trust fund to such child until such child shall attain the age of thirty (30) years, at which time Two Hundred Fifty Thousand ($250,000) Dollars of the then principal of the trust fund shall be paid over to such child; and thereafter shall (the next line is not clear) balance of the trust fund to such child until such child shall attain the age of thirty-five (35) years, at which time the entire balance of the principal of the trust fund shall be paid over to such child; and, if any child shall die before attaining any of the ages herein before set forth, then the trust fund of such deceased child shall be divided equally between the children surviving.

c) If any children of mine shall have attained any such respective ages at the time that such trust fund is directed to be set apart for such child, my Residual Trustees shall then pay over to such child such part, or parts, or all, as the case may be, of such fund instead of holding same in trust, as are directed to be paid over to such child upon attaining such respective ages.

SEVENTH: Anything herein contained to the contrary notwithstanding, my Residual Trustees May at any time or from time to time, pay over to any child of mine so much or all of the principal of the trust for the benefit of such child, as my Residual Trustees may in their discretion deem advisable, which payments shall be absolute and free from all trusts, and the judgment of my Residual Trustees as to the amount of such payment and the advisability thereof shall be final and conclusive upon all persons interested in or who may become interested in my estate or such trust. Trustees are authorized or directed to apply any income or principal to the support, education and maintenance of any person, my Residual Trustees, in determining the amount to be so applied, are authorized to disregard and not to take into consideration the amount of income received by such person from other sources or the amount of such person's independent property.

NINTH: Whenever, pursuant to this Will, my Residual Trustees are authorized and directed to apply any income or principal to the support, education, and maintenance of any minor, my Residual Trustees are authorized, among other methods, to pay all or any part of such income or principal at any time and from time to time to such minor, guardian of such minor or person with whom such minor may reside.

TENTH: I hereby nominate, constitute and appoint DAVID BEGELMAN, FREDDY FIELDS and ALLEN SUSSMAN as Literary Trustees under this, my Last Will and Testament. In the event any one of said Literary Trustees predeceases me, or for any reason fails to qualify or serve or continue to serve in such capacity, I hereby nominate, constitute and appoint MARVIN MEYERS as Alternate Literary Trustee.

ELEVENTH: I hereby nominate, constitute and appoint DAVID BEGELMAN, FREDDY FIELDS and ALLEN SUSSMAN as Residual Trustees under this, my Last Will and Testament. In the event any one of said Residual Trustees predeceases me, or for any reason fails to qualify or serve or continue to serve in such capacity, I hereby nominate, constitute and appoint MARVIN MEYERS as Alternate Residual Trustee.

(Provision #12 does not appear)

THIRTEENTH: I hereby give to my Residual Trustees and my Executor, in addition to the powers conferred upon them by law, the power to retain, deal with or dispose of it by public or private sale, or by lease, mortgage, conveyance or otherwise, any property subject to their control hereunder, and to invest and reinvest any such property, in any manner and at any time and under any terms, whether or not such investment or reinvestment is a legal investment or reinvestment for an Executor or Residual Trustee, in their sole discretion, as if they were sole individual owners of the same or of acting in respect to the same in a fiduciary capacity.

IN WITNESS WHEREOF, I have hereunto subscribed my name and affixed my seal this 30th day of June 1961, One Thousand Nine Hundred Sixty-One.

Signed JUDY GARLAND LUFT

SIGNED, SEALED, PUBLISHED, AND DECLARED by JUDY GARLAND LUFT, the Testatrix above-named, as and for her Last Will and Testament, in our presence, and in the presence and we, at her request, in her presence, and in the presence of each other, this attestation clause having first been read aloud to the Testatrix and to us, have hereunto subscribed our names as witnesses this 30th day of June One Thousand Nine Hundred Sixty-One.

Signed: Harriet ( ) residing at 10 West 86th St., New York

Daniel ( ) residing at 300 East 57th St., New York

H ( ) residing at 114 East Ave, New York

Appendix C

Judy's Address Book

The Listings in Judy Garland's last phone book, circa 1967–1969/red leather, *Judy* on front.

A:

Harold Arlen; Richard Avedon; ASCAP; J. Meyer (John Meyer.)

B:

Leslie Bricusse; Betty Bacall; Richard Belanger; Anne Bryant (She crafted new musical arrangements for Judy, late in 1968); Tony Bennett; Lenny Baren.

C:

CMA; Begelmen; C.M.A. Re London Irv Squires; Cumaro Rivers; Bobby & Delores Cole (Bobby was Judy's musical arranger/advisor from January 1964–March 1964, and her conductor during 1967; Delores was his wife); Harrison Carrol (Carrol was a newpaper columnist that Judy frequently spoke with); Johnny Carson c/o NBC Studios; Chase Manhattan; Manuafacturers Hanover Trust Co. New York; Marine Marshall Gave Trust, New York; Chris (Lawford, Joey's Friend); Prudential Cleaners (in Boston).

D:

Arthur Dillinger; Bill Doll (He ran Poster Company that made a 1967 Judy poster); Anthony DeFalco (Work/Home; He may have been the promotor who was reported keeping Judy's musical arrangements, as she apparently owed him money over a cancelled concert); John Derger; Arlene Dahl (the actress); Mr. Di's; Ken Darrell (Piano Procurer & Vocalist); Harold Davidson.

E:

Roger Edens; Eddie Fisher; Engelo, Maria; Esquire Limo.

F:

Fairfield Apts (Marlene Dietrich; Mr. Richardson); Ray Filiberti (Judy's "Group Five" boss); Hal Fishman (Office and home numbers); P. Friedman; W. Fuller (Wesley Fuller; close friend and musical advisor: see early June 1968 for more information); Freeman, Benjamin (Judy's attorney in Boston); Fuller's- Glaisfer.

G:

Garland-Boston Apt.; Prudential Buildings (Judy's apartment building complex in Boston, where she lived for a short while in the fall of 1968: see September 7, 1968 for more information); Richards; Ryan (these were people who lived in the complex with Judy); Peter Fall (another Boston friend); Berney Glassman (Home number listed; this was the head of Pathe Pictures, the man who had licensed Judy's television shows; For more information, see mid September 1966); Denise Gross; Tom Green; Lorna—Long Island; Marcy and Gary, Lowell, Mass.; Group 5: Ray Filiberti; Frank Gucci; Att; Lynn—Secretary for Jack Green.

H:

Hair Dressers: Bob La Ca; Raymond of London; Harvey Limassome; Marvin Hamlish.

J:

Robert Jordon; Jones, Judy; John Meyer; Jillys 52 St; Glyn Jones.

K:

Dirk Kaplan; Katz, Isadore (accountant, whom Judy refers to in one of her notes); Bob Kurman; Robert Kennedy; Dr. Binder; Dr. Kaufmann; The Kitchen: 23 Joy Street.

L:

Lee; Sid Luft; Irving Lazar; Liberace; Elenor Lambere; Liza & Peter Allen; Lorna Luft; Barry Leighton (home and office); Madeline Lorton (office); Chris Lawford—Joe Luft's Friend; Joe Luft; Lorna Luft.

M:

Mort Lindsey; Mort (Office); Mickey R.; Paul M; Madelin Lorton (two numbers); MGM; Liza, Calif.: Century Plaza Hotel; Liza; J. Meyer; Roddy McDowel; Martin Cleaners; Dr. Or.

P:

PJ Clarks (New York City restaurant); Dr. David Protech; Eite Priger; Palumbo, Gene (Judy's conductor); Prudential Apartments (Judy's Boston residence.)

R:

M. Rooney (Mickey Rooney), Calif.; ABC Printing Co., John M; Park Sheraton Pharmacy; Roberts, Ken, Peter Rogers; Mickey Rooney; Michael Butler; Richard Striker (Judy stayed with him in the fall of 1968 in his New York City apartment; he was a fan that had a large Garland collection.)

S:

Selma Scher; Bernie Scher (office number).

T:

Talk Of The Town; Tyler, Dr. (home and hospital numbers listed); Twentieth Century Fox.

W:

Wal G; Wai Wong; Jenny Wheeler (fan, and friend of Nancy Baar, Wheeler visited Judy's home on October 5, 1966: see that entry for more information; Jenny was frequently introduced—by Judy—as Judy's secretary in the fall of 1968); Welbarb.

*****

Receipts, cards, etc, inside phone book front cover pocket:

Lord & Taylor 12/2/68 $15.97 total (pink receipt)

Boston, Mass (Picked up by John Meyer as soon as he got into Boston to go see Judy in hospital); Paid by BC (Bank Card). There were 3 or 4 items here:

$9.00

$5.00 (2 at $2.50 each, I believe)

$1.50

——

.47 (tax)

$15.97 total

Appendix D

Recommended Movies and Music

While I have listed the performances that are available or exist within the entries for the date the work was originally done, here is a re-cap of some of the collections that contain some of Judy's best work currently available on CD and Home Video.

CD:

Judy (1998, 32 Records.) A box set that covers the 40 years of surviving Judy material (from 1929 at age 7, to 1969, including one of her last performances) on four CDs (two focus on her legendary television series), along with a videotape of highlights from the television series, and a 100-page color book with essays and thoughts by Will Friedwald, Camille Paglia, Aretha Franklin, Mort Lindsey, and this author, who coproduced the box set along with producers Grammy-winner Joel Dorn and his son Adam Dorn. Over nine months in the making, *Judy* contains recordings from Decca, Capitol, her MGM and Warner Brother movies, an outtake from the "Swanee" recording session for *Star Is Born,* radio, rehearsal, and "live" performances at Carnegie Hall and The London Palladium. It is a must for any Judy fan, either new or a long-time fan, mainly because it is the only audio release that spans the entire length of Judy's career.

Judy at Carnegie Hall: Fortieth Anniversary Edition (2001, Capitol Records.) Judy's biggest selling, and most famous recording, is this legendary two-record (and two-CD) set from 1961. Winner of five Grammy Awards—including *Best Female Vocal* and *Album of the Year*—this is the *ultimate* of Judy "live," and is at last now available complete, exactly the way it happened, with all of Judy's brilliant patter interspersed throughout her songs.

A Star Is Born Original Soundtrack (1988, Columbia Records.) This CD features all of Judy's songs in her 1954 masterpiece (except for her "Shampoo Commercial"), and they are taken from the *stereo* film tracks (except for the 2 "cut" songs, which are in mono.) A must-have, as Judy is in incredible voice.

Judy Garland in Hollywood, 1936–1963: Her Greatest Movie Hits (1998, TCM Music/Rhino Records): All of Judy's biggest movie hits on one CD, from *Pigskin Parade* in 1936 to *I Could Go On Singing* released in 1963. Excellent sound for the most part, and nice to have the original "Rainbow," "You Made Me Love You," "Trolley Song," "Get Happy," etc. all in one place.

The Complete Decca Masters, Plus from *MCA Records*, is a four-CD box set that contains all 79 singles Decca released during Judy's 1936–1947 years with the label, along with 11 alternate versions. Featuring a lavish and well-written booklet, and superb digital sound, this set is highly recommended.

There are many bootleg or small-label CDs on the market that feature performances from radio, TV, concert, or film appearances. Most of them offer inferior sound, so try to get a listen before you buy, and don't be shy about returning the disc if you're unhappy with the sound —unless you're a "hardcore" collector and must have any rare performance, regardless of sound.

VIDEO:

This area is easier to list, as: Every Judy Garland movie has been released on home video (VHS)—although several MGM films have been put on "hiatus." The last "hold-out," Judy's feature-film debut from 1936, *Pigskin Parade*, was released on June 3rd, 1997, by its studio, 20th Century Fox, on VHS. All of Judy's films have been issued on video cassette and laser disc, from MGM/UA Home Video, and starting in 1999, from Warner Home Video, which now controls the movies Judy made for MGM, through AOL-Time Warner's ownership of the Turner library, which includes those MGM musicals we all love. AOL-Time Warner/Warner Home Video also control *A Star Is Born* and *Gay Purr-ee.* MGM/UA Home Video controls *Judgment at Nuremberg*; *A Child Is Waiting*; and *I Could Go On Singing*, all of which were at one point issued on VHS and laser disc—but have not appeared on DVD as of this writing.

The only Judy movies on DVD currently, are *The Wizard of Oz, Till the Clouds Roll By* (in several inferior bootleg editions—Warner Home Video has not released it yet), *Annie Get Your Gun* (it contains the two songs Judy finished for the film), and *A Star Is Born. The Harvey Girls* is tentatively scheduled to be released in the first part of 2002—with audio commentary by director George Sidney, outtakes, and restored elements—from Warner Home Video.

Judy's non-film work in video—is basically her television work from 1962 to 1964, as any performer's concerts were rarely videotaped or filmed back in the 1950s and 1960s.

DVD:

The best work of Judy Garland's concert years that exists remains her 1963–1964 television series, which Pioneer Entertainment and Classic World Productions, Inc. have been releasing exclusively on DVD (VHS tapes are *hoped for* in 2002). These include *The Judy Garland Show—Volume One* and also Volumes Two through Five as well as the *Just Judy* and the *Songs For America* compilations, as well as *The Judy Garland Show Collection* DVD box set which contains the shows on Volumes One and Two, and ten additional (14 in all). A total of 21 of the 26 episodes have been released on DVD to date. The other two DVDs of Judy's concert years work is the 1962 Sinatra-Martin special that is the same colorized one as mentioned below, and *The Best of The Andy Williams Show*, which features the skit with Andy and Judy from her 1965 guest appearance in color.

Most of Judy's concert-era work on VHS can be found on the Delta Music/LaserLight label, a label that began licensing Judy videos from Sid Luft in 1995. The best of these include: *Judy, Frank, and Dean* (her 1962 special, colorized, from the 2-inch video master); *The Judy Garland Special* (her 1963 special with Robert Goulet and Phil Silvers: Hysterically funny); *The Judy Garland Christmas Show* (from 1963, and presented from the original video master air tape, complete with the vintage Commercials included; Classic World Productions also is working on their version of the show on VHS, which will use the original video tape and most likely will include Judy's Holiday Greetings that are on the DVD); *Judy Garland and Her Friends* (Barbra Streisand, Liza Minnelli, and Ethel Merman; This is a compilation from a few shows from Judy's television series); and *Judy Garland: The Concert Years.* (Although abridged from its original 85-minute length, this 59 minute tape still packs a powerful punch; and contains footage from nearly forty years of Judy—from 1929 to 1967.) Please keep in mind that all of the VHS tapes of Judy's television series shows listed in the VHS section above use inferior film prints and are not drawn from the original video source materials (with the exception of the Christmas show). So if you want to see Judy's best work in its best quality, then you'll want the DVD, which is quickly becoming "the" home video format anyway.

Bibliography

Clarke, Gerald: *Get Happy: The Life of Judy Garland*; New York: Random House, 2000.

Coleman, Emily: *The Complete Judy Garland*; New York: Harper and Row, 1990.

Dahl, David, and Barry Kehoe: *Young Judy*; New York: Mason/Charter, 1975.

Deans, Mickey, and Ann Pinchot: *Weep No More, My Lady*; New York: Hawthorn Books, Inc, 1972.

DiOrio, Al: *Little Girl Lost*; New Rochelle, New York: Arlington House, 1973.

Edwards, Anne: *Judy Garland*; New York: Simon and Schuster, 1975.

Finch, Christopher: *Rainbow*; New York: Grosset and Dunlap, 1975.

Fordin, Hugh: *The World of Entertainment*; Garden City, New York: Doubleday and Company, 1975. (Also available as a reprint from Da Capo Press.)

Frank, Gerald: *Judy*; New York: Harper and Row, 1975. (Also available as a reprint from Da Capo Press.)

Fricke, John: *World's Greatest Entertainer*; New York: Henry Holt and Company, 1992.

Harver, Ronald: *A Star Is Born*; New York: Alfred A. Knopf, 1988.

Meyer, John: *Heartbreaker*; Garden City, New York: Doubleday and Company, 1983.

Morella, Joe, and Edward L. Epstein: *Judy: The Films and Career of Judy Garland*; New York: The Citadell Press, 1969.

Sanders, Coyne Steven: *Rainbows End*; New York: William Morrow and Company, Inc., 1990.

O'Neil, Thomas: *The Emmys*; New York: Perigee/Berkley/A Variety Book, 2000.

———: *The Grammys*; New York: Perigee/Berkley/A Variety Book, 1999.

Scarfone, Jay, and William Stillman: *The Wizardry of Oz: The Artistry and Magic of the 1939 MGM Classic*; New York: Gramercy Books, 1999.

Watson, Thomas J. and Bill Chapman: *Judy: Portrait of an American Legend*; New York: McGraw-Hill Book Company, 1986.

* * *

Also helpful were the industry journals, and especially the journals issued by the various Judy clubs from 1955–1969, including Al Poland's and Pat McMath's (along with others) "Garland Gazette" (1955–1966); the British club's "Rainbow Review" (started by Lorna Smith in 1963, and still running); Max Preeo's (along with Dana Dial and others) "Garland News" (1964–1968), and Sonny Gallagher's "Judy NewsFlash" (1967–1969) and his "Beyond Rainbows" (1990–1995).

Acknowledgments

"Thank-You, Thank-You Very Much; I Can't Express It Any Other Way. . . ."

—Judy Garland, in *A Star is Born*

There are so many people involved in a project as vast as this one that it would be quite easy to fill all of the pages in this book with who just the gratitude I feel for them. Cherishing Judy has brought so many incredible people into my life over these many years, both personally and professionally.

To all those in the industry—including those who knew and worked with Judy that have shared what they experienced with me—and to those I've been fortunate enough to work with at AMC, Capitol Records, Classic World Productions, E! Entertainment, Pioneer Entertainment, and all the other companies that help keep her legacy alive through the CDs, DVDs, videos, TV shows, other projects, and those in the media who help spread the news of these events, I will always be grateful. In particular, I must thank: Gale Allen, Gordon Anderson, Army Archerd, Paul Atkinson, Jim Bailey, John Bailey, Nancy Baar-Brandon, Deborah Bancroft, Dee Baxter, Tom Beer, Mark Benardin, Ned Berkowitz, Steve Berkowitz, Brad Bessey, Marshal Blonstein, Danny Bennett, Tony Bennett, Robert Bianco, Buddy Bregman, Steve Brinberg, Wendy Brueder, Rick Bueler, Marcia Butler, Stephen Cambell, Rick Camino, Mario Cantone, Jim Caruso, Mike Clark, Gerald Clarke, Frank Collura, Barbra Cook, Steve Daly, Tom Danna, Heather David, everyone at DB Plus (including Gene, Bob, Tony, and my Jennifer), Dwight Dereiter, Dideau Duetch, Adam Dugas, Joel Dorn, Adam Dorn, Steve Dougherty, Brian Drutman, Denis Ferrara, Eileen Fitzpatrick, Hugh Fordin, Joe Franklin, Matt Friedman, Will Friedwald, Wesley Fuller, Jim Gallen, Tom Green, Joshua Greene, Merv Griffin, Dave Grumme, David Gurland, Michael Hartman, Greg Harvey, Susan Haskins, Frank Hendricks, Paul Hemstreet, Josselyne Herman, Howard Hersh, Robert Hilburn, Dave Hiltbrand, Steve Hoffman, Stephen Holden, David Horiuchi, Lena Horne, Marc Hulett, John Jimenez, Laurie Johnson, Diane Judge, Janet Keller, David Kenney, Bruce Kimmel, Susan King, Glen Korman, Steve Kmetko, Steve Jones, Gary Labriola, Garret Lee, Janet Leigh, Lee Lessack, David Levy, Irv Lichtman, Frank Lopez, Mort Lindsey, Lee Lodyga, Dave Lombard, David Lotz, Christopher Mason, Leonard Maltin, Rhonda Malmlund, Barry Manilow, Cary Mansfield, Michael Mayer, Andy McKaie, Bill

McCuddy, Audra McDonald, Ken Mendelbaum, John Meyer, Ann Miller, Dennis Millay, Toni Molle, Bill Moran, David Mucci, Michael Musto, Sidney Myer, Rebecca Myers, Ronald Neame, Basil Nester, Bob Norberg, Ron O'Brien, Rosie O'Donnell, Tom O'Neil, Robert Osborne, Michael Paoletta, Cheryl Pawelski, Joe Perrotta, Yvette Perry, Douglas Pratt, Max Preeo, Mike Ragogna, Fletcher Roberts, Bill Robinson, Michael Riedel, Rex Reed, Dan Revard, Mark Roche, Liz Rosenberg, Marion Rosenberg, Leah Rozen, Becky Rustuen, Jennifer Sanchez, Rich Sands, Tom Samiljan, Carl Samrock, Jay Scarfone, George Schlatter, Nancy Schwartz, Joel Siegel, Norma Sierra, Eric Shepard, Page Simon, Donald Smith, Liz Smith, Steven Smith, Mhammed Soumaya, John Springer, Cari Stausberg, David Patrick Stearns, Mike Stefanik, William Stillman, Billy Stritch, Elaine Stritch, Brian Swarth, Lily Tomlin, Peter Travers, Lawrence Turman, Sharon Weisz, Matthew West, Rob Wilcox, Dina White, Jamie White, Margaret Whiting, Bobby Williams, and Julie Wilson.

Special mention must go to everyone who has preserved Judy's work, especially George Feltenstein at Turner, and for her television shows I must thank everyone at Pioneer (their names are in the list above), for their kindness, heart, and support, and major kudos to Sid Luft, and also to Darryl Payne and his staff, especially Marilyn Diaz, at Classic World Productions, Inc., for believing in the importance of not having Judy's finest work—her television series—sit in vaults, but to make sure the shows are shared with the world.

My heart goes out, as it always has and as it always will, to Liza Minnelli, for all the kindness she's shown me over the last twenty years, for her incredible warmth and generosity. I can't imagine how painful it must be to read anything even the least bit unpleasant about your parent, and in a public vehicle like this, but she and her sister and brother have had to do that their entire lives. It wasn't easy to think of that while I was trying to present an entire life, and balance the overwhelming whites with the lesser grays and blacks that also were a part of their mother's life. I hope they feel I've succeeded in my quest to bring the focus to Judy Garland's art and body of work.

I have always felt that one of the greatest things about Judy has been the people she's brought together over so many years, just from sharing a similar passion for her artistry. The majority of those that love the lady carry on her qualities of warmth, compassion, strength, humor, and love that she demonstrated so well in everything she did. So, for the many years of over (and beyond) the rainbow Judy support, and personal kindness, I must thank the following from the "Judy World" (along with some friends-in-general): the generous Preston Blake for offering to set up and run my first website (www.garlandsforjudy.com); the vastly talented Lea Cantwell, who was my best friend in high school, and who remains one all these *many* years later (cough-cough), and who is so unbelievably supportive; Robert Carbone for being my dear "FS" in Judy Land; Marlin Peck Cruse for his vast ability to share and care; Russell Daisey and his "Cali" for making me smile always; My Ricky Demeo for opening his heart so easily and for always being there; Dana Dial for all the years and all the sharing; Al DiOrio for his wonderful book "Little Girl Lost," and mainly for being a dear friend; Ivan Farkas for his laughter and wisdom; to the late and great Sonny Gallagher for all he taught me; Ruth Ginther for opening her heart and her collection, and for all the laughter; Scott Gorenstein for decades of humor and wisdom; Sandra Grant for reading my mind and a million other things over a lifetime: I cherish her and her family so much; I can't say enough about Randy Henderson as a writer and especially as a person, but I am eternally grateful for him for so many things; Eric Hemphill for uncovering the fact that Judy was made an honorary corporal, and for sharing so much online; Steve Jarrett for his kindness and his superb website on Judy's concert years (visit it at http://users.deltacomm.com/rainbowz). To Jim Johnson for his warmth and for making the internet's most vast Judy website *The Judy Garland Database* (visit his site at www.jgdb.com); To "Judy's Gang" at

CBS—Judy, Eleanor, Margo, Ken, et Al.—thanks for the memories and friendship; Dave King for his heart and humor; Tom Lynch for the special sunshine he always exudes and for all the support and friendship; Dan Oldrati for my first Judy videotapes and twenty-plus years of humor and heart; Frank Marketti for the honesty and heart; Barry Monush for sharing his wisdom and laughter; Mari Rozanski for caring about me and my Wobbie; Tamara O'Leary for having one of the best voices and the biggest hearts I've ever known; Albert Poland for sharing and for giving Judy her first real fan club; to the brilliantly talented Carmine Red for his wonderful design work on our *Garlands For Judy* magazine and for his friendship and heart; Greg Rossi for the endless cheer; Ken Sawicki for twenty-plus years of important laughter, caring, sharing and " Sludge Fests"; the supremely talented Rick Skye, for coming through time and again; my incredibly beloved and dear Charles Triplett for twenty years of heart and support; Cliff Shenghit for answering the S.O.S. calls; Jerry Waters for being so generous over the years, and for preserving so much of Judy's work; Leo Weinberger for the support and ego-boosters; and Dave Zeliff for twenty years of being there. As I get older, I see more clearly what I got from both parents, and I hope they both know how much I love them and do think of them. My mom bought me my first Judy records—and would even let me stay home from school to watch Judy movies in the pre–VCR days, as long as I kept my grades up—so thanks, Mom, for your heavenly heart, for making me most of who I am, and for helping all of "this" to happen.

Finally, the people who worked on this project, often on a daily basis: The incredible mind, talent, and heart of Eric Stephen Jacobs: for his brilliant photography, his endless laughter, his huge heart, and his ability to make me look human in photos (plus all his computer help, to boot). The great people at Photofest, especially Howard and Ronald Mandelbaum for the endless hours of their time finding the right photos. Likewise to Ron Harvey and Zack Zito of the Everett Collection. The team at the University of Southern California Cinema-Televison Library—Ned Comstock and Noelle Carter—for arranging USC's vast material on the making of most of Judy's MGM and Warner Brothers movies to be available on short notice. The one-and-only show business expert, Tom O'Neil, who does friendship as well as does his books on the industry, and who never stopped cheering me on to finish this book. Justin Baker for his computer help. Allyson Wagner for going above-and-beyond in the research and work she did for me in California. No one does "above-and-beyond" like Russ Klein, who "lived-through" this book on a day-by-day basis yet never failed to offer his generosity, his gentleness, his faith, and his heart; I could never say how blessed I am to have him in my life, nor how much he means to me: I can only hope that he knows. Standing ovations to the great songwriter, record producer, agent, and all-around show-biz-wiz, Brian Gari (and all of his talented family, dating back to his grandfather Eddie Cantor, to his father Roberto Gari for his definitive Palace portrait of Judy, even his sister the great singer Amanda Abel for her heart—and for running across town with her computer): Brian made this book happen, by finding it the right home. I'll always be grateful for that, but am even more so for his laughter, advice, and heart. Lastly, I must thank the team at Cooper Square Press: Ross Plotkin, Hector DeJean, Michael Messina, my production editor Lynn Weber and her assistant, Brian Selzer, and most especially, my editor, Michael Dorr. He believed in this project from the very start, and has shared so much of his personal time, talents, and beautiful heart into making this be what we wanted. What a joy to work with someone who *is* a joy: I knew I'd love working with him when he offered a hug goodbye instead of a handshake at the end of our first meeting about the book. I am blessed to know him, as I am all of the people I've mentioned above. I must also say thanks to the lady herself: Judy Garland always said (to her children) to watch her; that she was "the perfect example of what *not* to do." She was also more often than not a perfect example of what *to* do, and I'm proud to learn and grow by loving a human being unlike any other. I'm grateful for "the Legend's Lessons," just as I am for "the Legend's Legacy."

Song Title Index

Notes to Index: Page numbers in *italic* refer to photographs

Subject Index

Notes to Index: *JG* refers to Judy Garland; all cities, unless major or noted otherwise, are in California; page numbers in *italic* refer to photographs

About the Author

Scott Schechter has devoted over a quarter of a century to researching the life and career of Judy Garland and is the only historian who is also an expert on the careers of her daughters Liza Minnelli and Lorna Luft. Mr. Schechter is proudest of his role as archivist, which has led to the recovery and release of rare or lost material—including Judy's complete Carnegie Hall concert and her long-lost television series.

CD projects he has produced, consulted on, and/or written liner notes for, include *Judy at Carnegie Hall: Fortieth Anniversary Edition* (Capitol Records); the four-CD/video/book box set *Judy* (32 Records), which spans the entire forty years of her recorded legacy; *Liza Minnelli: Ultimate Collection* (Hip-O Records/Universal Music); *Engelbert Humperdinck: You Belong to My Heart* (Varese Sarabande); *Miss Show Business/Judy* and *Judy: That's Entertainment!/I Could Go On Singing* (Collectable Records); and other upcoming compact discs, including the definitive audio compilation he produced and compiled of Garland's television series: *The Judy Garland Show: The Show That Got Away* (Hip-O Records/Universal).

As a writer, his words on Garland and family have appeared in the *Advocate*, TalkinBroadway.com, *Show Music* magazine, and the *New York Times*. He is also the publisher, editor, and writer of the *Garlands for Judy: The Legend's Legacy* tribute magazine, which he began in 1995 and has subscribers all over the world.

Television shows on which Mr. Schechter has consulted include ABC's *20/20*, AMC's *Behind the Screen*, and E! Entertainment Television's *True Hollywood Story* highly rated and critically acclaimed two-hour show on Judy, for which he served as consulting producer.

For his marketing and publicity efforts, Mr. Schechter has obtained the highest profile exposure for his clients—including MP3.com, Pioneer Entertainment, Classic World Productions, Inc., and Capitol Records. Media such as *Rolling Stone* magazine, *USA Today*, Fox News Channel, ABC, E! Entertainment, and TV Guide have been utilized.

Mr. Schechter is continuing work on the project of which he is proudest (along with the *Judy* box and the Carnegie reissues): *The Judy Garland Show* DVDs (Pioneer Entertainment/Classic World Productions, Inc.), which have been an astounding success. As well as being instrumental in getting the project approved, he has served as a consultant on the creative end—compiling the acclaimed *Just Judy* DVD of solo moments—and with marketing and publicity. The series DVD box set was honored with the Best Overall Presentation Award (non-theatrical) by the Video Software Dealer's Association (VSDA). He also conceived and compiled the *Judy Garland: Songs for America* DVD, from which all the proceeds benefit the American Red Cross.

Mr. Schechter's projects have received raves from the *New York Times*, *People*, *USA Today*, Liz Smith, Rex Reed, *Billboard*, *Los Angeles Times*, *Entertainment Weekly*, and the *New York Post*, which concluded its review of the *Judy* box by saying "music historian Scott Schechter's essay is an excellent read and will earn him a nomination for the prestigious Grammy Award for best liner notes."

Mr. Schechter resides in New York. He may be contacted via e-mail at Garlands63@aol.com; at www.garlandsforjudy.com; or www.scottschecter.com; or by sending an SASE to him at PO Box 2743, New York, NY 10163-2743.